SIMULATION

A Problem-Solving Approach

Stewart V. Hoover □ Ronald F. Perry

Digital Equipment Corporation   Northeastern University

 ADDISON-WESLEY PUBLISHING COMPANY

Reading, Massachusetts • Menlo Park, California • New York
Don Mills, Ontario • Wokingham, England • Amsterdam
Bonn • Sydney • Singapore • Tokyo • Madrid • San Juan

Library of Congress Cataloging-in-Publication Data

Hoover, Stewart V.
    Simulation : a problem-solving approach.

    Includes bibliographies and index.
    1. Digital computer simulation.   I. Perry, Ronald F.
II. Title.
QA76.9.C65H66   1989   001.4'34   88-16794
ISBN 0-201-16880-4

Addison-Wesley Publishing Company, Inc. makes no representations or warranties, express or implied, with respect to the software commands included in this text, including without limitations, any implied warranties of merchantability or fitness for a particular purpose, all of which are expressly disclaimed.

Many of the designations used by manufacturers and sellers to distinguish their products are claimed as trademarks. Where those designations appear in this book, and Addison-Wesley was aware of a trademark claim, the designations have been printed in initial caps or all caps.

To Mary Ellen, Stewart, and Amy
and
to Judy and Jeffrey

PREFACE

The objective of this book is to present the rudiments of discrete event simulation analysis in a clear and concise fashion. The orientation throughout is problem solving, with illustrative examples used extensively to promote a clear understanding of necessary simulation skills. We envision the book serving as an independent reference or as a text for a first course in simulation for undergraduate or graduate students.

Viewed as a course text, the book was designed for students of three different disciplines: Industrial Engineering, Computer Science, and Business Administration. The illustrative problems contain settings familiar to each of these audiences. The level of coverage was set to be comprehensible to all three audiences for those areas vital to the understanding and application of simulation analysis. However, some of the more theoretical and less vital sections may pose some problems for the student with an incomplete background in probability, statistics, and computer languages. We describe course designs below which are adapted to varied backgrounds. But first, we present a brief comment on a rather unique feature of the book and a digest of the material covered in the book.

SIMULATION LANGUAGE PRIMERS

In designing this book, our intent was to enable the user to construct and apply quite complex simulation models with little more than this text as a guide. The primary additional ingredients which must be supplied by the user are computer hardware and software. Simulation without a computer is not feasible; simulation without an appropriate special purpose simulation language is difficult—some would say impossible. To deal with the latter issue, we have included major appendixes to the book that are primers for three of the more widely used simulation languages: GPSS, SIMAN, and SIMSCRIPT.

Each primer covers a language in sufficient detail to permit quite realistic systems to be modeled and coded. As in the text, extensive use is made of illustrative examples to demonstrate the constructs of the language. The source code for all of the illustrative problems in the primers is available to adopters of the text on a floppy disk entitled Illustrative Problems for Simulation Language Primers. The disk is formatted for the IBM PC family of computers. Based upon personal experience in teaching simulation courses, we feel that this feature greatly enhances the utility of the book.

ORGANIZATION OF THE BOOK

The book is divided into four parts, each part dealing with a coherent group of simulation analysis tasks.

Part I: Simulation in Brief   In Chapter 1, we introduce the discipline of simulation and explain its utility in solving various types of real-world problems. Chapter 2 is in a sense a map for the remainder of the book; it describes in some detail the necessary steps for conducting a simulation analysis.

Part II: Modeling and Simulation   In this Part, we focus on the important role of modeling in simulation. Perhaps no other aspect of simulation analysis is as important as, and as little understood as, modeling. If there is such, modeling is certainly the keystone of simulation. In Chapter 3, we illustrate the process of modeling simple systems such that they can be solved using simulation, and in some cases also by analytic models. We demonstrate how simulation is of value when a system definition is extended so that assumptions of analytic models no longer hold.

Chapter 4 treats simulation languages and their use in coding models. The relative advantages and disadvantages of simulation languages versus general purpose languages are covered, and the essential characteristics of three popular languages (GPSS, SIMAN, and SIMSCRIPT) are presented. The same illustrative example is coded in all three languages to contrast their different world views. To complete our consideration of modeling and simulation, we compare, in Chapter 5, problem solutions using simulation and some of the more common analytic models such as queueing theory, inventory models, and Markov chains. The focus here is on ways to use analytic models to aid in the structuring and validating of simulation models. Thus, the analytic models are presented as an integral part of simulation analysis, not a dangling appendage, as in many simulation texts.

Part III: Building and Validating Simulation Models   This part consists of three chapters which deal with data collection and analysis, random variate generation and model verification and validation. Among the topics covered in connection with data collection and analysis are cost accuracy trade-offs as they relate to sample size, methods for selection of the appropriate probability distributions for input, and goodness of fit and contingency tests. Chapter 7 presents basic techniques of generating random numbers and random variates with emphasis on techniques for generating random variates for the most commonly used probability distributions.

The final chapter in Part III covers verification and validation of simulation models. This process is described in two stages. First, we must verify and validate the three models that comprise a simulation: conceptual model, logical model, and computer model. Then, we can validate our simulation as being representative of the real system behavior. Several techniques are suggested and illustrated for each step of the process. We feel that Chapter 8 makes a unique contribution to this aspect of simulation analysis by presenting the disparate notions on validation as a coherent rubric.

Part IV: Using Simulation Models   These three chapters concentrate on the payoff to be derived from simulation analysis. First, the unique statistical properties of simulation output are treated in Chapter 9. Statistical issues covered include: analysis of output from terminating, non-terminating, transient, and steady state simulations; and techniques for interval estimates of both statistically independent and dependent observations.

In Chapter 10, the use of simulation models to evaluate alternative system designs is covered. We describe and illustrate the methods available for experimental design and model optimization. From simple comparisons of output measures for two or three alternative system designs, the chapter progresses to experimental designs involving single and multiple measures, which can be used to compare many alternative system designs and also employ heuristic methods to seek optimal designs.

Finally, in Chapter 11 we attempt to provide an understanding of the implementation process and suggest strategies for successful installation of decision support systems stemming from simulation analysis. If implementation fails, then all of the effort in the simulation analysis was for naught. A review of the current state of the art of implementation, with reasons for lack of success, is presented. Suggested strategies for improving success address the roles of users and analysts in development, implementation, and integration of simulation results into the decision-making process. The inclusion of this chapter is unique in the genre of simulation texts we have seen.

COURSE DESIGNS FOR THE BOOK

As mentioned above, the book is intended to meet the needs of students in three disciplines: Industrial Engineering, Computer Science, and Business Administration. Given the foregoing description of the book's coverage, we may now define course designs suitable for these audiences.

Audience 1   Pragmatic users of simulation: possibly undergraduate or graduate business administration students who wish to know the rudiments of simulation and then apply them to problem solving for *not-too-complex* systems. These students should have *some* grounding in probability and statistics, and probably exposure to BASIC.

Chapters: 1, 2, 3 [Sections 3.1–3.4, 3.6], 4, 8, 9 [Sections 9.1–9.4, 9.7], 10 [Sections 10.1, 10.2, 10.6], and 11. Also, one of the language primers [GPSS, or SIMAN].

Sequence: 1–4, language primer, 8–11

Audience 2   Technically well-grounded students: Industrial Engineering or Computer Science undergraduate or graduate students who desire a reasonably thorough understanding of simulation methodology as well as applications. These students should have a good grasp of probability and inferential statistics and be conversant in at least a few computer languages.

Chapters: 1 2, 3, 4, 5 [Sections 5.1, 5.2, 5.4, 5.7], 6, 7, 8, 9, 10, 11 [optional]. Also, one or two of the language primers [GPSS, SIMAN, or SIMSCRIPT].

Sequence: 1 – 4, language primer(s), 5 – 11

Audience 3   Students who desire a thorough treatment of both simulation methodology and applications: Industrial Engineering graduate students and possibly Computer Science or Industrial Engineering undergraduate students. These students are equipped to fully understand the nuances of applying probability and statistical theory to simulation modeling and analysis.

Chapters: All. One or two of the language primers [GPSS, SIMAN, or SIMSCRIPT].

Sequence: 1 – 4, language primer(s), 5 – 11

The book will support a one or two semester course. However, Audiences 2 and 3 would appear to be the most likely candidates for the two semester course. For a one semester course, it is suggested that the appropriate chapters for the audiences identified above be covered to treat simulation methodology in conjunction with one simulation language to illustrate applications. Of necessity, treatment of the language features cannot be extensive in a one semester course. We recommend that SIMSCRIPT not be used since it is the most difficult to learn of the three languages treated.

For a two semester course, it is suggested that the first semester be devoted primarily to methodology (in much greater detail than the one semester course) and that one simulation language be introduced in a manner just sufficient to illustrate the role of such languages in simulation analysis. If SIMSCRIPT is to be covered, we suggest doing this in the second semester course.

The second semester is then used to develop the chosen language to a fuller potential and illustrate its use for modeling complex systems. A second and possibly even a third language could be covered during this course. It would be instructive to contrast the strengths and weaknesses of the languages for modeling various types of systems.

ACKNOWLEDGMENTS

As with any endeavor of this magnitude, it could not have come to fruition without the contributions and support of many people. To each we owe a debt of gratitude.

The reviewers of the manuscript performed a vital service. In particular, we would like to thank Dennis Pegden of Systems Modeling Corporation, whose careful critique of the SIMAN Primer improved its clarity and accuracy, and Edward Russell of C.A.C.I., who so meticulously reviewed the SIMSCRIPT Primer.

We also appreciate the many helpful suggestions of the following reviewers:

James W. Chrissis
Air Force Institute of Technology

Barry L. Nelson
The Ohio State University

Gary E. Whitehouse
Dean, College of Engineering
University of Central Florida

Bruce Schmeiser
Purdue University

William E. Biles
University of Louisville

Michael G. Ketcham
University of Massachusetts, Amherst

Roger Glassey
University of California at Berkeley

John Ballard
University of Nebraska, Lincoln

Kwangsoo Kim
Rochester Institute of Technology

The accuracy of the text was improved by many graduate students who used the draft manuscript in our courses. We are grateful for their comments.

We are also grateful to the Literary Executor of the late Sir Ronald A. Fisher, F.R.S., to Dr. Frank Yates, F.R.S., and the Longman Group Ltd., London, for permission to reprint the Table of Critical Values of the t-Distribution from their book *Statistical Tables for Biological, Agricultural, and Medical Research* (6th Edition, 1974).

Transforming a manuscript into a finished, polished book is a decidedly non-trivial task. For accomplishing this in a most proficient manner while making it relatively painless for the authors, we must thank Maura Burke, our copy editor, and Kazia Navas, Senior Production Supervisor, of Addison-Wesley.

And last, but certainly not least, we must thank our families for so generously tolerating the disruption of normal life caused by this project.

Nashua, NH   S. V. H.
Boston, MA   R. F. P.

BRIEF CONTENTS

CONTENTS

PART I

SIMULATION IN BRIEF

CHAPTER 1

SIMULATION ANALYSIS AND DECISION MAKING

What do voters at a polling place, patients in a hospital x-ray department, and office workers at a bank of elevators in the New York World Trade Center have in common? They all wait a shorter time for service thanks to problem analysis using simulation. The solutions obtained from simulation are often dramatic improvements over existing conditions. And, these examples are but an indication of the diverse problems that can benefit from simulation analysis.

1.1 INTRODUCTION

Today, simulation analysis is a powerful problem-solving technique. Its origins lie in statistical sampling theory and analysis of complex probabilistic physical systems. The common thread in both of these is the use of random numbers and random sampling to approximate an outcome or solution.

One of the more famous applications of random sampling occurred during the Second World War when simulation was used to study random neutron diffusion in connection with the development of the atom bomb. Since this research was top secret, it was given a code name appropriate for a process dealing with random events: Monte Carlo, referring to the world-famous gambling casino [9]. The name persisted, and was for a time used to refer to any simulation effort. But the term, Monte Carlo methods, now refers to that branch of experimental mathematics that deals with experiments on random numbers, while the term simulation, or system simulation, covers the more pragmatic analysis technique which is the subject of this book.

Although simulation analysis is eclectic in nature, the single most important contributor to its current power is the computer. High speed digital computers make it possible to describe and code models of large complex systems involving both animate and inanimate entities. In addition to computer programming skills, the technique of simulation also draws heavily on modeling ability, probability and statistics, and heuristic methods. Further discussion of the contribution made by these disciplines appears in the following sections.

Applications of simulation analysis historically have been found in the production sector, but increasingly, fruitful models are being developed for the service and government sectors. Notable areas where the technique has been profitably used in the production sector include corporate planning, inventory control systems, production lines, materials handling systems, and job shop scheduling. In the service and government sectors, simulation has been of value in the analysis of hospital admission systems, voter polling stations, transportation systems, and passenger elevator systems for high rise buildings, to name but a few applications.

A somewhat unique application of simulation is the area of gaming. Gaming has traditionally been important to military strategists and was used long before the availability of computers. In its current form, gaming permits the creation of an artificial environment that emulates a real one. Within this environment, participants engage in a competitive activity ranging from military conflict to more civilized business competition. Used in this way, simulation can be an effective training aid for future leaders in both industry and combat. Some of the most complex simulations ever undertaken are of a war game or war scenario nature.

In the balance of this chapter we more precisely define simulation analysis, and consider its advantages, disadvantages, and practice. Important concepts covered include: a definition of simulation, the important role modeling plays in simulation, and the value of simulation analysis from the practitioner's view point.

1.2   SIMULATION AND MODELING

1.2.1   MODELS VERSUS REALITY

One dictionary definition of the verb simulate is as follows:

"to assume or have the appearance or characteristics of." [15]

From the previous discussion, this would appear to be a reasonably accurate description of the technique. The key to a successful simulation, however, is not just the "appearance or characteristics," but rather the operation or behavior of the simulation model.

A useful working definition of simulation is the following:

The process of designing a mathematical or logical model of a real system and then conducting computer-based experiments with the model to describe, explain, and predict the behavior of the real system.*

In considering this definition, several points bear elaboration. First, an explicit model, mathematical or logical, is required. As we shall see, the ability to develop a "good" model is fundamental to the success of any simulation analysis. Next, it must be possible to express the model as an efficient, effective computer program. Further, since simulation models are descriptive in nature, one must ask the right questions using a well-devised experimental procedure to obtain useful results. Finally, the ultimate purpose of simulation analysis is to predict system behavior, thereby aiding decision makers in the evaluation of alternatives.

Implicit in the foregoing definition of simulation is the need for a specific set of skills. As mentioned earlier, these are: modeling, computer programming, probability and statistics, and heuristic methods. All of these topics are treated in this book, and all are important parts of the eclectic technique of simulation analysis. The area of modeling, however, is perhaps the least well defined of the set and the most vital to the success of simulation.

Models may be thought of as containing only the essentials of the real system. Those aspects of the system which do not contribute significantly to system behavior are not included since they would only obscure the relationships between inputs and outputs. At what point does one stop including realism in the model? It depends on the purpose for which the model is being developed. Models are not true or false, but rather they are useful and appropriate for the analysis at hand. More is said about this in Chapter 2.

---

* The kernel of this definition is due to Naylor et al. [11]

Models come in great variety. In form they may be iconic, analog, or symbolic. Iconic models resemble the real system physically, as a globe models the earth or a planetarium models the solar system and the stars. Analog models need resemble the real system only in their behavior, as the flow of water in pipes models the flow of electricity in wires. Symbolic models have no physical or analog relationship to the real system, but rather a logical one. They range from intuitive to verbal to logic flow to mathematical, in order of increasing specificity of structure. Since models for simulation analysis must be capable of being implemented on a computer, they must be very explicit: symbolic models at least at the level of logic flow.

The other skills involved in simulation analysis provide the ability to express the model in a usable form, and manipulate it to answer relevant system design and operating questions. The computer program translates the model into a usable form, while probability theory defines the random variables in the model, and statistical theory assists in design and analysis of the experiments used to answer the questions posed. Since neither statistics nor the simulation model itself is useful in achieving optimum solutions or answers, the final skill, heuristic methods, is employed to insure increasingly better, if not optimum solutions. Each of these skills is discussed and illustrated in one or more chapters of that book.

1.2.2   CLASSIFICATION OF MODELS

We stated above that models for simulation analysis must be symbolic. However, there are many different types of symbolic models. To make the perception of the model type we will be using more concrete, we consider several dichotomous model classifications. Models may be classified as:

- prescriptive or descriptive
- discrete or continuous
- probabilistic or deterministic
- static or dynamic
- open loop or closed loop

Prescriptive/Descriptive   Within the first dichotomy we can define prescriptive models which are used to formulate and optimize a given problem, thereby providing the one best solution. On the other hand, we can also define descriptive models which merely describe the system behavior and leave the optimization process totally in the hands of the analyst.

Discrete/Continuous   The discrete or continuous classification refers to the model variables. Continuous variables may take on the value of any real number, while discrete variables may assume only a limited, specified number of values. Particularly important in this distinction is the time variable in a simulation model. If alterations to the model occur continuously as time varies, we classify the model as continuous. If on the other hand, changes occur only at discrete points in time, the model is discrete.

In a chemical process, temperature and pressure would experience a rate of change continuously over time. Thus a continuous model would be appropriate. In a queueing system, such as supermarket checkout lanes, people arrive, begin service, and complete service at discrete points in time, so a discrete model is warranted. It should be noted that discrete models may treat time as a continuous variable. However, changes in the system do not occur continuously at a given rate, but rather at particular, discrete, event times. Hence they are commonly referred to as discrete event simulations.

Probabilistic/Deterministic   When distinguishing between probabilistic and deterministic models the focus is again on the model variables. If any random variables are present, we classify the model as a probabilistic model. Random variables must be defined by an appropriate probability function. If on the other hand, mathematical variables, variables whose values may be stated with certainty, are sufficient to describe the system behavior, we classify the model as deterministic. All systems involving humans and many systems consisting only of machines have random variation necessitating the use of random variables. A completely automated, robot staffed assembly line could adequately be described using a deterministic model. Our checkout example, however, is probabilistic since there is random variation in the arrival pattern of the customers, and the performance times of the cashiers and the baggers.

Static/Dynamic   Models are classified as either static or dynamic depending on whether or not the model variables change over time. Consider the layout of production departments in a factory where many different physical arrangements are possible, usually too many to evaluate all possible arrangements. One approach is to randomly assign departments to available locations and evaluate the layout based on a measure such as the total distance traveled. By selecting many such random samples one can quickly narrow consideration to only very good solutions which can be refined manually. This sampling approach defines a static model of the factory. Alternatively, the checkout system is an example of a dynamic system in that the model variables do change over time. For instance, the number of customers in the queue varies as new ones arrive and those already present complete the checkout process. All queueing models are classified as dynamic models.

Open Loop/Closed Loop   The notion of an open loop or a closed loop model is defined by the structure of the model rather than by the variables. Open loop models, which constitute the overwhelming majority of analytic and simulation models, have no provision for the output of the model to be fed back as input to modify subsequent outputs. In a closed loop model the output is fed back and compared to some desired level or goal to alter the system such that it maintains, or approximates, the desired value. Examples of open loop models of systems are numerous, and include all of the practical applications of simulation that are mentioned in Section 1.3, as well as our supermarket checkout example.

   The classic example of a closed loop system is a heating system. The output of the furnace is sensed by the thermostat which either turns the furnace on or off depending on a comparison of the temperature setting on the thermostat and that which is sensed, thus maintaining some desired temperature. An example of a closed loop system in an organizational context is a model of corporate decision making relative to some business growth goal. Decisions would be made and the resulting change in business growth would be observed and compared to the goal. If the goal were not being met, indicated changes in action would be taken and growth again would be observed, continuing in this manner to adjust and maintain growth at or near the goal. Examples of business oriented closed loop models may be found in Forrester [3].

Which Model for Simulation Analysis?   Using the five model dichotomies just described we could define 32 model types ($2^5 = 32$), 16 prescriptive and 16 descriptive. Quite a dizzying array of model possibilities! Many of the model types come under the purview of other analysis techniques, such as queueing theory, mathematical programming, and differential equations. But, even within the simulation discipline, which treats only descriptive models, a large number of possibilities exist. In this text we will deal primarily with discrete, probabilistic, dynamic, open loop models. The other model types, of course, have their strengths for particular applications. Of the many texts which deal with these other types of models, the following are noteworthy: Forrester [3], Roberts [16], and Speckhart [18].

1.3   SIMULATION AS A PROBLEM-SOLVING TECHNIQUE

In the discussion of any complex analysis technique it is important not to lose sight of the reason for its existence. Simulation analysis has the same goal as any other viable decision-aiding technique: to evaluate alternative decisions and select the best, or at least a very good, strategy for the decision maker. For an excellent discussion of the economics of simulation applied to decision making, see Godin [5].

Simulation has been widely employed by practitioners because of the degree of realism that can be included in simulation models, and the ease with which such models can be explained to non-technical decision makers. Compared with analytic techniques, such as queueing theory, simulation models do not require the sometimes stringent assumptions necessary for tractable solutions. Also, the logic and mathematical relationships associated with simulation models are generally more obvious to the uninitiated. On the other hand, simulation models can be less efficient and more cumbersome than analytic models. This has led some critics to say that simulation is a technique of last resort [21]. There is more to be said on this point in the following section.

Two national surveys of users suggest the practitioner's perception of simulation relative to other quantitative techniques. The first survey covered several aspects of Operations Research/Management Science (OR/MS) departments in corporate organizations, including the frequency of use of various OR/MS techniques [20]. Of the fourteen techniques mentioned simulation ranked second, bracketed by statistical analysis (ranked first) and linear programming (ranked third).

In another survey of both corporate and academic users, respondents were asked to rank various techniques, according to familiarity, and their desire to learn more about the technique [17]. In a group of twelve techniques, simulation ranked second in familiarity and first in utility and respondents' desire to learn more about the technique. Linear programming ranked first in familiarity, second in utility, but eighth in respondents' desire to learn more about the technique (see Table 1.1 for the rankings of all techniques). It is clear from these findings that simulation analysis is perceived to be a technique of definite usefulness by users of diverse backgrounds in corporate and academic settings.

Another perspective on the value of simulation to practitioners is evident from the annual prize competition of The Institute of Management Science for the best application of Management Science in an organization. A cash prize is awarded to the best paper reporting results with a verifiable, quantitative impact on the organization. In recent years simulation analysis has been a frequently used technique in the winning papers.

To better appreciate how simulation analysis can be of value to organizations, several actual simulation studies drawn from the literature and the authors' personal experience, and embracing both production and service sectors, will be described briefly. In each case the nature of the problem, the organization involved, and the benefits derived from the use of simulation are reported.

- Exxon Corporation built a model of a gasoline supply system at a refinery in less than one month. The model was used to control the inventories of several blends of gasoline and maximize storage tank utilization. Savings resulting from not building an additional storage tank amounted to $1.4 million [6].

- A simulation model of a multistage production system of assembled products was developed to examine the impact of operating rules on performance measures such as flow time, earliness and tardiness. The impact of the rules on inventory decisions was also explored [7].

- A corporate simulation model of Canterbury Timber Products, Ltd. was developed to improve planning for domestic and export operations. It was estimated that the ability to explore more alternatives with the model, the improved quality of decision making, and more timely information have resulted in savings in direct and opportunity costs of at least $10,000 annually [2].

- The authors developed a simulation model of an automated storage/retrieval/delivery system for a materials handling equipment manufacturer. The model permits evaluation of alternative operating rules and system design configurations. [14]

TABLE 1.1
QUANTITATIVE TECHNIQUES SURVEY RESULTS

Technique	Familiarity Rank	Utility Rank	Learning Rank
Linear Programming	1	2	8
Simulation	2	1	1
Network Analysis	3	4	2
Queueing Theory	4	7	10
Decision Trees	5	3	3
Integer Programming	6	6	6
Dynamic Programming	7	11	7
Nonlinear Programming	8	9	4
Markov Processes	9	10	11
Replacement Analysis	10	5	9
Game Theory	11	12	12
Goal Programming	12	8	5

- Using a model of a data center at General Dynamics Corporation, analysis of the impact of increased workload on tape drive utilization was conducted. Results indicated that replacement of existing tape drives with drives that were 60% faster was more economical than adding capacity in the existing drives [19].

- Consultants to the Federal Election Commission modeled the voting process at polling stations. The issues involved were voter waiting time and voting machine utilization. Analysis with the model enabled the machines to be allocated to minimize the need to purchase additional machines, reduced voter waiting time and increased voter turnout [8].

- A model of a diagnostic radiology department in a community hospital was constructed to evaluate patient and staff scheduling, and to assist in the planning of the department configuration over a five-year planning horizon. Analysis using the model indicated that changes in operating procedures could preclude the need for a major expansion in department size [13].

- A rather unique application of simulation analysis to the service sector was the elevator system design for the twin towers of the New York World Trade Center. The analysis permitted the assessment of service levels, in terms of passenger waiting time, before installation of the 95 elevators in each tower. A very detailed simulation of the elevators used extensive passenger arrival and departure data [1].

- A simulation model of a high volume consumer product manufacturing facility was developed to investigate the feasibility of manufacturing a second product using the same facility. The model suggested that with appropriate changes in the material handling system, the current facility could be expanded to include the second product. Thus, the need to build a second manufacturing facility was eliminated [4].

The foregoing examples should serve to illustrate the broad range of applications for which simulation is an effective problem solving technique. To provide a frame of reference for identifying potentially fruitful applications for simulation analysis, we can define applications in terms of the two dimensions, functional area and setting. Some functional areas are: inventory analysis, distribution systems, job shop scheduling, complex queueing systems, corporate planning, complex material handling systems, and business/war gaming. Settings, categorized previously as simply production and service, can be more completely described as: manufacturing, health care, criminal justice, government and public administration, and education. The studies described previously represent many different combinations of these two dimensions.

1.4 ADVANTAGES AND DISADVANTAGES OF SIMULATION ANALYSIS

Having described what simulation analysis is and illustrated where and how it can be used in problem solving, we now turn to the question of when it is advantageous to use simulation analysis. Given such an apparently powerful tool one is tempted to respond to the question with a resounding: **ALWAYS.** This is a naive response. There are those who would respond: only as a last resort [21]. The defensible answer lies somewhere between these two extremes.

Analytic models have definite advantages to be considered carefully when selecting a problem solving technique. These advantages include: conciseness in problem description, closed form solutions, ease of evaluating the impact of changes in inputs on output measures, and in some cases, the ability to produce an optimum solution. On the other hand, there are some disadvantages, such as assumptions regarding system description which may be unrealistic, and complex mathematical formulations which defy solution. For example, many systems can be modeled as queueing networks, but either the assumptions required for analytic solution are somewhat unrealistic (e.g., exponential interarrival and service times), or the mathematical formulation necessary to reflect the desired degree of realism is intractable. Simulation models can compensate for these disadvantages, but not without sacrificing some of the advantages of the analytic models.

Simulation models have their own superiorities and deficiencies some of which are quite unique. Simulation models can describe systems which are very complex. They can be used to experiment with systems which are not yet in existence, or to experiment with existing systems without actually altering the system. Analytic models can also be used in these ways only if the system is not too complex. Simulation models provide an effective training environment which will not impact on operations and will compress much simulated experience into a short time period. This is exemplified by business games and war gaming. Analytic models cannot do this. On the deficiency side of the ledger, there are no closed form solutions to simulation models; each change of input variables requires a separate solution or set of runs. Complex simulation models are costly and time consuming to build and run. It can be very difficult to establish the validity of the model (i.e., its correspondence to the real system).

There would then appear to be no clear cut answer to the question of when to use simulation. The technically correct answer is that simulation should be used when the advantages of using it outweigh the disadvantages of using it. This is not operationally very useful, however. Practically speaking, simulation analysis should be selected whenever either one or both of the following conditions prevail: the assumptions required by the appropriate analytic model are not sufficiently well satisfied by the real system, or the appropriately formulated model cannot be solved analytically. This might seem to severely reduce the range of problems for which simulation is appropriate, but as the illustrations of the previous section show, this is not the case. The complexity of real world problems and the power of analytic models are such that it is not difficult to encounter problems that satisfy the stated conditions.

Thus far simulation and analytic models have been presented as alternatives. A most fruitful, although limited, use of simulation analysis has been in conjunction with analytic models. This approach takes advantage of the best features of both methods while minimizing the disadvantages of either method used by itself. One such study involved the planning of ambulatory care facilities [10]. Using a recursive optimization-simulation approach, a mixed-integer programming model first generates optimal staffing and facility plans, and then a simulation model evaluates their effectiveness based on measures such as patient waiting time and staff utilization. If these measures are unsatisfactory, constraints are altered or developed for the mathematical programming model using regression analysis, and these are incorporated into a second round of optimization. The process continues in this fashion until an acceptable solution is achieved.

A second example uses this recursive approach to determine the size of the transportation forces for the Department of Defense [12]. A linear programming model provides allocation of mobility vehicles and schedules. Two simulation models, airlift and sealift models, are used to develop productivity estimates and tests of capability. The results from these models are used to suggest changes in the constraints of the linear programming formulation, thus completing one cycle of the analysis.

Using this approach takes advantage of the ability of the analytic model to efficiently produce optimum solutions, while using the simulation model to reflect the appropriate degree of realism and accuracy in system description. However, this combination approach does have the disadvantage of requiring a greater level of familiarity with analytic models and more ingenuity than the use of simulation analysis alone.

EXERCISES

1.1 Suggest at least two appropriate applications for simulation analysis in a business/manufacturing setting, and justify the use of simulation as opposed to analytic models. What aspects of simulation analysis are particularly advantageous for the applications selected?

1.2 Repeat Exercise 1.1 for applications in a service setting, for example, health care delivery or municipal government.

1.3 Suggest an application where the combination of optimization and simulation models might be profitably applied, and indicate how the two techniques would be linked.

1.4 Suggest at least two situations for which it would not be feasible to use analytic models, but where simulation analysis could be applied.

1.5 Review the technical literature to find one simulation study in a business/manufacturing setting and one in a service setting. In addition to the journals and proceedings referenced at the end of this chapter, consult: *Operations Research, Simulation, and Proceedings of the Institute of Industrial Engineers*. Briefly summarize each of the two articles and state why simulation was an appropriate choice of analysis technique.

REFERENCES

1. Browne, J. J., and Kelly, J. J., "Simulation of elevator system for world's tallest buildings," *Transportation Science*, Vol. 2, No. 1, 1968.
2. de Kluyver, C. A., and McNally, G. M., "Corporate planning using simulation," *Interfaces*, Vol. 10, No. 3, 1980.
3. Forrester, J. W., *Industrial Dynamics*, Cambridge, Mass.: MIT Press, 1961.
4. Freeman, D. R., Grossi, P., and Hoover, S. V., "Simulation of pack film manufacturing," *Proceedings of the 1971 Winter Simulation Conference*, New York, New York.
5. Godin, V. B., "The dollars and sense of simulation," *Decision Sciences*, Vol. 7, No. 2, 1976.
6. Golovin, L., "Product blending: A simulation case study in double time," *Interfaces*, Vol. 9, No. 5, 1979.
7. Goodwin, J. S., and Goodwin, J. C., "Operating policies for scheduling assembled products," *Decision Sciences*, Vol. 13, No. 4, 1982.

8. Grant, F. H., "Reducing voter waiting time," *Interfaces*, Vol. 10, No. 5, 1980.

9. Hammersley, J. M., and Handscomb, D. C., *Monte Carlo Methods*, New York: John Wiley and Sons, 1964.

10. Kropp, D. H., et al., *Planning of Ambulatory Health Care Settings Using Recursive Optimization-Simulation Modeling*, Technical Report 77-1, Department of Industrial Engineering, Stanford University, May 1977.

11. Naylor, T. H., et al., *Computer Simulation Techniques*, New York: John Wiley and Sons, 1966.

12. Nolan, R., and Sovereign, M., "A recursive optimization and simulation approach to analysis with an application to transportation systems," *Management Science*, Vol. 18, No. 12, 1972.

13. Perry, R. F., and Baum, R. F., "Resource allocation and scheduling for a radiology department," *Cost Control in Hospitals*, Ann Arbor, Michigan: Health Administration Press, 1976.

14. Perry, R. F., and Hoover S. V., "Simulation-aided design for an automated storage/retrieval/delivery system," *Proceedings of the 1983 Summer Computer Simulation Conference*, Vancouver, B. C., Canada.

15. *The Random House Dictionary of the English Language*, Unabridged Edition, New York: Random House, 1969.

16. Roberts, N., et al., *Introduction to Computer Simulation: A Systems Dynamic Modeling Approach*, Reading, Mass.: Addison-Wesley, 1983.

17. Shannon, R., et al., "Operation research methodologies in industrial engineering: A survey," *AIIE Transactions*, Vol. 12, No. 4, 1980.

18. Speckhart, H., and Green, W. H., *Guide to Using CSMP (Continuous System Model Program)*, Englewood Cliffs, N. J.: Prentice-Hall, Inc., 1976.

19. Taylor, R. J., and Evans, W. F., "Showing that the low-cost route to more data processing capacity will work," *Interfaces*, Vol. 12, No. 4, 1982.

20. Thomas, G., and DeCosta, J., "A sample survey of corporate operations research," *Interfaces*, Vol. 9, No. 4, 1979.

21. Wagner, H. M., *Principles of Operations Research*, Second Edition, Englewood Cliffs, New Jersey: Prentice-Hall, Inc., 1975.

CHAPTER 2

ELEMENTS OF
SIMULATION ANALYSIS

An old proverb states that a journey of a thousand miles begins with but a single step. To paraphrase, a simulation analysis begins with a single step and must proceed methodically through several steps if useful results are to be derived and implemented. But before beginning any significant journey, it is important to know something about the route and noteworthy milestones along the way. So, this chapter serves as a guide to the process of simulation analysis which is discussed in detail in the remainder of the book, presenting a brief description and purpose for each of the steps.

2.1　INTRODUCTION

Simulation analysis is a descriptive modeling technique. As such, it does not provide the explicit problem formulation and solution steps which are an integral part of optimization models, such as linear programming. Consequently, one must specify in some detail a procedure for the development and use of simulation models to assure successful outcomes from their application. In this chapter we describe such a procedure in sufficient detail to promote an appreciation of the skills required in simulation analysis. To a great extent, this chapter provides detailed guidance for conducting a study once the necessary skills have been acquired. Subsequent chapters provide a more complete discussion of each of the steps described.

The procedure described here is similar to some found in the literature [9,13], but we feel that this set of elements or steps is a particularly useful way of viewing simulation analysis. Although the elements are presented sequentially, the procedure in reality is iterative, as we will illustrate. The elements in a simulation study are:

1. Problem Formulation

2. Data Collection and Analysis

3. Model Development

4. Model Verification and Validation

5. Model Experimentation and Optimization

6. Implementation of Simulation Results

Figure 2.1 depicts these elements and the major iterative loops. Before explaining these simulation elements in subsequent sections of the chapter, we briefly summarize the main thrust of each of them. In the Problem Formulation step, we define the questions for which answers are sought, the variables involved, and measures of system performance to be used. Data Collection and Analysis is concerned with assembling the information and data necessary to further refine our understanding of the problem. Model Development involves building and testing the model of the real system, including selecting a computer programming language, coding the model, and debugging it. In the Model Verification and Validation step, we establish that the model is an appropriately accurate representation of the real system. Model Experimentation and Optimiza-

FIGURE 2.1   ELEMENTS OF SIMULATION ANALYSIS

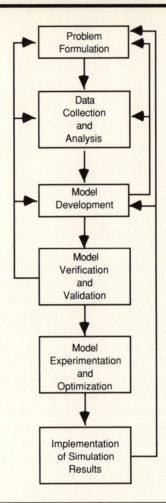

tion first treats issues of precision, such as how large a sample is necessary to estimate a system performance measure with a desired level of accuracy. Then, the design of effective experiments with which to answer the questions posed in the Problem Formulation stage is discussed. The final step, Implementation of Simulation Results, really begins early in any simulation analysis. It is concerned with ensuring acceptance of results by users and improved decision making stemming from the analysis.

2.2   PROBLEM FORMULATION

Problem formulation is, in a sense, the most important step in a simulation analysis. Appropriate solutions to inappropriately formulated problems cannot be achieved. But before a problem can be formulated, it must be identified or found. Problem finding is, in reality, choosing from among several problems which are competing for the same resources. Criteria for selection include technical, economic, and political feasibility, and the perceived urgency for a solution. Problem selection can have a significant impact on the ultimate success of the analysis and the implementation of the results. These issues are discussed further in the article by Urban [14].

A closer look at problem formulation reveals the following required tasks:

- identify decision and uncontrollable variables
- specify constraints on the decision variables
- define measures of system performance and an objective function
- develop a preliminary model structure to interrelate the system variables and the measures of performance

Each of these tasks is discussed and illustrated in the following paragraphs. In Chapter 3, the process of problem formulation is further illustrated with several detailed examples.

To explain problem formulation and subsequent steps we will use an example which is no doubt quite familiar to everyone: a supermarket checkout system consisting of several checkout lanes staffed by a cashier and possibly a bagger. The questions to be addressed deal with the effects of changes in certain staffing and operating policies on system performance. Figure 2.2 depicts the physical arrangement.

The system is entered when a customer selects a checkout queue and joins it, and it is departed when he leaves the lane after having paid for the purchases. The operations included in this system are: unloading the grocery cart (performed by the customer), tallying the purchases using a keyboard or laser scan device (performed by the cashier), paying for the purchases either by check or in cash (involving both the customer and the cashier), and the bagging of the purchases (performed either by a bagger or the cashier).

FIGURE 2.2   PHYSICAL ARRANGEMENT OF SUPERMARKET CHECKOUT SYSTEM

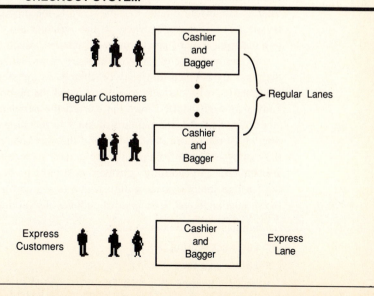

2.2.1   VARIABLES AND CONSTRAINTS

Having identified the specifics of the problem to be investigated, the first step in formulating a problem is the specification of variables that define the system and its outputs. Variables may be classified as either exogenous, or endogenous. Exogenous variables are sometimes referred to as input variables, and endogenous variables as output variables. Exogenous variables are external to the model and exist independently of the model. Endogenous variables, on the other hand, are internal to the model and are a function of the exogenous variables and the model structure. Exogenous variables can be further classified as being either controllable or uncontrollable. The former can be manipulated within some limits by the decision maker, while the latter are beyond the control of the decision maker. Controllable variables are often referred to as decision variables and uncontrollable variables are sometimes termed parameters. The designation of an exogenous variable as either controllable or uncontrollable depends to a large degree upon the resources under the control of the decision maker involved. Thus the model and subsequent analysis of the same system may be quite different depending on where in the organization the study is performed.

Returning to the supermarket example, exogenous variables for this system include:

- number of checkout lanes in the store
- number of lanes staffed with cashiers only
- number of lanes staffed with cashiers and baggers
- checkout equipment used
- policy variable designating one or more lanes as express lanes for a small number of purchases
- arrival pattern of customers
- salaries of the cashiers and the baggers

From the perspective of the store manager, the number of lanes in the store, the equipment used for checkout, the arrival pattern of the customers, and the personnel salaries are uncontrollable variables, while the others are decision variables. From the perspective of the store owner, all the variables are controllable except the arrival pattern of the customers, and perhaps the salaries, which may be fixed by union scale.

Even in the case of variables that are controllable, there are limits or constraints on the range over which they may be altered. At the store manager's level, the number of lanes staffed with cashiers may not exceed the number of lanes in the store. Also, the number of lanes staffed may not exceed the personnel available to staff them. At the store owner's level, the number of lanes in the store may not exceed some reasonable fraction of total store floor space, and the checkout equipment may not exceed in cost the money available from profits to purchase such equipment. In formulating a problem, it is important to carefully consider constraints on decision variables, since they define the feasible solution space within which to search for good or optimum solutions using the simulation model. Examples of endogenous variables in this system include:

- number of customers waiting
- customer waiting time
- cashier idle time
- bagger idle time
- customer checkout time

The first four variables must be treated as functions of the exogenous variables and the model structure, while the last may or may not be treated as such. These variables are directly a function of all the exogenous variables defined above, with the exception of personnel salaries. For example, as more lanes are staffed, waiting time will decrease and idle time will increase, all other things being equal. But, customer checkout time may be thought of as a random variable with a mean and probability distribution which can be determined during the data collection stage of the study and inserted into the model as an exogenous variable. On the other hand, checkout time may be viewed as a function of some of the exogenous variables already defined, such as the presence of a bagger and the efficiency of the checkout equipment, with some random variation. More is said about this in our discussion of which variables to include in a model and which to exclude.

2.2.2   SYSTEM PERFORMANCE MEASURES AND OBJECTIVE FUNCTIONS

To evaluate the effectiveness of a system, we must identify a measure or measures of performance by which to judge it. Measures of system performance are selected from the endogenous system variables. The measure or measures which we choose to minimize or maximize in configuring the system are referred to as the objective function. For the checkout system, we might decide that minimization of customer waiting time is a desirable measure of system performance since this provides a good perceived level of service. But what about cashier and bagger idle time? If these are excessive, costs will be noncompetitively high.

When selecting multiple measures of performance, often they cannot all be optimized simultaneously. It would seem desirable to have a system with both minimum customer waiting time and minimum cashier and bagger idle time. But, this is not possible since minimizing one tends to produce a large value for the other. There are three approaches to this dilemma: make implicit trade-offs among the measures, make explicit trade-offs by combining all of the measures using some common dimension such as cost, or select the measure of most concern to optimize while constraining the others to be within some minimum acceptable range. Use of implicit trade-offs will not be considered, since it is very subjective and can be improved upon by either of the two remaining approaches.

The techniques for making explicit trade-offs among several measures of system performance are designated as multiple-attribute or multiple-objective decision making analysis. Chapter 10 treats this topic more fully; a complete discussion of the theory behind these techniques is found in Keeney and Raiffa [4]. But, for now, a conceptual discussion will suffice. If one is fortunate, dominance may be shown for the multiple objectives. That is, one alternative system design will have values of the measures of performance which are better than, or dominate, those for all other alternatives for all measures considered. In the checkout system, a dominant configuration would have shorter customer waiting time, shorter cashier and bagger idle time, and shorter checkout time than any other configuration.

When dominance cannot be shown, which is more often the case, we must deal with the problem of combining the measures included in the objective function. To do this we must decide on a common dimension for all of the measures, weighting factors for aggregating them, and the form of the aggregating function. In the checkout example, we might use the total cost of customer waiting time and cashier idle time as the objective function. Figure 2.3 shows hypothetical cost curves as a function of the number of cashiers, and indicates the optimum range of cashiers to minimize total cost. In assigning costs to these times, idle time of employees could be assessed from salary costs, but what is a minute of customer waiting time worth? Is a linear combination of these costs appropriate? Practical difficulties such as these often lead one to focus on a single measure of performance while constraining the others.

At first consideration, the approach of optimizing only one measure of performance while constraining the others to be within acceptable ranges may appear to severely curtail the ability to achieve optimal, or at least very good solutions. However, once the constrained solution is obtained, we may relax one or more of the constraints. The decision maker can then weigh the cost of relaxing the constraint against the resulting improvement in the objective function. For example, we could strive to minimize customer waiting time while constraining cashier idle time to be less than some specified value, thus remaining competitive in service level and costs. If we permit idle time to increase beyond the specified upper limit by adding a cashier, customer waiting time will decrease. The question to be answered by the store manager is: will the increase in service level produce sufficient increased sales to more than offset its additional cost? That is, is it worth it?

2.2.3   DEVELOPING AN APPROPRIATE MODEL

The model developed thus far in this problem formulation phase includes seven exogenous variables (see the list in Section 2.2.1) to describe the checkout system. Are these sufficient to completely describe the behavior of the system? This question raises the issue of adequacy of a model. Models are abstractions of the essentials of real systems. To include all of the detail of the real system would obscure the relationships between decision variables and measures of performance which we are trying to understand. Models, however, are not right or wrong, true or false, but rather appropriate or inappropriate, sufficiently accurate or not sufficiently accurate. But how much detail is

FIGURE 2.3   COST RELATIONSHIPS FOR SUPERMARKET CHECKOUT SYSTEM

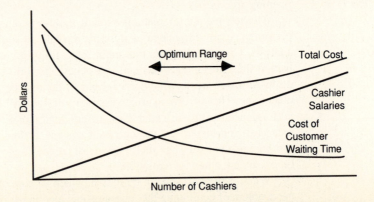

to be included in the model of a system? It depends upon the purpose for which the model is being developed and the marginal contribution of the additional detail. The first notion is easy to justify. A model being developed for a corporate strategic plan over a three year horizon need not, indeed cannot, contain very detailed production schedules for all products on all machines. On the other hand, a model to evaluate alternative production schedules to meet next week's quotas must contain a detailed description of the process including times on all machines for all products, and priority rules for different products. To discuss the marginal contribution of additional model detail, we return to the checkout system example.

We stated above that customer checkout could be treated as either an exogenous random variable with a known probability distribution, or as an endogenous variable that is a function of the presence of a bagger and the efficiency of the checkout equipment, with some random variation. Viewing checkout time as an endogenous variable would appear to lead to a more precise estimation of checkout time, but what are the exogenous variables that affect checkout time? A list of candidates would include: the number of items purchased, the experience of the cashier, the length of the queue at the checkout lane, and the disposition or mood of the cashier. These are listed more or less in order of diminishing contribution to checkout time. The number of items purchased is a variable with an obviously significant impact, but the mood of the cashier would not likely be of major importance.

When to stop including variables in a model must be based on a subjective, trial and error derived assessment of the marginal cost of obtaining the necessary data and including the required relationship in the model, versus the additional accuracy with which estimates of system performance measures can be made. The ultimate goal of any simulation model is to assist in decision making, and this must dictate the problem formulation.

When the task of problem formulation is completed, we have identified and defined decision variables, uncontrollable variables, measures of system performance, an objective function, and a preliminary model structure to relate measures of performance to decision variables. We can now turn to the problem of collecting and analyzing the data to more precisely define the developing model.

2.3   DATA COLLECTION AND ANALYSIS

Although data collection is placed second in the discussion of simulation analysis elements, it is quite likely that some data collection will have already been done to facilitate problem formulation. It is during this step, however, that the bulk of the data is collected, reduced, and analyzed to make the model more explicit. Since these topics are the subject of Chapter 6, it is our purpose here simply to give an overview of the process.

2.3.1   DATA COLLECTION

Data collection methods are as varied as the problems to which they have been applied, ranging from unsophisticated, manual approaches to very sophisticated high technology techniques. This is not accidental. The data collection method should be tailored to the particular system setting if the data are to be collected efficiently and accurately. In selecting a method, the following issues should be considered: ability to record the data quickly enough to achieve the desired level of accuracy, impact of the data collection process on the behavior of system attribute being measured, ease of conversion of the data to computer processable form, and cost of the method.

For many situations simple direct observation and manual recording of the attribute of interest will suffice. But, if it is a person being measured, often the presence of an observer may influence his behavior. Also, the action may be happening so quickly that it is not possible for a human observer to record it accurately, as in the collection of vehicular traffic data. Observers make errors even when the action is only moderately paced. Two additional shortcomings with direct observation are data conversion and cost. The traditional keypunching of data from observers' forms is error prone and slow. Selection of a better data collection medium can alleviate this problem, as we shall discuss. The cost of observers is often higher than alternative semiautomated or automated methods.

Returning to the checkout system example, suppose we desired to collect data which could be used to express the customer checkout time as a function of the number of items purchased, presence of a bagger, and experience level of the cashier. All of these data, as well as the elapsed checkout time, could be collected by direct observation, but it is unlikely that an observer could consistently record it all without error. One could take advantage of the technology already present in the checkout process itself. If a computer terminal/cash register is being used, the number of items in a customer's order is captured for inventory control and cash flow purposes. Also, using an internal computer clock, the time could be linked to employee shift assignments and thus obtain cashier experience and bagger presence. A further peripheral benefit of this approach is that the data are, for the most part, already in computer processable form.

Turning to less sophisticated automated data collection techniques, time stamping clocks could be used to track an entity through a system. This approach was used to track patients through a diagnostic radiology department [11]. The data were subsequently used to develop examination performance and film developing times. This approach requires the full cooperation of the personnel involved, and does have the drawback of requiring keyboard data entry. Keyboard entry of data can be eliminated by careful attention to the data collection medium used by the observers. For example, use of preprinted observation forms on perforated punch cards permits a punch card to be generated at the observation site. The hole next to the appropriate observation is simply removed by the observer. Alternatively, a preprinted form with provisions for darkening in a space next to the appropriate observation may be used at the site and then optically read into the computer. Other automated data collection methods include movie and video cameras, and automatic light or pressure sensing equipment.

Regardless of the method used to collect the data, the decision of how much to collect remains. In determining the sample size, a trade-off between cost and accuracy must be made. Larger sample sizes lead to more accurate estimates of population characteristics, but require more time to collect and convert to computer processable form, and therefore cost more. Statistical theory can define the precision of an estimate associated with a given size sample to permit a qualitative assessment of whether the added cost is warranted.

2.3.2   DATA ANALYSIS

Some of the data used to define models is deterministic, that is, known with certainty, but much of it is probabilistic. Given a set of probabilistic data, there are basically two ways to include it in a model: use the actual sample data to represent the probability distribution, or determine a theoretical probability distribution which is appropriately similar to the sample, and use it in the model. Often the use of an appropriate theoretical distribution is both revealing in the understanding of the system behavior and efficient in the running of the model. In Chapter 6 we discuss some statistical tests for determining whether a given probability distribution is a good fit to the sample data.

In our checkout system, the arrival pattern of customers is an example of a probabilistic variable required as a model input. To determine the time between successive arrivals at the checkout lanes in our model, we could use the actual interarrival times collected, or we could search for a theoretical probability distribution which would be a good match. Empirical evidence about systems such as this, where arrivals occur at random with no pre-scheduling, suggests that the exponential distribution is often a good fit.

At the conclusion of this step in a simulation analysis, we should be ready to proceed to model development, and produce a computer program into which we will assimilate our data and derived probability distributions. However, discoveries made while collecting data may prompt a return to the Problem Formulation step to recast the original problem.

2.4   MODEL DEVELOPMENT

In the model development step we make the description of the system being modeled explicit by quantifying the relationships among all of the variables and the performance measures. In order to develop an accurate computer program which implements our model, we must fully understand the system and all of its intricacies. In this section we discuss and illustrate approaches to achieving this level of understanding, as well as the various types of models which may be used to describe a system and the necessary tasks for model construction. In Chapter 3, we apply these concepts and techniques to build models of several systems.

2.4.1   UNDERSTANDING THE SYSTEM

Acquiring sufficient understanding of a system to develop an appropriate model is one of the most difficult tasks in a simulation analysis. Approaches for doing this vary greatly. Some are almost innate and defy clear description. We present here two commonly used objective techniques which, with practice, can be very effective: physical flow approach and state change approach.

Physical Flow Approach   To use the physical flow approach, one identifies the physical entities for which processing or transformation constitute the main purpose of the system. These entities are then tracked through the system, noting the points of processing and the branching decision rules that determine their route. A diagram of the entity flow and the system processing elements then provides the representation of the system from which the model and its associated computer program can be developed. Although not as tangible as people or products, information often may constitute a relevant entity for tracking, for example, an insurance claims processing system. Some simulation programming languages provide nearly perfect isomorphism between such a flow chart and the computer program so that when the flow chart is complete, the program is essentially done.

Although relatively simple, the checkout system example provides an instructive illustration of this approach. There are two possibilities for entities to track: customers and purchases. However, customers are the main concern, while purchases are of secondary importance. We begin tracking customers when they approach the checkout lanes. At this point a customer decides which queue to join based on some rationale such as selecting the shortest one. This decision determines the route through the remainder of the system. The customer resides in the system element designated as a checkout queue until he/she reaches the system element designated cashier. Here three processes occur: purchases are tallied, paid for, and bagged. The customer then leaves the system. Figure 2.4 depicts the flow chart for the checkout system.

State Change Approach   In order to describe the state change approach, we must define an additional endogenous variable classification, state variables, and introduce a new modeling concept, the event. State variables describe the status of the system in some meaningful way, such as the number of people in a queue or the number of people currently being served. Given the current values of state variables, coupled with exogenous variables and the model structure, one can determine the future system status. Such variables may be used in calculating measures of performance, such as customer waiting time.

An event is a particular point in time when the status of the system changes. For example, when a person arrives at the checkout lanes and joins a queue, the state vari-

FIGURE 2.4   FLOW CHART FOR SUPERMARKET CHECKOUT SYSTEM

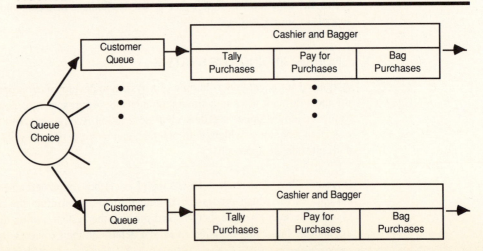

able that tracks the number of people in that queue is altered. By incorporating into the model the ability to update these variables as time advances and events occur, we can completely describe the system behavior.

For the checkout example we focus on a particular checkout lane since they are all identical in operation. The major state variables are the number of people in the system, and the number of people in each of the queues. Other state variables are concerned with the busy or idle status of the cashiers and baggers. Some events that change the status of the system, and hence the values of state variables, are an arrival to the checkout system, the selection of a queue to join, and a checkout completion and subsequent departure from the system. The model for a checkout lane must then contain a procedure to represent the arrival of customers, the checkout process, and the changing of the state variable values as events occur.

A useful approach to represent this diagrammatically is the event graph. Events are represented as nodes and progression from event to event as arrows. Figure 2.5 depicts an event graph for our supermarket checkout system. In Chapter 3 we describe how to create such a graph for any system being modeled.

2.4.2   MODEL CONSTRUCTION

With an understanding of the system and of the type of model that is to be developed, we can now turn to some issues in the actual model construction. Again, each of these issues will be treated in detail in subsequent chapters so our goal here is to provide a broad perspective of model construction. The major tasks in model construction are: (1) developing a computer program flow chart for the model; (2) selecting a programming language; (3) providing for generation of random numbers and random variates, and collection of performance measure values in the program; and (4) writing and debugging the program code.

Computer Program Flow Chart   A first step in writing the computer program is to produce a logic flow chart or block diagram. If a physical flow approach was taken to understand the system, this flow chart could be refined to evolve into the program flow chart. If the state change approach was taken, the flow chart developed should describe the procedure to accomplish changing state variables over time. Two other factors

FIGURE 2.5   EVENT GRAPH FOR SUPERMARKET CHECKOUT SYSTEM

Events

1. Customer arrives
2. Customer selects cashier
3. Cashier begins checkout
4. Cashier finishes checkout
5. Bagger begins packing
6. Bagger finishes packing
7. Customer leaves

Note: ⌣ = Conditional link

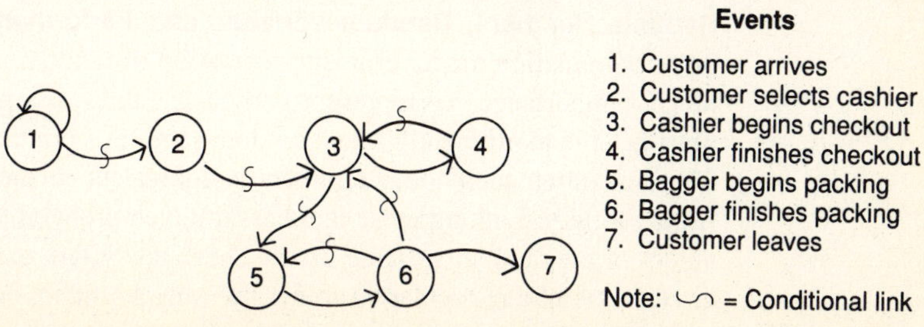

impinge on program flow chart construction: the time flow control mechanism chosen and the programming language selected.

There are fundamentally two ways to keep track of advancing time in a simulation model: fixed time step and event tracking. Each of these leads to a different logic flow chart and a different computer program. In fixed time step, the status of the model is checked after advancing some constant time increment. Any necessary changes in system variables are then made, for example the number of people in the queue, or the number being served. The simulation continues in this fashion, checking system status every time increment until a statistically determined period of time has been simulated. Using event tracking, the simulation logic notes when events, and hence changes in the system status, occur and only checks the system at these times, changing the affected variables. Note that state variables play an important role in both of these methods. Although there are some obvious advantages to the event oriented technique, discussion of the relative merits of each approach is postponed until Chapters 3 and 4.

Programming Language Selection   An increasingly large number of programming language options are becoming available for the implementation of simulation models. Prominent simulation languages include: GPSS (General Purpose Simulation System) [3], SLAM (Simulation Language for Alternative Modeling) [12], SIMAN (Simulation Analysis) [10], and SIMSCRIPT [5]. Many general purpose languages are quite adequate for simulation analysis, for example, FORTRAN, PASCAL, and BASIC. But, special purpose simulation languages provide features that make programming, debugging, and experimentation more efficient of user time and effort, although they consume more computer time in execution. Perhaps the single most important advantage of simulation languages is the correspondence of system elements to language elements. For instance, in GPSS there is a flow chart block and program statement set called QUEUE which processes entities through a waiting line and accumulates data on output variables such as waiting time in line.

It should be noted that the language selected may influence the exact form of the computer program flow chart. Some special purpose simulation languages use different flow chart block shapes to represent sets of program steps (e.g., GPSS, SLAM, and SIMAN). General purpose languages, such as FORTRAN, are the least restrictive in this regard. Thus one should actually have selected the programming language to be used before serious flow charting or block diagramming begins.

A full discussion of simulation languages for modeling and the selection of the "right" language is contained in Chapter 4.

Random Numbers, Random Variates, and Performance Statistics   In any probabilistic simulation model efficient generation of random numbers and random variates is of vital importance. To represent particular values of a probabilistic input variable, one must be able to efficiently select random samples from the given probability distribution. The generation of random numbers is equivalent to the drawing of winning numbers from a lottery. Linking these numbers to given probability distributions yields particular values of the random variable. In the checkout system example, we would determine the arrival time of a particular customer by using a random number to sample from the probability distribution of interarrival times.

Although we refer to the numbers used in the simulation for sampling as random, they are not truly random, since they are produced from a deterministic algorithm. However, the properties of the numbers produced can be made to be sufficiently close to random to make them quite serviceable for simulation analysis. If the model is programmed in a general purpose language, one must select and include in the program the algorithms necessary to generate the required random variates. But if a simulation language is used these algorithms are included and easily accessed by the user. A complete discussion of random number and random variate generating algorithms is presented in Chapter 7, and the use of such algorithms embedded in various simulation languages is covered in Chapter 4.

No matter how well devised and detailed the simulation model may be, it is all for naught if careful and complete collection of performance measure statistics is not provided to evaluate alternatives. The appropriate analogy is a very attentive spectator at a sporting event who cannot recall any of the outstanding plays, or even the final score when the event is over. Again, if the model is programmed in a general purpose language, the analyst must program in detail the collection of all performance statistics. In the checkout example we might collect information on the average waiting time at each lane, and the average idle time of all cashiers. If a more detailed picture of the system performance were desired, we might accumulate frequency tables or histograms for waiting time and idle time. To do this in a language such as FORTRAN is very tedious and time consuming. On the other hand, simulation languages permit copious statistics collection using simple program statements. Further discussion of this feature is contained in Chapter 4.

Programming and Debugging the Model   It should be evident by now that the choice of programming language pervades all aspects of model construction. Many issues discussed are resolved for better or for worse by the selection of the programming language. General purpose languages tend to leave the analyst largely to his own devices, providing little assistance in constructing a logically correct program to represent the model. Simulation languages, however, facilitate the coding of the computer program, and also possess features that ease the debugging task. But, the advantages are not all for simulation languages. This difficult choice is fully discussed in Chapter 4.

With a fully debugged program that implements the model we should now be able to consider whether the model is an appropriate representation of the real system. That is, do we have a valid model? However, at this point it may be discovered that insufficient data exist to structure the model as planned, necessitating a retreat to step 2, Data Collection and Analysis. Or, it may be decided that the model is too complex and a return to step 1, Problem Formulation, to redefine the problem, is in order.

2.5   MODEL VERIFICATION AND VALIDATION

Model verification and validation actually is concerned with three models: a conceptual model, a logical model, and a computer model. Chapter 8 defines these models and discusses several approaches for their verification and validation. Verification focuses on internal consistency of a model, while validation is concerned with the correspondence between the model and reality.

As an example, consider verifying the computer model for a queueing system. One approach is to assess output measures for appropriate behavior. Do the queues grow and diminish with the passage of time? Does the server experience both busy periods and idle periods? Notice that this is quite different from validating the overall simulation model, where the question would focus on things such as correspondence of queue sizes generated by the model with those of the real system.

A model is be said to have validity if its output measures have appropriately close correspondence to the same measures for the real system. How one defines correspondence, and determines if it is sufficient is not universally agreed upon. See, for example, Law and Kelton [6] and Shannon [13].

The ultimate test of a model's validity must be how well the model accurately predicts future events. In the checkout system example, the model should tell the store manager what the customer waiting time and cashier idle time will be if he provides cashiers for two lanes to accommodate the estimated customer arrival pattern. This is a severe test to pass, however. Consider the possible sources of error in the prediction.

First, to predict future system behavior we must predict the value of input variables. In predicting customer arrival pattern next week or next month, we experience forecast errors. During the time that elapses between the prediction and the actuality, unanticipated changes in the system could occur that would not be reflected in the model. If experienced cashiers were present when the model was developed but a large amount of turnover occurred during the prediction lead time, the model's prediction could contain a considerable error. Errors in the estimation of model input variables that do not change over time could be present. The rate at which cashiers can tally the customer purchases is a random variable which could be subject to large sampling error. Finally, the actual model structure could be incorrect.

All of these sources of prediction error are heavily confounded with each other. Any one of them could cause us to declare the model not valid, but it would be difficult to isolate the cause or causes. Therefore we are forced to seek more pragmatic, operationally feasible definitions of model validity. One such definition focuses on the correspondence of performance measures provided by the model and those exhibited by the real system. This approach to validation is illustrated in Figure 2.6. After the model is developed, we observe the real system for a period of time, collecting data for all exogenous variables and performance measures. The exogenous variables are then used as model inputs which yield performance measures from the model. A decision on model validity is based on the degree to which the performance measures produced by the model and those observed in the real system are similar.

In the checkout system, we would note the settings of the decision variables, such as the number of cashiers and the presence of baggers, and collect data on the uncontrollable input variables: arrival pattern of customers and the random variation in customer checkout time. We would also observe and collect data on performance measures such as customer waiting time and cashier idle time. Having done this for a statistically sufficient data collection period, the input variables are supplied to the model, and the computer program is run. The resulting performance measures are then compared to those observed during the study period for similarity. This comparison is discussed in detail, including applicable statistical tests, in Chapter 8.

Given a debugged, validated model of the real system, the next step is to consider how the output from such models should be interpreted. However, if we fail to demonstrate validity it may be necessary to return to the previous step of Model Development, or earlier in the simulation analysis, to make revisions that will produce a valid model.

FIGURE 2.6   AN APPROACH TO MODEL VALIDATION

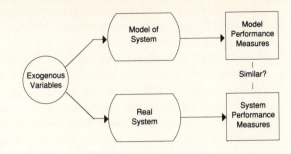

2.6   MODEL EXPERIMENTATION AND OPTIMIZATION

It is in this phase of simulation analysis that we begin to reap the benefits of the preceding arduous tasks. We can now provide answers to the questions posed when the problem was originally formulated. By evaluating alternative system designs according to the measures of performance produced by our simulation model, we can select the best, or at least a very good system design. However, the nature of simulation model outputs is such that they need the proper statistical treatment to give us valid comparisons of alternatives. We briefly describe these issues in Section 2.6.1 before covering experimental design and optimization in Section 2.6.2.

2.6.1   OUTPUT ANALYSIS

There are some aspects in the interpretation of model outputs that are unique to simulation analysis. While probabilistic analytic models provide solutions with completely defined measures of performance, simulation models yield estimates of the measures that are subject to sampling error. For example, analytic queueing results provide the population mean and variance, and exact probability distribution for measures such as number of people in the system and waiting time in the system. Simulation results contain the sample mean and variance, and the frequency distribution of waiting times in the sample. From these we must estimate the population parameters and probability distribution.

Since simulation model outputs are samples, all concerns regarding statistical inferences from samples apply here as well. The major issues in obtaining useful estimates from samples are: that the sample be representative of the typical system behavior, and that the sample size be large enough to provide some stated level of precision for the performance measure estimates. Sample size is well defined, but representative system behavior depends on the nature of the questions being asked of the model. An excellent conceptual discussion of these issues is found in Conway [2].

We can envision two types of analysis being performed with a simulation model: a terminating analysis and a steady state analysis [6]. The former analysis is designated terminating because the model run is ended by some specific event. For example, we may wish to study the checkout system from store opening to store closing with no customers present. The terminating event is the instant of time after closing when the last customer leaves. Or, we may concentrate on a peak period, say from noon to 1:00 P.M. The terminating event here is the end of the one hour interval of interest. The focus in this type of study is on aggregate system performance over the entire day, or any portion of it, and the performance measures would reflect any variability of activity level present during that time.

In steady state analysis we are interested in long run averages of performance measures after the system has passed through any transient behavior period. Steady state measures can be defined as the value of the measure in the limit, as run length approaches infinity. If our checkout system experienced a buildup of customers during the first hour of business which then remained more or less steady for the remainder of the day, a steady state analysis to determine average waiting time would be appropriate.

In both terminating and steady state analyses, the initial conditions, that is, the state of the system at the beginning of the simulation run, will influence the estimates of performance measures. In a terminating analysis of the one hour peak period referred to above, an empty system would not be a reasonable expectation of initial conditions in reality. To make the sample obtained representative we must approximate the actual conditions at noon before we begin data collection in the model run.The initialization, or transient behavior, period for a system initialized as empty does not produce typical or long-run average values of a performance measure. To obtain good steady state estimates we must either eliminate this period or diminish its effect on the estimates. Chapter 9 discusses alternative approaches to this problem.

Sample size is important since the precision of estimates is dependent upon the variance of the sample mean, and the variance changes inversely with the sample size. If the size of a sample is quadrupled, the standard deviation will be halved. The definition of the sample size for a simulation analysis is dependent upon the type of analysis being performed. For a terminating analysis one would replicate the period of interest, beginning with appropriate initial conditions, a sufficient number of times to achieve the desired precision of estimate. Each replication would be one point in a random sample. With a steady state analysis the sample size is closely tied to the model run length or the amount of simulated time. For instance, a sample size of 400 customers where the average arrival rate to the checkout lanes is 0.5 customers per minute is equivalent to a run length of 800 minutes. This time period may not include the initialization period. Whether the run length is treated as one sample point or divided into many sample points is one of several statistical issues reserved for discussion in Chapter 9.

2.6.2 MODEL EXPERIMENTS

Having dealt with the foregoing preliminaries, we may now turn to the ultimate purpose of model experimentation: to derive information about system behavior helpful in decision making. When considering system performance we may wish to know how well a system behaves in an absolute sense, or comparatively, in contrast with one or more alternative system configurations. We may focus on one measure of performance, or wish to consider several simultaneously. For example, in staffing the checkout system we could compare average customer waiting time for four, five, or six lanes staffed. And, we might vary the ratio of cashiers to baggers for each of those staffing levels. Or, both customer waiting time and cashier idle time may be of concern and we would wish to deal with both measures simultaneously.

It should be evident from these proposed experiments with the checkout system model that the number of possibilities for exploration can become extremely large, very quickly. Even for modest experimental designs, enumeration of all possible solutions is not recommended nor feasible in searching for the best, or very good solutions. Consequently we need a more directed, structured approach to seeking worthwhile solutions. We will consider two different approaches to this problem: predetermined sets of experiments and optimum-seeking techniques.

The first approach is that of classical experimental design, which is so predominantly illustrated in the literature with corn plants and alternatively fertilized and watered plots. Essentially, the approach entails identifying treatments or factors which would affect some output measure, and performing the experiment with the factors set at particular values or combinations of values. Statistical techniques, often referred to as analysis of variance (ANOVA), are then applied to discern whether the factor or factors selected have any impact on the output measure. The output measures of simulation analyses can be adapted so that the statistical assumptions of this technique are reasonably well-satisfied, and therefore it can be applied in model experimentation by considering the factors to be the decision variables in the model. A good description of the philosophy of this approach may be found in Cox [1].

A particularly general experimental design is the factorial design. In it, two or more factors are considered with each being set at two or more levels. In the checkout system experiment described, we defined two factors: number of cashiers and the ratio of cashiers to baggers. One could set each of these factors at three levels, and conduct the experiment using total cost of customer waiting time plus employee idle time as the measure of performance. To provide the data for this design the model would be run nine times for some specified run length. The ANOVA would then be used to determine if these decision variables made a statistically significant impact on total cost and which combination of factors produced the lowest cost.

The use of a predetermined set of model experiments is effective in identifying good solutions if one can approximate the region of optimality from previous experimentation or experience with the problem. However, this technique cannot lead one toward an overall best solution (a global optimum), nor can it even guarantee one of several very good solutions (a local optimum). There are iterative techniques, however, which produce local optima. These techniques cannot guarantee a global optimum, but each successive solution is as good or better than the previous one.

A useful set of optimum-seeking techniques is referred to as response surface methodology (RSM). The response surface is the function that describes the relationship of a performance measure to the factors or decision variables. A two factor experiment defines a surface in three dimensions which may be thought of as terrain to be climbed. In fact, the two dimensional representation of the response surface looks much like contour lines on a topographic map, as illustrated in Figure 2.7. By using various strategies one can reach high points in the terrain, and perhaps even the summit. One fruitful strategem is the method of steepest ascent. It requires that sufficient model runs be made to determine which direction (changes in decision variable values) seems to yield the greatest increase in altitude (increase in the performance measure). The decision variables are changed accordingly, and the process continues until one can go no higher. At this point a local or global optima has been achieved. Discussions of the concepts of optimum-seeking and RSM techniques are found in Wilde [15] and Myers [8]. Detailed treatment of optimum-seeking methods, including RSM approaches, is contained in Chapter 10.

To illustrate with the checkout system, start with values for cashiers and cashier to bagger ratio both at the low end of their ranges and explore the surrounding terrain. Since we seek to minimize cost, the appropriate analogy is to select the direction of steepest descent on each iteration until a low or lowest point in a valley is reached.

2.7 IMPLEMENTATION OF SIMULATION RESULTS

At this point we have concluded all of the steps in the simulation analysis dealing with the creation and experimentation with the model. All that remains is the implementation of the chosen solution. This final step is at once the most important and the most neglected one in the entire procedure. It should be obvious that the benefits of a lengthy and costly analysis will not be realized without proper implementation and acceptance by the users. Since it is last chronologically, it is often the case that implementation is not thought about, or dealt with until the final solution has been developed. An ever growing body of empirical evidence suggests that this approach will almost assure failure.

We review in this section some of the reasons for implementation difficulties and suggest possible strategies for successful efforts. In Chapter 11 we pursue these topics in more detail, to better understand implementation and how it is viewed by all participants—simulation analysts, managers, and the users themselves.

Reasons for unsuccessful implementation efforts often include the following: a communications gap, or the inability of users and managers to understand the technical jargon of the analyst; the undertaking of implementation too late in the analysis procedure; and resistance to change, or a lack of coincidence of personal and organizational objectives. In dealing with these potential obstructions, the general approach is adapted from techniques used in developing and implementing information systems, namely treating the entire project as a change process and viewing the analyst as a change agent [7]. This approach requires full involvement of users and analysts from the inception of the simulation analysis project.

FIGURE 2.7   RESPONSE SURFACE FOR TWO DECISION VARIABLES

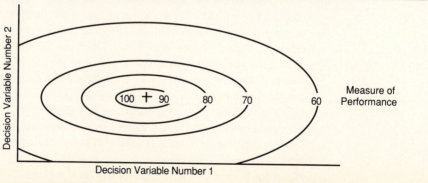

2.8 CONCLUSION

In this chapter we have defined the necessary steps in the conduct of a simulation analysis as:

1. Problem Formulation

2. Data Collection and Analysis

3. Model Development

4. Model Verification and Validation

5. Model Experimentation and Optimization

6. Implementation

This broad overview was presented so that the reader may grasp the scope of such analyses. Also, the chapter provides a framework into which to integrate the more detailed coverage of these topics as it is presented in subsequent chapters. Finally, the chapter may serve as a detailed guide for the analyst in conducting simulation studies when the necessary skills have been acquired.

EXERCISES

2.1 For each of the following systems, execute the tasks specified in the Problem Formulation step of a simulation analysis, namely: Specify the question to be investigated by the study, identify decision and uncontrollable variables, specify constraints on the decision variables, define measures of system performance, define an objective function, and suggest a relationship between the measures of performance and the variables.

  a) A two-island gas station (two pumps per island) with one attendant

  b) A single elevator in a five-story building

  c) A traffic control signal system at the intersection of two streets (traffic flows in four directions)

  d) A police patrol beat where cars follow predetermined routes when not responding to calls

  e) An ambulance service with four ambulances which are in stationary locations while awaiting calls

  f) An ambulatory care health clinic with several different medical specialties and ancillary services, such as radiology and clinical laboratory

  g) A man-paced, progressive assembly line for light-weight, small products

  h) A time-shared, multi-user computer system consisting of many terminals, a high-speed disk, and a processor

2.2 For each of the systems described in Exercise 2.1, suggest an appropriate method of data collection, justify it, and describe how you would execute it.

2.3 For each of the systems described in Exercise 2.1, use the physical flow approach to describe the system. In each case, identify the entity or entities to be tracked and construct a block diagram to indicate the route or routes through the system.

2.4 For each of the systems described in Exercise 2.1, define state variables and events that would be useful in developing the simulation model.

REFERENCES

1. Cox, D. R., *Planning of Experiments*, New York: John Wiley and Sons, 1958.
2. Conway, R. W., "Some tactical problems in digital simulation," *Management Science*, Vol. 10, No. 1, 1963.
3. Gordon, G., *The Application of GPSS V to Discrete System Simulation*, Englewood Cliffs, N. J.: Prentice-Hall, Inc., 1975.
4. Keeney, R. L., and Raiffa, H., *Decisions with Multiple Objectives: Preferences and Value Tradeoffs*, New York: John Wiley and Sons, 1976.
5. Kiviat, P. J., et al., *The SIMSCRIPT II Programmming Language*, Englewood Cliffs, N. J.: Prentice-Hall, Inc., 1969.
6. Law, A. M., and Kelton, W. D., *Simulation Modeling and Analysis*, New York: McGraw-Hill Book Company, 1982.
7. Lucas, H., *Toward Creative Systems Design*, New York: Columbia University Press, 1974.
8. Myers, R. H., *Response Surface Methodology*, Boston: Allyn and Bacon, 1971.
9. Nance, R., "Model representation in discrete event simulation: The conical methodology," Technical Report CS81003-R, Department of Computer Science, Virginia Polytechnic Institute and State University, March 1981.
10. Pegden, C. D., *Introduction to SIMAN*, State College, Penn.: Systems Modeling Corp., 1982.
11. Perry, R. F., and Baum, R. F., "Resource allocation and scheduling for a radiology department," *Cost Control in Hospitals*, Ann Arbor, Michigan: Health Administration Press, 1976.
12. Pritsker, A. A., and Pegden, C. D., *Introduction to Simulation and SLAM*, West Lafayette, Indiana: Systems Publishing Corp., 1979.
13. Shannon, R. E., *Systems Simulation: The Art and Science*, Englewood Cliffs, N. J.: Prentice-Hall, Inc., 1975.
14. Urban, G., "Building models for decision makers," *Interfaces*, Vol. 4, No. 3, 1974.
15. Wilde, D. J., *Optimum Seeking Methods*, Englewood Cliffs, N. J.: Prentice-Hall, Inc., 1964.

PART II

MODELING AND SIMULATION

CHAPTER **3**

DEVELOPING SIMULATION MODELS

Models have been used for centuries to better understand the world around us. One of the simplest but perhaps most consequential models is a sphere with labeled land masses and oceans being used to represent the earth. The construction of such physical models is comparatively easy. When building models of less tangible and more complex systems, the relationships between the elements are far less obvious than the positions of continents and oceans. For example, in a supermarket checkout line, exactly what factors determine how long we wait? Which factor or factors will most improve the situation? These are some of the questions our models must be able to answer.

3.1 INTRODUCTION

Our purpose in this chapter is to illustrate the process of modeling simple systems such that they can be analyzed using discrete-event simulation. With the general understanding of simulation analysis provided by Chapters 1 and 2, we are now ready to illustrate the technique using some specific examples. All aspects of modeling are discussed: formulating the simulation model based on the description of the real system, sampling from probability distributions of model variables, coding the model using two common simulation time-control approaches, and using equivalent analytic model results to assess the precision of estimates derived from simulation results.

We begin with a static model, the classic Buffon Needle problem, which is used to illustrate the modeling of a simple system and to focus on the random sampling aspects of simulation analysis. We then turn our attention to discrete event systems that are dynamic, that is, the values of state variables change over time. Starting with a simplified, generic, single-server queuing system, we progress to an inventory system, and finally, to a time-shared computer system. Several models of this system are developed, including an analytic queuing model. The assumptions of the analytic model are relaxed and a more general, realistic model is developed, pointing out the flexibility of simulation models.

Finally, certain programming considerations are presented, including the mechanism for advancing time and event management, and scheduling. Several types of data structures which are particularly useful in the construction of efficient simulation models are presented.

3.2 A SIMPLE SIMULATION MODEL

A simulation model must reflect the most important features of the real system. How to construct such a model is often not obvious. To introduce the process of modeling, the classic Buffon needle problem of probability theory was chosen [1]. The physical aspects of this experiment are easy to represent in a simulation model and, since a theoretical solution exists, we can consider the precision of the estimates obtained by the model. Thus Buffon's needle provides a good vehicle for introducing both modeling and the random sampling that is necessary for probabilistic simulations. An interesting aspect of this experiment is that it provides a way of empirically estimating the value of the constant, π. We shall see how this is done when we present the theoretical solution.

3.2.1 A SIMULATED EXPERIMENT

In Buffon's needle experiment, a needle of length l is dropped at random onto a plane ruled with a series of parallel lines a distance d apart, which might be represented by a plank floor (see Fig. 3.1). To facilitate the theoretical solution, the length of the needle is constrained to be equal to or less than the distance d. If this experiment is performed repeatedly, an estimate of the probability of the needle touching or intersecting a line, P, can be obtained from the ratio of the number of trials on which a line was touched or intersected, NI, to the total number of trials, NT, as: $P = NI/NT$. From this procedure we can see that Buffon's needle experiment is an example of a Monte Carlo simulation, as defined in Chapter 1, since we are using random numbers and random sampling to approximate the outcome.

To simulate this experiment, we must be able to locate the position of the needle randomly, relative to the parallel lines. If a physical experiment were performed, this would present no problem because we could simply drop the needle, observe where it landed and note whether it intersected any lines. But how can we concisely express this in computer code for our simulation? A little thought reveals that to fix the position of the needle uniquely, we need only the location of a specified point on the needle, say the midpoint m and the angle θ, which the needle makes with the parallel lines. To accomplish random positioning, these variables are treated as random variables that are uniformly distributed.

Before making this procedure specific, it is helpful to reduce the physical sample space, and thus, the range of the variables that must be considered. We need only consider one "plank" or two parallel lines, since all other lines merely duplicate this situation. Once the location of the midpoint m has been fixed, we must determine which of the two lines it is closest to, since the needle would have the greater chance of touching or intersecting that line. But the random positioning is symmetric, therefore, we need only consider one-half the distance between lines. Thus a, the distance from m to the line, is a random variable uniformly distributed over the range 0 to $d/2$. Also, because of

FIGURE 3.1   BUFFON NEEDLE EXPERIMENT

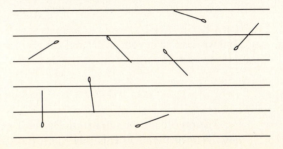

FIGURE 3.2   REDUCED PHYSICAL SAMPLE SPACE FOR SIMULATION OF BUFFON NEEDLE EXPERIMENT

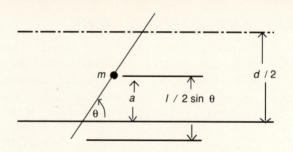

symmetry, θ is a random variable uniformly distributed over the range 0 to π radians (see Fig. 3.2).

Given randomly-determined a and θ, the method of deciding if the needle touches or intersects the line is as follows. Calculate the vertical projection of the distance from m to the end of the needle as $(l/2)\sin\theta$, and compare to the distance a. If $a \le (l/2)\sin\theta$, the needle touches or intersects the line, as shown in Fig. 3.2. If $a > (l/2)\sin\theta$, the needle does not intersect. To complete the model development, we must specify a means of randomly selecting values of a and θ.

When selecting a random sample for experimental purposes, random numbers are often mapped into the items to be sampled. For example, from a set of 1000 checking accounts, a sample of 50 is to be audited. If we assign the numbers 1 to 1000 to the accounts and arbitrarily select 50 random numbers from a random number table with a range from 1 to 1000, we will have the desired sample. In simulation analysis, this is the approach taken, except that it is cumbersome to store random number tables. Efficient algorithms have been developed to produce pseudo-random numbers with properties that resemble very closely those of true random numbers. (See Chapter 7 for further discussion of this topic.)

To obtain random samples of a and θ, it is convenient to use pseudo-random numbers, r, such that $0 \le r \le 1$. Then we can define values of a and θ for particular trials of the experiment as:

$$a = (d/2)\, r$$

$$\theta = \pi\, r.$$

And we have achieved the desired ranges of a and θ as:

$$0 \le a \le d/2$$

$$0 \le \theta \le \pi.$$

The procedure for simulating Buffon's needle problem can now be specified in the flow chart of Fig. 3.3. This procedure was programmed in FORTRAN and 3000 trials were run for a needle length, $l = 10$, and a distance between lines, $d = 20$. The source code appears in Appendix 3A of this chapter. The results of the simulation provide an

FIGURE 3.3   FLOW CHART FOR BUFFON NEEDLE EXPERIMENT

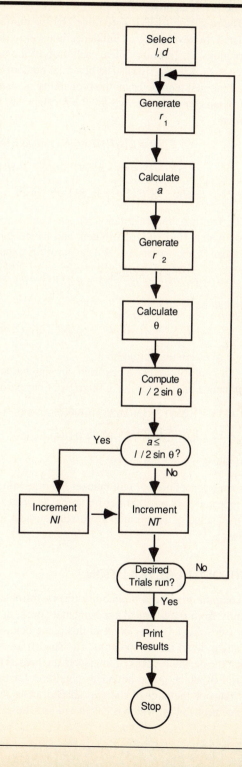

estimate of the probability of touching or intersecting the line, P, as 0.3133. But how accurate is this estimate?

The precision for P is determined by the number of trials of the experiment that are simulated. In developing a confidence interval to determine this precision, the following observations are relevant. Since each drop of the needle is a Bernoulli trial, the number of successes, NI, in NT trials is a binomial random variable, and $P = NI/NT$ is an estimate of the binomial parameter, p, the probability of success. Using the conventional notation for a parameter estimate, we let $P = \hat{p}$. Then, we may make the following probability statements:

$$E[\hat{p}] = E[NI/NT] = p \quad \text{since } E[NI] = p \times NT$$

$$VAR[\hat{p}] = p(1-p)/NT \text{ since } \quad VAR[NI] = NT \times p(1-p)$$

$$\text{and} \quad Z = (\hat{p} - p)/(p(1-p)/NT)^{\frac{1}{2}}.$$

To facilitate the calculation of our confidence interval, we may assume that $\hat{p}$ is approximately normally distributed, and hence Z is assumed to be normally distributed with mean 0, and variance 1. We can now write the following probability statement:

$$P[-Z_{.025} \le (\hat{p} - p)/(p(1-p)/NT)^{\frac{1}{2}} \le Z_{.025}] = 0.95$$

which can be written as:

$$P[\hat{p} - Z_{.025}(\hat{p}(1-\hat{p})/NT)^{\frac{1}{2}} \le p \le \hat{p} + Z_{.025}(\hat{p}(1-\hat{p})/NT)^{\frac{1}{2}}] = 0.95$$

using $\hat{p}$ to estimate p throughout.

If we substitute the values from our simulation into this expression we may compute a confidence interval for the 3000 trials of our particular experiment as:

$$P[0.3133 - 1.96(0.3133(0.6867)/3000) \le p \le 0.3133 + 1.96(0.3133(0.6867)/3000)] = 0.95$$

$$P[0.3133 - 0.0166 \le p \le 0.3133 + 0.0166] = 0.95$$

$$P[0.2967 \le p \le 0.3299] = 0.95.$$

This confidence interval will bracket the true value of p 95 percent of the time when we run repeated sets of 3000 needle drops. However, for this experiment we can compute the true value of p, to compare to our estimate, using probability theory, as explained below.

3.2.2 A THEORETICAL SOLUTION

To compute p using a probability-theory formulation, the sample space is defined differently from the physical experimental space, as a rectangle d units wide by π radians long (see Fig. 3.4). Any point in this plane defines a unique needle position in terms of the angle θ and the midpoint m. The shaded areas of Fig. 3.4 define those positions for which the needle touches or intersects the lines. The curve is described by the expression $(l/2)\sin\theta$, which is the boundary condition for the needle point to just touch the lines. The ratio of the sum of the two shaded areas to the area of the rectangle is then the desired probability, which is calculated as follows:

$$p = 2 \int_0^\pi \frac{(l/2)\sin\theta \; d\theta}{\pi \, d}$$

$$= \frac{2\,l}{\pi \, d}.$$

Two things are obvious from this solution. First, it is clear that one's intuitive guess that the probability of intersecting a line increases as the ratio of l/d increases, is indeed correct. That is, the longer the needle relative to the width of the planks of the floor, the more likely it is to touch or cross a crack between planks. Second, by repeating this experiment a large number of times, we may estimate the value of the constant π from the equation:

$$\pi = 2\,l/pd$$

where l and d are given, and p is estimated from NI/NT.

An enlightening graph can be plotted using the simulation results and the theoretical probability. As can be seen in Fig. 3.5, as the number of trials increases, the estimate $\hat{p}$ approaches the theoretical value. Also, the confidence interval widths decrease with increasing numbers of trials. The data is from the example cited above, with $l = 10$, $d = 20$, and $p = 0.3183$. With a plot of this type, we can consider trade-offs between simulation run time and precision of estimates in a rudimentary way. Further discussion of this important topic is contained in Chapter 9, Output Analysis.

In this section, we have introduced the notions of modeling and random sampling in simulation analysis using a very simple, real world system. In subsequent sections of this chapter, more complex real systems are modeled, converted to computer programs, and simulated to further illustrate this approach to problem solving.

**FIGURE 3.4   SAMPLE SPACE FOR ANALYTIC SOLUTION OF
                              BUFFON NEEDLE EXPERIMENT**

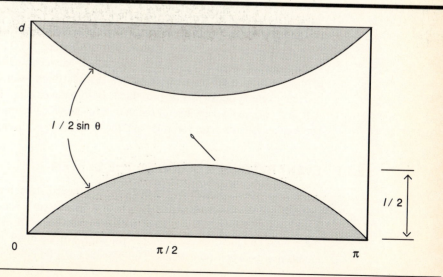

**FIGURE 3.5   PROBABILITY OF INTERSECTION WITH
INCREASING NUMBER OF TRIALS**

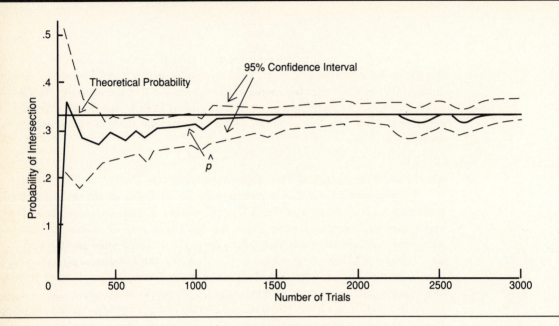

3.3   DYNAMIC DISCRETE-EVENT MODELING

The Buffon Needle simulation was a static discrete-event simulation in the sense that it consisted of a series of random events with each event unaffected by the prior events. The passage of time was not part of the simulation. The dropping of the needle was replicated again and again, giving better and better estimates of the probability of the needle intersecting the line, but the simulation would have been the same if 3000 needles were dropped all at once or if one needle was dropped 3000 times. More often than not, simulations are dynamic, in that the interaction between random events and the passage of time is part of the simulation. In this section, three examples of modeling dynamic discrete-event systems will be presented. Before developing these models, however, we will first consider a very useful technique for graphically representing the relationships between a system's state variables and the occurrence of discrete events.

3.3.1   EVENT REPRESENTATION OF THE SYSTEM

A discrete-event simulation model can be viewed as a model of the interaction of discrete events occurring in the system and the system's state variables. These interactions can be represented as a graph with the nodes (or vertices) of the graph representing the events, and the directed branches (or edges) of the graph representing a direct causal connection between two events. The branches can be either conditional, indicating that the event will occur only when certain conditions hold, or unconditional. We will use the following symbols to construct the graph.

Event *i*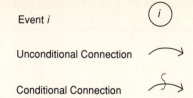

Unconditional Connection

Conditional Connection

If the branch connecting two events is a broken line it implies that the occurrence of one event may lead to the cancellation of another event. If there is a time delay between two connected events, the delay is shown on the branch between the two events. If the occurrence of an event is conditional, reference to the necessary conditions are shown on the connecting branch. For example,

implies that event *i* will lead to event *j*, after a delay of *t*, provided condition 1 holds. A more complete development of this method of representing the conceptual model can be found in Schruben [4].

As an example of representing a discrete-event system as an event graph, consider a collection of machines being attended by a group of operators. Every so often a machine breaks down and needs to be serviced by an operator. After the operator has serviced the machine, it starts up again. Here, the state variables of the system are:

$M(i)$ the status of machine *i*
        0 = waiting for service
        1 = being serviced
        2 = running

$O(j)$ the status of operator *j*
        0 = idle
        1 = busy

The discrete events that occur are:

$1(i)$ Machine i requests service
        $M(i)$ set to 0

$2(ij)$ Operator j begins to service Machine i
        $M(i)$ set to 1
        $O(j)$ set to 1

$3(ij)$ Operator j completes service on Machine i
        $O(j)$ set to 0

$4(i)$ Machine i starts to run
        $M(i)$ set to 2

The conditions are:

$C(1)$:   Some $O(j) = 0$ (an operator is idle)
$C(2)$:   Some $M(i) = 0$ (a machine is waiting)

**FIGURE 3.6   EVENT GRAPH REPRESENTATION OF
MACHINE ATTENDANCE SYSTEM**

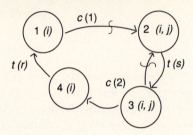

The delays in the occurrence between events are

$t(r)$:   The time a machine runs between calls for service

$t(s)$:   The time required to service a machine

The event graph representation of this system is shown in Fig. 3.6.

From this graph we see that when a machine needs to be serviced, the service will begin, conditional on an operator being available. Similarly, the graph shows that when an operator completes service on one machine, a service-initiation event will occur if any machine is waiting.

When developing event graphs, we should bear in mind that each system does not have a unique event-graph representation. Rather, the event graph serves as a method of identifying the relationships between the state variables and discrete events within a system.

3.3.2   A MODEL OF A SINGLE-SERVER QUEUE

As our first example of a simulation model of a dynamic-discrete event system, consider a system in which customers arrive at random points of time and are processed by a server. If, upon arrival, a customer finds the server is available, service commences immediately, but if the server is processing a previous arrival, the customer must "queue up" and wait until the server is available. Examples of such systems are numerous, including the customer checkout system described in Chapter 2, sales of tickets at a theater box office, requests for disk I/O in a computer system, and jobs arriving at a special-purpose machine.

In this initial attempt at discrete-event simulation we will take a "pencil and paper" approach to simulating this system. The time each customer arrives and the associated processing time is tabulated in Table 3.1. All times are assumed to be in minutes.

The event graph representation of this system is:

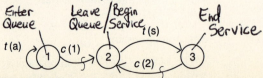

TABLE 3.1
ARRIVAL TIMES AND SERVICE TIMES $t(a)$ $t(s)$

Arrival	Time of Arrival	Wait Until Next Arrival	Length of Service
1	4	6	3
2	10	3	5
3	13	6	6
4	19	1	4
5	20	9	7
6	29	2	3
7	31	3	6
8	34	9	7
9	43	4	2
10	47	4	6
11	51	7	3
12	58	5	8

where

STATE VARIABLE

n = number of customers in the system
(waiting or being serviced)

EVENTS

1   customer arrival
2   service begins
3   service completed

CONDITIONS

$C(1)$: $n = 0$
$C(2)$: $n > 0$

DELAYS

$t(a)$ = time until next arrival
$t(s)$ = time to service a customer

To simulate this sequence of arrivals and service, we need to keep track of how the state of the system, defined as the number of customers in the system (including the customers being serviced and any customers waiting), changes over time. Two discrete events will cause an instantaneous change in the state of the system. Event 1, an arrival, causes the state to increase by one and Event 3, a service, will cause the state of the system to decrease by one. Notice that Event 2, the start of service, does not cause the state variable, n, to change. If, however, we were to add a new state variable, n_q, defined as the number of customers waiting, then Event 2 would also cause a change in a state variable. For the example data in Table 3.1, the value of our state variable, the number of customers in the system, is shown in Table 3.2 and Fig. 3.7.

TABLE 3.2
STATE VARIABLE $n(t)$

Time	Event	No. in System After Event
4	arrival of customer 1	1
4	service begins for customer 1	1
7	service complete on customer 1	0
10	arrival of customer 2	1
10	service begins for customer 2	1
13	arrival of customer 3	2
15	service complete on customer 2	1
15	service begins on customer 3	1
19	arrival of customer 4	2
20	arrival of customer 5	3
21	service complete on customer 3	2
21	service begins for customer 4	2
25	service complete on customer 4	1
25	service begins for customer 5	1
29	arrival of customer 6	2
31	arrival of customer 7	3
32	service complete on customer 5	2
32	service begins for customer 6	2
34	arrival of customer 8	3
35	service complete on customer 6	2
35	service begins for customer 7	2
41	service complete on customer 7	1
41	service begins for customer 8	1
43	arrival of customer 9	2
47	arrival of customer 10	3
48	service complete on customer 8	2
48	service begins for customer 9	2
50	service complete on customer 9	1
50	service begins for customer 10	1
51	arrival of customer 11	2
56	service complete on customer 10	1
56	service begins for customer 11	1
58	arrival of customer 12	2
59	service complete on customer 11	1
59	service begins for customer 12	1

FIGURE 3.7   PROFILE OF CUSTOMERS IN THE SYSTEM

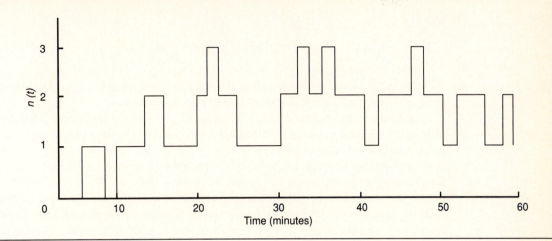

In a manner similar to the Buffon Needle simulation, we can conduct a simulation of the arrivals and service over a 60-minute interval and estimate properties of the system, such as the mean number of customers in the system and the mean time a customer spends in the system. The area under the profile of the number of customers in the system (Fig. 3.7) represents the number of minutes all customers spend in the system. If we divide this quantity by the number of customers who entered the system, we have an estimate of the mean time a single customer spends in the system. Similarly, if we divide the number of customer minutes by the length of the simulation, we have an estimate of the mean number of customers in the system. More formally:

let $n(t)$ = number of customers in the system at time t
k = number of arrivals
T = length of the simulation
$\bar{n}$ = mean number of customers in the system
$\bar{w}$ = mean time a customer is in the system

then

$$\bar{n} = \frac{1}{T}\int_0^T n(t)\,dt$$

$$\bar{w} = \frac{1}{k}\int_0^T n(t)\,dt$$

where the integral operation is equivalent to measuring the area under the profile of the state variable, $n(t)$.

If the demand for service does not exceed the capacity for service, it can be shown that under very general circumstances, the following hold [3]:

$$\lim_{k \to \infty} \{P(\,|\,\overline{w} - E(w)\,|\,) < \varepsilon\} = 1.0$$

and

$$\lim_{T \to \infty} \{P(\,|\,\overline{n} - E(n)\,|\,) < \varepsilon\} = 1.0.$$

That is, by increasing the length of the simulation we become more and more certain that w and n will be within ε units of their expected values.

Simulations are seldom carried out using such a ''pencil and paper'' approach. Instead, the logical steps of the simulation are encoded in a computer programmed simulation model which can execute the events of the system being simulated again and again, building up very accurate estimates of the system's properties. The general logic for executing a discrete-event simulation is shown in Fig. 3.8. Before the simulation begins, the parameters of the system and simulation variables are read or initialized. After this initialization, we can begin to iteratively execute the simulation. First we must determine if the simulation is to be continued, and if not, we print out the statistical results. If execution of the simulation is to continue, we must determine the most

FIGURE 3.8   LOGIC OF SIMULATION MODELS

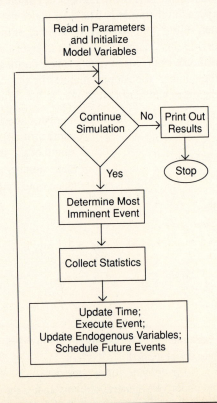

imminent discrete event and build up the time-integral of the variables on which we are collecting time integral statistics. We can now "advance the simulation clock" by setting the variable representing time to the scheduled time of occurrence of the next event. This event is then executed, updating any state variables and simulation variables (such as the count of the number of arrivals). If the occurrence of this event leads to future discrete events, these events and their time of occurrence are added to the list of future events. We now repeat this cycle, first checking if the simulation should continue.

An expansion of this overall logic to the simulation of a simple single-server queuing system is shown in Fig. 3.9. The variables used to define the model are:

N = Number of customers currently in the system

T = Current time

T_{max} = Length of time the simulation is run

T_s = Service completion time

T_a = Time of arrival of next customer

K = Total number of arrivals during simulation

TN = Time integral of N.

In this model the decision to continue the simulation is based on the length of time we have been simulating the system. We could have just as easily ended the simulation after a certain number of customers had arrived, or when the number of customers in the system reached some upper limit. In the simulation model, when the event to be executed is an arrival, the time of the next customer arrival must be added to the list of future events. Notice, however, that the length of time required to service the customer is not determined until service begins, in contrast to our "pencil and paper" approach in which each arrival carried its own service time.

If this model is properly developed, it can be used to gain a better understanding of the relationship between the customer arrival rates, service times, and the time customers wait for service, including both the mean waiting time and the distribution of waiting time. A FORTRAN implementation of the logic in Fig. 3.9 can be found in Appendix 3B.

3.3.3 AN INVENTORY MODEL

As a second example of a simulation model of a dynamic system, consider an inventory system in which a distributor maintains an inventory of a particular item, drawing off from inventory to meet customer orders. If the distributor is out of stock, the customer will seek another source for the unfilled demand, rather than wait for a back order. When the inventory falls below a certain level, the distributor orders additional inventory from the manufacturer. The distributor has an inventory policy described by the size of the replenishment order and the level of inventory, or reorder point, which triggers a new order to the manufacturer. The distributor, when selecting an inventory policy, attempts to trade off the costs of carrying inventory, C_I, costs of ordering, C_R, and penalty costs, C_P, associated with not being able to satisfy a customer's order.

Without getting into the problems of actually establishing these costs, let us assume that the distributor has found that

FIGURE 3.9   LOGIC FOR ONE-SERVER QUEUEING SYSTEM

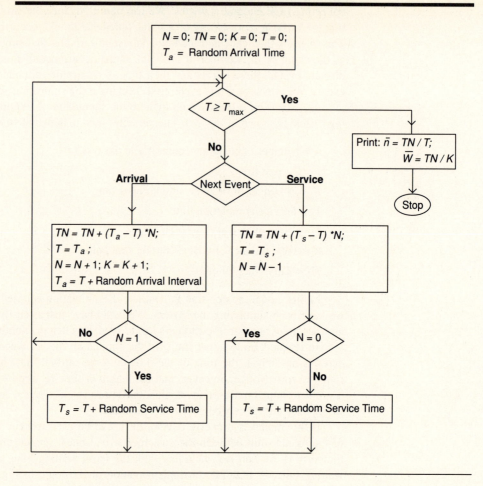

C_I = $0.40/unit/year

C_R = $5.00/order

C_P = $1.00/unit.

Each day the distributor receives orders from customers and at the end of the day takes inventory to determine if additional stock should be ordered from the manufacturer. If a customer's order cannot be completely filled, a partial order is sent out but no backordering occurs. From day to day, it is not possible to predict customer orders although the relative frequency of daily orders has been collected and is summarized in Table 3.3. Orders come in only on Monday through Friday. Although no business is conducted on Saturday or Sunday, the cost of carrying inventory is incurred on these two days as well.

If the distributor places an order to the factory, it is equally likely to arrive 4, 5, or 6

TABLE 3.3
DISTRIBUTION OF DEMAND

Daily Demand	Relative Frequency
0	0.14
1	0.27
2	0.27
3	0.18
4	0.09
5	0.05

working days later. The objective of the distributor is to minimize the total of the carrying, ordering, and penalty costs.

Simulating this system merely requires stepping through time day by day, adjusting the level of inventory (the system's state variable) to reflect customer demand and orders arriving from the factory.

The event graph representation of this system is:

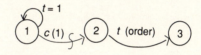

where

STATE VARIABLES

Inv = The inventory on hand
O = order placement status
    1 = A new order has been placed
    0 = A new order has not been placed

EVENTS

1   demand for item
2   item re-ordered
3   re-order arrives

CONDITION

$C(1)$: Inv less than Re-order Point and $O = 0$

DELAYS

t(order) = time until re-order arrives

A possible sequence of customer orders is shown in Table 3.4 and a plot of inventory over time is shown in Fig. 3.10.

In order to construct a computer program for the simulation model of this inventory system, we need to program the computer to step through the logic that is followed in building up Table 3.4. Figure 3.11 shows the logic necessary to simulate the inventory

TABLE 3.4
DAILY INVENTORY AND DEMAND

Day	Opening Inventory	Customer Orders	(Notes)
1	20	5	Assume day 1 is Monday
2	15	3	
3	12	2	Reorder 30 units to
4	10	4	arrive in 5 days
5	6	1	
6	5	0	Saturday
7	5	0	Sunday
8	5	2	
9	3	2	
10	1	3	Short two units
11	30	2	Order arrived
12	28	1	
13	27	0	Saturday
14	27	0	Sunday
15	27	3	
16	24	5	
17	19	4	
18	15	2	
19	13	4	

system using the variable definitions below. A FORTRAN implementation of this logic can be found in Appendix 3C.

To define this problem fully, we need the following variables.

EXOGENOUS VARIABLES—UNCONTROLLABLE

DEMAND	Current day's customer demand
C_INV	Cost of carrying one unit of inventory for one year
C_ORDER	Cost of placing an order to the manufacturer
C_PENALTY	Cost/unit of unfilled customer demand

EXOGENOUS VARIABLES—CONTROLLABLE (DECISION VARIABLES)

Q	Quantity ordered from factory
S	Reorder point

ENDOGENOUS VARIABLES—STATE VARIABLES

INV	Current inventory
T_ORDER_ARRIVE	Time the next factory order arrives
O	Order placement status

FIGURE 3.10 INVENTORY PROFILE

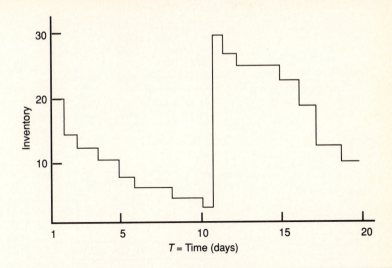

T = Time (days)

ENDOGENOUS VARIABLES—MEASURES OF PERFORMANCE

`CUM_INV`	Cumulation of inventory over time or
`CUM_LOST`	Cumulative customer orders not filled to date
`N_ORDERS`	Number of factory orders placed to date
`TOTAL_COST`	`C_INV*CUM_INV + C_ORDER*N_ORDERS + C_PENALTY*CUM_LOST`
`ANNUAL COST`	`TOTAL_COST/(T_FINAL/365)`

SIMULATION MODEL VARIABLES

`T`	Time in days, T = 1,2...
`T_FINAL`	Number of days the system is simulated

To simulate the inventory system, we would need to step through the logic shown in Fig. 3.11 and upon completion of the simulation (when `T = T_FINAL`), we would have an estimate of the measure of performance, namely, total annual cost. We could also use the simulation model to estimate other characteristics of the system such as

$$\text{Average Inventory} = \frac{1}{T}\int_0^T INV \ dt.$$

That is, the area under the inventory profile in Fig. 3.10, divided by T, gives us the average number of units in inventory. Notice how this compares to finding the average number of customers in the queuing system. Other quantities that could be found include:

$$\text{Average orders/year} = \text{N\_ORDERS}/(\text{T}/365)$$

and

$$\text{Average lost demand/year} = \text{CUM\_LOST}/(\text{T}/365).$$

FIGURE 3.11   LOGIC FOR INVENTORY SIMULATION

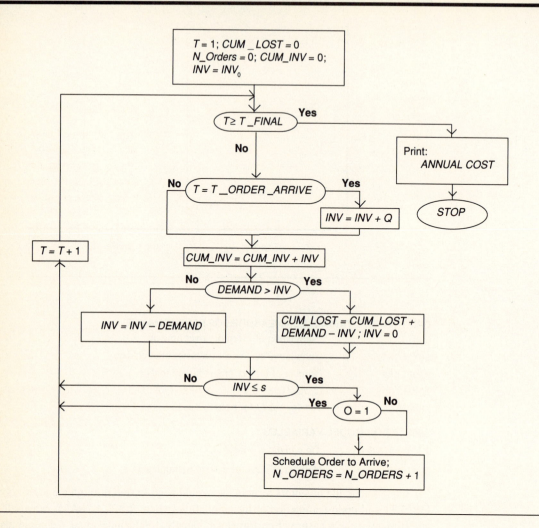

When the logic of Fig. 3.11 is implemented as a computer program and the inventory system is simulated for three years, using the above costs and inventory policy, we find that:

Average inventory = 19.25 units

Average orders/year = 20.075 orders

Average lost demand/year = 5.47 units

Average annual cost = $113.55.

This model is a good illustration of aggregating several measures of performance into a single measure with a common denominator such as dollars. The model could be used as a decision-support tool for selecting optimum inventory policies. The model could also be expanded to collect statistics on the probability of not completely filling a customer's order and the average stock on hand when an order from the factory arrives (safety stock). With this model, we could then go on to observe how the total cost and the various component costs change as we adjust the two decision variables, Q and S.

3.4   A TIME-SHARED COMPUTER SYSTEM

As a third example of a dynamic discrete-event system, consider a time-shared computer system in which users connect to the system through dial-up telephone lines. There are a limited number of ports for these dial-up connections, and if all the ports are being used when a call is placed, the user receives a busy signal and must try to make a connection at a later time. Once a connection is made, the port is unavailable to other users until the current user breaks the connection by hanging up the telephone. A schematic of the system is show in Fig. 3.12.

In order to simplify our initial analysis of this system we will assume that users attempt to connect to the computer at random times throughout the day at an average rate of 35 calls per hour.

FIGURE 3.12   TIME-SHARED COMPUTER SYSTEM

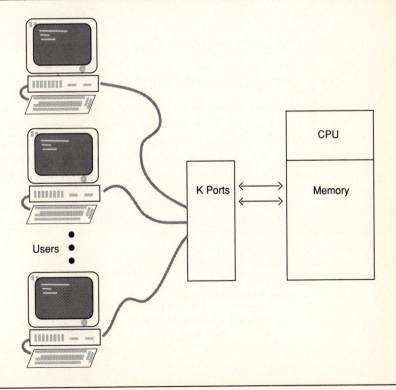

There is some historical data available on the times users connect to the system and the times at which they disconnect. An average session length, including both computing and noncomputing time is 25 minutes. Although there are currently 14 ports, it is not unusual for a user, when calling in, to find all the ports busy. There have been frequent requests to enlarge the CPU memory and to increase the number of ports and speed of transmission, in order to improve the level of service.

The ports are relatively expensive because of the hardware costs and the monthly cost of telephone service. The hardware costs for each port is approximately $4000, and the cost of telephone service and maintenance for each port is $25 per month. Further, the computer system can only support 32 ports and the computing capacity of the system is limited.

It is believed that by increasing the transmission rate between the computer system and the dial-up users from 120 cps (characters per second) to 960 cps, the session lengths could be reduced. It is believed that the average time per session could be reduced by three minutes using the higher transmission rate. Upgrading from 120 cps to 960 cps would cost $400 for each of the 100 terminals that can connect to the system.

Preliminary studies indicate that the performance of the system would improve if the CPU memory were enlarged. The effect of such an upgrade would be a more responsive session in which a user would be connected to the system for a shorter time. The CPU memory is currently 1M (million) bytes but could be expanded to either 2M bytes or 3M bytes. Table 3.5 shows the cost and reductions in connect times for 1M, 2M, and 3M bytes of memory.

In order to evaluate the utility of adding more ports, increasing the transmission speed, or adding memory, it has been suggested that the system performance and associated cost be studied with the aid of an analytic model, a simulation model or both.

3.4.1   PROBLEM FORMULATION

As discussed in Chapter 2, careful formulation of the problem is essential when modeling a system. Thus before proceeding further with the description and analysis of the system, we should stop and ask a very fundamental and important question. Namely, what do we hope to learn by constructing a simulation model of this system? What answers do we want the simulation to provide? In the two previous examples of simulation modeling, we did not explicitly raise these questions. All too often, in the practice of simulation, this critical question is not explicitly raised but, rather, some vague and general questions are in the back of the analyst's mind which, hopefully, the simulation

TABLE 3.5
MEAN COMPUTING TIME

Average Computing Time (minutes)	Cost (dollars)	Upgrade
10	0	Current configuration
8	20,000	1M-byte memory
7	30,000	2M-byte memory

model can answer. It is our experience that the success or failure of analysis using simulation models rests, to a great extent, upon how clearly the objectives of the simulation model have been stated.

We can use the simulation model to predict the system's performance as the parameters of the system change or, more desirably, we can use the simulation model to guide us in optimizing some objective, subject to certain constraints. In the former case, by trying different system configurations, we can observe measures of performance of the system. Our questions might be something like:

1. What is the probability of connecting to the system as a function of the number of terminal connections (ports)?

or

2. What is the average number of busy ports, as a function of memory, terminal connections and transmission speed?

or

3. What is the level of user satisfaction as a function of increased resources?

Many other questions could (and should) be raised, each helping the analyst to focus upon the goal of the simulation model.

Alternatively, as discussed in Chapter 2, we can state an objective function which we would like to optimize along with any constraints that must be met in order to have a feasible solution. For example, we might select as objectives and constraints any of the following:

1. Maximize (User Satisfaction)
   subject to: Total Cost of Expenditures $< C_0$

or

2. Minimize (Total Expenditures)
   subject to: User Satisfaction $> S_0$

or

3. Minimize (Mean Length of a User Session)
   subject to: Total Cost $< C_0$

or

4. Minimize (Total Cost)
   including User Costs and Resources Costs.

Several of these objectives and constraints need further clarification, which is an important step in formulating the problem. For example, for user satisfaction we need to consider both the probability that a user makes a connection on the first try and the time a user, once connected, remains on the system. For measuring the delay of users, we must consider the delay on first getting on the system and the subsequent delays, while contending with other users for the resources of the system. The expenditures on resources include the cost of additional hardware, such as memory, as well as the cost of additional connections to the system, including the monthly cost of leasing telephone lines. The costs should also include the price of maintaining the resources and reflect the expected useful life of the resources.

Without identifying clearly and early in the analysis the questions that are to be answered via the simulation model, the process of building the simulation model becomes an end in itself and the analyst can too easily lose sight of the eventual purpose of the model. Further, the detail and level of complexity of the model should reflect the eventual use of the model. The model should be no more complex or detailed than necessary to answer the questions posed at the beginning of the analysis. In later chapters, we will take up as separate topics the issues of design of simulation experiments and the analysis of output; both are very dependent upon the clarity of the questions to be answered by the simulation model.

To facilitate the formulation of the problem and subsequent model development and analysis, we should define the variables and parameters of the system.

EXOGENOUS VARIABLES—UNCONTROLLABLE

k_0 Current number of ports
$\lambda(t)$ Mean arrival rate at time t
C_T Monthly cost for each additional telephone line
C_H Hardware cost per additional port
C_U Cost of upgrading all users to 960 cps
L Expected life of hardware

EXOGENOUS VARIABLES—CONTROLLABLE (DECISION VARIABLES)

k_1 Number of additional ports
C_R Investment in additional computing resources
K Total number of ports
        $k_0 + k_1$
U Cost of upgrading users to 960 cps, C_U
        [0 if users not upgraded]
$E(T)$ Expected user connect time per session

ENDOGENOUS VARIABLES—STATE VARIABLES

$n(t)$ Number of users connected to the system at time t

ENDOGENOUS VARIABLES—MEASURES OF PERFORMANCE

TC Total annual cost
        $C_R + k_1 C_H + U/L + 12 k_1 C_T$
P_K Probability a user will attempt to connect and find all K ports occupied
P_C Probability a user will attempt to connect and find fewer than K ports occupied
        (also referred to as the Service Level)
P_C $= 1 - P_K$

Since the objective of the model being developed is to provide decision support, we must then consider the decision criteria including both our goal or the objective function and any constraints which must be met. Many possible decision criteria exist, but if we limit our choice to measures that reflect costs and level of service, we might consider such criteria as:

1. Minimize TC

2. Minimize TC
     subject to: $P_K < P_0$

3. Minimize P_K
     subject to: $TC < TC_0$

4. Minimize total system cost
>   including both the value of users' time, and the hardware and telephone costs.

The last criteria is certainly the most global, but adds several levels of complexity to the model which we may prefer to avoid at this point. Particularly difficult in this last model is the problem of determining the value of the users' time.

A reasonable criteria to settle upon would be the second candidate

$$\text{Minimize } TC$$
$$\text{subject to: } P_K < P_0$$

For the rest of this chapter we will set P_K to 0.02, and our objective will be to minimize the total annual cost, while maintaining the service level at least 0.98.

Measuring the Total Cost, TC, is straight forward since there are well defined hardware and telephone costs, but there is a problem finding P_K. The approach we will take is to model the system in such a way that P_K can be predicted for various hardware alternatives.

3.4.2   AN ANALYTIC MODEL

Before developing a simulation model of a system, one should always consider whether the system can be modeled analytically. Typically, analytic models are much less expensive to develop and use than simulation models, and even if a perfect fitting analytic model does not exist, an approximate analytic model may be very useful for analyzing the system. An analytic model may be a close enough fit to the real system that it can distinguish between alternative solutions to the problem being considered or it can assist the analyst in understanding the behavior of the more complex and detailed simulation model.

An analytic model of our time-shared system can be developed if certain assumptions are made about the behavior of the system, including:

a) The connect times are exponentially distributed random variables with a constant mean.

b) The time between calls to the system is exponentially distributed with a constant mean.

c) The effect of the initial number of users connected to the system at the beginning of the day vanishes quickly.

d) The distribution of the time between calls does not change (substantially, at least) when all ports are occupied.

These assumptions may seem to be very restrictive, but without them either it would not be possible to develop an analytic model or, if a model were developed, it would be very complex and difficult to use. When a simulation model is developed later in this section, these assumptions will be relaxed and the results of our analysis using this analytic model will be compared to the analysis using the more general simulation model.

The model we will develop is called a queueing model. In Chapter 5 a more complete treatment of this model and others like it will be presented. An excellent reference on queuing models is Kleinrock [2]. For now, however, we will restrict ourselves to only stating the equations describing the probability of 0,1,...K users connected to the system.

Let P_i = P(exactly i users connected to the system) $i = 0,1..K$

λ = 1/(mean time between arrivals)

μ = 1/(mean connect time)

then

$$P_0 = \left[\sum_{i=0}^{K} \left(\frac{\lambda}{\mu} \right)^i \Big/ i! \right]^{-1} \tag{3.1}$$

$$P_i = P_0 \left(\frac{\lambda}{\mu} \right)^i \Big/ i! \quad 1 \le i \le K. \tag{3.2}$$

In this model, P_K is the probability that all the ports will be occupied or, equivalently, the probability that a user calling into the system will not be connected. Combining equations (3.1) and (3.2)

$$P_K = \left[\left(\frac{\lambda}{\mu} \right)^K \Big/ K! \right] \Big/ \sum_{i=0}^{K} \left(\frac{\lambda}{\mu} \right)^i \Big/ i! \tag{3.3}$$

Altogether there are 108 different alternative choices (2 transmission speeds, 3 memory sizes, and up to 18 more ports). From the perspective of a queueing model, however, each alternative can be represented by the mean connect time $(1/\mu)$ and the number of ports K. Using equation (3.3), the service level P_C can then be calculated for each of the 108 alternatives. Table 3.6 shows the mean connect times for a subset of two transmission speeds and the three memory choices.

Given a particular transmission speed and memory size, the resultant cost and service level can be calculated as a function of the number of ports. In Fig. 3.13, the cost and service level for a 120 cps, 3M-byte memory system is shown as a function of the number of additional ports.

It can be seen from Fig. 3.13 that when the number of ports is increased to 19 (5 additional ports), the service level is at the required 98 percent at an annual cost of $11,500. If a similar analysis is done for each of the remaining configurations of transmission speed and memory, the queuing model would point to the optimum solution

TABLE 3.6
MEAN CONNECT TIMES

Transmission Speed (cps)	Memory		
	1M byte	2M byte	3M byte
30	25	22	20
120	22	19	17

FIGURE 3.13   TOTAL ANNUAL COST AND P_K VS. NUMBER OF ADDITIONAL PORTS

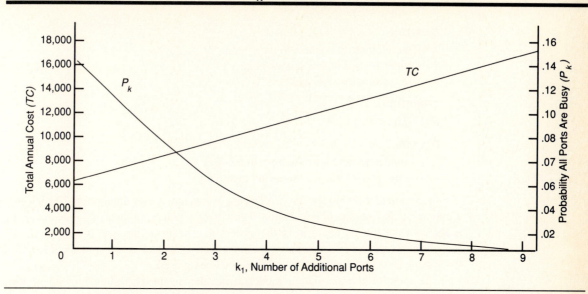

as being 20 ports with 2M memory transmitting at 120 cps costing $10,600. The achieved service level would be 0.984. That is, about 98 percent of the time a port will be available when a user attempts to connect.

It is important to remember that this solution was found using a model that made many assumptions about the system's behavior and characteristics that do not hold exactly. In the next section, a simulation model will be developed that will reflect more of the details and nature of the system.

3.4.3   A SIMULATION MODEL

As an alternative to the analytic model, we can construct a simulation model of the time-shared system. An advantage of the simulation model is that we do not need to make the assumptions we made in the analytic model. The price we must pay, however, for relaxing the assumptions is increased modeling and computational effort. The event graph representation of the system is shown in Fig. 3.14 where

FIGURE 3.14   EVENT GRAPH FOR TIME SHARED COMPUTER SYSTEM

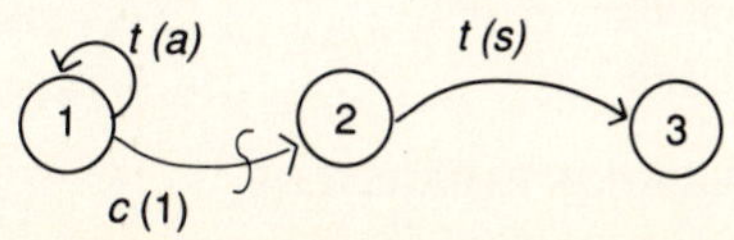

STATE VARIABLE:

$n(t)$ = The number of busy ports

EVENTS:

1   User attempts to connect to the system
2   Connection made and session begins
3   User completes a session.

CONDITION:

$C(1)$: $n(t) < K$

DELAYS:

$t(a)$ = time until next user attempts to connect
$t(s)$ = time a user remains connected to system.

In this simulation model, the two driving events are: a user attempting to connect to a port and a user completing a session. These events will be replicated again and again, along with the logical changes in the system that occur as the events take place. By recording the appropriate statistics, we can estimate P_k as well as other characteristics of the system, such as the average number of ports being used.

The logic of the simulation model, using the event scheduling method of time advance, is shown in Fig. 3.15. The variables in the model are defined as follows, and the logic of Fig. 3.15 is implemented in a FORTRAN program which can be found in Appendix 3D.

EXOGENOUS VARIABLES—UNCONTROLLABLE

MEAN_CALL_TIME	Expected time between user calls

EXOGENOUS VARIABLES—CONTROLLABLE (DECISION VARIABLES)

K	Total number of ports
MEAN_CONNECT_TIME	Expected length of user session

ENDOGENOUS VARIABLES—STATE VARIABLES

N	Number of ports currently being used
T_NEXT_CALL	Time of the next user call
T_CALL_END(I)	Time connection ends at port I
PORT_STATUS(I)	Indicates if port is busy or idle

ENDOGENOUS VARIABLES—MEASURES OF PERFORMANCE

CUM_CONNECT_TIME	Cumulation of user minutes connected to system
N_CALLS	Total number of user calls to system
N_CONNECT	Total number of calls that resulted in a connect
N_FAIL_CONNECT	Total number of calls that failed to connect
PROB_CONNECT	N_CONNECT/N_CALLS
PROB_FAIL_CONNECT	N_FAIL_CONNECT/N_CALLS
AVE_NUM_USERS	CUM_CONNECT_TIME/T_FINAL

SIMULATION PARAMETERS

T	Current time
SEED1	Random number seed for calls to system

FIGURE 3.15   LOGIC FOR TIME SHARED COMPUTER SYSTEM MODEL

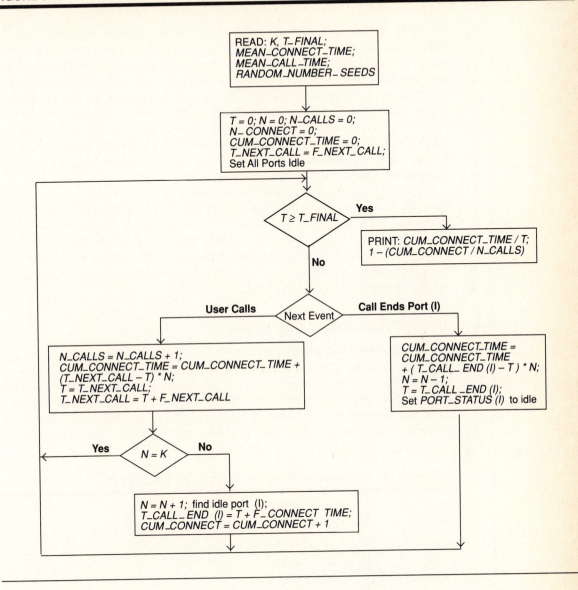

SEED2	Random number seed for connect times
T_FINAL	Length of simulation

FUNCTIONS AND SUBROUTINES

F_NEXT_CALL	Calculates the time until the next user call
F_CONNECT_TIME	Calculates the length of the user session
FREE_PORT	Locates a port that is available

NEXT_CALL_END   Locates the port with the earliest session finish

RANDOM   Returns a uniformly distributed random number (0,1).

In the simulation program, the length of time the users remain connected to the system and the times between users attempting to connect to the system are generated according to an exponential distribution. Although the simulation program could generate almost any type of random variable to represent the times between calls and connect times, by using exponentially-distributed random variables, we can compare the results of the simulation model to the analytic model. In Chapter 7, we will take up in more detail the methods of generating random variables and sampling from specific probability distributions, including the methods used in this simulation program. For now, we may simply say that the approach is to map random numbers r, $0 \leq r \leq 1$, into the exponential cumulative distribution function.

Figure 3.16 shows the progressive estimates of P_K as the length of the simulation increases. In this simulation, the mean connect time was 20 minutes (120-cps transmission speed, 3M-byte memory, and 18 ports). Using the analytic queuing model, P_K was found to be 0.022. As the length of simulation increases, the estimated value found through the simulation model appears to be converging to the analytic or theoretic value. Since both models are representations of the same system, built upon the same set of assumptions, we would certainly expect similar results!

3.4.4   AN EXPANDED SIMULATION MODEL

The advantage of a simulation model is its versatility in representing a very broad spectrum of parameters and assumptions. In our simulation model of the time-sharing system, we can relax the assumption that the distribution of the connect times and time between user calls is exponentially distributed. Even more importantly, the simulation model is capable of including many real world aspects of the problem which could not be incorporated in an analytic model. To illustrate this point let us take a more realistic

FIGURE 3.16   ESTIMATES OF P_K VS. LENGTH OF SIMULATION

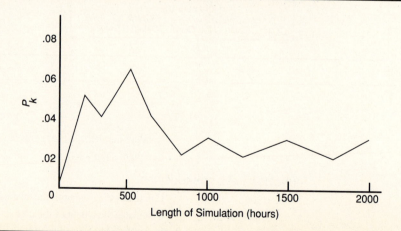

view of the rate at which users attempt to connect to the system, as well as what a user does if all the ports are occupied. We would expect that the rate at which users attempt to connect to the system to be related to the working hours of the users. Few calls would be expected before 8 a.m. and after 5 p.m. During the lunch hour, we would also expect to see a reduction in the number of users attempting to connect. Further, if a user attempts to connect to the system and fails, it is very likely that another attempt will be made a short time later. This is sometimes called "crash dialing," in that the user keeps trying to connect at a rapid rate until the connection is made or until he becomes discouraged and abandons this strategy, trying later as any other user might.

Let us assume that the mean call rate between 8 a.m. and 5 p.m. is as shown in Fig. 3.17 and that when a user fails to connect to the system, the average time until another attempt is made is 3 minutes, exponentially distributed. Let us further assume that each time a call is made and fails, the probability that the user will abandon "crash dialing" is 0.15, thereby returning to the general group of callers. Let us also assume that at the beginning of the day (8 a.m.), there are no users on the system, leaving all K ports available.

Our analytic model cannot accommodate most, if any, of these real world considerations, but it has been very useful for a first pass simplified analysis. The simulation model, however, is much more robust, and with relatively few modifications, can still be used to model the time-shared system as now described. The changes in the simulation model will include:

1. The time between calls will be generated in such a way that the mean call rate follows the call rate shown in Fig. 3.17.

2. Arrival of calls from users "crash dialing" will be included as a third type of event.

3. The model will simulate the system for 9 hours each day (8 a.m. to 5 p.m.) for more than one day, starting each day with no users connected to the system.

FIGURE 3.17   ARRIVAL RATE BETWEEN 8:00 A.M. AND 5:00 P.M.

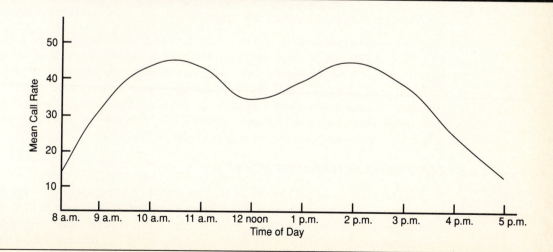

**FIGURE 3.18   EVENT GRAPH FOR EXPANDED TIME-SHARED
                COMPUTER SYSTEM**

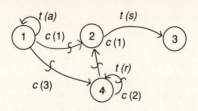

The event graph for this extended model of the time sharing system is shown in Fig.
3.18 where

STATE VARIABLES:

$n(t)$ = The number of busy ports
$m(t)$ = The number of users crash dialing

EVENTS:

1 User attempts to connect to the system
2 Connection made and session begins
3 User completes a session
4 Rejected user tries again to connect to the system

CONDITIONS:

$C(1)$: $n(t) < K$
$C(2)$: user has not tired of crash dialing
$C(3)$: $n(t) = K$

DELAYS:

$t(a)$ = Time until next user attempts to connect
$t(s)$ = Time a user remains connected to system
$t(r)$ = Time until a crash dialer tries again

The logical modifications needed to include these new assumptions is shown in Fig.
3.19. Appendix 3E lists the modified FORTRAN program and additional subroutines for
the new version of our simulation model. In order to simulate the system for 100 days,
the model should not be executed 900 hours, but rather, we should repeat the simulation
100 times, each simulation lasting 9 hours (8 a.m. to 9 p.m.). Upon doing so, we find that
P_K, the probability a user finds all K ports occupied, is 0.14. In order to reduce P_K to 0.02
or less, we would need to increase the number of ports to 22.

3.4.5 COMPARING ALTERNATIVE MODELS

We have now developed three models of our time-shared system. Each model was used
to solve the problem of allocating the least costly set of resources in order to meet the
required level of service. The queueing model and the first simulation model were really
the same model, except the first was analytic and the second was numeric. For both of

FIGURE 3.19 LOGIC FOR EXPANDED TIME-SHARED COMPUTER SYSTEM SIMULATION MODEL

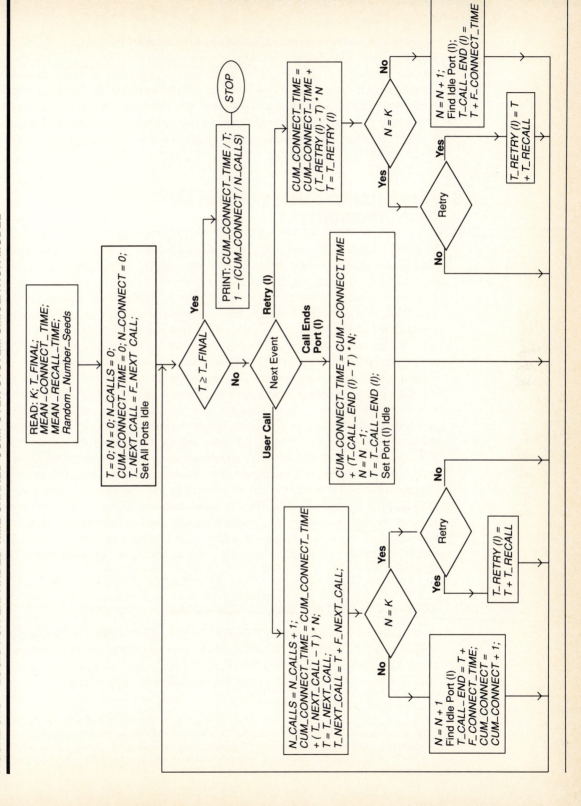

these models, we were restricted in our assumptions about the pattern of users calling into the system and about the behavior of users if they failed to connect. We then saw that the advantage of the simulation model was its capability of being expanded to include more realistic assumptions about the rates of arrival of the users and about the behavior of a user if a connection is not made. It is this flexibility that makes simulation such a powerful tool. The increased flexibility does not come free, however, but requires considerable effort in the development of the model and subsequent interpretation of the model output.

3.5   PROGRAMMING CONSIDERATIONS AND DATA STRUCTURES *

In a typical simulation, much of the computational effort is associated with the management of the events to be executed, such as identification of the most imminent event and the scheduling of future events. Once the next event is identified, usually very little computation is required to update the state variables to reflect its occurrence and update time. The use of simulation languages such as those described in Chapter 4, rather than a general purpose programming language, relieves the user of this burden.

   To illustrate the nature of the problem, consider our time-sharing simulation. When a user attempted to connect to the system, a counter and an accumulator were incremented, and if a port were available, the number of users connected to the system was increased by one. Similarly, when a user completed a session, the number of busy ports was decremented by one, the accumulated user connect time was incremented, and the port was set idle. Finding the next event, however, required examining every location of the arrays containing the status of the ports and the times when the connection was scheduled to end. Further, the entire array containing the times of the next re-try for users crash dialing had to be examined. The simulation program would be much more efficient if the events to be executed were sorted by the time of next occurrence, rather than stored as an unsorted array. That is, rather than search the set of future events in order of physical location in the computer memory, we should access them in logical order. By such methods of "data structuring," the efficiency of a computer simulation can be increased significantly, especially when a simulation has many future events scheduled.

3.5.1   ADVANCING TIME IN A SIMULATION MODEL

In the simulation of the inventory system, the variable T (time) was incremented or stepped by a fixed increment, *DELTA*. A check was then made to determine whether any events (a customer order or stock arriving from the factory) occurred that caused the state of the system to change. Although this mechanism of stepping is simple and direct,

---

* This section may be omitted without any loss of continuity in the chapters to follow. However, analysts planning to build simulation models using a general-purpose programming language such as FORTRAN, C, or PASCAL should become familiar with these methods of managing time and events and techniques of structuring data.

FIGURE 3.20   ADVANCING TIME USING THE FIXED-TIME STEP METHOD

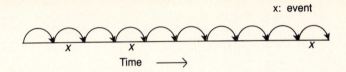

it has several drawbacks. First, in many cases T will be updated to $T + DELTA$ with no events occurring during the interval $(T, T + DELTA)$, causing the scanning for events during the interval to be a waste of effort. Secondly, there may be some loss of accuracy if the events are allowed to occur only at times that are multiples of $DELTA$. If $DELTA$ is increased, the first problem is reduced, but at the expense of accuracy. Conversely, if the size of $DELTA$ is reduced, accuracy improves, but the frequency of updating (and subsequent scanning for events) increases, making the model computationally less efficient. A representation of fixed-time stepping is shown in Fig. 3.20.

An alternative method of updating T, or stepping through time, is to examine all scheduled future events and step T forward to the most imminent event. This method of stepping is shown in Fig. 3.21.

By stepping forward to the nearest scheduled event, both the problems of unnecessary updating and accuracy are eliminated, but at the cost of slightly more complex logic. In most discrete-event simulations, event tracking is the preferred method of advancing in time and is the method used in most simulation languages. There are situations, however, where fixed-time stepping is preferable and this method should not be dismissed as universally inferior to event scheduling.

3.5.2   EVENT MANAGEMENT: LINKED LISTS

In the last example, in order to update time, T, it was necessary to examine the session-completion times for all ports. If the number of ports is large, the computational effort associated with this scan of completion times can become considerable. If, however, the ports could be sorted by the times the current sessions end (leaving out the ports that are idle), it would not be necessary to search for nearest completion time, but rather the completion time for the first port on the sorted listed would determine the next most imminent completion. The data structure necessary for accomplishing this is called a

FIGURE 3.21   ADVANCING TIME USING THE EVENT-SCHEDULING METHOD

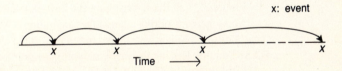

FIGURE 3.22   SESSION-COMPLETION TIMES STRUCTURED AS A LINKED LIST

PORT	TIME	LIST ELEMENT (PORT)	SESSION COMPLETION TIME	NEXT ELEMENT (POINTER)
1	6	1	6	5
2	10	2	10	6
3	IDLE	3	IDLE	
4	2	4	2	1
5	7	5	7	7
6	13	6	13	
7	8	7	8	2
8	IDLE	8	IDLE	

3.22a   **3.22b**

linked list. For purposes of illustration, let us assume that our time-shared system has only eight ports with six of the eight ports currently occupied. Further, let us assume that the times to complete the sessions are 6,10,idle,2,7,13,8,idle, as shown in Fig. 3.22(a). If the set of times were stored as a sequential list, we would need to search through all eight times to know that port 4 has the most imminent completion time. Suppose, however, that each port carried with it a pointer indicating the port with the next largest completion time, as shown in Fig. 3.22(b).

Once the location of the first or head element (relative to a sorted sequence) is known, the list can be searched or traversed in sequence. In simulation models, however, we must have a method of adding and deleting elements (events) to and from the list. If the first sorted element is removed (element 4), the new head element becomes the element to which the current head is pointing. In our example, the head would be changed from element 4 to element 1. If a new element is added to the list, the list pointers must be changed to include the new element in the linked sequence. For example, if port 8 is added with a session completion time of 9, then element 7 will point to element 8 and element 8 will point to element 2 (the old pointer value for element 7). Notice that the insertion of a new element into the list required three operations:

a) Locate where the new element fits in the list.

b) Reset the pointer of the preceding element so it now points to the new element.

c) Set the pointer of the new element so it points to the element to which its predecessor was pointing.

Figure 3.23 shows the list with the new element added and element 4 removed.

Many general purpose languages including PASCAL, Modula 2, Ada, C, and PL/1 have built-in pointer variables, but many older languages such as FORTRAN and BASIC do not, leaving the implementation of pointers to the user.

In the time-sharing FORTRAN simulation model, the inclusion of a linked list for maintaining the times of all three types of events could be accomplished through the use of three arrays, EVENT_TIME, EVENT_TYPE, and NEXT where

FIGURE 3.23   LINKED LIST IMPLEMENTED AS AN ARRAY STRUCTURE

PORT	TIME	LIST ELEMENT (PORT)	SESSION COMPLETION TIME	NEXT ELEMENT (POINTER)
1	6	1	6	5
2	10	2	10	6
3	IDLE	3	IDLE	
4	IDLE	4	IDLE	
5	7	5	7	7
6	13	6	13	
7	8	7	8	8*
8	9	8	9	2*

* pointer changes

EVENT_TIME(I) = the time of the event associated with element I

EVENT_TYPE(I) = The type of event associated with element I

NEXT(I) = A pointer to the next element in the list.

Some form of encoding the type of event is needed, such as 0 representing a new call arriving, 1 to K representing the completion of a session at port K, and $K+1$ and beyond, representing a user making repeated attempts to connect.

The logic of the simulation would need to be changed to allow for the new method of locating the most imminent event (selecting the element at the head of the list) and inserting future events (next call arriving or a service completion) into the linked list. In all other ways, however, the simulation program would be unchanged.

3.5.3   IMPLEMENTING QUEUES IN SIMULATION MODELS

So far we have focused our attention on the events in the simulation and ignored the arrivals, or customers. If we were simulating a system in which the arrivals were allowed to queue up, waiting for an available facility, it might be desirable to gather information on the arrivals' experiences, such as the mean, variance, and range of the time the arrivals wait. This requires that we maintain information on each arrival, such as the time they arrive and their priority in the queue. There are several methods of maintaining this information including:

1) An unsorted array containing the priority of each arrival

2) A linked list with arrivals sorted in order of priority.

3) An array of arrivals sorted in order of priority.

The first approach is easy to implement but inefficient if the array is long, since the entire array must be searched in order to find the next arrival to be served. The second approach is very similar to keeping the list of future events sorted as a linked-list, but the information representing the arrivals is now linked according to the priority of the each arrival. Most simulation languages use this method for implementing queues. Since we have already considered the linked list data structure in the previous section we will not discuss this approach any further.

When the queue discipline is first-in-first-out, an alternative to an unsorted array is an array data structure in which entries are added to the tail of the queue and removed from the head of the queue. The length (number of elements) of the queue can change over the course of the simulation and, when the queue is empty, the head and tail will not point to any element. In order to implement such a queue structure in a high-level language, we must create an array to store the arrival times of users and have pointers to the elements in the array corresponding to the head and tail of the queue. In addition, we must maintain a count of the number of elements in the queue. An example of a queue data structure is shown in Fig. 3.24.

Notice that it is possible for the tail to be located before the head, and that some of the elements in the queue structure are not used since the queue contains less than 10 elements. If an attempt is made to enter more than 10 elements onto the queue, the queue overflows and the elements are lost. In such a case, a warning message should be issued and the program should halt. (The problem of queue overflow can, of course, be avoided using a linked-list structure.)

3.5.4   MEMORY MANAGEMENT IN SIMULATION MODELS

In many simulation models it is difficult to predict the maximum number of future of events that will be scheduled, the maximum lengths of each of the queues in the model, or the maximum number of entities, such as customers, that will be present. One solution to this problem is to allocate such large amounts of memory for lists, queues, and entities that there is little chance the allocated memory will be exceeded during the simulation. The shortcomings of this approach are obvious and, many times, a more sophisticated approach is required. As an alternative we could allocate memory as needed while the simulation is executing. That is, when an element is to be added to a list, we allocate from a general store of unused memory the number of units of memory needed. Simi-

FIGURE 3.24   IMPLEMENTATION OF A QUEUE DATA STRUCTURE

ELEMENT	TIME OF ARRIVAL	
1	30	
2	36	← Q_TAIL = 2
3	--	
4	--	
5	18	← Q_HEAD = 5
6	20	
7	21	
8	21	NO_IN_QUEUE = 8
9	26	
10	28	

FIGURE 3.25   INITIAL ARRANGEMENT OF STACK

```
              LOCATION        CONTENTS
              1               --
              2               1
              3               2
              .               .
              .               .
              L               L-1
                 stack_pointer = L
```

larly, when this memory is no longer needed, it is returned to the general store of memory for future use. In this way memory does not have to be dedicated to a particular use, but can be allocated as needed.

The data structure that allows us to allocate and de-allocate memory space from the general store is a stack. A stack is simply a set of memory locations linked together on a last-in-first-out order (LIFO). Initially the stack contains L elements with element 2 pointing to element 1, element 3 pointing to element 2, etc. A variable called the stack pointer is set to (or points to) the last element on the list. Initially the stack pointer is set to L, or points to the last element on the list which in turn points to element L-1, and so on. Figure 3.25 shows a stack before any elements have been added or removed.

Removing an element from the stack is commonly referred to as popping the stack, and adding an element to the stack is commonly called pushing the stack. Figure 3.26 shows a stack containing six elements before and after location 15 is popped (removed) from the stack and location 9 is pushed (added) onto the stack.

When an element is needed from the stack for scheduling a future event, element L is selected and the stack pointer is set to the value of the element. In order to return an element to the stack after an event is executed, we need only set the value of the returned element to the value of the stack pointer and then set the stack pointer to the index of the element being returned.

FIGURE 3.26   BEFORE AND AFTER POPPING AND PUSHING THE STACK

LOCATION	CONTENTS (POINTER)	LOCATION	CONTENTS
10		10	
12	10	12	10
14	12	14	12
11	14	11	14
15	11	9	11

```
      stack_pointer = 15           stack_pointer = 9
          3.26a                        3.26b
```

Most simulation languages dynamically allocate memory as needed, in a manner that is transparent to the user. Newer general-purpose languages, programming languages such as PASCAL, C, Modula-2, Ada, and Pl/1 directly provide a mechanism for dynamically allocating memory. In older languages such as FORTRAN and BASIC, however, it is up to the programmer to manage the general store of memory.

3.6 CONCLUSION

In this chapter we have considered in some detail the process by which a discrete-event system can be represented through simulation models. The first example we considered, the Buffon Needle problem, was a static simulation, in which the passage of time was not part of the simulation. We next turned our attention to dynamic discrete-event systems in which the passage of time was an inherent part of the process. Three different systems were modeled, each increasing in complexity. For two of the systems, the inventory system and time-shared system, we went so far as to formulate the problem in terms of an objective, or goal, and constraints on the set of solutions that can be used to meet our objective. We stressed the importance of clearly identifying the question(s) that the simulation model should answer. For each of the systems considered, the state variables of the system were identified, the discrete events that cause these state variables to change were defined, and logical relationships between the state variables and the discrete events were described through event graphs and logic diagrams. Finally, we considered the problems of programming these logical relationships in a high-level general-purpose language, including the issue of advancing through time and the data structures necessary to efficiently execute the discrete events many number of times. In subsequent chapters, we model discrete-event systems in special-purpose simulation languages, which make many of these programming considerations transparent to the analyst. The next chapter considers the advantages of such languages and describes three of the more widely used simulation languages.

EXERCISES

3.1 A popular dice game called Craps involves tossing two dice. On the first toss of the dice if the sum is 2,3, or 12, the player loses whatever he bets. If the sum is 7 or 11, he wins the amount he bets. If the sum of the dice is 4,5,6,8,9, or 10, this sum becomes the "point" and the player continues tossing the dice until either the point is tossed again or a 7 is tossed. If the "point" is tossed, the player wins whatever is bet, while if the 7 is tossed, the player losses whatever is bet. Using an absorbing Markov chain, this game can be modeled analytically, with the absorbing states being WIN or LOSE and the nonabsorbing states being BEGIN, 4,5,6,8,9,10.

    a) Construct an event graph for the game.

    b) Construct a simulation model of the game.

3.2 A bus driver must carry a certain amount of change for passengers who do not have the exact fare. If the driver cannot provide the correct change the passenger is allowed to ride free. The fare for the bus is 35 cents and previous experience has shown that passengers will board the bus with the following money for the fare:

1 quarter,1 dime	0.20
1 quarter, 2 nickels	0.10
3 dimes, 1 nickel	0.05
2 dimes, 3 nickels	0.03
2 quarters	0.25
4 dimes	0.07
1 dollar bill	0.25
1 five dollar bill	0.05

a) Formulate this problem in terms of an objective function and constraints.

b) Construct an event diagram for this system.

c) Construct the logic for a simulation model that can be used to determine the best mixture of change the driver should be given when she begins the route. Assume that over the course of the day approximately 100 passengers will board the bus.

3.3 A distributor of plastic bags sells relatively small quantities of a certain type of bag to small-volume customers, but in addition has three volume customers who will order very large quantities. Every four weeks the distributor reorders from the manufacturer in order to bring the inventory of bags up to the desired level. Assume that the demand for the bags on the part of the smaller customers is typically 100 per day, plus or minus 10, while the larger customers will order quantities according to the table.

Customer	Mean Order Size	Std. Dev.	Mean Time Between Orders	Std. Dev.
A	1000	200	20 days	10 days
B	2000	400	15 days	5 days
C	3000	200	20 days	8 days

a) Construct a model of this inventory system identifying an appropriate objective function and constraints. Identify the decision variables and the parameters of the system.

b) Construct an event diagram for this system.

c) Construct the logic of a simulation model for this system that can be used to evaluate any inventory policy the distributor may want to consider.

3.4 In a remote part of the country five radar units are used to give early warning of any unauthorized planes coming into the area. A particular component of the radar is subject to frequent failures and, in order to keep all five units operational, extra components are kept on hand. When one of the radars has such a component failure, a spare component is installed, if available. The failed component is sent off for repair and will be returned or replaced. Assume that the times between failures of these components is exponentially distributed with a mean of 20 days, and when a component is sent off for repair, it will take exactly 15 days until it is returned to the radar center. The component is very expensive, and therefore it is desirable to have no more on hand than necessary.

a) What are the decision variables and objective function for this system?

b) Construct an event diagram for this system.

c) Construct the logic for a simulation model of this system that can be used to determine the "optimum" number of spare units.

3.5 Reconsider the simulation of the time-shared system of Section 4.4. Now assume, upon failing to connect, the user is placed in a queue and connects to the first available port.

a) Modify the event-stepped simulation model to accommodate this type of system.

3.6 Consider the problem of estimating how many fish of a particular species are in a lake. A common approach is to net n fish, mark them in some harmless way and then release them. Subsequently if n fish are again netted and k are found to be marked, then an estimate of the number of fish in the lake can be made using the approximation

$$\frac{\text{total fish marked}}{\text{total fish in lake}} = \frac{\text{fish in sample found marked}}{\text{total fish in sample}}$$

In order to improve the estimate, all the unmarked fish caught could be marked and released. By repeating this procedure again and again, better estimates of the number of fish can be obtained.

a) Identify the variables that need to be included in a simulation model of this process.

b) Construct an event diagram for this system.

c) Construct the logic diagram for a simulation model of this process.

3.7 An automatic packaging machine requires operator intervention periodically for such tasks as clearing jams, restocking packing materials, alignment, and periodic maintenance. One operator can keep several machines operating, but if a machine needs attendance when the operator is busy with another machine, it becomes idle, causing a loss in production. On the other hand, if too few machines are assigned to an operator, the cost of operating the machines may be excessive. Consider a machine that requires operator intervention on the average of three times per hour and the mean length of time the operator must attend the machine is 2.5 minutes per instance. Assume the times between calls for operator assistance and the length of assistance are random variables.

a) Formulate this problem in terms of an objective function and constraints.

b) Construct an event diagram for this system.

c) Identify the variables in the system.

d) Construct a logic diagram that could be used to build a simulation model of the system.

3.8 The spread of a rumor (or similarly a disease or a joke) through a population of fixed size is a common phenomenon. As a simplification of the spread of the rumor, assume the population consist of three groups characterized by:

> Group I has not heard the rumor.
>
> Group II has heard the rumor and is actively spreading it.
>
> Group III has heard the rumor but is no longer spreading it.

When members of Group I hear the rumor they tell it to everyone they meet (joins Group II), until they meet up with someone who already knows the rumor and then they stop spreading it (join Group III).

Simulation models of this process have been used to measure the spead of the rumor and the final sizes of the three groups when the rumor is no longer being spread.

a) Identify the variables that would be used to simulate this process.

b) Construct an event diagram for this system.

c) Identify the events in the simulation model.

d) Construct a logic flow diagram that could be used to simulate this process.

3.9 In a data-base management system, users request records from a disk file for reading and processing. Because it takes considerable time and effort to retrieve a record from a disk file, once the record is retrieved it is kept in a "buffer area" of memory and will be kept in memory until it becomes the oldest record and its memory space is needed for storing a newer record.

Users retrieve records at the rate of 1 record per minute and once a record is retrieved the likelihood that it will be referenced again is (0.50) $(1/k)$ where k is the cumulative number of records the user has retrieved during a session. The total number of records a user retrieves in any one session is a random variable K.

a) Formulate this problem in terms of an objective function and constraints.

b) Construct an event diagram for this system.

c) Identify the decison variables in this system.

d) Draw a logic flow diagram that could be used for constructing a simulation model of this system.

3.10 A famous problem in probability theory is the St. Petersburg Paradox. The paradox concerns a game of chance in which a fair coin is tossed repeatedly until a head appears. The number of times the coin must be tossed until the first head is a random variable X distributed according to the geometric distribution. The payoff in the game is 2 raised to the power x. That is,

$$PAYOFF = 2^x, \quad x = 1, 2...$$

a) Using the geometric distribution, find the game's expected payoff.

b) Simulate the game 10,000 times to find the average payoff.

c) How do you reconcile the dramatically different payoffs as suggested by the analytic and the numeric model of the game?

3.11 In Boston, the MBTA provides bus service between Boston and Cambridge with buses scheduled every 20 minutes. The bus schedule is such that a bus never arrives at a stop early, but can be anywhere from 0 to 10 minutes late. At the bus stop on the corner of Massachusetts Ave. and Huntington Ave., passengers arrive randomly at the rate of one passenger every minute. When the bus arrives it may have anywhere from 20 to 45 passengers already aboard. The capacity of the bus is 50 passengers, which cannot be exceeded by law. When a bus's capacity is reached, the remaining passengers must wait until another bus arrives.

a) Identify the events that can be associated with the above transportation system.

b) Construct an event diagram for this system.

c) Formulate this problem in terms of an objective function and constraints.

d) Construct a logic diagram that could be used to simulate the system.

3.12 A business man is considering setting up an automatic wash and wax operation for automobiles on a corner lot. To be competitive he must charge no more than $2.00 for washing a car and $3.00 for a combination wash and wax.

The equipment necessary to wash and wax cars comes in two configurations:

a) wash only costing $30,000 and

b) wash and/or wax costing $36,000.

The equipment is capable of washing a car in 1.0 minutes and washing and waxing a car in 1.25 minutes. Based on some preliminary surveys and observing the level of business at operations with similar locations, he believes the opportunities for washing and waxing cars at his location are dependent on the day of the week and time of day, as follows:

MONDAY—FRIDAY

9 a.m. — 4 p.m.	35
4 p.m. — 6 p.m.	50
6 p.m. — 9 p.m.	40

SATURDAY—SUNDAY

9 a.m. — 12 a.m.	90
12 a.m. — 4 p.m.	110
4 p.m. — 6 p.m.	90
6 p.m. — 9 p.m.	40

About 40 percent of customers arriving want to have their cars washed and waxed with the remaining 60 percent desiring a wash only. The lot he plans to build on is such that, at most, four units can be installed, leaving room for up to 20 cars to form a waiting line. When a car is within two car lengths of the wash/wax units, the driver must decide which unit will be selected (based upon length of line ahead and whether waxing is desired). Once a unit is selected, the driver cannot move to another line. A single operator can handle up to two units. The operators will be paid $6.00 per hour. The cost for detergent, energy, and water is 20 cents per cycle while the cost of wax is 30 cents per cycle.

a) Formulate this problem in terms of an objective function and constraints.

b) Construct an event diagram for this system.

   c) Identify the events that would be included in a discrete-event simulation model of this problem.

   d) Draw a logic diagram that could be used to program the model in a high-level general-purpose language.

3.13 A time shared computer system has a single 200M-byte (million bytes) disk. The average access time of the disk is 40 ms (milliseconds). The disk contains user files which are requested relatively infrequently and system files such as compilers and editors, which are accessed very frequently. The system is currently disk – I/O bound with approximately 1500 disk I/Os per minute. Approximately 20 percent of these requests are for system files and the remaining 80 percent are for user files. The operating system is designed to share the CPU among a maximum of 25 users. Each user is given a fixed quantum of CPU time, but if during any quantum an I/O occurs, the quantum ends. The operating system then initiates the next job on the CPU. About 30 percent of the I/Os are to the disk. When a job is awaiting I/O, the operating system does not give it a quantum of time. The current quantum time is 0.01 seconds. During any quantum there is a 50 percent chance that an I/O will occur, equally likely anywhere during the quantum. In order to improve the system performance, it has been suggested that a fixed-head high-speed disk be used to store all system files. The average access time for this type of disk is 10 msec.

   a) Formulate this problem in terms of an objective function and constraints.

   b) Construct an event diagram for this system.

   c) Identify the variables in this system.

   d) Construct a logic diagram that could be used to simulate this system.

3.14 A community is considering a second fire department and must decide where it should be located. For planning purposes the community has been divided into six areas. Estimates of the frequency of fires and calls for assistance has been compiled from past records. Further, estimates of the time for emergency vehicles to travel from one area to another have been made. Each fire department will have two fire engines and two emergency vehicles. Calls are always handled by the nearest fire department. If a fire department cannot respond to a call because both engines and emergency vehicles are on call, the other station answers the call. About 50 percent of the calls require a fire engine, 25 percent require an emergency vehicle and 25 percent require both a fire engine and an emergency vehicle.

Assume that the mean time a vehicle is at the scene of a fire is 45 minutes and the times to travel beween the areas of the community are:

	Mean Travel Time					
Area	1	2	3	4	5	6
1	5	8	10	12	6	7
2	8	5	9	8	7	7
3	10	9	5	15	8	9
4	12	8	15	5	9	13
5	6	7	8	9	5	10
6	7	7	9	13	10	5

Further, assume that the daily frequency of fires or emergencies for the six areas average 2, 4, 6, 3, 5, and 6, respectively. The location of the current fire station is in area 5.

a) Formulate this problem in terms of an objective function and constraints.

b) Construct an event diagram for this system.

c) Identify the variables in the system.

d) Construct a logic diagram that could be used to build a simulation model of the system.

3.15 An important consideration when designing a multi-floor building is the elevator system. If it is incapable of moving sufficiently large numbers of people in short periods of time, considerable congestion and delays may result. On the other hand, elevators are very expensive and take up space in a building that could be put to other uses. Most elevator systems are designed to handle the peak load, typically in the early morning when employees in the building are arriving (or in the case of an apartment building when the occupants are leaving for work). The load placed on the system can be described in terms of the mean number of people on floor i desiring to be transported to floor j. The capacity of the elevator is measured by its carrying capacity (passengers) and the time required to travel various numbers of floors. The travel time is a nonlinear function of the number of floors traveled before stopping because of acceleration and deceleration.

a) Formulate the problem of designing an elevator system in terms of an objective function and constraints.

b) Construct an event diagram for this system.

c) If a discrete event simulation model of an elevator system was to be developed, identify the events in the model.

3.16 Blood banking has been a problem for which simulation models have proved to be useful, particularly as an aid in setting minimum and maximum levels for whole blood of a specific type. After whole blood has been collected, it can be stored for only a limited number of days (typically 21) before it must be reduced to blood serum. When the level of whole blood rises above the maximum desired level, some of the older blood is reduced to serum or sent to a central facility where it can be used by other blood banks. If the level falls below the minimum level, additional amounts will need to be obtained from the central facility (serving a region of the state) or specific donors may be contacted for immediate donations of blood. In either case, considerable cost and effort will be required to raise the level of blood beyond the minimum.

a) Formulate this problem in terms of an objective function and constraints.

b) Construct an event diagram for this system.

c) If a discrete-event simulation model of the blood bank were to be developed, identify the events in the model.

d) Develop a logic flow diagram that could be used to construct a simulation model of the blood bank.

e) A similiar problem exists for the regional facility. Go through steps a) thru c) for the regional facility.

REFERENCES

1. Gnedenko, B.V., *The Theory of Probability, Fourth Edition*, New York: Chelsea Publishing Co., 1968.

2. Kleinrock, L., *Queuing Systems, Volume 1*, New York: John Wiley and Sons, 1975.

3. Little, J.D.C., "A proof of the queuing formula L = W," *Operations Research*, Vol. 9, 1961.

4. Schruben, L., "Simulation modeling with event graphs," *Communications of the ACM*, Vol. 26, No. 11, 1983.

APPENDIX 3A

FORTRAN Code for Buffon Needle Example

```
C BUFFON NEEDLE PROBLEM
      TYPE *, 'ENTER: NEEDLE LENGTH, BOARD WIDTH, NO. OF TRIALS'
      TYPE *,
      READ *, FNEEDLE,DIST,NTRIALS
      TYPE*, 'NEEDLE LENGTH=   ',FNEEDLE, 'BOARD WIDTH=    ',DIST,
     1      'NO. OF TRIALS= ',NTRIALS
      WRITE (6,100) FNEEDLE,DIST,NTRIALS
  100 FORMAT (' NEEDLE LENGTH=   ',F7.0,'BOARD WIDTH=   ',F7.0,
     1      'NO. OF TRIALS',I6)
      DO 1 I=1,NTRIALS
      Y=RAN(ISEED)
      A=Y*DIST/2
      Y=RAN(ISEED)
      THETA=Y*3.1416
      IF(A.LE.(FNEEDLE/2.)*SIN(THETA)) THEN
              CROSS=CROSS+1.
      END IF
      IF(MOD(I,50) .EQ.0) THEN
              TYPE *,'TRIAL NO.=  ',I,'FRACTION CROSSING=  ',CROSS/FLOAT( I)
  101 FORMAT('   TRIAL NO.=  ',I,'    FRACTION CROSSING=  ',F5.4)
      END IF
  1   CONTINUE
      THEO_PROB=2.*FNEEDLE/(3.1416*DIST)
      TYPE *,'THEORETICAL PROB=   ',THEO_PROB
      WRITE(6,102) THEO_PROB
  102 FORMAT('   THEORETICAL PROB=   ',F6.5)
      END
```

APPENDIX 3B

FORTRAN Code for Simulating a One-Server Queue

```
      TYPE *,'INPUT MEAN INTER-ARRIVAL AND SERVICE TIMES'
      READ *,X_ARRIVAL,X_SERVICE
      TYPE *,'INPUT LENGTH OF SIMULATION'
      READ *,TMAX
      TYPE *,'INPUT RANDOM NUMBER SEED'
      READ*,ISEED
      T=0
      TN=0
      K=0
      N=0
      BIG=TMAX**2
      T_SERVICE=BIG
      T_ARRIVAL=RANDOM_ARRIVAL(X_ARRIVAL,ISEED)
      DO 20 WHILE (T .LT. TMAX)
      IF (T_ARRIVAL .LT. T_SERVICE) THEN
           TN=TN+N*(T_ARRIVAL-T)
           N=N+1
             K=K+1
           T=T_ARRIVAL
           T_ARRIVAL=T+RANDOM_SERVICE(X_ARRIVAL,ISEED)
           IF (N .EQ. 1) THEN
               T_SERVICE=T+RANDOM_SERVICE(X_SERVICE,ISEED)
           ENDIF
      ELSE
           TN=TN+N*(T_SERVICE-T)
           N=N-1
           T=T_SERVICE
           IF (N .GT. 0) THEN
               T_SERVICE=T+RANDOM_SERVICE(X_SERVICE,ISEED)
           ELSE
               T_SERVICE=BIG
           ENDIF
      ENDIF
20    CONTINUE
      TYPE *,'MEAN NUMBER OF CUSTOMERS IN SYSTEM WAS',TN/T
      TYPE *,'MEAN TIME CUSTOMERS WERE IN SYSTEM WAS',TN/K
      END

      FUNCTION RANDOM_SERVICE(X,ISEED)
      RANDOM_SERVICE=-X*ALOG(RAN(ISEED))
      END

      FUNCTION RANDOM_ARRIVAL(X,ISEED)
      RANDOM_ARRIVAL=-X*ALOG(RAN(ISEED))
      END
```

APPENDIX 3C

FORTRAN Code for Simulating an Inventory System

```
LOGICAL ORDER_PLACED
TYPE *,'INPUT C_INV,C_ORDER,C_PENALTY'
READ *,C_INV,C_ORDER,C_PENALTY
TYPE *,'INPUT RE_ORDER POINT AND ORDER QUANTITY'
READ *,S,Q
TYPE *,'INPUT INITIAL INVENTORY'
READ *,INV0
TYPE *,'INPUT NO. OF DAYS TO BE SIMULATED'
READ *, T_FINAL
TYPE *,'INPUT RANDOM NUMBER SEED'
READ *,ISEED
CUM_LOST=0
N_ORDERS=0
CUM_INV=0
INV=INV0
T=1
T_ORDER_ARRIVE=0
ORDER_PLACED=.FALSE.
DO 20 WHILE (T .LT. T_FINAL)
IF (T_ORDER_ARRIVE .EQ. T) THEN
     INV=INV+Q
     ORDER_PLACED=.FALSE.
ENDIF
CUM_INV=CUM_INV+INV
DEMAND=RANDOM_DEMAND(ISEED,T)
IF (DEMAND .GT. INV) THEN
   CUM_LOST=CUM_LOST + (DEMAND-INV)
   INV=0
ELSE
   INV=INV-DEMAND
ENDIF
IF (INV .LE. S .AND. .NOT. ORDER_PLACED) THEN
   ORDER_PLACED=.TRUE.
   T_ORDER_ARRIVE=T+RANDOM_ORDER_TIME(ISEED)
   N_ORDERS=N_ORDERS+1
ENDIF
T=T+1
20    CONTINUE
T_YEARS=T/365
TYPE *,'AVERAGE _INVENTORY=',CUM_INV/T
TYPE *,'AVERAGE NO. ORDERS/YEAR=',N_ORDERS/T_YEARS
TYPE *,'AVERAGE LOST DEMAND/YEAR=',CUM_LOST/T_YEARS
AVE_ANNUAL_COST=N_ORDERS/T_YEARS*C_ORDER
1       +CUM_INV/T*C_INV+CUM_LOST/T_YEARS*C_PENALTY
TYPE *,'AVERAGE ANNUAL COST=',AVE_ANNUAL_COST
END

FUNCTION RANDOM_DEMAND(ISEED,T)
IDAY=MOD(IFIX(T),7)
IF (IDAY .GT. 5) THEN
     RANDOM_DEMAND=0
RETURN
ENDIF
X=RAN(ISEED)
IF (X .LT. .14) THEN
```

```
            RANDOM_DEMAND=0
            RETURN
      ENDIF

      IF (X. LT. .41) THEN
            RANDOM_DEMAND=1
            RETURN
      ENDIF

      IF (X .LT. .68) THEN
            RANDOM_DEMAND=2
            RETURN
      ENDIF

      IF (X .LT. .86) THEN
            RANDOM_DEMAND=3
            RETURN
      ENDIF

      IF (X .LT. .95) THEN
            RANDOM_DEMAND=4
            RETURN
      ENDIF

            RANDOM_DEMAND=5
            RETURN
END

FUNCTION RANDOM_ORDER_TIME(ISEED)
RANDOM_ORDER_TIME=4+IFIX(RAN(ISEED)*3)
RETURN
END
```

APPENDIX 3D

FORTRAN Program for Simulation of a Time-Shared Computer System

```
        COMMON T_CALL_END(64),PORT_STATUS(64),T,T_FINAL,N,
     1        T_NEXT_CALL,MEAN_CONNECT_TIME,MEAN_CALL_TIME,
     2        IDLE,BUSY,NCALLS,CUM_CONNECT,CUM_FAIL_CONNECT,
     3        SEED1,SEED2,N_PORTS
        INTEGER PORT_STATUS,IDLE,BUSY,NCALLS,CUM_FAIL_CONNECT,
     1        SEED1,SEED2,N_PORTS,N
        REAL    T_CALL_END,T,T_FINAL,MEAN_CONNECT_TIME,MEAN_
     1        CALL_TIME,CUM_CONNECT
        DATA IDLE/0/,BUSY/1/
        CALL READ_DATA
        CALL INITIALIZE
        DO 100 WHILE (T.LT.T_FINAL)
          CALL FIND_NEXT_EVENT(K,J)            !K=EVENT TYPE,J=PORT
          GO TO (10,20) K                      !K=1 CALL ARRIVES
10        CALL ARRIVAL                         !K=2 SESSION COMPLETED
          GO TO 100
20        CALL END_SESSION(J)
          GO TO 100
100     CONTINUE
        CALL OUTPUT
        END

        SUBROUTINE READ_DATA
        COMMON  T_CALL_END(64),PORT_STATUS(64),T,T_FINAL,N,
     1        T_NEXT_CALL,MEAN_CONNECT_TIME,MEAN_CALL_TIME,
     2        IDLE,BUSY,NCALLS,CUM_CONNECT,CUM_FAIL_CONNECT,
     3        SEED1,SEED2,N_PORTS
        INTEGER PORT_STATUS,IDLE,BUSY,NCALLS,CUM_FAIL_CONNECT,
     1        SEED1,SEED2,N_PORTS,N
        REAL    T_CALL_END,T,T_FINAL,MEAN_CONNECT_TIME,MEAN_
     1        CALL_TIME,CUM_CONNECT
        WRITE(6,*) 'INPUT NUMBER OF PORTS, MEAN_CONNECT_TIME AND MEAN_
     1CALL_TIME'
        READ(5,*)N_PORTS,MEAN_CONNECT_TIME,MEAN_CALL_TIME
        WRITE(6,*) 'INPUT LENGTH OF SIMULATION AND 2 RANDOM NUMBER SEEDS'
        READ(5,*) T_FINAL,SEED1,SEED2
        RETURN
        END

        SUBROUTINE INITIALIZE
        COMMON  T_CALL_END(64),PORT_STATUS(64),T,T_FINAL,N,
     1        T_NEXT_CALL,MEAN_CONNECT_TIME,MEAN_CALL_TIME,
     2        IDLE,BUSY,NCALLS,CUM_CONNECT,CUM_FAIL_CONNECT,
     3        SEED1,SEED2,N_PORTS
        INTEGER PORT_STATUS,IDLE,BUSY,NCALLS,CUM_FAIL_CONNECT,
     1        SEED1,SEED2,N_PORTS,N
        REAL    T_CALL_END,T,T_FINAL,MEAN_CONNECT_TIME,MEAN_
     1        CALL_TIME,CUM_CONNECT
        N=0
        T=0
        CUM_CONNECT_TIME=0.0
        CUM_FAIL_CONNECT=0
        NCALLS=0
```

```
      DO 10 I=1,N_PORTS
      PORT_STATUS(I)=IDLE
10    CONTINUE
      T_NEXT_CALL=ARRIVE_TIME(MEAN_CALL_TIME,SEED1)
      RETURN
      END


      SUBROUTINE FIND_NEXT_EVENT(K,J)                    !K=TYPE OF EVENT
      COMMON   T_CALL_END(64),PORT_STATUS(64),T,T_FINAL,N,
     1         T_NEXT_CALL,MEAN_CONNECT_TIME,MEAN_CALL_TIME,
     2         IDLE,BUSY,NCALLS,CUM_CONNECT,CUM_FAIL_CONNECT,
     3         SEED1,SEED2,N_PORTS
      INTEGER PORT_STATUS,IDLE,BUSY,NCALLS,CUM_FAIL_CONNECT,
     1         SEED1,SEED2,N_PORTS,N
      REAL     T_CALL_END,T,T_FINAL,MEAN_CONNECT_TIME,MEAN_
     1         CALL_TIME,CUM_CONNECT
      LOGICAL FOUND
      IF (N.GT.0) THEN
       I=1
       FOUND=.FALSE.
       DO 20 WHILE (.NOT. FOUND)
        IF (PORT_STATUS(I).EQ.IDLE) THEN
         I=I+1
        ELSE
         FOUND=.TRUE.
        ENDIF
20     CONTINUE
       J=I                                          !J=BUSY PORT INDEX
       I1=I+1
       DO 30 I=I1,N_PORTS
       IF (PORT_STATUS(I).EQ.BUSY) THEN
        IF (T_CALL_END(I).LT.T_CALL_END(J)) J=I
       ENDIF
30     CONTINUE                                     !J=INDEX OF BUSY PORT
       IF (T_NEXT_CALL.LT.T_CALL_END(J)) THEN !  NEXT TO FINISH
        K=1
       ELSE
        K=2
       ENDIF
      ELSE
       K=1
      ENDIF
      RETURN
      END


      SUBROUTINE ARRIVAL
      COMMON   T_CALL_END(64),PORT_STATUS(64),T,T_FINAL,N,
     1         T_NEXT_CALL,MEAN_CONNECT_TIME,MEAN_CALL_TIME,
     2         IDLE,BUSY,NCALLS,CUM_CONNECT,CUM_FAIL_CONNECT,
     3         SEED1,SEED2,N_PORTS
      INTEGER PORT_STATUS,IDLE,BUSY,NCALLS,CUM_FAIL_CONNECT,
     1         SEED1,SEED2,N_PORTS,N
      REAL     T_CALL_END,T,T_FINAL,MEAN_CONNECT_TIME,MEAN_
     1         CALL_TIME,CUM_CONNECT
      LOGICAL FOUND
      NCALLS=NCALLS+1
      CUM_CONNECT=CUM_CONNECT+(T_NEXT_CALL-T)*N
      T=T_NEXT_CALL
      T_NEXT_CALL=T+ARRIVE_TIME(MEAN_CALL_TIME,SEED1)
```

(Continued)

```
        IF (N.LT.N_PORTS) THEN
          N=N+1
          FOUND=.FALSE.                                !BEGIN SEARCH FOR
          I=1                                          !IDLE PORT
          DO 20 WHILE (.NOT. FOUND)
            IF (PORT_STATUS(I).EQ.BUSY) THEN
              I=I+1
            ELSE
              FOUND=.TRUE.
            ENDIF
20        CONTINUE
          T_CALL_END(I)=T+T_CONNECT_TIME(MEAN_CONNECT_TIME,SEED2)
          PORT_STATUS(I)=BUSY
        ELSE
          CUM_FAIL_CONNECT=CUM_FAIL_CONNECT+1
        ENDIF
        RETURN
        END


        SUBROUTINE END_SESSION(J)                      !J=PORT ENDING
        COMMON  T_CALL_END(64),PORT_STATUS(64),T,T_FINAL,N,
       1        T_NEXT_CALL,MEAN_CONNECT_TIME,MEAN_CALL_TIME,
       2        IDLE,BUSY,NCALLS,CUM_CONNECT,CUM_FAIL_CONNECT,
       3        SEED1,SEED2,N_PORTS
        INTEGER PORT_STATUS,IDLE,BUSY,NCALLS,CUM_FAIL_CONNECT,
       1        SEED1,SEED2,N_PORTS,N
        REAL    T_CALL_END,T,T_FINAL,MEAN_CONNECT_TIME,MEAN_
       1        CALL_TIME,CUM_CONNECT
        CUM_CONNECT=CUM_CONNECT+(T_CALL_END(J)-T)*N
        N=N-1
        T=T_CALL_END(J)
        PORT_STATUS(J)=IDLE
        RETURN
        END


        SUBROUTINE OUTPUT
        COMMON  T_CALL_END(64),PORT_STATUS(64),T,T_FINAL,N,
       1        T_NEXT_CALL,MEAN_CONNECT_TIME,MEAN_CALL_TIME,
       2        IDLE,BUSY,NCALLS,CUM_CONNECT,CUM_FAIL_CONNECT,
       3        SEED1,SEED2,N_PORTS
        INTEGER PORT_STATUS,IDLE,BUSY,NCALLS,CUM_FAIL_CONNECT,
       1        SEED1,SEED2,N_PORTS,N
        REAL    T_CALL_END,T,T_FINAL,MEAN_CONNECT_TIME,MEAN_
       1        CALL_TIME,CUM_CONNECT
        WRITE(6,1) T,NCALLS,FLOAT(CUM_FAIL_CONNECT)/NCALLS
1       FORMAT(1X,'TIME=',F6.1,'   TOTAL CALLS= ',I6,
       1       'PROB. FAIL CONNECT=',F5.3)
        WRITE(6,2) CUM_CONNECT/T
2       FORMAT(1X,'AVE. NUMBER OF BUSY PORTS=',F6.2)
        RETURN
        END


        FUNCTION ARRIVE_TIME(XMEAN,SEED)
C **THIS FUNCTION GENERATES AN EXPONENTIALLY DISTRIBUTED R.V. WITH MEAN
XMEAN**
        INTEGER SEED
        CALL RANDOM(X,SEED)
        ARRIVE_TIME=-ALOG(X)*XMEAN
        RETURN
        END
```

```
      FUNCTION T_CONNECT_TIME(XMEAN,SEED)
C **THIS FUNCTION GENERATES AN EXPONTIALLY DISTRIBUTED R.V. WITH  MEAN
XMEAN**
      INTEGER SEED
      CALL RANDOM(X,SEED)
      T_CONNECT_TIME=-ALOG(X)*XMEAN
      RETURN
      END

      SUBROUTINE RANDOM(X,SEED)
      INTEGER SEED
      X=RAN(SEED)                        !RANDOM NUMBER
      RETURN                             !GENERATOR FOR
      END                                !VAX 11/780
```

APPENDIX 3E

FORTRAN Program for the Simulation of the Expanded Time-Shared System

```
       COMMON  T_CALL_END(64),PORT_STATUS(64),T,T_FINAL,N,N_WAIT,
      1         T_NEXT_CALL,MEAN_CONNECT_TIME,MEAN_CALL_TIME,MEAN_
      2         RECALL,IDLE,BUSY,NCALLS,CUM_CONNECT,CUM_FAIL_CONNECT,
      3         T_RECALL(100),MAX_RECALL,SEED1,SEED2,SEED3,N_PORTS,
      4         PROB_RENEG,N_SIM
       INTEGER PORT_STATUS,IDLE,BUSY,NCALLS,CUM_FAIL_CONNECT,
      1         SEED1,SEED2,SEED3,N_PORTS,N,MAX_RECALL
       REAL    T_CALL_END,T,T_FINAL,MEAN_CONNECT_TIME,MEAN_
      1         CALL_TIME,CUM_CONNECT,MEAN_RECALL,PROB_RENEG
       DATA IDLE/0/,BUSY/1/,MAX_RECALL/100/
       CALL READ_DATA
       TYPE *, 'TURN ON DEBUG?, 1=YES, 0=NO'
       READ *,IDEBUG
       CUM_CONNECT=0.0
       CUM_FAIL_CONNECT=0
       NCALLS=0
       DO 1000 KKK=1,N_SIM
       CALL INITIALIZE
       DO 100 WHILE (T.LT.T_FINAL)
         CALL FIND_NEXT_EVENT(K,J)              !K=EVENT TYPE,J=PORT
       IF (IDEBUG.EQ.1) TYPE *,'T=',T,'  N=',N,'  N_WAIT=',NWAIT,'  K=',K
         GO TO (10,20,30) K                     !K=1 CALL ARRIVES
10         CALL ARRIVAL                         !K=2 SESSION COMPLETED
           GO TO 100                            !K=3 USER RETRY
20         CALL END_SESSION(J)
           GO TO 100
30         CALL RETRY(J)
           GO TO 100
100    CONTINUE
1000   CONTINUE
       CALL OUTPUT
       END


       SUBROUTINE READ_DATA
       COMMON  T_CALL_END(64),PORT_STATUS(64),T,T_FINAL,N,N_WAIT,
      1         T_NEXT_CALL,MEAN_CONNECT_TIME,MEAN_CALL_TIME,MEAN_
      2         RECALL,IDLE,BUSY,NCALLS,CUM_CONNECT,CUM_FAIL_CONNECT,
      3         T_RECALL(100),MAX_RECALL,SEED1,SEED2,SEED3,N_PORTS,
      4         PROB_RENEG,N_SIM
       INTEGER PORT_STATUS,IDLE,BUSY,NCALLS,CUM_FAIL_CONNECT,
      1         SEED1,SEED2,SEED3,N_PORTS,N,MAX_RECALL
       REAL    T_CALL_END,T,T_FINAL,MEAN_CONNECT_TIME,MEAN_
      1         CALL_TIME,CUM_CONNECT,MEAN_RECALL,PROB_RENEG
       WRITE(6,*) 'INPUT NUMBER OF PORTS, MEAN_CONNECT,MEAN_
      1CALL,MEAN_RECALL TIMES'
       READ(5,*)N_PORTS,MEAN_CONNECT_TIME,MEAN_CALL_TIME,MEAN_RECALL
       WRITE(6,*) 'INPUT LENGTH OF SIMULATION AND 3 RANDOM NUMBER SEEDS'
       READ(5,*) T_FINAL,SEED1,SEED2,SEED3
       WRITE(5,*) 'INPUT PROB. OF RENEGING ON RECALL AND NO. OF SIMULATIONS'
       READ(6,*) PROB_RENEG,N_SIM
       RETURN
       END
```

```
      SUBROUTINE INITIALIZE
      COMMON  T_CALL_END(64),PORT_STATUS(64),T,T_FINAL,N,N_WAIT,
     1        T_NEXT_CALL,MEAN_CONNECT_TIME,MEAN_CALL_TIME,MEAN_
     2        RECALL,IDLE,BUSY,NCALLS,CUM_CONNECT,CUM_FAIL_CONNECT,
     3        T_RECALL(100),MAX_RECALL,SEED1,SEED2,SEED3,N_PORTS,
     4        PROB_RENEG,N_SIM
      INTEGER PORT_STATUS,IDLE,BUSY,NCALLS,CUM_FAIL_CONNECT,
     1        SEED1,SEED2,SEED3,N_PORTS,N,MAX_RECALL
      REAL    T_CALL_END,T,T_FINAL,MEAN_CONNECT_TIME,MEAN_
     1        CALL_TIME,CUM_CONNECT,MEAN_RECALL,PROB_RENEG
      N=0
      N_WAIT=0
      T=0
      DO 10 I=1,N_PORTS
      PORT_STATUS(I)=IDLE
10    CONTINUE
      DO 20 I=1,MAX_RECALL
20    T_RECALL(I)=2.*T_FINAL
      T_NEXT_CALL=ARRIVE_TIME(T,SEED1)
      RETURN
      END


      SUBROUTINE FIND_NEXT_EVENT(K,J)                        !K=TYPE OF EVENT
      COMMON  T_CALL_END(64),PORT_STATUS(64),T,T_FINAL,N,N_WAIT,
     1        T_NEXT_CALL,MEAN_CONNECT_TIME,MEAN_CALL_TIME,MEAN_
     2        RECALL,IDLE,BUSY,NCALLS,CUM_CONNECT,CUM_FAIL_CONNECT,
     3        T_RECALL(100),MAX_RECALL,SEED1,SEED2,SEED3,N_PORTS,
     4        PROB_RENEG,N_SIM
      INTEGER PORT_STATUS,IDLE,BUSY,NCALLS,CUM_FAIL_CONNECT,
     1        SEED1,SEED2,SEED3,N_PORTS,N,MAX_RECALL
      REAL    T_CALL_END,T,T_FINAL,MEAN_CONNECT_TIME,MEAN_
     1        CALL_TIME,CUM_CONNECT,MEAN_RECALL,PROB_RENEG
      LOGICAL FOUND
      IF (N.GT.0) THEN
       I=1
       FOUND=.FALSE.
       DO 20 WHILE (.NOT. FOUND)
        IF (PORT_STATUS(I).EQ.IDLE) THEN
         I=I+1
        ELSE
         FOUND=.TRUE.
        ENDIF
20     CONTINUE
       J=I                                                   !J=BUSY PORT INDEX
       I1=I+1
       DO 30 I=I1,N_PORTS
       IF (PORT_STATUS(I).EQ.BUSY) THEN
        IF (T_CALL_END(I).LT.T_CALL_END(J)) J=I
       ENDIF
30     CONTINUE                                              !J=INDEX OF BUSY PORT
       IF (T_NEXT_CALL.LT.T_CALL_END(J)) THEN !  NEXT TO FINISH
        K=1
       ELSE
        K=2
       ENDIF
      ELSE
       K=1
      ENDIF
      IF (N_WAIT.GT.0) THEN
        FOUND=.FALSE.
        I=1
        DO 40 WHILE (.NOT. FOUND)
```

(Continued)

```
            IF (T_RECALL(I).LT.2.0*T_FINAL) THEN
             FOUND=.TRUE.
            ELSE
             I=I+1
            ENDIF
40      CONTINUE
        L=I
        I1=I
        DO 50 I=I1,MAX_RECALL
        IF (T_RECALL(I).LT.T_RECALL(L)) L=I
50      CONTINUE
        GO TO (60,70)K
60      IF(T_RECALL(L).LT.T_NEXT_CALL) THEN
        K=3
        J=L
        ENDIF
        RETURN
70      IF(T_RECALL(L).LT.T_CALL_END(J)) THEN
        K=3
        J=L
        RETURN
        ENDIF
        ENDIF
        RETURN
        END

        SUBROUTINE ARRIVAL
        COMMON   T_CALL_END(64),PORT_STATUS(64),T,T_FINAL,N,N_WAIT,
     1           T_NEXT_CALL,MEAN_CONNECT_TIME,MEAN_CALL_TIME,MEAN_
     2           RECALL,IDLE,BUSY,NCALLS,CUM_CONNECT,CUM_FAIL_CONNECT,
     3           T_RECALL(100),MAX_RECALL,SEED1,SEED2,SEED3,N_PORTS,
     4           PROB_RENEG,N_SIM
        INTEGER PORT_STATUS,IDLE,BUSY,NCALLS,CUM_FAIL_CONNECT,
     1           SEED1,SEED2,SEED3,N_PORTS,N,MAX_RECALL
        REAL     T_CALL_END,T,T_FINAL,MEAN_CONNECT_TIME,MEAN_
     1           CALL_TIME,CUM_CONNECT,MEAN_RECALL,PROB_RENEG
        LOGICAL FOUND
        NCALLS=NCALLS+1
        CUM_CONNECT=CUM_CONNECT+(T_NEXT_CALL-T)*N
        T=T_NEXT_CALL
        T_NEXT_CALL=T+ARRIVE_TIME(T,SEED3)
        IF (N.LT.N_PORTS) THEN
         N=N+1
         FOUND=.FALSE.                              !BEGIN SEARCH FOR
         I=1                                        !IDLE PORT
         DO 20 WHILE (.NOT. FOUND)
          IF (PORT_STATUS(I).EQ.BUSY) THEN
           I=I+1
          ELSE
           FOUND=.TRUE.
          ENDIF
20       CONTINUE
         T_CALL_END(I)=T+T_CONNECT_TIME(MEAN_CONNECT_TIME,SEED2)
         PORT_STATUS(I)=BUSY
        ELSE
         CUM_FAIL_CONNECT=CUM_FAIL_CONNECT+1
         FOUND=.FALSE.
         I=1
         DO 30 WHILE(T_RECALL(I).LT.2.0*T_FINAL)
30       I=I+1
         CALL RANDOM(X,SEED3)
         IF (X.GE.PROB_RENEG) THEN
```

```
      N_WAIT=N_WAIT+1
      T_RECALL(I)=T+T_RECALL_TIME(MEAN_RECALL,SEED3)
    ENDIF
  ENDIF
  RETURN
  END


  SUBROUTINE END_SESSION(J)                      !J=PORT ENDING
  COMMON  T_CALL_END(64),PORT_STATUS(64),T,T_FINAL,N,N_WAIT,
 1        T_NEXT_CALL,MEAN_CONNECT_TIME,MEAN_CALL_TIME,MEAN_
 2        RECALL,IDLE,BUSY,NCALLS,CUM_CONNECT,CUM_FAIL_CONNECT,
 3        T_RECALL(100),MAX_RECALL,SEED1,SEED2,SEED3,N_PORTS,
 4        PROB_RENEG,N_SIM
  INTEGER PORT_STATUS,IDLE,BUSY,NCALLS,CUM_FAIL_CONNECT,
 1        SEED1,SEED2,SEED3,N_PORTS,N,MAX_RECALL
  REAL    T_CALL_END,T,T_FINAL,MEAN_CONNECT_TIME,MEAN_
 1        CALL_TIME,CUM_CONNECT,MEAN_RECALL,PROB_RENEG
  CUM_CONNECT=CUM_CONNECT+(T_CALL_END(J)-T)*N
  N=N-1
  T=T_CALL_END(J)
  PORT_STATUS(J)=IDLE
  RETURN
  END


  SUBROUTINE RETRY(J)
  COMMON  T_CALL_END(64),PORT_STATUS(64),T,T_FINAL,N,N_WAIT,
 1        T_NEXT_CALL,MEAN_CONNECT_TIME,MEAN_CALL_TIME,MEAN_
 2        RECALL,IDLE,BUSY,NCALLS,CUM_CONNECT,CUM_FAIL_CONNECT,
 3        T_RECALL(100),MAX_RECALL,SEED1,SEED2,SEED3,N_PORTS,
 4        PROB_RENEG,N_SIM
  INTEGER PORT_STATUS,IDLE,BUSY,NCALLS,CUM_FAIL_CONNECT,
 1        SEED1,SEED2,SEED3,N_PORTS,N,MAX_RECALL
  REAL    T_CALL_END,T,T_FINAL,MEAN_CONNECT_TIME,MEAN_
 1        CALL_TIME,CUM_CONNECT,MEAN_RECALL,PROB_RENEG
  LOGICAL FOUND
  CUM_CONNECT=CUM_CONNECT+(T_RECALL(J)-T)*N
  T=T_RECALL(J)
  IF(N.LT.N_NPORTS) THEN
  N=N+1
  FOUND=.FALSE.
  I=1
  DO 20 WHILE (.NOT.FOUND)
   IF (PORT_STATUS(I).EQ.BUSY) THEN
   I=I+1
  ELSE
  FOUND=.TRUE.
  ENDIF
20  CONTINUE
  T_CALL_END(I)=T+T_CONNECT_TIME(MEAN_CONNECT_TIME,SEED2)
  PORT_STATUS(I)=BUSY
  T_RECALL(J)=T_FINAL
  N_WAIT=N_WAIT-1
  ELSE
  CALL RANDOM(X,SEED3)
   IF(X.LT.PROB_RENEG) THEN
    T_RECALL(J)=T_FINAL
    N_WAIT=N_WAIT-1
   ELSE
    T_RECALL(J)=T+T_RECALL_TIME(MEAN_RECALL,SEED3)
   ENDIF
  ENDIF
  RETURN
  END
```

(Continued)

```
      SUBROUTINE OUTPUT
      COMMON   T_CALL_END(64),PORT_STATUS(64),T,T_FINAL,N,N_WAIT,
     1         T_NEXT_CALL,MEAN_CONNECT_TIME,MEAN_CALL_TIME,MEAN_
     2         RECALL,IDLE,BUSY,NCALLS,CUM_CONNECT,CUM_FAIL_CONNECT,
     3         T_RECALL(100),MAX_RECALL,SEED1,SEED2,SEED3,N_PORTS,
     4         PROB_RENEG,N_SIM
      INTEGER PORT_STATUS,IDLE,BUSY,NCALLS,CUM_FAIL_CONNECT,
     1         SEED1,SEED2,SEED3,N_PORTS,N,MAX_RECALL
      REAL     T_CALL_END,T,T_FINAL,MEAN_CONNECT_TIME,MEAN_
     1         CALL_TIME,CUM_CONNECT,MEAN_RECALL,PROB_RENEG
      WRITE(6,1)T,NCALLS,FLOAT(CUM_FAIL_CONNECT)/NCALLS
1     FORMAT(1X,'TIME=',F6.1,'   TOTAL CALLS= ',I8,
     1         '    PROB. FAIL CONNECT=',F5.3)
      WRITE(6,2) CUM_CONNECT/(T*N_SIM)
2     FORMAT(1X,'AVE. NUMBER OF BUSY PORTS=',F6.2)
      RETURN
      END
      FUNCTION T_CONNECT_TIME(XMEAN,SEED)
      INTEGER SEED
      CALL RANDOM(X,SEED)
      T_CONNECT_TIME=-ALOG(X)*XMEAN
      RETURN
      END

      FUNCTION T_RECALL_TIME(XMEAN,SEED)
      INTEGER SEED
      CALL RANDOM(X,SEED)
      T_RECALL_TIME=-ALOG(X)*XMEAN
      RETURN
      END



      FUNCTION ARRIVE_TIME(T,SEED)
      DIMENSION ARR_RATE(10)
      INTEGER SEED
      DATA ARR_RATE/15.,37.,45.,45.,37.,40.,48.,40.,25.,10./
      I=T/60+1
      RATE=ARR_RATE(I)+(ARR_RATE(I+1)-ARR_RATE(I))*(IFIX(T)-T)/60.
      CALL RANDOM(X,SEED)
      ARRIVE_TIME=-ALOG(X)/RATE*60.
      RETURN
      END

      SUBROUTINE RANDOM(X,SEED)
      INTEGER SEED
      X=RAN(SEED)
      RETURN
      END
```

CHAPTER 4

SIMULATION LANGUAGES FOR MODELING

It is possible to write simulation models in programming languages such as FORTRAN, BASIC, or PASCAL; or even in languages like C, PROLOG, or LISP. To construct and use a simulation model written in one of these languages, however, requires extensive programming skill. An appropriate analogy would be the need for a thorough understanding of the internal combustion engine before being able to drive an automobile. But, a person can certainly understand the essentials of driving without knowing the technical intricacies of engine repair. Similarly, a user may have a thorough understanding of the problem and wish to focus attention on the description of the system components and their inter-relationships, and not on the technical details of a programming language. Simulation languages permit modelers to do just that. So, the model developer need not be an expert programmer to produce useful models.

4.1   INTRODUCTION

With the knowledge of model development obtained from Chapter 3, we are now ready to consider the construction of the computer code needed to implement our models. In focusing on the creation of code, we will postpone consideration of some facets of modeling, such as data collection, random-variate generation, and model validation, until Part III: Building and Validating Simulation Models. Consequently, in our illustrative examples we will make some assumptions about probability distributions for arrivals and service times, but this will in no way impair our ability to adequately consider the use of simulation languages for modeling.

The selection of a programming language in which to code a simulation model has far-reaching effects on the ultimate success or failure of a simulation analysis. It is the intent of this chapter to provide sufficient knowledge of simulation languages in general, and three more popular languages in specific, to permit the analyst to make this choice fully aware of its probable consequences.

We begin with an overview of simulation languages, considering the justification for such languages, the structure and features of currently available languages, and scenarios for simulation modeling in the future. The issue of selecting any simulation language, rather than a general-purpose language, is closely scrutinized. We consider some relevant factors in language selection, from the ability to support the necessary simulation tasks of random variate generation and statistics collection, and the very pragmatic concern about the transport of models from one computer to another.

Three of the more popular discrete event simulation languages, GPSS, SIMAN, and SIMSCRIPT, are described and illustrated with example problems in Section 4.3. When describing the structure of these languages, we draw heavily on the Primers found in Appendixes A, B, and C. In addition, some other languages are briefly described to provide a sense of the scope of problems that can be addressed by simulation languages.

Finally, to provide a more specific basis for comparing different languages, a single problem is coded in the three simulation languages and in FORTRAN. Comparisons are drawn in terms of measures such as the number of source statements and the model running time. This comparative analysis is intended to provide some insight into the choice of modeling language: simulation versus general-purpose, and one simulation language versus another. The problem selected is the time-shared computer system described in Section 3.4 of Chapter 3.

4.2   ANATOMY OF SIMULATION LANGUAGES

4.2.1   SIMULATION LANGUAGES: EARLY BEGINNINGS

Simulation analysis is an eclectic technique that depends heavily on the skill and ingenuity of the analyst for success. Executing the steps of the analysis described in Chapter 2 can be a costly, time-consuming exercise. In particular, the model development phase of a simulation analysis is often protracted because of the long, complex computer code necessary to represent the model. The judicious selection of a computer language can greatly facilitate this, and other phases of the analysis.

The elements and structure of most general-purpose computer languages, such as FORTRAN or PASCAL, are not closely aligned with those of systems we wish to simulate. For example, these languages do not provide convenient data structures for event processing. This is an essential logical element in simulation modeling. There is no statement in FORTRAN that explicitly increments or decrements queues of people or objects. There is no statement in FORTRAN that tallies the number of objects in a queue and computes the mean to provide all-important statistical output. Advance of the time variable, essential to running a simulation model, is also missing from FORTRAN and other general-purpose languages.

In order to include these functions, and others essential to the model structure in the computer program, extensive, often complex and difficult to debug code must be written. Thus the motivation for the development and use of simulation languages stems from the desire to shorten the time needed to develop valid models that are relatively easy to debug and that conveniently provide the statistical output so necessary for decision making. It should be noted that these objectives have been accomplished at some expense of efficiency in model execution. Further discussion of this issue is contained in Section 4.4.

The first language to address the unique requirements of simulation model coding was GPSS (General Purpose Simulation System), developed by Geoffrey Gordon and first published in 1961 [2]. The language has evolved through many versions, most of them produced by IBM. An independently developed version of GPSS, GPSS/H, permits interactive debugging of code [4]. Today, GPSS is available for most mainframe and minicomputers, and two versions exist for the IBM PC microcomputer.

The elements of the GPSS language are defined to have a high degree of isomorphism with the elements of discrete systems. For example, the QUEUE element in GPSS tracks objects as they wait for service and computes statistics on waiting time. The SEIZE block permits an object to take control of the facility that will provide the required service. This close correspondence of language to the real world makes the tasks of learning the language and coding the models in it much easier and much quicker.

Shortly after the appearance of GPSS, a simulation language called SIMSCRIPT, developed at the RAND Corporation, was introduced in 1963 [9]. This language possessed a more general world view that permitted the modeling of more complex systems. To do this, the elements of the language were less explicitly linked to elements of the real world. The use of sets, events, processes, and resources figure heavily in the structure and operation of SIMSCRIPT programs. This requires the modeler to provide more of the model structure, necessitating a longer time to become proficient in using the language.

The modeling of more complex, and usually very large systems confined SIM-SCRIPT to minicomputers and mainframe computers until recently. The advancing computer technology has now made possible a version of SIMSCRIPT for the IBM PC microcomputer.

These pioneer languages were soon followed by a spate of simulation languages which appeared over the next 25 years. Some of these attempts endured, others did not. Some addressed a very small class of simulation modeling, others a broad range of systems. In Section 4.3, we discuss some of the survivors, with emphasis on those that are still evolving. Of particular note are SLAM [13] and SIMAN, [10] which are perhaps the most all-inclusive of simulation languages, addressing not only discrete-event models, but also continuous and combined continuous discrete-event models.

4.2.2 STRUCTURE OF SIMULATION LANGUAGES

As suggested in the previous section, each simulation language may take a different world view, where world view refers to the way in which the language represents the real system. The concern of this section is the way these world views are implemented in the structure of the language. A useful framework for this discussion is contained in a paper by Kiviat [7], which also appears in [8] as Appendix C. Kiviat defines the static structure of a simulation language to have three parts: identification of objects and object characteristics, relationships between objects, and generation of objects. He defines the dynamic structure of the language in terms of the method for advancing simulated time.

Objects are the things in the system and the model that are the main concern of the analysis: customers in a bank, or parts on an assembly line. Different languages refer to objects using terms such as entities (SIMAN) or transactions (GPSS). The characteristics of objects serve to differentiate among objects. For example, bank customers wishing to cash checks, versus customers making deposits to several accounts, would presumably be processed in dissimilar ways in the model. Characteristics are variously referred to as attributes (SIMAN, SIMSCRIPT), parameters (GPSS), properties, etc.

To make the discussion more specific, we compare the structure of three simulation languages: GPSS, SIMAN, and SIMSCRIPT. These languages were also selected for detailed coverage in Section 4.3 and the Primers of Appendixes A, B, and C because of their preeminence and widespread usage. Table 4.1 contrasts the approaches taken by these languages in defining objects and object characteristics.

Even though objects may have unique characteristics, for purposes of processing them in the model, it may be advantageous to group them into classes. For example, bank customers having more than one transaction may be grouped according to the number of transactions as:

Group 1: 2-3 transactions

Group 2: 4-6 transactions

Group 3: more than 6 transactions.

Each language may have a different mechanism for accomplishing this. Table 4.2 describes the relationship mechanisms used by GPSS, SIMAN, and SIMSCRIPT for grouping objects.

TABLE 4.1
OBJECTS AND OBJECT CHARACTERISTICS

Language	Object, Characteristic	Example	
GPSS	Transaction, Parameter	P1	First parameter of a transaction
SIMAN	Entity, Attribute	A(I)	Ith attribute of an entity
SIMSCRIPT	Entity, Attribute	AGE(MAN)	The AGE of an entity coded MAN

Even in the case of a relatively small system, maintaining all objects to be dealt with by the model for the entire run length could be prohibitive in terms of computer memory required. Consequently, a means of generating objects when needed and disposing of them when their role in the system has been completed must be provided.

The manner in which different simulation languages implement this varies widely. In many cases the mechanism used may be traced back to the characteristics of the root compiler language upon which the simulation language was initially built, rather than the world view of the particular simulation language. For example, SIMSCRIPT was initially rooted in FORTRAN, and SIMAN is also currently rooted in FORTRAN. Thus the analyst defines the model in statements that serve as input to a FORTRAN program, which is ultimately compiled and run.

Simulation languages that are tied less closely to the data-structure conventions of a particular compiler generate objects in a manner closely related to the world view of the language. GPSS is one such language; it was originally written in the assembly language

TABLE 4.2
RELATIONSHIPS BETWEEN OBJECTS

Language	Relationship Mechanism	Example
GPSS	User chain	LINK I,FIFO Place a transaction first on Chain I
	Group	JOIN 10 Join Group 10
SIMAN	Set	GROUP:3 Aggregate groups of 3 entities
SIMSCRIPT	Set	FILE MAN FIRST IN CUSTOMERS Insert MAN into a set called CUSTOMERS

of each individual machine. As the capabilities of general-purpose computer languages have improved, most simulation languages have been recoded in assembly-like, machine-independent languages, such as C. But the initial structure for object generation persists in the simulation languages. Table 4.3 describes the object generation mechanisms used by GPSS, SIMAN, and SIMSCRIPT.

The static structure of a simulation language places the objects in the model in space, that is, where the objects are located physically in the system. A dynamic structure is needed to place the objects in time and to permit progression from one point in time to another. As described in Chapter 2, there are fundamentally two approaches: fixed-time step, and event-tracking.

The first approach examines the system at fixed-time intervals to determine if its status has changed. The status will change whenever a customer arrives at a queueing system, for example. If the status has changed, the appropriate variables are altered. If the status remains the same, the time variable is incremented by the fixed-time interval. Figure 4.1 illustrates this approach for a single-server queueing system. Although logically simple to implement, this method is inherently very inefficient. There will be many points in time when the system will not change status, and hence many unnecessary system examinations by the model. Consequently, there are no discrete-event simulation languages that use this approach for dynamic structure.

The event-tracking approach examines the system only when its status changes. Logic is included in the model to determine when events or system status changes occur, and the time variable is advanced to precisely these points before the system is examined. Figure 4.2 shows this method for the single-server queueing system. The logic needed to do this is considerably more complicated than that of the fixed-time step method, but the savings in model execution time overwhelmingly justify it. As explained in Chapter 3, the use of lists, pointers, and stacks can greatly simplify the implementation of event tracking in a model.

A special case of the event-tracking approach is referred to as process interaction, where a process is defined as a sequence of events ordered in time. Rather than focusing on the changes in system state, this method is centered on the progress of an object through the model elements. The interacting processes may be thought of as the series of

TABLE 4.3
GENERATION OF OBJECTS

Language	Generation Mechanism	Example
GPSS	Create a new transaction with a specified time between successive generations	`GENERATE 20` 20 time units between successive generations
SIMAN	Create a new entity with a specified time between successive generations	`CREATE:EX(1,1)` Exponential intervals between generations
SIMSCRIPT	Schedule an event whenever one is needed	Schedule a `MAN.CREATION IN 10 MINUTES`

FIGURE 4.1   FIXED-TIME STEP APPROACH TO TIME ADVANCE

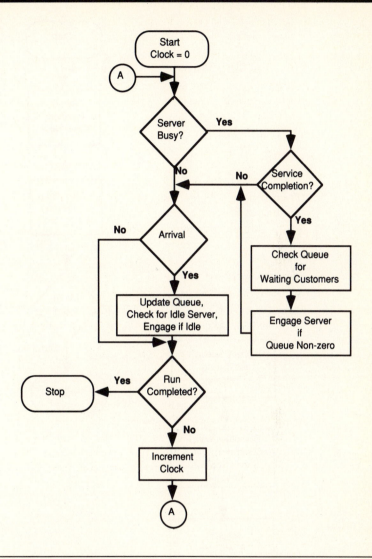

events necessary to follow arriving objects from system entry to system exit. For example, each arrival to a single-server queueing system has a series of events that correspond to implementing its arrival, joining the queue, leaving the queue, being served, and leaving the system. This series of events constitutes a process for each arrival. Figure 4.3 illustrates this approach for a single-server queueing model.

Notice that we must now distinguish between unconditional and conditional waits in our model logic. For example, the block that contains "Advance Clock by Service Time" implements an unconditional wait: the duration of the service time. However, the "Wait Until Selected for Service" block implements a conditional wait: the object's

FIGURE 4.2 EVENT TRACKING APPROACH TO TIME ADVANCE

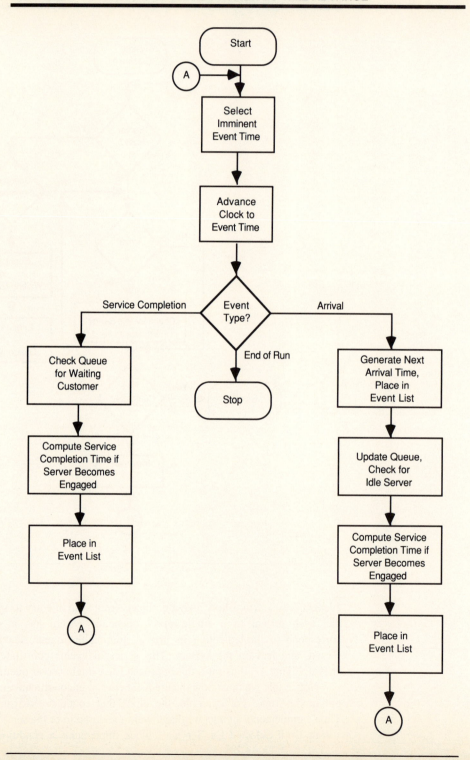

FIGURE 4.3   PROCESS-INTERACTION APPROACH TO TIME ADVANCE

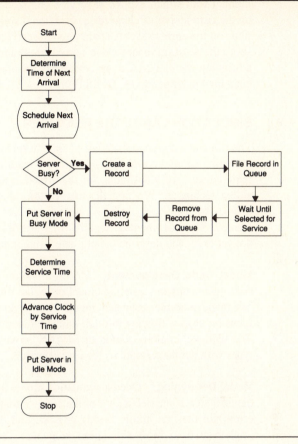

time in the queue while waiting for a free server. This wait is conditioned upon the status of the server.

As was the case for static-language structure, our three example simulation languages differ in their dynamic structure as well. GPSS adopts the process interaction approach, while SIMAN and SIMSCRIPT permit the use of either event tracking or process interaction within the same model framework.

The implementation of the process interaction approach by GPSS is somewhat different from that of SIMAN, SIMSCRIPT, and other simulation languages that use this approach. The GPSS process is closely focused on the object flowing in the model, and thus it is more accurately described as a transaction-flow orientation. Events in GPSS are tracked by placing transactions in either of two lists, or chains: the current-events chain and the future-events chain.

Transactions on the first chain are due to progress in the model at the current moment in time, while those on the second are not scheduled to move until some future time. Each transaction on the current-events chain is advanced as far as possible in the model before the next transaction on the chain is dealt with. Among the situations that may stop a transaction's progress are a delay for service time or a queue in front of a

server. In the first case, the transaction is placed on the future-events chain for an unconditional wait which expires at service completion time, while in the second, it remains
on the current-events chain for a conditional wait until a server is free. When all transactions on the current-events chain have progressed as far as possible, the time variable is
set to the most imminent move time of the transactions on the future-events chain, thus
advancing the clock. A more detailed description of the dynamic structure of GPSS is
contained in Appendix A, GPSS Primer.

4.2.3   SIMULATION LANGUAGE FEATURES

The static and dynamic structure of simulation languages provide the bare necessities for
executing simulation models. Many other features provided by simulation languages are
required, or highly desirable, for the effective use of simulation analysis as a decision-
aiding technique. We first discuss features that are currently available in simulation
languages, using our three example languages to illustrate how they can be implemented. Then we mention features that are desirable in simulation languages but may
not yet exist, and describe the ultimate ''Integrated Simulation Environment'' [5].

Model Code Development   Most simulation languages still require the entering of
code statements to create the model code, but the graphics capability of microcomputers
has made possible graphical input. This is particularly well-suited to languages that
focus on objects flowing through model elements or blocks, such as GPSS and SIMAN.
The IBM PC implementation of SIMAN provides graphical input by displaying block
types with parameter options for user selection.

Model Debugging   Once a simulation model has been coded in the selected language,
the next step is the debugging of the code so that it runs to a normal termination. Syntax
errors are the first hurdle in this process, and the diagnostics to detect these are well
implemented in most simulation languages. Some IBM PC versions of GPSS and
SIMAN will not accept syntactically incorrect code. They do not, however, suggest how
to correct the errors.

Far more difficult to correct are errors that occur during execution of the code. The
diagnostics of most simulation languages are not totally adequate in this regard. Upon
encountering an error, the program often terminates, providing no reason in terms of
model logic for the termination. GPSS, SIMAN, and SIMSCRIPT do permit the user to
perform a trace as the program is running. The additional output provided during the run
for values of specified variables is designed to assist the analyst in uncovering the error.
GPSS/H and SIMAN provide further help by permitting the user to debug interactively.
The values of specified variables may be watched during execution and even changed
mid-run.

Random Variate Generation   For any probabilistic simulation, the ability to extract
random samples from specified probability distributions is most important. In Chapter 7
we describe techniques for generating random numbers and random variates from
specific distributions, many of which require extensive computer code. Simulation
languages greatly simplify this task. All three of our example languages permit sampling
from a wide range of common probability distributions as well as the specification of
user-defined distributions.

Collection of Statistics   The execution of a simulation model without collection of data on system performance measures may be likened to an inattentive observer of a real system. The observer was present during the system operation but cannot recount what happened, and therefore is useless for the assessment of possible system changes. Statistics on system-performance measures accumulated while running the simulation model are what justifies all that computer time. A simulation language should permit the user to easily specify a wide variety of statistics to be collected during model execution.

Also, to aid in the interpretation of the simulation output, graphical portrayal and statistical inference capabilities are desirable. For example, a frequency distribution of the waiting time in a queue may give more insight into the level of service being provided than a simple mean waiting time. If 10 percent of the customers wait in excess of 15 minutes, service may be deemed poor even with a low mean waiting time. Since all data collected during the model run are samples, one needs to use inferential statistics to interpret them. For example, placing a confidence interval around the mean waiting time would indicate how precise the estimate is.

All of the example simulation languages have extensive capabilities for the collection of statistics. GPSS is perhaps the most inflexible, in that a standard set of output statistics is provided, whether requested or not. Both SIMAN and SIMSCRIPT permit the user wide latitude in the specification of output reports. SIMAN has modest statistical inference capability.

Experimental Design   Since simulation analysis is a descriptive, rather than prescriptive, technique, its successful application depends heavily on model experimentation. Effective, efficient experimental designs do much to enhance the ultimate quality of solutions obtained from a simulation model. The simulation language can contribute to this by facilitating changes to the model, since each data point in the experiment requires a separate model run.

GPSS is probably the least helpful in this regard; even simple changes in initial values require the entire program to be re-assembled. SIMAN has addressed the problem by totally divorcing the model logic from the experimental design logic. In this way, a particular model structure may be employed using many different sets of data, or experimental design configurations, without re-compiling the model code. For complex models this can result in appreciable savings of computer time. SIMSCRIPT facilitates altering of data through flexible input/output options contained within the model code.

Graphical Animation and Dynamic Output   The ability to use simulation languages on microcomputers permits the graphics capability of these machines to illustrate, in some fashion, the running of the simulation model or its output. Illustration of objects flowing through elements of a model is referred to as animation. Animations usually employ color monitors and easily-recognizable symbols for objects and model elements. It is believed that by observing such flow, the analyst can discern the causes of operational problems, and alter the model to correct them.

As would be surmised, animating a model decreases the speed at which it will execute. Because of this, adequate animations are usually only accomplished on the fastest microcomputers with a large complement of memory. However, simple models can be animated on smaller microcomputers to provide insights, as illustrated in Hoover and Perry [6].

In an attempt to aggregate the events occurring during a model run, graphs of output measures are altered as the run progresses. A typical graph is a bar chart representing the length of a queue. As the time is updated, the size of the bar increases and decreases with changes in queue length. Such graphs are often included in a corner of the screen so they may be observed along with the animation.

The increasing power of microcomputers, as exemplified by the IBM PC/AT and compatibles, has made very detailed color graphics animation possible. A product that takes full advantage of this power is the SIMAN language animation package, CINEMA. This software allows the user to create both the static setting for the animation and the icons that represent the movable objects in the simulation. When the simulation model is executed, a color graphics portrayal of the action and selected output measures pass before the user.

Features Yet to Come   A review of simulation languages from the user's point of view performed by Perry [11] approximately 20 years ago shows a marked similarity in some areas to a more recent review by Henriksen [5]. The need for automated model-code generation, effective interactive-debugging capability, and facile means for changing the experimental design still exist. This is not to say that simulation languages have not made great strides in the intervening two decades in areas such as language constructs to accommodate more complex systems, better error diagnostics, efficient object-code production, and implementation of languages on smaller and smaller machines. But the current state of the art is quite far from the ''Integrated Simulation Environment'' described by Henriksen.

This environment envisions a large common knowledge base that allows easy communication and transition among the software elements of the environment. These elements are: model editor, input-preparation subsystem, statistics-collection definition facility, experimental design facility, output-definition facility, program editor, compiler, and run-time support. Figure 4.4 shows the explicit relationships among the software components. Under this environment, a user could move easily from one phase of model development and execution to another, greatly reducing the time and effort required to produce usable results from the simulation model.

It is possible to embody in this integrated-simulation environment an approach perhaps too pervasive to refer to as a feature of a simulation language: artificial intelligence. The concepts of artificial intelligence are just beginning to be included in simulation models.

An assessment of what these concepts can contribute to simulation analysis is provided by Shannon [17]. He describes the major differences between conventional simulation models and those using the artificial intelligence, or AI, approach as follows.

First, the AI models distinctly separate the model, experiment, and output analysis aspects of the analysis. Also, certain characteristics of the model itself are different. For example, conventional models tend to be numeric in their description of the system being modeled, have explicit steps for model execution, and cannot do anything not planned by the analyst. By contrast, AI models use symbolic descriptions and processes, include heuristic search techniques, and permit the model to ''learn'' from experience and thereby alter its operation.

This brief description of the differences between the conventional and AI approaches to simulation greatly oversimplifies the matter. But one thing is certain from our discussion of simulation languages: effective implementation of the AI approach depends heavily on the language structure and features.

FIGURE 4.4 INTEGRATED SIMULATION ENVIRONMENT

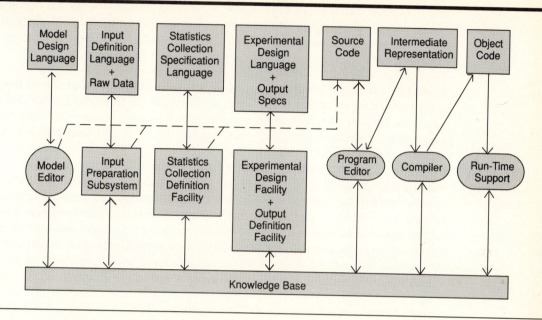

4.2.4 SELECTING THE "RIGHT" SIMULATION LANGUAGE

Selecting the right simulation language is analogous to the problem of developing the right simulation model. The answer to the question, "Which is right?," is the same in either case: "It depends." Just as the model content depends heavily on the purpose for which it is intended, the language chosen depends to a great extent on the particular circumstances of the users. Certainly the features discussed above are relevant. But beyond that, there are pragmatic issues to be considered. In the following paragraphs we will suggest but a few of these issues, not necessarily in order of relative importance.

Ease of Learning   Some languages are inherently more complex than others, even though the complexity may be necessary to deal with more involved systems. In general, the more isomorphic the language elements are to real-world elements, the easier a language is to learn. For example, GPSS transactions flow through model elements with names such as QUEUES, FACILITIES, and STORAGES. If a language is not easily self-taught, then training should be readily available by competent experts. The creators of SIMSCRIPT and SIMAN offer regularly scheduled short courses in the languages.

Ease of Explanation to Nontechnical Individuals   Closely related to the issue of learning to use the language is that of explaining how a simulation model functions to the manager who is paying for it, and who may not be interested in the nuances of computer languages. A language such as GPSS or SIMAN, with its graphical portrayal of system elements as blocks, can be easily explained. SIMSCRIPT, with its statements close to a narrative description of the problem, is certainly easier to explain than an equation-oriented language.

Cost   The assessment of the cost of a simulation language should include the cost of initial purchase, maintenance of the software, training, and developing and executing models coded in the language. An inexpensive language may not run as efficiently as a more expensive one. Constant expansion and correction of dormant bugs by a vendor is expensive, but it maintains the currency and usefulness of the language.

Standard Code for All Computers   Initially, simulation languages were closely linked to the machine for which they were written. To run the model on another machine meant significant recoding. As general-purpose computer languages became more machine-independent, so did simulation languages. But the degree of standardization does not approach that of the ANSI languages such as FORTRAN. Each implementation of a language such as GPSS has minor variations across machines.

A new challenge of standardization is to permit the identical source code statements to be accepted by the mainframe, minicomputer, and microcomputer implementations of the language. SIMAN is one language that has accomplished this. Standardization across microcomputer and larger machine versions permits convenient model development and code debugging on a personal computer, and ultimate production runs on the larger, faster machine without any code changes. The debugged model code can easily be uploaded from the personal computer to the mainframe.

Scope of Problems Addressable by the Language   To be truly useful, a simulation language should be able to model a wide variety of real systems: inventory management, job shops, material handling systems, and local area networks, to name just a few applications. Most general-purpose simulation languages such as our three example languages can easily do this. But some languages have been devised to solve a fairly small class of problems, for example, job shops. As the size of the class shrinks, these so-called languages become more application programs in fact. We will mention a few of these briefly in Section 4.3.4. Such "languages" may have the advantage of being easy to learn and use, but if the solution of a broader range of problems is ever contemplated, a more general-purpose simulation language should be considered.

4.3   SOME POPULAR SIMULATION LANGUAGES

In the sections that follow, the three example simulation languages, GPSS, SIMAN, and SIMSCRIPT, are discussed in some detail. The world view of each language is described briefly, a nuclear set of language elements is discussed, and a simple illustrative problem is provided for each language. The reader is referred to specific sections of the Primers of Appendixes A (GPSS), B (SIMAN), and C (SIMSCRIPT) for detailed definitions of language elements and further example problems.

If one seeks a minimum understanding of the structure of each language, then the discussion in the following sections will suffice. But if it is desired to construct the simulation models in the exercises at the end of the chapter using one of the languages, at least some of the material from the Primers must be consulted.

4.3.1   GPSS

GPSS, or more fully, General Purpose Simulation System, is a process-interaction or transaction-flow-oriented language. The fundamental language elements, which are called entities, may be collected into six categories: basic, equipment, statistical, computational, reference, and chain. The two basic entities are transactions, which are the objects flowing in the model, and blocks, which are the model elements through which transactions flow. In addition to the entities, which describe the model structure, GPSS contains control statements. These are used to specify the manner in which the simulation model is to be executed: for example, initializing variables and fixing the length of the run.

A fundamental set of GPSS blocks is: GENERATE, TERMINATE, SEIZE, RELEASE, ADVANCE, QUEUE, and DEPART. In addition, the following control statements are needed to execute even the simplest model: SIMULATE, START, and END. Each block in GPSS has a unique flow chart symbol. When the flow of transactions in the model is described using these symbols, converting the flow chart to computer code is accomplished by simply recording the corresponding statement for each symbol.

The format of a GPSS statement is divided into four fields as shown in the table.

Col. 1–6	Col. 8–18		Col. 19–71
Block Location	**Block Name (or Control Statement)**	**Operands**	**Comments**
	GENERATE	10	CUSTOMER ARRIVES
BLOC1	SEIZE	MACH	CAPTURE MACHINE
	START	200	
	ADVANCE	10,4	PROCESS PART

Fields must be separated by blanks or tab characters, and operands by commas. The Block Location and Comments fields are optional. Block Location is analogous to a statement label in general-purpose programming languages, and is used for transaction routing.

In the first example statement, transactions representing customers arrive every 10 time units, precisely. The SEIZE block permits a transaction to take control of the equipment entity named MACH and it is not relinquished until the transaction passes through a RELEASE block. The START statement initializes a counter which can be used to set the number of transactions to pass through the model before it is terminated. In the last example, the ADVANCE block holds a transaction to represent the processing of a part. The holding time is uniformly distributed over the interval 10 ± 4, or from 6 to 14.

Having established the flavor of the language, a simple system model using GPSS is now presented and used as a vehicle to explain the fundamental blocks and the output provided by GPSS. The system chosen is a single-server queue such as might be encountered in a small grocery store, a one-stall car wash, or a small-town bank. The model comments view the system as a bank. The flow chart appears in Fig. 4.5 and the GPSS statements in Fig. 4.6.

The first statement is a comment statement, denoted by the * (asterisk) as the first character, which is ignored by the GPSS assembler. The SIMULATE statement tells the GPSS assembler to execute this program, rather than just perform a syntax check, which it would do if the statement were omitted. The GENERATE block creates customers at intervals of 10 ± 5 minutes, uniformly distributed, who join a queue named LINE if the single teller is busy.

FIGURE 4.5   GPSS FIOW CHART FOR SINGLE-SERVER QUEUE

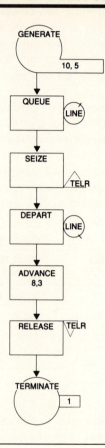

FIGURE 4.6   GPSS CODE FOR SINGLE-SERVER QUEUE

```
Block     Block Name     Operands          Comments
Location
------------------------------------------------------------------
*   CUSTOMER SERVICE EVALUATION MODEL - SMALLTOWN BANK
          SIMULATE
          GENERATE       10,5              CUSTOMERS ARRIVE
          QUEUE          LINE              JOIN LINE
          SEIZE          TELR              CAPTURE TELLER
          DEPART         LINE              LEAVE THE LINE
          ADVANCE        8,3               TRANSACT BUSINESS
          RELEASE        TELR              RELINQUISH TELLER
          TERMINATE      1                 COUNT  CUSTOMERS LEAVING
          START          200               RUN 200 CUSTOMERS THRU
          END
------------------------------------------------------------------
```

When a customer reaches the head of the line, the facility called TELR is engaged to process the required bank transactions by using the SEIZE block. The customer then leaves the queue named LINE. It is necessary to seize the facility before departing the queue because we wish to collect statistics on the waiting time that ensues when the SEIZE block refuses the transaction entry. If the transaction passed through the DEPART block first, the statistics would not be accumulated.

The ADVANCE block represents the time required to process a customer's business. In this model, that time is uniformly distributed over the interval 8 ± 3 minutes. At the completion of his business, the customer relinquishes the teller by passing through a RELEASE block, and leaves the model via a TERMINATE block. The "1" in the operands field of the TERMINATE block decrements a preset counter by 1 every time a transaction passes through the block. The run length can thus be controlled by the number of customers processed. The counter is set by the control statement START, and for this run a value of 200 customers was used. Finally, the control statement END returns control to the operating system at the conclusion of the run.

The output for this model is shown in Fig. 4.7. The first section displays the GPSS statements and their associated line numbers and block numbers. The next section begins with the clock value at the conclusion of the run. Following this is a listing of the model block numbers, the current number of transactions in each block, and the total number of transactions that passed through each block during the run. This information is often helpful in debugging errors that affect transaction flow. The final section of the output contains statistics collected for each entity. In this case, there are but two: the queue LINE and the facility TELR.

The foregoing discussion presents a very brief, and simplified view of the GPSS language. Even the statements illustrated can be formulated to model much more complex situations. The reader is referred to the Primer of Appendix A for a much fuller description of these and other features of the language. Sections 1.0 through 4.0 describe in detail the blocks used in our simple bank model, and provide a fundamental understanding of the language structure and operation. Further examples using a slightly augmented set of blocks are included in Section 3.2 of Appendix A. The remaining sections of the Primer treat intermediate and advanced modeling concepts and the associated GPSS blocks. Four additional problem sets illustrate the use of these blocks. For an even more complete description of the GPSS language than that provided by the Primer, the reader is referred to texts such as Gordon [3], or Schriber [16].

4.3.2   SIMAN

SIMAN (SIMulation ANalysis) is a simulation language suitable for modeling discrete-event, continuous, and combined continuous/discrete-event systems. We limit our coverage here and, in the Primer of Appendix B, to discrete-event models formulated using SIMAN block diagrams. This approach may be described as process-interaction or entity-flow oriented, and is similar to GPSS. SIMAN uses a directed block diagram consisting of several block types, each of which has a unique function. The world view assumed is that of entities flowing through the blocks, which define system components.

Unlike GPSS, SIMAN explicitly recognizes and separates three major phases of simulation analysis: model definition, model experimentation, and output analysis. This permits several alternative systems to be evaluated without altering the model code.

FIGURE 4.7   GPSS OUTPUT FOR SINGLE-SERVER QUEUE

```
LINE    BLOCK  BLOCK    BLOCK NAME      OPERANDS COMMENTS
NUMBER  NUMBER LOCATION
--------------------------------------------------------------------
 1             *  CUSTOMER SERVICE EVALUATION MODEL - SMALLTOWN BANK
 2                         SIMULATE
 3        1              GENERATE        10,5       CUSTOMERS ARRIVE
 4        2              QUEUE           LINE       JOIN LINE
 5        3              SEIZE           TELR       CAPTURE TELLER
 6        4              DEPART          LINE       LEAVE THE LINE
 7        5              ADVANCE         8,3        TRANSACT BUSINESS
 8        6              RELEASE         TELR       RELINQUISH TELLER
 9        7              TERMINATE       1          COUNT CUSTOMERS LEAVING
10                       START           200        RUN 200 CUSTOMERS THROUGH


RELATIVE CLOCK 1987    ABSOLUTE CLOCK 1987

    BLOCK   CURRENT      TOTAL
       1       1         201
       2       0         200
       3       0         200
       4       0         200
       5       0         200
       6       0         200
       7       0         200
```

QUEUE	MAXIMUM CONTENTS	AVERAGE CONTENTS	TOTAL ENTRIES	ZERO ENTRIES	PERCENT ZEROS
LINE	1	0.152	200	109	54.50

AVERAGE TIME/TRANS	$AVERAGE TIME/TRANS
1.51	3.330

FACILITY	AVERAGE UTILIZATION	NUMBER ENTRIES	AVERAGE TIME/TRANS	SEIZING TRANS. NO.	PREEMPTING TRANS. NO.
TELR	0.816	200	8.110		

Further distinguishing SIMAN from GPSS and other block diagram languages, is the ability to readily model complex material-handling systems using special-purpose blocks.

A fundamental set of SIMAN blocks consists of: CREATE, SEIZE, RELEASE, DELAY, QUEUE, and TALLY. Each block in SIMAN has an identifying flow chart symbol. When the flow of entities is described using these symbols, converting the flow chart to computer code for the model frame of SIMAN is simply a matter of recording the corresponding statement for each symbol. In addition, a basic set of experimental frame elements are needed to define the particular run of the model. These are: PROJECT, DISCRETE, RESOURCES, PARAMETERS, TALLIES, and REPLICATE.

The syntax of model-frame and experimental-frame element statements are shown in the table.

MODEL-FRAME ELEMENTS

col. 1–8	col. 10–74	
Label	*Blockname,Operands:Modifiers;*	*Comments*
	CREATE,5:UN(3,2):MARK(2);	CUSTOMERS ARRIVE
	SEIZE:MACHINE;	CAPTURE MACHINE
	DELAY:EX(2,2)	PROCESS PART

EXPERIMENTAL-FRAME ELEMENTS

col. 1–74	
Elementname,Operands:Modifiers;	*Comments*
PROJECT,JOBSHOP A,J. SMITH,3/5/85;	TITLE LINE
DISCRETE,5,2,3;	DEFINE MODEL SIZE
RESOURCES:1,MACHINE;	MACHINE CAPACITY =1

The delimiters for separating fields (i.e., Label, Blockname, Operands, Modifiers, and Comments) and entries within fields cannot be described briefly, but one universal delimiter is the semicolon (;), used to separate the executable part of the statement from comments. The Label and Comments fields are optional. Label is used to route entities to specific blocks. For the experimental frame statements, the Label field is not used, and the statement itself begins in the first column. Section 2.5 of Appendix B describes the formats for both model- and experimental-frame statements in detail.

The first three statements above are for model-frame definition, while the last is for experimental-frame definition. In the first example statement, entities are created in batches of five. The interarrival times are described by a uniform probability distribution defined by parameter set 3 and random-number stream 2, UN(3,2), which are included in the experimental frame. Also, arrival times are saved in attribute number 2 of each entity, MARK(2). The second statement captures a resource named MACHINE. Control of this resource must be relinquished by means of a RELEASE block. The DELAY statement, which represents the processing of a part, holds the part for a random time described by an exponential distribution defined by parameter set 2 and random-number stream 2, EX(2,2). The last statement is part of the experimental frame; it defines the capacity of the RESOURCE called MACHINE to be 1.

With these brief examples as background, a simple system model using SIMAN is now developed and used as a vehicle to explain the fundamental model- and experimental-frame elements, and the output provided by SIMAN. The system used is the same one modeled in GPSS in the previous section: a single teller bank. The flow chart for the model appears in Fig. 4.8, and the model and experimental-frame statements are listed in Fig. 4.9a and 4.9b.

The first and last statements for the model and experimental frames must be BEGIN and END; they define the limits of the code for the SIMAN processor. Comment statements, such as the second and third lines of the program, begin with a semicolon (;) and are ignored by the processor. The CREATE statement produces customers according to a uniform distribution described by parameter set 1, defined in the experimental frame,

FIGURE 4.8   SIMAN FLOW CHART FOR SINGLE-SERVER QUEUE

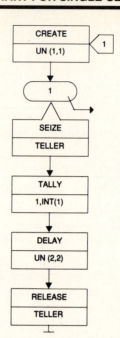

and random-number stream 1, UN(1,1). The modifier MARK records the arrival time of a customer in attribute 1 of the entity. This information is used to collect statistics on waiting times.

When the resource TELLER is found to be occupied, the customer joins the QUEUE 1. When the TELLER is free, the customer advances to transact business, SEIZE:TELLER. At the moment the customer begins service, the TALLY statement records the waiting time, current time minus arrival time recorded in attribute 1, in a TALLY designated 1, TALLY:1,INT(1). The time to transact business is represented by a DELAY statement. These service times are described by a uniform distribution defined by parameter set 2, specified in the experimental frame, and random-number stream 2, UN(2,2). Finally, when service is completed, the customer relinquishes the TELLER in the RELEASE block, and leaves the bank, by way of the DISPOSE modifier.

Turning now to the experimental frame, PROJECT is an optional statement used to provide a heading for the model output. It includes a title, the analyst's name, and the date. The DISCRETE statement defines the size of the model in terms of the maximum number of active entities permitted, the number of attributes each entity shall have, and the number of queues in the model. The TALLIES statement simply assigns a title to each numbered TALLY block in the model frame. RESOURCES assigns a capacity to each named resource in the model frame.

PARAMETERS is a very flexible way of assigning specific values to attributes and variables in the model frame. In this example, PARAMETERS is used to make two uniform probability distributions specific: one for the arrival process (parameter set 1

FIGURE 4.9   SIMAN CODE FOR SINGLE-SERVER QUEUE

```
Label    Blockname,Operands:Modifiers; Comments
-------------------------------------------------------------
BEGIN;
; CUSTOMER SERVICE EVALUATION MODEL  - SMALLTOWN BANK
;
        CREATE:UN(1,1):MARK(1);      CUSTOMERS ARRIVE
        QUEUE,1;                     JOIN LINE
        SEIZE:TELLER;                CAPTURE TELLER
        TALLY:1,INT(1);              TALLY CUSTOMER WAIT
        DELAY:UN(2,2);               TRANSACT BUSINESS
        RELEASE:TELLER:DISPOSE;      RELEASE TELLER, LEAVE
END;
-------------------------------------------------------------


Elementname,Operands:Modifiers;    Comments
-------------------------------------------------------------
BEGIN;
PROJECT,SMALLTOWN BANK,JONES,1/20/85;
DISCRETE,50,1,1;              50 ENTITIES,1 ATTRIBUTE, 1 QUEUE
TALLIES:1,CUSTOMER WAIT;      TALLY CUSTOMER WAITING TIME
RESOURCES:1,TELLER;           1 TELLER IN BANK
PARAMETERS:1,5,15:            !CUSTOMER ARRIVALS
          2,5,11;             TIME TO TRANSACT BUSINESS
REPLICATE,1,0,2400;           1 RUN,START=0 FOR 5 480 MIN DAYS
END;
-------------------------------------------------------------
```

{1,5,15}), and one for the service time (parameter set 2 {2,5,11}). The interarrival times are distributed over the range 5 to 15 minutes, and their service times over the range 5 to 11.

Finally, the REPLICATE statement defines the number of runs, the starting time for the first run, and the run length. For this example, a single run is made starting at time zero and continuing for 2400 minutes, or five 480-minute days.

The standard output for a SIMAN run is illustrated in Figure 4.10 for this example. In addition to the heading, the figure shows the ending time of the run, the TALLY block statistics, and the computer time required to execute the run. The TALLY block statistics are quite minimal, showing only measures such as the mean, and standard deviation. Additional output describing the distribution of waiting times, the number of customers in the queue, as well as printer graphs for these data are available from SIMAN using model frame blocks and special post processing of data collected during the model run.

The description of SIMAN and the example problem discussed above provide but a hint of the capabilities of the language. The reader is referred to the Primer of Appendix B for a full discussion of the language features. Sections 1.0 through 3.0 describe in detail the fundamental set of blocks used in the bank model and provide an understanding of the language structure and operation. Further examples, using a slightly augmented set of blocks, are included in Section 3.5. The remaining four sections of the

FIGURE 4.10   SIMAN OUTPUT FOR SINGLE-SERVER QUEUE

```
                        SIMAN Summary Report

                        Run Number   1 of  1

Project:   SMALLTOWN BANK
Analyst:   JONES
Date   :   1/20/1985

Run ended at time :    .2400E+04

                        Tally Variables
                        ---------------

Number Identifier     Average    Standard   Minimum    Maximum    Number
                                 Deviation  Value      Value      of Obs.
-------------------------------------------------------------------------
   1  CUSTOMER WAIT    2.10803    3.94398   .00000     20.83658     249

Run Time :  8 Second(s)
```

Primer treat intermediate and advanced concepts of the language. Of particular note are Section 5.0, which deals with the implementation of submodels in SIMAN, and Section 6.0, which covers the material-handling systems concepts. For a complete description of the SIMAN language, the reader is referred to Pegden [10].

4.3.3 SIMSCRIPT

SIMSCRIPT is both a structured general-purpose programming language and a simulation language. More correctly, the language is referred to as SIMSCRIPT II.5, which is a major revision of the original language. For brevity, we shall use SIMSCRIPT. In contrast to special-purpose simulation languages, in SIMSCRIPT the analyst can construct most any data structure needed, declare variables to be integer, real, alpha, or text, and include in the model user-written subroutines and functions. In SIMSCRIPT even pointer variables and recursion are provided.

There is no fixed format to SIMSCRIPT statements and they may start in any column and go across as many lines as necessary. It is also possible for multiple SIMSCRIPT statements to occupy the same line of the program. For clarity, however, each statement should be confined to a single line, unless the statement is too long to fit on a single line. SIMSCRIPT has no reserved words but every statement begins with a key word and continues across as many lines as necessary, until the statement is complete.

At first glance SIMSCRIPT appears bewilderingly complex, containing well over 150 key words and qualifiers, as well as a large collection of system variables and functions. Because the syntax of SIMSCRIPT statements is more variable and less obvious than either GPSS or SIMAN, potential users of the language are often discouraged from learning it. This is unfortunate, since once the initial investment in time and effort to learn the language is made, the modeler has an extremely powerful modeling resource at his or her disposal.

The principle elements the SIMSCRIPT language provides for simulation modeling are entities, sets, events, resources, and processes. Initially SIMSCRIPT did not include processes or resources but they were added to allow for process interaction modeling to be included in the capabilities of the language. In principle, resources are an extension of entities and processes are an extension of events. A model consists of SIMSCRIPT statements describing how these elements should be manipulated and processed over the course of the simulation. In a SIMSCRIPT model events and process are scheduled, and when they occur, entities are created and destroyed, put into and removed from sets, are given and returned control of resources and schedule other processes and events.

Included as part of SIMSCRIPT is a rich library of mathematical and statistical functions, making linkages to routines written in other languages unnecessary. Since SIMSCRIPT is a compiler language calls to system services provided by the operating system are also possible. Unlike GPSS there is only one vendor of SIMSCRIPT, namely CACI, who supports the language on most American mainframe computers, as well as on the IBM PC.

Unlike GPSS and SIMAN, SIMSCRIPT provides no automatic collection or display of statistics. To collect statistics on any variable, entity, set, or resource, the user must specify in the first section of the program what statistics should be collected, and then at any point in the simulation, the user can print out or reference the current values of the statistics.

The general structure of a SIMSCRIPT program is:

```
PREAMBLE section
MAIN program
ROUTINES
```

All entities, processes, events, routines, resources, and sets are declared in the Preamble section. Global variables are also declared in the Preamble section along with any statistics, that are to be collected. The Preamble sets the environment and declares the elements of the simulation model.

The Main program is usually very short. Typically, in this section, the initial processes and events are scheduled and entities that are permanently present in the model (permanent entities) are created. The simulation is then started by passing control of program execution to the first scheduled event or process. Control does not return to the Main program until there are no further processes or events to be executed. Typically, when control returns to the main program, the statistical measures that were being built during the simulation are printed out.

The Routines are the heart of the simulation model; they describe the actions that occur during the simulation. A Routine may describe an Event Routine which occurs with no time delays or a Process Routine which can be delayed or interrupted. While a Routine is executing, new Processes or Event Routines can be scheduled for future execution, or routines scheduled in the future can be cancelled.

Upon reading over the SIMSCRIPT statements that make up the program of Fig. 4.11, it is fairly easy to fathom the logic of the program. The output from this program is shown in Fig. 4.12. One particular strength of SIMSCRIPT is the absence of any significant limitations on the name of variables, requiring only that they begin with a letter and contain no blanks. However, to help understand this model, certain of the statements in each of the sections (Preamble, Main, and Process) will be discussed.

FIGURE 4.11   SIMSCRIPT II.5 CODE FOR SINGLE-SERVER QUEUE

```
PREAMBLE
''THIS IS A SIMSCRIPT MODEL OF A SINGLE SERVER QUEUE
''IN THIS MODEL THERE IS ONLY ONE PROCESS CALLED
''CUSTOMER.  WHEN THIS PROCESS BEGINS A NEW CUSTOMER
''PROCESS IS INITIATED
NORMALLY MODE IS UNDEFINED
PROCESSES INCLUDE CUSTOMER
RESOURCES INCLUDE SERVER
ACCUMULATE UTIL.SERVER AS THE AVERAGE OF N.X.SERVER
ACCUMULATE AVE.QUEUE.LENGTH AS THE AVERAGE OF N.Q.SERVER
ACCUMULATE MAX.QUEUE.LENGTH AS THE MAXIMUM OF N.Q.SERVER
DEFINE NO.OF.ARRIVALS AND MAX.NO.ARRIVALS AS INTEGER VARIABLES
END

MAIN
PRINT 1 LINE THUS
INPUT NUMBER MAXIMUM NUMBER OF ARRIVALS
READ MAX.NO.ARRIVALS
CREATE EVERY SERVER(1)
LET U.SERVER(1)=1
ACTIVATE A CUSTOMER IN EXPONENTIAL.F(10.0,1) MINUTES
START SIMULATION
PRINT 4 LINES  WITH TIME.V*24*60, UTIL.SERVER(1),
             AVE.QUEUE.LENGTH(1) AND MAX.QUEUE.LENGTH(1) THUS
CLOCK TIME = *******.** MINUTES
THE UTILIZATION OF THE SERVER WAS ****.**
THE AVERAGE LENGTH OF THE QUEUE WAS ***.**
THE MAXIMUM LENGTH OF THE QUEUE WAS ****
END

PROCESS CUSTOMER
ADD 1 TO NO.OF.ARRIVALS
IF NO.OF.ARRIVALS < MAX.NO.ARRIVALS
ACTIVATE A CUSTOMER IN EXPONENTIAL.F(10.0,1) MINUTES
ALWAYS
REQUEST 1 UNIT OF SERVER(1)
WORK EXPONENTIAL.F(8.0,2) MINUTES
RELINQUISH 1 UNIT OF SERVER(1)
END
```

FIGURE 4.12   SIMSCRIPT II.5 OUTPUT FOR SINGLE-SERVER QUEUE MODEL

```
INPUT NUMBER MAXIMUM NUMBER OF ARRIVALS
II.5> 1000

CLOCK TIME =   10008.36 MINUTES
THE UTILIZATION OF THE SERVER WAS      .80
THE AVERAGE LENGTH OF THE QUEUE WAS    2.65
THE MAXIMUM LENGTH OF THE QUEUE WAS    12
```

In the Preamble of the model, using the MODE statement, we force explicit typing of all variables in the model. A default type could be declared but a good programming practice is to require all variables to be explicitly declared. The process, CUSTOMER, and the resource, SERVER, are declared. The ACCUMULATE statements set up the mechanisms in the model for the collection of statistics on the average number of customers waiting for the server, the utilization of the server, and the maximum number of customers in the queue. In SIMSCRIPT the prefix N.Q and N.X refer to, respectively, the number of entities currently waiting for a resource and, number of entities using the resource. The variables NO.OF.ARRIVALS and MAX.NO.ARRIVALS are global integer variables, which can be referenced or modified anywhere in the model.

In the MAIN section of the model, the user is prompted to input the value of MAX.NO.ARRIVALS which will be used to control the length of the simulation. Next, the resource, SERVER, is created with the suffix (1) indicating only one such resource is present. The capacity (maximum number of available units) of the resource is declared as 1.0 in the statement: LET U.SERVER(1) = 1. An instance of the process CUSTOMER is scheduled to occur at a random exponentially-distributed time in the future. The START SIMULATION transfers control to the SIMSCRIPT event management routines which will activate processes and events at their scheduled times. Control will not return to the Main program until there are no longer any processes or events to be executed. When control is eventually returned to the Main program, the PRINT statement will be executed, printing out on four lines the values of the current time, TIME.V, and the three statistics declared in the Preamble-UTIL.SERVER, AVE.QUEUE.LENGTH, and MAX.QUEUE.LENGTH.

The process CUSTOMER contains the logic for processing a customer. When this process begins, the number of arrivals is incremented by one and if the maximum number of arrivals has not been reached, a new CUSTOMER is scheduled for some random time in the future. The process then requests one unit of the resource SERVER and if it is not available, the process is suspended until one unit of the resource becomes available. Statistics on the number of processes waiting for the resource are gathered and stored in the statistical variables AVE.QUEUE.LENGTH and MAX.QUEUE.LENGTH. When a process is given the requested number of resources the process resumes. In our example, after a request for 1 unit of the resource is granted, the process is immediately suspended through the WORK statement for a random time, representing the servicing of the customer.

After the specified delay in the WORK statement is completed, the process is resumed and the requested unit of the resource is RELINQUISHed and the process ends.

The foregoing example provides only a very brief introduction to SIMSCRIPT II.5. The Primer of Appendix C provides a much more complete description of the language, illustrating its features with many example problems. But to fully understand the capabilities of the language, a reference such as Russell [15] is recommended.

4.3.4   OTHER LANGUAGES

The availability of discrete-event simulation languages did not increase dramatically during the last two decades. Review of a survey of continuous and discrete-event simulation languages conducted in 1966 by Teichrow and Lubin [18] shows that of the six discrete-event languages compared, three are currently supported in either the original form or as revisions. They are: GPSS, SIMSCRIPT, and SLAM. The last language resulted from a major revision of GASP, one of the six languages from the 1966 study, into a form which now permits modeling of continuous, discrete, or combined continuous/discrete-event systems. SLAM is a proprietary language which is described by its developers in reference [13].

Most of the discrete-event languages appearing recently, or new implementations of existing languages, have been created primarily in response to the increase in the computing power of microcomputers, which now can execute the complex code required for simulation models almost as quickly as some mainframe computers. There is a growing spate of microcomputer simulation languages for discrete-event modeling. Of the established languages, GPSS, SIMSCRIPT, and a version of SLAM have been introduced in forms suitable for microcomputers, most notably the IBM PC family. Among the new languages is SIMPAS, a notable attempt to capitalize on the favorable reception PASCAL has received. SIMPAS is implemented as a preprocessor that accepts an extended version of PASCAL as input and produces a standard PASCAL program as output [1].

Many more so-called special-purpose simulation languages have appeared than true general-purpose languages. These languages are designed to readily solve a class of problems of a specific nature, such as job-shop scheduling or manufacturing systems. Their syntax is designed to correspond closely to the parameters in which the problem would be stated by knowledgeable users in a given field. The use of such languages may be justified in terms of the cost of the software, but more importantly, the cost and time for model development may be drastically reduced. The danger is that as the model evolves, it may outgrow the limited capability of the language, necessitating recasting in a more powerful language.

Two examples of such languages that address diverse problem areas are INS [14] and SPEED [19]. The first language, INS, is designed for the simulation of ambulatory-care facilities. The world view is one of entities flowing through a network of resources. Although health care is the focus of this language, its elements are sufficiently general to permit modeling of many other types of systems.

The second language, SPEED, addresses manufacturing systems. The model is constructed by forming statements with operands that describe the entities and resources of the system. Complex model structures, such as routings through a job shop, are easily defined using SPEED statements. Unlike INS, the SPEED elements are couched in terms closely related to manufacturing processes, such as STATION, PART, and TRANSPORTER. Thus use in other problem settings may require a somewhat contrived view of reality.

4.4 SIMULATION LANGUAGES VS. FORTRAN: A COMPARISON EXAMPLE

In this section we focus on the manner in which the three simulation languages we have described model the same system. By so doing, we intend to point out the relative advantages of the languages in terms of some of the factors discussed as relevant in the selection of a simulation language. Further, since the system chosen is also modeled in FORTRAN, we can compare the use of a general-purpose language to simulation languages in general.

The problem chosen for this comparative analysis is the time-shared computer system of Chapter 3. Specifically, we model the expanded system described in Section 3.4.4. Recall that this system consists of a computer system with a number of ports for remote telephone access by the user population.

The particular characteristics of the system being simulated are as follows. There are currently 18 input ports to the computer. Users attempt to call the system at a mean rate which varies by hour of the day as shown in Fig. 3.17 of Chapter 3. The intervals between arriving calls are described by an exponential distribution with an appropriate mean. If a user fails to connect because all ports are occupied, he begins "crash" dialing. That is, the time between successive attempts is 3 minutes, exponentially distributed. Each time a user fails to connect in this mode, there is a 0.15 probability that he will cease calling. Once connected, the time on the system is exponentially distributed with a mean of 20 minutes. Our concern in this analysis is the probability that a user will find all ports occupied when calling the system.

In order to compare the four implementations of this model we refer to some of the factors cited in Section 4.2.4 as relevant in selecting a simulation language. Some of these can be measured more exactly than others, but they are all important. The factors selected are: cost, ease of explanation to nontechnical individuals, and standard code for all computers. The first factor is expanded as follows: program development effort, program length, program execution time, and ease of altering the program.

The code and output for the implementations in GPSS, SIMAN, and SIMSCRIPT appear in Appendix 4A. The FORTRAN code appears in Appendix 3E to Chapter 3. Except for the comments contained in the programs, little will be said to explain the details of the code. The reader is referred to the language Primers of Appendixes A, B, and C for explanations of unfamiliar statements. Then, in Table 4.4, the four implementations are compared relative to the factors cited above.

Before discussing the comparisons embodied in Table 4.4, some explanation of how the entries were determined is in order. First, all programs were run using VAX-11/780 implementations of the languages. Each of the four simulations used a run length of one day of simulated time. Program development time is an estimate of the time required to enter and debug the code. Program length is the number of lines of executable statements. Execution time includes only model run time, not compilation or assembly time. Ease of change indicates whether or not a change in model inputs requires that the model be recompiled or reassembled. Ease of explanation refers to similarity of model entities to system elements and the degree to which words rather than symbols are used to describe the model structure. Finally, standard computer code indicates whether the model may be transferred among machines without *any* change to the code. A "no" entry indicates that minor changes are required in such things as variable name lengths, random-number-generating routines, or input/output specification.

Turning now to the comparative analysis summarized in Table 4.4, it is apparent that the simulation languages as a group perform quite similarly, but differ markedly from the general-purpose language in all aspects compared. Program development time for the general-purpose language is four to five times longer than that of any simulation language. A somewhat correlated factor, program length, is approximately six times that of the average length of the simulation-language programs.

But a most important measure of language performance, program execution time, indicates that the general-purpose language is executed more quickly by a factor of five.

TABLE 4.4
COMPARISON OF FOUR IMPLEMENTATIONS OF A
TIME-SHARED COMPUTER SYSTEM

| Language | Cost | | | Ease of Change | Ease of Explanation | Standard Computer Code |
	Program Development Effort	*Program Length*	*Program Execution Time*			
GPSS	1–2 Hours	30 Lines	2.80 Sec.	Program change required	Good, some symbolic notation	No
SIMAN	1.5–2 Hours	22 Lines	2.48 Sec.	Change experimental frame only	Good, but considerable symbolic notation	Yes
SIMSCRIPT	1.5–2 Hours	85 Lines	2.13 Sec.	Program change required	Very good, little symbolic notation	Yes
FORTRAN	8–9 Hours	280 Lines	0.50 Sec.	Only data file requires change	Poor, all symbolic notation	Yes, only if ANSI standard observed

Also, when comparing ease of program change, the general-purpose language is superior in that data files may be readily changed to evaluate alternative policies with the already compiled model. The difficulties in explaining code written in a general-purpose language, such as FORTRAN, to persons with little computer background are well known. The intensive use of symbols and lack of correspondence between real world and model elements combine to confuse anyone not comfortable in dealing with abstractions. Finally, when comparing the factor, standard code, FORTRAN may be superior to at least one of the simulation languages if ANSI conventions are observed in writing the code.

As noted above, the differences among the simulation languages compared are far less than the differences between such languages and general-purpose languages. Nonetheless, some significant contrasts among the languages compared can be cited. Perhaps the most notable is the number of lines of executable code required. SIMSCRIPT lives up to its reputation of being a language that relies heavily on narration to define models. It uses 85 lines of code, compared to 30 and 22 lines for GPSS and SIMAN, respectively, to define the same model. It would appear that this is the price one pays for a self-documenting, easily explained language. One other factor in which these languages differ is their level of standardization. GPSS is the most difficult to transport among computers, perhaps because it is not a proprietary language. The other two languages are proprietary, and thus control over their development is total.

In all other respects (program development effort, program execution time, and ease of program change) these languages are not significantly different. GPSS has the longest execution time, and for more complex models this margin may be significant. All of the languages except SIMSCRIPT require some recompiling or reassembling in order to make even the simplest data changes. As mentioned in Section 4.2.3, facilitating efficient model alteration is one important area to be addressed by the ''Integrated Simulation Environment.''

How much can reliably be concluded from this modest comparative analysis? It is certainly not the definitive study by which a language selection should be guided. Rather, it is intended to provide a sense of the differences between general-purpose languages and simulation languages as a group, and to a lesser extent, the contrasts among simulation languages. This analysis, coupled with the brief explanations and illustrative problems for each of the languages contained in Section 4.3, should serve as a foundation for the further investigation necessary to make an informed judgment on a language for real-world applications.

4.5   CONCLUSION

The selection of a simulation language is a decision that has a major impact upon the ultimate success of a simulation analysis. To make a proper selection, one needs to understand how simulation languages seek to facilitate the process of transforming a logical model into acceptable computer code, and the specific language features available to support model development and experimentation. In addition, there are many pragmatic considerations in the selection of a language such as ease of learning, the ability to run on many different computers, and the scope of problems addressed. We have provided this background early in the chapter.

With these issues presented, an assessment of specific languages can be made. In particular, GPSS, SIMAN, and SIMSCRIPT were covered in sufficient detail to provide the flavor of the language, and illustrated with a simple example problem. The Primers of Appendixes A, B, and C are recommended for those needing to actually implement models in these languages.

The comparison of a model of a time-shared computer system implemented in the three example simulation languages and in FORTRAN provided a more detailed understanding of the value of simulation languages to the simulation analyst. Comparison measures include lines of code, and model run time.

EXERCISES

The following problems may be coded in one or more of the simulation languages discussed in this chapter and described in detail in the Primers of Appendixes A, B, and C, namely, GPSS, SIMAN, and SIMSCRIPT.

4.1 A small grocery store consists of three aisles and a single checkout station. Shoppers arrive at the store according to an exponential distribution of interarrival times with a mean of 50 seconds. After arriving, each customer takes a shopping cart and may go down one or more of the three aisles, selecting items to purchase as he/she proceeds. The probability of going down each aisle is given in the table below. The time required to shop each aisle is a uniformly-distributed random variable. Information on these variables is also shown in the table below.

Aisle	Probability of Going Down Aisle	Time Required to Shop Aisle (sec.)	Number of Items Selected
1	.75	120 ± 60	10
2	.55	150 ± 30	5
3	.82	120 ± 45	8

When shopping is complete, customers queue up in FIFO order at the checkout station. A customer's checkout time depends on the number of items purchased, each item requiring one second to check out. Also, 60 percent of the customers pay by check and this requires an additional five seconds to process. After checking out, the customer departs the store.

a) Construct and run a simulation model to simulate five 8-hour days of operations.

b) We are concerned with the availability of shopping carts. As described, the model assumes an infinite number of carts, but of course, they are finite, and expensive. Also, customers will balk (refuse to join the line) if there are more than three people waiting. Experiment with several quantities of carts and examine the impact on throughput under these more realistic assumptions.

4.2 The following transition matrix describes the career advancement path for a certain organization. Position 1 = entry level programmer, 2 = systems analyst, 3 = group manager, 4 = vice president, and 5 = leave the organization. Each row of the matrix contains the probabilities of being promoted to position j, or leaving the organization, given you currently hold position i. Promotions are made after annual reviews.

	1	2	3	4	5
1	.20	.70	.00	.00	.10
2	.00	.70	.22	.00	.08
3	.00	.00	.60	.35	.05
4	.00	.00	.00	.97	.03
5	.00	.00	.00	.00	1.00

If an employee remains with the organization, he/she retires after 35 years. Simulate career transitions for a group of 1000 entering employees. Collect information on the frequency distribution of positions held at retirement and the number of employees leaving the organization before retirement.

4.3 To facilitate customers with only check cashing needs, a certain bank has assigned one teller to perform just this function. About 40 percent of arriving customers are of this nature. The remaining 60 percent have additional transactions to process, and must use one of the other four tellers in the bank. When a customer arrives, he assesses the situation, and determines the shortest queue for which he is eligible, or engages a free teller. Note that check cashing customers are not obliged to use the dedicated teller. If the line selected contains more than three people, the customer will balk, and leave the bank. Otherwise, the customer joins the line and remains there without jockeying or changing lines (unlike the real situation) until served.

a) What decisions could be addressed by this simulation?

b) What statistics should be collected in the model to address these decisions?

c) Construct a model of this system. Assume customers arrive according to an exponential probability distribution with a mean interarrival time of 2 minutes. Check cashing customers require an average of one minute to transact their business, while all others require an average of 6 minutes. Service times are also exponentially distributed. Include in the model the statistics identified in b).

4.4 In a certain communications system, messages arrive at a switching center at the rate of 7 ± 3 seconds, uniformly distributed. From there, they are sent to one of four destinations with the following probabilities: destination 1, 0.35; destination 2, 0.25, destination 3, 0.15, and destination 4, 0.25. The link to each destination may transmit only one message at a time. If necessary, the switching center may store messages to await an available line. The messages are uniformly distributed in size over the range 10 to 100 characters. Each line can transmit messages at the rate of 100 characters per second.

a) Develop a model to simulate 1000 messages being transmitted. Collect statistics on congestion in the system.

b) Since storage capacity is limited at the switching center, explore the impact of varying capacity by changing the GPSS code appropriately and making several runs to evaluate alternatives.

4.5 Assembled television sets pass through inspection stations upon completion. If a set does not pass inspection, it is diverted to one of several adjustment stations. After adjustment, the set is sent back to one of the inspection stations where it is inspected again. Sets that pass inspection, initially or subsequently, are routed to a packing area.

Sets arrive at the four inspection stations at intervals of 3.5 ± 2 minutes, uniformly distributed. Sets are routed to the inspection station with the shortest queue [optional, may use a single queue for all inspection stations]. Inspection requires 11 ± 3 minutes. The number of defects requiring adjustment follows a Poisson distribution with a mean of 6. About 85 percent of the sets pass inspection, the remaining 15 percent are routed to one of two adjusters.

At an adjustment station it requires an average of 6 minutes per defect to repair the sets. The total repair time is exponentially distributed. Sets are selected from the queue for repair based on the number of defects to be repaired. The set with the fewest defects is selected first. If a set must be returned for adjustment more than once, the number of defects is assumed to be one (1) on all subsequent trips to an adjuster.

a) Specify the model code necessary to simulate this operation. Use the model to assess the amount of storage space required in front of the inspection stations and the adjustment stations. Run the model for five 8-hour days.

b) Add appropriate code to the model to tabulate the number of sets that pass inspection the first time, second time, third time, and after four or more times through the inspection process.

c) A more realistic model of this operation would determine whether a TV passes inspection based upon the number of defects present. Incorporate this into the simulation by assuming that a TV must have zero (0) defects to be passed. Instead using the 85 percent/15 percent pass/fail probabilities, assume that there is a 90 percent chance that any defects present will be corrected when processed by an adjuster.

4.6 An automatic packaging machine requires operator intervention periodically for such tasks as clearing jams, restocking packaging materials, alignment and maintenance. One operator is capable of servicing several machines, but if a machine needs attention when the operator is busy with another machine, it becomes idle, causing a loss in production. On the other hand, if too few machines are assigned to an operator, the cost of operating the machines may be excessive.

Machines require operator attention on the average three times per hour, and the mean service time for each instance is 2.5 minutes. The times between calls for operator assistance and the length of service time are both exponentially distributed. The question to be answered is: how many machines should one operator tend?

a) Identify the decision and uncontrollable variables, and performance measures associated with this problem.
b) Construct a model for this system which provides statistics for the selected measures of performance.

4.7 A car wash has six stalls (S1, S2, S3,..., S6) S1—S3 can perform wash *only*, while S4—S6 can do wash *and* wax. A "wash only" customer may enter *any* of the six stalls. Cars arrive at a mean rate of 2.5 per minute. The times between arrivals are exponentially distributed. Assume 25 percent of the arriving cars desire wash *and* wax. Cars enter an empty stall upon arrival, or join the shortest queue for which they are eligible. However, the available space is such that no more than three cars may queue in front of a stall. Arriving cars finding this situation balk (refuse to join the queue). Wash rate is 0.5 car per minute, while wash and wax rate is 0.45 car per minute. Service times follow the exponential distribution.

The management is trying to decide whether to add more queueing space or additional stalls, or both queueing space and stalls to the car wash. Queueing space costs $200 each while stalls cost $2500 each. Washing is priced at $4.00 per car, and washing and waxing is $6.00 per car.

a) Construct a model to simulate this system for one week's operations (7 days, 10 hours per day).
b) Devise an experiment to evaluate the impact of alternative configurations of queueing space and numbers of stalls on revenue. Run the model and contrast the results.

4.8 A certain time-shared computer system has 10 dial-up input ports and 20 users who connect to the system. Users call the computer at random with a mean rate of 0.5 calls per minute and remain connected to the system an average of 3 minutes, exponentially distributed. If all ports are busy when an attempt to connect is made, the caller is placed in a queue to await an available port. If at the end of 10 minutes a port is not free, the caller is removed from the queue and returned to the calling population. All callers have the same priority and are treated on a first-come-first-served basis.

a) Construct a simulation model of this system.
b) Compile statistics on the average waiting time to gain access to a port, and the probability of not gaining access to a port on a given trial.

4.9 For this exercise, refer to the exercises following Chapter 3.

   a) Construct and run a simulation model for exercise 3.2.

   b) For exercise 3.3.

   c) For exercise 3.4.

   d) For exercise 3.8.

   e) For exercise 3.9.

4.10 Refer to the example problem of Section 4.4.

   a) Make any necessary changes to the code of the GPSS version to permit the simulation to be run for more than one day.

   b) Repeat a) for the SIMSCRIPT version.

4.11 Consider the following GPSS program:

```
GENERATE        10,5
QUEUE           LINE
SELECT LE       1,1,5,2,S
QUEUE           P$1
ENTER           P$1
DEPART          LINE
ADVANCE         30
LEAVE           P$1
GENERATE        480
TERMINATE       1
START           1
END
```

   a) What does this program appear to be trying to do?

   b) Will the program be executed by GPSS? Why or why not? If not, what changes would you make.

   c) Assuming that the program is executing, do you foresee any problems in its operation? What? What changes would you recommend?

4.12 A communications complex has the following characteristics. Messages are created at the rate of one every 30 ±10 seconds. They are sent over a communications channel one at a time. Twenty percent of them require a reply, which returns over the same channel after a delay of 60 ±30 seconds. Original messages are 6000 ±100 characters long, and replies are 4000 ±100 characters long. Assume that both messages and replies may be stored for transmission if the channel is not available when needed.

The system to accommodate these messages may be designed to operate in a half-duplex fashion (send or receive messages, but not both simultaneously), or in a full-duplex fashion (send and receive messages simultaneously). If half-duplex is used, replies have priority over messages. Also, transmissions may be made at three speeds: 300 baud (30 characters per second [cps]), 1200 baud (120 cps), or 9600 baud (960 cps).

The relative cost for each of these features is as follows:

Half-duplex	50
Full-duplex	100
300 baud	100
1200 baud	400
9600 baud	4000

Thus, total relative cost of a full duplex, 9600 baud system would be $4100.

The selected measure of performance is total relative cost. There are constraints on waiting time to transmit a message or reply and on channel idle time so that the decision criteria for the system design are as follows.

Minimize:	Total Relative Cost
Subject to:	Average waiting time to transmit < 30 seconds
	Channel idle time <20%

Build a simulation model that can be used to evaluate each of the six possible systems defined by the combinations of duplex mode and transmission speed described above. Run each version of the model to simulate the transmission of 1000 messages and determine which system is optimal using the problem statement above.

4.13 Consider the following GPSS program:

```
SIMULATE
GENERATE      4,3
QUEUE         1
SEIZE         1
DEPART        1
ADVANCE       4
RELEASE       1
TERMINATE     1
START         5
END
```

The following string of random numbers is associated with the GENERATE block: 0.143, 0.286, 0.143, 0.429, 0.714. (Recall the GPSS convention is such that the GENERATE block will produce interarrival times over the interval 1 to 7 with equal likelihood.)

a) When the clock is equal to 9, specify the contents of the current events and future events chains (number the transactions to identify them).

b) At the conclusion of the program run, compute the following:

- Average waiting time for QUEUE 1, given a wait greater than zero
- Average waiting time for QUEUE 1 for all transactions
- Maximum queue length for QUEUE 1
- Average time spent in facility 1
- Utilization of facility 1.

4.14 A computer terminal cluster has five terminals for use by both graduate and undergraduate students. Undergraduate students arrive at the rate of 5 ±2 minutes. If a terminal is available, it is occupied; if not, the student joins the shortest of the five queues in front of the terminals, provided that the shortest queue is no longer than four people. Queue lengths of all queues are observed continuously, and if a shorter line exists, the student will switch to it. Also, if a terminal does not become available within 10 minutes of joining the first queue, the student leaves. Graduate students arrive at intervals of 15 ±5 minutes. If a terminal is available, it is occupied; if not, the student goes to the *head* of the shortest line where he remains until a terminal is free. All sessions require 10 ±3 minutes to complete.

a) Construct a model to simulate operation of an 8-hour day and answer the following questions:

1) How long do graduate students wait for terminals?

2) How long do undergraduate students wait?

3) How long do all users wait?

4.15 A large supermarket has 10 aisles, five checkout lanes, and a conveyor system to transport the groceries to a pick-up station for loading into the customer's car. Customers arrive at intervals of average length three minutes exponentially distributed. Each customer enters the supermarket and travels through each aisle placing items in his/her shopping cart. The number of items selected from each aisle follows a uniform distribution over the range 0 to 15. It requires 15 seconds to select an item.

When the last aisle has been shopped, customers select one of the checkout lanes according to the naive rule of shortest queue. It requires 10 seconds per item to tally and bag purchases, and paying for them requires another 45 seconds. Bagged purchases are placed in tote bins for transport via conveyor to the pick-up station. It may be assumed that a supply of tote bins is always available. Each tote bin holds no more than forty items. It requires 15 seconds to place each bin on the conveyor. Customers leave immediately after paying for the groceries to retrieve their cars and drive to the pick-up station.

The conveyor is L-shaped, consisting of a 48-foot length in the store and a 45-foot length outside of the store. The five checkout lanes are spaced uniformly along the 48-foot section in the store (i.e., 12 feet between each checkout lane). It is a one-way conveyor so that empty tote bins must be returned manually. Tote bins measure two feet in length and require a buffer of one foot between each bin. The conveyor travels at a rate of three feet per second. The conveyor is not totally reliable; the time between failures is exponentially distributed with a mean of one hour. It requires an average of 10 minutes, exponentially distributed, to repair the conveyor.

When tote bins arrive at the pick-up station at the end of the conveyor, they accumulate automatically on a roller conveyor of unlimited capacity to await the arrival of the customer's car. Customers take an average of two minutes, uniformly distributed over the interval one to three minutes, to retrieve their cars and drive to the pick-up station where they queue up to have their groceries loaded by a bag loader. The bag loader requires an average of 50 seconds per tote bin to load bags into customers' cars. The load time is normally distributed with a standard deviation of 10 seconds.

In evaluating the store's performance, the management is concerned with several things, but of primary importance is the ability of the conveyor to deliver tote bins to the pick-up station in a timely manner, and the amount of accumulator conveyor required at that station. Measures of performance of interest include: waiting time of customers at the pick-up station, number of bins on the conveyor awaiting pick-up, waiting time of customers to check out, and utilization of the checkout clerks and the bag loader.

Construct a SIMAN model for this supermarket and simulate its performance for two 10-hour shopping days.

4.16 For this exercise, refer to the exercises following Chapter 3.

a) Construct and run a simulation model for exercise 3.11.

b) For exercise 3.12.

c) For exercise 3.13.

d) For exercise 3.14.

REFERENCES

1. Bryant, R., *SIMPAS User Manual*, Computer Sciences Technical Report #391, University of Wisconsin-Madison, Madison, Wisconsin, June 1980.

2. Gordon, G., "A General Purpose Systems Simulator Program," *Proceedings of the Eastern Joint Computer Conference*, Washington, D.C., 1961.

3. Gordon, G., *The Application of GPSS V to Discrete System Simulation*, Englewood Cliffs, N. J.: Prentice-Hall, 1975.

4. Henriksen, J., *The GPSS/H User's Manual*, Falls Church, VA: Wolverine Software, 1983.

5. Henriksen, James, "The Integrated Simulation Environment (Simulation Software of the 1990s)," *Operations Research*, Vol. 31, No. 6, (1983).

6. Hoover, S. and Perry, R., "Concurrent Graphical Display of GPSS Simulations," *Proceedings of the 1983 Summer Computer Simulation Conference*, Vancouver, B. C., Canada, July 1983.

7. Kiviat, P. J., "Digital Computer Simulation: Computer Programming Languages," The RAND Corporation, RM-5883-PR 1969.

8. Kiviat, P. J., "Simulation Languages," in Naylor, T. (Ed.), *Computer Simulation Experiments with Models of Economic Systems*, New York: John Wiley & Sons, 1971.

9. Markowitz, H., Hausner, B., and Karr, H., "SIMSCRIPT: A Simulation Programming Language," The RAND Corporation, RM-3310-PR 1962.

10. Pegden, C. Dennis, *Introduction to SIMAN*, State College, Pennsylvania: Systems Modeling Corporation, 1984.

11. Perry, R., "Simulation from the User's Point of View," unpublished paper, April 1966.

12. Perry, R. and Hoover S., "Simulation-Aided Design for an Automated Storage-Retrieval-Delivery System," *Proceedings of the 1983 Summer Computer Simulation Conference*, Vancouver, BC, Canada, July 1983.

13. Pritsker, A., and Pegden, C., *Introduction to Simulation and SLAM*, West Lafayette, IN: Systems Publishing Corp., 1979.

14. Roberts, S. and Sadlowski, T., "INS: A Simulation Language for Analyzing Operational Issues in Ambulatory Care," Paper presented at the ORSA/TIMS Joint National Meeting, Miami, FL, November 1976.

15. Russell, Edward, *Building Simulation Models with SIMSCRIPT*, Los Angeles, CA: C.A.C.I., 1983.

16. Schriber, T., *Simulation Using GPSS*, New York: John Wiley & Sons, 1974.

17. Shannon, R., "Keynote Address: Artificial Intelligence and Simulation," *Proceedings of the 1984 Winter Simulation Conference*, Dallas, TX, November, 1984.

18. Teichroew, D. and Lubin, J., "Computer Simulation—Discussion of the Technique and Comparison of Languages," *Communications of the ACM*, Vol. 9, No. 10 (1966).

19. *User's Guide to SPEED*, Boston, MA: Horizon Software, Inc., 1982.

APPENDIX 4A

GPSS, SIMAN, and SIMSCRIPT Code for Time-Shared Computer System

```
*TIME-SHARED COMPUTER SYSTEM  --TIME IN TENTHS OF MINUTES
        SIMULATE
*
*INITIALIZATION
*
        INITIAL         XH$ARATE,40            ARRIVAL RATE, START OF DAY
        INITIAL         XH$MEAN,200            MEAN CONNECT TIME
  PORTS STORAGE         18                     DEFINE NO. OF PORTS
  PORTS TABLE           S$PORTS,2,2,10         TALLY PORT OCCUPANCY
  ARATE FUNCTION        C1,C10                 MEAN ARRIVAL RATE BY
*                                              HR OF DAY
0.,40./600.,16.22/1200.,13.3/1800.,13.3/2400.,16.22/3000.,15./3600.,12.5
4200.,15./4800.,24./5400.,60.
  EXPON FUNCTION        RN5,BE                 BUILTIN EXPONENTIAL DIST.
*
*MODEL LOGIC
*
        GENERATE        XH$ARATE,FN$EXPON      CALLS TO SYSTEM
        SAVEVALUE       ARATE,FN$ARATE,XH      SET HOURLY ARRIVAL RATE
        QUEUE           PORTQ                  WAIT FOR AVAIL PORT
        TEST G          R$PORTS,0,RDIAL        TEST FOR AVAIL PORT
  LOGON ENTER           PORTS                  CAPTURE PORT
        DEPART          PORTQ                  LEAVE QUEUE
        ADVANCE         XH$MEAN,FN$EXPON       CONNECT TIME TO COMPUTER
        LEAVE           PORTS                  RELINQUISH PORT
        TERMINATE
*
*DETERMINE IF "CRASH" DIALING OR REGULAR INTERVAL
*
  RDIAL TEST E          R$PORTS,0,LOGON        PORT AVAILABLE?
        TRANSFER        .150,,STOP             GIVE UP "CRASH" DIALING?
        ADVANCE         30,FN$EXPON            CONTINUE "CRASH" DIALING
        TRANSFER        ,RDIAL                 TRY TO CONNECT
  STOP  SAVEVALUE       GIVUP+,1,XH            COUNT NO. OF TURN-AWAYS
        TERMINATE                              GIVE UP THIS ATTEMPT
*
*COLLECT STATISTICS ON PORT OCCUPANCY
*
        GENERATE        30                     TRANSACTION EVERY 3 MIN
        TABULATE        PORTS                  TALLY NO. PORTS OCCUPIED
        TERMINATE
*
*MODEL RUN LENGTH CONTROL
*
        GENERATE        5400                   TRAN AT END OF EACH DAY
        TERMINATE       1                      DECREMENT START COUNTER
        START           1                      RUN FOR 1 DAYS
        END
```

QUEUE	MAXIMUM CONTENTS	AVERAGE CONTENTS	TOTAL ENTRIES	ZERO ENTRIES	PERCENT ZEROS	AVERAGE TIME/TRANS	$AVERAGE TIME/TRANS
PORTQ	14	3.550	333	276	82.883	57.565	336.298

(Continued)

STORAGE	CAPACITY	AVERAGE CONTENTS	TOTAL ENTRIES	AVERAGE TIME/TRANS	AVERAGE UTILIZ.	MAXIMUM CONTENTS
PORTS	18	11.929	327	197.0	0.663	18

NON-ZERO HALFWORD SAVEVALUES

SAVEX	VALUE
GIVUP	6

TABLE PORTS

ENTRIES	MEAN ARGUMENT	STANDARD DEVIATION
179	11.950	5.013

UPPER LIMIT	OBSERVED FREQUENCY	PER CENT OF TOTAL	CUMULATIVE PERCENTAGE
2	13	7.26	7.26
4	5	2.79	10.06
6	11	6.15	16.20
8	18	10.06	26.26
10	17	9.52	35.75
12	16	8.94	44.69
14	27	15.08	59.77
16	32	17.99	77.76
18	40	22.35	100.00

SIMAN CODE: MODEL FRAME

```
BEGIN;
            CREATE:EX(1,1)/(TF(1,TNOW)/60.0);
;                                       GENERATE A CALL
            COUNT:1;                    INCREMENT NO. ARRIVALS
            BRANCH,1:
            IF,NR(1) .LT. MR(1),CONNECT:
            ELSE,RETRY;                 PORT OPEN, OR TRY LATER
CONNECT     QUEUE,1;
            SEIZE:PORT;                 CONNECT TO PORT
            COUNT:2;                    INCR. NO. CONNECT 1S TRY
            DELAY:EX(2,2);              DURATION OF CONNECTION
            RELEASE:PORT:DISPOS         RETURN PORT AND EXIT
;
RETRY       BRANCH,1:
            IF,NR(1) .LT. MR(1),CONNECT:
            WITH,P(3,1),QUIT:
            ELSE,TRYLTR;                STOP RETRYING OR TRY LATER
TRYLTR      DELAY:EX(1,3)*P(4,1):NEXT(RETRY);
;                                       WAIT AND RETRY
QUIT        COUNT:3:DISPOSE;            COUNT NO. STOPPED RETRYING
END;
```

SIMAN CODE FOR EXPERIMENTAL FRAME

```
BEGIN;
PROJECT,TIMESHARE SYSTEM,HOOVER PERRY,2/2/85;
DISCRETE,200,0,1,0;
REPLICATE,1,0,540;
RESOURCES:1,PORT,18;
PARAMETERS:1,1.0:
            2,20.0:
            3,0.15:
            4,3;
```

```
COUNTERS:1,NO. OF ARRIVALS:
         2,NO. CNCT 1ST TRY:
         3,NO. QUIT RETRYING;
DSTAT:1,NR(1),PORT UTILIZATION;
TABLES:1,0.0,60.0,15.0,37.0,45.0,45.0,37.0,40.0,48.0,40.0,
      25.0,10.0;
END;
```

OUTPUT FOR SIMAN MODEL

SIMAN SUMMARY REPORT

RUN NUMBER   1 OF   1

PROJECT: TIMESHARE SYSTEM
ANALYST: HOOVER PERRY
DATE   :   2/ 2/1985

RUN ENDED AT TIME : 0.5400E+03

DISCRETE CHANGE VARIABLES

NUMBER	IDENTIFIER	AVERAGE	STANDARD DEVIATION	MINIMUM VALUE	MAXIMUM VALUE	TIME PERIOD
1	PORT UTILIZATION	0.1046E+02	0.4715E+01	0.0000E+00	0.1800E+02	0.5400E+03

COUNTERS

NUMBER	IDENTIFIER	COUNT	LIMIT
1	NO. OF ARRIVALS	317	INFINITE
2	NO. CNCT 1ST TRY	304	INFINITE
3	NO. QUIT RETRYIN	13	INFINITE

SIMSCRIPT CODE

```
''SIMSCRIPT SIMULATION MODEL OF A TIMESHARING SYSTEM
''WITH K PORTS
PREAMBLE
NORMALLY MODE IS UNDEFINED                ''FORCE DECLARATION OF ALL VARIABLES
PROCESSES INCLUDE CALL.FOR.PORT
RESOURCES INCLUDE PORTS
DEFINE N.CALLS,N.CONNECT.FIRST.TRY AND
      N.SUCCESSFUL.RETRY AS INTEGER VARIABLES
DEFINE HOURLY.ARRIVE.RATE AS A REAL 1-DIM ARRAY
DEFINE LENGTH.DAY AND MEAN.CONNECT.TIME AS A REAL VARIABLES
DEFINE PROB.RETRY AS A REAL VARIABLE
DEFINE INITIALIZE AND END.SIM AS REAL ROUTINES
DEFINE ARRIVAL.F AS A REAL ROUTINE GIVEN 1 ARGUMENT
ACCUMULATE AVE.NO.PORTS.BUSY AS THE AVERAGE OF N.X.PORTS
ACCUMULATE MAX.NO.PORTS.BUSY AS THE MAXIMUM OF N.X.PORTS
END
```

(Continued)

```
MAIN
CALL INITIALIZE
CREATE EVERY PORTS(1)
PRINT 1 LINE THUS
INPUT NUMBER OF PORTS
READ U.PORTS(1)
PRINT 1 LINE THUS
INPUT THE MEAN CONNECTION TIME
READ MEAN.CONNECT.TIME
ACTIVATE A CALL.FOR.PORT IN EXPONENTIAL.F(ARRIVAL.F(TIME.V),1) MINUTES
START SIMULATION
END


ROUTINE END.SIM
PRINT 5 LINE WITH AVE.NO.PORTS.BUSY(1),MAX.NO.PORTS.BUSY(1),N.CALLS,
    N.CONNECT.FIRST.TRY/N.CALLS AND N.SUCCESSFUL.RETRY THUS
THE AVERAGE NUMBER OF BUSY PORTS WAS              ***.**
THE MAXIMUN NUMBER OF BUSY PORTS WAS              ***.**
THE NUMBER OF CALLS WAS                           ***
THE PROBABILITY OF CONNECTING WITHOUT A RETRY WAS *.**
THE NUMBER OF UNSUCCESSFUL RETRYS WAS             ***
STOP
END


PROCESS CALL.FOR.PORT
DEFINE SUCCESSFUL.RETRY AS AN INTEGER VARIABLE
ADD 1 TO N.CALLS
IF 24*TIME.V LT 9.0
   SCHEDULE A CALL.FOR.PORT IN
            EXPONENTIAL.F(60.0/ARRIVAL.F(TIME.V),1) MINUTES
ELSE
CALL END.SIM
ALWAYS
IF U.PORTS(1) > 0
   REQUEST 1 UNIT OF PORTS(1)
   ADD 1 TO N.CONNECT.FIRST.TRY
   WAIT EXPONENTIAL.F(MEAN.CONNECT.TIME,2) MINUTES
   RELINQUISH 1 UNIT PORTS(1)
ELSE
   LET SUCCESSFUL.RETRY=0
   WHILE RANDOM.F(3)<PROB.RETRY AND SUCCESSFUL.RETRY =0 DO
   WAIT 3 MINUTES
   IF U.PORTS(1) > 0
   ADD 1 TO N.SUCCESSFUL.RETRY
   REQUEST 1 UNIT OF PORTS(1)
   WAIT EXPONENTIAL.F(MEAN.CONNECT.TIME,2) MINUTES
   RELINQUISH 1 UNIT PORTS(1)
   LET SUCCESSFUL.RETRY=1
   LOOP
   ALWAYS               ''IF U.PORTS(1)>0 {FOR RETRY}
ALWAYS                  ''IF U.PORTS(1)>0 {FOR ORIGINAL CALL}
END


ROUTINE ARRIVAL.F GIVEN T
DEFINE I AS AN INTEGER VARIABLE
DEFINE T AS A REAL VARIABLE
LET I = TRUNC.F(T*24) +1          ''CALCULATE THE TIME IN INTEGER HOURS
RETURN WITH (HOURLY.ARRIVE.RATE(I) +
      (I-T*24)*(HOURLY.ARRIVE.RATE(I+1)-HOURLY.ARRIVE.RATE(I)))
END
```

```
ROUTINE INITIALIZE
RESERVE HOURLY.ARRIVE.RATE(*) AS 10
LET HOURLY.ARRIVE.RATE(1)=15.0        ''ARRIVALS PER HOUR 8
LET HOURLY.ARRIVE.RATE(2)=37.0        ''ARRIVALS PER HOUR 9
LET HOURLY.ARRIVE.RATE(3)=45.0        ''ARRIVALS PER HOUR 10
LET HOURLY.ARRIVE.RATE(4)=45.0        ''ARRIVALS PER HOUR 11
LET HOURLY.ARRIVE.RATE(5)=37.0        ''ARRIVALS PER HOUR 12
LET HOURLY.ARRIVE.RATE(6)=40.0        ''ARRIVALS PER HOUR 1
LET HOURLY.ARRIVE.RATE(7)=48.0        ''ARRIVALS PER HOUR 2
LET HOURLY.ARRIVE.RATE(8)=40.0        ''ARRIVALS PER HOUR 3
LET HOURLY.ARRIVE.RATE(9)=25.0        ''ARRIVALS PER HOUR 4
LET HOURLY.ARRIVE.RATE(10)=10.0        ''ARRIVALS PER HOUR 5
LET LENGTH.DAY=9 ''HOURS
LET PROB.RETRY=0.15
RETURN
END
```

OUTPUT FOR SIMSCRIPT MODEL

```
INPUT NUMBER OF PORTS

II.5> 18

INPUT THE MEAN CONNECTION TIME

II.5> 20

THE AVERAGE NUMBER OF BUSY PORTS WAS          12.16
THE MAXIMUN NUMBER OF BUSY PORTS WAS          18.
THE NUMBER OF CALLS WAS                        339
THE PROBABILITY OF CONNECTING WITHOUT A RETRY WAS  .92
THE NUMBER OF UNSUCCESSFUL RETRYS WAS            3
```

CHAPTER 5

ANALYTIC MODELS AND SIMULATION

Statistician George Box reminds us that "all models are false but some models are useful." Analytic models can give us quick and meaningful insights into the behavior of a complex system. Simple analytic models of a system can often be constructed in a few days or even hours while simulation models often require weeks or months to construct. It is false economy to go forward in the development of a very expensive and time consuming simulation model without first investigating if a useful analytic model of the system can be constructed.

5.1 INTRODUCTION

Although the focus of this text is on discrete-event numerical models, practitioners of simulation should be familiar with certain classes of analytic models. Development of an analytic model should not be considered as the alternative to the development of a simulation model, but rather an integral part of simulation analysis. Practitioners of simulation are often criticized for resorting to complex and expensive simulation models too quickly, without first considering alternative analytic models. Whenever we construct a model of a system we should keep in mind the advice of the statistician George E. Box: ''All models are false, but some models are useful.'' Analytic models can give a quick and meaningful insight into the behavior of complex discrete-event systems. In addition, analytic models are helpful in the construction, validation, verification, and statistical analysis of discrete-event simulation models.

In this chapter we first briefly discuss the relative advantages and disadvantages of analytic and numeric models. Then we present a class of state-change models known as Markov Chains. Following this, three common model types are discussed: queueing models, which are used to describe the properties of a broad class of congestion systems, inventory models, and analytic investment models. In each of these sections we will present examples of modeling discrete-event systems with both analytic and simulation models and will consider the relative advantages of each type of model.

Although we will present many important properties of these analytic models, these properties will not be formally derived. The reader should keep in mind that this is a very brief treatment of these models. For a more complete and detailed treatment, reference should be made to the vast body of literature broadly classified as Operations Research.

5.2 ANALYTIC MODELS VERSUS SIMULATION MODELS

A mathematical model is an abstraction of a real system. Mathematical expressions are used to describe the relationships between elements of the system which the analyst believes are relevant to the questions of interest. The formulation of the model should reflect the questions that the analyst wants answered about the real system. If the model can be used to answer these questions by applying analytic methods of mathematics (such as algebra or calculus), then we call the model an analytic model. If the questions the model is intended to answer can only be obtained by numerical analysis methods, then we call the model a numeric or simulation model. There is seldom a clear choice between modeling a system with an analytic or simulation model. It is often the case that much insight is obtained using both types of models, with each model giving different perspectives of the system being modeled.

ILLUSTRATIVE
PROBLEM
5.1

As an example of a system that can be modeled with both an analytic model and a simulation model, consider the famous St. Petersburg Paradox. The paradox centers about a game of chance in which the player tosses a fair coin until a head appears. The payoff to the player is $\$2^x$, where x is the number of tosses made until the coin comes up heads. The question to be answered is: What is a fair price to pay, in order to play the game? One should be willing to pay at least \$2.00 since that is minimum payoff. In the next two sections we will use both an analytic and simulation model to arrive at an answer.

5.2.1   ADVANTAGES AND DISADVANTAGES OF ANALYTIC MODELS

In analytic models the relationships between the elements of the system are expressed through mathematical equations. These equations are then used to determine properties of the system. When constructing the equations of the analytic model, assumptions are often made about the system which may limit the application of the model to more general cases. Analytic models are expressed in terms of the parameters of the system, allowing us to examine how changes in parameters of the system change the system's properties.

A major disadvantage of analytic models is that they are often difficult to build unless one has considerable mathematical skills. Analytic models can become very esoteric and lack credibility in the eyes of decision-makers who can not fully understand the basis of the model or the mathematics that supports it. There are, however, many well documented mathematical models that have been applied in a variety of environments. This is particularly true for models of congestion systems, finite-state systems, inventory systems, and financial systems.

A major use of analytic models is in the verification of simulation models. Often the parameters and assumptions of the simulation model can be set to correspond with a simpler analytic model. Under these conditions we can judge the correctness of the simulation model's logic by comparing the output of the simulation model to the theoretic results of the analytic model. Analytic models can also be used to determine general directional changes in the system's performance as parameters of the system change. If the simulation model does not exhibit the general properties that hold for the analytic model, we may have reason to question the correctness of the simulation model and should investigate carefully the reasons for the simulation model's unexpected behavior. One may, upon further investigation find a proper explanation for the model's unexpected behavior, in which case the analytic model aided in the validation of our model.

ILLUSTRATIVE PROBLEM 5.2   In order to determine a fair price to pay to play the game we will build a model of the game which will give a player's expected payoff. If x is the number of tosses until the first head then

$$p(x) = p(\text{tail})^{x-1}p(\text{head}), \qquad x=1,2...$$

and

$$E(\text{payoff}) = E(2^x)$$

$$= \sum_{x=1}^{\infty} 2^x p(\text{tail})^{x-1} p(\text{head})$$

If the coin is fair then

$$E(\text{payoff}) = \sum_{x=1}^{\infty} 2^x (1/2)^x$$

$$= \sum_{x=1}^{\infty} 1 = \infty.$$

Thus the paradox: even though half the time we would win only $2.00 the expected winnings are unbounded. The analytic model suggests that there is no amount too large to pay in order to play the game. A counter argument is that the game must last forever in order to realize such winnings. This is however, a weak argument, for if we modify the payoff to:

$$\text{Payoff} = 2^x \qquad x = 1,2,...1,000,000$$

$$= 0 \qquad x>1,000,000.$$

then the expected payoff is still $1,000,000. Would you pay even half this amount to play the game?

   The analytic model has given us something to think about. It is one view of the game that is valuable, but is it a complete view? In the next section we will model the problem using a simulation model.

5.2.2   ADVANTAGES AND DISADVANTAGES OF SIMULATION MODELS

In simulation models the relationships among the elements of the system are expressed using an algorithm encoded in a computer program. To determine the state of the system at some future time we use the computer program to execute the algorithm. Simulation models do not provide direct answers but reveal the system's properties as the computer program executes the algorithm. If the algorithm includes the stochastic nature of the system, then the output of computer program must be statistically analyzed before conclusions can be made about the system's properties.

   A major advantage of simulation models is their flexibility. Since simulation models are encoded in computer programs, they can include many of the elements and characteristics of the system that could not be included in analytic models. In simulation models the properties of the system are not determined by direct mathematical analysis, thereby allowing the simulation model to include elements and relationships that would make an analytic model mathematically intractable. An additional advantage of simulation models is their algorithmic nature. It is often easier for a non-mathematical audience to understand how a model works when the model is an algorithm than when it is a system of equations. This can be very important when it is time to validate and implement the model. That is, in order for the model to have credibility in the eyes of the decision-makers, the model should not be beyond their grasp.

Modeling a system with a simulation model does, however, have its disadvantages. Simulation models are often very expensive to build and validate, and considerable time may pass between the initial inception of the simulation model, and the eventual construction and validation of the model. Analyzing the output of a simulation model is also often difficult, especially if the model includes many stochastic elements. In addition, simulation models give us only an estimate of the properties of the system, requiring the use of statistics to draw proper conclusions about the system.

ILLUSTRATIVE PROBLEM 5.3

In the previous section we saw that the expected winnings in the St. Petersburg Paradox were either unbounded or could be made arbitrarily large. Although this is an interesting feature of the game, it does not help us decide what is a fair price for the game. Notice that when the game is played, half the time the winnings are only $2.00. An alternative approach to setting a price on the game is to construct a simulation model of the game and then play the game many times, keeping a record of the amount won each time the game is played. Table 5.1 shows the results of simulating the game various numbers of times.

The simulation model sheds a different light on the game. Although the potential winnings are very large, the probability of realizing large winnings is so small that when the game is played 10,000 times, the average amount won is barely over $12.00. Using

TABLE 5.1
SIMULATION OF THE ST. PETERSBURG PARADOX

No. Games Played	Average Winnings	Maximum Winnings
10	$5.60	$32
50	4.90	1024
100	13.56	256
500	21.48	4096
1000	11.94	1024
10000	12.56	8192

both models of the game we now have a better understanding of the game and can make a much better judgment on what is a fair price for the game. Although no upper bound can be placed on the expected amount a player will win, a judicious player would not pay much more than $12.00 for a chance to play.

5.3 ANALYTIC STATE-CHANGE MODELS (MARKOV CHAINS)

Many discrete-event systems can be modeled as systems that make transitions between a finite set of states. Examples of such systems are shown in Table 5.2.

The state of a system may be more than one dimensional; if it is greater than 2, analytic models of the system are often impractical to develop. If, however, the state of the system is one dimensional and the system has the Markov property, then analytic models are often easily constructed and can be very useful in understanding the system.

Let E_i, $i = 1,2,...$ be the set of states the system can occupy, let t_n, $n = 0,1,2,...$ be the times at which the system makes a state transition, and let $X(t_n)$ be the state of the system at time t_n.

A system is Markovian if

$$P[X(t_{n+1}) = E_i | X(t_n), X(t_{n-1}),...X(t_0)] = P[X(t_{n+1}) = E_i | X(t_n)]. \quad (5.1)$$

Equation (5.1) simply means that the probability of the system making its next transition to state E_i depends only on the current state of the system. Such systems are sometimes called memoryless, indicating that the system cannot "remember" the path it took to reach its current state. If equation 5.1 holds then we can define the transition probabilities

$$p_{ij} = P[X(t_{n+1}) = E_j | X(t_n) = E_i].$$

and

$$p_{ij}^k = P[X(t_{n+k}) = E_j | X(t_n) = E_i].$$

If the number of states of the system is finite then we can define the transition matrix P as

TABLE 5.2
EXAMPLES OF STATE TRANSITION SYSTEMS

System	State
Building elevator	Floor number
Inventory system	Number of units of inventory
Game of chance	Money player has accumulated
Computer system	Number of active processes
Job shop	Number of jobs at each center
Epidemic	Number infected and susceptible
Competitive market	Customer preference
Hospital	Number of beds occupied

$$P = \begin{bmatrix} p_{11} & p_{12} \cdots & p_{1n} \\ p_{21} & p_{22} & p_{2n} \\ \cdot & \cdot & \cdot \\ \cdot & \cdot & \cdot \\ p_{n1} & p_{n2} \cdots & p_{nn} \end{bmatrix}$$

ILLUSTRATIVE PROBLEM 5.4

A used-car dealer will keep up to two cars of a desirable sports model. On any given day the probability that there will be one buyer for this model sports car is .20, and the probability of two buyers is .04. Similarly, each day the probability that the dealer will have the opportunity of buying one model of the car is .30 and the probability that he can buy two cars is .09. Once the dealer has two cars in stock, he stops buying. The dealer cannot sell cars he does not have in stock. When the dealer buys a car, he cannot sell it until the next day. We can model this system as a Markov Chain, letting the states of the system correspond to the number of cars the dealer has in stock. The transition matrix, P, for this system is

	STATE AT $t+1$		
	0	1	2
STATE AT t 0	.6100	.3000	.0900
1	.1464	.5572	.2964
2	.0400	.2000	.7600

The transition diagram for this system is

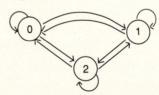

These probabilities are calculated by considering, for each state, the possible events that could occur during the day. For example, the probability that the system would make a transition from state 1 to state 0 is the probability of one or two buyers and no cars becoming available (.24 × .61 = .1464). Similarly, the probability of making a transition from state 1 back to state 1 is the probability of one or more buyers and one or more cars becoming available, or no buyers and no cars becoming available (.39 × .24 + .61 × .76 = .5572).

5.3.1 CLASSIFICATION OF MARKOV CHAINS AND SUMMARY OF THEIR PROPERTIES

Before summarizing the properties of Markov Chains, we must first define several classes of Markov Chains.

Definition: A Markov Chain is regular if for some k, $p_{ij}^k > 0$ for all i, j. That is, a Markov Chain is regular if, after k or more transitions, it is possible to be in any state.

Definition: A Markov Chain is absorbing if there is one or more states such that $p_{ii} = 1.0$. That is, a Markov Chain is absorbing if it is possible to enter a state that cannot be exited.

The probability of the system occupying any of its n states after k transitions is defined as the probability vector

$$\pi^k = P(X(t_k) = E_1, X(t_k) = E_2, \ldots X(t_k) = E_n) \tag{5.2}$$

$$= (\pi_1^k, \pi_2^k \cdots \pi_n^k).$$

It is easily shown that

$$\pi^{k+1} = \pi^k \mathbf{P} \tag{5.3}$$

which leads to

$$\pi^k = \pi^0 \mathbf{P}^k \tag{5.4}$$

where

$$\mathbf{P}^k = \mathbf{P} \times \mathbf{P} \times \ldots \mathbf{P} \quad (k \text{ self products of the transition matrix } \mathbf{P})$$

and the ijth element of $\mathbf{P}^k$ is

$$p_{ij}^k = P[X(t_k) = j \mid X(t_0) = i]. \tag{5.5}$$

That is, p_{ij}^k is the probability that the system is in state j at end of the kth transition, given the system was initially in state i.

We will not develop here the many properties of Markov Chains, but rather summarize some of the more important results. For a more detailed treatment of Markov Chains we refer the reader to Kemeny and Snell [6].

Properties of Regular Markov Chains   If a Markov Chain is a regular chain then the limiting distribution of the state of the system, π is the solution to the set of equations:

$$\pi = \pi \mathbf{P} \tag{5.6}$$

$$\sum_{i=1}^{n} \pi_i = 1.0. \tag{5.7}$$

The n equations in $\pi = \pi P$ are not independent and one of the equations can be eliminated.

A second property of regular Markov Chains is the expected number of transitions required to change from state i to state j or the first-passage times.

To find the matrix of first-passage times we first define

$$\mathbf{F} = (\mathbf{I} - \mathbf{Z} + \mathbf{E}\mathbf{Z}_{dg})\mathbf{D} \tag{5.8}$$

where

$$\mathbf{I} = \text{the identity matrix}$$

$$\mathbf{Z} = [\mathbf{I} - (\mathbf{P} - \mathbf{W})]^{-1} \tag{5.9}$$

with each row of W being the stationary distribution of the system found using equations 5.6 and 5.7.

$\mathbf{Z}$ is referred to as the fundamental matrix.

$\mathbf{E}$ is an n by n matrix with each $e_{ij} = 1$.

$\mathbf{D}$ is a diagonal matrix with $q_{ii} = 1/\pi_i$.

$\mathbf{Z}_{dg}$ is diagonal matrix whose ith diagonal element is z_{ii}.

Properties of Absorbing Markov Chains   We can partition an absorbing Markov Chain's transition matrix $\mathbf{P}$ into

$$\mathbf{P} = \frac{\mathbf{I} \mid \mathbf{O}}{\mathbf{R} \mid \mathbf{Q}} \tag{5.10}$$

where

$\mathbf{I}$ is the identity matrix of order r.

$\mathbf{O}$ is an r by s matrix of zeros.

$\mathbf{R}$ is an s by r matrix containing the one-step transition probabilities from the non-absorbing states to the absorbing states.

$\mathbf{Q}$ is the s by s matrix containing the one-step transition probabilities between the non-absorbing states.

Two properties of particular interest in systems modeled as an absorbing Markov Chains are the probabilities of being absorbed in a particular state and the mean number of transitions before making a transition to an absorbing state. The key to both of these questions is found in the fundamental matrix $\mathbf{N}$ where

$$\mathbf{N} = (\mathbf{I} - \mathbf{Q})^{-1}. \tag{5.11}$$

It can be shown that for the matrix $\mathbf{N}$, n_{ij} is the mean number of times a system, when initially in non-absorbing state i, will be in non-absorbing state j, before making a transition to one of the r absorbing states. The sum of the s elements in row i give us the mean number of transitions before absorption.

To determine the probability of entering the rth absorbing state from an initial non-absorbing state, we again use the fundamental matrix to form

$$\mathbf{A} = \mathbf{NR}. \tag{5.12}$$

Here a_{ir} gives the probability of being absorbing in state r, given the system was initially in state i.

5.3.2   A MARKOV CHAIN AND SIMULATION MODEL OF MARKET SHARE

To illustrate how Markov Chains can be employed to gain insight into the behavior of state-change systems, we will analyze a marketing problem using first a Markov Chain model and then a simulation model.

ILLUSTRATIVE PROBLEM 5.5   The AAA Company produces a consumable product and is considering a new promotional campaign. This promotional campaign is intended to reduce the likelihood that customers who currently use their product will switch to a competitor's product. In addition, it is hoped that the promotion will also increase the likelihood that users of a competitor's products will switch to their product. It is assumed that customers will switch products only when they have consumed all of the product they currently use and are about to purchase again. There are currently two competing suppliers, designated here as B and C. The market is evenly shared by all three suppliers. Preliminary estimates indicate that, as a result of the campaign, the likelihood that a consumer making a purchase will switch to a competitor's product are:

		Next Supplier		
		AAA	B	C
Current Supplier	AAA	.60	.20	.20
	B	.40	.30	.30
	C	.40	.30	.30

In addition, the package size of each product is different and consequently the time between purchases varies by supplier. The distribution of the time between purchases is shown below.

Supplier	Time Between Purchases (days)
AAA	35 ± 10
B	30 ± 8
C	25 ± 5

The firm wants to know what fraction of the market it will have 100 days after initiating the promotional campaign.

The two alternative models of this problem are a Markov Chain model and a simulation model. We will first model the problem as a Markov Chain and then consider a simulation model of the problem.

This problem can be modeled as a Markov Chain if we make the simplifying assumption that within the next 100 days a consumer will make three purchases. The transition matrix for the Markov Chain model is then:

$$\mathbf{P} = \begin{bmatrix} .60 & .20 & .20 \\ .40 & .30 & .30 \\ .40 & .30 & .30 \end{bmatrix}$$

and

$$\pi^0 = (1/3 \ \ 1/3 \ \ 1/3).$$

Then

$$\pi^3 = \pi^0 \mathbf{P}^3$$

$$= .498 \ \ .251 \ \ .251.$$

A simulation model of the problem can include the variation in the time between purchases for both the next purchase and subsequent purchases. Based on a simulation of 10000 customers, after 100 days firm AAA will have 50.2% of the market while firms B and C will each have 24.9% of the market. A listing of the Pascal code for the simulation model is included in Appendix 5A.1.

Although these two models gave different answers, both of them are useful in trying to predict the supplier's share of the market after 100 days of promotion. The simulation model includes more of the relevant aspects of the problem, but is more difficult to construct. The advantage of the analytic model is that is was easily constructed and quickly gives some preliminary answers. The analytic model can also be used to verify the simulation model. If the simulation model had given dramatically different answers than the analytic model, we would need to question the validity and internal integrity of each of the models. In this sense the models are complementary. We will take up the issue of model validation and verification in Chapter 8, but can see from this example that one model can be used to verify the other.

5.3.3　A MARKOV CHAIN AND SIMULATION MODEL OF COMBATIVE TACTICS

As a second example of using Markov Chains to model discrete-event systems we consider a model of combat between three opponents.

ILLUSTRATIVE PROBLEM 5.6

Three tanks, A, B, and C are engaged in combat. The strength of each tank is measured by the probability that it can disable an opponent when it fires. The probability that tank A will knock out an opponent in one firing is .50 while the probabilities of B and C knocking out an opponent are .40 and .30, respectively. The time between firings is an exponentially-distributed random variable with a mean of 1.0 minute. A tank always fires at the strongest remaining opponent. Combat continues until one or no tanks remain.

A Markov Chain model of this system can be constructed if we assume that the tanks all fire at the same time. That is, we will not include in the model the fact that the time between firings is a random variable. Under this assumption it is possible for the combat to end with all three tanks disabled. The transition matrix, **P**, for the Markov Chain model can be directly derived from the above probabilities as:

	–	A	B	C	ABC	AB	AC	BC
–	1.0	0	0	0	0	0	0	0
A	0	1.0	0	0	0	0	0	0
B	0	0	1.0	0	0	0	0	0
C	0	0	0	1.0	0	0	0	0
ABC	0	0	0	.29	.21	0	.21	.29

	–	A	B	C	ABC	AB	AC	BC
AB	.20	.30	.20	0	0	.30	0	0
AC	.15	.35	0	.15	0	0	.35	0
BC	.12	0	.28	.18	0	0	0	.42

where A is the state with only tank A remaining, ABC is the state with all three tanks remaining, "-" is the state with no tanks remaining, etc.

The fundamental matrix **N** for this Markov Chain is:

	ABC	AB	AC	BC
ABC	1.27	0.00	0.41	0.63
AB	0.00	1.43	0.00	0.00
AC	0.00	0.00	1.54	0.00
BC	0.00	0.00	0.00	1.72

and the probabilities of being absorbed **A** are:

	–	A	B	C
ABC	.137	.143	.177	.543
AB	.286	.428	.286	.000
AC	.231	.538	.000	.231
BC	.206	.000	.482	.312

This analysis would indicate that the weakest tank, C, has the greatest chance of winning. That is, the probability of going from nonabsorbing state ABC to absorbing state C is .543. The analysis also suggests that the mean number of firings before combat ends is 2.31 (1.27 + 0.41 + 0.63).

In the simulation model the tanks do not fire simultaneously. This eliminates the possibility of all three tanks being hit when combat ends. Our model does not give us any guidance on how to redistribute the probability of this event to tanks A, B, or C winning.

When a simulation model of the combat is constructed and used to simulate 30,000 episodes we find:

$$P \text{ (A wins)}=.258, \; P(\text{B wins})=.335, \text{ and } P(\text{C wins})=.407.$$

The mean time before the combat ended with one tank remaining was 2.19 minutes. The major difference between the analytic model and the simulation model is that in the simulation model, we included the fact that the time between firings is a random variable, rather than fixed at 1.0 minutes. Thus in the simulation model, the tanks cannot simultaneously disable one another. Appendix 5A contains a Pascal listing of the simulation model for this combat system.

From this analysis we again see that two different models of the same system can be very useful and complementary. The Markov model was very easy to construct and yielded answers by simple matrix operations. The simulation model allowed more aspects of the combat to be included, but required developing a computer model. Both the Markov Chain model and the simulation model indicate that combat will be very short and that the strongest of the three tanks has the least chance of surviving.

5.4   ANALYTIC CONGESTION MODELS

A congestion system may broadly be described as a system in which there is a demand for the resources of a system, and when the resources are not available, those requesting the resource wait for them to become available. That is, the system becomes congested with requests for its resources. The level of congestion in such systems is often measured by the waiting line, or queue, of resource requests. For this reason models of congestion systems are often referred to as waiting-line or queueing models. We will use the terms congestion models, queueing models and waiting-line models interchangeably. Examples of such systems include customers requesting the services of tellers at a bank, customers checking out of a supermarket, jobs awaiting processing a in factory, and processes in a computer system waiting for the CPU. Although discrete-event simulation models are often used to analyze congestion systems, simpler analytic models of congestion systems can help explain the behavior of more complex congestion systems. In addition, knowledge of analytic congestion models is often helpful in the design and validation of simulation models and in the statistical analysis of the output of simulations of congestion systems. In this section we will consider a number of classical models of congestion systems, particularly paying attention to the properties of these models that will be helpful in understanding more complex systems, that must be modeled using discrete-event simulations.

5.4.1   ELEMENTS OF A QUEUEING SYSTEM

Every queueing system consists of three elements:

1. An arrival process
2. A service process
3. A queueing discipline

In a queueing system the arrival process is characterized by the distribution of the time between the arrival of successive customers. Although analytic models have been developed for different arrival processes, two of the most important cases are when the times between arrivals are exponentially distributed and when they are constant.

If the time between arrivals is exponentially distributed, its probability density function is

$$f(t) = 1/\theta e^{-t/\theta} \qquad t > 0.$$

The expected time between arrivals is θ and the variance of the time between arrivals is θ^2. The exponential distribution plays a central role in queueing models because it is a memoryless distribution. That is,

$$P(t > a + b \mid t > a) = P(t > b).$$

For an arrival process this property means that the probability of an arrival during the next b time units is independent of when the last arrival occurred. For example, if an arrival just occurred or if we have been waiting 20 minutes for an arrival, the probability of an arrival during the next 5 minutes remains the same. It can be shown that the only continuous random variable that is memoryless is the exponentially distribution. It can also be shown that if the time between arrivals is exponentially distributed with mean θ, then the distribution of the number of arrivals during the unit time interval is a Poisson distributed with mean $1/\theta$.

Other characteristics of an arrival process include whether the customer population is finite or infinite and whether the mean time between arrivals is constant or changing over time. If the population of customers is finite, the rate of customer arrivals diminishes as the number of customers in the system increases. When the mean time between arrivals is changing over time, we have a much more complex queueing system, and often must resort to discrete-event simulation models to analyze the system.

The service process is characterized by the distribution of the time to service an arrival and the number of servers. Models of congestion systems often assume the service time is exponentially distributed, thereby facilitating the development of analytic models of the congestion system. The number of servers may be one or more, possibly infinite, and it is most often assumed that the rate at which customers can be serviced is greater than the rate at which customers arrive. Analytic congestion models most often assume that the service times for all servers are identically distributed.

An important parameter of every congestion system is its traffic intensity, ρ, defined broadly as

$$\rho = \frac{\text{rate at which customers arrive}}{\text{rate customers can be served}}.$$

For many congestion systems an equivalent definition of ρ is

$$\rho = \frac{\text{mean service time}}{(\text{mean time between arrivals})\,(c)}$$

$$\rho = \frac{\text{arrival rate}}{(\text{service rate})\,(c)}.$$

where c is the number of servers.

However, to use this definition we must assume that the arrival rate and service rate are not functions of other system variables such as the number of customers in the system, and are not time dependent.

If the traffic intensity of a congestion system exceeds 1.0, the congestion in the system will grow without bound. In the analysis of any congestion system, using either an analytic model or simulation model, one should always know if the traffic intensity is less than 1.0. When the traffic intensity in a congestion system is greater than 1.0 the analysis of the system become much more difficult.

The queue discipline describes the order in which arrivals are serviced. Common queue disciplines are FIFO (first-in-first-out), priority queues, shortest service time first, and random selection for next service. The queue discipline also includes characteristics of the system such as a maximum queue length (when the queue reaches this maximum, arrivals turn away or balk) and customer reneging (customers waiting in line become impatient and leave the system before service).

Kendall [7] developed a system for the classification of queueing system models of the form

$$A/B/s$$

where A specifies the arrival process, B specifies the service process, and s specifies the number of servers. This classification system has been extended to

$$A/B/s/K/E$$

where K is the maximum number of customers allowed into the system and E is the queue discipline.

Commonly used symbols for this classification system are:

M: Exponentially-distributed service or arrival times
D: Constant service or arrival times
E_k: Erlang-k distributed service or arrival times
G: General service or arrival times
$FIFO$:   First-in-first-out queue discipline
$SIRO$:   Serve in random-order queue discipline
PRI: Priority queue discipline
GD: General queue discipline

Using this classification system, an M/D/3/50/PRI would be a queueing system with exponentially-distributed arrivals, constant service time, three servers, a limit of 50 customers in the system, and customers are serviced according to some priority measure.

Although there are many ways that the performance characteristics of a congestion system can be measured, the most commonly used measures are:

L_s: Expected number of customers in the system
L_q: Expected number of customers in queue
W_s: Expected time a customer is in the system, including the time for service
W_q: Expected time a customer waits for service
P_i: Probability of exactly i customers in the system, $i=0,1....$
$P(W_q > t)$:   Probability a customer waits t or longer.

5.4.2   THE *M/M/1* QUEUEING MODEL

Queueing models are most easily developed when the arrival times and service times are exponentially distributed. Although the assumption of exponentially-distributed arrival and service times may seem unrealistic, this group of models has wide application and can also serve as a useful first pass in the analysis of more complex congestion systems.

The development of the model begins with the observation that, for exponentially-distributed arrival times and service times,

$$P \text{ (one arrival during the interval } t, \ t + \Delta) = \lambda \Delta t$$

and

$$P \text{ (service completed the interval } t, \ t + \Delta) = \mu \Delta t$$

where $1/\lambda$ is the mean time between arrivals and $1/\mu$ is the mean service time. Alternatively λ is the rate at which customers arrive into the system and μ is the rate at which customers can be serviced.

Letting $P_n(t)$ = Probability of exactly n customers in the system at time t, it follows that

$$P_0(t + \Delta t) = \mu \Delta t P_1(t) + (1 - \lambda \Delta t) P_0(t) \tag{5.13}$$

$$P_n(t + \Delta t)T = \lambda \Delta t P_{n-1}(t) + \mu \Delta t P_{n+1}(t) + (1 - \lambda \Delta t)(1 - \mu \Delta t) P_n(t) \tag{5.14}$$

That is, the probability that there are n customers in the system at time $t + \Delta t$ is the sum of the probabilities of the three events:

1. One arrival during Δt
2. One service during Δt
3. No arrival or service during Δt.

We exclude the probability of multiple events occurring during Δt, such as two arrivals or both a service and an arrival, because we are assuming that Δt is so narrow that the probability of such events becomes negligible.

Rearranging the terms, and dividing by Δt we have

$$\frac{P_0(t + \Delta t) - P_o(t)}{\Delta t} = -\lambda P_0(t) + \mu P_1(t) \tag{5.15}$$

$$\frac{P_n(t + \Delta t) - P_n(t)}{\Delta t} = \lambda P_{n-1}(t) - (\lambda + \mu) P_n(t) + \mu P_{n+1}(t) \quad n = 1, 2, \ldots$$

and then taking limit as $\Delta t \to 0$ we have

$$\frac{dP_0(t)}{dt} = -\lambda P_0(t) + \mu P_1(t) \tag{5.16}$$

$$\frac{dP_n(t)}{dt} = \lambda P_{n-1}(t) - (\lambda + \mu) P_n(t) + \mu P_{n+1}(t) \quad n = 1, 2, \ldots \tag{5.17}$$

In this development we could have both λ and μ be time- and system-state dependent, resulting in the more general set of equations

$$\frac{dP_0(t)}{dt} = -\lambda_0(t) P_0(t) + \mu_1(t) P_1(t) \tag{5.18}$$

$$\frac{dP_n(t)}{dt} = \lambda_{n-1}(t) P_{n-1}(t) - [\lambda_n(t) + \mu_n(t)] P_n(t) + \mu_{n+1}(t) P_{n+1}(t). \tag{5.19}$$

If there is a limit on the maximum value of n, this system of differential equations can be solved using commonly available numerical analysis routines. The probabilities provided by this solution are exact (within the numerical accuracy of the routine being used) as compared to estimates of the state probabilities obtained from a discrete-event simulation. If no upper bound can be placed on the maximum number of customers in the system, we can always impose an upper bound and obtain an approximate numeric solution to equations 5.16, 5.17.

ILLUSTRATIVE PROBLEM 5.7

In a job shop two attendants are assigned to eight machines. The machines periodically need servicing by the attendants. If a machine needs servicing but the attendants are busy, the machine must wait until an attendant is available. When a machine is running, the rate of service requests is one per hour. The mean time to service a machine is 30 minutes (i.e., the service rate per attendant is two per hour).

In order to develop the differential equations associated with this system we first determine that the arrival rates λ_n and service rates μ_n are:

n	λ_n	μ_n
0	8	0
1	7	2
2	6	4
3	5	4
4	4	4
5	3	4
6	2	4
7	1	4
8	0	4

The differential equations for this system become

$$\frac{dP_0(t)}{dt} = -8P_0(t) + 2P_1(t)$$

$$\frac{dP_1(t)}{dt} = 8P_0(t) - 9P_1(t) + 4P_2(t)$$

$$\frac{dP_2(t)}{dt} = 7P_1(t) - 10P_2(t) + 4P_3(t)$$

$$\frac{dP_3(t)}{dt} = 6P_2(t) - 9P_3(t) + 4P_4(t)$$

$$\frac{dP_4(t)}{dt} = 5P_3(t) - 8P_4(t) + 4P_5(t)$$

$$\frac{dP_5(t)}{dt} = 4P_4(t) - 7P_5(t) + 4P_6(t)$$

$$\frac{dP_6(t)}{dt} = 3P_5(t) - 6P_6(t) + 4P_7(t)$$

$$\frac{dP_7(t)}{dt} = 2P_6(t) - 5P_1(t) + 4P_8(t)$$

$$\frac{dP_8(t)}{dt} = 1P_7(t) - 4P_8(t).$$

The time-dependent solutions for this system of equations can be obtained using numerical methods. Once we find the time-dependent values of $P_i(t)$, $i = 0,1,,.8$, we can consider the time-dependent behavior of the system. Figure 5.1 shows $N_q(t)$, the expected number of machines waiting for repair, for the first four hours of operation, where

$$N_q(t) = \sum_{i=2}^{8} (n - 2)P_i(t).$$

FIGURE 5.1   TIME DEPENDENT BEHAVIOR OF *M/M/2* MODEL

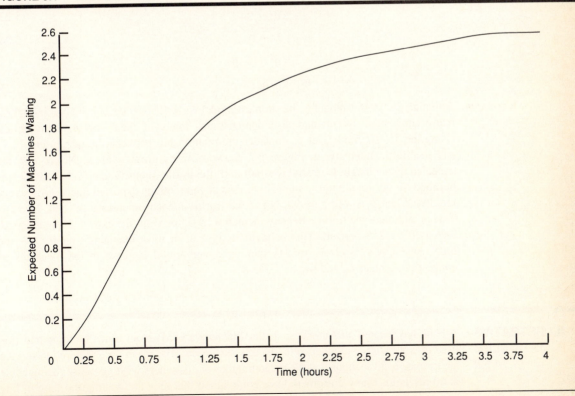

5.4.3   STEADY-STATE *M/M/s* QUEUEING MODELS

A queueing system is said to be in steady state when

$$\frac{dP_n(t)}{dt} = 0$$

for all n. When an *M/M/s* is in steady state we can rewrite equations 5.16, 5.17 as

$$\lambda_0 P_0 = \mu_1 P_1 \tag{5.20}$$

$$(\lambda_n + \mu_n)P_n = \lambda_{n-1}P_{n-1} + \mu_{n+1}P_{n+1} \quad n = 1,2... \tag{5.21}$$

This relatively simple set of equations provides the analytic solutions to a large number of queueing systems. Since the intent of this chapter is expository, rather than an in-depth analysis of queueing models, we will not develop analytic solutions. Instead we will present the performance measures of a number of *M/M/s* systems that are often useful as a first-pass model of more complex congestion systems. We will also use these models as a guide to the performance of more complex queueing systems. It is our opinion that before one tries to model and analyze complex congestion systems, it is important that one understands how simpler and more elementary systems behave.

***M/M/1/∞/∞* Model**   In this model we will define $\rho = \lambda/\mu$.

$$P_n = (1 - \rho)\rho^n \qquad n = 0,1,... \tag{5.22}$$

$$L_s = \rho/(1 - \rho) \tag{5.23}$$

$$L_q = L_s - \rho \tag{5.24}$$

$$= \rho^2/(1 - \rho)$$

$$W_q = \rho/\mu(1 - \rho). \tag{5.25}$$

Although the *M/M/1* model is the simplest model we will consider, it is a good model for many congestion system and also demonstrates many of their important properties. Using the *M/M/1* model, let us consider the relationship between the queue length, L_q and the traffic intensity, ρ. Figure 5.2 shows how L_q grows with ρ. Notice that the expected queue length is relatively small until the traffic intensity approaches the neighborhood of .60. As the traffic intensity grows beyond .60 the expected queue grows very rapidly. When ρ is .60, $L_q = .90$, but if the traffic intensity increases to 0.80, $L_q = 3.2$. That is, although the traffic intensity increased by 33 percent, the expected queue length increased by 255 percent. This behavior is typical of most queueing systems. As the traffic intensity gets closer to 1.0, there is a very rapid increase in the measures of congestion, such as L_q and W_q.

ILLUSTRATIVE PROBLEM 5.8   A bank has located an Automatic Teller Machine (ATM) in an office building and it is used by a very large number of the bank's customers. The mean time required to service a customer is 50 seconds and the mean number of customers wishing to use the machine is 60 per hour. Many customers have complained that they are waiting too long in line and believe a second ATM is justified. Both the time between customer arrivals and the

FIGURE 5.2 E (CUSTOMERS IN SYSTEM) VS. TRAFFIC INTENSITY: *M/M/2* MODEL

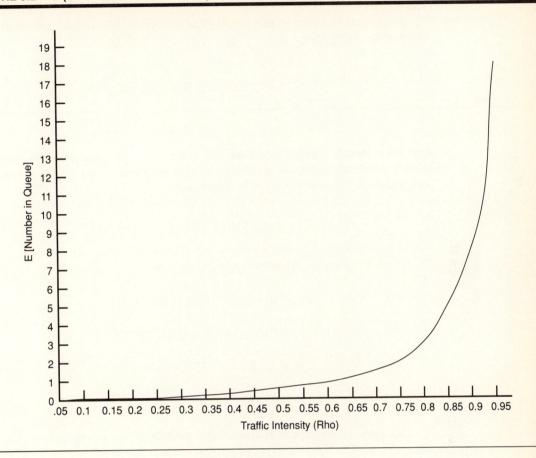

customer service time are exponentially-distributed random variables. In order to determine if a second machine is needed, the bank would like to know the probability that a customer must wait in line and the mean time a customer waits for a machine to become available.

For this system the arrival rate is 60/hour and the service rate is 72/hour. The traffic intensity, ρ, is 60/72=.8333. Using the steady-state performance measures for the *M/M/1* model

$$P_0 = 1 - \rho = .1667$$

and

$$W_q = \rho/\mu(1 - \rho)$$

$$= .8333/(72)(.1667)$$

$$= .0694 \text{ hours}$$

$$= 4.167 \text{ minutes.}$$

Thus we find that about 83 percent of customers must wait in line and the average wait is about 4 minutes.

As additional measure of the congestion in this system, we can calculate the average length of the waiting line

$$L_q = \rho^2/(1-\rho)$$

$$= 4.2 \text{ customers waiting in line.}$$

M/M/s/∞/∞ Model: In this model we will define $\rho = \lambda/s\mu$ since the service capacity is the service rate of each server times the number of servers. Using the steady-state balance equations 5.20 and 5.21 it can be shown that:

$$P_0 = (1/[\sum_{i=1}^{s-1}(s\rho)^i/i! + (s\rho)^s/(c!(1-\rho))] \tag{5.26}$$

$$P(n \geq s) = (s\rho)^s P_0/(s!(1-\rho)) \tag{5.27}$$

$$L_s = s\rho + (s\rho)^{s+1}P_0/[s(s!)(1-\rho)^2] \tag{5.28}$$

$$L_q = P_0(s^{s+1}\rho^{s+1}/s)/(s!(1-\rho)^2 \tag{5.29}$$

$$W_s = L_s/\lambda \tag{5.30}$$

$$W_q = L_q/\lambda. \tag{5.31}$$

This model extends the *M/M/1* model to a model allowing for multiple but identical servers. Figure 5.3 shows the expected number of customers in the system, L_s as a function of the traffic intensity, ρ, for $s = 2, 4, 5,$ and 10. Again, like the case of the *M/M/1* model, as the traffic intensity approaches 1, the congestion builds rapidly. Notice also that, for a fixed traffic intensity, as the number of servers increases, the number of customers in the system increases. That is, congestion is reduced by having a few very fast servers rather than many slower servers.

Implicit in this model is the assumption that there is only one waiting line and customers will always move to an idle server. If each server has a separate waiting line, and switching lines is not permitted, the expected number of customers in the system is greater than presented in this model.

ILLUSTRATIVE PROBLEM 5.9   A supermarket is being designed with four checkout lanes. At peak hours it is expected that customers will arrive at the rate of 100 per hour and the mean time to checkout a customer is expected to be two minutes. The designers of the supermarket would like to know the mean time a customer will have to wait in line and the probability that a customer will not have to wait.

FIGURE 5.3   E (NUMBER IN QUEUE) VS. TRAFFIC INTENSITY: *M/M/s* Model

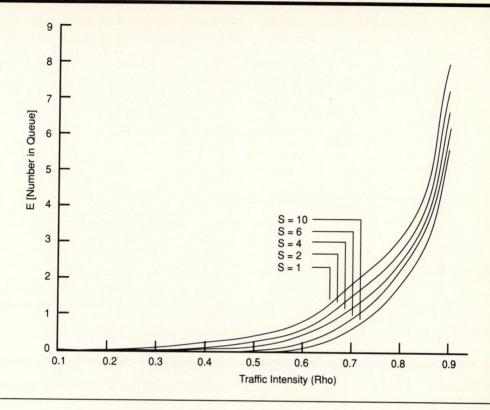

Using the *M/M/s* queueing model with $s = 4$:

$\lambda = 100$ customers per hour

$\mu = 30$ customers per hour per server

$\rho = \lambda/(s\mu) = .8333$

From equations 5.26 through 5.31

$$L_q = 3.29$$

and

$$P(wait) = 1 - P(n \geq 4)$$

$$= .658$$

As an additional measure of congestion in the supermarket we can use

$$L_s = 6.62$$

M/M/1/K **Model:**   In this model we will define $\rho = \lambda/\mu$, but when there are K customers in the system, additional arrivals are turned away. In this system there is a nominal arrival rate λ, but when the state of the system is K, the arrival rate, λ, becomes 0.0. Because the arrival rate is 0.0 when there are K customers in the system, this queueing system will have a steady-state solution even when the nominal arrival rate exceeds the service rate. Using the steady-state balance equations 5.20 and 5.21 it can be shown that

$$P_0 = (1 - \rho)/(1 - \rho^{k+1}) \qquad \rho \neq 1 \tag{5.32}$$

$$= 1/(K + 1) \qquad\qquad \rho = 1$$

$$P_n = P_0 \rho^n \qquad\qquad n = 1, 2, \dots K$$

$$L_s = \rho/(1 - \rho) - (K + 1)\rho^{k+1}/(1 - \rho^{k+1}) \qquad \rho \neq 1 \tag{5.33}$$

$$= K/2 \qquad\qquad\qquad \rho = 1$$

$$L_q = L_s - (1 - P_o) \tag{5.34}$$

$$\lambda_{eff} = \lambda(1 - P_k) \tag{5.35}$$

$$= \lambda(1 - P_0)\rho^k$$

$$W_q = L_q/\lambda_{eff} \tag{5.36}$$

$$W_s = L_s/\lambda_{eff} \tag{5.37}$$

In this model the effective arrival rate λ_{eff}, is a weighted average of an arrival rate of λ when the system is not full and an arrival rate of 0.0 when there are K customers in the system.

ILLUSTRATIVE PROBLEM 5.10

A barber shop has only one barber chair and a small waiting room with four chairs. The mean time for a hair cut is 20 minutes and customers arrive at the rate of four customers per hour. If an arriving customer finds all five chairs are full he will not enter the shop. The barber is interested in knowing how much extra business he will receive if he expanded his shop to six chairs. He would also like to know how much longer customers will have to wait if the waiting room is expanded to six chairs.

In this problem

$\mu = 3$ per hour

$\lambda = 4$ per hour

and

$\rho = 4/3$

Using equations 5.32 through 5.37 we find that with four chairs in the shop

$P_0 = .072$

$\lambda_{eff} = 2.78$

$W_q = .852$

and if the waiting room is expanded

$P_0 = .051$

$\lambda_{eff} = 2.848$

$W_q = 1.1$

indicating that his business will increase by 0.54 customers per day (assume 8 hours/day) but his customers will wait on the average 15 minutes more.

5.4.4   NON-MARKOVIAN QUEUEING MODEL

When the time between customer arrivals and the service times are not exponentially distributed, we cannot use the balance equations 5.20 and 5.21 to derive the properties of the queueing system. For certain queueing systems it is still possible to derive analytic expressions for the properties of the system such as L_s and L_q. Because our treatment of queueing models is primarily expository, we will not derive these results but rather state them compactly and consider their implications as to the general behavior of congestion systems.

M/G/1 **Model**   In this queueing model the assumptions of the *M/M/1* model are relaxed to allow the service time to follow an arbitrary distribution with a mean of $1/\mu$ and variance σ^2. Like the *M/M/1* model, the traffic intensity is defined as $\rho = \lambda/\mu$. It can be shown that when $\rho < 1.0$

$$P_0 = 1 - \rho \tag{5.38}$$

$$L_s = \rho + \rho^2 (1 + \sigma^2\mu^2)/2(1 - \rho) \tag{5.39}$$

$$L_q = L_s - \rho$$
$$= \rho^2(1 + \sigma^2\mu^2)/2(1 - \rho) \tag{5.40}$$

$$W_q = L_q/\lambda$$
$$= \lambda(1/\mu^2 + \sigma^2)/2(1 - \rho). \tag{5.41}$$

The *M/G/1* model brings out the important property of congestion systems that, as the variance of the service time decreases, congestion decreases. For the case of an *M/D/1* queueing system ($\sigma^2 = 0$)

$$L_s = \rho + \rho^2/2(1 - \rho) \tag{5.42}$$

$$L_q = \rho^2/2(1 - \rho)$$

which is one half the number of customers in an *M/M/1* queueing system.

M/D/s **and** *D/M/s* **Models**   Analytic models of multiple-server queueing systems have been developed only for special cases of the arrival and service distributions. Two special case of particular interest in the analysis of congestion systems are the *M/D/s* model (constant service times) and the *D/M/s* model (constant interarrival times). Extrapolating from the *M/G/1* model we would expect that the expected waiting time in a system with constant service times or constant interarrival times would be less than in an *M/M/s* system. This is in fact the case. The development of the expressions for the waiting times in each of these models goes beyond our intended level of treatment but are shown in Figure 5.4 for 1, 3, 5, and 10 servers. For a complete comparison of queueing systems see Dietrich [1]. From these graphs we see several important properties of queueing systems.

FIGURE 5.4   WAITING TIMES FOR *M/M/1*, *M/D/1*, AND *D/M/1* Queueing Systems

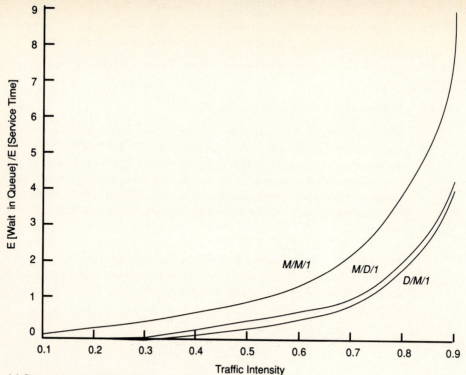

(a) Comparison of M/M/1, M/D/1, and D/M/1

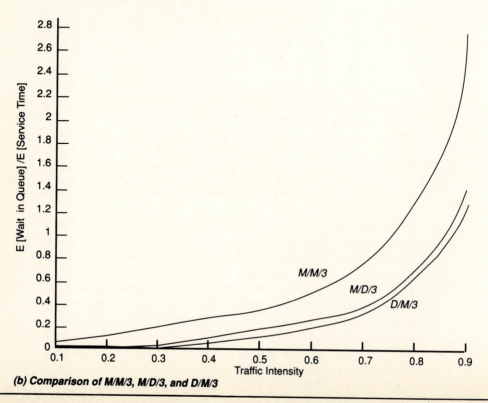

(b) Comparison of M/M/3, M/D/3, and D/M/3

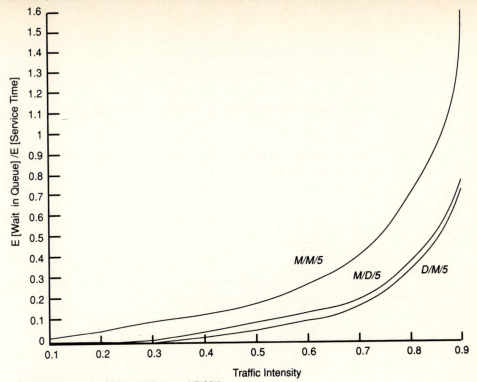

(c) Comparison of M/M/5, M/D/5, and D/M/5

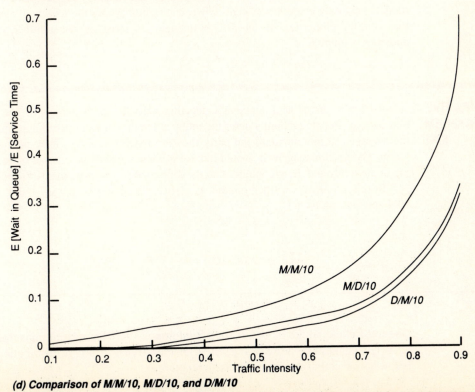

(d) Comparison of M/M/10, M/D/10, and D/M/10

1. Constant service or interarrival times have a significant effect on the mean waiting time, typically reducing the waiting time by half or more.

2. A constant interarrival time reduces the waiting time more than a constant service time.

3. When the traffic intensity exceeds .70 the expected wait in the queue escalates very rapidly.

M/G/∞ Model   In this model we assume that the customers themselves are the servers. For this model we will define $\rho = \lambda/\mu$. It can be shown that when the interarrival times are exponentially distributed and for an arbitrary service distribution

$$P_0 = e^{-\rho} \tag{5.43}$$

$$P_n = P_0 \rho^n / n! \qquad n = 1, 2, \ldots$$

$$= e^{-\rho} \rho^n / n!$$

That is, the distribution of the number of customers in the system is Poisson distributed, with a mean of ρ. It then follows that

$$L_s = \rho \tag{5.44}$$

$$L_q = 0 \tag{5.45}$$

$$W_s = 1/\mu. \tag{5.46}$$

In this system customers never wait for service since they service themselves. This model is not only useful for systems where the customers are the servers, it also gives us the limiting properties of an $M/G/s$ queueing system as the number of servers approaches infinity.

ILLUSTRATIVE PROBLEM 5.11   A hotel lobby serves as a convenient meeting place for both patrons of the hotel and non-patrons. People randomly enter the lobby at the rate of eight per minute and wait, on the average, 10 minutes until the party they are meeting arrives. They then depart the lobby. The hotel management would like to estimate the average number of people waiting in the lobby and the probability that the lobby will fill to more than 100 people.

In this problem $\lambda = 8$ per minute, $\mu = .10$ per minute and $\rho = 80$. Using equations 5.44 and 5.46 we have

$$L_s = 80$$

and

$$P(n > 100) = 1 - \sum_{i=0}^{100} P_n = .013.$$

General Relationships in Congestion Systems   There are relationships that hold for all $G/G/s$ congestion systems, regardless of the service or arrival distributions. Listed below are several of the more important relations.

1) E(number in system) = λE(time in system):

$$L_s = \lambda W_s$$

$L = \lambda W$

Little's Law

2) E(number in queue) = λE(wait in the queue):

$$L_q = \lambda W_q$$

3) E(time in system) = E(wait in queue) + $1/\mu$

$$W_s = W_q + 1/\mu$$

4) E(number in system) = E(number in queue) + λ/μ

$$L_s = L_q + \lambda/\mu$$

When building and analyzing simulation models of congestion systems, these relationships should always be kept in mind.

5.4.5 QUEUEING NETWORKS

Congestion systems often are a network of queueing systems, with departures from one queueing system becoming the arrivals at another queueing system. Such systems can become very complex and difficult to analyze, except in the case of a network of $M/M/s$ queues. It can be shown that the steady-state distribution of times between departures from an $M/M/s$ queueing system is an exponential distribution [5]. Since the time between departures is exponentially distributed, it follows that the number of departures per unit time is Poisson distributed. Surprisingly, the queueing discipline does not effect the distribution of the time between departures. The significance of this property of $M/M/s$ queueing systems is that each system in the network can be analyzed separately, using the elementary models we have presented.

It can further be shown that if the departures are randomly routed to one of several different queueing systems in the network, then the time between arrivals is still exponentially distributed. An example of such a system is a job shop in which jobs arrive and are routed through various processing centers in the shop. Although it is unlikely that processing times at the centers are exponentially distributed, as a first-pass model of a job shop, a network queuing model is often very useful and easily constructed.

The time between departures from an $M/M/s$ queueing system is not exponentially distributed if the servers are not immediately available after service completion. This is the case when there is a finite queue between components of the network. With finite queues, "blocking" can occur, whereby one queueing system can block service from continuing at another system, because the customer cannot depart. If blocking is prevalent in a queueing system, simulation may be the only method of analysis.

5.4.6 A QUEUEING AND SIMULATION MODEL OF A BANK

As our first illustration of how a queueing model can be used for a preliminary model of a congestion system, we will model a three-teller bank.

ILLUSTRATIVE PROBLEM 5.12

A bank opens at 9:00 a.m.in the morning and closes at 5:00 p.m. The time between customer arrivals at the bank is uniformly distributed between 10 and 110 seconds and the time required for a teller to service a customer is uniformly distributed between 62 and 262 seconds. When customers arrive at the bank they select the teller with the shortest line.

We will first model this system using an *M/M/3* model with a traffic intensity of .90. (arrival rate = 1 per minute and a service time of 2.70 minutes per customer.) Using equations 5.22 and 5.24 we would predict the expected time a customer would wait in line to be 7.35 minutes. Before considering the simulation model, we should consider the assumptions that were made in the analytic model to decide if the analytic model will over or under estimate the time a customer waits. The analytic model uses the correct mean interarrival and service time. However, since the analytic model assumes exponentially-distributed times for interarrival and service, the variances are much larger than in the real system. Further, the analytic model assumes that the system has become stationary, at which point the expected waiting times are the largest. Since both of these assumptions lead to an over estimation of the wait, we would expect the actual waiting times to be somewhat less than 7.35.

Using a simulation model, we simulate this system for 10 different 8-hour days and find the mean average waiting time to be 5.46 minutes. A listing of the GPSS code for the simulation model can be found in Appendix 5A.3. As in the case of Markov Chain models, we find that an analytic model gives us some preliminary estimates of the properties of the system which could be tempered by an understanding of the assumptions of the analytic model. This is not to say that we do not need to build a simulation model of the bank, but rather, before going into simulation modeling, we should look for simpler models that can give an early and preliminary indication of the system's behavior.

5.4.7   A QUEUEING AND SIMULATION MODEL OF AN ASSEMBLY LINE

As a second illustration of modeling a system first with both an analytic queueing model and simulation, we will consider a simple two-stage assembly line.

ILLUSTRATIVE PROBLEM 5.13

An assembly is manufactured in two stages. In the first stage, an operator fits parts together and then passes them on to the next station where they are inspected. If they are found defective, they are returned to be corrected. There is limited space between the operator and the inspector and a maximum of four parts can build up between the two workers. The mean time to fit the parts together is 70 seconds with a spread of ±50 seconds. The mean time to inspect the parts is exactly 50 seconds. The inspector returns 10 percent of the parts for correction. The mean time to correct a rejected part is 10 ± 5 seconds. We would like to know how many good parts we can expect each hour from this process.

A first-pass analytic model of this process would be a *M/D/1* queue model. This model can be useful in predicting the likelihood the first operator will have to stop because eight parts have built up before the inspector. Assume that approximately 90 percent of the parts require, on the average, only 1 minute of the operator's time while 10 percent requires 1 minute and 10 seconds. We will then estimate the mean time between arrivals as 70 seconds $\times$ .90 + 10 seconds $\times$ .10 = 64 seconds and the service time as 50 seconds. That is, the traffic intensity, ρ, is 50/64 = .78. Given this traffic intensity we can use a simple *M/D/1* model to estimate the average queue length. Given the average queue length we then have some idea of the likelihood of the operator becoming idle. If we know what fraction of time the operator is idle we can estimate the number of assemblies completed each hour.

From equation 5.40 we find the average length of the queue before the inspector is 1.36. Assuming the standard deviation is about the same as the mean (a rather extreme assumption), then the likelihood of more than three parts building up should be very low (less than 2 percent for most distributions). That is, our analytic model indicates that about 98 percent of the time the assembly operator will be busy. Equivalently, the number of parts produced in one hour should be approximately 3600/71 $\times$ .98 = 49.69. (Notice that we are allowing for 1 out of every 10 parts needing an extra 10 seconds of the operator's time.)

In this model we have made a number of very general assumptions to allow for an analytic model that fits our system. We can, however, capture more detail of the system by building a simulation model. A listing of an appropriate simulation model that includes all the aspects of the system can be found in Appendix 5A. When this model is run for 100 hours we find the average number of parts produced is 50.72 parts per hour. There is some difference between our two models, but the analytic model gave us some very good initial estimates.

5.5 ANALYTIC INVENTORY MODELS

The proper management of inventory systems has been a subject of investigation since the beginning of Operations Research. Like congestion systems, a set of analytic inventory models have been developed that are often good approximations to the reality of complex inventory systems and have proven useful for setting optimal policies for the management of these systems.

5.5.1 ELEMENTS OF AN INVENTORY SYSTEM

The emphasis of most inventory models is on either the cost of operating the inventory system or on the customer service level. Analytic inventory models describe inventory systems as a function of:

1. Inventory system cost parameters
2. Uncontrollable external variables
3. Inventory policy

Before presenting specific models of inventory systems, we should first describe each of these elements.

The cost parameters that are often included in an inventory model are:

C: The unit purchase cost of the item being inventoried

C_H: The cost of carrying one unit of inventory for one unit of time (typically 1 year)

C_R: The cost of placing a replenishment order

C_P: The penalty cost for being short or backordering

C_S: The salvage value of unsold inventory.

The unit cost, C, may be fixed or depend upon the quantity ordered. The cost of carrying inventory, C_H, is often expressed as a fraction, i, of the C. The carrying cost often includes the cost of capital tied up in inventory, and may also include the cost of warehousing the item. The cost of placing a replenishment order, C_R, is incurred each time the item is re-ordered and includes costs such as the administrative cost of placing the order, of inspecting an incoming order, and possibly of expediting the order. The cost of being short, C_P, includes costs such as lost revenue, possible substitution of another item, loss of customer goodwill, and the administrative cost of processing a backorder.

Uncontrollable variables include:

D: The customer demand for the item

L: The lead time, or time required for a replenishment order to arrive.

The customer demand, D, may be modeled as a constant rate of demand or it may be modeled as a random variable. If the demand for the item is a random variable, the distribution of demand may be modeled as a discrete random variable, or as a continuous random variable. In either case, the models are basically the same, except that, with a discrete demand distribution, the model is formulated using discrete summations of demand. If the demand is a continuous random variable, methods of calculus are used to formulate the model.

The lead time, L, may be constant for every replenishment order, or may be a random variable. When the customer demand or the lead time is a random variable, we risk shortages during the time in which the replenishment order is placed and the order arrives.

The management of an inventory system is characterized by an inventory policy. The inventory policy is expressed in terms of:

Q: The replenishment order quantity

Re-Order Rule: The rule used to trigger a replenishment order.

The quantity ordered, Q, may be a fixed quantity or may depend upon the current level of inventory. The re-order rule governs when a replenishment order should be made. Two common rules are to place an order when the inventory level falls below a preset level, or to periodically review the inventory level and if the level is too low, place a replenishment order.

Finally, inventory models are either static or dynamic models. In static models only one ordering cycle is considered, while dynamic models are used to model systems in which inventory is reordered. We will first consider the static model and then go on to dynamic-inventory models.

5.5.2 A STATIC-INVENTORY MODEL

In a static-(single-period) model the decision variable is the number of units of inventory on hand at the beginning of the period. During the period, the demand for the inventory is uncertain, but the probability distribution of the demand is known. The single-period inventory model can be formulated as an expected-cost model or as an expected-revenue model. The expected-cost model includes C, the cost of purchasing the inventory at the beginning of the period, C_P, the penalty for running out of stock during the period, and C_S, the salvage value of the inventory remaining at the end of the period. The penalty cost, C_P, is often expressed as the difference between the selling price of the item and the purchase cost. An expected-revenue model includes all the elements of the expected-cost model and also includes the expected revenue from the sale of the inventoried item.

We will first formulate an expected-revenue model for the case of discrete demand. Where S is sale price of the item

E(Revenue) = E(Sales) − Purchase Costs − E(Penalty Cost) + E(Salvage Income)

$$= \underbrace{\sum_{k=1}^{Q} SkP_k + QS \sum_{k=Q+1}^{\infty} P_k}_{E(Sales)} - \underbrace{CQ}_{\substack{Purch. \\ Cost}} - \underbrace{\sum_{k=Q+1}^{\infty} C_P(k-Q)P_k}_{E(Penalty)} + \underbrace{\sum_{k=0}^{Q-1} C_s(Q-k)P_k}_{E(Salvage)} \quad (5.47)$$

ILLUSTRATIVE PROBLEM 5.14

Our first example of a single period inventory problem will be the classic "Newspaper Boy Problem." Assume a newspaper boy can purchase newspapers for 15 cents and sells them for 25 cents. Any unsold newspapers can be returned for a refund of 10 cents. The newspaper boy has kept records on the demand for the newspaper at his location. The distribution of demand is:

Demand	Probability
12	.05
13	.10
14	.20
15	.30
16	.20
17	.10
18	.05

In this problem we will assume that there is no penalty for being short, other than the implicit loss of sales. The objective of the newspaper boy is, of course, to maximize his daily profits. To find the ordering policy that maximizes profits, he can calculate the expected profits for any inventory level from 12 to 18.

These calculations are shown in Table 5.3, indicating that 16 is the optimal number of papers to purchase each day.

TABLE 5.3
EXPECTED PROFIT CALCULATION

Q	Expected Sales	Expected Salvage	Purchase Cost	E(Profit)
12	$3.00	$0.00	$1.80	$1.200
13	$3.24	$0.01	$1.95	$1.293
14	$3.45	$0.03	$2.10	$1.380
15	$3.61	$0.06	$2.25	$1.418
16	$3.70	$0.12	$2.40	$1.420
17	$3.74	$0.21	$2.55	$1.393
18	$3.75	$0.30	$2.70	$1.350

In the above problem we used the distribution of daily demand to determine the expected profits at each inventory level. This approach is sometimes called total-value analysis. An alternative method of determining the optimal inventory policy is through an incremental analysis. In this method we determine the largest inventory such that there is an incremental expected profit on the last unit of inventory. The incremental expected profit is

$$\Delta \text{Profit}_Q = S[P(\text{Demand} \geq Q)] + C_S[P(\text{Demand} < Q)] - C.$$

When ΔProfit is 0.0 we have

$$S[P(\text{Demand} \geq Q)] + C_S[P(\text{Demand} < Q)] = C$$

and since

$$P(\text{Demand} < Q) = 1 - P(\text{Demand} \geq Q)$$

we find the optimal inventory is at the point where

$$P(\text{Demand} \geq Q) = \frac{C - C_s}{S - C_s}$$

In the newspaper boy example, the optimal inventory level is when

$$P(\text{Demand} > Q) = (.15 - .10)/(.25 - .10)$$

$$= .333.$$

Table 5.4 shows $P(\text{Demand} \geq Q)$.

When the inventory level is set at $Q = 16$, the incremental profit from the 16th unit is positive. However, if we increase the inventory to 17, the incremental profit is negative. Therefore, we would not move up to this higher inventory level. The optimal inventory policy using an incremental analysis is, of course, the same as the optimal policy using a total value analysis.

5.5.3   A CONTINUOUS REVIEW DYNAMIC INVENTORY MODEL

In dynamic inventory systems the inventory is reviewed and if the inventory is too low, a replenishment order is placed. The inventory level may be reviewed continuously or periodically. We will first consider the continuous review system. In this system, the

TABLE 5.4
DEMAND DISTRIBUTION

Q	P(Demand = Q)	P(Demand ≥ Q)
12	0.05	1.00
13	0.10	0.95
14	0.20	0.85
15	0.30	0.65
16	0.20	$0.35 \leftarrow P(D>Q) = 0.333$
17	0.10	0.15
18	0.05	0.05

inventory policy is characterized by the reorder quantity Q and the reorder point R_P. When the inventory falls below R_P, an order of size Q is placed. The time for a replenishment order to arrive is defined as the lead time. If, during this lead time, the demand exceeds the inventory, a shortage occurs. If the demand is deterministic and the lead time does not vary from order to order, then the reorder point can be set so that no shortages occur and the inventory is just exhausted when the replenishment order arrives. Figure 5.5 shows a typical continuous review, dynamic inventory system with a deterministic demand.

A total cost model for this system is

$$\text{Total Annual Cost} = C_H C Q / 2 + C_R D / Q \tag{5.48}$$

where D is the annual rate of demand for the item.

FIGURE 5.5   CONSTANT DEMAND/LEAD TIME INVENTORY SYSTEM

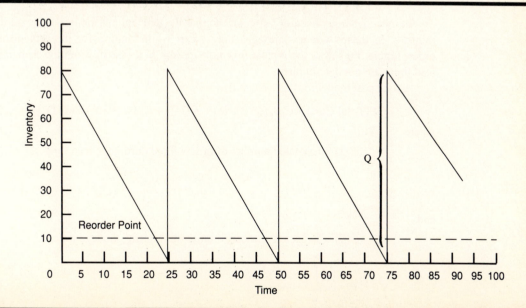

By taking the derivative of equation 5.48 and setting it to zero, we can determine the optimal value of Q is

$$Q = \sqrt{2DC_R/C_H C} \qquad (5.49)$$

The reorder point should be $L \times D$ where L is the lead time for a replenishment order.

ILLUSTRATIVE PROBLEM 5.15

A supplier of electronic parts carries inventory for a component that has yearly a demand of 10,000 units. Each unit costs the manufacturer $1.00 and the annual cost of carrying inventory is 12 percent of the purchase price. The cost of ordering the component from the supplier is $10.00. The lead time to receive an order is 10 days. Currently the supplier is ordering 2000 units. He is wondering what it currently costs to inventory the item and what is the optimal order size.

Using equation 5.48 we find the inventory cost of the component is

$$(0.12)\,(\$1.00)\,(2000/2) + (\$10.00)\,(10{,}000/2000) = \$170.00$$

and using 5.49 the optimal order size is

$$\sqrt{(2)\,(10000)(\$10.00)/(0.12)(\$1.00)} = 1290$$

and the cost of this optimal inventory policy is

$$(0.12)\,(1.00)\,(1290/2) + (\$10.00)\,(10{,}000/1290) = \$154.92$$

with a reorder point of

$$(10000/365)\,(10) = 274.$$

In most dynamic inventory systems, neither the demand nor the lead time are deterministic. In these systems shortages may occur while waiting for the replenishment order. Figure 5.6 shows the typical inventory profile in a system when the demand and lead times are not deterministic.

A total cost model for this system is

$$E(\text{Total Cost}) = C_H C(Q/2 + R_P - E(U)) + C_R D/Q + C_P E(S)D/Q \qquad (5.50)$$

where

$$E(U) = \text{Expected number of orders filled during the lead time}$$

$$= \int_0^{R_P} x f(x)\,dx$$

and

$$E(S) = \text{Expected number of units short during the lead time.}$$

$$= \int_{R_P}^{\infty} (x - R_P) f(x)\,dx$$

FIGURE 5.6   VARIABLE DEMAND/LEAD TIME INVENTORY SYSTEM

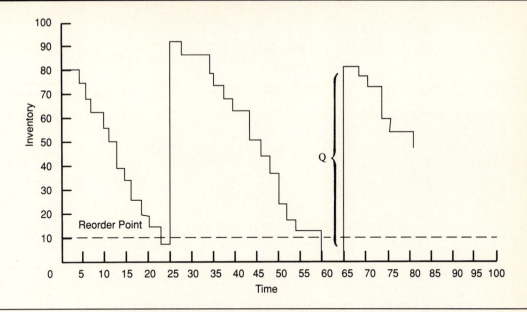

with $f(x)$ being the probability density function of the demand during the lead time. It can be shown that the optimal policy is when

$$Q = \sqrt{2E(D)(C_R + C_P E(S))/C_H C}$$ (5.51)

and

$$P(D > R_p) = Q C_H C / C_P E(D)$$ (5.52)

These two equations can be solved iteratively by first assuming that $E(s)$ is zero, solving for Q in equation (5.51), then solving for R_p in equation (5.52). Once R_p is found, an improved estimate of Q can be found, leading to an improved estimate of R_p, etc. In most cases the optimal policies can be found within reasonable accuracy using only three or fewer iterations.

ILLUSTRATIVE   In the previous example we assumed that the demand and the lead time were constant. A
PROBLEM   more realistic assumption is that the demand during the lead time is a random variable
5.16   and C_P the penalty cost for being short, is $0.50 per unit. For illustration purposes, we will assume that the demand during the reorder period is uniformly distributed between 200 and 400 units. We can now iteratively solve for the optimal order quantity and reorder points using equations 5.51 and 5.52.

Our first estimate of Q is

$$Q = \sqrt{(2)1000(10+0)/(.12)(1)} = 1291$$

and to find R_P note that

$$P(D > R_p) = \frac{1}{200} \int_{R_P}^{400} dx = \frac{400 - R_P}{200}$$

we find R_p by solving

$$\frac{400 - R_p}{200} = (1291)(.12)(\$1.00)/(0.50)(10,000)$$

$$R_p = 393.00$$

and

$$E(S) = \frac{1}{200} \int_{393}^{400} (x - 393) dx$$

$$= .1225$$

If we refine our estimate of Q using $E(S)$, we find the optimal value of Q is now 1295. A second iteration would show that the optimal value of R_p remains at 393.

5.5.4   A PERIODIC REVIEW DYNAMIC INVENTORY MODEL

In a periodic review inventory system the level of inventory is not monitored continuously, but reviewed at the end of every period. The size of the re-order is not fixed but is the difference between the current inventory and S. Figure 5.7 shows a typical profile of inventory in a periodic review system. In this inventory system there are two decision variables, the length of the review period, T, and the target inventory, S. The expected annual cost of this system is

$$E(\text{Total Cost}) = R_p/T + C_H(S - DT/2 - LD) + C_P E(s)/T \tag{5.53}$$

where L is the lead time and $E(s)$ is the expected shortage during each period.

$$E(s) = \int_s^{\infty} (x - S) f(x) dx \tag{5.54}$$

where $f(x)$ is the distribution of the demand during the review period.

Solving equations 5.53 and 5.54 for the optimal values of S and T is difficult because $f(x)$ depends upon the length of the review period. As a first approximation to the optimal policy, we use the optimal solution, Q, for the continuous review model to find $T = D/Q$, and set $S = DT$. By direct search we can then find the optimal values of T and S. For a more complete treatment of this inventory system see Hadley and Whitin [3].

5.5.5   AN ANALYTIC AND SIMULATION MODEL
          OF AN INVENTORY SYSTEM

In order to illustrate how an analytic model can be used to provide some early and quick insights into the behavior of inventory systems, we consider two models of an inventory system.

FIGURE 5.7   PERIODIC REVIEW INVENTORY SYSTEM

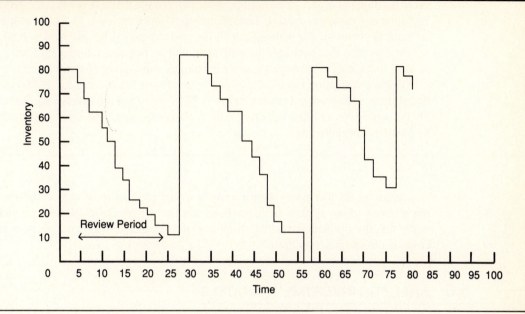

ILLUSTRATIVE PROBLEM 5.17

A retailer stocks an item whose demand varies by day of the week. On each day the demand is uniformly distributed but the mean and range of the demand differs. The store is open for only five days of the week. When the inventory falls below 20 units a replenishment order of 100 units is placed and will be received exactly four days later. Customer orders cannot be backordered, resulting in lost sales when there is not sufficient inventory. Listed below is the mean, spread, and variance of the demand by day of the week.

Day	Mean	Spread	Variance
Monday	4	± 3	3.00
Tuesday	6	± 3	5.33
Wednesday	10	± 6	12.00
Thursday	12	± 10	33.33
Friday	6	± 4	5.33
Saturday	0	± 0	0.00
Sunday	0	± 0	0.00
Average	5.43		8.43

We would like to know the expected time between orders and the expected number of lost sales during each re-order period.

Using the simple re-order point model we can estimate the mean time between orders to be $100/5.43 = 18.4$ days. Further, since the average demand per day is 5.43 and the lead time is 4 days, the average demand during re-order period is 21.72. In addition the standard deviation of the demand during the re-order period is $\sqrt{(8.43)(4)} = 5.80$. Thus we can conclude that over half the time there will be lost demand ranging from 0 to 10 or more units. As a very rough guess we could pick a mid-point of about 5 units.

When a simulation model of this system is constructed and run for 10,000 days we find that the average time between orders is 19.92 days, and the average number of orders lost during the re-order period is 7.22. A Pascal listing of the simulation model can be found in Appendix 5A.

Again we see that a very simple analytic model gives us some early estimates about the behavior of the system. In addition we can use the results of the analytic model to verify that the simulation model is behaving in a reasonable way (i.e., are there coding errors in our computer program?).

5.6   ANALYTIC INVESTMENT MODELS

Simulation models are often used to analyze systems in which financial receipts and expenditures occur over time. In financial analysis it is a common practice to apply a discount factor to receipts or expenditures that occur in future times. That is, a dollar spent or received today is not to be equated in value to a dollar several years hence. The discount factor to be applied to future dollars is based on the Minimum Rate of Return which reflects both the cost of borrowing money, inflation, and the alternative opportunities for investment.

The basic formula for discounting future cash flows is the same formula that is used in finance to determine the future worth of an investment. If each year an investment grows by i, then after 1 year it will have grown to $(1 + i)$ times the original investment. After the second year it will have grown by $(1 + i)^2$. In general, after n years, the investment will have grown to $(1 + i)^n$ times the original investment. The relationship between an initial investment of P dollars today and its future value, F, is then

$$F_n = P(1 + i)^n. \tag{5.55}$$

The reciprocal relationship between P and F_n shows how future dollars are to be discounted.

$$P = F_n \frac{1}{(1 + i)^n} \tag{5.56}$$

ILLUSTRATIVE PROBLEM 5.18   To show the difference in values of an investment at different times, consider the future value of $100, invested for 10 years, growing in value by .10 each year (a 10 percent annual rate of return). Using equation 5.55 we have

$$F_n = \$100(1+i)^{10}$$
$$= \$100(2.593)$$
$$= \$259.30.$$

Alternatively, the present value of $100, 10 years away is

$$P = \$\frac{100}{(1 + .10)^n}$$
$$= \$\frac{100}{2.593}$$
$$= \$38.57.$$

That is, although we will receive $100, 10 years hence, its value in present day dollars is only $38.57. Equivalently, we could invest $38.57 today (at 10 percent interest) and have $100, 10 years later.

5.6.1   CASH FLOW DIAGRAMS

A convenient method of describing an investment is through the use of a cash flow diagram in which expenditures and receipts are drawn, showing the time at which they occur. For example the cash flow diagram

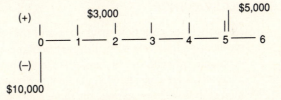

depicts an investment in which $10,000 is initially invested and then, for the next six years, the investor receives payments of $3000. At the end of the sixth year, a single payment of $5000 is also received.

When drawing a cash flow diagram, the most commonly used notation is:

P: The initial investment at the beginning of the project

F_n: A future receipt or expense n years into the project

A: An annual series of end of year receipts or payments

5.6.2   DISCOUNTING CASH FLOWS

We have already shown the relationship between P and F_n. The relationship between a series of n end of year payments of amount A and F is found using

$$F_n = A[(1 + i)^{n-1} + (1 + i)^{n-2} .. + 1] \qquad (5.57)$$
$$= A[(1 + i)^{n-1}]/i.$$

TABLE 5.5
DISCOUNTED CASH FLOW FORMULAS

Term	Formula
Compound Amount Factor ($F\|P,i,n$)	$F_n = P(1+i)^n$
Present Worth Factor ($P\|F,i,n$)	$P = F_n/(1+1)$
Capital Recovery Factor ($A\|P,i,n$)	$A = P(i(1+1)^n/[(1+i)^n - 1)]$
Series Present Worth Factor ($P\|A,i,n$)	$P = A([(1+i)^n - 1]/[i(1+i)])$
Series Compound Amount Factor ($F\|A,i,n$)	$F_n = A[(1+i)^n - 1]/i$
Sinking Fund Factor ($A\|F,i,n$)	$A = F_n i/[(1+i)^n - 1]$

Table 5.5 shows the relationships between an initial investment P, an annual series of size A, and a future payment F.

Tables in Appendix 5B contain discounting factors for interest rates of 5 percent, 10 percent, 15 percent, and 20 percent. For a complete set of tables see Grant [2].

5.6.3   EQUIVALENCE

Not only is the cash flow diagram useful for describing an investment, it also provides a mechanism for evaluating different economic alternatives. When evaluating different economic alternatives, an important concept is that of equivalence. Two investment alternatives are considered equivalent at discount rate i if they can be equated to a common cash flow. For example, the three alternatives shown

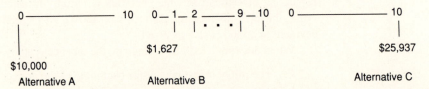

are equivalent at a discount rate of 10 percent since the initial investment of $10,000 in Alternative A could produce a final value of $25,937 shown in Alternative C, if invested at 10 percent, for ten years. Equivalently, the $25,937, when discounted at a rate of 10 percent, is viewed at the present time as worth only $10,000. Similarly, if the first of the $1,627 payments was discounted for one year, the second $1,627 discounted for two years, etc., the present value of the 10 payments would be $10,000. Also, if each of the $1,627 payments shown in B were allowed to gather 10 percent interest, at the end of 10 years, we would have $25,937. Using this principle of equivalence of cash flows, we can compare one or more economic alternatives by reducing each of the alternatives to a simpler but equivalent cash flow.

ILLUSTRATIVE PROBLEM 5.19

A manufacturer is considering two different testing machines. The machines differ in their initial cost, the cost of maintenance, and the salvage value at the end of their useful life. Machine A costs initially $200,000 and will require $10,000 in annual maintenance. It will have a salvage value of $50,000 after 10 years. Machine B cost $240,000 but will require only $5,000 in annual maintenance and will have a salvage value of $100,000. The discount rate used by the manufacturer is 10 percent. The cash flow diagrams for each of the alternatives is:

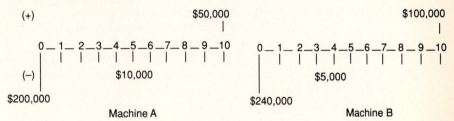

Using our formulas for discounting cash flows to their present value we can find the present value of Machine A and Machine B.

$$\text{Present Value}_A = \$200,000 + (\$10,000)(P|A, 10\%, 10yr) - (\$50,000)(P|F, 10\%, 10yr)$$
$$= \$200,000 + (\$10,000)(6.1446) - (50,000)(.38554)$$
$$= \$242,169$$

$$\text{Present Value}_B = \$240,000 + (\$5,000)(P|A, 10\%, 10yr) - (\$100,000)(P|F, 10\%, 10yr)$$
$$= \$240,000 + (\$5,000)(6.1446) - (\$100,000)(.38554)$$
$$= \$232,169$$

That is, purchasing Machine A is equivalent to spending $242,169 in a single payment while Machine B is equivalent to spending $232,169. From this analysis we would conclude, all other considerations being equal, that Machine B is economically a better choice.

When comparing two alternatives that have unequal lives, we cannot compare them using equivalent present values, but must compare them using equivalent annual payments.

ILLUSTRATIVE PROBLEM 5.20

The two alternative investments in the previous problem can be compared on an equivalent annual cost by finding the annual series of payments that are equivalent to their actual cash flows.

$$\text{Annual Cost}_A = (\$200,000)(A|P, 10\%, 10yr) + 10,000 - (\$50,000)(A|F, 10\%, 10yr)$$
$$= (\$200,000)(.16275) + \$10,000 - (\$50,000)(.06275)$$
$$= \$39,413$$

$$\text{Annual Cost}_B = (\$240,000)(A|P, 10\%, 10yr) + 5,000 - (\$100,000)(A|F, 10\%, 10yr)$$
$$= (\$240.000)(.16275) + \$5,000 - (\$100,000)(.06275)$$
$$= \$37,785$$

5.6.4   CALCULATING THE RATE OF RETURN ON AN INVESTMENT

To understand the meaning of "the rate of return on an investment," consider an investment which, when discounted at rate i has a present worth of 0.0. An investor expecting rate i would be indifferent toward the investment. An investor expecting a rate higher than i would view the investment as having a negative present worth. An investor expecting a rate of return less than i would view the investment as having a positive present worth. That is, the rate of return on an investment is the discount rate for which the present worth of the income from the investment is equal to the present worth of the expenditures.

ILLUSTRATIVE PROBLEM 5.21

An investment opportunity requires an initial expenditure of $35,000. Over the next five years the investment will yield an income of $6000 and at the end of five years, $20,000 of the original investment can be recovered. A potential investor would like to know the effective rate of return.

The rate of return on the investment can be found by trial and error calculation of its present worth at various discount rates. Using

$$\text{Present Worth} = \$35,000 + (\$6000)(P|A, i\%, 5yrs) + (\$20,000)(P|F, i\%, 5yr)$$

we have

Discount Rate	Present Worth
5%	$6,647
8%	2,568
10%	163
11%	- 956

That is, at a discount rate of slightly more than 10 percent, but less than 11 percent, the present value of the investment is zero. Using straight line interpolation between 10 percent and 11 percent we can estimate the effective rate of return on the investment to be 10.15 percent.

5.6.5   THE EFFECT OF UNCERTAINTY IN CASH FLOWS

In most cases the cash flows associated with an investment alternative are uncertain. Future cash flows are usually stated in terms of their expected values but when the cash flow occurs, it seldom is equal to its expected value. If the cash flows in an investment are considered to be random variables, then its equivalent present value, annual cost, and rate of return are random variables. When analyzing cash flows with uncertainty, we are often interested in finding the mean and variance of their equivalent cash flows, or the rate of return, and if possible, the probability distribution of these measures. Our analysis is facilitated by the following properties of the sums of random variables:

If

$$Y = a_1X_1 + a_2X_2 + ... + a_nX_n$$

then

$$E(Y) = a_1E(X_1) + a_2E(X_2) + ... + a_nE(X_n) \tag{5.58}$$

$$\text{Var}(y) = a_1^2 \text{Var}(X_1) + a_2^2 \text{Var}(X_2) + ... + a_n^2 \text{Var}(X_n)$$

$$+ \sum a_i a_j \text{Cov}(X_i X_j) \qquad\qquad i \neq j \tag{5.59}$$

and if all X_i are independent random variables then

$$\text{Var}(y) = a_1^2 \text{Var}(X_1) + a_2^2 \text{Var}(X_2) + ... + a_n^2 \text{Var}(X_n) \tag{5.60}$$

If all X_i are normally distributed, then Y is normally distributed. Further, from the central limit theorem, even though all X_i are not normally distributed, as the number of terms in the summation Y increases, Y converges to a normally-distributed random variable. For our purposes, the a_i's are the discounting terms used to calculate an investment's equivalent present worth or annual cost.

From equation 5.58 we see that if the cash flows in an investment alternative are random variables, we can use their expected values to determine the expected equivalent present value or annual cost. If, however, we want to obtain a measure of the variation in the equivalent present value or annual cost, we must know the variance and possibly covariance of the cash flows.

ILLUSTRATIVE PROBLEM 5.22 An investor has the opportunity of purchasing two bonds which will cost initially $15,000. After 5 years one bond will be sold at market value, while the second bond will be held for 10 years and then be sold for its market value. The probability distributions of the estimated distributions of market values of the two bonds after 5 and 10 years are:

Value Bond 1	Probability	Value Bond 2	Probability
$12,000	.20	$8,000	.25
$13,000	.30	10,000	.25
$14,000	.30	12,000	.25
$15,000	.20	14,000	.25

Using these probabilities, the mean and variance of the redemption value of the two bonds are

$$E(\text{Bond 1}) = \$13.5 \times 10^3 \quad \text{Var(Bond 1)} = 1.05 \times 10^6$$

$$E(\text{Bond 2}) = \$11.0 \times 10_3 \quad \text{Var(Bond 2)} = 5.0 \times 10^6$$

Using equations 5.58 and 5.59 we can find the mean and variance of the present value of the investment

$$E(\text{Present Worth}) = (P|F,i\%,5\text{yrs})E(\text{Bond 1}) + (P|F,i\%,10\text{yrs})E(\text{Bond 2})$$

$$\text{Var(Present Worth)} = (P|F,i\%,5\text{yrs})^2\text{Var(Bond 1)} +$$

$$(P|F,i\%,10\text{yrs})^2\text{Var(Bond 2)} +$$

$$(P|F,i\%,5\text{yrs})(P|F,i\%,10\text{yrs})\,\text{Cov(Bond 1, Bond 2)}$$

If we assume that the redemption values of the two bonds are independent, then the last term in the Var(Present Worth) is zero.

Using a discount rate of 10%,

$$E(\text{Present Worth}) = (.62092)(13.5 \times 10^3) + (.38554)(11.0 \times 10^3)$$

$$= \$12,623$$

$$\text{Var(Present Worth)} = (.62092)^2(1.05 \times 10^6) + (.38554)^2(5.0 \times 10^6)$$

$$= 1.148 \times 10^6$$

and the standard deviation of the Present Worth of the investment is

$$\text{Std.Dev (Present Worth)} = \sqrt{1.148 \times 10^6}$$

$$= \$1,071$$

Finding the mean and variance of the rate of return on an investment is more difficult than finding the mean and variance of the present value or annual cost, and simulation may be the only practical method. However, it is possible to show that

$$E(\text{Rate of Return}) \leq \text{Rate of Return of Expected Cash Flows}$$

That is, if any of the cash flows in the investment alternatives are random variables, then the expected rate of return on the investment will be less than the rate of return found using the expected values of the cash flows.

ILLUSTRATIVE PROBLEM 5.23   In order to illustrate the effect of uncertainty on the rate of return on an investment alternative consider an investment of $10,000. After five years the investment will be equally likely to have a value of $12,000 or $18,000.

The expected value of the investment, after five years is

$$(\$12,000)(0.50) + (\$18,000)(0.50) = \$15,000.$$

To find the rate of return on this type of investment we must find i such that

$$F = P(1 + i)^n$$

Thus

$$i = {}^n\sqrt{F/P} - 1$$

$$= .0845.$$

The rate of return on expected future value of the investment is

$$ {}^5\sqrt{\$15,000/\$10,000} - 1 $$

$$= .0845.$$

However, our investment will not be worth \$15,000 in five years, but rather it will be worth either \$12,000 or \$18,000. If the investment is worth \$12,000, then the rate of return will be

$$ {}^5\sqrt{\$12,000/\$10,000} - 1 $$

$$= .037$$

while if the investment is worth \$18,000, then the rate of return is

$$ {}^5\sqrt{\$18,000/\$10,000} - 1 $$

$$= .125$$

Thus

$$E(\text{rate of return}) = .037*.50 + .125*.05$$

$$= .081.$$

which is less than the rate of return based on the expected values of the cash flows.

5.6.6   AN ANALYTIC AND SIMULATION MODEL OF AN INVESTMENT

In order to illustrate how analytic and simulation models of investments complement each other, we will analyze a simple investment using both types of models.

ILLUSTRATIVE PROBLEM 5.24   An investor is considering investing \$7000 for 5 years. At the end of five years the expected value of the investment will be \$12,000 with a spread of $\pm\$5000$. The investor would like to know the expected rate of return on this investment as well as the likelihood of achieving a rate of return of less than 8 percent.

An analytic model of this investment can be based on equation 5.55. That is,

$$F_5 = P(1 - i)^5$$

or

$$i = (F_5/P)^{1/5} - 1$$

Solving for i we find $i = .114$.

From the previous section, however, we know that using the expected cash flows overstates the expected rate of return. Further, we do not know the probability of obtaining a rate of return below 8 percent. An alternative model is, of course, a simulation model that estimates the mean rate of return, as well as the likelihood of the rate of return falling below 8 percent. Appendix 5A.6 contains a Pascal listing of a simulation model of this problem. When the simulation model is run for 500 samples we find the average rate of return is .106, and 35 percent of the time the investment returns less than 8 percent.

Again, we see that the simpler analytic model gave us a quick but approximate answer while the simulation model gave us more detailed information, but with considerably more effort.

5.7 CONCLUSION

In this chapter we have presented a number of analytic models of systems that are often modeled using discrete-event simulation models. Although these analytic models make many assumptions about a system, they often provide a very good first-pass model of more complex systems. An integral part of simulation modeling is the identification of any analytic models that may serve as a simple, initial model. The analytic model then can be used to give the analyst early insights and estimates of the more complex system's behavior.

EXERCISES

5.1 In the St. Petersburg Paradox the expected winnings were shown to be unbounded. If we incorporate utility theory, an alternative solution is available. The underlying idea in utility theory is that the value of money is not linear. For example, a million dollars may not have 1000 times the utility of a thousand dollars. As the dollars amount increases, the utility of the amount begins to level off. An example utility function might be

$$U = (1 - e^{-x/1,000,000}) \qquad x>0$$

a) Using utility as a measure of winnings, what is the expected amount a player will win?

b) Based on the expected winnings, as measured by the above utility function, what is a fair price to pay, in order to play the game?

5.2 The Gambler's Ruin problem was modeled as a Markov Chain in Problem 4.7. When the probability of winning the toss is equal for each gambler, we can calculate the probability of Gambler A winning or Gambler B winning by using the fact that the game is fair. A game is fair when the expected winnings of each player is 0.0.

a) If Gambler A brings A dollars to the game and Gambler B brings B dollars to the game, show $P(\text{Gambler A wins}) = A/(A+B)$.

5.3 The process of hiring a new employee can be modeled as a Markov Chain. Assume that the personnel department has arranged interviews with three candidates. At the end of each interview the department head must either offer the candidate the job or go to the next candidate. If the job has not been offered to either the first or second candidate, the third candidate, by default, will get the job. Each candidate is graded as either 1, 2, or 3 with 3 being the highest rating. The probabilities a candidate will be a 1, 2, or 3 are 0.30, 0.50, and 0.20, respectively. If the object is to end up with the highest rated hire, what is the optimal policy for selection of a candidate? That is, should the ith candidate be offered the job, if her rating is a 1 or 2? (Obviously, when a 3 is interviewed the candidate should be hired.)

5.4 A tennis game can be modeled as an absorbing Markov Chain with the score of the game being equivalent to the game's state. In order to win a game in tennis, a player must win at least four points and be ahead by two points. That is, once both players have won three points, the score can be stated in terms of the number of points a player is ahead or behind, with the game ending when one player is ahead by two points.

  a) Construct the transition matrix for this absorbing Markov Chain.

  b) If the probability of one player winning any single point is 0.55, what is the probability of that player winning the game?

  c) A set in tennis can also be modeled as a Markov Chain. To win a set a player must win at least six games and be ahead by two games. Construct the transition matrix for a set of tennis. Using the results from part a), what is the probability the player will win the set?

  d) To win a tennis match a player must win two out of three games. Using the results of part c), what is the probability the player will win the match?

5.5 Exercise 3.1 described the rules for the game of Craps. Using these rules, model the game as an absorbing Markov Chain.

5.6 At a military base the bursars cash checks for both officers and enlisted personnel. There is a separate window for officers and a separate window for enlisted personnel. The mean time to cash a check is 40 seconds. Officers arrive at their window at a rate of 60 per hour while enlisted men arrive at a rate of 70 per hour.

  a) What is the mean time officers wait in line?

  b) What is the mean time enlisted personnel wait in line?

  c) What would be the waiting times if officers and the enlisted personnel shared the two windows? That is, the system becomes one two-server queue rather than two one-server queues.

5.7 For an *M/M/1* queueing system with a traffic intensity of 0.80, which is more effective for reducing the length of the queue—a 10 percent increase in the service rate or a 40 percent reduction in the variance of the service time? (Notice, if ρ remains at .90 and the variance in the service time is reduced by 40 percent, the system is no longer an *M/M/1*.)

5.8 When planning the size of a new hospital, it is assumed that a patient that needs to be admitted will never be turned away. Based on the population the hospital will be serving, the expected admission rate of patients is 20 per day and the expected length of stay in the hospital is 8 days.

   a) How many beds should be in the hospital in order that only one percent of the patients admitted will not have a bed available?

5.9 A spare-parts inventory system can be modeled using a queueing model. Consider the case of five machines that occasionally need a spare part. Only 2 such spare parts are kept in inventory. When a part is used, a replacement order is made. The mean time for a replacement part to arrive is 10 days. Each machine will need the spare part about once every 25 days.

   a) Using an M/M model, what is the probability that a machine will need the spare part but none will be available?

   b) What is the mean number of spare parts kept in inventory?

5.10 In Chapter 3 a simulation model of a time-shared computer system was developed. A queueing model of the system can be developed, letting the number of servers correspond to the number of ports and allowing no queue to develop.

   a) Construct the balance equations for this system.

   b) Using this system of equations, derive an expression for P_i, $i=0...K$.

   c) Assuming the rate users attempt to connect to the system is 20 per hour, the mean connect time is 20 minutes, and there are 10 ports. What is the probability all the ports are busy?

5.11 Consider a system that makes transitions between states 1 and 2. The probabilities of making a transition from state i to state j is dependent upon the current and previous state as shown in the following table.

Current State	Previous State	Transition Probability
1	1	$P(1\rightarrow1) = .4; P(1\rightarrow2) = .6$
1	2	$P(1\rightarrow1) = .5; P(1\rightarrow2) = .5$
2	1	$P(2\rightarrow1) = .3; P(2\rightarrow2) = .7$
2	2	$P(2\rightarrow1) = .6; P(1\rightarrow2) = .4$

   a) Construct the transition matrix for this system which includes both the current and previous state of the system.

   b) Using the transition matrix in a), determine the steady-state probabilities and first-passage times between states.

   c) Construct a transition matrix for this system which reflects only the current state of the system and then calculate the steady-state probabilities and first-passage times.

5.12 A computer system is being designed and a choice must be made between having two disks with an average retrieval time of 40 milliseconds or a single fast disk with an average retrieval time of 20 milliseconds. Assume the requests for access to the disk arrive at the rate of 40 requests per second. The times between requests for retrievals is exponentially distributed and the retrieval times have such a small variance that they can be modeled as being constants. If a disk is busy when a request arrives it is placed in a queue and must wait until the disk becomes available. For the two-disk system, the requests are evenly distributed between each disk.

    a) What is the average time required to complete a retrieval for each of the two systems?

    b) What is the average length of the queue for each system?

5.13 An item costing $20 is inventoried. The expense for carrying the item in inventory is 15 percent of its cost. It costs $25 each time an order is placed and the cost of being short one item is $10. The demand for the item is Poisson distributed with a mean demand of 2000 per year. The lead time for receiving an order is exactly 10 days. Assume a year is 300 working days.

    a) What is the optimal order quantity and re-order point?

    b) Suppose the company is currently ordering 1000 items each time an order is placed, and the company places the order when inventory falls below 100 units. How much will they save in ordering, carrying, and shortage costs by using the optimal inventory policy?

5.14 A merchant is considering how many Christmas trees he should purchase. Because of the shortness of the season only one order can be placed. The trees cost the merchant $5.00 and they can be sold for $15.00. They have no salvage value. The merchant estimates the demand for Christmas trees to be normally distributed with a mean of 200 and a standard deviation of 50 trees.

    a) What is the optimal number of trees to be ordered?

    b) What is the expected profit when an optimal order is placed?

5.15 A purchaser of a new automobile has narrowed his choice to two models. The relevant costs for each of the two models is shown in the following table.

	Model I	Model II
Original cost	$10,000	$15,000
Annual maintenance cost	2,000	1,500
Annual fuel cost	3,000	5,000
Expected life	4 yrs	6 yrs
Salvage value	1,000	3,000

    a) For a discount rate of 15 percent, what is the most economical choice?

    b) As the discount rate increases, which model becomes more and more attractive?

5.16 An investor is considering the purchase of rental property. The initial cost of the property is $1,000,000. The annual income from rental is estimated to be $200,000 and the resale value of the building in 10 years is expected to be $2,000,000. The rental income is not certain to be $200,000 every year and can be modeled as a normally-distributed random variable with a standard deviation of $50,000. Similarly, the resale value of the building is estimated to be normally distributed with a standard deviation of $800,000. The investor has a discount rate of 10 percent.

a) What is the expected present worth of the investment?

b) What is the standard deviation of the investment's present worth?

c) Set a 95 percent confidence interval on the present worth of the investment.

5.17 Consider an investment requiring an initial investment of $1000. After two years the investment will be worth F dollars. F is a random variable uniformly distributed between $1200 and $1600. That is,

$$f(F) = \frac{1}{400} \qquad \$1200 \leq F \leq \$1600$$

a) What is the probability distribution of the rate of return for this investment?

b) What is the expected rate of return?

c) What is the rate of return using the expected cash flows?

5.18 In our development of interest formulas, it is assumed that interest payments occur at the end of each period. An alternative model assumes that interest is computed continuously. Show that for continuous compounding, the formula for the future worth, F, of an initial investment of P is

$$F = Pe^{it}$$

REFERENCES

1. Dietrich, S.: *Comparison Methods for Queues and Other Stocastic Models.* John Wiley and Sons, New York, 1983.

2. Grant, Ireson: *Engineeering Economy*, Ronald Press, N.Y., 1960.

3. Hadley, G. and Whitin, T.: *Analysis of Inventory Systems*, Prentice Hall, Englewood Cliffs, N.J., 1963.

4. Hillier, F.S. and Lieberman, G.J.: *Introduction to Operations Research*, 4th Edition, Holden-Day Inc., Oakland, Ca., 1986.

5. Kemeny, J.G. and Snell, J.L.: *Finite Markov Chains*, D. Van Nostrand Company, Inc., Princeton N.J., 1960.

6. Kendall, D.G.: "Stochastic Processes Occurring in the Theory of Queues and their Analysis by the Method of Imbedded Markov Chains," *Annals of Mathematical Statistics, 4* (1953).

APPENDIX 5A.1

Simulation Model of a Competitive Market

```
PROGRAM MARKET(INPUT,OUTPUT);
{This program simulate a market in which customers making a purchase select
  between 3 brands: A,B and C.  The time between purchases is a  a random
  variable and depends on the last brand selected. The model simulates the
  behaviour of a customer for 100 days.  The input is the current brand
  preference and the out put is the probablity of brand A, B and C being the
  latest purchase 100 days later. This program is compiled by Turbo Pascal}

TYPE BRAND_TYPE=(A,B,C);

VAR P:ARRAY[A..C,A..C] OF REAL;          {matrix of trans. probablities}
    MEAN:ARRAY[A..C] OF REAL;            {mean time between purchases   }
    SPREAD:ARRAY[A..C] OF REAL;          {range in time between purchases}
    F_STATE,XSTATE,STATE:BRAND_TYPE;     {customer state}
    T,T_MAX:REAL;                        {Time variables}
    CUM_STATE:ARRAY[A..C] OF INTEGER;    {statistical accumulators}
    I,ISTATE,N:INTEGER;

FUNCTION NEXT_STATE(S:BRAND_TYPE):BRAND_TYPE;
VAR X:REAL;
BEGIN
X:=RANDOM;
IF X <=P[S,A] THEN NEXT_STATE:=A
ELSE
IF X <= (P[S,A] + P[S,B]) THEN NEXT_STATE:=B
ELSE
NEXT_STATE:=C;
END;

PROCEDURE INIT;
{Initialize transition probablities, means and spreads of transition times}
BEGIN
P[A,A]:=0.60; P[A,B]:=0.20; P[A,C]:=0.20;
P[B,A]:=0.40; P[B,B]:=0.30; P[B,C]:=0.30;
P[C,A]:=0.40; P[C,B]:=0.30; P[C,C]:=0.30;
MEAN[A]:=35; SPREAD[A]:=10;
MEAN[B]:=30; SPREAD[B]:=8;
MEAN[C]:=25; SPREAD[C]:=5;

{initialize statistical accumulators}
CUM_STATE[A]:=0; CUM_STATE[B]:=0; CUM_STATE[C]:=0;

{input current brand preference}
WRITELN('INPUT CURRENT STATE 1,2,3');
READLN(ISTATE);
IF ISTATE=1 THEN F_STATE:=A
ELSE
IF ISTATE=2 THEN F_STATE:=B
ELSE
F_STATE:=C;

{input number  days to simulate}
WRITELN('INPUT NO DAYS');
READLN(T_MAX);
END;
```

(Continued)

```
{MAIN}
BEGIN
INIT;
{input number times the simulation should be run}
WRITELN('INPUT NUMBER OF SIMULATIONS');
READLN(N);

FOR I:=1 TO N DO
BEGIN
  STATE:=F_STATE;
  T:=0;
  WHILE T<T_MAX DO
    BEGIN
    T:=T+MEAN[STATE] - SPREAD[STATE] +2*SPREAD[STATE]*RANDOM);
    STATE:=NEXT_STATE(STATE);
    END;
  CUM_STATE[STATE]:=CUM_STATE[STATE]+1;
END;

{output number of times final state is A, B or C}
FOR XSTATE:=A TO C DO
WRITELN('CUM_STATE =',ORD(XSTATE), '     ',    CUM_STATE[XSTATE]);
END.
```

APPENDIX 5A.2

Simulation Model of Tank Combat

```
PROGRAM TANK_PROB(INPUT,OUTPUT);
{This program simulates combat between three tanks.   The tanks fire
 successively until disabled.  The combat ends with only one  tank
 remaining.}

CONST BIG=100000.0;

TYPE TANK_TYPE=(A,B,C);

VAR P_HIT:ARRAY[A..C,A..C] OF REAL;    {array of prob. of tank hitting target}
    TANK_SET:SET OF TANK_TYPE;         {set of remaining tanks}
    NEXT_TANK:TANK_TYPE;
    T:REAL;
    T_FIRE:ARRAY [A..C] OF REAL;       {time tank next fires}
    N_WINS:ARRAY [A..C] OF INTEGER;    {number of times tank wins}
    I,N:INTEGER;
    N_TANKS:INTEGER;

FUNCTION NEXT_SHOT:REAL;
{This function calculates the time between firings}
BEGIN
NEXT_SHOT:=-LN(RANDOM);
END;

PROCEDURE SHOOT(T1,T2:TANK_TYPE);
{Determines whether tank hits target and if so removes tank from set
 The time of next firing also is set in this procedure              }
BEGIN
IF RANDOM <=P_HIT[T1,T2] THEN
BEGIN
N_TANKS:=N_TANKS-1;
TANK_SET:=TANK_SET -[T2];
T_FIRE[T2]:=BIG;
END;
T_FIRE[T1]:=T+NEXT_SHOT;
END;


PROCEDURE FIRE(TANK:TANK_TYPE);
BEGIN
{This procedure determines which target a tank selects}
    CASE TANK OF
A:  IF B IN TANK_SET THEN
    SHOOT(A,B)
    ELSE
    SHOOT(A,C);
B:  IF A IN TANK_SET THEN
    SHOOT(B,A)
    ELSE
    SHOOT(B,C);
C:  IF A IN TANK_SET THEN
    SHOOT(C,A)
    ELSE
    SHOOT(C,B);
    END;
END;
```

(Continued)

```
PROCEDURE INIT;
BEGIN
P_HIT[A,B]:=0.50; P_HIT[A,C]:=0.50;
P_HIT[B,A]:=0.40; P_HIT[B,C]:=0.40;
P_HIT[C,A]:=0.30; P_HIT[C,B]:=0.30;
TANK_SET:=[A,B,C];
N_TANKS:=3;
T_FIRE[A]:=-LN(RANDOM);
T_FIRE[B]:=-LN(RANDOM);
T_FIRE[C]:=-LN(RANDOM);
END;

{MAIN}
BEGIN
WRITELN('INPUT NUMBER OF GAMES');
READLN(N);
N_WINS[A]:=0;N_WINS[B]:=0;N_WINS[C]:=0;
FOR I:= 1 TO N DO
BEGIN
INIT;
WHILE N_TANKS >1 DO
BEGIN
NEXT_TANK:=A;
IF T_FIRE[B] < T_FIRE[NEXT_TANK] THEN NEXT_TANK:=B;
IF T_FIRE[C] < T_FIRE[NEXT_TANK] THEN NEXT_TANK:=C;
T:=T_FIRE[NEXT_TANK];
FIRE(NEXT_TANK);
END;
IF A IN TANK_SET THEN N_WINS[A]:=N_WINS[A]+1;
IF B IN TANK_SET THEN N_WINS[B]:=N_WINS[B]+1;
IF C IN TANK_SET THEN N_WINS[C]:=N_WINS[C]+1;
END;
WRITELN('P WIN TANK A=',N_WINS[A]/N);
WRITELN('P WIN TANK B=',N_WINS[B]/N);
WRITELN('P WIN TANK C=',N_WINS[C]/N);
END.
```

APPENDIX 5A.3

Simulation Model of a Bank

```
* This is a simulation of a three teller bank.  Customers enter
* the bank and select the teller with the shortest queue. Customers
* do not switch to another queue.  The time between arrivals is
* is 60 +/- 50 seconds, and the time it takes a customer to transact
* their banking is 162 +/- 100 seconds.  The bank  is open for
* 8 hours each day.
        SIMULATE
FIRST EQU             1,Q
LAST  EQU             3,Q
BANK  EQU             4,Q
      GENERATE        60,50                 Customers arrive
      QUEUE           BANK                  Enter bank queue
REGLR SELECT MIN      3,FIRST,LAST,,Q       Select shorest queue
      QUEUE           P3                    Join queue and wait
      SEIZE           P3                    Obtain teller services
      DEPART          P3                    Leave queue of waiting custrs.
      ADVANCE         162,100               Transaction processing time
      RELEASE         P3                    Free up teller
      DEPART          BANK                  Depart the bank
      TERMINATE                             End of customer in system
      GENERATE        28800                 After 8 hours in seconds
      TERMINATE       1                     End timing transactions
      START           1
      END
```

APPENDIX 5A.4

Simulation of an Assembly and Inspection Process

```
* This is a simulation model of an assembly operation.  After a part
* is assembed it is inspected.  If it fails inspection it must be
* adjusted by the the assembly operator.
 LINE STORAGE             4                     storage between oper. and inspct.
      SIMULATE
      GENERATE           0,0,,1                 generate one part to start process
 OPER QUEUE              OPER                   wait for operator to come avail.
      SEIZE              OPER                   seize the operator
      SPLIT              1,OPER                 generate a next part and send to queue
      ADVANCE            70,40                  assemby time
 AAA  ENTER              LINE                   attempt to enter line for inspection
      RELEASE            OPER                   free up operator
      SEIZE              INSPECT                seize the inspector
      LEAVE              LINE                   leave space between oper. and inspect.
      ADVANCE            50                     time for inspection
      RELEASE            INSPECT                free up inspector
      TRANSFER           900,REDO,DONE          route 10% parts back to oper.
 REDO QUEUE              OPER                   wait for the operator
      SEIZE              OPER                   seize operator
      ADVANCE            10                     adjust part
      TRANSFER           ,AAA                   go back to inspector
 DONE TERMINATE          1                      good part leaves system
      START              10000                  simulate for 10000 good parts
      END
```

APPENDIX 5A.5

Simulation Model of an Inventory System

```
PROGRAM INVEN(INPUT,OUTPUT);
{This is a simulation model of an inventory system in which the mean demand
 changes from day to day. In addition the replenishment time is a random
 variable.  Customer orders that cannot be met are lost.}

VAR SPREAD,MEAN:ARRAY[1..7] OF INTEGER; {mean and spread of daily demand}
    INVENTORY,          {inventory on hand}
    Q,                          {order quanatity}
    REORDER,            {re-order point}
    ORDER_TIME,         {mean time to recieve order}
    N_ORDER,            {number of orders placed
    TOT_INVENTORY,      {accumulation statistic for inventory}
    T_LOST:INTEGER;     {total order lost}
    T_MAX,              {number of days in simulation
    I,                          {working index}
    DAY:INTEGER;        {index indicating the day of the simulation}
    T_ARRIVE,   {time of order arrival}
    X:INTEGER;          {working variable}
    ORDER:BOOLEAN;      {indicator that an order has been placed}


FUNCTION DEMAND(DAY:INTEGER):INTEGER;
{This function generates the demand for a particular day}
VAR I:INTEGER;
BEGIN
I:=DAY MOD 7 + 1;
DEMAND:=MEAN[I] - SPREAD[I] + TRUNC(RANDOM*SPREAD[I]*2);
END;

PROCEDURE INIT;
{initialization and input of parameters}
BEGIN
WRITELN('INPUT INITIAL INVENTORY');
READLN(INVENTORY);
WRITELN('INPUT ORDER SIZE');
READLN(Q);
WRITELN('INPUT REORDER POINT');
READLN(REORDER);
WRITELN('INPUT LEAD TIME');
READLN(ORDER_TIME);
WRITELN('INPUT NUMBER OF DAYS TO RUN');
READLN(T_MAX);
MEAN[1]:=4; SPREAD[1]:=3;
MEAN[2]:=6; SPREAD[2]:=4;
MEAN[3]:=10; SPREAD[3]:=6;
MEAN[4]:=12; SPREAD[4]:=10;
MEAN[5]:=6; SPREAD[5]:=4;
MEAN[6]:=0; SPREAD[6]:=0;
MEAN[7]:=0; SPREAD[7]:=0;
TOT_INVENTORY:=0;
N_ORDER:=0;
T_LOST:=0;
ORDER:=FALSE;
END;
```

(Continued)

```
{main}
BEGIN
INIT;
FOR I:=1 TO T_MAX DO
BEGIN
TOT_INVENTORY:=TOT_INVENTORY+INVENTORY;        {accumlate inventory stat.}
X:=DEMAND(I);                                  {determ. demand for this day}
IF X <=INVENTORY THEN                           {check if enough inventory}
INVENTORY:=INVENTORY -                          {reduce inventory by order}
ELSE                                            {else if not enough inventory}
BEGIN
T_LOST:=T_LOST+(X-INVENTORY);                   {accumulate lost orders}
INVENTORY:=0;                                   {set inventory to 0}
END;

IF (NOT ORDER) AND (INVENTORY <= REORDER) THEN{if no order out, place order}
BEGIN
ORDER:=TRUE;                                    {set order flag}
T_ARRIVE:=I+ORDER_TIME-3 + TRUNC(RAND(SEED)*3) + 1;
                                                {calc. time of order arrival}
N_ORDER:=N_ORDER+1;                             {incr. number of orders}
END
ELSE
IF I = T_ARRIVE THEN                            {check if order has arrived}
BEGIN
ORDER:=FALSE;                                   {reset order flag}
INVENTORY:=INVENTORY+Q;                         {increase inventory}
END;
END; {FOR}

WRITELN('AVERAGE INVENTORY=', TOT_INVENTORY/T_MAX);
WRITELN('NUMBER OF ORDERS=',N_ORDER);
WRITELN('AVERAGE SALES LOST PER CYCLE=',T_LOST/N_ORDER);

END.
```

APPENDIX 5A.6

Simulation Model of an Investment

```
PROGRAM RATE_RETURN(INPUT,OUTPUT);
{This program simulates an investment of $7000 which will be worth $12000 ±
 $5000 in 5 years. The simulation also estimates the probability of a return
 below a minimum rate}
CONST MEAN_F=12000;                            {mean final value}
      SPREAD_F=5000;                           {spread of final value}
      P=7000;                                  {initial investment}
VAR SEED:INTEGER;
    PROB:REAL;
    LOW_RATE:REAL;                             {lowest acceptable rate of
return}
    N_LOW:INTEGER;                             {counter of low return}
    N_TRIALS:INTEGER;                          {no. of times inv. simulated}
    XRATE:REAL;                                {calculated rate of return}
    N_YEARS:INTEGER;                           {length of investment}
    I:INTEGER;                                 {working variable}
    SUM_RATE:REAL;                             {accumulator of rates of
return}

FUNCTION RATE(P,F:REAL;N:INTEGER):REAL;
{This function calculates the rate of return}
BEGIN
RATE:=EXP(LN(F/P)/N) - 1;
END;

FUNCTION RANDOM_F(VAR SEED:INTEGER):REAL;
{This function randomly generates the final value of the investment}
BEGIN
RANDOM_F:=MEAN_F - SPREAD_F + 2*SPREAD_F*RANDOM;
END;

{MAIN}
BEGIN
WRITELN('INPUT NUMBER OF YEARS IN INVESTMENT'); {prompt for length of inv.}
READLN(N_YEARS);
WRITELN('INPUT NUMBER OF SIMULATIONS');         {prompt for no. of simlations}
READLN(N_TRIALS);
WRITELN('INPUT MINIMUM RATE');                  {prompt for lowest allow. rate}
READLN(LOW_RATE);
N_LOW:=0;
FOR I:=1 TO N_TRIALS DO
   BEGIN
   XRATE:=RATE(P,RANDOM_F(SEED),N_YEARS);       {get rate for 1 inv.}
   SUM_RATE:=SUM_RATE+XRATE;                     {accum. rate of return}
   IF XRATE < LOW_RATE THEN                      {check if below minimum}
   N_LOW:=N_LOW+1;
   END;
WRITELN('PROBABLILTY OF RETURN BELOW MINIMUM=',N_LOW/N_TRIALS);
WRITELN('AVERAGE RATE OF RETURN = ',SUM_RATE/N_TRIALS);
END.
```

APPENDIX 5B

Discounted Cash Flow Factors

RATE = 5 Percent

n	Cmpnd.Amt. Factor F/P	Prsnt.Wrth. Factor P/F	Cap.Recvr. Factor A/P	Ser.P.W. Factor P/A	Ser.C.Amt. Factor F/A	Sink.Fund Factor A/F
1	1.0500	0.9524	1.0500	0.9524	1.0000	1.0000
2	1.1025	0.9070	0.5378	1.8594	2.0500	0.4878
3	1.1576	0.8638	0.3672	2.7232	3.1525	0.3172
4	1.2155	0.8227	0.2820	3.5460	4.3101	0.2320
5	1.2763	0.7835	0.2310	4.3295	5.5256	0.1810
6	1.3401	0.7462	0.1970	5.0757	6.8019	0.1470
7	1.4071	0.7107	0.1728	5.7864	8.1420	0.1228
8	1.4775	0.6768	0.1547	6.4632	9.5491	0.1047
9	1.5513	0.6446	0.1407	7.1078	11.0266	0.0907
10	1.6289	0.6139	0.1295	7.7217	12.5779	0.0795
11	1.7103	0.5847	0.1204	8.3064	14.2068	0.0704
12	1.7959	0.5568	0.1128	8.8633	15.9171	0.0628
13	1.8856	0.5303	0.1065	9.3936	17.7130	0.0565
14	1.9799	0.5051	0.1010	9.8986	19.5986	0.0510
15	2.0789	0.4810	0.0963	10.3797	21.5786	0.0463
16	2.1829	0.4581	0.0923	10.8378	23.6575	0.0423
17	2.2920	0.4363	0.0887	11.2741	25.8404	0.0387
18	2.4066	0.4155	0.0855	11.6896	28.1324	0.0355
19	2.5270	0.3957	0.0827	12.0853	30.5390	0.0327
20	2.6533	0.3769	0.0802	12.4622	33.0660	0.0302
21	2.7860	0.3589	0.0780	12.8212	35.7193	0.0280
22	2.9253	0.3418	0.0760	13.1630	38.5052	0.0260
23	3.0715	0.3256	0.0741	13.4886	41.4305	0.0241
24	3.2251	0.3101	0.0725	13.7986	44.5020	0.0225
25	3.3864	0.2953	0.0710	14.0939	47.7271	0.0210
30	4.3219	0.2314	0.0651	15.3725	66.4388	0.0151
35	5.5160	0.1813	0.0611	16.3742	90.3203	0.0111
40	7.040E+00	1.420E-01	0.0583	17.1591	1.208E+02	8.278E-03
45	8.985E+00	1.113E-01	0.0563	17.7741	1.597E+02	6.262E-03
50	1.147E+01	8.720E-02	0.0548	18.2559	2.093E+02	4.777E-03
100	1.315E+02	7.604E-03	0.0504	19.8479	2.610E+03	3.831E-04

RATE = 10 Percent

n	Cmpnd.Amt. Factor F/P	Prsnt.Wrth. Factor P/F	Cap.Recvr. Factor A/P	Ser.P.W. Factor P/A	Ser.C.Amt. Factor F/A	Sink.Fund Factor A/F
1	1.1000	0.9091	1.1000	0.9091	1.0000	1.0000
2	1.2100	0.8264	0.5762	1.7355	2.1000	0.4762
3	1.3310	0.7513	0.4021	2.4869	3.3100	0.3021
4	1.4641	0.6830	0.3155	3.1699	4.6410	0.2155
5	1.6105	0.6209	0.2638	3.7908	6.1051	0.1638
6	1.7716	0.5645	0.2296	4.3553	7.7156	0.1296
7	1.9487	0.5132	0.2054	4.8684	9.4872	0.1054
8	2.1436	0.4665	0.1874	5.3349	11.4359	0.0874
9	2.3579	0.4241	0.1736	5.7590	13.5795	0.0736
10	2.5937	0.3855	0.1627	6.1446	15.9374	0.0627
11	2.8531	0.3505	0.1540	6.4951	18.5312	0.0540
12	3.1384	0.3186	0.1468	6.8137	21.3843	0.0468
13	3.4523	0.2897	0.1408	7.1034	24.5227	0.0408
14	3.7975	0.2633	0.1357	7.3667	27.9750	0.0357
15	4.1772	0.2394	0.1315	7.6061	31.7725	0.0315
16	4.5950	0.2176	0.1278	7.8237	35.9497	0.0278
17	5.0545	0.1978	0.1247	8.0216	40.5447	0.0247
18	5.5599	0.1799	0.1219	8.2014	45.5992	0.0219
19	6.1159	0.1635	0.1195	8.3649	51.1591	0.0195
20	6.7275	0.1486	0.1175	8.5136	57.2750	0.0175
21	7.4002	0.1351	0.1156	8.6487	64.0025	0.0156
22	8.1403	0.1228	0.1140	8.7715	71.4027	0.0140
23	8.9543	0.1117	0.1126	8.8832	79.5430	0.0126
24	9.8497	0.1015	0.1113	8.9847	88.4973	0.0113
25	10.8347	0.0923	0.1102	9.0770	98.3471	0.0102
30	17.4494	0.0573	0.1061	9.4269	164.4940	0.0061
35	28.1024	0.0356	0.1037	9.6442	271.0244	0.0037
40	4.526E+01	2.209E-02	0.1023	9.7791	4.426E+02	2.259E-03
45	7.289E+01	1.372E-02	0.1014	9.8628	7.189E+02	1.391E-03
50	1.174E+02	8.519E-03	0.1009	9.9148	1.164E+03	8.592E-04
100	1.378E+04	7.257E-05	0.1000	9.9993	1.378E+05	7.257E-06

RATE = 15 Percent

n	Cmpnd.Amt. Factor F/P	Prsnt.Wrth. Factor P/F	Cap.Recvr. Factor A/P	Ser.P.W. Factor P/A	Ser.C.Amt. Factor F/A	Sink.Fund Factor A/F
1	1.1500	0.8696	1.1500	0.8696	1.0000	1.0000
2	1.3225	0.7561	0.6151	1.6257	2.1500	0.4651
3	1.5209	0.6575	0.4380	2.2832	3.4725	0.2880
4	1.7490	0.5718	0.3503	2.8550	4.9934	0.2003
5	2.0114	0.4972	0.2983	3.3522	6.7424	0.1483
6	2.3131	0.4323	0.2642	3.7845	8.7537	0.1142
7	2.6600	0.3759	0.2404	4.1604	11.0668	0.0904
8	3.0590	0.3269	0.2229	4.4873	13.7268	0.0729
9	3.5179	0.2843	0.2096	4.7716	16.7858	0.0596
10	4.0456	0.2472	0.1993	5.0188	20.3037	0.0493
11	4.6524	0.2149	0.1911	5.2337	24.3493	0.0411
12	5.3503	0.1869	0.1845	5.4206	29.0017	0.0345
13	6.1528	0.1625	0.1791	5.5831	34.3519	0.0291
14	7.0757	0.1413	0.1747	5.7245	40.5047	0.0247
15	8.1371	0.1229	0.1710	5.8474	47.5804	0.0210
16	9.3576	0.1069	0.1679	5.9542	55.7175	0.0179
17	10.7613	0.0929	0.1654	6.0472	65.0751	0.0154
18	12.3755	0.0808	0.1632	6.1280	75.8364	0.0132
19	14.2318	0.0703	0.1613	6.1982	88.2118	0.0113
20	16.3665	0.0611	0.1598	6.2593	102.4436	0.0098
21	18.8215	0.0531	0.1584	6.3125	118.8101	0.0084
22	21.6447	0.0462	0.1573	6.3587	137.6316	0.0073
23	24.8915	0.0402	0.1563	6.3988	159.2764	0.0063
24	28.6252	0.0349	0.1554	6.4338	184.1678	0.0054
25	32.9190	0.0304	0.1547	6.4641	212.7930	0.0047
30	66.2118	0.0151	0.1523	6.5660	434.7451	0.0023
35	133.1755	0.0075	0.1511	6.6166	881.1702	0.0011
40	2.679E+02	3.733E-03	0.1506	6.6418	1.779E+03	5.621E-04
45	5.388E+02	1.856E-03	0.1503	6.6543	3.585E+03	2.789E-04
50	1.084E+03	9.228E-04	0.1501	6.6605	7.218E+03	1.385E-04
100	1.174E+06	8.516E-07	0.1500	6.6667	7.829E+06	1.277E-07

RATE = 20 Percent

n	Cmpnd.Amt. Factor F/P	Prsnt.Wrth. Factor P/F	Cap.Recvr. Factor A/P	Ser.P.W. Factor P/A	Ser.C.Amt. Factor F/A	Sink.Fund Factor A/F
1	1.2000	0.8333	1.2000	0.8333	1.0000	1.0000
2	1.4400	0.6944	0.6545	1.5278	2.2000	0.4545
3	1.7280	0.5787	0.4747	2.1065	3.6400	0.2747
4	2.0736	0.4823	0.3863	2.5887	5.3680	0.1863
5	2.4883	0.4019	0.3344	2.9906	7.4416	0.1344
6	2.9860	0.3349	0.3007	3.3255	9.9299	0.1007
7	3.5832	0.2791	0.2774	3.6046	12.9159	0.0774
8	4.2998	0.2326	0.2606	3.8372	16.4991	0.0606
9	5.1598	0.1938	0.2481	4.0310	20.7989	0.0481
10	6.1917	0.1615	0.2385	4.1925	25.9587	0.0385
11	7.4301	0.1346	0.2311	4.3271	32.1504	0.0311
12	8.9161	0.1122	0.2253	4.4392	39.5805	0.0253
13	10.6993	0.0935	0.2206	4.5327	48.4966	0.0206
14	12.8392	0.0779	0.2169	4.6106	59.1959	0.0169
15	15.4070	0.0649	0.2139	4.6755	72.0351	0.0139
16	18.4884	0.0541	0.2114	4.7296	87.4421	0.0114
17	22.1861	0.0451	0.2094	4.7746	105.9306	0.0094
18	26.6233	0.0376	0.2078	4.8122	128.1167	0.0078
19	31.9480	0.0313	0.2065	4.8435	154.7400	0.0065
20	38.3376	0.0261	0.2054	4.8696	186.6880	0.0054
21	46.0051	0.0217	0.2044	4.8913	225.0256	0.0044
22	55.2061	0.0181	0.2037	4.9094	271.0307	0.0037
23	66.2474	0.0151	0.2031	4.9245	326.2369	0.0031
24	79.4968	0.0126	0.2025	4.9371	392.4842	0.0025
25	95.3962	0.0105	0.2021	4.9476	471.9811	0.0021
30	237.3763	0.0042	0.2008	4.9789	1181.8816	0.0008
35	590.6682	0.0017	0.2003	4.9915	2948.3411	0.0003
40	1.470E+03	6.804E-04	0.2001	4.9966	7.344E+03	1.362E-04
45	3.657E+03	2.734E-04	0.2001	4.9986	1.828E+04	5.470E-05
50	9.100E+03	1.099E-04	0.2000	4.9995	4.550E+04	2.198E-05
100	8.282E+07	1.207E-08	0.2000	5.0000	4.141E+08	2.415E-09

BUILDING AND VALIDATING SIMULATION MODELS

CHAPTER 6

DATA COLLECTION AND ANALYSIS

What sort of tailor would cut out a suit without first taking the customer's measurements? What sort of builder would construct a house without first taking samples of the soil or researching the area's weather and flood conditions? What sort? Amateurs of course! Similarly, when constructing a simulation model a professional analyst would not begin to sew and hammer the model together until good data has been gathered on the system that the model is intended to represent.

6.1 INTRODUCTION

The collection and analysis of data is a critical step in the development of a discrete-event simulation model. The collected data becomes a major underpinning of the simulation model and errors in the collection or analysis of the data can invalidate the model.

Given data gathered by observing the processes of the system to be simulated, we must specify the probability distributions that will be used to represent these processes in the simulation model. When selecting a probability distribution we have two alternatives:

1) Use an empirical distribution based upon our direct observations of the system

2) Use the data collected as a basis for choosing a theoretical distribution that will represent the random processes of the system.

We will first take up in Section 6.2 the notion of data collection as both an art and science, and then present in Section 6.3 commonly used descriptive measures of a set of data. In Section 6.4 we will present statistical procedures for analyzing the data collected, including tests for independence, randomness, homogeneity, and goodness of fit to a theoretical distribution. In Sections 6.5 and 6.6 we present a number of theoretical discrete and continuous distributions which often serve as good models of random processes. In Section 6.7 we take up the problem of estimating parameters of these theoretical distributions, using the collected data.

6.2 THE ART AND SCIENCE OF DATA COLLECTION

Typically, texts and courses in statistics pay little attention to the actual process of gathering data. Rather, the starting point in statistical analysis is a random sample $(x_1, x_2, ... x_n)$ which is implicitly assumed to consist of independent observations obtained from a common population. In practice, however, obtaining such a "pure" sample may be very difficult, and the quality of the sample may depend more on the skill of the data gatherer than the data analyst.

Gathering data on a process that is to be simulated is a tedious and inglorious task, but we should keep in mind that the data obtained acts as a foundation for the rest of the simulation project. If data are not carefully gathered, the random processes in the simulation model will not be representative of the processes in the real system. Part of the skill of gathering data is knowing what to record and when to record it. To illustrate this, let us again consider the supermarket example from Chapter 2.

In order to simulate the supermarket we would need to know how long it takes for a customer to be checked out at the cash register. How should we go about recording data that would define checkout times? The uninitiated might stroll into the market and, with a stop watch, begin to measure the times to checkout customers. Before accepting the data gathered in such a manner, however, we might consider the effect the observer has on the checkout clerk. The clerk, upon realizing he/she is being observed, may react to being timed and work at an unrepresentative pace. The clerk may not be typical of most clerks in the market. The customers being checked out may not be representative of the rest of the market's customers. To avoid such problems, and also improve our understanding of the process to be modeled, we should record more than a single attribute of the process. In the case of the supermarket we would minimally want to record:

- The time to check out the customer
- The date and time of day the observation was made
- The number of items checked out (at least an estimate)
- The sex and approximate age of the customer
- The name of the checkout clerk
- Whether a bagger was assisting
- Any unusual events such as a malfunction in the cash register or price checks on purchased items
- The number of bags needed to carry the purchases

Although this list may seem long, it may not be long enough. After the data are gathered and analyzed, many questions about the process may arise that can often be answered if supporting data is available. The marginal cost of making one additional recording is small compared to the cost of not having an accurate picture of the process.

As a precaution against collecting unrepresentative data we should not make all our observations in a single session, but rather, data should be collected over a span of time. As a case in point, one of the authors was planning to construct a simulation model of a bank in a metropolitan area and began gathering data on customer arrival times to the bank during the day, and the time to process each customer. On the first day of data collection there was a large influx of customers and short processing times. Further investigation disclosed that many of the customers of the bank were retired and the day selected for data collection was the day that Social Security checks had been received in the mail. If a single long session had been used to gather data, an unrepresentative sample would have been obtained. However, by sampling across many days of the month and at different times of the day, a more accurate composite picture of the bank was obtained.

A technique borrowed from the field of quality control can be very useful in analyzing data. Using "control charts" to record groupings of data, we can detect when the process being observed is no longer "under control" (i.e., whether its statistical properties have changed). A control chart consists of upper and lower limits which a process under control will exceed only α percentage of the time (usually α is 5% or 1%).

The control limits are established by doing some preliminary sampling of the process and then, as subsequent samples are taken, they are plotted on a control chart. The points plotted on the control chart are not generally based on just one observation, but rather on k sequential observations. The most common control charts plot the sample averages and the sample variances. In quality control applications, when a point falls outside the control limits, the process is halted and re-calibrated. When using control charts to monitor the data gathering for a process to be simulated, one cannot halt the process, but rather, the analyst is made aware that a shift in the process has taken place and that the data being gathered may not be homogeneous. If several points fall outside the limits, it may also signal that the control chart limits should be reset to reflect a change in the mean or variance of the process being observed.

The initial control limits are set using n samples of k sequential observations and calculating

$$\bar{x}_i = \sum_{j=1}^{k} x_{ij}/k \qquad\qquad i = 1,2,...n$$

$$s_i^2 = \sum_{j=1}^{k} (x_{ij} - \bar{x}_i)^2/(k-1) \qquad\qquad i = 1,2,...n$$

$$\bar{X} = \sum_{i=1}^{n} \bar{x}_i/n$$

$$\bar{s}^2 = \sum_{i=1}^{n} s_i^2/n.$$

When plotting the sample mean of k sequential observations, the control limits are:

$$\bar{X} \pm 1.96\,\bar{s}/\sqrt{k}$$

for

$$\alpha = 5 \text{ percent}$$

and

$$\bar{X} \pm 2.58\bar{s}/\sqrt{k}$$

for

$$\alpha = 1 \text{ percent.}$$

For plotting the sample variance, the corresponding control limits are

$$\bar{s}^2 \chi^2_{df=k-1,\alpha/2}/(k-1)$$

and

$$\bar{s}^2 \chi^2_{df=k-1,1-\alpha/2}/(k-1).$$

The preliminary sampling that establishes $\bar{X}$ and $\bar{s}^2$ should be carefully conducted since it establishes the initial control limits. If these limits are consistently exceeded they should be reviewed and reset.

TABLE 6.1
SUBGROUPING OF 80 SAMPLES INTO SETS OF 4

i	x_{i1}	x_{i2}	x_{i3}	x_{i4}	Sample Mean $\bar{x}_i$	Sample Variance s_i^2
1	5.8	4.4	6.8	5.7	5.7	1.0
2	4.2	2.9	8.2	2.8	4.5	6.4
3	9.4	6.0	4.7	4.1	6.0	5.7
4	8.5	8.5	5.1	6.5	7.1	2.8
5	6.8	10.0	4.7	4.5	6.5	6.4
6	6.2	6.2	8.0	8.0	7.1	1.02
7	6.0	7.0	6.3	5.4	6.2	0.4
8	9.7	6.4	1.2	4.7	5.5	12.7
9	5.3	8.0	6.5	7.2	6.7	1.3
10	3.1	6.3	2.8	10.2	5.6	11.9
11	7.3	6.3	4.3	8.3	6.6	2.8
12	9.5	6.3	5.0	10.0	7.7	5.8
13	3.9	2.7	5.5	6.5	4.6	2.8
14	5.5	7.5	5.3	1.7	5.0	5.8
15	4.6	3.6	4.4	5.9	4.6	0.9
16	9.0	6.1	4.9	6.7	6.7	3.0
17	7.2	4.6	5.4	7.1	6.1	1.6
18	6.2	7.2	7.7	5.4	6.6	1.1
19	6.4	5.3	3.6	4.8	5.0	1.3
20	4.1	4.2	4.5	6.6	4.8	1.4

As an example of using control charts for the analysis of sampling values, consider the sample data shown in Table 6.1 with the data grouped into sets of four.

Calculating the mean of the sample means and the mean of the sample variances we have $\bar{X} = 5.93$ and $\bar{s}^2 = 3.80$, $\bar{s} = 1.95$. The 1 percent upper and lower control limits for $\bar{X}$ then become

$$\bar{X}_{lc} = 5.93 - (2.58)(1.95)/\sqrt{4} = 3.41$$

and

$$\bar{X}_{uc} = 5.93 + (2.58)(1.95)/\sqrt{4} = 8.45,$$

while the 1 percent control limits for s^2 are

$$\bar{s}_{lc}^2 = (3.80)(.070)/(4-1) = .091$$

and

$$\bar{s}_{uc}^2 = (3.80)(12.1)/(4-1) = 15.3.$$

The control charts for this example are shown in Fig. 6.1 and Fig. 6.2.

FIGURE 6.1 CONTROL CHART ON SAMPLE MEANS

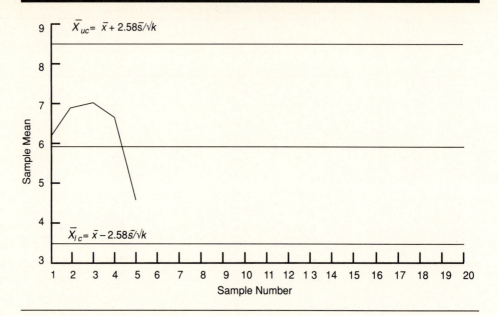

As sampling continues, the mean and variance of each set of four samples can be plotted on the two control charts, and if points start to exceed the upper and lower control limits we are alerted that a shift or change in the process has occurred.

To continue this example, assume the next five sets of four data are:

i	x_{i1}	x_{i2}	x_{i3}	x_{i4}	Sample Mean $\bar{x}_1$	Sample Variance s_i^2
1	5.8	6.2	5.5	7.2	6.2	0.4
2	4.4	6.1	6.1	9.1	6.4	2.9
3	6.8	7.2	5.8	8.2	7.0	0.7
4	5.7	6.0	6.3	8.5	6.6	1.2
5	6.4	5.7	5.9	1.1	4.8	6.1

When these five sets of data are plotted against the limits of Figs. 6.1 and 6.2, we see that both the mean and the sample variance remain well within the control limits.

In the final analysis there is still much room for judgment and discretion on the part of the analyst, but having displayed the data on control charts, we can gain significant insights into the process being observed as well as detect statistically-aberrant samples.

FIGURE 6.2   CONTROL CHART ON SAMPLE VARIANCE

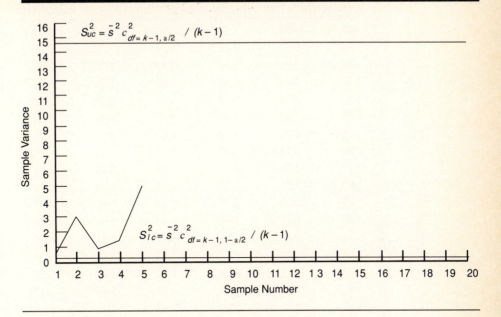

6.3   DATA ANALYSIS USING DESCRIPTIVE STATISTICS

The purpose of descriptive statistics is to reduce a large set of data to a small number of descriptors, thereby revealing characteristics of the data which may not otherwise be apparent. There is always the risk of missing important characteristics of the process if we substitute a few measures for the entire data set. We strongly recommend the entire set of data be examined for patterns and cycles, which descriptive or inferential statistics may gloss over. Although descriptive statistics is more of an art than a science, there are standard descriptors that can give us substantial insight into the process from which the data came.

One method of reducing a set of data is to graphically display it using frequency and cumulative frequency distributions, often referred to as histograms. The frequency distribution is formed by dividing the real line into equal intervals (except for the last and first which are generally open) and then recording the frequency of observations which fall into each interval. The cumulative frequency distribution records the frequency of observations that are equal to or less than an interval boundary. The frequency distribution and cumulative frequency distribution are analogous to the probability distribution function $f(x)$ and cumulative distribution function $F(x)$. An example set of data which we will use throughout this section to demonstrate the analysis of input data is shown in Table 6.2. The data represent 200 random samplings of the number of seconds of CPU time to compile programs in a multi-user computer system.

A frequency distribution and cumulative frequency distributions are shown in Table 6.3 and Figs. 6.3 and 6.4. From the table and figures one can see the data in better perspective. Several important characteristics of the data become apparent, such as a

TABLE 6.2
COMPILATION TIMES (SECONDS OF CPU TIME) FOR 200 PROGRAMS

1.92	5.76	1.37	5.63	2.45	3.34	2.38	2.08
1.94	6.57	1.67	5.94	1.72	3.90	2.78	4.77
1.62	2.02	2.32	12.92	2.36	2.97	2.78	2.40
3.36	3.16	1.38	1.32	1.19	3.23	2.40	3.08
5.40	2.29	6.12	1.02	1.26	2.55	3.62	6.23
5.95	1.05	1.03	0.63	8.16	1.38	6.29	6.17
1.68	0.52	1.42	0.69	3.60	1.36	3.49	5.37
2.80	1.25	2.32	2.49	1.25	4.83	1.95	1.81
2.05	2.21	1.46	1.56	3.79	1.81	4.17	3.64
0.93	3.93	3.36	6.05	6.92	1.21	1.16	4.90
1.85	2.25	0.73	2.47	2.05	1.73	1.32	5.09
3.23	2.07	3.66	3.40	2.00	4.86	3.17	3.35
6.71	4.41	1.06	3.29	0.83	0.95	0.90	0.82
2.01	0.84	2.57	7.58	3.13	5.25	1.19	0.96
1.77	1.32	7.18	1.42	4.43	1.20	3.24	0.93
3.91	1.70	2.63	0.45	2.89	3.63	1.37	3.29
3.53	2.77	5.49	1.47	2.01	1.63	1.63	1.14
2.59	2.17	1.52	7.19	1.15	3.01	2.49	2.05
0.58	4.33	2.44	3.33	3.27	5.02	2.28	9.99
1.23	2.38	5.84	2.06	2.89	4.36	0.75	3.03
0.98	3.68	2.23	4.91	1.89	1.04	7.81	1.92
1.62	1.78	3.28	1.03	0.18	2.10	1.84	2.26
1.61	5.00	3.27	2.16	1.22	1.66	1.73	2.61
3.57	2.12	3.93	5.32	0.99	7.42	2.34	3.84
6.37	1.76	3.51	3.63	0.07	1.91	1.88	0.99

clustering about intervals between 1.0 to 3.0, and a definite leaning (skew) to the right with fewer than 5% of the observations exceeding 7.0. The shape of the frequency distribution often suggests a specific distribution that may be used to model the process being observed. As a further compression of the data set $\{x_i\}$ we can find measures of central tendency, dispersion, and shape.

The most common measures of central tendency are:

1. the mean: $\bar{X} = \sum_{i=1}^{n} x_i / n$ (6.1)

$\bar{X}$ is often referred to as the sample mean or sample average

2. Median: $X_m = x_{(n+1)/2}$ when n is odd and

$$\frac{x_{n/2} + x_{n/2+1}}{2} \quad \text{when } n \text{ is even}$$ (6.2)

TABLE 6.3
FREQUENCY AND CUMULATIVE FREQUENCY DISTRIBUTIONS OF COMPILATION TIMES

Interval	Frequency	Cumulative Frequency
0.0–1.0	20	20
1.0–2.0	58	78
2.0–3.0	45	123
3.0–4.0	37	160
4.0–5.0	10	170
5.0–6.0	13	183
6.0–7.0	9	192
7.0–8.0	5	197
8.0–9.0	1	198
9.0–10.0	1	199
10.0–11.0	0	199
11.0–12.0	0	199
12.0 or over	1	200

where $\{x_i\}$ are first sorted in ascending order. The median is a value such that half the data falls below X_m and half above.

3. Mode: $X_d = x_i$ which occurs most frequently in the sample.

FIGURE 6.3   FREQUENCY HISTOGRAM FOR COMPILATION TIMES

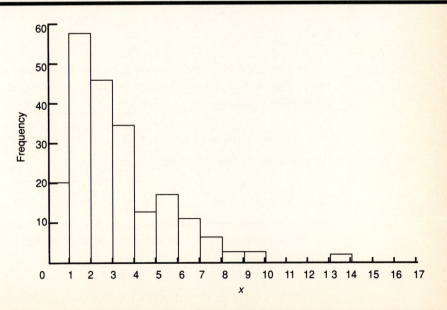

FIGURE 6.4   CUMULATIVE FREQUENCY HISTOGRAM FOR COMPILATION TIMES

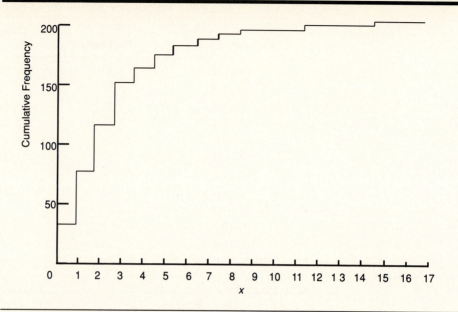

For continuous data, X_d is often set at the mid-point of the interval of the frequency distribution with the greatest number of entries.

For our sample data in Table 6.2 we have

$$\overline{X} = 2.89$$

$$x_m = 2.06$$

$$x_d = 1.50.$$

In addition to measuring the central tendency of a data set, it is important to measure its dispersion or spread. The most frequently used measure of dispersion is the sample standard deviation:

$$s = \sqrt{\sum_{i=1}^{n}(x_i - \overline{X})^2/(n - 1)}. \tag{6.3}$$

An equivalent method of calculating s is:

$$s = \sqrt{(\sum_{i=1}^{n}x_i^2 - (\sum_{i=1}^{n}x_i)^2/n)/(n - 1)} \tag{6.4}$$

which is computationally more efficient and has a smaller round-off error.

An important measure of dispersion relative to the mean is the coefficient of variation

$$C_v = s/\overline{X}. \tag{6.5}$$

The merit of using C_v to describe the dispersion in a sample is that it puts the size of the dispersion in perspective relative to the sample values. For example, if $s = 1000$ we might have the impression that there is great dispersion across the sample, but if

$\bar{X} = 1,000,000$ we see that the dispersion, relative to the mean, is very low with $C_v = .001$.

For the sample data in Table 6.2

$$s = 1.94$$

and

$$C_v = 0.67.$$

Two other descriptors of data are the skew and kurtosis (peakedness) measures. The skew is measured by

$$\delta_1 = \frac{\sum_{i=1}^{n}(x_i - \bar{X})^3/n}{s^3} \qquad (6.6)$$

and the kurtosis is measured by

$$\delta_2 = \frac{\sum_{i=1}^{n}(x_i - \bar{X})^4/n}{s^4}. \qquad (6.7)$$

The skew measure δ_1 will be close to zero if the data are symmetric and will be positive as the data become skewed to the right and negative as the data become skewed to the left.

The kurtosis measure δ_2 will be small for distributions that are very peaked and grow as the distribution loses central tendency.

For a normally distributed population

$$E(\delta_1) = 0$$

and

$$E(\delta_2) = 3$$

and these measures are sometimes used as a criteria for deciding whether the data were drawn from a normally distributed population.

For the sample data in Table 6.2 we have

$$\delta_1 = 1.546$$

and

$$\delta_2 = 6.461$$

6.4 DATA ANALYSIS USING INFERENTIAL STATISTICS

The power of descriptive statistics is that it condenses a large volume of data to a few measures and descriptors. On the other hand, descriptive statistics cannot detect subtle relationships within the data set or provide an explicit criteria for accepting or rejecting hypotheses about the statistical properties of the process from which the data came. The purpose of inferential statistics is to test hypotheses about the process's statistical properties, including independence or randomness of successive values of the process, homogeneity, time invariance, and goodness of fit to theoretical distributions. The statistical tests presented in this section are nonparametric in that they do not depend upon an assumption that the data came from any specific distribution. For a more complete treatment of nonparametric statistics the reader is referred to Hollander and Wolfe [2].

6.4.1   TESTS OF INDEPENDENCE

Very often, when building a simulation model of a system, multivariate data is collected. That is, we record more than a single measure when observing the process. For the case of the observation consisting of two measures, A and B, the hypothesis of independence is:

H_0:   Measure A is independent of Measure B.

H_1:   Measure A and B are not independent.

As an example, if we were going to build a simulation model of an inventory system, we would need to gather data on the daily number of orders for an item. The observer could also record the day of the week when an order is received, and before we build a simulation model, we would want to test whether the daily number of orders is independent of the day of the week. As a second example, suppose we were to build a simulation model of a computer system, including disk I/O and memory management. We might like to know if the number of times a job requires disk I/O is independent of the job's memory requirements. That is, does a relationship exist between memory requirements and disk I/O?

A common test for independence is the Chi Square Contingency Test in which a cross tabulation, or contingency table (as shown in Fig. 6.5), is made of the two measures A and B. The contingency table is constructed by defining n_A and n_B intervals for the measures A and B. The two-way table is then developed with n_A rows and n_B columns where

o_{ij} =   The observed number of elements in the data set with measure A in interval i and measure B in interval j.

$N_{i.}$ =   total of row i.

$N_{.j}$ =   total of column j.

N =   the total number of observations.

To better understand this test, notice that $N_{i.}/N$ is an estimate of $P(A_i)$, the probability that an observation falls into category A_i while $N_{.j}/N$ is an estimate of $P(B_j)$, the probability that an observation falls into category B_j.

If A and B are independent, then $P(A_iB_j) = P(A_i)P(B_j)$, which we can estimate by $(N_{i.}/N)(N_{.j}/N)$.

Letting

e_{ij} = The expected number of elements with measure A in interval i and measure B in interval j.

If H_0 is true we can estimate the expected number of observations falling into category ij by

$$e_{ij} = P(A_iB_j)N$$

$$= N_{i.}N_{.j}/N \tag{6.9}$$

FIGURE 6.5 n_A BY n_B CONTINGENCY TABLE

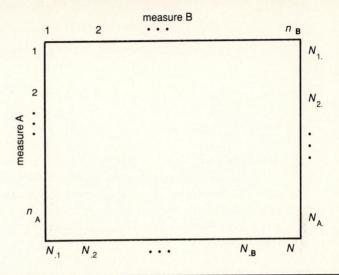

It can be shown that if A and B are independent and $e_{i,j}$ is greater than 5 for all cells, then

$$\chi^2 = \sum_{i=1}^{n_A}\sum_{j=1}^{n_B}(o_{ij} - e_{ij})^2/e_{ij} \tag{6.10}$$

is approximately Chi Square distributed with $(n_a - 1)(n_b - 1)$ degrees of freedom.

ILLUSTRATIVE PROBLEM 6.1

A simulation model of a medical laboratory is being constructed. The model will be used to predict the effect of changing admission patterns and case mixes upon the laboratory technicians' work load. As part of the data collected, the number of laboratory tests ordered at the time of admission was recorded for 300 randomly-selected patients. The patients were classified as medical, surgical, pediatric, or obstetric. The distribution of tests for each medical classification is:

| | Number of Tests | | | | | |
	0	1–3	4–6	7–10	>10	Total
Medical	14	29	55	31	21	150
Surgical	8	10	18	27	7	70
Pediatric	10	16	14	8	2	50
Obstetric	8	15	13	4	0	40
Total	40	70	100	70	30	310

Our hypothesis is

H_0:   the number of tests is independent of the type of patient.

H_1:   the number of tests is dependent upon the type of patient.

When a Chi Square contingency test is performed

$$\chi^2 = \sum_{i=1}^{4} \sum_{j=1}^{5} (o_{ij} - e_{ij})^2 / e_{ij}$$

$$= 36.34$$

as compared to $\chi^2_{.05, df=12} = 21.0$.

Since the calculated χ^2 value exceeds the tabulated value, we reject H_0. This indicates that the number of tests performed is dependent upon the type of admission. The implication of rejecting the null hypothesis is that a simulation model of the laboratory will require separate probability distributions of the number of tests ordered for each type of patient.

6.4.2   TESTS OF RANDOMNESS

A sequence of random variables, $x_1, x_2, \ldots x_n$, is considered to be independent or random if

$$f(x_i \mid x_j) = f(x_i) \qquad \text{for all } i \neq j$$

The hypothesis of randomness is:

$$H_0: f(x_i \mid x_j) = f(x_i) \qquad \text{for all } i \neq j$$
$$H_1: f(x_i \mid x_j) \neq f(x_i) \qquad \text{for any } i \neq j.$$

In simulation it is often important to determine if a random process to be included in a simulation model can be represented as a random or independent sequence. For example, when simulating a production process in which the items can be either defective or good, it would be important to know if successive items are randomly defective with repetitions of good items followed by runs of defective items. For continuous random variables we should be concerned whether the process has a tendency to run up or run down. For example, when building a simulation model of a data-base management system, it would be important to know if the times to locate a data element are truly random, or if they tend to be serially dependent. Many statistical tests have been suggested for detecting whether a sample is random. Here we will present only two such tests, the Runs Test and the Runs Up and Runs Down Test.

The Runs Test is intended to detect a lack of randomness in the interweaving of runs of two outcomes, A and B, such as our example of defective and good items coming off a production process. It is a very simple test to perform, requiring the sequence be divided into runs of A and B.

Letting

$$n_1 = \quad \text{The number of A elements in the sample}$$

$$n_2 = \quad \text{The number of B elements in the sample}$$

$$R = \quad \text{Sum of the number of runs of A and runs of B}$$

it can be shown that if the sequence is truly random then

$$E(R) = 2n_1 n_2 / (n_1 + n_2) + 1 \qquad (6.11)$$

and

$$\text{Var}(R) = \frac{2n_1 n_2 (2n_1 n_2 - n_1 - n_2)}{(n_1 + n_2)^2 (n_1 + n_2 - 1)} \qquad (6.12)$$

If $n_1, n_2 > 10$, R is approximately normally distributed.

ILLUSTRATIVE PROBLEM 6.2

In a simulation model of air traffic, incoming flights were classified as commercial (C) or private (P). Based upon 50 successive incoming flights the sequence of arrivals was:

CCPCPPCCCPCPPCCPCCCCPCCPPPPCCCCCCPPPCCPPCCPPCCCCPC

Our hypothesis is

H_0:   The occurrence of a commercial or private flight is independent of the previous occurrences of commercial or private flights.

H_1:   The occurrence of commercial or private flights are not independent of previous occurrences.

Upon counting the number of cases of C and P and the numbers of runs, we have 30 commercial flights, 20 private flights, and 23 runs of C or P. Notice that a run may be only one instance of C or P.

Thus

$$n_1 = 30, \ n_2 = 20, \text{ and } R = 23.$$

Using equations 6.11 and 6.12 we have

$$E(R) = 25 \text{ and } \sigma_R = 3.36$$

and upon normalizing R we get

$$Z = [R - E(R)]/\sigma_R$$

$$= (25 - 23)/3.36 = .60$$

When Z is compared to the critical value of $Z_{.05} = 1.96$ we cannot reject H_0. Thus, we have no evidence of a lack of randomness of the occurrences of private and commercial aircraft.

The Runs Up and Runs Down Test is used when observations cannot be dichotomized as A or B but instead occur across a continuum. The test is based upon the number of ascending and descending runs, indicated by the sign of the difference between successive elements in the sample.

For example, in the sequence:

$$10.1, 12.2, 9.7, 6.1, 4.2, 5.9, 6.8, 5.5$$

the sign of the differences are:

$$+ - - - + + -$$

thus giving 2 runs up and 2 runs down or a total of 4 runs.

Letting R be the total number of runs in the sample, it can be shown that if the elements in a sample are randomly selected, then:

$$E(R) = (2n - 1)/3 \qquad (6.13)$$

and

$$\text{Var}\,(R) = (16n - 29)/90. \qquad (6.14)$$

As the sample size, n, increases, R becomes normally distributed [3].

ILLUSTRATIVE PROBLEM 6.3

A simulation model is being constructed to represent an assembly line in which the assembly operations are performed manually. The hypothesis to be tested is:

H_0:   The assembly times form a random sequence or sample.

H_1:   The assembly times are not a random sequence.

The times for 25 successive assemblies are:

$$10.0, 10.1, 10.5, 10.9, \ 11.0, 10.5, 10.4, 10.6, \ 10.3, 10.2$$
$$9.0, \ \ 9.4, \ \ 9.5, \ \ 9.6, 10.1, 10.2, 10.1, 10.0, \ \ 9.6, \ \ 9.7$$
$$10.2, 10.5, 10.8, \ \ 9.9, \ \ 9.6$$

giving a signed sequence of:

$$+ + + + - - + - - - + + + + + - - - + + + + - -$$

or $R = 8$ and from equations 6.13 and 6.14:

$$E(R) = 16.3, \ \text{Var}\,(R) = 4.1$$

Upon normalizing R we have:

$$Z = [R - E(R)]/\sigma_R$$

$$= (8 - 16.3)/2.02 = -4.11$$

Comparing this value with the critical value of 1.96 at the 5% significance level, we reject H_0. Thus, we conclude that the assembly times are not occurring randomly, but rather there are more runs up and down than should occur by chance.

6.4.3   TESTS OF HOMOGENEITY

When building a simulation model one often gathers multiple sets of data from populations that are separated by time or distance. For example, when constructing a simulation model of a computer system the number of CPU seconds per user session may be available by time of day and day of week. It would be important to know whether the distribution of CPU time is the same (homogeneous) across the hours of the day and days of the week. As a second example, consider constructing a simulation model of operators attending multiple machines. Data should be obtained on the times between machine failures and times to repair machines, and it could be important to know if the machines have similar failure and repair characteristics. Tests for whether multiple sets of data can be considered as coming from identical populations are generally referred to as tests of homogeneity.There are many tests of homogeneity available, with some goodness-of-fit tests designed for specific families of distributions, such as the normal or Poisson, while others are distribution free. For distributions that are normal, or approximately normal, the Analysis of Variance (ANOVA) tests are equivalent to testing for homogeneity of the means and the F statistic can be used to test for homogeneity of the variance of pairs of populations. In this section, we will take up two distribution-free tests for homogeneity, the Kolmogorov-Smirnov two-sample test and the Chi Square test of homogeneity.

Kolmogorov-Smirhov Two-Sample Test   Given samples from two populations, $G(x)$ and $H(x)$ the Kolmogorov-Smirnov two-sample test can be used to test the hypothesis:

$$H_0: \quad G(x) = H(x)$$
$$H_1: \quad G(x) \neq H(x)$$

To perform the test the two sets of data are used to construct the two-sample cumulative-distribution functions $G(x)$ and $H(x)$. The test statistic is the maximum of the absolute value of the difference between the empirical cumulative distributions $H(x)$ and $G(x)$. That is, the test statistic D is:

$$D = \sup_{\text{all } x} |G(x) - H(x)| \tag{6.15}$$

In this test we must measure the difference between $G(x)$ and $H(x)$ whenever either function changes (see Fig. 6.6). The critical values of D have been derived by F.J. Massey [4]. For large n_1 and n_2 ($n_1, n_2 > 15$) the critical values of D for $\alpha = .05$ and .01 are

$$D_{.05} = 1.36 \sqrt{(n_1 + n_2)/n_1 n_2}$$

and

$$D_{.01} = 1.63 \sqrt{(n_1 + n_2)/n_1 n_2}. \tag{6.16}$$

ILLUSTRATIVE PROBLEM 6.4   The number of seconds of CPU time per job were gathered for two classes of batch users in a computer system. The hypothesis to be tested is:

H_0:   The distributions of the CPU times for class I and II users are identical.

H_1:   The distributions of CPU times are not identical for class I and II.

For class I users the times for 50 jobs are, in sorted order:

1.86	2.59	2.75	2.82	2.99	2.99	3.24	3.26
3.29	3.44	3.69	3.91	4.09	4.13	4.15	4.18
4.19	4.26	4.32	4.80	4.92	4.96	5.45	5.46
5.96	6.08	6.11	6.15	6.20	6.21	6.34	6.66
6.88	7.01	7.16	7.26	7.62	8.03	8.24	8.28
8.30	8.42	9.04	9.24	10.03	10.48	10.91	11.36
12.77	14.42						

while for 50 class II jobs the times are, in sorted order:

0.14	0.23	0.41	0.45	0.49	0.60	0.61	1.00
1.01	1.08	1.50	1.53	1.63	1.64	2.12	2.14
2.21	2.41	2.45	2.50	2.72	2.96	3.02	3.43
3.70	3.94	3.95	4.73	4.86	5.16	5.31	5.80
6.23	6.96	7.65	7.89	8.57	9.83	10.79	10.95
11.35	14.10	14.22	15.27	16.25	17.08	21.12	22.76
23.30	38.30						

The sample cumulative distribution functions are shown in Figure 6.6. For this set of data we find

$$D = sup \mid G_{50}(x) - H_{50}(x) \mid = .380$$
$$\text{all } x$$

occurring at the point $x = 2.59$.

Thus, with D exceeding $D_{.05} = .272$ we reject the hypothesis that the samples are from identical distributions.

If we calculate measures of central tendency and dispersion for the above samples we find some similarities and some differences. The means of the samples are very close with $\overline{X}_I = 6.14$ and $\overline{X}_{II} = 6.77$ while the medians and sample standard deviations are very different with $\overline{X}_{Im} = 6.02$, $\overline{X}_{IIm} = 3.82$, and $s_{xI} = 2.82$, $s_{xII} = 7.666$. The Kolmogorov-Smirnov test has provided a statistical basis for concluding whether two distributions differ by more than sampling error would allow.

Chi Square Test   The Chi Square test of homogeneity can be used to test whether K sets of data have the same distribution. That is,

H_0: $F_1(x) = F_2(x)... = F_K(x)$

H_1: $F_i \neq F_j$,   for some i, j $i \neq j$

FIGURE 6.6   CUMULATIVE FREQUENCY HISTOGRAMS FOR CLASS I AND II JOBS

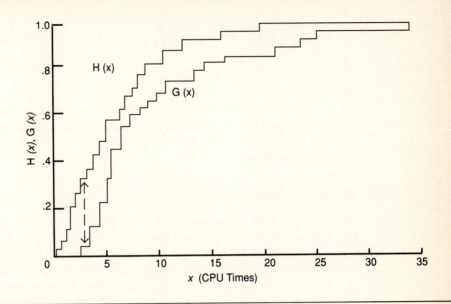

In this test, the real line is divided into N subintervals forming an N by K contingency table. The table contains $o_{i,j}$, the number of observations from distribution i, falling into interval j. The test used is the standard Chi Square contingency table statistic (see equation 6.10) with $(K-1)(N-1)$ degrees of freedom. The subintervals need not be of equal size, but like the contingency table test for independence, the expected frequency e_{ij} should be 5 or greater in every cell.

ILLUSTRATIVE PROBLEM 6.5

Using the data from Illustrative Problem 6.4, for the seconds of CPU time for the two classes of users, we can set up a χ^2 contingency table to test the hypothesis that the distribution of CPU times are identical (the same hypothesis that was tested using the Kolmogorov-Smirnov two-sample test).

Forming the contingency table:

Data Set	Interval					
	0.00–3.00	3.01–6.00	6.01–9.00	9.01–12.00	12.00 +	
1	6 (14)	19 (14.5)	17 (11)	6 (5)	2 (5.5)	50
2	22 (14)	10 (14.5)	5 (11)	4 (5)	9 (5.5)	50
	28	29	22	10	11	100

where $e_{ij} = (\ )$

We calculate the χ^2 statistic using equations 6.9 and 6.10 to find $\chi^2 = 23.3$ as compared to a critical value of

$$\chi^2_{.05, df = 4} = 9.49$$

indicating that the two classes of users do not have identical distributions of CPU time.

There is some evidence [4] that when K, the number of populations to be compared for homogeneity, is two, the Kolmogorov-Smirnov two-sample test is more powerful than the Chi-Square test, but the Chi-Square test can be more broadly applied since K can be two or more.

6.4.4   GOODNESS-OF-FIT TESTS

Goodness-of-fit tests are designed to test whether a collection of data can be considered as a sample from a specified probability distribution. The two most frequently used goodness-of-fit tests are the Pearson's Chi-Square Goodness-of-fit test and the Kolmogorov-Smirnov (K-S) goodness-of-fit test [4]. Each of these tests have their own merits and, in particular situations, one test may be more appropriate or powerful than the other. A limitation of the Kolmogorov-Smirnov test is that it can only be used on continuous distributions and the data cannot be used to estimate the parameters, θ_i of the hypothesized distribution. The goodness-of-fit test hypothesis is:

$$H_0: \qquad F(x) = F_0(x \mid \theta_1, \theta_2, ..\theta_n)$$
$$H_1: \qquad F(x) \neq F_0(x \mid \theta_1, \theta_2, ..\theta_n)$$

Chi-Square Test   In the Chi-Square Goodness-of-fit test the elements in the sample are divided into k intervals with

$o_i =$ The number of observations in interval i, $i = 1, 2...k$.

$e_i =$ The expected number of observations in interval i, when H_0 is true, $i = 1, 2,...k$.

The test statistic is:

$$\chi^2_{df} = \sum_{i=1}^{k} (o_i - e_i)^2 / e_i. \qquad (6.17)$$

In this test the degrees of freedom are:

$$df = k - 1 - (\text{number of parameters estimated from the data})$$

Like the Chi-Square contingency table test it is recommended that $e_i > 5$.

ILLUSTRATIVE PROBLEM 6.6   As an example of a Chi Square goodness-of-fit test consider the data on the next page, which describes the daily number of sales of a specialty item in a gourmet food shop for 50 days.

8	6	4	2	4	5	6	7	6	11
0	5	5	4	7	7	5	4	3	9
6	8	5	6	1	7	6	3	4	5
4	4	7	3	3	5	8	6	4	8
3	6	4	5	3	2	3	2	1	3

To test the hypothesis that the daily sales are Poisson distributed, we first estimate the mean of the distribution from the data and find $\overline{X} = 4.9$.

For the Poisson distribution

$$f(x) = \lambda^x e^{-\lambda} / x! \qquad x = 0, 1, 2, \ldots$$

The most commonly used estimate of λ is $\overline{X}$. Based on the hypothesis that the distribution of sales is Poisson distributed we can tabulate the observed and expected number of observations falling into the intervals shown in the table.

Interval	Observed	Probability	Expected	$(o_i - e_i)^2 / e_i$
0–2	6	.1332	6.6	.055
3	8	.1460	7.3	.067
4	9	.1788	8.9	.001
5	8	.1752	8.8	.073
6	8	.1430	7.2	.089
7 or more	11	.2238	11.2	.004
				.289

From the χ^2 tables in Appendix D $\chi^2_{.05, df=4} = 9.49$, thus the hypothesis that daily sales are Poisson distributed cannot be rejected. Further, since the value of the test statistic is very small relative to the critical value, the test suggests that the data is more than a marginally good fit to the Poisson.

Kolmogorov-Smirnov Test   The Kolmogorov-Smirnov goodness-of-fit test is very similar to the two-sample K-S test of homogeneity, using the test statistic:

$$D^+ = \max_{\text{all } x_i} \{i/n - F^*(x_i)\} \qquad (6.18)$$

$$D^- = \max_{\text{all } x_i} \{F^*(x_i) - (i-1)/n\} \qquad (6.19)$$

$$D = \max \{D^+, D^-\} \qquad (6.20)$$

where $F^*(x_i)$ is the theoretical cumulative distribution to which we fit the observations $\{x_i\}$.

TABLE 6.4
$F^*(x_i)$, D^+, D^- **FOR KOLMOGOROV-SMIRNOV TEST**

i	x_i	$F^*(x_i)$	$i/n - F^*(x_i)$	$F^*(x_i) - (i-1)/n$
1	0.01	0.010	0.040*	0.010
2	0.11	0.104	-0.004	0.054
3	0.20	0.181	-0.031	0.081
4	0.33	0.281	-0.081	0.131
5	0.36	0.302	-0.052	0.102
6	0.38	0.316	-0.016	0.066
7	0.46	0.369	-0.019	0.069
8	0.58	0.440	-0.040	0.090
9	0.87	0.581	-0.131	0.181
10	1.07	0.657	-0.157	0.207
11	1.07	0.657	-0.107	0.157
12	1.20	0.699	-0.099	0.149
13	1.91	0.852	-0.202	0.252**
14	2.01	0.866	-0.166	0.216
15	2.27	0.897	-0.147	0.197
16	2.84	0.942	-0.142	0.192
17	3.10	0.955	-0.105	0.155
18	3.92	0.980	-0.080	0.130
19	4.65	0.990	-0.040	0.090
20	4.74	0.991	0.009	0.041

* D^+
** D^-

For $n \geq 20$ an approximation for the critical values of D is

$$D_{.05} = 1.36/\sqrt{n} \tag{6.21}$$

and

$$D_{.01} = 1.63/\sqrt{n}. \tag{6.22}$$

ILLUSTRATIVE PROBLEM 6.7

As an example of the Kolmogorov-Smirnov test consider the following sample of 20 values from a distribution which is assumed to be exponentially distributed with a mean of 1.0.

That is

$$H_0: \quad F(x) = 1 - e^{-x}.$$
$$H_1: \quad F(x) \neq 1 - e^{-x}.$$

To facilitate the K-S test the data is presented sorted.

0.01	0.11	0.20	0.33	0.36	0.38	0.46	0.58	0.87	1.07
1.07	1.20	1.91	2.01	2.27	2.84	3.10	3.92	4.65	4.74

In Table 6.4 we calculate $F^*(x_i)$, D^+, and D^- for all x_i.

In this example $D = \max (0.040, 0.252) = 0.252$ and using equation 6.21 we find

$$D_{.05, n=20} = 0.304.$$

A comparison of the calculated value of the test statistic $D = 0.252$ to the critical value indicates that we cannot reject the null hypothesis that the data is drawn from an exponentially distributed population with a mean of 1.0.

6.5   THEORETICAL DISCRETE DISTRIBUTIONS

When building a simulation model, one must eventually decide whether to represent a process with a theoretical distribution that can pass a goodness-of-fit test, or whether to use the empirical data and form a distribution that is unique to the process. The advantage of using theoretical distributions can be appreciated when we begin to experiment with the model, examining its sensitivity to changes in the process, such as shifts in the mean or changes in the variance. Theoretical distributions can easily be adjusted to accommodate these changes. For example, if we were representing a process using the Gamma distribution, we can change the mean and variance of the process by adjusting the parameters α and β to better fit the data. Signs of sensitivity to small changes in parameters would suggest the need for more accurate estimates.

Adjusting empirical distributions is much more difficult since we must adjust all the data values that were used to establish the empirical distribution. For most random processes the most important characteristics to capture are the mean, variance, and upper and lower limits. If we can find a theoretical distribution whose first and second moments and limits match the process, as evidenced by our input data, there is a strong case for using the theoretical distribution. One should keep in mind that just as there may be some error in representing a real process using a theoretical distribution, the same errors can occur when using an empirical distribution. In the final analysis, the choice of how to represent a process rests with the analyst and one should look ahead to later steps in the modeling process, especially model validation, experimentation, and implementation, before a final choice is made.

In this section and the section to follow, we will present a number of theoretical discrete and continuous distributions which are often appropriate models of random processes found in real systems. The selection of a particular distribution should finally be made based on the degree to which it fits the data, as determined by the tests of the previous section. We first consider four models of discrete random variables and then in Section 6.6 we consider models which may be used to represent continuous random variables.

6.5.1   THE BERNOULLI DISTRIBUTION

The distributions presented in this section are used to model processes where the underlying event is a trial in which an event will occur with probability p, and not occur with probability $1 - p$. Such an event is sometimes referred to as a Bernoulli trial. Letting

$x = 1$ when the event occurs (success) and $x = 0$ when the event fails to occur (failure), the probability distribution can be expressed as

$$f(x) = \begin{cases} p^x(1-p)^{1-x} & x = 0,1 \\ 0 & \text{elsewhere.} \end{cases} \quad (6.23)$$

It is easily shown that

$$E(x) = p$$

and

$$\text{Var}(x) = p(1-p)$$

A Bernoulli distribution with $p = 0.60$ is shown in Fig. 6.7. Examples of processes that could be represented using the Bernoulli distribution are whether:

- an employee calls in ill or not
- a part is defective or non-defective
- a user connected to a computer system will print a file or not.

6.5.2   THE BINOMIAL DISTRIBUTION

The binomial distribution is an extension of the Bernoulli distribution in which n independent Bernoulli trials $\{x_1, x_2, \ldots x_n\}$ are summed to form

$$x = x_1 + x_2 + \ldots + x_n.$$

That is, x is the number of occurrences of Bernoulli events, or successes in n trials. Letting $p = P(x_i = 1)$, for all i, it is easily shown that:

$$f(x \mid p, n) = \begin{cases} \binom{n}{x} p^x(1-p)^{n-x} & x = 0, 1, \ldots n \\ 0 & \text{elsewhere} \end{cases} \quad (6.24)$$

and since x is a sum of Bernoulli trials it follows that

$$E(x) = np$$

and

$$\text{Var}(x) = np(1-p)$$

FIGURE 6.7   BERNOULLI DISTRIBUTION WITH $p=0.60$

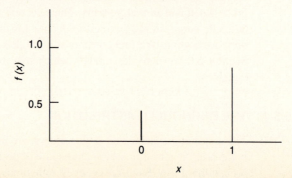

FIGURE 6.8   BINOMIAL DISTRIBUTION WITH _p_=0.30 and _n_=6

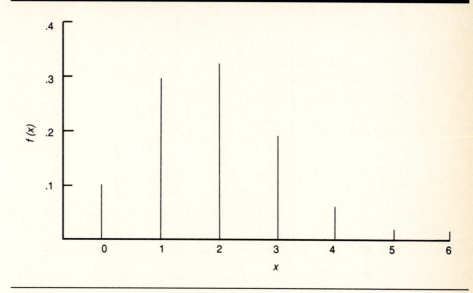

The binomial distribution with $p = 0.30$ and $n = 6$ is shown in Fig. 6.8. Examples of phenomena that might be represented by the binomial distribution are the number of employees in a department of n calling in sick (assuming that all employees are equally likely to be ill and act independently), the number of defective items in a lot n, and the number of users on a local area network attempting to transmit data. For the binomial distribution to be a valid model of a process it is important that for each trial, the probability of the event occurring remains the same and that all trials are independent of one another.

6.5.3   THE POISSON DISTRIBUTION

The Poisson distribution plays a very active role in simulation modeling. Its probability distribution can be derived by considering the limiting case of the binomial distribution when $p \rightarrow 0$ and $n \rightarrow \infty$ but with $E(x) = np$ remaining constant at λ. That is

$$f(x) = \lim_{n \to \infty} \binom{n}{x} p^x (1-p)^{n-x} \qquad np = \lambda \tag{6.25}$$

$$= \frac{\lambda^x e^{-\lambda}}{x!} \cdot \qquad x = 0, 1, 2, \ldots$$

It is a straight forward algebraic exercise to show that

$$E(x) = \lambda$$

and

$$\text{Var}(x) = \lambda.$$

Fig. 6.9 shows the Poisson distribution for $\lambda = 4$.

FIGURE 6.9   POISSON DISTRIBUTION WITH $\lambda = 4.0$

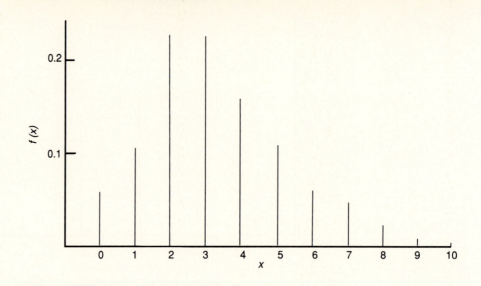

As an example of a process that could be modeled using the Poisson distribution, consider the distribution of the number of customers entering a supermarket in one minute. The probability that any one of the supermarket's customers would enter during this minute is very small but the customer base is very large (ie, $p \to 0$, $n \to \infty$). Thus we should not be surprised to find that the distribution of customers coming into the market during this interval of time is Poisson distributed. Other examples of processes which could potentially be modeled by the Poisson distribution are the number of interrupts the CPU receives each second, the daily sales of an item, and the number of defects in a printed-circuit board.

6.5.4   THE GEOMETRIC DISTRIBUTION

The binomial and Poisson distribution are models of the number of occurrences of an event, but in some processes we are interested the number of trials until the event occurs for the first time. If p is the probability of the event occurring on any single trial and x is the number of trials until a success occurs then:

$$f(x) = \begin{cases} (1-p)^{x-1}p & x=1,2,... \\ 0 & \text{elsewhere} \end{cases} \tag{6.26}$$

$$E(x) = 1/p$$

and

$$\text{Var}(x) = (1-p)/p^2$$

Figure 6.10 shows the geometric probability distribution.

FIGURE 6.10   GEOMETRIC DISTRIBUTION WITH $p=0.5$

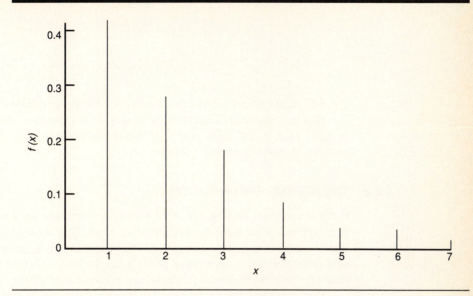

As an example of the geometric distribution consider an automobile salesman attempting to sell a car. The number of customers to whom he must show the car until the sale is made would be geometrically distributed, provided that the probability that any potential customer buys the car is p, and that all trials (sales presentations) are independent. Other examples of processes that could be modeled using the geometric distribution are the number of times a disk is accessed until it fails, the number of job applicants to be interviewed until a qualified applicant is found, and the number of children born to a family until the first female offspring.

6.6   THEORETICAL CONTINUOUS DISTRIBUTIONS

Random variables that can take on a continuum of values are commonplace, but the mechanisms underlying these processes are difficult to identify. Most often, for continuous random variables, the likelihood of an observation taking on an extreme value is small, with most values occurring in a central region. One should bear in mind, when attempting to match a theoretical distribution to a set of data, we often have a choice of several candidates, any one of which could pass a goodness-of-fit test. In this section we describe several theoretical continuous distributions and their properties along with examples of processes for which they can often serve as models.

6.6.1   THE UNIFORM DISTRIBUTION

The uniform distribution is used to describe a process in which the outcome is equally likely to fall between the values a and b. The probability density function for the uniform distribution is

$$f(x) = \frac{1}{b-a} \qquad a \le x \le b$$

$$E(x) = \frac{a+b}{2} \qquad\qquad\qquad (6.27)$$

$$\text{Var}\,(x) = \frac{(b-a)^2}{12}$$

Fig. 6.11 shows the probability density function for the uniform distribution.

Although uniformly distributed processes are not common, the uniform distribution is often used in the early stages of simulation analysis as a convenient and well-understood source of random variation.

6.6.2   THE NORMAL DISTRIBUTION

Random processes that appear to be normally distributed are frequently encountered. One explanation for data so often appearing normally distributed is based on the central limit theorem, in that, within any observation we make, there are many independent random processes whose cumulative effect gives the final value we observe. Figure 6.12 shows the probability density function for the normal distribution.

The probability density function for the normal distribution can be expressed as

$$f(x) = \frac{1}{\sqrt{2\pi}\,\sigma} e^{-(x-\mu)^2/2\sigma^2} \qquad -\infty < x < +\infty \qquad (6.28)$$

$$E(x) = \mu$$

and

$$\text{Var}\,(x) = \sigma^2$$

FIGURE 6.11   UNIFORM DISTRIBUTION

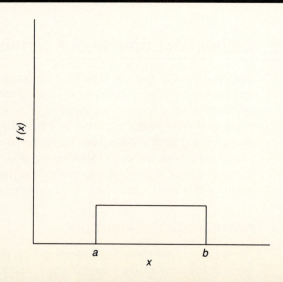

FIGURE 6.12   THE NORMAL DISTRIBUTION

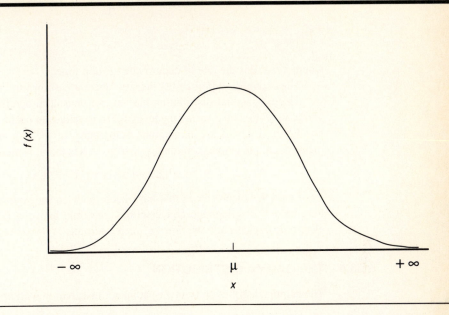

Processes whose values are symmetrically distributed around a point of central tendency and whose extreme values are unbounded are often good candidates for being modeled as normal random variables. The distribution of the physical dimensions of objects are often normally distributed. The normal distribution can also serve as a good approximation to the binomial and Poisson distributions when np or λ are large. For example, in a poll of a large group of citizens the number of respondents holding a particular opinion would technically be binomially distributed but the normal distribution could serve as a good approximation. In this approximation we would let

$$E(x) = np$$

and

$$\text{Var}(x) = np(1-p)$$

where p is the probability any one respondent would hold the opinion of interest, and n would be the total number of citizens polled.

6.6.3   THE EXPONENTIAL DISTRIBUTION

The exponential distribution plays a strong role in the theory of congestion systems. It can be shown that if the number of arrivals during an interval is Poisson distributed, then the time between successive arrivals is exponentially distributed with probability density

$$f(x) = \begin{cases} \dfrac{1}{\theta}\, e^{-x/\theta} & x > 0 \\[2mm] 0 & \text{elsewhere} \end{cases} \tag{6.29}$$

$$E(x) = \theta$$

and

$$\text{Var}(x) = \theta^2$$

$E(x)$ and Var (x) often stated as:

$$E(x) = 1/\lambda$$

and

$$\text{Var}(x) = 1/\lambda^2$$

where $\lambda = 1/\theta$ is the rate of occurrence per unit time.

The exponential probability density function is shown in Fig. 6.13.

The exponential distribution has several unusual properties including a coefficient variation of 1.0 and a strong tendency for most values to occur near the extreme left with no clustering about a central point. A property of the exponential distribution which makes it unique among continuous distributions is that it is memoryless. That is

$$P(X > x + x_0 \mid x > x_0) = P(X > x).$$

Examples of processes that have been modeled by exponential distribution include the duration of telephone conversations, the time between failures of certain types of electronic devices, and the time between interrupts of the CPU in a computer system.

6.6.4   THE GAMMA DISTRIBUTION

The gamma distribution is a two-parameter distribution with probability density function

$$f(x) = \begin{cases} \dfrac{x^{\alpha-1}e^{-x/\beta}}{\beta^\alpha \Gamma(\alpha)} & x > 0 \\ 0 & \text{elsewhere} \end{cases} \tag{6.30}$$

when α is integer $\alpha = (\alpha - 1)!$

$$E(x) = \alpha\beta$$

and

$$\text{Var}(x) = \alpha\beta^2.$$

The shape of the gamma distribution is determined by the parameters α and β. By selecting particular values of α and β the distribution can take on a wide variety of shapes. Figure 6.14 shows the two general shapes of the gamma distribution.

Because of its ability to assume many shapes the gamma distribution is a popular candidate for modeling processes. Examples of processes that have been found to be gamma distributed are the time to perform a manual task, the monthly sales of an item, the seconds of CPU time a job will require, and the deviation of a trajectory from its intended target. A particularly important case of the gamma distribution when α is an integer is referred to as the Erlang distribution. The Erlang distribution is sometimes used to model the service process in queueing systems. A useful property of the Erlang is that it may be expressed as the sum of α independent exponential distributions.

6.6.5   THE WEIBULL DISTRIBUTION

Like the gamma distribution the Weibull distribution is a multi-parameter distribution that can take on a variety of shapes. A graph of the Weibull distribution is shown in Fig. 6.15.

FIGURE 6.13   THE EXPONENTIAL DISTRIBUTION

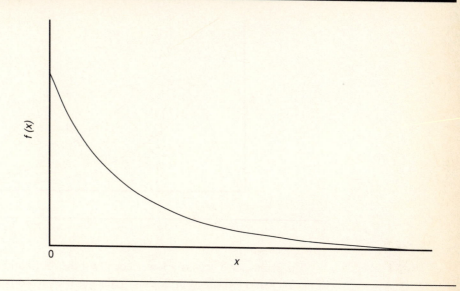

The probability density function of the Weibull distribution is

$$f(x) = \begin{cases} \dfrac{\alpha\,(x-\delta)^{\alpha-1}\exp\,(-(x-\delta/\beta)^{\alpha})}{\beta^{\alpha}} & x>\delta \\[2mm] 0 & \text{elsewhere} \end{cases} \qquad (6.31)$$

$$E(x) = \delta + \beta \mid (1 + 1/\alpha)$$

$$\text{Var}\,(x) = \beta^{2}(\Gamma(1+2/\alpha) - \Gamma^{2}(1 + 1/\alpha))$$

FIGURE 6.14   THE GAMMA DISTRIBUTION

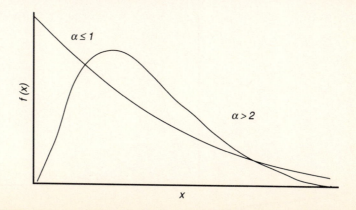

FIGURE 6.15   THE WEIBULL DISTRIBUTION

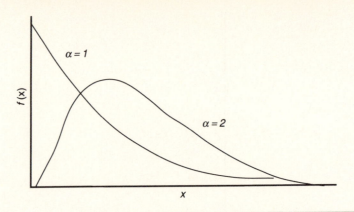

The parameter δ acts as a lower bound for the distribution and in many treatments of the Weibull is assumed to be zero, reducing it to a two-parameter distribution. The Weibull distribution has often been used in reliability theory to model the distribution of the time until failure, particularly for devices where wear or usage is a factor such as vacuum tubes, ball bearings, and springs.

6.6.6   THE LOGNORMAL DISTRIBUTION

The lognormal distribution is a two-parameter distribution over the interval $(0, \infty)$. The lognormal distribution can be derived by starting from a normally distributed random variable Y with mean μ and variance σ^2 and then defining $x = \ln Y$. The lognormal distribution is shown in Fig. 6.16 and its probability density function is

FIGURE 6.16   THE LOGNORMAL DISTRIBUTION

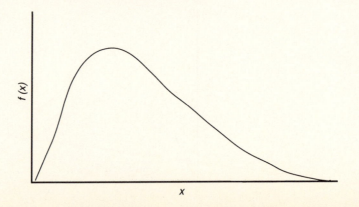

$$f(x) = \frac{1}{\sqrt{2\pi}\ \sigma} \exp\left(-\ln(x-\mu)^2/2\sigma^2\right) \qquad x>0 \qquad (6.32)$$

$$E(x) = \exp\left(\mu + \sigma^2/2\right)$$

$$\text{Var}\,(x) = \exp\left(2\mu + \sigma^2\right)\left(\exp\left(\sigma^2\right) - 1\right)$$

The lognormal is often used as a model of the time to perform manual tasks such as assembly, inspection, or repair, and has also been used as a model of the time until failure (Gupta[1]).

6.6.7   THE BETA DISTRIBUTION

The Beta distribution is a two-parameter distribution defined over the interval (0,1). The Beta distribution is shown in Fig. 6.17; its density function is

$$f(x) = \begin{cases} \dfrac{\Gamma(\alpha+\beta)x^{\alpha-1}(1-x)^{\beta-1}}{\Gamma(\alpha)\Gamma(\beta)} & 0 \leq x \leq 1 \\[2mm] 0 & \text{elsewhere} \end{cases} \qquad (6.33)$$

$$E(x) = \alpha/(\alpha+\beta)$$

$$\text{Var}(x) = \frac{\alpha\beta}{(\alpha+\beta)^2(\alpha+\beta+1)}$$

The Beta distribution can take on an unusually large variety of shapes by varying α and β. An attractive feature of the Beta distribution is that by a simple transformation it can be used to model a random process Y defined over any interval (a,b) by letting $Y = X(b-a) + a$.

$$E(y) = (b-a)E(x) + a$$

and

$$\text{Var}\,(y) = (b-a)^2\text{Var}\,(x)$$

FIGURE 6.17   THE BETA DISTRIBUTION

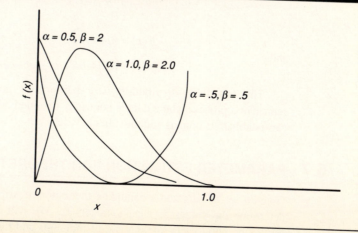

FIGURE 6.18   THE TRIANGLUAR DISTRIBUTION

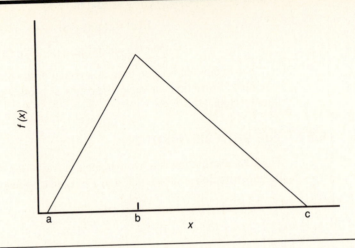

A commonly cited example of a process that can be modeled using the Beta distribution is the time to complete an activity in a project consisting of multiple activities (PERT networks). The Beta distribution is also used for sampling and estimation in Bayesian statistical analysis.

6.6.8   THE TRIANGULAR DISTRIBUTION

Although the triangular distribution is not easily identified with any physical process, it is a useful model for communication, conceptualization, and approximation. The triangular distribution is shown in Fig. 6.18 with the parameters of the distribution being its minimum, mode, and maximum values signified by a, b, and c, respectively.

The probability density function of the triangular distribution is defined by Lindgren [3] as

$$f(x) = \begin{cases} 2(x-a)/(b-a)(c-a) & a \leq x \leq b \\ 2(c-x)/(b-a)(c-a) & b \leq x \leq c \\ 0 & \text{elsewhere} \end{cases} \tag{6.34}$$

$$E(x) = (a+b+c)/3$$

and

$$\text{Var}(x) = (a^2 + b^2 + c^2 - ab - ac - bc)/18$$

The triangular distribution is a particularly good model when attempting to represent a process where data is not easily obtained but knowledge of its characteristics can establish its bounds and most likely value.

6.7   PARAMETER ESTIMATION FOR THEORETICAL DISTRIBUTIONS

Given a set of data and a candidate theoretical distribution, $f(x \mid \theta_1, \theta_2, ... \theta_n)$ we must determine the values of the parameters θ_i. We will consider two general methods of estimating parameters, the method of moments and the method of maximum likelihood

(MLE). Although the two methods appear to be very different, they often give the same value for θ_i. In this section we will give a brief description of each method and a more complete treatment can be found in Lindgren [3].

6.7.1   THE METHOD OF MOMENTS

The method of moments is the most easily understood method of estimating parameters. When this method is used for a k parameter distribution, the first k moments U_1, $U_2...U_k$ are expressed as a function of the k unknown parameters θ_1, $\theta_2...\theta_k$. We then use the sample data to estimate each moment and solve for estimates of the unknown parameters.

ILLUSTRATIVE PROBLEM 6.8

The two parameters α and β of the gamma distribution can be estimated by the method of moments using the data to estimate the mean and variance. From Section 6.6.4 we have $E(x) = \alpha\beta$ and Var $(x) = \alpha\beta^2$ and by equating sample moments we have:

$$\bar{X} = \hat{\alpha}\hat{\beta}$$

and

$$s^2 = \hat{\alpha}\hat{\beta}^2$$

Solving for $\hat{\alpha}$ and $\hat{\beta}$ we get $\hat{\alpha} = \bar{X}^2/s^2$ and $\hat{\beta} = s^2/\bar{X}$.

Using the data in Table 6.2 we found $\bar{X} = 2.89$ and $s^2 = 3.76$ and if we assume that the data comes from a gamma distribution, or establish this, using a goodness-of-fit test, we can use as estimates of α and β, $\hat{\alpha} = 2.22$ and $\hat{\beta} = 1.30$. In fact, this data was drawn from a gamma distribution with $\alpha = 2.25$ and $\beta = 1.33$.

6.7.2   THE METHOD OF MAXIMUM LIKELIHOOD ESTIMATORS

In concept the maximum likelihood estimator method (MLE) is very simple. Using the probability distribution $f(x \mid \theta_1, \theta_2,...\theta_k)$ a likelihood function, L, is formed in terms of the unknown parameters $\{\theta_1, \theta_2,...\theta_k\}$ and the sample points $\{x_1, x_2,...x_n\}$

$$L = f(x_1, x_2,...x_n \mid \theta_1, \theta_2,...\theta_k).$$

The principle behind the MLE method is that the estimators of $(\theta_1, \theta_2,...\theta_k)$ should be chosen so that the probability (or probability density) of the sample $(x_1,x_2,...x_n)$ will be maximized. That is:

$$\underset{(\theta_1, \theta_2,...\theta_k)}{\text{Max}} \quad (L)$$

The maximization of L is in most cases accomplished by taking the partial derivatives of L, or partial derivatives of a monotonic transformation of L such as $\ln L$, setting these derivatives to zero and then solving for $(\theta_1, \theta_2,...\theta_k)$. That is:

$$\frac{\delta L}{\delta \theta_i} = 0 \qquad i = 1,2,...k$$

ILLUSTRATIVE PROBLEM 6.9

The normal distribution is a two-parameter distribution with θ_1 and θ_2 being μ and σ. For a sample (x_i) the likelihood function is

$$L = \frac{1}{\sigma^n (2\pi)^{n/2}} \, \exp \left(-\sum_{i=1}^{n} (x_i - \mu)^2 / 2\sigma^2 \right)$$

and upon taking the natural logrithm of L we have

$$\ln L = -n/2(\ln 2\pi + \ln \sigma^2) - \sum_{i=1}^{n} (x_i - \mu)^2 / 2\sigma^2$$

Taking partial derivatives yields

$$\frac{\delta \ln L}{\delta \mu} = \sum_{i=1}^{n} (x_i - \mu)/\sigma^2 = 0$$

$$\frac{\delta \ln L}{\delta \sigma^2} = -n/2\sigma^2 + \sum_{i=1}^{n} (x_i + \mu)^2 / 2\sigma^4 = 0$$

and upon solving for estimates of μ and σ^2 we have

$$\hat{\mu} = \sum_{i=1}^{n} x_i / n$$

$$\hat{\sigma}^2 = \sum_{i=1}^{n} (x_i - \overline{X})^2 / n$$

If we had used the method of moments we would have arrived at the same estimate for μ and

$$\hat{\sigma}^2 = \sum_{i=1}^{n} (x_i - \overline{X})^2 / (n-1).$$

6.8 CONCLUSION

In this chapter we have presented elements of the art and the science of data collection and analysis. Methods of analyzing or monitoring data as it is collected were presented, as well as some common descriptive statistics. We then considered some of the more common inferential statistical tests including tests of independence, randomness, homogeneity, and goodness of fit. A number of commonly used discrete and continuous theoretical distributions were presented. Finally, we considered methods of estimating parameters of theoretical distribution from the collected data. In the next chapter we will take up the problem of generating random variates from the distribution we have selected to represent the random processes in the system being modeled.

EXERCISES

6.1 Using your local telephone directory select a particular exchange and then count the number of sequential listings until this exchange occurs. Plot the distribution and cumulative distribution of the data. Select an appropriate theoretic distribution for modeling this process and perform a goodness-of-fit test for this data.

6.2 Using the method of maximum likelihood, find the parameter estimates of α and β for the Gamma distribution.

6.3 The times to assemble components onto an integrated circuit board were collected for 50 boards.

8.6	11.2	9.1	12.4	11.0
12.0	7.7	8.9	11.1	8.3
9.1	9.1	10.0	11.1	9.6
10.4	9.6	10.2	4.0	12.0
12.3	9.0	12.3	9.0	8.5
11.6	8.0	7.3	5.1	12.1
9.6	14.2	10.4	13.4	10.5
7.9	8.0	10.6	12.1	10.5
13.0	12.0	10.3	9.9	6.0
7.7	10.7	8.0	7.2	11.5

Grouping the data into 10 sets of 5, set up control limits for the mean and variance of future samples. Suppose the next 50 samples were:

14.7	12.4	11.1	14.0	12.5
11.5	11.3	13.3	13.0	11.8
13.0	11.5	13.1	12.1	11.7
13.5	11.1	11.5	11.5	13.3
12.4	10.7	12.9	12.9	11.3
11.3	10.1	12.8	12.8	13.1
10.5	13.6	12.7	14.0	13.7
12.8	11.1	12.4	11.7	13.1
10.0	13.3	12.2	13.7	13.6
11.4	14.1	12.1	12.7	12.3

Using the above control limits is there some question concerning the homogeneity of the data?

6.4 As an example of a process to be tested for randomness, observe at a cafeteria the sex of successive customers as they are checked out by the cashier. Perform a runs test to determine if the occurrence of male and female customers is random.

6.5 A simulation model of a plastic molding operation is to be constructed which will include the effect of the molding machines failing during the day's operation. Based on 20 days of data the number of times each of three machines failed per day is as follows:

NUMBER OF FAILURES PER DAY

Machine	0	1	2	3	4	5	6 or more
I	3	4	6	2	1	3	1
II	2	3	5	4	3	3	0
III	1	0	6	4	4	3	2

Apply the appropriate tests for goodness of fit and homogeneity.

6.6 Using the first set of data in problem 6.3, test for randomness.

6.7 Fifty observations were made on the time between customers arriving at a bank. The times were (in seconds):

5	2	6	2	1	3	4	6	8	10
1	4	15	5	7	1	2	1	4	3
2	4	1	6	8	1	3	5	2	12
13	1	3	1	2	3	6	9	1	6
9	3	6	1	1	2	3	1	7	2

a) Use the Chi Square goodness-of-fit test to test the hypothesis that the times between arrivals is exponentially distributed.

b) Using the Kolmogorov-Smirnov test, test the hypothesis that the times between arrivals is exponentially distributed with a mean of 4.0 seconds.

6.8 Observations were taken on the times to complete customer orders at a fast-food restaurant. The times (in seconds) for two servers are shown below, sorted in ascending order.

Server 1:   25,30,34,40,45,46,52,60,65,75,80,82,83,95,96,107,140,165,201,252

Server 2:   15,23,45,47,49,50,55,68,89,95,100,105,115,200

Using the Kolmogorov-Smirnov two-sample test, test the hypothesis that the service times for the two servers are identically distributed.

6.9 Show that like the exponential distribution, the geometric distribution is also "memoryless."

6.10 Consider the problem of estimating the parameter A for the uniformly distributed random variable with probability density function

$$f(x \mid A) = 1/A \qquad 0 < x < A$$

a) using the method of moments find an estimate for A based on the sample

$$(1\ 2\ 1\ 3\ 2\ 4\ 3\ 8\ 4\ 1)$$

b) Comment on the apparent contradictory estimate of A.

c) Using the method of maximum likelihood estimation, find an estimate for A.

6.11 Using the method of maximum likelihood, find estimators for A and B for the Gamma distribution.

6.12 When using control charts to monitor if a set of observations were taken under the same conditions we can group N samples into n groups of size k ($nk - N$), where k can be anywhere from 1 to N. Assume the population being sampled is normal.

    a) What are the trade-offs for selecting larger or smaller values of k?

    b) If the mean shifts by 1 standard deviation, and N is 1000, what is the optimum value of k that maximizes the probability of detecting the shift?

    c) For the $k=1,4,8,16$ plot the expected number of samples taken before the shift is detected.

6.13 In the hyper-exponential distribution, the random variable will be distributed as an exponential with mean $T_a/2s$ with probability s, or as an exponential with mean $T_a/2(1 - s)$ with probability $1 - s$.

    a) Find the expected value of a hyper-exponentially distributed random variable.

    b) Find the variance and coefficient of variation of a hyper-exponential distribution.

    c) Derive the probability density function of the hyper-exponential distribution.

6.14 For a random variable uniformly distributed on the range A,B:

    a) show that the variance is $(B - A)/12$.

    b) Derive C_v, the coefficient of variation.

    c) If the the lower bound A must be positive, find the maximum value of C_v.

REFERENCES

1. Gupta, S. Order Statistics from the Gamma Distribution, *Technometrics* 2, 243–262, 1962.

2. Hollander and Wolfe, *Nonparametric Statistical Methods*, John Wiley and Sons, New York, 1972.

3. Lindgren, B.E. *Statistical Theory, 3rd Edition*, MacMillan Publishing Co., New York, 1976.

4. Massey, F. J., "Distribution Table for the Deviation Between Two Sample Cumulatives," *Ann. Math. Stat. 23*, 435–41, 1952.

7

RANDOM NUMBERS AND RANDOM-VARIATE GENERATION

It isn't necessary to be a mechanic to drive a car. Nor is it necessary to understand optics or chemistry to take pictures. Yet every professional driver knows how an automobile works and can make simple repairs, and a professional photographer has some understanding of optics and the chemistry of photography and knows how to develop and enlarge photographs. Simulation languages tend to shield us from the mechanics of generating random numbers and random variates, but if we are to be well-rounded professionals, we should know something about the turbines that drive the simulation.

7.1   INTRODUCTION

In Chapter 3, several simulation models were developed which incorporated random sampling from distributions of random variates. Sampling from distributions of random variates is central to discete-event simulation. In this chapter we will present various methods for generating random numbers and random variates. A prerequisite to generating random variates is the ability to generate uniformly-distributed random numbers, most often uniformly distributed between 0 and 1. We then use the uniformly-distributed random numbers to generate random variates from the appropriate distribution. In Section 7.2 methods of generating true and pseudorandom numbers are presented, as well as the desirable properties of random numbers. In Section 7.3 statistical tests for determining how well-generated random numbers conform to the theoretical uniform distribution are taken up, and in Section 7.4 we consider four different ways of using random numbers to generate random variates. Finally, in Sections 7.5 and 7.6 methods for generating certain families of random variates are presented.

7.2   GENERATING RANDOM NUMBERS

The history and theory of random numbers is a rich and fascinating branch of applied mathematics, but we will limit ourselves here to the more practical aspects, with only a brief overview of the associated history. The reader interested in a more complete treatment should refer to Hull and Dobell [8], and Nance and Overstreet [16]. To better understand the importance of uniform random numbers in the generation of random variates, consider the tossing of a fair six-sided die with the faces of the die numbered 1 through 6. If we had access to a source of uniformly-distributed random numbers between (0,1) we could simulate the toss of the die by mapping the uniformly-distributed random numbers into (1,2,3,4,5,6) as shown in Table 7.1.

We were not limited to simulating the toss of a fair die, but could have simulated a biased die by merely changing the random-number intervals corresponding to particular values of the die. For example, if we had wished to simulate a die that usually comes up 2, we could have used a mapping like that in Table 7.2.

When we sample from this second distribution, we will map the random numbers we generate into the die value of 2 about 75 percent of the time, provided that random

TABLE 7.1
PROBABILITY DISTRIBUTION FOR FAIR DIE TOSS

Random Number	Value of Die
.000 – .166	1
.167 – .333	2
.334 – .500	3
.501 – .667	4
.668 – .833	5
.834 – .999	6

numbers are uniformly distributed across the interval (0,1). This table look-up method can, of course, be used to generate any finite discrete random variable. Before presenting any further ways of using random numbers to generate random variates, we will first consider several methods of generating random numbers as well as their relative merits and faults.

7.2.1   TRUE VS. PSEUDORANDOM NUMBERS

True uniformly-distributed random numbers are random variables with the probability density function

$$f(u) = \begin{cases} 1 & 0 \leq u \leq 1 \\ 0 & \text{elsewhere.} \end{cases} \tag{7.1}$$

This probability density function is shown in Fig. 7.1.

Further, if $u_1, u_2, \ldots u_n$, is a sample from this distribution, each u_i should be independent of the other members of the sample. In practice it is very difficult, if not impossible, to generate true random numbers but there are methods for generating random numbers which have many of the statistical properties of true uniformly-distributed random numbers.

There are two general methods of generating random numbers: physical methods

TABLE 7.2
PROBABILITY DISTRIBUTION FOR BIASED DIE TOSS

Random Number	Value of Die
.000 – .100	1
.101 – .850	2
.851 – .900	3
.901 – .904	5
.905 – .999	6

FIGURE 7.1 UNIFORM DISTRIBUTION

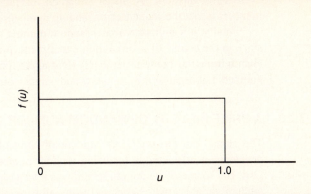

and arithmetic methods. Arithmetic methods are based upon some mathematical algorithm while physical methods are governed by the laws of physical chance. Random numbers generated using arithmetic methods are often referred to as pseudorandom numbers. It should be pointed out, however, that although random numbers that are generated using physical methods are more obviously dependent upon the laws of chance, it does not follow that they are any more equivalent to sampling from the probability density function of equation (7.1).

7.2.2 DESIRABLE PROPERTIES OF RANDOM NUMBERS

In order that a random-number generator be useful it should be:

1. Statistically equivalent to sampling from a uniform distribution
2. Capable of generating sequences of random numbers that can be reproduced
3. Computationally efficient.

Given that it is not practical to produce random numbers that are true samples from the probability density function of equation (7.1), the generated random numbers should at least exhibit the same statistical properties as true random numbers. The properties that are of particular concern are independence and full uniform coverage across the interval (0,1). In Section 7.3 we will present a number of statistical tests for determining if these properties are present.

In simulation experiments it is desirable, and sometimes required, to be able to reproduce the same sequence of random events in order to measure the effect of changing a decision variable. For example, in the simulation model of the time-sharing system in Chapter 3, it would be desirable to simulate the same sequence of user calls and user connect times while changing the number of ports. This can only be done by mapping the same sequence of random numbers into the random variables representing the times between user calls and connect times. By using the same sequence of random numbers, we would know that any changes in the system's measures of performance are due to changes in the number of ports and not attributable to chance variations in the number of calls or length of user connect times. In Chapter 10, when the issue of model experimentation is taken up, the importance of reproducing a sequence of random numbers will be even more apparent. A major weakness of physical methods of generating random numbers is that the sequences of random numbers are not reproducible.

Finally, it is important that a random-number generator be computationally efficient, since in the course of a simulation experiment, it is not unusual to generate millions (or even billions) of random numbers. Here again, physical methods of generating random numbers fail because they are slow and cumbersome to interface with a computer.

7.2.3   A BRIEF HISTORY OF RANDOM-NUMBER GENERATORS

The statistician Gosset (alias Student of Student's t test) is credited with the early development of methods for using random numbers for sampling of random variables [20]. His source of random numbers was a well-shuffled deck of cards. For many years, random variables were generated using all sorts of mechanical generators, ranging from decks of cards, to urns of numbered balls, to 20-sided dice. In some cases the random numbers generated were published for use by other researchers, the most widely used set being the RAND Corporation's *A Million Random Digits and 100,000 Normal Deviates* [17].

With the advent of digital computers the interest in using random sampling methods in applied mathematics increased and the emphasis in generating random numbers shifted from physical methods to mathematical algorithms (i.e., generation of pseudorandom numbers). The mathematician von Neuman is credited with one of the earliest arithmetic algorithms using a middle-square method. In this algorithm, random numbers are generated by extracting the middle digits from the square of the previously-generated number. Although this was the most commonly used algorithm in the 1940s, it has the undesirable property of degenerating when the middle digits are close to zero and the method is computationally slow [5]. The middle-square method is seldom used today, having been replaced by linear congruential methods introduced by Lehmer in 1951 [11]. This algorithm is amazingly simple, involving only a multiplication, an optional addition, and a division operation.

7.2.4   LINEAR CONGRUENTIAL METHOD

The linear congruential method uses the simple recursive formula

$$Z_i = (AZ_{i-1} + C) \mod M. \tag{7.2}$$

After Z is generated it can be normalized over the interval $(0,1)$, denoted $U(0,1)$, by

$$U_i = Z_i/M.$$

The reasoning behind this algorithm is the common observation that in multiplication and division, the lower, order digits are more difficult to predict, exhibiting no obvious pattern or sequence. The same reasoning is used by bookmakers when establishing the daily lottery number, basing it upon the last few digits of the total amount bet at a particular race track. The number appears to be random because it is based upon the digits that are least predictable and changing most rapidly.

Congruential methods have been shown to produce sequences of random numbers that appear to be statistically random, provided the coefficients A and C are properly chosen. At first this may seem surprising since the successive values of Z are easily predicted.

It can be shown by recursive substitution that:

$$Z_i = [A^i Z_0 + C(A^i - 1)/(A - 1)] \mod M. \qquad (7.3)$$

From equation (7.2) we can see that when Z_i equals Z_0, the sequence of random numbers repeats itself. The length of the sequence is referred to as the period and the theoretic maximum length is M. It can be shown that a full period (length M) can be obtained provided:

1. C is relatively prime to M (C and M do not have a common factor)

2. Every prime factor of M is also a prime factor $A - 1$

3. If M is a power of 4 then 4 is also a factor of $A - 1$

Using a generator with a full period is, however, no assurance that the numbers generated will be statistically random. For example if $A = 1$, $M = 11$, and $C = 3$, the above conditions are satisfied, yet starting with $Z = 1$ the full sequence of numbers produced is 4, 7, 10, 2, 5, 8, 0, 3, 6, 9, 1, 4, 7, etc. Hardly random!

Despite the relatively simple form of equation (7.2), some computational efficiency can be gained by letting $C = 0$, thereby eliminating an operation, and by letting M be a power of 2 and then using masking operations to replace division by M.

Knuth [10] shows that if C is zero, the maximum period can still be $M - 1$ provided M and A are chosen correctly, and if $M = 2^k$, the maximal period is $M/4$ provided $A \mod 8$ is 3 or 5.

There is no general agreement on the best choice of A, M, and C and today there are many linear congruential generators in use. Table 7.3 lists some of the more common choices.

The selection of a particular random-number generator is usually based on a number of factors, including characteristics of the hardware and software available, user's confidence, and convenience of use. Most simulation languages provide a random-number generator, but if there is any doubt as to the statistical randomness of a particular random-number generator, it should be subjected to a sequence of statistical tests to assure its validity. In the next section we will describe some of the more commonly used tests.

TABLE 7.3
COMMON RANDOM-NUMBER GENERATORS

Generator	A	M	C
RANF CDC 60000 FTN compiler	44485709377909	2^{48}	—
GGUBS IMSL Routine	7^5	2^{31}	—
RANDU IBM Scientific Subroutine	$2^{16} + 3$	2^{31}	—
GGL IBM Subroutine Lib.-Math.	7^5	2^{31}	—

7.3   STATISTICAL TEST OF PSEUDORANDOM NUMBERS

Although pseudorandom-number generators may not be truly random, the sequence of numbers they generate may be statistically indistinguishable from independent random variables with the probability density function of equation (7.1). In this section we consider three groups of tests for evaluating the statistical properties of sequences of pseudorandom numbers. We first consider a set of measures that may detect obviously poor random-number generators. We then present some statistical tests for independence or randomness of the numbers generated, and finally we consider some statistical tests for determining if the numbers generated are distributed uniformly over the unit interval. It is suggested that tests be performed in this order since relatively simple measures may raise serious doubts about a generator, and the tests for uniformity assume the numbers being tested are independent. Each of the tests will be described and applied to a set of 10,000 random numbers which have been generated using the linear congruential generator

$$Z_i = [25173 Z_{i-1} + 13849] \bmod 65536 \tag{7.4}$$

$$Z_0 = 23311.$$

This generator has been suggested by Grogono [6] as an acceptable random-number generator for 16-bit computers.

7.3.1   SOME QUICK AND CURSORY INDICATORS

The following procedures are not posed in terms of a null and alternative hypothesis, but are easily performed, and can give the analyst some confidence (or may raise some serious questions) about a random-number generator.

If x_i is distributed according to equation (7.1) then

$$E(x) = 1/2$$

$$\text{Var}(x) = 1/12$$

and if x_i and x_{i+1} are independent then the expected value of the autocorrelation factor $x_i x_{i+1}$ is:

$$E(x_i x_{i+1}) = E(x_i) E(x_{i+1})$$
$$= 1/4.$$

When a large sample of random numbers is generated, very accurate estimates of the mean, variance, and autocorrelation factor can be obtained and compared to the theoretic values above.

ILLUSTRATIVE PROBLEM 7.1

When 10,000 numbers are generated using equation (7.4) and normalized to the unit interval we find

$$\bar{X} = .5019$$

$$s^2 = .08412$$

and
$$\frac{1}{10,000} \sum_{i=1}^{9999} x_i x_{i+1} = .2526$$

which are very close to the theoretic values. One could, of course, formally test the hypothesis that the mean of the sampling distribution was 0.50.

7.3.2   TESTS OF RANDOMNESS

In this section we will consider two commonly used tests for randomness or independence, the Serial Correlation Test and the Runs Test.

The Serial Correlation Test is a relatively easy test to apply and quite similar to the quick measures described by Knuth [10]. The serial correlation coefficient is defined as:

$$C = \frac{n \sum_{i=1}^{n-1} x_i x_{i+1} - \left[\sum_{i=1}^{n} x_i \right]^2}{n \sum_{i=1}^{n} x_i^2 - \left[\sum_{i=1}^{n} x_i \right]^2}. \tag{7.5}$$

If random variables are independent, the expected value of their correlation coefficient is zero, but in this case the adjacent terms in the summation are not independent since any two successive products $(x_i)(x_{i+1})$ and $(x_{i+1})(x_{i+2})$ share a common term. It can be shown, however, that if a set of normal variates are serially independent then

$$E(C) = -1/(n-1) \tag{7.6}$$

and

$$\sigma_c^2 = \sqrt{n(n-3)/(n+1)}/(n-1) \tag{7.7}$$

and for uniform random numbers, the approximation is considered to be good when n is large [10].

ILLUSTRATIVE PROBLEM 7.2

For the 10,000 random numbers generated, we find from equations (7.5) through (7.7)

$$C = -.002741$$

which leads to

$$Z = [C - E(C)]/\sigma_c = -.0264$$

which is not significant.

There are several versions of the Runs Test which differ somewhat in procedure and power. Here we will consider two such tests: the Runs Up test and the Runs Up and Down test.

In the Runs Up test, a run is defined as a sequence of ascending numbers. For example the sequence:

$$.12, .14, .65, .18, .33, .77, .89, .72, .66, .43, .70, .81, .94, .98, .03$$

can be partitioned into the ascending sequences:

$$|.12, .14, .65|\quad |.18, .33, .77, .89|\quad |.72|\quad |.66|\quad |.43, .70, .81, .94, .98|\quad |.03|.$$

For this sequence there are three runs of length 1, one run of length 3, one run of length 4, and one run of length 5. In practice it is common to discard the first and last runs, although we did not in this example.

In the Runs Test, the theoretic number of runs, when the sample elements are independent, is compared to the actual number of runs in the sample. At first glance it would appear that the Chi-Square test, based on the difference between the observed and expected number of runs of length i, could be used, but this is not a correct procedure since the length of successive runs are not independent. Long runs are typically followed by short runs causing covariance between the number of runs of length i [12]. For a Runs Up test, Knuth suggests avoiding this covariance problem by discarding the number that immediately follows a run up, thereby establishing runs of independent length. Using Knuth's procedure, the probability distribution of k, the length of a run, can be shown to be:

$$f(k) = k/(k + 1)! \qquad k = 1,2,... \tag{7.8}$$

ILLUSTRATIVE PROBLEM 7.3

For our sample set of 10,000 random numbers, after discarding the value ending each run to avoid covariance problems there are 3665 runs distributed as:

Run Length	Probability	Observed	Expected	$(o_i - e_i)^2 / e_i$
1	1/2	1826	1832.5	0.020
2	1/3	1223	1221.6	0.001
3	1/8	451	458.1	0.107
4	1/30	126	122.2	0.131
5	1/144	32	25.5	1.715
6+	1/720	7	5.1	1.252
				3.226

Based on $\chi^2_{.05, df = 5} = 11.071$ there is no evidence for rejecting the hypothesis that the sequence of numbers is random.

A second Runs Test that can be used to test for randomness is based on the number of ascending and descending sequences (runs up and runs down). This test was used in Chapter 6 to test the independence of observations on a process. A convenient method for counting the number of runs up and down is to use the sign of the difference of adjacent numbers. For our sequence:

.12, .14, .65, .18, .33, .77, .89, .72, .66, .43, .70, .81, .94, .98, .03

the signed differences are:

$$+ + - + + + - - - + + + + -.$$

Counting both runs up and runs down there are six runs: two runs of length 1, one run of length 2, two runs of length 3, and one run of length 4.

It can be shown that

$$E(R) = (2n - 1)/3 \tag{7.9}$$

$$\text{Var}(R) = (16n - 29)/90 \tag{7.10}$$

and for large n, R is approximately normally distributed.

ILLUSTRATIVE PROBLEM 7.4

For our sample of 10,000 random numbers there are 6602 runs (alternating up and down). Using equations (7.9) and (7.10) we find

$$E(R) = 6666.3, \ \text{Var}(R) = 1777.5$$

and

$$Z = (6602 - 6666.3)/\sqrt{1777.5}$$

$$= -1.52$$

giving no evidence for rejecting the hypothesis that the sequence of numbers is random.

7.3.3   TESTS OF UNIFORMITY

Although a full period linear congruential generator will give the fullest possible coverage across the interval (0,1) the period may be so long that only a small part of the cycle of random numbers will be generated. The behavior of a generator over a portion of the cycle is important since, in a simulation, only a limited portion of the cycle is generally used. For example, if $M = 2^{32} - 1$ and $C = 0$, the length of the period is approximately 1.1 billion. Thus it is important to be able to test whether a random-number generator gives uniform coverage across the interval (0,1). The most commonly used tests for uniformity are the Chi-Square goodness-of-fit test and the Kolmogorov-Smirnov test.

The Chi-Square test requires the unit interval be divided into k subintervals each of width $1/k$. The width of each interval must be such that $n/k > 5$ where n is the length of the random number sequence being tested. The Chi Square test described in Chapter 6, is used to test for the uniformity of a set of random numbers. The test statistic is:

$$X^2_{df=k-1} = \sum_{i=1}^{k} (o_i - n/k)^2/(n/k), \tag{7.11}$$

where

$$o_i = \text{the count of the random numbers in interval } i.$$

When the degrees of freedom exceed 100 it is common to approximate χ^2 by the normal distribution with $\chi^2_{1-\alpha,\,df} = df + z_{1-\alpha}\sqrt{2df}$.

ILLUSTRATIVE PROBLEM 7.5   When the 10,000 random numbers generated by equation (7.4) are subjected to a Chi Square test, using 2000 intervals (1999 degrees of freedom) each of width .0005, $\chi^2 = 853.4$. Using the normal approximation

$$\chi^2_{.95,\,1999} = 1999 + 1.65\sqrt{2 \times 1999}$$

$$= 2103.3.$$

Thus we cannot reject the hypothesis that the distribution is uniformly distributed across the unit interval.

A second frequently-used test for uniformity is the Kolmogorov-Smirnov test. The test statistic is:

$$D = \max\{D^+, D^-\} \qquad (7.12)$$

where

$$D^+ = \max_{1 \le i \le n} \{i/n - F^*(u_i)\} \qquad (7.13)$$

$$D^- = \max_{1 \le i \le n} \{F^*(u_i) - (i - 1)/n\} \qquad (7.14)$$

and $F^*(u_i)$ is the theoretical distribution function of the set of random numbers u_i. This test was discussed in Chapter 6, Section 6.4.4.

For large n Massey [15] suggests as approximations for the critical values of D:

$$D_{.05} = 1.36/\sqrt{n} \qquad (7.15)$$

and

$$D_{.01} = 1.63/\sqrt{n}. \qquad (7.16)$$

ILLUSTRATIVE PROBLEM 7.6   When the Kolmogorov-Smirnov test is applied to the 10,000 random numbers generated by equation (7.4), we find $D = .007612$ versus a critical value of $D_{.05,\,n=10,000} = .0136$, thus showing no significant evidence of non-uniformity.

7.3.4   ADDITIONAL TESTS AND CONSIDERATIONS

We have considered just a few of the many statistical tests for independence and uniformity of a sequence of random numbers. Other tests that have often been suggested are the gaps test, serial test, and poker test. Each test has its own particular merits and capabilities for detecting sequences that are not random or uniform. Two excellent references of testing random number sequences are Knuth [10] and Fishman [4]. Despite the large number of investigations and analyses of random-number generators, there does not appear to be any one generator that emerges as clearly preferable to all others. In most cases the analyst uses a generator that he/she is familiar with or uses a random-number generator supplied by the programming language or operating system being used. The tests we have presented should detect poor generators but very subtle patterns or deviations from randomness can be very hard to detect. For most applications if such subtle variations occur they will have little effect on the validity of the simulation model, but caution is always advised when using pseudorandom numbers.

7.4   METHODS OF GENERATING RANDOM VARIATES

Given a means of producing pseudorandom numbers, we can now address the problem of generating random samples from specified probability distributions for our simulations.

The four general methods for generating random variates are the:

Inverse method

Acceptance/Rejection method

Composition method

Convolution method.

The relative ease of application and the computational cost of these methods vary greatly among families of random variables. We will first describe each method in general, and then for commonly used random variables, give specific algorithms for generating variates. In the sections that follow $f(x)$ can be a discrete probability function or a continuous probability density function and we will refer to either type of function as a probability function.

7.4.1   THE INVERSE METHOD OF GENERATING RANDOM VARIATES

In Section 7.2, the inverse method was used for generating values of a discrete random variable representing the toss of a die. In theory, this method can be generalized to any random variable for it can be shown that if u is a random variable uniformly distributed over the unit interval and x is a random variable with distribution function $F(x)$ when

$$F(x) = u$$

then

$$x = F^{-1}(u)$$

is a random variable with distribution function $F(x)$. For a mathematical proof of this method see Knuth [10]. As shown in Fig. 7.2, first a value of $F(x)$ is selected using a random number between 0 and 1. The corresponding value of x is then taken as the value of the random variable x.

From Fig. 7.2 we can see that the steeper the ascent of $F(x)$ (or equivalently the greater is $f(x)$) the more likely F^{-1} will map into x. The utility of the inverse method depends upon how easily the inverse function, $F^{-1}(u)$, can be found.

FIGURE 7.2 GENERATING X BY THE METHOD OF INVERSION

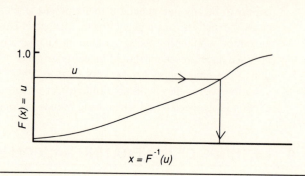

ILLUSTRATIVE PROBLEM 7.7

In this example we will generate a random variate with probability density function

$$f(x) = \begin{cases} 2x & 0 \leq x \leq 1 \\ 0 & \text{elsewhere} \end{cases}$$

using the method of inversion.

For this probability density function the cumulative distribution is:

$$F(x) = \begin{cases} 0 & x \leq 0 \\ x^2 & 0 \leq x \leq 1 \\ 1 & x \geq 1. \end{cases}$$

The inverse function

$$x = F^{-1}(u)$$

$$= \sqrt{u}.$$

Generating a random number, u, we set the inverse $F(u)^{-1} = x$ and then solve for x. For example if $u = .3245$ then

$$x = \sqrt{.3245}$$

$$= .5696.$$

7.4.2 THE ACCEPTANCE/REJECTION METHOD

The acceptance/rejection method is generally credited to Von Neumann [24] and is based on a two-step algorithm in which a sample is first taken from a probability distribution $h(x)$, and x is then accepted or rejected as a sample from $f(x)$, based upon a second sample from $U(0,1)$. The method requires that $f(x)$ be represented as

$$f(x) = Ch(x)g(x)$$ (7.17)

where

$$C \geq 1.0$$

$h(x)$ is a probability density function whose $H^{-1}(x)$ is easily found,

$$0 \leq g(x) \leq 1 \text{ for all } x.$$

This implies that $Ch(x) > f(x)$, where $Ch(x)$ is often referred to as the majorizing function, while $g(x)$ can be viewed as a scaling function in that it scales $Ch(x)$ back to $f(x)$. See Fig. 7.3.

Generating $u_1 = U(0,1)$ and using $x = H^{-1}(u_1)$ we can select a point $[x, Ch(x)]$. Next we generate $u_2 = U(0,1)$ and accept x as a sample from the space defined by $f(x)$ if $u_2 Ch(x) < f(x)$, otherwise reject x and repeat the process. Notice that since $g(x) = f(x)/Ch(x)$, an equivalent acceptance criteria is: accept if $u_2 < g(x)$. It is also important to notice that for a given value of x the probability of accepting x is $1/C$. Since the distribution of the number of samples taken until acceptance is geometrically distributed, the expected number of times the method must be applied is C.

A formal proof of this method can be found in Rubinstein [18] but the algorithm also has a geometric interpretation. The set of all pairs $[x, Ch(x)]$ will form a profile of points following the upper curve in Fig. 7.3, and by accepting only a portion $p = f(x)/Ch(x)$, we have a set of points corresponding to the profile defined by $f(x)$.

The formal algorithm is:

S1: $u_1 = U(0,1)$

S2: $x = H^{-1}(u_1)$

S3: $u_2 = U(0,1)$

S4:   accept if $u_2 < g(x)$, $[u_2 Ch(x) < f(x)]$

else

S5:   go to S1.

FIGURE 7.3 $f(x)$ AND $Ch(x)$ FOR THE ACCEPTANCE/REJECTION METHOD

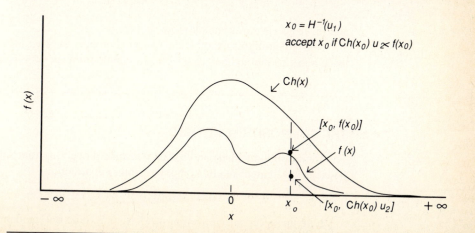

ILLUSTRATIVE PROBLEM 7.8

We will illustrate the acceptance/rejection method for generating a continuous random variable with probability density

$$f(x) = \begin{cases} \sin x & 0 \le x \le \pi/2 \\ 0 & \text{elsewhere.} \end{cases}$$

For a majorizing function $Ch(x)$ we will use

$$Ch(x) = x$$

letting

$$h(x) = 8x/\pi^2 \qquad 0 \le x \le \pi/2$$

$$C = \pi^2/8$$

· Then

$$H(x) = 4x^2/\pi^2$$

and

$$H^{-1}(u) = \pi\sqrt{u}/2.$$

Assume that $u_1 = .40$ and $u_2 = .88$ then

$$x = H^{-1}(u_1)$$
$$= .9934.$$

Calculating

$$u_2 Ch(x) = (.888)(.9934)$$

which is greater than

$$\sin(.9934)$$

and so we reject x as a sample from $\sin x$. Upon repeating the procedure assume that $u_1 = .65$ and $u_2 = .12$ then

$$x = H^{-1}(u_1)$$
$$= 1.27.$$

Calculating

$$u_2 Ch(x) = (.12)(1.27)$$

which is less than

$$\sin(1.27)$$

and so we accept x as a sample from $\sin(x)$.

Notice that in this example the expected number of times we must apply the acceptance rejection method before selecting a sample from $\sin(x)$ is $C = \pi^2/8 = 1.233$.

7.4.3   THE COMPOSITION METHOD

The composition method can be used when the probability function $f(x)$ can be decomposed as a weighted sum of k other probability distributions

$$f(x) = p_1 f_1(x) + p_2 f_2(x)...p_k f_k(x) \tag{7.18}$$

Like the acceptance/rejection method, more than one random number is needed to

S1: $x = 0; f = e^{-\lambda}; F = f$

S2: $u = U(0,1)$

S3:   if $u < F$ return x

else

$x = x + 1; f = f\lambda/x$

S4: $F = F + f$

S6:   go to 3.

When λ is large both the above algorithms can be inefficient and a normal distribution with a mean and variance of λ is often used for approximating the Poisson distribution. As in the case of the normal approximation to the binomial, a correction factor of 1/2 should be applied.

7.5.4 EMPIRICAL DISCRETE DISTRIBUTIONS

When the probability distribution of a discrete random variable is represented through a set of empirical probabilities, the most common method of generation is the inverse method, using a table look-up on $F(x)$, as shown in Section 7.1 for a die. The algorithm is:

S1: $u = U(0,1); i = 1$

S2:   if $u \leq F(x_i)$ return x_i

else

$i = i + 1$

S3:   go to $S2$.

ILLUSTRATIVE PROBLEM 7.14

A discrete random variable has the probability distribution

x_i	$f(x_i)$	$F(x_i)$
0	.2	.2
3	.5	.7
6	.2	.9
8	.1	1.0

Using the table look-up method

S1: $u = .6282; \quad i = 1;$

S2:   since $u > F(x_1) \quad i = i + 1 = 2;$

S3:   go to $S2;$

S2:   since $u \leq F(x_2)$ return $x = 3$.

If the empirical distribution can be majorized very closely by a uniform distribution with the same limits, the acceptance/rejection method is an efficient alternative.

7.6 GENERATING CONTINUOUS RANDOM VARIATES

In this section we present some of the more commonly-used methods for generating continuous random variates for discrete-event simulation models.

7.6.1 THE CONTINUOUS UNIFORM DISTRIBUTION

The continuous uniform distribution provides a convenient and efficient method for introducing random variation in a process being simulated. The mean and variance of the distribution can be easily adjusted by changing the limits (A,B) of the distribution, thereby providing a simple mechanism for studying the effect of changes in the first two moments of a random process in a simulation model. The computational effort is minimal, using the following algorithm:

S1: $u = U(0,1)$

S2: $x = A + (B - A)u$

S3:   return x.

7.6.2 THE NORMAL DISTRIBUTION

Because of the theoretical importance and the frequent use of the normal distribution to represent random processes, there have been many methods suggested for generating normal variates. Here we present two algorithms, the first exact but requiring heavy computing, and a second, more efficient algorithm which uses the convolution method to generate approximately normally-distributed random variates. Algorithms for generating normal variates generate a standard normal variate ($\mu = 0$, and $\sigma = 1$) which is then scaled to a normal with any mean μ and standard deviation σ using:

$$y = \mu + \sigma x.$$

The cumulative form of the normal distribution cannot be expressed in closed form using Cartesian coordinates, but the cumulative form of the bivariate normal can be expressed using polar coordinates. It is this transformation that is the basis of several popular methods for generating normal variates.

An inversion method developed by Box and Muller [3] is:

$$x_1 = [-2 \ln u_1]^{1/2} \sin 2\pi u_2 \tag{7.26}$$

and

$$x_2 = (-2 \ln u_1)^{1/2} \cos 2\pi u_2.$$

The algorithm is then

S1: $u_1 = U(0,1); \quad u_2 = U(0,1)$

S2: $r = (-2 \ln u_1)^{1/2}$

S3: $a = 2\pi u_2$

S4: $x_1 = r \sin a;$
        $x_2 = r \cos a;$

S5:   return x_1, x_2.

ILLUSTRATIVE PROBLEM 7.15

Using the above algorithm we will generate two samples from a normal distribution.

S1: $u_1 = .0682;\quad u_2 = .8702$

S2: $r = (-2 \ln (.0682))^{1/2} = 1.7689$

S3: $a = 2\pi (.8702) = 5.4676$

S4: $x_1 = 1.7689 \sin (5.4676) = -1.288;$

$x_2 = 1.7689 \cos (5.4676) = 1.212$

S5:   return $-1.288, 1.212.$

Marsaglia and Bray [14] have shown a slight improvement in the algorithm by letting

$$v_1 = 2u_1 - 1$$

and

$$v_2 = 2u_2 - 1$$

and if

$$s = v_1^2 + v_2^2 < 1$$

then

$$c = (-2 \ln s / s)^{1/2}$$

and

$$x_1 = cv_1; \quad x_2 = cv_2.$$

In recent years a number of more efficient, but more complex algorithms using the acceptance/rejection method and the composition method have been developed, including Kinderman and Rampage [9].

A very efficient but approximate method, which avoids computing logarithms and trigonometric functions, is based on convolutions of uniform variates between $(0,1)$. From the central limit theorem we know that as the number of elements in the convolution increases, the sum becomes more normally distributed. Since the variance of a uniform random variate over $(0,1)$ is $1/12$, twelve convolutions are often taken. The algorithm is:

S1: $i = 0; x = 0;$

S2: $u = U(0,1);$

S3: $x = x + u$

S4: $i = i + 1;$

S5:   if $i < 12$ go to $S2$

else

S6: $x = x - 6$

S7:   return $x.$

The approximation is very good for the central portion of the standard normal, but at the extremes of the tails, it is subject to some error.

7.6.3 THE EXPONENTIAL DISTRIBUTION

The form of the distribution function of the exponential distribution

$$F(x) = 1 - e^{x/\theta} \qquad x \geq 0 \qquad (7.27)$$

makes it an ideal candidate for the inverse method, for by setting $F(x) = u$ we have

$$u = 1 - e^{x/\theta}$$

or

$$x = -\theta \ln(1 - u)$$

and since $(1 - u)$ is also a a random number we can write

$$x = -\theta \ln(u).$$

The algorithm is then:

S1: $u = U(0,1)$

S2: $x = -\theta \ln(u)$

S3:   return x.

ILLUSTRATIVE PROBLEM 7.16

Using the above algorithm we will generate a sample from an exponential distribution with a mean of 10.0.

S1: $u = .5418$

S2: $x = -10 \ln(.5418) = 6.1286$

S3:   return 6.1286.

More complex algorithms which are marginally faster using acceptance/rejection and composition methods have been developed (see Ahrens and Deiter [1], and MacLaren, Marsaglia, and Bray [13]), but most often the above algorithm is used.

7.6.4 THE GAMMA DISTRIBUTION

The gamma distribution is frequently used in simulation models because of the role it plays in the theory of statistics and because of the variety of shapes it can assume.

Three properties of the gamma distribution that are often used when generating random variates are:

1. The exponential distribution is a gamma distribution with $\alpha = 1$.
2. If X_1 is gamma (α_1, β) and X_2 is gamma (α_2, β) then $Y = X_1 + X_2$ is gamma $(\alpha_1 + \alpha_2, \beta)$.
3. If X is gamma $(\alpha, 1)$ then βX is gamma (α, β).

The first two properties mean that we can generate high order gamma distributions (large values of α) by using convolutions of gamma random variates. The third property means that we only need to develop methods of generating gamma random variables with $\beta = 1$.

Most methods for generating gamma variates are developed for either $\alpha<1.0$ or $\alpha>1.0$, but if one can generate a gamma variate for $\alpha<1.0$ then, by convolutions of gammas with $\alpha=1.0$ (the exponential distribution), any other gamma-distributed random variable can be generated. If α is large, however, using convolutions of exponentials can be inefficient, and here we will present two acceptance/rejection methods for generating gamma variates, the first for the case $\alpha<1.0$ and the second for $\alpha>1.0$.

One of the most popular methods for generating gammas with $\alpha<1.0$ was developed by Aherns and Deiter [2] using the acceptance/rejection method. In this algorithm the gamma density $f(x)$ is expressed as

$$f(x) = Ch(x)G(x). \tag{7.28}$$

Letting $C = b/\alpha\Gamma(\alpha)$, with $b = (e+\alpha)/e$
for $0 < x < 1$

$$h(x) = ax^{\alpha-1}/b$$

$$g(x) = e^{-x}$$

$$H(x) = x^{\alpha}/b$$

while for $x>1$

$$h(x) = \alpha e^{-x}/b$$

$$g(x) = x^{\alpha-1}$$

$$H(x) = 1 - \alpha e^{-x}/b.$$

Inverting $H(x)$ we have

$$H^{-1}(u) = (bu)^{1/\alpha}, \qquad u < 1/b$$

$$= -\ln(b(1-u)/\alpha), \qquad u > 1/b.$$

The algorithm is then

S1:   generate u_1

S2:   if $u_1 \leq 1/b$ then $x = (bu)^{1/\alpha}$

  else

  $x = -\ln(b(1-u)/\alpha)$

S3:   generate u_2

S4:   if $x \leq 1$ then

  if $u_2 < e^{-x}$ accept x

  else go to $S1$

  else

  if $u_2 < x^{\alpha-1}$ accept x

  else go to $S1$.

ILLUSTRATIVE PROBLEM 7.17   Using the above algorithm we will generate a sample from a gamma distribution with $\alpha = .5$ and $\beta = 6$. The first step is to generate a sample from a gamma distribution with $\alpha = .5$ and $\beta = 1$.

For

$$\alpha = .5, \, b = (e + .5)/e$$
$$= 1.184$$

S1:   Assume $u_1 = .2315$.

S2:   Since $u_1 \le 1/b$ $(.2315 < 1/1.184)$
       then $x = (.2315)(1.184)^{1/.5}$
       $= .0751$

S3:   Assume $u_2 = .1121$

S4:   (Case of $x \le 1$, test if $u_2 \le e^{-x}$).

Since

$$.1121 < e^{-.0751} \quad \text{accept } x.$$

We now scale x to a gamma variate with $\beta = 6$ by multiplying x by β yielding

$$x = (.0751)(6) = .4506.$$

Several efficient algorithms have been developed for when $\alpha > 1$ by Tadikamalla [21, 22]. We will present his algorithm based on an Erlang maximizing function using the acceptance/rejection method. For large values of α, Tadikamalla [21, 22] has developed a more efficient, but more complex algorithm, and we will not present it here. In this algorithm the gamma density function is written as

$$f(x) = Ch(x)g(x)$$

with

$$h(x) = B^{-m}x^{m-1}e^{x/(B(m-1)!)}$$
$$g(x) = (x/\alpha)^d e^{-d(x/(\alpha-1))}$$
$$C = \frac{\alpha^m m^m e^{-B(m-1)!}}{\Gamma(\alpha)}$$

where

$$m = \langle \alpha \rangle$$
$$d = \alpha - m$$
$$B = \langle \alpha/m \rangle.$$

In this algorithm notice that $h(x)$ is the Erlang probability density function which can be sampled by using m convolutions of exponentially distributed random variates with mean B. The algorithm is then:

S1:   Let $x = -B \ln(\sum_{i=1}^{m} u_i)$

S2:   generate u_{m+1}

S3:   if $u_{m+1} < g(x)$ accept x

       else go to $S1$.

A special case of the gamma is the Erlang distribution in which α is an integer. When α is small, the Erlang is generated by convolutions of exponentials.

7.6.5   THE BETA DISTRIBUTION

The beta distribution is often used to represent random variables which are constrained over the interval (0,1). The density function of the beta random variable can assume a variety of shapes, depending upon the parameters of the distribution α, β. One of the most common and simplest methods of generating beta random variables is to use the relationship between the beta and gamma distributions:

if x_1 is a gamma $(\alpha, 1)$

and

x_2 is a gamma $(\beta, 1)$

then

$y = x_1/(x_1 + x_2)$ is beta (α, β).

It is easy to implement such an algorithm, but because methods for generating gamma variates can be inefficient, other algorithms have been developed using acceptance/rejection methods (see Ahrens and Dieter [1]) and use-of-order statistics. For descriptions of other methods of generating beta variables, the reader should refer to Fishman(4).

7.6.6   THE TRIANGULAR DISTRIBUTION

The triangular distribution with minimum a, mode b, and maximum c can be transformed to a simpler form with a minimum 0.0, mode S, and maximum T using:

$s = b - a$

and

$T = c - a.$

The transformation is shown in Fig. 7.5. Using the composition method we can represent the density function $f(x)$ as

FIGURE 7.5   TRIANGULAR DISTRIBUTION

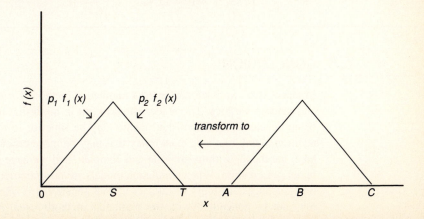

$$f(x) = p_1 f_1(x) + p_2 f_2(x) \qquad 0 \leq x \leq T \tag{7.29}$$

with

$$p_1 = S/T; p_2 = 1 - p_1$$

and

$$f_1(x) = 2x/S^2; \qquad\qquad 0 \leq x \leq S;$$

$$f_2(x) = 2(x - S)/(T - S)^2 \qquad S \leq x \leq T.$$

It can be easily shown that

$$F_1(x) = x^2/S^2; \; F^{-1}(u) = S\sqrt{u} \tag{7.30}$$

and

$$F_2(x) = 1 - (T - x)^2/(T - S)^2; \; F^{-1}(u) = T - (T - S)\sqrt{u}. \tag{7.31}$$

The algorithm is then

S1: $S = b - a ; T = c - a$

S2: $u_1 = U(0,1); u_2 = U(0,1)$

S3: if $u_1 \leq S/T$ go to $S6$

else

S4: $x = T - (T - S)\sqrt{u_2} + a$

S5: return x

S6: $x = S\sqrt{u_2} + a$

S7: return x.

ILLUSTRATIVE
PROBLEM
7.18

Using the above algorithm we will generate a sample from a triangular distribution with parameters $a = 10$, $b = 15$, $c = 25$.

S1: $S = 15 - 10 = 5; \; T = 25 - 10 = 15;$

S2: Assume $u_1 = .2346$ and $u_2 = .8672;$

S3: since $u_1 \leq S/T$ (.2345 < 5/15)
go to S6;

S6: $x = 5\sqrt{.86772} + 10 = 12.42.$

7.7 CONCLUSION

In this chapter we have presented a number of methods for generating random numbers and random variates. The reader should keep in mind that new methods are constantly being developed and published which may be superior to those we have described. In addition, many methods exist today that may be more efficient than the ones presented here, but the algorithms are long and complex, and we have elected not to include them in our presentation. When simulation models are programmed in special-purpose simulation languages, a library of random variate generators is often available and the analyst may not be concerned with the particular methods used. Some caution is necessary, however, for there are cases where inefficient and even incorrect algorithms (Houle [7]) have been included in such libraries.

EXERCISES

7.1 A possible source of random numbers is a telephone directory.

a) Using the last four digits of 1000 telephone numbers, test for randomness and uniformity.

b) What are the advantages and disadvantages of this source of random numbers?

7.2 Consider the "random number" generator

$$z_{i+1} = |\langle \sin(az_i + c)(10000)\rangle| \bmod 1000, \text{ with } a = 100 \text{ and } c = 0.$$

a) Generate 1000 such numbers and subject them to tests for randomness and uniformity.

b) What are the merits or disadvantages of this generator?

7.3 The principle of a linear congruential random number generator can be generalized to

$$z_i = (a_1 z_{i-1} + a_2 x_{i-2} + \ldots + a_n z_{i-n}) \bmod M$$

a) What would be the advantages and disadvantages of such a generator?

b) Implement such a generator for n=2 and test for randomness and uniformity.

7.4 List the steps in an acceptance/rejection algorithm for generating discrete random variables from an empirical distribution

$$f(x_i), \ i = 1,2,\ldots n$$

7.5 Using the method of convolutions for generating normal random variates, generate 1000 standardized variables (mean $= 0$ and variance $= 1$) and test for normality using both the Chi Square test and K-S test.

7.6 For the standardized normal variate z

$P(|z|>1.645) = .10$
$P(|z|>1.960) = .05$
and
$P(|z|>2.576) = .01$

a) Use the method of convolution and method of inversion to generate two sets of 10,000 variates and compare how each method performs at the tails of the normal distribution.

b) Use an appropriate statistical test on each set of data to test the hypothesis that these tail-end data points came from a normal distribution.

7.7 The maximum of the beta probability density function occurs at $x = (\alpha-1)/\alpha+\beta-2$.

a) Using the uniform distribution $h(x) = 1 \quad 0<x<1$, describe an acceptance/rejection algorithm for generating beta random variables.

b) What is the expected number of samples from $h(x)$ until x is accepted as a sample from the beta distribution?

7.8 Consider the random variable z with density function

$$f(z) = \begin{cases} 1 - z & -1 < z < 0 \\ z & 0 < z < 1 \\ 0 & \text{otherwise} \end{cases}$$

a) Construct a composition algorithm for generating z.

b) Construct an inverse algorithm for generating z.

c) Construct an acceptance/rejection algorithm for generating z.

d) Which of the above algorithms is computationally most efficient?

7.9 Construct two inversion algorithms for generating a geometrically-distributed random variable. Compare the computational efficiency of these two algorithms.

7.10 Construct two algorithms for generating Chi-Square random variables and compare their computational efficiencies.

7.11 An approximate method for generating continuous random variables is to represent the distribution function as a series of piecewise linear functions and by interpolation find $x = F^{-1}(u)$. See the figure below:

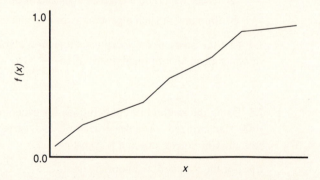

Construct such an approximation for the standardized normal distribution, including criteria for selecting the end points of the linear approximations.

7.12 An alternative to linear congruential random number generators is the Tausworthe [23] generator in which a series of binary digits are generated using the recurrence function

$$b_i = a_1 b_{i-1} + a_2 b_{i-2} + \ldots + a_n b_{i-n}.$$

Most often all but two or three of the coefficients a_j are zero.

a) Construct an algorithm for generating binary k digit random numbers.

b) Using this algorithm, generate 10000 such numbers and test for randomness and uniformity.

c) Compare the merits and properties of this method to the congruential multiplier method.

REFERENCES

1. Ahrens, J.H. and Dieter, U., "Computer Methods for Sampling from the Exponential and Normal Distributions," *Comm. ACM 15*: 873 – 882, 1972.

2. Aherns, J.H., and Dieter,U., "Computer Methods for Sampling from Gamma, Beta, Poisson and Binomial Distributions," *Computing 12*: 223 – 246, 1974.

3. Box,G.E.P., and Muller, M.E., "A Note on the Generation of Random Normal Deviates," *Annals of Math. Statistics*, 29: 610 – 611, 1958.

4. G. S. Fishman, *Principles of Discrete Event Simulation*, John Wiley and Sons, New York, 1978.

5. Forsythe, G. E., "Generation and Testing of Random Digits at the National Bureau of Standards, Los Angeles," Monte Carlo Method, Nat. Bur. Stand.,

6. Grogono, P., *Introduction to Pascal*, 2nd Edition, Addison-Wesley, Reading, Mass., 1980.

7. Houle, P.A., "Comment on Gamma Deviate Generation," *Comm. ACM*, 15:747 – 748, 1982.

8. Hull, T.E. and A.R. Dobell: "Random Number Generators," *SIAM Review*, 4:230 – 254, 1964.

9. Kinderman, A.J. and Ramage, J.G. "Computer Generation of Normal Random Variables," *Journal of the American Statistical Association*, 71: 893 – 896, 1976.

10. Knuth, D. E., *The Art of Computer Programming*, Vol. 2, Addison-Wesley, Reading, Mass. 1969.

11. Lehmer, D. H., "Mathematical Methods in Large Scale Computing Units," *Ann. Comp. Laboratory*, Harvard University 26:141 – 146, 1951.

12. Levine, H and Wolfowitz, J. "The Covariance Matrix of Runs Up and Down," *Annals of Math. Stat.* 15: 58 – 66, 1944; Applied Math. Series 12:34 – 35, 1951.

13. MacLaren, M.D., Marsaglia, G., and Bray, T.A., "A Fast Procedure for Generating Exponential Random Variables," *Comm. ACM 7*:298 – 300, 1964.

14. Marsaglia, G., and Bray, T. A., "A Convenient Method for Generating Normal Variates," *SIAM Review* 6:620 – 624, 1964.

15. Massey, F. J., "The Kolmogorov-Smirnov Test for Goodness of Fit," *J. Am. Stat. Assn.* 47:425 – 41, 1952.

16. Nance, R.C. and Overstreet, C., "A Bibliography on Random Number Generator," *Computing Review Vol.* 13, 1972.

17. RAND Corporation, *A Million Random Digits with 100,000 Normal Deviates*, Free Press, Glencoe, Ill. 1955.

18. Rubinstein, R. Y., *Simulation and the Monte Carlo Method*, John Wiley and Sons, New York, 1981.

19. Schmeiser, B. W., *Random Variate Generation, Simulation with Discrete Models: A State of the Art View*, (T.I Oren, et al, editors) IEEE, 1980.

20. Student (Gossett, W.S.) "The Probability Error of a Mean," *Biometrica* 6:1 – 25, 1908.

21. Tadikamalla, P.R. "Computer Generation of Gamma Random Variables," *Comm. ACM*, 21: 925 – 928, 1978.

22. Tadikamalla, P.R. "Computer Generation of Gamma Random Variables II," *Comm. ACM*, 21: 925 – 928, 1978.

23. Tausworthe, R. C., "Random Numbers Generated by Linear Recurrence Modulo 2," *Math. Comput.*, 19:201, 201 – 209, 1965.

24. Von Nuemann, J., *Various Techniques Used in Connection with Random Digits*, U.S. Nat. Bur. Stand. Applied Math. Ser. No. 12:36 – 38, 1951.

CHAPTER 8

MODEL VERIFICATION AND VALIDATION

The authors surveyed over 200 applications of simulation, and a count was made of the number of articles that even mentioned the words ''verification'' or ''validation.'' Less than 33 percent of the applications even brought up the issue of verification or validation and less than 10 percent gave any evidence that their models were verified or validated. Do less than 10 percent of the physicians check if the patient is cured? Does only one out of ten architects observe if the building remains standing? Do only 10 percent of the tailors check to see if the suit fits?

8.1 INTRODUCTION

Since any simulation model we develop is only an abstraction of the real system being studied, we should always retain a healthy skepticism about the correspondence between the real system and the model. In this chapter, we consider the process of establishing the credibility of a simulation model. Although this issue is taken up toward the end of the book, one should not infer that testing and measuring the credence of the model is a last step in developing a simulation model. Quite to the contrary; querying and testing the model's relevance to the real system should be going on throughout the simulation project.

The terms most often used for the process of establishing that the simulation model is a credible representation of the real system are model verification and model validation. Fishman and Kiviat [2] are most often credited with first using these two terms and differentiating between the two processes. Verification is the process of determining whether the operational logic of the model (the computer program) corresponds to the flow chart logic. In simplest terms: Are there errors in the program? Validation, on the other hand, is the process of determining whether the model, as a conceptualization or an abstraction, is a meaningful and accurate representation of the real system. Other terms used to describe the process of establishing the model's credibility are internal/external validation and logical/technical/operational validation. In this chapter we will stay with the more standard terms of verification and validation.

Starting with Section 8.2 we show how verification and validation fit into the overall process of simulation modeling, and in Section 8.3 we discuss some of the methods that practitioners of simulation have found helpful in validating conceptual models. Section 8.4 presents methods of verifying logical models and in Section 8.5 we present methods of verifying the computer model. In Section 8.6, we take up the issues and methods involved in validating the simulation model. Throughout this chapter the reader should keep in mind that verifying and validating a simulation model are more art than science, and the methods and techniques used depend to a great extent upon the process being modeled and the intended use of the model.

8.2   THE ROLE OF VERIFICATION AND VALIDATION IN SIMULATION

When building a simulation model of a real system, we must pass through several stages or levels of modeling. As shown in Fig. 8.1, starting with the real system, we first form a conceptual model of the system that contains the elements of the real system which we believe should be included in our model. From this conceptualization of the system we form a logical model that contains the logical relationships among the elements of the system, as well as the exogenous variables that affect the system. This second model is sometimes referred to as a flow chart model. Using this logical model we then develop a computer model, also referred to as the simulation model, which will execute the logic contained in the flow chart model. This computer model may be written in a general-purpose language or in a special-purpose simulation language, the relative merits of each having been discussed in Chapter 4.

Developing a simulation model is an iterative process with successive refinements at each stage. The basis for iterating between the different models is the success or failure we have when verifying and validating each of the models. One does not move progressively from the real system to the conceptual model, then to the logical mode, and finally to the computer model. In the process of developing and verifying or validating the model at one stage, we cannot avoid raising questions about the correctness of the models developed in prior stages. The interdependence between the adjacent stages of modeling should be apparent, but there is also a strong interrelationship between the conceptual model and the computer model. Although the final stage in modeling is the writing of the code to represent the logical model, it is neither realistic nor desirable to develop the conceptual model or logical model without first looking ahead to the computer model. An experienced simulation analyst will have a repertoire of languages for modeling the real system, with each language having a world view which may or may not map into the real system. For example, if the real system is a material-handling system with products being moved about a factory, the world view of GPSS or SIMAN (transactions flowing through the model, vying for entities such as conveyors or workers) may be very useful in the development of the conceptual model. Similarly, if the system is one of concurrent processes sharing a common resource, the SIMSCRIPT world view may be advantageous in developing the simulation model.

When we validate a model we establish that the model is a credible representation of the real system, when we verify a model we determine that the logic of the model is correctly implemented. Because the objectives of validation and verification are dif-

FIGURE 8.1   THE THREE MODELS OF SIMULATION ANALYSIS

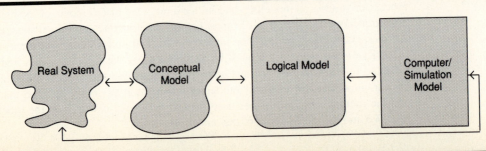

ferent, the techniques that have proven useful for one task are not always helpful for the other. We will therefore put forth methods for verifying a model's logic and its implementation through a computer program, and then take up methods for validating the model.

To either verify or validate a simulation model, we need to establish a set of criteria to judge whether the model's flow chart and internal logic are correct, and whether the conceptual model is a valid representation of the real system. Along with these criteria for evaluating the model, we need to specify who will apply the criteria and judge how well they have been met. In the best of circumstances, validation or verification is a team effort, drawing upon the technical skills of the simulation analyst, and the knowledge and insights of the users and managers of the real system. In practice, however, it is not always possible to form such a team. It is often left to the simulation analyst to verify that the computer model is working correctly and then to convince the managers and users of the real system that the model is a credible representation of their system.

An often-cited criterion for judging a model's validity is the ability of the model to duplicate the past, the present, and possibly the future behavior of the real system. This may not be a very useful operational criterion and can, in some cases, be an inappropriate criterion for judging the model. Simulation models often exclude certain real world aspects of the system because they do not bear directly upon the questions the model is intended to answer. By not including these parts of the real system, the model becomes a much more useful decision making tool. There is no one set of universal criteria for evaluating a simulation model, but whatever criteria are finally selected, they should reflect the intended use of the simulation model and the questions that the simulation model is expected to answer.

It is most important to establish the criteria and methods for verifying and validating a simulation model early in the simulation project. It is all too common for the analyst to become enamored with the sophistication of the model and the computer code. Validation and verification then become a concession to the less technical participants. It is possible the criteria will change as we gain a greater understanding of the real system, but the verification and validation criteria should constantly be applied to all three forms of the model throughout the life of the simulation project, rather than left as a last task.

To illustrate the process of verifying and validating a simulation model, let us once more take up the supermarket example that was first presented in Chapter 2. Before we begin to develop a simulation model of the supermarket, we need to identify what questions the simulation model is expected to answer. The manager and users of the system should be involved in developing these questions, along with the analyst serving in a consultative role, rather than, as is so often the case, the analyst alone deciding what important questions are to be answered by the model. If we proceed without having agreed upon such a set of questions, we run the risk of developing a model that is unrelated to the decisions at hand, and might thus validate and verify an inappropriate model. Let us assume, after consulting with the managers and users of the supermarket, we decide that the following questions are to be answered by the model:

1. What is the relationship between the number of baggers and cashiers to the time customers wait in line?

2. What effect does one or more express checkouts have upon customer waiting time?

3. What effect do two or more cashiers sharing a bagger have upon the time customers wait in line?

4. What would be the effect of having one or more cashiers who open and close as the number of customers waiting grows and decays?

These questions are still not as sharp as we will eventually want them to be, but they set the stage for the first step in modeling, the formulation of a conceptual model. Building the conceptual model requires us to identify those elements of the real system we will include in the model, as well as the events that occur in the system. At this stage in the modeling process we should also be identifying the endogenous and exogenous variables, including external events, state variables, and measures of performance. After identifying the elements, events, and variables to be included in the model, we should go back to the users and managers of the system to establish that the model contains all of the elements that must be included to answer the questions previously posed. That is, validation should be ongoing, even in this first stage of model development.

After the conceptual model has been developed, we next develop the logical or flow chart model which incorporates the elements, events, and variables included in the conceptual model. During the development of the logical model, it is not unusual to find faults or weaknesses in the conceptual model, resulting in a revised conceptual model. As before, when we change the conceptual model, we should continue to have the participation of the users and managers of the real system to ensure that our conceptual model is a valid representation of the real system.

The process of comparing the conceptual model to the logical model involves both validation and verification. The flow chart model must be a valid representation of the conceptual model and must also correctly represent the logic of the conceptual model. When modeling the supermarket, we may include in the conceptual model certain behavioral characteristics of the customers, such as going to the cashier with the shortest line, but this concept must then be correctly translated to the logical model. The form of the logical model should reflect the world view and capabilities of the computer language that will be used to code the logical model. In the supermarket example, selecting the cashier with the shortest line can be done with one or many operations, depending upon the language used. Again, we see a two-way relationship between adjacent models of the system.

After the logical model has been programmed, we must verify that this computer program is a correct implementation of the logical model. In a following section we will present a number of methods for verifying the computer program. Program verification is primarily a task the simulation analyst must perform, in order to build his/her confidence in the computer model. The users and managers of the system play little or no role in program verification.

When the simulation analyst is confident the computer model has been verified as a correct representation of the logical model, we come full circle and validate the computer model as a representation of the real system which will accurately answer the questions first posed when building the conceptual model. For our supermarket example we might validate the model by showing that the lines, waiting times of the customers, and utilization of the clerks and baggers in the computer model are meaningful representations of what happens in the real system as decision variables change. There is no one method or set of techniques for verifying and validating a simulation model and the process is as much art as science.

As a summary of the roles validation and verification play in simulation modeling, Table 8.1 presents the validation and verification issues for the conceptual, logical, and

TABLE 8.1
ISSUES IN MODEL VERIFICATION AND VALIDATION

Model	Verification	Validation
Conceptual Model		Does the model contain all relevant elements, events, and relationships?
		Will the model answer the questions of concern?
Logical Model	Are events represented correctly?	Does the model contain all events included in the conceptual model?
	Are mathematical formulas and relationships correct?	Does the model contain all the relationships of the conceptual model?
	Are statistical measures formulated correctly?	
Computer Model/ Simulation Model	Does the code contain all aspects of the logical model?	Is the computer model a valid representation of the real system?
	Are the statistics and formulas calculated correctly?	Can the computer model duplicate performance of the real system?
	Does the model contain coding errors?	Does the computer model output have credibility with system experts and decision makers?

computer model. In the next four sections we will present a number of methods and approaches that have been found useful in establishing the simulation model as a credible representation of the real system.

8.3 VALIDATING THE CONCEPTUAL MODEL

The first step in constructing a simulation model of a system is the formulation of the conceptual model. This model is the basis for the logical model and computer model which follow. The conceptual model should be carefully thought out, with a great deal of interaction among the decision makers, the manager and users of the real system. If the conceptual model of the system is not a valid representation of the real system, the remaining activities in the simulation project become fruitless.

Validating the conceptual model is the process of establishing the relevance of our abstraction of the real system to the questions the simulation model is expected to answer. Validating the conceptual model can be thought of as a binding process in which the simulation analyst, the decision makers, and the manager of the system agree upon which aspects of the real system will be included in the model, and on what information the model will provide as output. Since there is no standard method of validating the conceptual model, we can only present a number of approaches which have been found useful for establishing the relevance of the conceptual model to the real system.

8.3.1   EVENT REPRESENTATION OF THE SYSTEM

In Chapters 2 and 3 event graphs are suggested as a method for graphically describing the events and elements of discrete-event systems. The event graph is also very useful in validating the conceptual model.

A discrete-event simulation model can be viewed as a model that simulates the interaction of the events occurring in the system. These interactions can be represented as a graph with the nodes or vertices of the graph representing the events, and the directed branches or edges of the graph representing a direct causal connection between two events. The branches can be either conditional, indicating that the event will occur only when certain conditions hold, or unconditional. We will use the following symbols to construct the graph:

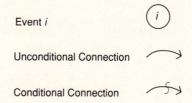

Event i

Unconditional Connection

Conditional Connection

A fuller development of the method of representing the conceptual model can be found in Chapters 2 and 3, and in Schruben [11].

Returning to our supermarket problem, we could conceptually model the system as the interaction of events.

1. Customer arrives at the cashiers' area
2. Customer selects a cashier
3. Cashier begins to check out customer
4. Cashier finishes checking out customer
5. Bagger begins to pack customer purchases
6. Bagger finishes packing customer purchases
7. Customer departs supermarket

A graphical representation of the system is shown in Fig. 8.2.

We should clearly state the conditional relationships between the events. For example, when the cashier finishes checking out a customer he/she does not begin to check out another customer unless there is a customer waiting in line, and the bagger is nearly finished packing the current customer's purchases.

Graphical representation can be used as a bridge to the logical model (flow chart model) as well as serving as a powerful graphical aid for communication between the simulation analyst, decision makers, and the managers. Closely related to event graphs are flow diagram models, representing the flow of entities through the system. A number of simulation languages (see GPSS and SIMAN primers of Appendixes A and B) have

FIGURE 8.2 EVENT GRAPH FOR SUPERMARKET CHECKOUT SYSTEM

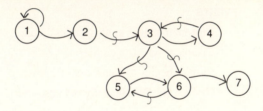

developed diagram representation of the flow of entities and these diagrams can be very useful in developing the conceptual model, as well as being a bridge to the logical model and computer model.

8.3.2 EXPLICIT IDENTIFICATION OF THE ELEMENTS TO BE IN THE MODEL

The conceptual model cannot, in most cases, include every detail and nuance of the real system, but rather the conceptual model should include the elements of the real system which are relevant to the questions the model is expected to answer. It is important when forming the conceptual model, to explicitly identify those elements in the real system that will be included in our simulation model. That is, we should identify all events, facilities, equipment, operating rules, state variables, decision variables, and measures of performance that will be part of the simulation model. We should also explicitly identify those elements of the real system that will not be included in the simulation model. In this part of the modeling process, the decision makers, managers, and the simulation analyst must jointly agree upon how much of the real system should be included in the model to bring about a valid representation of the real system.

Two extreme philosophies for deciding on how much of the real system should be included are:

- Include every aspect of the system that can have an effect on its behavior and then simplify the model as one gains insights to the relevant elements of the system.
- Start first with a simple model of the system and then let the model grow in complexity as it becomes apparent that additional elements of the real system must be included in the model to answer the question posed.

We believe a more sound philosophy to follow when constructing the conceptual model is:

- Spend a great deal of effort and time with those most familiar with the real system, identifying all the elements of the real system that will have a significant impact upon the answers to the questions the model is expected to answer.

Before going on to build the logical model there should be strong agreement among those expert in the real system and the simulation analyst that the conceptual model is a valid abstraction of the real system. That is, the conceptual model should have a high degree of face validity.

Using this approach for our supermarket problem, we can identify the following elements which should be included in a conceptual model of the system:

EVENTS

Customer arrives at the cashiers' area

Customer selects a cashier

Cashier begins to check out customer

Cashier finishes checking out customer

Bagger begins to pack customer's purchases

Bagger finishes packing customer's purchases

Customer departs supermarket

FACILITIES

Cashiers

Baggers

STATE VARIABLES

Number of customers in line at each cashier

State of cashiers (busy or idle)

State of baggers (busy or idle)

MEASURES OF PERFORMANCE

Waiting times of customers

Utilization of cashiers

Utilization of baggers

DECISION VARIABLES

Number of cashiers

Number of baggers

Number of express checkout lanes

Maximum number of items for use of express checkout lanes

OPERATIONAL RULES

Customers always select the cashier with the shortest line

No jockeying occurs (switching cashiers after initial selection)

Cashiers do not get too far ahead of baggers

ASPECTS OF REAL SYSTEM NOT INCLUDED

Jockeying between cashiers

Noncompliance with rules for using express checkout lanes

Bulk arrivals of customers (example, senior citizen bus)

Equipment failures

Absenteeism of cashiers and baggers

Customers selecting items in aisles of market

8.4   VERIFYING AND VALIDATING THE LOGICAL MODEL

The logical model (flow chart model) serves as a bridge from the conceptual model to the computer model. The format of the logical model depends upon the programming language that will be used to implement the logical model. If the conceptual model has been well constructed, verifying the logical model is not a complex process. There are, however, a number of questions that should be answered before we can be confident the logical model is a valid representation of the conceptual model.

One approach to verifying the logical model is to focus on:

1. Are the events within the model processed correctly?

2. Are the mathematical formulas and relationships in the model valid?

3. Are the statistics and measures of performance calculated correctly?

8.4.1   VERIFYING AND VALIDATING THE PROCESSING OF EVENTS

To be a valid implementation of the conceptual model, the logical model must contain all the events included in the conceptual model, as well as the logic for correctly scheduling the future events. If a graph representation of the events within the conceptual model has been constructed as described in Section 8.3.1, the logical model can be compared to the event graph. We should validate that the logical model contains all the events in the conceptual model as well as verify the connections between events. We should also verify that the logical model processes simultaneous events in the correct order. Finally, we should verify that all the state variables which are changed by the occurrence of an event are correctly updated.

A common method for verifying and validating the event processing within the logical model is a structured walk-through in which the developer of the logical model must explain (walk through) the detailed logic of the model to other members of the simulation project. It often happens that those who take the structured walk-through detect errors in the logical model, but more often errors in the logical model are found by the developer of the logic as the detailed logic of each section of the model is verbalized. The structured walk-through is not unique to validating simulation models but has been widely used as a technique for verifying and validating broad classes of software. For a more detailed treatment of the structured walk-through technique see Yourdon [14]. In Section 8.7 we will present the more salient points of the structured walk-through method.

8.4.2   VERIFICATION OF FORMULAS AND RELATIONSHIPS

Embedded in a simulation model are a number of explicit or implicit mathematical relationships and functions. The generation of random numbers and random variates is mathematically based, and in most simulation models there are laws of conservation that must be met. When the logical model is constructed, care must be taken that correct mathematics is part of the model and that conservation relationships are preserved. Some of these logical errors can be detected when the logical model is implemented as a computer program, but even at this stage care must be taken so that mathematical functions and relationships are correct.

As an example of a relationship that must hold throughout the simulation of a system, consider the supermarket model. In this model the number of customers being checked out or waiting to be checked out should equal the total number of customers who have entered the market less the number of customers departed.

The method of detecting errors in mathematical calculations or formulas is not much different than detecting errors in semantics or spelling in natural language. That is, careful scrutiny by the analyst and proofing by someone else may detect many such errors.

8.4.3 VERIFICATION OF STATISTICS AND MEASURES OF PERFORMANCE

In simulation models, statistical performance measures are developed as the events in the simulation model occur. A common error in simulation modeling is to fail to update all relevant statistics and measures when an event occurs. One method of verifying that statistics and measures of performance are updated correctly is the use of the event graph. With an event graph we can associate with each event a complete list of all statistics and measures that will change when the event occurs. In many simulation languages (for example GPSS, SIMAN, and SIMSCRIPT) some types of statistical measures can be collected automatically as the simulation executes. That is, statistical measures are built up in a method that is transparent to the analyst, thereby reducing the chance of erroneous statistics.

When the logical model is constructed, it is most important to validate that the statistics and performance measures are the ones needed to answer the questions the model is expected to address. For example, in our supermarket model, when we collect waiting times of the customers, we should separate the waiting times by customers who use the express checkout lanes versus customers using the regular checkout lanes. We should also separate waiting time of the customers in line from the time customer are being checked out by the cashier versus time spent waiting for purchases to be bagged. The logical model should also separate waiting times of customers for different periods of the day if the rate at which customers arrive is not the same throughout the day.

8.5 VERIFICATION OF THE COMPUTER MODEL

Once the logical or flow chart model has been verified, the programming of the computer model can begin. The computer model is verified by showing the computer program is a correct implementation of the logical model. Verifying the computer model is quite different from showing the computer model is a valid representation of the real system and a verified model does not guarantee a valid model. In Section 8.6 we take up methods of validating the simulation model.

Some methods of verifying the computer model are unique to simulation, while other methods of verification are the same as those used in any software development endeavor. The effort required to verify the computer model is heavily dependent upon the programming language used and there is no agreed-upon general verification methodology. Verifying the computer model often requires a great deal of imagination and ingenuity on the part of the analyst, and is one of the few activities in the simulation project that is best done without the aid of the decision makers or managers.

In this section we will discuss six general approaches to verifying the computer model. These methods are:

1. Structured programming methods
2. Tracing the simulation
3. Program testing
4. Logical relationship checks
5. Comparison to analytic models
6. Graphics

In addition to these six methods, there is also the methodology of structured walk-throughs which will be presented separately in Section 8.7.

8.5.1   STRUCTURED PROGRAMMING METHODS

There is a large body of literature devoted to structured programming methodology. For a complete discussion of structured programming the reader should see Yourdon [12]. At its very least, structured programming is an explicit citing of good programming practices. Many advocates of this methodology argue that it is the most effective method known for generating correct and maintainable program code. Regardless of either point of view, however, when a program is poorly structured it is very difficult to verify, correct erroneous code, or modify. Briefly, the principles of structured programming include:

1. **Top-Down Design:** The program is designed starting with the highest level processes which are then decomposed into subsidiary modules which themselves can be further decomposed.

2. **Modularity:** Each subsidiary module is responsible for a single function.

3. **Stepwise Refinement:** Each module is developed using a step-by-step refinement of the module's function ending with language-specific code. Some of the stepwise refinement should have occurred in the development of the logical model.

4. **Compact Modules:** Modules should be short in length. Fifty (50) lines of code is often suggested as an upper limit for any one module.

5. **Structured Control:** All control code should be highly structured using `IF-THEN-ELSE`, `WHILE`, `REPEAT-UNTIL`, `FOR` and `CASE` statements. The use of `GOTO` statements should be avoided.

By constructing a simulation model in well structured modules, segments of the model can be verified separately, thereby simplifying the verification process. It is always easier to verify 20 modules averaging 25 lines of code than it is to verify one module of 500 lines.

Simulation languages like SIMSCRIPT II.5 lend themselves to the methods of structured programming more readily than process interaction languages such as GPSS and SIMAN. However, even when the language used to implement the logical model is transaction oriented, the principles of top-down design, stepwise refinement, and modularity can still be employed to great advantage.

8.5.2 SIMULATION TRACES

Many simulation languages provide built-in capabilities for tracing the simulation as it occurs. GPSS and SIMAN can display the flow of entities through the model, while SIMSCRIPT will print out the sequence of processes and event execution as well as user-coded traces. When a simulation model is programmed in a general-purpose language, the analyst must, of course, build tracing capacities into the code. When the logical model is programmed, mechanisms for tracing the simulation should be included as part of the program design and not patched in when there appear to be errors in the computer program. Traces should be capable of being turned on and off and provide concise but intelligible diagnostics.

One mechanism the authors have often used when programming the logical model in languages such as FORTRAN, PASCAL, or SIMSCRIPT is to include a print statement at the beginning of each function or subprogram which conditionally will print out all parameters being passed as well as the simulation time. A global Boolean trace variable can be turned ON or OFF to activate the trace. In FORTRAN the code would be something like:

```
SUBROUTINE SERVICE(I)
COMMON TRACE,TIME,N,T_SER(10), etc.
LOGICAL TRACE
IF (TRACE.EQ.TRUE) THEN
PRINT *, 'ENTERING ROUTINE SERVICE AT',TIME
PRINT *, 'SERVICE COMPLETED BY SERVER',I
ENDIF
{body of SUBROUTINE SERVICE}
RETURN
END
```

Although traces can provide a detailed record of the execution of the model, the volume of output can be overwhelming. A variation of the trace is a break feature, or interactive debugging whereby the model will cease execution; allowing the analyst to query the values of the variables in the model and then resume execution. Breaks are much more efficient than traces and produce fewer lines of output but may require much more coding. In some operating systems breaks and traces can automatically be included in the compiled code. Many simulation languages provide interactive debugging facilities. It has been our experience that debugging utilities are invaluable aids and provide a highly effective mechanism for verifying the computer model.

The code for tracing and breaks should not be removed from the computer model when the analyst believes that the computer model has been verified, for as the model is used, additional errors or questions will in all probability arise. The trace and break features included in the initial development of the model are often very helpful for program maintenance or enhancements and subsequent verifications.

8.5.3 TESTING

Testing is defined as the controlled exercise of the computer model. The two most common approaches to testing are bottom-up and top-down testing. In bottom-up testing the lowest, most basic modules are tested and verified first. This is sometimes referred to as unit testing. In the bottom-up method, after the basic modules have been tested, integration tests are performed in which the interfaces between two or more modules are tested. This bottom-up approach continues until the model can be tested as a single system.

A most critical part of testing is the selection of test data. The advantage of testing the lowest modules first is that they typically require a smaller set of test data than a larger integration of modules. Modules can be tested using drivers that generate test data, and then call the module to be executed. The choice of test data is critical, since code not exercised is code not tested.

In top-down testing, the testing begins with the main module and incrementally moves down to lower modules. In top-down testing, stubs or dummy routines are required to simulate the function of lower-level modules. An advantage of the top-down method is that the process progresses logically, parallel with the program flow, rather than against it, as in the bottom-up method. Programmers and managers often feel more comfortable with top-down testing because it gives the appearance that progress is being made. After the model has been tested, using either a structured bottom-up or top-down approach, the model should be exercised using extreme conditions. If carefully selected, the results of the simulation under some extreme conditions can be predicted. For example, in the supermarket problem, if we test the model when the arrival rate of customers is much greater than the capability of the checkout clerks, we can predict the line lengths and utilization of the checkout clerks and baggers. Similarly, we could simulate the supermarket with very low arrival rates and again be able to predict line lengths and utilization.

8.5.4   CHECKING LOGICAL RELATIONSHIPS

For almost any simulation model there are logical relationships that must be maintained throughout the execution of the model's logic. These relationships may be based on laws of conservation or may be statistical in nature. If these relationships are not maintained, we know the program is not a correct implementation of the logical model. A convenient point for checking such relationships is when the model steps forward in time. Some general-purpose languages, such as PASCAL, allow for variables that can only assume a limited range and if this range is exceeded, program execution ends. As an example of using logical checks the authors modeled a material-handling system and found a series of coding errors by checking whether the number of tote bins remained constant, and whether the number of tote bins on a conveyor was always between 0 and the conveyor capacity.

Typically, programming errors are not randomly or uniformly distributed throughout the computer model, but cluster together. By detecting one logically-erroneous relationship we often come across a colony of bugs.

8.5.5   VERIFYING WITH ANALYTIC MODELS

In Chapter 5 a number of analytic models were presented which are often useful for gaining insights into more complex systems. Although simulation models are most often used to analyze systems that cannot be modeled using these analytic models, one can often, by properly selecting data and parameters for the simulation model, make the simulation model equivalent to an analytic model. By comparing the output of the simulation model, under these special conditions, to the analytic model, we can get an indication of whether the simulation model is correct. We will see in Chapter 9, however, that the output of simulation models must be carefully interpreted before we make any conclusions about the system's behavior.

As an example of using an analytic model to verify a simulation model, our supermarket could be made identical to an M/M/s queueing system by making the interarrival times and service times exponentially distributed with constant means, having no baggers in the system and a single queue for all customers waiting. By comparing the average number of customers in the system, the utilization of the checkout clerks, and the average waiting time of the customers for both the analytic model and simulation model, we could assess the correctness of the computer model.

8.5.6   VERIFYING USING GRAPHICS

On-line animation of the execution of a simulation has an intrinsic appeal, and has been used in a number of simulation applications [6,7]. If properly implemented, the analyst can watch the simulation unfold or step through the simulation one event at a time. This sometimes leads to the detection of errors which would otherwise go undetected. The problem of animation, however, is if the animation is slow enough for the analyst to follow the simulation, the amount of time required to observe an entire simulation can be exceedingly long. On the other hand, if the animation is sped up, the analyst may fail to see certain graphic images that indicate the simulation model is not a valid implementation of the logical model. With the advent of inexpensive high-resolution color graphics and windowing, graphics may in time become a powerful tool for both verifying the computer model and interpreting the simulation output.

8.6   VALIDATING THE SIMULATION MODEL

When the computer model has been verified we must next determine if its output is an accurate, and therefore valid, representation of the real system. Unless the simulation model is validated, it is at best a correctly-executing computer program. Validating the simulation model should be done with the participation of analyst, decision makers, and managers of the system. A test of model validation is whether the decision makers in the system have enough confidence in the model to use it as part of their decision-making process. That is, does the decision maker believe that the model is correctly answering the questions that it was intended to address?

As with verifying the computer model, there is no single or predominantly used technique for validating the simulation model. We will describe a number of frequently used approaches, but the procedure for validating the simulation model depends upon the system being modeled and the modeling environment. For example, validating a model of an operating system for a computer currently being designed is a very different problem than validating a simulation model of a material-handling system that currently exists.

The methods of validation we will discuss are:

1. Comparison of the output of the model to the real system
2. The Delphi Method
3. The Turing Test
4. Extreme behavior

8.6.1   COMPARISONS OF THE MODEL OUTPUT TO THE REAL SYSTEM

Comparing the performance measures output by the simulation model to the equivalent performance measures taken from the real system is the most often suggested method of validating a simulation model. If sufficient data is available on a performance measure of the real system, a commonly used statistical test is the Student's t test, in which we test the hypothesis of equality of means. Sometimes an F test can also be employed to test the equality of variances of the real system and simulation model. Also, some non-parametric tests, such as ChiSquare and Kolmogorov-Smirnov are useful. There are, however, a number of problems that generally arise when one attempts to use this method of validation.

The comparison between the model and the real system is a statistical comparison and the differences in performance measures must be tested for statistical significance. This comparison is not a simple one to make since the model performance measures are based upon simulations of very long time periods, perhaps several years. The performance measures of the real system, on the other hand, are based upon much shorter time frames, perhaps weeks or months at most. An additional complication is that those initial conditions of the system, which will have an effect on the performance of the system, are generally not known for the real system. In Chapter 9, statistical methods for interpreting the output of a simulation model will be presented and we will find that the statistical analysis of simulation models can be difficult.

A further problem in making a statistical comparison between the real system and the simulation model is that the performance measures taken from the real system may reflect many elements or effects in the system that were intentionally excluded from the model. For example, a performance measure for a production system may include effects such as labor unrest, holidays, and industrial accidents. These effects would most likely be left out of the simulation model because their effect would be constant for any alternatives the simulation model is expected to evaluate. Identifying the presence of such effects are often difficult, or even when identified it is difficult to adjust the performance measures of the real system to reflect their presence.

In many simulation projects the system being simulated does not yet exist. In such cases no real system performance measures can be used for comparison to the simulation model's performance measures. At best, one may find systems similar to the one being simulated, but such comparisons are only tenuous.

One should not conclude that comparisons between the real system and the simulation model can never be made. The authors [3,9] have built simulation models of a number of systems where this method of validation was used. However, if the performance measures of the real system and the simulation model are not statistically similar, one should not conclude the simulation model is invalid. Rather, accept that serious questions about the model's validity have been raised and, if they cannot be satisfactorily answered, the model should be reviewed for its lack of similarity to the real system.

8.6.2   THE DELPHI METHOD

The Delphi Method was developed as an approach to problem analysis when very little hard data is available on the problem or system being considered. In the Delphi Method, a carefully selected group of experts form a panel which will arrive at consensus answers to questions put to them. In a simulation environment, the panel may consist of managers and users of the system being modeled and the questions are about the behaviors or performance of the system under specified operating conditions. The Delphi Method excludes face-to-face group discussion of the questions, thereby avoiding the pitfalls of group discussion such as band wagon effects, domination by the loudest or most eloquent participant, defensiveness toward one's original position, and submission to those in the group of greater organizational authority. The method was developed by the RAND Corporation [8] and has been used in a variety of settings [1,4,5].

In the Delphi Method, a panel of experts is polled several times using a questionnaire and controlled data input, including opinion feedback and statistical analysis. The Delphi Method consists of the following interactive procedures:

1. A questionnaire is sent to each member of the panel. For validating a simulation model the question would deal with the real system's response to certain inputs or structural changes.

2. Based on the responses to the questions in Step 1, new questions are formed which will elicit more specific responses from the panel.

3. The new questions are sent to the panel, along with a distillation of the panel's response to the previous round of questions.

Steps 1 through 3 are repeated two or more times at which point the analyst should have an expert's prediction of the system's response to the inputs or structural changes being considered.

A first criticism of the Delphi Method is that it is time consuming and expensive. This may not, however, be a fair criticism. The Delphi Method of validating the model does not need to cause a delay in the simulation project since it can be performed simultaneously with the construction of the computer model. The Delphi Method can be expensive, but for many simulation projects the cost may be small relative to other methods of validating the model. Further, validation of simulation models in general can be lengthy and expensive, but much less costly than using a model that is an incorrect representation of the real system.

A second criticism of the Delphi Method is that, if it is so effective a method of predicting the behavior of the real system, why not use the Delphi Method in lieu of simulation modeling? In some situations, the Delphi Method may, in fact, be a more cost-effective method. However, it is not generally practical to keep a panel of experts on hand to predict the system's response to changes being considered. Even if such a panel could be kept on hand, the delay in response from the panel would be very long and the panel would eventually become fatigued.

8.6.3   THE TURING TEST

A frequently suggested method for validating a simulation model is the Turing Test. This test was suggested by Alan Turing as a test of artificial intelligence. In this test an expert, or panel of experts, is presented summary descriptions or reports based on the real system and the simulation model. If the experts cannot identify the reports based on the output of the simulation model, the credibility of the model is increased.

The Turing Test is, in spirit, the reverse of the Delphi Method. That is, in the Turing Test, a panel of experts is asked to identify in retrospect the simulated system, while in the Delphi Method a panel is asked to predict the response of the system. Although the Turing Test is intuitively appealing, there have been few reports of its use [10] and the method requires considerable effort in massaging and formatting the performance statistics of the real system to create Turing reports. A major difficulty in validating a model using the Turing Test is the adjustment of the performance measures of the real system so that effects not intended to be part of the simulation model are removed. The Turing Test also requires a statistical analysis of the panel's selection of real versus simulated reports, determining whether the differentiation of reports is statistically significant.

8.6.4 VALIDATION BY BEHAVIOR AT EXTREMES

Occasionally the real system can be observed under extreme conditions whereby an unusual situation arises. This is sometimes an ideal situation for gathering data on the performance measures of the real system for comparison to the output of the simulation model, run under similar conditions. It is also possible that the managers of the system can predict how the real system will behave under extreme conditions more easily than they can predict the system's behavior under normal conditions. By comparing the predictions of the system's behavior under extreme conditions to the model's performance under these same conditions, we can validate the model.

As an example of using extreme conditions for validation, consider the supermarket problem. We might know, or be able to predict, how the lines of customers would build up if only one cashier were available and the rate of customers arriving greatly exceeded the rate at which customers could be checked out. The lines should grow steadily and then drop off as additional cashiers are added to the system. If the simulation model showed the same relative growth and decay of customers waiting, the credibility of the model is increased.

8.7 THE STRUCTURED WALK-THROUGH

The structured walk-through is a technique that is used for many programming applications and is not restricted to simulation models. The technique has been espoused by Yourdon [13] as the best method for producing well structured and correct computer programs. In simulation modeling, structured walk-throughs can be done when the logical model is being developed, as well as when the computer model is being written. In essence, the structured walk-through is a peer review, allowing those not directly constructing the model or writing the code to review the analyst's or programmer's work. In order for this review process to be maximally successful, a series of guidelines has been proposed. These guidelines include:

1. Walk-throughs can be either formal or informal. Informal walk-throughs are typically more spontaneous and few, if any, minutes are recorded. Formal walk-throughs are more structured and require more planning and preparation. Both informal and formal walk-throughs should be used during the development of a large software product.

2. The members of the team for a structured walk-through are:

   • The Producer: The person who has developed and will present the model or computer code to be reviewed.

   • The Coordinator: The person who schedules and makes arrangements for the review, and acts as meeting chairperson during the review.

- The Secretary/Scribe: The person who takes notes and makes a permanent record of the meeting.
- The Maintenance Oracle: The person who reviews the product being presented from the vantage of maintenance. For simulation models, maintenance is equivalent to modification of the program to include additional features of the real system.
- The Standards Bearer: The person who reviews whether the product being developed is adhering to standards of good programming practice.
- The User Representative: The person who reviews the product from the vantage of whether it is a model of the real system.
- Other Reviewers: Individuals who can contribute materially to the review of the product.

There is no strict demarcation of the responsibilities of any members of the review team, and any member may raise questions about any issue, regardless of his/her special function in the team. These roles are set up, however, to insure that specific areas such as maintenance and standards are of special concern to one member of the team.

3. During structured walk-throughs, errors in logic or code are not corrected, but rather noted, and the producer is responsible for their correction after the review.

4. Structured walk-through should not be long, typically lasting less than an hour.

5. The emphasis in structured walk-throughs should be finding fault with the logic or code, not finding fault with the producer.

6. Everyone on the structured walk-through team should be on the same peer level, and the supervisor of the producer or participants should not be present at the reviews.

The structured walk-through can be difficult to apply when building a simulation model. The number of participants in the project is generally small, especially few on the same peer level, but the principles of this review technique can be a useful tool for developing valid logical models and correctly executing computer models.

8.8   CONCLUSION

Verification and validation occur on several levels and at several stages in the simulation project. It is a critical step in the building of a simulation model and in this chapter, issues of verifying and validating the simulation have been taken up as well as some of the approaches used in validation and verification. It is at best an inexact science and the practitioner of simulation must be very resourceful and imaginative when establishing the credibility of the simulation model. In practice, because of time pressures and the inexact nature of verification and validation, this most important step in model development is given short treatment. The authors believe this is a serious error and no model should be accepted as a representation of the real system until it has been properly verified and validated.

After the model has been validated and verified, it can be used to answer the questions it is intended to answer. In Chapters 9 and 10, we will take up the problem of statistically interpreting the output of simulation models.

EXERCISES

8.1. In Chapter 5 (Section 5.3.4) both an analytic and simulation model of combat between three tanks was developed.

   a) Develop a conceptual and logical model that would be useful in developing the simulation model.
   b) How can the simulation model of this system be verified?
   c) How can the simulation model of this system be validated?

8.2. Simulation models of traffic congestion systems are often constructed, in order to better understand the cause of the congestion. Suppose we were to construct a simulation model of two major roads intersecting, with traffic controlled by signal light.

   a) Construct a conceptual model of this system.
   b) Draw the event graph for the logical model of this system.
   c) How would you verify the simulation model of this system?
   d) How would you validate the simulation model?

8.3. The following remark was made during a presentation at a simulation conference:

   "The computer simulation model has been run using a variety of data sets and it seems to be able to handle any values we throw at it. This has given us a great deal of confidence in the validity of our model."

Is the process described above validation, verification, both or neither validation nor verification?

8.4. A simulation of a single server queueing system was conducted. In this simulation customers arrived at a constant rate of 10 customers per hour, with the times between successive arrivals exponentially distributed with a mean of 6 minutes. The service time per customer is always 4.5 and 5.5 minutes. When the system was simulated for 500 hours (about 5000 arrivals) the average time a customer waited in line (exclusive of service time) was 1 hour.

   Does the result of this simulation suggest that the model needs to be further verified or raise any questions about the validity of the model?

8.5. In Chapter 1 (Section 1.3) reference was made to a simulation of the elevator system for the New York World Trade Towers.

   a) Suggest several ways this simulation model could have been verified.
   b) How could the model have been validated?

8.6. Models of systems can be broadly classified as, conceptual models, physical models, analytic models, and simulation models. What are the similiarities and differences in the verification and validation of these four types of models?

8.7. What impact, if any, does the choice of a simulation language have on the verification and validation process?

8.8. Select from a professional journal, a reported application of simulation.

   a) How was the simulation model verified?
   b) How was the simulation model validated?
   c) Does the author(s) make a distinction between validation and verification?

REFERENCES

1. Basu S., Schroeder, R., Incorporating Judgments in Sales Forecasts: Application of the Delphi Method at American Hoist & Derrick, *Interfaces:7* May, 1977.

2. Fishman, G.S. and Kiviat, P. J., The Statistics of Discrete Event Simulation, *Simulation 10* 185 – 195 (1968).

3. Freeman, D., Grossi, P., and Hoover, S., Simulation of Pack Film Assembly, *Proceedings of the 1971 Winter Simulation Conference, SCS,* LaJolla, Ca.

4. Linstone, H. and Turoff, M., *The Delphi Method: Techniques and Applications*, Addison-Wesley, Reading Ma., 1975.

5. Helmer, O., The Use of the Delphi Technique—Problems of Educational Innovation. The RAND Corp. December, 1966.

6. Hoover, S., MICRO-SIM, *Proceedings of the 1983 MultiConference in Simulation*, SCS, LaJolla, Ca.

7. Hoover, S. and Perry, R., Concurrent Graphical Display of GPSS Simulations, *Proceedings of the 1983 Summer Simulation Conference*, SCS, LaJolla, Ca.

8. Norman, D. and Helmer, O., An Experimental Application of the Delphi Method to the Use of Experts RM-727, The RAND Corporation, July 1962.

9. Perry, R. and Hoover, S. Simulation-Aided Design for an Automated Storage/Retrieval/Delivery System, *Proceedings of the 1983 Summer Simulation Conference*, SCS, LaJolla, Ca.

10. Schruben, L., ''Establishing the Credibility of Simulations,'' *Simulation 34*, 1980.

11. Schruben, L. ''Simulation Modeling with Event Graphs,'' *Comm. of the ACM 26*, 957 – 963 (1983).

12. Yourdon, E., *Techniques of Program Structure and Design*, Prentice-Hall, Englewood Cliffs, NJ, 1975.

13. Yourdon, E., *Structured Walkthroughs*, Yourdon Inc. New York, N.Y. 1978.

PART IV

USING SIMULATION MODELS

CHAPTER 9

OUTPUT ANALYSIS

Pollsters can predict the outcome of an election within 2 or 3 percentage points by polling only 1000 voters. Quality control inspectors can predict with amazing accuracy the fraction of a lot that is defective by sampling only a few hundred items. In contrast, when using a simulation model of a bank to estimate the mean time customers wait in line, we can simulate the system for many months of activity, recording the waiting time of thousands of customers, and still under or over estimate the waiting time by 20 percent or more. Why is this? Data collected during a simulation is highly correlated and must be analyzed using specialized methods.

9.1   INTRODUCTION

Discrete-event simulation models are different from most other types of models. Because a discrete-event simulation model brings together the confluence of many random variables, the output of the model is, itself, a random variable. Using the output of a discrete-event simulation model to answer questions about the behavior and properties of the system it represents can be a difficult task. The output of a simulation model can easily be misinterpreted, resulting in false conclusions about the system it represents.

To illustrate this point, consider a simulation model of a single-server queue. Let us assume that customers arrive at the rate eight per hour and the mean service time is 6.0 minutes. Let us further assume that both the times between customer arrivals and times to service customers are exponentially distributed. From elementary queueing theory we can show that the expected number of customers waiting in line is 3.2 and the expected time a customer waits in line is 24 minutes. Using a simulation model, we estimate the mean number of customers waiting in line and the mean time a customer waits. The results of simulating the system five times, each simulation representing 240 hours of operation are shown in the accompanying table.

Simulation	Number of Arrivals	Mean No. of Customers Waiting	Mean Customers Waiting Time	Error of Waiting Time Estimate
1	1814	2.11	16.75	-30%
2	1919	2.60	19.52	-19%
3	1961	3.51	25.77	+ 7%
4	1983	4.35	31.59	+32%
5	1883	3.96	30.28	+26%
Average	1912	3.31	24.78	+ 3%

These simulations exemplify the difficulty of drawing conclusions about the properties of such a system, using a simulation model. Each simulation is equivalent to observing the system for 24 hours a day, for 10 days. In each simulation, the waiting time for over 1800 customers was recorded and then averaged. Despite such large samples, the estimates of the mean waiting times and the mean number of customers waiting are in substantial error in four out of the five simulations. If we had naively accepted the results of the first simulation, we would have a very inaccurate estimate of the mean time customers wait in line. Only after simulating the system a number of times do we begin to get a more accurate estimate of the mean waiting time in the queue.

In this chapter we take up the problem of analyzing the output of simulation models. We first consider the purpose of output analysis in Section 9.2 and then in Section 9.3 we show why the statistics produced from simulation models are intrinsically different from classical statistics. In Section 9.4 we divide the analysis of simulations into two cases, terminating and nonterminating simulations, and give examples of each type. In Sections 9.5 and 9.6 we present the more commonly used methods of analyzing the output of each of these two types of simulations.

9.2   THE PURPOSE OF OUTPUT ANALYSIS

Throughout this book we have taken the point of view that the first and most important step in a simulation analysis is to clearly define the questions the simulation model is expected to answer. The analyst should always have a clear understanding of what questions should be answered when the analysis is completed and use these questions as a guide throughout data analysis, model development, validation, and the analysis of output. The purpose of output analysis is to correctly answer the questions originally posed. The form of the questions indicate if these questions should be answered using hypotheses tests, confidence intervals, or point estimates.

To illustrate how the questions the model should answer affect the form of the analysis, consider a simulation model of a bank with several tellers. Let us assume that the bank opens at 9 A.M. and closes its doors at 4 P.M. Any of the following questions might be of interest to an analyst simulating this system.

1. What is the average time customers wait in line?
2. What fraction of the customers wait?
3. What is the probability a customer will wait more than 10 minutes in line?
4. What is the average number of customers waiting in line?
5. What is the effect on waiting times when there is a single line for all tellers versus one line per teller?
6. Will adding one more teller reduce the mean waiting time by 5 minutes?
7. What is the average number of customers inside the bank when the doors close at 4 P.M.?
8. What is the mean length of a teller's idle period?
9. By how much will the mean waiting time increase if the customer arrival rate increases by 10 percent?
10. For what fraction of the day will the number of customers waiting exceed 12?

If the model is properly designed, any of these questions can be answered, but each question requires different data to be gathered during the simulation of the bank and once the data is gathered, it must be analyzed in different ways. To correctly or accurately answer any of these questions, the analyst must decide on the number of times the bank will be simulated, the control exercised on the arrival stream and service times, and the statistical precision of the answers. Some of these questions will require point and interval estimates, and some questions may be posed as hypotheses, while other questions are open-ended and exploratory. Before taking up the various ways of analyzing the output of simulation models, we will first consider why the output of simulations models is different from most other kinds of statistical data.

9.3   THE PROBLEMS OF ANALYZING SIMULATION MODEL OUTPUT

To illustrate the problems encountered when analyzing data gathered from a discrete-event simulation, let us consider a very simple but representative simulation of a single-server queueing system. This simulation model could represent a bank, a supermarket, or any number of congestion systems.

In this simulation, let us assume we want to estimate the mean time that arrivals (customers) wait in line for service. We will assume that at the beginning of the simulation there is no waiting line. That is, the first arrival does not experience any wait, but subsequent customers will have to wait whenever they arrive and find the server busy. Let us further assume that customers arrive at the rate of 10 per hour, the customer's mean service time is 4.8 minutes and both the time between customers arriving and the service times are exponentially distributed random variables.

Using a simulation model written in SIMSCRIPT II.5, the waiting times for the first 100 customers are recorded. These waiting times are listed in Table 9.1 and plotted in Fig. 9.1.

Whenever we analyze statistical data, we must make assumptions about the process from which the data is collected, and about the observations made on the process. If the assumptions we make about the process and our observations of the process are incorrect, we run a very high risk of drawing incorrect conclusions about the characteristics and behavior of the process. When analyzing statistical data, it is common to assume the following:

1. The observations are independent.
2. The process is time invariant.
3. When the number of observations is large (30 or more), the sample mean is a normally distributed random variable.

If these assumptions are true, we can use for point estimators of the mean and the variance of the time customers wait in line

$$\overline{W} = \frac{1}{n}\sum_{i=1}^{n} w_i \tag{9.1}$$

and

$$s^2 = \frac{1}{n-1}\sum_{i=1}^{n}(w_i - \overline{W})^2 \tag{9.2}$$

where w_i is the time the ith customer waits in line.

TABLE 9.1
WAITING TIMES FOR THE FIRST 100 CUSTOMERS

Arrivals					
(1–5)	0.000	0.000	0.220	8.529	8.083
(6–10)	14.916	7.689	8.787	7.404	10.737
(11–15)	13.821	16.479	23.897	10.745	11.087
(16–20)	11.886	13.818	10.640	8.619	0.000
(21–25)	0.000	0.000	0.000	5.000	15.898
(26–30)	15.616	0.000	1.961	1.261	0.000
(31–35)	1.111	0.165	0.000	0.000	8.651
(36–40)	12.764	22.930	21.011	15.516	14.818
(41–45)	11.458	16.464	18.694	30.921	32.283
(46–50)	29.001	23.111	16.115	8.439	14.333
(51–55)	11.179	11.569	8.021	7.082	6.879
(56–60)	6.138	5.533	7.967	6.545	0.000
(61–65)	2.532	0.000	0.515	6.209	6.762
(66–70)	0.000	0.000	0.543	3.787	4.193
(71–75)	0.000	6.147	8.273	18.130	19.895
(76–80)	18.024	6.404	23.089	27.518	24.216
(81–85)	22.394	20.876	17.264	17.233	2.865
(86–90)	0.000	2.681	0.000	13.892	13.309
(91–95)	14.332	0.000	0.000	0.000	1.037
(96–100)	0.049	0.000	0.000	9.232	10.234

FIGURE 9.1   CUSTOMER WAITING TIMES

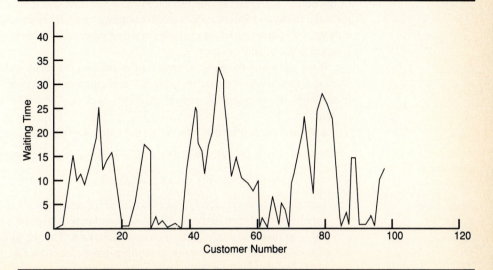

If n is large (30 or more) we can set a 95 percent confidence interval on the mean time a customer waits using

$$P(E(W) = \overline{W} \pm 1.96s/\sqrt{n}) = .95. \tag{9.3}$$

Unfortunately, in a discrete-event simulation, all of these assumptions are generally not true, or in order to make them true, we must be willing to face a considerable computational expense.

From either Table 9.1 or Fig. 9.1 it is obvious the customers experience successive runs of both long waits and short waits. For example, customers 78 through 84 experienced waits averaging over 20 minutes while customers 92 through 98 experienced little or no wait. From this data it appears that a good predictor of a customer's waiting time is the time the previous arrival waited. That is, the waiting times of customers are highly serially correlated. This is, of course, just as we would expect, since once the waiting line builds up, every customer who joins the line faces a long wait. Conversely, during the periods of time when there is a small or no waiting line, all arrivals wait for short periods, or do not wait at all.

Before continuing with the analysis of the customer waiting times produced from this simulation, let us take advantage of the fact that, since the arrival and service times were exponentially distributed, we can find the mean, variance, and confidence intervals for customer waiting times using an analytic queueing model. The queueing model that corresponds to our simulation is an $M/M/1$ model as described in Chapter 5. Rather than redeveloping the differential equations of this model, we will limit ourselves to presenting, in graph form, the properties of the system that are important for this discussion. Figure 9.2 shows the expected time a customer waits in line, as a function of the time of arrival, and Figure 9.3 shows the standard deviation of the time a customer waits in line, as a function of the time of arrival. From these figures it appears that the mean and variance of the waiting times are changing over the course of the simulation, exhibiting a transient behavior, but ultimately stabilizing at some steady state value. This nonstationarity of the mean and variance of the waiting times further complicates the analysis of the output of the simulation model. We can see now that it would be incorrect to estimate the mean and variance of customer waiting times by equations (9.1) and (9.2). Not only are our observations on customer waiting times highly correlated, they do not share a common mean and variance.

If we had taken the naive approach of estimating the mean and variance of customer waiting times, using the data in Table 9.1 and equations (9.1) and (9.2), we could have incorrectly set as point estimators of $E(W)$ and σ_w, $\overline{W} = 9.16$ minutes and $s = 8.45$ minutes.

A 95 percent confidence interval on the mean waiting time using equation (9.3) is

$$P(9.16 - (1.96)(8.45)/\sqrt{30} < E(W) < 9.16 + (1.96)(8.45)/\sqrt{30})$$

$$= P(7.51 < E(W) < 10.82) = .95.$$

This confidence interval clearly makes no sense for most regions of Fig. 9.2.

An obvious solution to the problems of correlated data and the nonstationarity of the process is to make multiple, independent simulations. This is, in fact, commonly done. Let us consider this solution more carefully, however. From Fig. 9.3 we see that after two hours the standard deviation of the waiting time, $\sigma_{t=2}$, is 15.2. If we are willing to

FIGURE 9.2   MEAN WAIT IN QUEUE

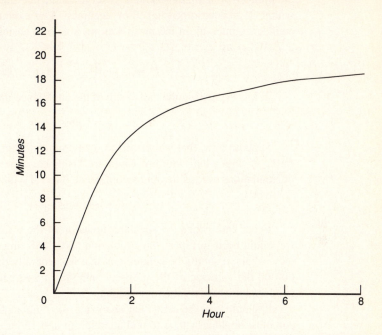

FIGURE 9.3   STANDARD DEVIATION OF WAIT IN QUEUE

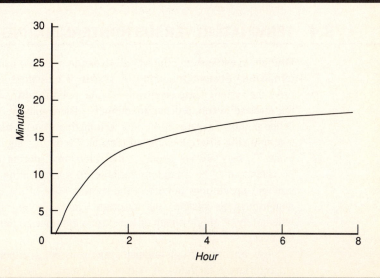

assume that the distribution of waiting times is somewhat normal we can then estimate the number of samples required to set a confidence interval on the mean waiting time within a predetermined level of accuracy. For example, we can set a 95 percent confidence interval on the mean waiting time of a customer arriving at the start of hour 2, $E(W_{t=2})$, as

$$P(E(W_{t=2}) = \overline{W}_{t=2} \pm 1.96\sigma_{t=2} / \sqrt{n}) = .95.$$

In this expression the half width of the confidence interval is

$$I = 1.96\sigma_{t=2} / \sqrt{n}. \tag{9.4}$$

Suppose now, that we wished to set a confidence interval on the mean waiting time, $E(W_{t=2})$, with a half width of 1 minute. Using equation (9.4) we can find n, the number of simulations needed to yield a confidence interval with the desired half width. That is,

$$n = (1.96\sigma_{t=2} / I)^2.$$

In our case, since the standard deviation of the waiting time is approximately 15.2, we would need to repeat the simulation about 888 times to achieve this level of accuracy. Again, it should be pointed out that we generally do not have this kind of information on the variance of the property being estimated, since in most simulation projects good analytic models are not available.

It should now be clear that analyzing the output of simulation models is complex and must be done with care and attention to underlying statistical concepts. In this section we have analyzed the output of a simulation model of a process whose properties are well understood. Most often, however, we model processes for which analytic models are not available to guide us in our analysis. In the next section, we present a number of general methods for analyzing the output of a simulation model. No one approach is always dominant. The choice of method depends very much on the objectives of the simulation and the resources available to the analyst.

9.4 TERMINATING VERSUS NONTERMINATING SYSTEMS

Discrete-event systems (in fact all dynamic systems) can be categorized as being either terminating or nonterminating. A system is classified as terminating if the events that drive the system cease occurring at some point in time, while in nonterminating systems the discrete events reoccur indefinitely. There may be reoccurring epochs, sometimes called points of regeneration, in a terminating system, but each epoch starts off fresh. In a terminating discrete-event system, an event, T_E, signals the end of one epoch. The event T_E may always occur at the same time, during each epoch, or the time of its occurrence may be a random variable. In a terminating system, the ending state of the previous epoch does not affect the starting state of the current epoch. By contrast, in a nonterminating system, the discrete events driving the system continue to occur indefinitely. A single epoch of the system continues indefinitely and there is no terminating event.

It is important to distinguish systems as being either terminating or nonterminating since different methods of output analysis are used for each case. In the simulation literature the terms terminating, nonterminating, transient, and steady state are often used to describe both dynamic systems and simulations of these systems. The intermixing of these terms has led to some confusion. A distinction should be made between the system and the simulation of the system. Every simulation is a terminating process but not all systems are terminating. Often, authors in the simulation literature divide simulations into terminating simulations and steady-state simulations. It is our view that we must first classify the system as being terminating or nonterminating and then consider whether the system reaches a steady state or only has a transient state.

The way we analyze output of a simulation model should depend upon the nature of the system (terminating or nonterminating) and the characteristics of its behavior (steady state or transient). Examples of terminating systems are:

1. Bank: The bank opens each day at 9 A.M., with no customers in the bank, and locks its doors at 4 P.M., completing service for the customers currently in the bank. Here the length of each epoch differs but each epoch always begins with no customers in the system and ends with no customers in the system. The terminating event is the departure of the last customer. In this simulation we would most likely select measures of performance that would estimate the mean time all customers wait, as well as the mean waiting time of customers arriving at different times of the day.

2. Computer System: The computer system starts up in the morning when the first user logs on to the system, and when the last user during the day logs off, the system comes to rest. Although during the late evening and very early morning hours an occasional user may log on to the system, the interval of concern is only during normal working hours and the performance of the system during the off hours is not of concern. Here each epoch may start at 8 A.M. with a random number of users (early arrivals already on the system) and the epoch ends when the last user signs off after 5 P.M. The terminating event is the last user signing off after 5 P.M. Possible measures of performance include the mean number of users connected to the system at different times in the day, the probability a user cannot log on to the system at different times in the day, the mean number of users connected to the system across the entire day, and the overall probability a user cannot log on to the system.

3. Game of Chance: Two gamblers toss coins. When both coins are either heads or tails, the first gambler wins a dollar. When one head and one tail occur, the second gambler wins a dollar. The game continues until an hour passes or until one of the gamblers wins all of the other's money. The duration of the epoch is either one hour or until the system reaches a state in which one of the gamblers cannot continue. The terminating event occurs when one of the gamblers wins the last dollar of the other gambler or one hour has elapsed. Measures of performance include the mean length of the game and the probability of winning the game.

4. Spare Parts Inventory: A manufacturer buys a special-purpose machine along with five replacements for a critical part. The machine will be used for the next two years. If the critical part fails, it is replaced. The manufacturer cannot obtain any replacements after the initial purchase without a substantial delay and cost. The length of an epoch is two years or until all five replacement parts have been used. The terminating event is either the passage of two years time or the failure of the fifth spare part, whichever event occurs first. Likely measures of performance would be the probability of the spare parts lasting the entire two-year interval and the mean length of time the system operated.

5. Data Base System: In a computerized data base the data is distributed across several disks. The data is linked together using key fields and pointers. When a query to the data base occurs, a search is made across the various disks containing the data, using the pointers and key fields to locate the data item requested. The length of the epoch is the time required to access the data. The terminating event is the location of the desired data item. Measures of performance would include the mean number of disk accesses and the mean time required to locate a data item.

Examples of nonterminating systems are:

1. Jobshop: A manufacturing facility consists of several work centers. When work arrives at the facility it is routed through the various centers until it is completed. Although the shop may operate only one shift and not operate on Saturdays or Sundays, this is still a nonterminating system. When operations cease (such as on a Friday evening) the ending state of the system will be the starting state when operations resume. The life of the system is indefinite, and we simulate the system for as long as necessary to accumulate statistics on the performance measure. Possible performance measures would include the mean time a job is in the shop, the utilization of various centers in the jobshop, and the mean work in process.

2. Inventory System: A retailer stocks merchandise and re-orders when the level of inventory falls to or below some threshold level. Although the retailer does business for only eight hours a day, five days a week, the ending inventory one day is the opening inventory on the next day. The discrete events driving this system continue indefinitely, and the measures of performance could include the mean inventory, the fraction of orders that have to be backordered or turned away, and the mean number of orders placed each year.

3. An Airport: For twenty-four hours a day, planes arrive and depart at a municipal airport. Although there are periods of light and heavy activity, the state of the airport in the morning depends upon how well air traffic was managed during the evening with no termination of the system. Possible measures of performance are the mean time an arriving plane must wait for a runway or terminal, and the mean number of planes waiting for runways or terminals.

4. Hospital: Patients are admitted to a hospital provided a bed is available. Once the patient is admitted, the bed he/she occupies is unavailable until the patient is discharged. Patients not admitted because of lack of bed space are either referred to another hospital if immediate care is required or placed on a waiting list until space becomes available. The number of patients admitted and discharged each morning clearly depends on the number of patients in the hospital and the length of the waiting list on the previous evening. Possible measures of performance are the mean time patients are in the clinic and the mean time patients wait for care.

5. A Tenure System: Faculty are hired by a university and given a number of years credit toward tenure. After each year of teaching and research the faculty receives another year of credit toward tenure. When the number of years credit reaches six, the faculty member is reviewed and either recommended for tenure or given a final one-year contract. During the period of earning credit toward tenure, the faculty member may decide to leave. After receiving tenure, the faculty member may stay on until retirement or leave for another position outside the university. This is a non-

terminating system (except for the faculty who do not receive tenure) since the university has an indefinite life. At the end of any given year, the number of faculty at the university depends on the number at the beginning of the year as well as their tenure status and years toward tenure. Measures of performance would be the number of tenured and untenured faculty members and the probability that a faculty member becomes tenured.

Closely related to the issues of terminating or nonterminating systems are the transient and steady-state properties of a system. When analyzing the output of a simulation model, it is necessary to differentiate between data gathered when the system was in a transient phase and when it was in steady state. The difference between the transient and steady-state properties of a system are often misunderstood and confused as being equivalent to a system that is terminating or nonterminating. When simulating a terminating system, it is possible that during most of the simulation, the system is in the steady-state phase. For example, in an $M/M/1$ queueing system, when the traffic intensity is .60 or less, after 40 arrivals, the state probabilities are, for most practical purposes, at their steady-state values. But it is also not unusual to simulate a nonterminating system that has no steady-state phase. For example, if the rate of occurrence of events changes over time, the system can never reach a steady-state condition.

In order to understand the difference between the transient and steady-state properties of a discrete-event system we should define these terms more rigorously.

Let $s(t)$ be the state of the system at time t.

Let $P_s(t)$ be the probability that the system is in state s at time t.

The system is in steady state relative to state variable s when

$$\frac{dP_s(t)}{dt} = 0.$$

Otherwise, the system has not achieved steady state and is said to exhibit transient behavior.

In Chapter 5 this definition was applied to a steady-state queueing system, but the definition is more general and can be applied, in general, to all state variables in a discrete-event system. When the probability distribution of the state variable is no longer changing over time, then we say the state variable has reached steady state or, more correctly, reached its steady-state distribution.

To illustrate this definition with an example, let us consider the standard example of a single-server queueing system with exponential interarrival times and exponential service times (the $M/M/1$ model). The state of the system is completely described by $n(t)$, the number of customers in the system at time t. Figures 9.4 and 9.5 show $P_n(t)$ (for $n = 0$, 1, and 5) and $E[n(t)]$ when the customer arrival rate is 8.0 per hour and the service rate is 10.0 per hour. Although, technically, the steady-state probability distribution $P_n(\infty)$ is only an asymptotic limit; in a very short time the system, as measured by both $P_n(t)$ and $E[n(t)]$, is near steady-state behavior.

The term steady state can be misleading, suggesting the system becomes more tranquil, making fewer radical changes in its state. We should not be lulled into thinking the system settles down after a substantial period of operation. Although the state variable's probability distribution is stabilizing over time, the system is switching from state to state as actively in the steady-state phase as when it was in the transient phase. In fact, the variance of the state of the system is greater at steady state than during the transient

FIGURE 9.4 TRANSIENT PROBABILITIES FOR *M/M*/1 QUEUE

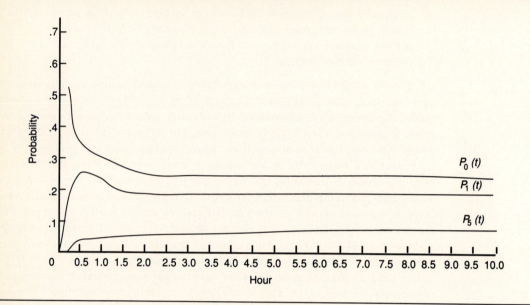

FIGURE 9.5 EXPECTED NUMBER IN SYSTEM FOR *M/M*/1 QUEUE

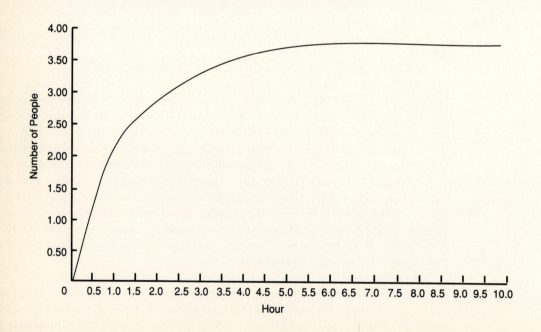

FIGURE 9.6   PROFILE OF NUMBER IN SYSTEM

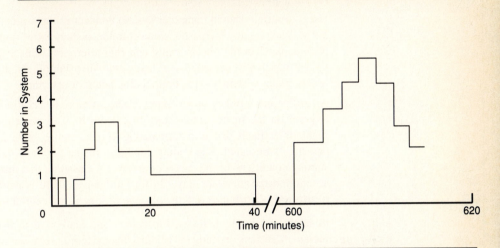

phase. Figure 9.6 shows a simulation of an *M/M/1* system during it's first 8 state transitions and 8 transitions after 10 hours of simulated time. We see that the system is changing states as rapidly during the steady-state phase as it is during its transient phase, the difference being that when the system is in steady state, the probability distribution of the states of the system is no longer changing.

Examples of systems that achieve steady state are:

1. A jobshop receives orders at a constant mean rate. Initially, in the simulation, the jobshop may have no jobs in process. The assumption is that the shop continues in operation indefinitely. This system is nonterminating and achieves a steady-state behavior.

2. A blood bank collects and stores blood, dispensing it to member hospitals as needed. Provided the demand for blood is uniform throughout the year, there will be a steady-state distribution of inventoried blood. The system is nonterminating.

3. Fares are collected at a set of toll booths at the entrance to a highway during the rush hour from (7 A.M. to 9 A.M.). If the intensity of the traffic does not change over the two hours, and the arrival rate is substantial, the system will pass through its transient phase very quickly and a steady-state analysis is appropriate, even though the simulation covers just a two-hour period. When analyzed in this fashion, the system is terminating and the terminating event is the conclusion of the rush hour period.

Examples of systems that will not achieve steady state are:

1. An urban walk-in health center schedules the number of physicians staffing the center to reflect the patient arrival pattern throughout the 24-hour day. Since the clinic is open continuously, this is a nonterminating simulation. The state variables in the system, however, can never reach a steady-state distribution since the mean

rate that patients arrive, and number of physicians on staff, are changing throughout the simulation.

2. Users of a time-shared computer system connect to the system between 8 A.M. and 5 P.M. The rate at which users connect to the system varies throughout the day, with peak demand in the mid-morning and mid-afternoon. This system is a terminating system which will not achieve a steady-state distribution, due to the varying demand for computer system and the limited nine hours of operation.

3. An airline has a policy of accepting 5 percent more reservations for seats than actually are on the plane, anticipating that some booked passengers will not show at flight time. Each day is a terminating epoch, ending with a random number of passengers unseated. The ending condition of the previous day does not affect the starting conditions of the succeeding day. (We assume that unseated passengers are accommodated the same day.) In this simulation there is neither a transient nor a steady-state distribution and the passage of time is not central to the simulation.

In summary, the methods used to collect and analyze data from a simulation of a discrete-event system depends on whether the system is terminating or nonterminating, and whether or not the distribution of the states of the system approaches a steady-state distribution. For either terminating or nonterminating systems, we may see transient behavior, steady-state behavior, or both. It is generally the case that in terminating simulations, we are interested in the transient behavior, but the terminating event may occur when the system is behaving nearly as it would in steady state. It is usually the case that in nonterminating simulations, we are interested in the steady-state behavior. Often, however, nonterminating systems never achieve a steady-state behavior. In the next section we consider methods of collecting and analyzing data from simulations of terminating systems, and in Section 9.6 we consider how data should be collected and analyzed when simulating a nonterminating system.

9.5   OUTPUT ANALYSIS FOR TERMINATING SYSTEMS

The most common method of estimating a characteristic of a system, using a simulation model, is to collect instances or samples of the characteristic as the simulation model executes. Once this data is collected we can use it to establish point and interval estimates of the characteristic. For example, if we wanted to estimate the mean time a customer waits in line in a bank, we could simulate the bank's customers arriving, waiting in line, and eventually being served, recording for several simulated days the amount of time each customer waited.

Before considering how this data should be analyzed, however, let us consider the properties of the two most commonly used point estimators: $\overline{X}$ the sample mean, and s the sample standard deviation.

For the sample $(x_i, \ i=1,2..n)$

$$\overline{X} = \sum_{i=1}^{n} x_i / n$$

$$s = \sqrt{\sum_{i=1}^{n} (x_i - \overline{X})^2 / (n-1)}\ .$$

It can be easily shown that if

$$E(x_i) = \mu \text{ for all } i \text{ then } E(X) = \mu.$$

Notice, that is not necessary that each x_i be an independent observation, but only that they all have a common expected value.

In order that

$$E(s^2) = \sigma^2,$$

however, it is necessary that each x_i have a common expected value and all x_i are independent.

For terminating simulations, the most commonly used method of insuring that the observations x_i are independent and have a common expected value is replication. That is, the simulation is executed a number of times, with each replication independent of the other replications. During the course of each simulation, observations are made at designated points in time or upon the occurrence of designated events.

It is often suggested in the simulation literature that an overall performance be accumulated over the course of each replication of the simulation, ignoring the behavior of the system at intermediate points in the simulation. We believe this is too simple an approach to collecting statistics when simulating a terminating system. It reminds us of the statistician who had his head in the refrigerator and feet in the oven, commenting that on the average he was quite comfortable. Typically, the characteristics and behavior of a terminating system are different during the initial phase of any epoch than at the end of the epoch. For example, in a queueing system, the first few arrivals would expect to experience shorter waits than later arrivals. For this reason, we suggest that intermediate statistics be accumulated when simulating terminating systems. If we must characterize the performance or nature of the system with a single measure, we may well use the overall performance measure, but it would be short-sighted to fail to collect statistics on the system at intermediate points in the simulation.

For a simulation replicated R times, with K intermediate observations in each simulation let

$$x_{ij} = j\text{th observation on the } i\text{th replication,}$$

where

$$i=1,2...R \text{ and } j=1,2...K$$

and let

$$y_i = \text{some overall performance measure during } i\text{th replication.}$$

Then

$$\overline{X}_j = \sum_{i=1}^{R} x_{ij}/R \qquad j=1,2,...K, \tag{9.5}$$

$$\overline{Y} = \sum_{i=1}^{R} y_i/R, \tag{9.6}$$

$$s_j^2 = \sum_{i=1}^{R} (x_{ij} - \overline{X}_j)^2/(R-1) \tag{9.7}$$

and

$$s_y^2 = \sum_{i=1}^{R}(y_i - \overline{Y})^2/(R-1). \tag{9.8}$$

For example, in the ith simulation of a queueing system, we would measure the waiting time of an arriving customer at each of K different time points, x_{ij}, and Y_i, the overall waiting time of all customers arriving during the simulation.

We now have independent and unbiased estimates of the expected value and variance of the system's performance at K different points in time, as well as an unbiased estimate of the mean and variance of the overall performance measure. Notice, however, that we cannot conclude that Y_i and the set $\{X_i\}$ are independent.

Once the mean and point estimators have been established using equations (9.5) through (9.8), we can set approximate confidence intervals for $E(x_{ij})$ and $E(y_i)$ using

$$P(\mu_j = \overline{X}_j \pm t_{\alpha/2,(R-1)}\, s_j/\sqrt{R}\,) = 1 - \alpha \tag{9.9}$$

and

$$P(\mu_Y = \overline{Y} \pm t_{\alpha/2,(R-1)}\, s_y/\sqrt{R}\,) = 1 - \alpha.$$

The half width of the confidence interval is

$$I = t_{\alpha/2,(R-1)}\, s/\sqrt{R} \tag{9.10}$$

and indicates how accurately we have estimated the performance measure in question.

These confidence intervals are approximate intervals since they are based on the assumption that x_{ij} and y_i are normally distributed. If this is not true, the precision of the confidence interval may not be $(1-\alpha)$. From the central limit theorem, however, we know that as the number of replications increases, the sample means become more and more normally distributed.

ILLUSTRATIVE PROBLEM 9.1

As a first example of setting point and interval estimates, let us consider a simulation of the classic $M/M/1$ queueing system. In this simulation we assume that the arrival rate is 10 arrivals per hour and the mean service time is 4.8 minutes (a service rate of 12.5 per hour), resulting in a traffic intensity of .80. Since the behavior of the $M/M/1$ queueing system is well understood, we can compare our estimates of the mean waiting times to the true values.

Table 9.2 shows x_{ij}, the sample waiting times for the customers, arriving immediately after hour 1,2,...8, and Y_i, the average waiting time for all customers, for each of 25 replications. Using the data in Table 9.2 and equations (9.5) through (9.9) we can set point estimates and 95 percent confidence intervals on the expected times customers will wait in the queue. These point and interval estimates are shown in Table 9.3. In this table the confidence interval is expressed in terms of its half width, I and the resulting lower-limit $(\overline{W} - I)$ and upper-limit $(\overline{W} + I)$. Fig. 9.7 shows how well the confidence intervals enclose the expected waiting times. The width of the confidence intervals will, of course, get smaller as we increase the number of replications.

TABLE 9.2
WAITING TIMES FOR 25 REPLICATIONS OF AN M/M/1 QUEUEING SYSTEM ($\rho = 0.8$)

Rpl	X_{i1} Hour 1	X_{i2} Hour 2	X_{i3} Hour 3	X_{i4} Hour 4	X_{i5} Hour 5	X_{i6} Hour 6	X_{i7} Hour 7	X_{i8} Hour 8	Y_i Overall
1	1.27	8.65	8.43	0	0	3.54	0	27.16	6.15
2	7.06	.82	0	0	24.06	0	15.81	35.3	11.36
3	.09	0	19.01	4.74	44.12	40.69	68.65	47.65	40.38
4	7.21	2.35	0	0	2.36	0	0	2.51	5.32
5	7.84	3.23	26.02	29.96	35.58	0	0	0	18.01
6	7.84	0	23.87	.85	0	2.61	6.58	0	8.38
7	0	0	6.51	0	0	.04	0	35.38	7.11
8	22.84	12.75	16.78	0	12.65	0	0	4.49	8.12
9	34.07	38.26	.58	13.02	0	0	0	1.37	13.67
10	0	0	13.25	0	19.46	2.89	0	0	7.56
11	9.79	2.91	0	0	0	0	0	76.87	10.73
12	0	0	0	2.6	0	0	0	0	3.86
13	0	0	21.19	4.61	0	0	34.17	.84	12.56
14	15.17	5.87	6.85	1.93	13.04	0	1.98	0	7.83
15	6.37	2.67	0	0	0	56.63	46.23	35.41	22.58
16	6.05	0	0	22.19	10.94	0	0	0	9.09
17	0	0	0	16.9	0	0	2.76	17.06	3.64
18	7.24	10.78	0	3.61	0	0	7.77	0	5.93
19	0	3.08	23.09	57.19	51.26	15.45	0	0	29.92
20	11.65	0	0	8.83	6.57	0	42.52	24.96	13.14
21	0	0	0	4.88	0	65.04	90.2	62.6	31.64
22	2.12	0	0	24.81	.44	0	0	0	4.03
23	13.07	12.57	28.79	0	0	0	34.08	0	10.42
24	7.14	0	18.08	27.95	20.26	0	15.68	23.22	16.91
25	16.82	0	1.97	54.29	30.55	6.31	0	34.92	19.43

TABLE 9.3
ANALYSIS OF 25 REPLICATIONS OF AN M/M/1 QUEUEING SYSTEM SIMULATION

	Hour 1	Hour 2	Hour 3	Hour 4	Hour 5	Hour 6	Hour 7	Hour 8	Overall
$\bar{X}_j$	07.34	04.95	08.57	12.33	10.85	07.72	14.65	17.18	13.11
s_j	08.31	09.05	10.26	17.09	15.40	18.14	24.46	22.26	09.42
I	03.42	03.72	04.22	07.04	06.34	07.47	10.07	09.17	03.88
$L\ lmt$	03.91	01.22	04.34	05.29	04.50	00.25	04.57	08.01	09.22
$U\ lmt$	10.77	08.68	12.80	19.37	17.19	15.20	24.73	26.36	16.99

FIGURE 9.7 CONFIDENCE INTERVALS: E(WAIT IN QUEUE)

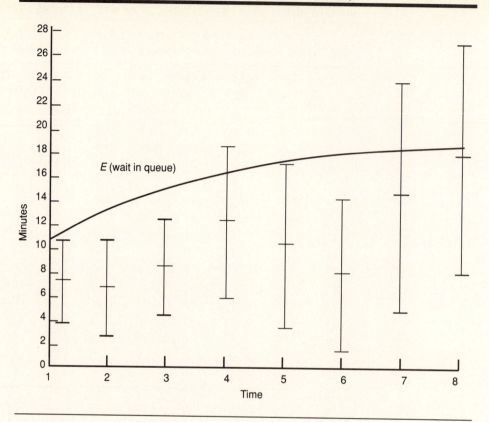

In Table 9.2, x_{ij} is the time the customer arriving at the jth hour, of the the ith simulation waited for service while y_i is the mean waiting time of all customers during the ith simulation.

A common misinterpretation of a confidence interval is that it sets probability limits on the value of the process. From the data in Table 9.3 we are 95 percent confident that the expected waiting time of a customer arriving at the first hour is 7.34 ± 3.42. This should not be interpreted as meaning that 95 percent of the customers arriving at the first hour will wait between 3.91 and 10.77 minutes. In order to state the probability that a customer will wait between 3.91 and 10.77 we need to know the probability distribution of the customer waiting times. Reliably estimating the probability distribution of a measure of a system typically requires a very large number of simulations, and is seldom done. If, however, we are willing to assume that the distribution of the random variable being estimated is unimodal, we can estimate with some confidence the variance of customer's waiting times, and then make use of the fact that for most random variables, 95 percent of the distribution is within two standard deviations of the mean. We should make such statements with caution, however, since it takes a considerable number of observations to reliably estimate the variance. In our example, a sample size of 25 obser-

FIGURE 9.8   TRUE VS. ESTIMATED STANDARD DEVIATION

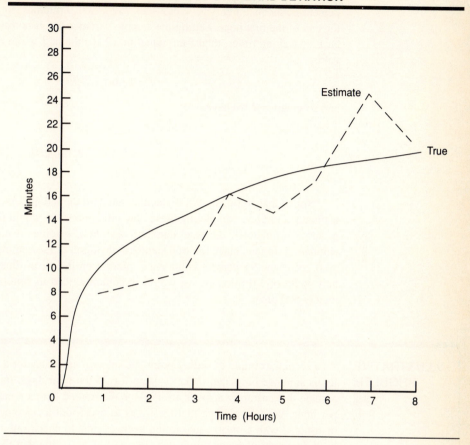

vations is not nearly large enough. As an illustration of the degree of error we can have in our estimates of the variance, Fig. 9.8 shows the actual and estimated standard deviation of waiting times for our 25 replications of an *M/M/1* queueing system simulation.

In this simulation we also collected statistics on the average waiting time of all customers who pass through the system. This statistic is the arithmetic mean of the waiting times for the first through last customer in the system. The statistic serves as an overall measure of the waiting time in the system, but does not represent any individual arrival. Notice that, although this statistic is based on 80 arrivals (on the average), as compared to a single arrival for the hourly points, its standard deviation is only reduced by about one-half. The explanation for this surprisingly small reduction in the standard deviation of the estimate, despite a sample 80 times larger, lies in the lack of independence between the successive observations that comprise the statistic.

In practice, this system should be simulated hundreds of times before drawing any firm conclusions about the mean and variance of the waiting times, or even the number of simulations needed to set confidence intervals with the intended half width. As a first guess at the number of simulations required to establish reasonable confidence intervals on mean waiting times, let us estimate the number of observations required to set a 95 percent confidence interval, with a half width of 1.0 minutes, for a customer arriving at the end of the first hour. Letting the sample variance act as an estimate for the true variance of waiting times, then from equation (9.10) the half width of the confidence interval is:

$$I = 1.96\sigma_{t=1}/\sqrt{R}$$

and solving for R we have

$$R = (1.96s/I)^2$$
$$= \{(1.96)(8.31)/1.0\}^2$$
$$= 265.$$

Notice that from Fig. 9.8 the actual standard deviation is much larger than our first estimate, and upon completing these 256 simulations we would most likely have a more accurate estimate of the true standard deviation, leading to more replications of the simulation. In fact, since the true standard deviation of the waiting time is approximately 13.0, to set the 95 percent confidence interval on the mean time a customer waits, at a half width of 1.0 minutes, we would in actuality need to simulate the system approximately 600 times.

ILLUSTRATIVE PROBLEM 9.2

As a second example of setting point and interval estimates for a terminating simulation, let us simulate our supermarket system for 25 ten-hour days. In this simulation we will assume that customer arrivals are Poisson distributed with a mean rate of 120 customers per hour. We will assume that the times to check out a customer's purchases is Erlang distributed with a mean equal to the average time to check out a single item, multiplied by the number of items purchased. We will also assume that the factor k of the Erlang distribution is equal to the number of items the customer purchases. In this example the average time to check out a single item is .1 minutes, and the number of items a customer purchases is Poisson distributed with a mean of 15 items. In addition to the checkout time, it takes an average of 20 seconds, exponentially distributed, to collect payment and make change. The supermarket being simulated has three regular checkouts and one express checkout which will be used only by customers with 12 or fewer purchases.

During the simulation we will gather observations on the times designated customers wait in line before being checked out, and also accumulate for each simulation the overall mean waiting time for all customers. In each replication, the customer arriving immediately after the jth hour will be designated as the customer to generate the observation x_{ij}, $i=1,2...25$ and $j=1,2...9$. Notice that since the simulation ends at exactly 10 hours, we cannot record the waiting time for a customer who arrives at exactly the 10th hour. A summary of the observations collected is shown in Table 9.4

In addition to estimating the mean time customers wait until being checked out, we can also estimate the probability that a customer has any wait in line.

TABLE 9.4
DATA GATHERED FROM 25 REPLICATIONS OF THE SUPERMARKET SIMULATION

Rpl.	Hr. 1	Hr. 2	Hr. 3	Hr. 4	Hr. 5	Hr. 6	Hr. 7	Hr. 8	Hr. 9	Overall
1	1.86	1.56	0	2.07	.89	4.55	2	1.93	1.53	2.17
2	2.19	4.26	3.81	10.69	8.86	0	0	4.19	5.46	2.63
3	0	3.83	2.1	0	1.11	4.71	1.51	0	.29	2.09
4	.27	4.94	2.16	1.5	.11	9.59	16.81	0	18.17	6.67
5	6.97	0	0	0	.47	0	0	1.47	.33	2.23
6	0	1.31	.75	8.79	1.33	11.86	11.19	15.22	16.63	6.80
7	0	2.85	0	0	17.91	1.92	.95	0	0	3.77
8	.74	.79	.4	.82	0	0	2.41	3.69	.91	2.12
9	1.05	0	8.42	7.78	1.67	4.4	3.13	4.07	6.96	2.93
10	1.37	2.41	0	0	10.31	1.17	8.84	18	7.39	5.06
11	6.28	2.89	0	0	2.85	4.72	0	0	2.29	2.16
12	6.71	1.89	.79	0	3.17	0	.85	0	0	2.04
13	1.69	0	4.67	1.8	3.93	8.3	1.28	0	.14	2.70
14	6.67	.68	3.94	12.12	0	1.5	2.15	0	0	2.72
15	2.30	.43	5.37	16.27	4.8	0	1.08	2.83	3.73	4.41
16	2.38	0	4.24	3.15	3.63	0	2.61	4.61	2.21	2.47
17	0	.16	7.59	0	5.15	0	2.57	.1	1.51	2.86
18	2.22	2.78	4.83	.5	10.28	0	0	1.59	1.52	3.44
19	0	3.24	4.29	.78	2	0	0	4.83	0	1.94
20	6.7	.52	3.52	0	5.32	0	0	2.31	0	3.34
21	0	0	0	3.55	0	11.27	2.6	5.07	2.42	3.17
22	5.82	15.71	12.88	13.58	17.87	.04	8.85	1.21	3.74	8.03
23	3.13	3.82	0	0	0	1.59	9.19	11.8	6.57	3.46
24	0	1.02	2.71	1.42	3.1	5.02	1.6	1.42	0	2.53
25	3.22	.18	.1	1.27	.47	2.2	0	0	2.36	2.16

Let

$$u_{ij} = \begin{cases} 1 & \text{if } x_{ij} > 0 \\ 0 & \text{if } x_{ij} = 0 \end{cases}$$

and

$$p_j = 1/25 \sum_{i=1}^{25} u_{ij} \qquad j = 1, 2 \ldots 9$$

Here u_{ij} will be 0 if the customer arriving at the jth hour of the ith simulation does not wait, and 1 if the customer does experience a wait. Then, p_j gives us an unbiased estimate of the probability that a customer arriving on the jth hour will have to wait in line.

TABLE 9.5
ANALYSIS OF 25 REPLICATIONS OF SUPERMARKET SIMULATION

	Hr. 1	Hr. 2	Hr. 3	Hr. 4	Hr. 5	Hr. 6	Hr. 7	Hr. 8	Hr. 9	Overall
$\bar{X}_i$	02.47	02.21	03.90	03.44	04.20	02.91	03.18	03.37	03.36	03.35
s_j	02.56	03.20	03.25	04.95	05.13	03.76	04.32	04.80	04.81	01.64
I	01.05	01.32	01.34	02.04	02.11	01.55	01.78	01.97	01.98	00.67
$L\ lmt$	01.41	00.88	01.56	01.40	02.09	01.36	01.40	01.39	01.38	02.67
$U\ lmt$	03.52	03.53	04.24	05.48	06.32	04.46	04.96	05.35	05.35	04.03
p	0.72	0.80	0.72	0.64	0.84	0.60	0.72	0.68	0.76	
I_p	0.18	0.16	0.18	0.19	0.14	0.19	0.18	0.18	0.17	

Note: I_p is the half width of the confidence interval on P (waiting).

In this simulation we do not have the advantage of an analytic model to test against our estimates of the mean time customers wait. Since u_{ij} is a binomial variable interval estimates for $E(p_j)$ can be established using

$$P(E(p_j) = p_j \pm z_{\alpha/2}\sqrt{p(1-p)/n}\,) = 1 - \alpha$$

Table 9.5 shows the point and interval estimates on the mean waiting times and probability that a customer waits. Notice that the sample variances are large and result in extremely wide confidence intervals. We can always reduce the size of the confidence interval by increasing the number of replications.

As in the case of the $M/M/1$ queueing simulation, notice that half width of the confidence interval, I, is smaller for the overall measure than I for a single sampling point, but not in proportion to the number of samples comprising the overall measure. During each replication only one sample was taken each hour, while the overall measure was based on the waiting times of approximately 1200 customers. Once more we see the effect of observations not being independent.

9.6 OUTPUT ANALYSIS FOR NONTERMINATING SYSTEMS

When analyzing the output of simulation models of nonterminating systems, we must deal with several problems which are not present in terminating simulations. These problems are:

Initial Condition Bias. The data collected during the early part of the simulation may be biased by the initial state of the system. The behavior of the system during this early phase of the simulation may be misleading, or irrelevant to the questions we expect the simulation model to answer.

Covariance between Samples. Groups or sets of data gathered during the simulation are generally not independent of one another. If the sample sets are not independent, our variance estimates will be biased.

Run Length. Although the system itself may be nonterminating, the simulation of the system must eventually be terminated. If we terminate the system too early, we may not have a representative simulation. For very complex systems, however, it is often impractical to make extremely long runs of the simulation model.

Our previous analysis of the *M/M/1* queueing system, in Section 9.4, illustrates these problems. From Fig. 9.2 we see that it can take several hours before the expected wait in the queue begins to level out to its steady-state value. In Fig. 9.5 we see that after 40 arrivals, the mean number in the system is approximately 3.5 while the steady-state expected number in the system is 4.0. Since the number of customers in the system can differ by only one, for two successive state changes, there is a strong covariance between successive observations on the state of the system. Finally, for our *M/M/1* queueing system, we have seen that the system never reaches the steady-state condition, but moves asymptotically toward steady state.

In this section we will present four commonly used methods for analyzing the output of a simulation model of a nonterminating system. These methods are:

1. Replication
2. Batching
3. Autocorrelation
4. Regeneration states

Each method has its own advantages and shortcomings. We will demonstrate the application of each of these methods, using the output of a simulation model of a blood bank inventory system.

ILLUSTRATIVE PROBLEM 9.3

A blood bank maintains an inventory of whole blood of a specific type. The blood is collected from voluntary donors, who come to the blood bank randomly, at the mean rate of two donors per day. Each donor contributes exactly one unit of blood (1 pint). The mean number of blood recipients is one per day and is also randomly distributed. Each recipient will request at least one unit of blood. The number of units requested after the first unit, is Poisson distributed with a mean of 1.0. Blood has a limited storage life and any blood that is older than 21 days cannot be used. The blood bank does not place an upper limit on the number of units kept in inventory, but lets the supply rise and fall by the random occurrence of donor and recipients. If the supply falls to zero, blood is obtained from a second source but at a considerable expense. The simulation model will estimate the average blood inventory, the mean number of units that become outdated each year, and the mean number of blood units that must be obtained from the second source each year. For a complete simulation model of this system see Section 4.6 of the SIMSCRIPT II.5 Primer in Appendix C.

9.6.1 THE METHOD OF REPLICATION

The output of a nonterminating simulation model can be analyzed using methods similar to those used for terminating simulations. For nonterminating simulations, however, we must avoid (or at least minimize) the effect of the initial conditions on the output of the model. The most common way of avoiding the effect of the initial conditions is to discard the observations gathered during the early phase of the simulation and use only data gathered when the system has reached a steady-state condition. Although in principle this is a relatively simple method, in practice a number of problems arise. First, we must have some way of deciding when to discard the start-up data and begin collecting the steady-state data. That is, we must decide when steady-state conditions begin. Secondly, the computational cost of discarding the data during the initial phase may be considerable. To illustrate these two problems, let us revisit the classic $M/M/1$ queueing system, using a unit interarrival time and an initial state of zero customers in the system. Fig. 9.9 shows the mean number of arrivals required before the expected wait in the queue reaches 70% of the steady state wait, as a function of traffic intensity ρ. Letting $E\left[w_q(t)\right]$ act as a surrogate measure of steady-state behavior, notice that for low traffic intensities, the system approaches steady state very quickly. On the other hand, when the traffic intensity is 0.95, we need to wait for over 4000 arrivals before the expected number in the system is within 70 percent of the steady-state value.

As a first example of using the replication method for a nonterminating simulation, we have simulated an $M/M/1$ queueing system with an arrival rate of 10 per hour and a mean service time of .08 hours (here ρ, or the traffic intensity, equals 0.80). In this simulation, statistics are gathered on the mean time customers wait in the queue during the first 50 hours and between the hours 50 through 500. After simulating 50 hours of operation of the system, the statistical counters in the model are reset and statistics are accumulated for an additional 450 hours of simulation time. When the statistical measures are reset, after 50 hours, the number of customers in the queue is also recorded. Table 9.6 shows the statistics collected for 25 replications. Notice that although the number of customers in the queue varied from 0 to 19, when the collection of steady-state statistics started, the mean number in the system was 3.84. For an $M/M/1$ queueing system, with ρ equal to 0.80, the expected number of customers in the system at steady state is 4.0. That is, after 50 arrivals, the mean number of customers in the system seems to be close to the

FIGURE 9.9   NUMBER OF ARRIVALS UNTIL $L(t) = 0.7L$

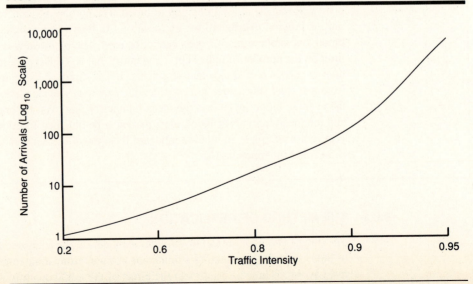

TABLE 9.6
NUMBER IN THE QUEUE AND WAITING TIMES FOR
25 REPLICATIONS OF *M/M/*1 QUEUE ($\rho = 0.8$)

Replication	$N_q(50)$	$W_q t < 50$	$W_q t > 50$
1	17	25.916	27.731
2	5	13.686	20.07
3	11	20.466	15.193
4	0	6.617	17.261
5	0	35.71	38.409
6	1	11.627	9.529
7	2	11.059	17.224
8	14	34.183	23.596
9	19	18.577	21.91
10	1	5.014	15.262
11	0	8.844	16.491
12	0	9.363	26.924
13	0	30.97	13.371
14	5	5.633	12.172
15	4	6.542	12.691
16	5	31.921	17.368
17	0	6.466	8.342
18	0	17.092	20.013
19	1	9.286	14.873
20	1	5.829	19.671
21	1	6.527	16.471
22	0	18.705	16.635
23	3	4.554	19.56
24	6	5.422	15.492
25	0	5.833	13.848
Mean	3.84	14.233	18.004
Std. Dev.	5.57	10.160	6.313

expected number in the queue during steady state. Based on these 25 replications we can set a confidence interval on the mean time a customer waits in the queue.

$$P(E(W_q) = \overline{W}_q \pm t_{\sigma/2,(n-1)} s / \sqrt{n}) = 1 - \alpha$$

or

$$P(E(\overline{W}_q) = 18.004 \pm (2.064)(6.313)/\sqrt{25}) = .95.$$

Thus, based on 25 replications, we can set a 95 percent confidence interval with a half width of 2.61. If a narrower interval is desired, more simulations will be needed.

More often than not, there is no analytic model to help us decide when the system is approaching steady state, but with some exploratory simulations, we may be able to find how long the simulation must run before the initial conditions no longer have a major effect on the state of the system. To illustrate the use of such exploratory simulations, we return to the blood bank simulation of Illustrative Problem 9.3.

ILLUSTRATIVE PROBLEM 9.4

Let us run the blood bank simulation model for 1000 days (approximately three years) recording the average inventory every 100 days. The results of two typical replications of the simulation and the average across 25 replications are plotted in Fig. 9.10. From these simulations it would appear that the system should be simulated for about 500 days before collecting statistics to estimate the steady-state properties of the blood bank.

Based on these exploratory simulations, the simulation of the blood bank is now replicated 20 times, (run length of 2000 days) discarding statistics gathered during the first 500 days, and then collecting statistics during the next 1500 days. The results of these 20 replications of the simulation are shown in Table 9.7.

Using these results we can set a 95 percent confidence interval on the average number of blood units on hand as well as the expected number of units short and outdated each year. For illustration purposes we will set a 95 percent confidence interval on the average number of units short per year. Based on a 1500-day simulation an unbiased estimate of the mean number of units short per year is

$$\text{Average short per year} = (365/1500) \text{ Average short per 1500 days}$$

And, since

$$\text{Variance(Shortage/Year} = (365/1500)^2 \text{ Variance(Shortage/1500 days)}$$

we will estimate the variance of the annual number of units short as

$$s_{365}^2 = (365/1500)^2 s_{1500}^2$$

If we assume that the distribution of the number of units short per year is normal, we can set a 95 percent confidence interval on units short per year using

$$\bar{X}_{\text{shortage/year}} = 14.13$$

$$S_{\text{shortage/year}}^2 = 1.20$$

$$P[E \text{ (annual units short)} = \bar{X} \pm t_{\alpha/2,(n-1)} s/\sqrt{n}] = .95.$$

or

$$P[E \text{ (annual units short)} = 14.13 \pm 2.093 \sqrt{1.2/20}\,] = .95.$$

9.6.2 THE METHOD OF BATCH MEANS

Two problems associated with the method of replication are the computational cost of repeating an initial warmup of the simulation and the uncertainty of the length of the transient phase. The batch method reduces, but does not eliminate, both of these problems. In the batch method, one long simulation is performed and we periodically record and then reset the statistical measures. These statistical resettings may be based on either

FIGURE 9.10   SIMULATION OF BLOOD BANK

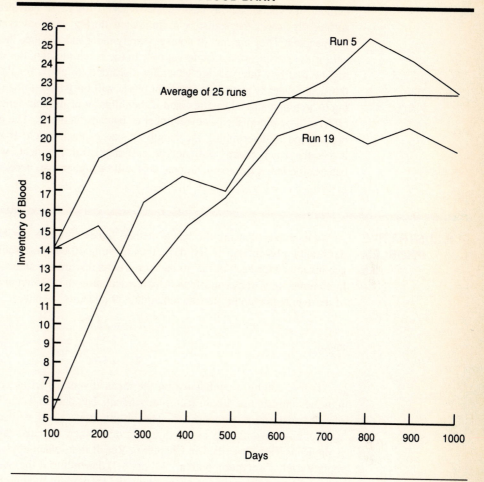

TABLE 9.7
STATISTICS FOR 20 REPLICATIONS OF BLOOD BANK SIMULATION

Measure	0—500 days	501—2000 days
Average inventory	21.186	21.047
Ending inventory	18.567	19.521
Std. dev. average inventory	6.230	2.435
Average units short	54.050	58.050
Std. dev. units short	6.411	4.501
Average units outdated	47.100	126.500
Std. dev. units outdated	31.520	57.517

the passage of a certain number of simulated units of time, or the occurrence of a certain number of events, such as customer arrivals. If the lapse between successive resets is sufficiently large, the statistics accumulated during each interval may be considered independent. They are not, of course, strictly independent since the ending state of interval i is the starting state of interval $i+1$. In the batch method, the statistics gathered during the first few intervals are generally discarded, to allow for the system to pass from transient to steady state. The transient phase will only have to be traversed once, resulting in a computational savings, and if the duration of the transient is underestimated, its effect will be diminished as the number of batches increases. The difficulty of the batching method is determining the length or size of each batch. If we select too small a batch, the batch means will not be sufficiently independent, while if we make the batches too large, the computational cost will be higher than necessary.

ILLUSTRATIVE PROBLEM 9.5

As an example of using the batch method let us simulate our blood bank for 20,000 days, with a batch size of 500 days, thus forming 40 batches. Table 9.8 shows the average inventory for each of the 40 batches. Let us discard the statistics from the first batch to eliminate any transient effects. Upon calculating the mean and the standard deviation of the average inventory for the remaining 39 intervals we have:

$$\bar{X}_{inv} = 22.22$$

and

$$S_{inv} = 5.74.$$

Before setting a confidence on the mean inventory let us consider what evidence indicates the batches are, in fact, independent. The data in Table 9.8 do not display any obvious patterns of dependence. The observations seem to oscillate back and forth without any obvious runs in one direction or another. A statistical test for independence is the Runs Test, described in Chapter 6. Recall that, when applying the Runs Test, we replace each observation with a "+" or "−" depending if the observation is greater (+) or less than (−) the previous observation and then count the number of runs, R, of "+" and "−." If the observations are independent then

$$E(R) = (2n-1)/3 \tag{9.11}$$

and

$$Var(R) = (16n - 29)/90.$$

With 40 observations $E(R) = 26.3$ and $Var(R) = 6.78$.

Transforming the observation to the signed runs we have

$$+ - + + + - - + + - + - + - + - - + - - + - + + + - + + - - + - + - + - + - + - -$$

or $R = 28$.

Forming the Z statistic we have

$$Z = \frac{R - E(R)}{\sigma_R}$$

$$Z = (28 - 26.3)/2.60 = .65.$$

Thus, based on the Runs Test, we can accept the hypothesis that the 40 observations are a sequence of independent random variables.

Since we can accept the hypothesis that the observations are independent, we may set a confidence interval on the expected number of units of blood in inventory. The 95 percent confidence interval is

$$P(\mu_{inventory} = \overline{X}_{inv} \pm t_{\alpha/2,(n-1)} s/\sqrt{n}) = 1-\alpha$$

or

$$P[\mu_{inventory} = 22.17 \pm (1.96)(5.68/\sqrt{39})] = .95$$

TABLE 9.8
BLOOD BANK SIMULATION BATCHED OUTPUT

Days	Avg. Inventory	Days	Avg. Inventory
500	15.57	10500	20.4
1000	17.70	11000	31.70
1500	13.42	11500	12.68
2000	20.02	12000	14.06
2500	28.58	12500	20.91
3000	29.06	13000	26.59
3500	26.54	13500	10.40
4000	17.72	14000	14.20
4500	26.92	14500	33.18
5000	27.70	15000	19.92
5500	18.11	15500	17.17
6000	20.23	16000	28.14
6500	18.99	16500	27.39
7000	21.66	17000	29.86
7500	17.02	17500	20.72
8000	24.38	18000	25.04
8500	20.31	18500	24.67
9000	17.81	19000	30.04
9500	25.75	19500	25.05
10000	23.04	20000	24.30

9.6.3 THE SEQUENTIAL BATCH METHOD

In order to reduce the half width of our confidence interval we need to either reduce the variance of our observations or increase the number of observations. We can increase the number of observations by either simulating the system for a longer period of time or by reducing the size of the batches. If we reduce the size of the batch, however, the batch means may not be statistically independent. The sequential batch procedure suggested by Law and Carson [4] attempts to determine the smallest batch size such that the adjacent batch means appear to be statistically independent. As a measure of the independence of adjacent batches they suggest using the lag correlation coefficient

$$p_1 = \sum_{i=1}^{L-1} [B_i - \bar{B}][B_{i+1} - \bar{B}] / \sum_{i=1}^{L} [B_i - B]^2 \tag{9.12}$$

where B_i is the mean of the ith batch $(i=1,2,...L)$ and

$$\bar{B} = \sum_{i=1}^{L} B_i / L.$$

To reduce the bias of p_1 they suggest using the jacknifed estimator

$$p_1' = 2p_1 - (p_1^1 + p_1^2)/2$$

where p_1^1 is calculated from equation (9.12), using only the first $L/2$ batch means while p_1^2 uses the last $L/2$ batch means.

To use the sequential batch procedure we iteratively:

1) Simulate the system until L batches of k observations are formed.

2) Using p_1', test if the batch means may be considered independent.

3) If the batch means appear to be independent set the confidence interval and if the width of the confidence interval is within the desired precision stop. Otherwise increase k, the batch size and go to step 1.

4) If the batch means do not appear to be independent increase k, the batch size. Go to step 1.

In this procedure, past observations are not discarded on each iteration. Rather, additional observations are added to the past observations. We then partition the observations according to the new batch size. We continue to increase the batch size, make additional observations, and then partition the observations into larger batches until the batches statistically appear to be independent and the confidence interval is small enough.

A specific implementation of this procedure, is suggested by Law and Carson [4]. In their implementation the number of batches remains constant while the size of the batches increases on each iteration. The batch size on the ith iteration is m_i/L where m_i is the total number of observations through the ith iteration. However, the final confidence interval is set by combining the m_i/L batches into n large batches.

1. Set $i=1$, $n=40$, $f=10$, $m_0=600$, $m_1=800$, $L=400$, $u=0.4$;
   Define $nf=L$ where $n=40$, $f=10$. (n and f are needed in step 5.)

2. Simulate until m_i observations are made. Divide the m_i observations into L batches of size k. Calculate p_1'.

3. If $p_1' > u$ go to step 6   {batches are not independent}
   else if $p_1' < 0$ go to step 5   {can set trial confidence interval}
   else go to step 4.

4. Divide the m_i observations into $L/2$ batches of size $2k$. Recalculate p_1'.
   If the new value of p_1' is less than the previous value of p_1' (found in step 2)
   go to step 5
   else go to step 6.

(Note: In this step we are checking if doubling the batch size decreases the lag correlation.)

5. Divide the m_i observations into n batches of size m_i/n. Calculate

$$s_B^2 = \sum_{i=1}^{n}(B_i - \bar{B})^2/(n-1)$$

and set a confidence interval with half width of

$$t_{\alpha/2,(n-1)}s_B/\sqrt{n}$$

If the confidence interval is within the desired precision stop,
otherwise go to step 6.
(Note: In this step we are increasing the batch size by a factor of f and reducing the number of batches by a factor of f. That is, when we set the final confidence interval we will have 40 batches and each batch will be $10L$ in size.)

6. Increment i; Set $m_i = 2m_{i-2}$
Go to step 2.
(Note: When returning to step 2 only $m_i - m_{i-1}$ new observations will be necessary.)

In the above algorithm we would sample as follows

Sequence	m_i	Batch Size for p'ₗ (m_i/L)	Batch Size for Confidence Interval (m_i/n)
1	800	2	20
2	1200	3	30
3	1600	4	40
4	2400	6	60
5	3200	8	80
6	4800	12	120
7	6400	16	160
8	9600	24	240
9	12800	32	320
	etc.		

9.6.4   AUTOCORRELATION METHODS

While batch methods attempt to reduce or eliminate the correlation between adjacent samples, auto correlation methods include the effect of correlation between observations to estimate the variance of the process being simulated.

Recall that for a sequence of random variables, $\{X_1,X_2...X_n\}$, the definition of covariance is

$$\text{Cov}(X_i,X_j) = E[(\bar{X}_i - E(X_i))(\bar{X}_j - E(X_j))] \qquad i,j=1,2...n$$

and if $i=j$ then

$$\text{Cov}(X_iX_j) = \text{Var}(X_i)$$

Throughout this section we will assume that the process being simulated is mean stationary and covariance stationary. That is

$$U = E(X_i),$$

$$\text{Var}(X) = \text{Var}(X_i) \qquad \text{all } i$$

and

$$\text{Cov}(X_i, X_{i+k}) = \text{Cov}(X_j, X_{j+k}) \qquad \text{for all } i, j.$$

That is, all observations have a common mean and variance and the covariance between any two observations, in the sequence of observations, depends only on their separation in the sequence and not upon their position in sequence.

In the previous section we defined the lag 1 correlation coefficient. Let us now make a more general definition of the lag k covariance for a covariance stationary process. The lag k covariance is

$$R_k = \text{Cov}(X_i, X_{i+k}) \text{ for } \qquad 0 \le k \le n-1$$

Notice that by this definition

$$\text{Var}(X) = R_0.$$

To understand how covariance is incorporated into our estimate of the variance, consider the expression for the mean of n batches

$$\bar{\bar{X}} = \sum_{i=1}^{n} \bar{X}_i / n$$

where $\bar{X}_i$ is the mean of the ith batch. Then

$$\mu = E(\bar{X})$$

and

$$\text{Var}(\bar{\bar{X}}) = E(\sum_{i=1}^{n} \bar{X}_i / n - \mu)^2$$

$$= E[\sum_{i=1}^{n} (\bar{X}_i / n - \mu) \sum_{i=1}^{n} (\bar{X}_i / n - \mu)] / n^2$$

$$= E[\sum_{i=1}^{n} \sum_{j=1}^{n} (\bar{X}_i - \mu)(\bar{X}_j - \mu)] / n^2$$

$$= [n \text{Var}(\bar{X}) + \sum_{\substack{i=1 \\ i \ne j}}^{n} \sum_{j=1}^{n} \text{Cov}(\bar{X}_i, \bar{X}_j)] / n^2. \qquad (9.13)$$

but since we are assuming the process is covariance stationary, the last equation can be reduced, with some effort, to

$$\text{Var}(\bar{X}) = \frac{1}{n} R_0 + 2 \sum_{k=1}^{n-1} (1 - k/n) R_k \qquad (9.14)$$

Most commonly, R_k gets smaller as k increases and in practice only the first few terms in the sequence are used. A common practice is to include only the first s terms which are significantly different from 0.0. To estimate R_k we substitute for μ the batch mean, $\bar{X}$, and let

$$R_k = \sum_{i=1}^{n-k} [(\overline{X}_i - \overline{X})\,(\overline{X}_{i+k} - \overline{X})]/(n-k-1) \qquad k=0,1...n-1. \qquad (9.15)$$

Notice that $R_0 = s^2$.

As a test of the hypothesis that $E(R_i) = 0$ we can use the statistic

$$D_k = \sqrt{n}\; R_k/R_0. \qquad (9.16)$$

When $\overline{X}_i$, $\overline{X}_{i+k}$ are independent, D_k is normally distributed with mean 0 and variance 1.0 [3].

ILLUSTRATIVE PROBLEM 9.6

To demonstrate the use of covariance in establishing a confidence interval, let us simulate the blood bank for 3000 days collecting batch means every 100 days. Table 9.9 shows the 30 sample means, and Table 9.10 the covariance estimates, R_k, and the test statistic, D_k. Since the only significant lag covariance is at $k=1$ we will use only the first lag covariance term when estimating the variance of the mean inventory. That is

$$\text{Var}\,(\overline{X}) = R_0 + 2(1 - 1/30)R_1$$

$$= 102.195 + 2(1 - 1/30)54.00$$

$$= 206.595.$$

Thus, we can set a 95 percent confidence interval on the mean inventory of the blood bank using

$$P[E(\overline{X}) = \overline{X} \pm 1.96\sigma/\sqrt{n}] = .95$$

or

$$P[E(\overline{X}) = 16.027 \pm (1.96)\,\sqrt{206.595}/\sqrt{30}] =$$

$$P[E(\overline{X}) = 16.027 \pm 5.143] = .95.$$

9.6.5   THE REGENERATIVE METHOD

Methods previously presented for estimating steady-state properties of a system attempted to eliminate the initial bias by discarding the statistics gathered during the initial warm-up stage and then continuing the simulation with the system in a more representative state. Using these methods, each batch mean is affected, of course, by the state of the system when the collection of data begins. For many queueing systems, the most probable state is the state with no customers present. If the collection of batch statistics is begun in the same state as when the simulation first started, the initial warm-up accomplished nothing.

TABLE 9.9
AVERAGE INVENTORY FOR INTERVALS OF 100 DAYS

Day	Average Inventory
100.	3.327
200.	12.242
300.	6.609
400.	4.783
500.	5.667
600.	8.926
700.	5.107
800.	10.513
900.	27.699
1000.	21.592
1100.	26.068
1200.	11.243
1300.	8.384
1400.	5.366
1500.	26.937
1600.	31.503
1700.	30.294
1800.	34.840
1900.	27.686
2000.	4.793
2100.	8.415
2200.	21.681
2300.	9.708
2400.	17.949
2500.	10.138
2600.	4.123
2700.	15.874
2800.	22.154
2900.	34.213
3000.	22.981
Average	16.027

The regenerative method avoids the problem of initial bias by using regeneration points. A regeneration point (sometimes referred to as a renewal point) is a system state in which the future behavior of the system is independent of the system's past history. It is not possible to identify regeneration points for every system, but when a system does have a regeneration point, it can be exploited to yield point and interval estimates of the system's properties. Examples of systems with regeneration points are:

SYSTEM	REGENERATION POINT
Queueing system with exponential Interarrivals	When there are no customers in the queue or in service.
Inventory system based on a fixed re-order point and re-order quantity.	When the inventory is restored to its maximum level.
Blood bank	When the inventory goes to zero.
An elevator in an office building	When the elevator returns to the main floor and no one is waiting.

To illustrate the use of the regenerative method consider Fig. 9.11 depicting a system changing states, and eventually returning to a state that is a regeneration point. The passage of the system from one regeneration point to another is a regeneration cycle. For the ith cycle let us use as an estimate the system's property X, the ratio of two random variables Y_i and T_i, such that

$$E(X) = E(Y)/E(T).$$

The choice of Y and T is dependent upon the property X that is to be estimated. Examples of X, Y and T for various systems are:

SYSTEM	X	Y	T
Queueing system	Mean customer waiting time	Total waiting time of all customers during cycle	No. of customers arriving in cycle
Queueing system	Mean number customers in the queue	Time integral of number customers in the queue	Length of cycle
Blood bank	Mean inventory	Time integral of inventory	Length of cycle

TABLE 9.10
LAG k COVARIANCE ESTIMATES AND TEST OF SIGNIFICANCE

k	R_k	D_k
0	102.195008	
1	54.005607	2.894 (significant at $\alpha = .01$)
2	15.743086	.843
3	−11.323526	− .606
4	−26.416090	−1.415
5	−14.880568	− .797
6	12.766665	.684
7	14.630002	.784
8	−15.301385	− .820
9	−18.515762	− .992
10	−20.180513	−1.081

FIGURE 9.11   REGENERATION CYCLES

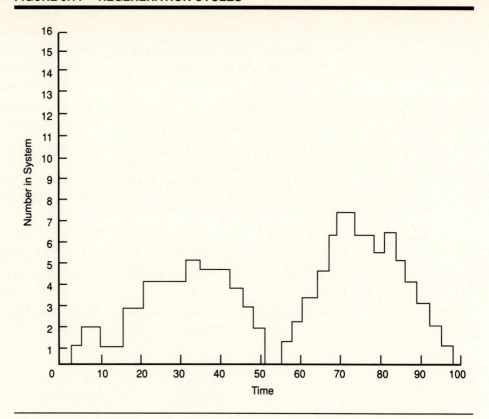

Let n = number of cycles observed,

$$Y = \sum_{i=1}^{n} Y_i / n$$

$$T = \sum_{i=1}^{n} T_i / n$$

and

$$\bar{X} = Y/T. \qquad (9.17)$$

Although $\bar{X}$ is, in most cases, a biased estimate of $E(X)$, under most conditions $\bar{X} \rightarrow E(X)$ as $n \rightarrow \infty$.

In order to set a confidence interval on $E(X)$ we must determine the variance of $\bar{X}$. The trick to finding the Var $(\bar{X})$ is to define a new variable

$$D_i = Y_i - E(X)T_i. \qquad (9.18)$$

Then

$$E(D) = 0$$

and

$$\text{Var}(D) = \text{Var}(Y) + E(X)^2 \text{Var}(T) - 2E(X)\,\text{Cov}(Y,T). \qquad (9.19)$$

The statistical ratio

$$t = D/\sqrt{\text{Var}(D)}/\sqrt{n} \qquad (9.20)$$

will approach a standard normal as $n \rightarrow \infty$. Then by substituting $D = Y - E(X)T$, in equation (9.20) and using our sample data for the n cycles to estimate Var (Y), Var (D) and Cov (Y,T), and dividing the ratio by T we have

$$\frac{\bar{X} - E(X)}{T\sqrt{\text{Var}(D)/n}} \rightarrow N(0,1). \qquad (9.21)$$

A confidence interval on $E(X)$ can be set using equation (9.20) as

$$P(E(X) = \bar{X} \pm z_{\alpha/2}/(\text{Var}(D)/n)^{1/2}). \qquad (9.22)$$

TABLE 9.11
FIFTY REGENERATIVE CYCLES FOR THE BLOOD BANK INVENTORY SIMULATION

Cycle	Cumulative Inventory	Cycle Length	Cycle	Cumulative Inventory	Cycle Length
1	18.881	6.754	26	215.728	30.385
2	187.094	24.416	27	.426	1.163
3	11509.231	337.683	28	23.304	5.320
4	.868	2.440	29	21.779	7.708
5	8.543	4.329	30	640.367	45.564
6	.918	.691	31	1.474	1.383
7	.164	.665	32	168.883	23.466
8	4.869	2.190	33	6.873	4.152
9	.016	.441	34	15.061	4.179
10	2.129	1.299	35	.536	1.612
11	.402	.555	36	1.338	.817
12	264.472	27.815	37	2.310	2.067
13	1.070	.933	38	.207	.209
14	1372.348	93.503	39	1.092	2.602
15	.911	1.338	40	6.858	4.410
16	6.741	2.045	41	1.611	1.257
17	1.147	1.773	42	6.363	3.779
18	.470	1.123	43	.990	.971
19	4.969	3.371	44	7.508	4.364
20	10.062	3.864	45	6.196	4.552
21	1351.671	61.555	46	2010.875	109.319
22	1.499	1.449	47	373.796	34.293
23	51.159	10.289	48	12.583	4.260
24	20.419	6.083	49	.128	.252
25	8.410	3.871	50	.964	.988

ILLUSTRATIVE
PROBLEM
9.7
To demonstrate the use of the regenerative method the blood bank inventory system is simulated for 50 cycles. For each cycle we measured the cumulative inventory (Y_i) and the length of each cycle (T_i). The data is shown in Table 9.11. Using this data we get

$$Y = 367.114$$

$$\text{Var}(Y) = 2,684,256$$

$$T = 17.991$$

$$\text{Var}(T) = 2,579$$

and

$$\text{Cov}(Y,T) = 81,070.$$

Using equation (9.19) we have

$$\text{Var}(D) = 449,394$$

and from equation (9.22)

$$P[E(X) = 20.40 \pm (1.96)(5.26)] = .95.$$

That is, after simulating the system for 50 cycles, across 900 days we set a confidence interval on expected inventory with half width of 10.31 blood units.

9.7 CONCLUSION

An important first step in the analysis of the output of a simulation model is identifying the questions the simulation model is expected to answer. Once we have a clear understanding of what answers the model is expected to provide we can correctly determine the data that is to be gatherd during the simulation and how the data should be analyzed.

The output of a simulation model requires careful analysis. Classical statistical techniques seldom directly apply. The observations collected during the simulation are often not independent nor time invariant. When analyzing the output of simulation models we must distinguish between terminating and nonterminating simulations, and between simulations that reach a steady-state condition versus simulation in which a steady-state condition cannot be achieved.

For terminating simulations, the model can be run a number of times, with each run being an independent observation. For nonterminating simulation, we must let the model warm up and pass through any transient conditions. We then collect the data in a manner that will allow us to establish point and interval estimates on the measures of performance needed to answer our questions concerning the system being simulated.

New statistical techniques for analyzing the output of simulation models are frequently published in simulation and statistics literature. We expect additional and more powerful methods of analyzing the output of simulation models will be developed. The current state of the art, however, requires that extensive runs of the simulation models be made before tight estimates of the system's characteristics can be established.

EXERCISES

9.1 Described below are five different systems. Classify each of these systems as terminating or nonterminating and as transient or steady state.

a) An investor takes out a loan and purchases an apartment building. He continues to hold the investment as long as the net income from the building (income less expenses and interest on the loan) is at least 15 percent of the building's current value. Although the building is increasing in value each year, the gross rental income and expenses increase each year as well. The investor is interested in knowing what his eventual return will be, using this policy. He is also interested in knowing how long he should expect to hold the investment.

b) At a busy street intersection there is a traffic control light that regulates the flow of traffic. During the week days, there is a heavy build up of traffic between the hours of 7 A.M. and 9 A.M. Cars approach the intersection from four directions and there is concern about the length of time automobiles wait at the intersection.

c) A restaurant is open from 6 P.M. to 12 P.M. for serving dinner. The restaurant is capable of seating up to 120 people. If no seats are available arriving customers either wait for a seat or decide to go elsewhere. The management is considering adding more tables to the restaurant.

d) A pharmacy stocks a medicine that is in low demand. Whenever the medicine is sold, a replacement order is made, to bring the inventory back to its previous level. It takes two to three weeks for the replacement order to arrive. The pharmacy would like to know how many units of the medicine should be kept in stock.

e) A local charity is putting on a "Las Vegas Night" and will run a roulette table. They must start the night with enough cash on hand to insure that no early winners "break the bank" but do not want to have an excessive amount of cash at the start of the evening. There is some history on the distribution of the sizes and kinds of bets gamblers will make.

9.2 In each of the examples in Exercise 9.1 state what statistical measures should be used in order that the simulation model can answer the relevant questions. Indicate also, what statistical methods should be used in analyzing the statistics and how interval and point estimations on the system's properties should be set.

9.3 Table 9.2 shows the waiting time of the customer arriving just after the jth hour.

a) Are the observations in any one column independent? Why?

b) Are observations across any one row independent? Why?

9.4 Using a Runs Test on the average inventory in the blood bank during each 100 day interval (Table 9.9), test the hypothesis that the average inventory during successive 100-day periods are independent random variables.

9.5 Listed below are the total minutes customers spent waiting in a queue for 30 regenerations and the length of each of the regeneration intervals. Using this data, set point and interval estimates on the mean time customers wait in the queue.

Cycle	Waiting Times	Length of Interval	Cycle	Waiting Times	Length of Interval
1	25.2	4.2	16	34.2	5.2
2	4.2	1.2	17	100.5	10.5
3	45.2	10.9	18	47.8	6.8
4	609.8	56.4	19	14.6	1.7
5	245.9	42.3	20	234.6	12.1
6	334.6	20.5	21	49.0	2.5
7	867.9	103.5	22	5.1	0.4
8	37.9	12.5	23	1008.9	102.3
9	2.1	1.2	24	0.1	1.1
10	775.6	94.2	25	345.7	11.2
11	23.1	1.7	26	55.8	3.8
12	84.2	5.6	27	765.4	15.2
13	9.2	1.2	28	51.4	4.9
14	37.6	2.8	29	77.7	5.1
15	443.0	177.6	30	2.1	.1

9.6 When using the regeneration method to estimate the mean and variance of the wait in a queueing system we form the ratio

$$V_i = W_i/T_i$$

where W_i is the total minutes of waiting time during the ith cycle and T_i is the length of the ith cycle. It is necessary that W_is are independent and that the T_is are independent. Using both the Runs Test and autocorrelation test, test this hypothesis of independence for the data in Exercise 9.5.

9.7 In a simulation of a bank, data was collected on the mean time customers waited for an available teller as well as the number of customers that had to wait for a teller. Listed below are the results of simulating the bank for 20 days.

Day	Aver. Wait	Number of Arrivals	No. that Waited	Day	Aver. Wait	Number of Arrivals	No. that Waited
1	3.4	100	10	11	5.6	120	13
2	5.5	89	21	12	9.2	133	43
3	6.7	105	15	13	13.2	112	31
4	9.2	115	20	14	10.2	99	12
5	5.5	85	6	15	33.2	135	46
6	6.5	113	11	16	12.3	110	12
7	3.4	116	9	17	14.3	115	10
8	6.9	93	9	18	21.2	124	16
9	5.0	103	12	19	25.1	127	26
10	5.9	119	9	20	24.2	132	31

a) Assuming that each day is an independent simulation of the bank, set point and interval estimates on the expected waiting time and probability that a customer waits.

b) Is there a relationship between the number of arrivals, the mean wait, and the number of customers who had to wait?

9.8 Show that if X_i, X_{i+k} are covariance stationary $[E(X_iX_{i+k})$ are equal for all $i]$ then

$$\mathrm{Var}\,(\bar{X}) = \frac{1}{n}R_0 + 2\sum_{k=1}^{n-1}(1-k/n)R_k.$$

9.9 The antithetic method of simulation takes advantage that if U is uniformly distributed between $(0,1)$, then $U^1 = 1 - U$ is also uniformly distributed between $(0,1)$. The system can be simulated first using the set of random numbers (U_i) and simulated again using the set $(1 - U_i)$.

a) Are the two simulations independent? Why?

b) How can the antithetic method be used to set confidence intervals on a performance measure.

Hint: Recall that $\mathrm{Var}\,(X+Y) = \mathrm{Var}\,(X) + \mathrm{Var}\,(Y) + 2\mathrm{Cov}(X,Y)$ and that X and Y may have a negative covariance.

c) Use the antithetic method to simulate a single-server queue and then set a confidence interval on the mean time customers wait, first using just the runs based on the set (U_i) and then the pairs of runs using (U_i) and $(1 - U_i)$.

9.10 In a simulation of a jobshop the average work-in-process during each week is recorded. Shown below are the results of a 30-week simulation:

$$\begin{array}{cccccccccc}
23.4, & 33.4, & 13.4, & 25.2, & 24.6, & 33.5, & 10.2, & 8.9, & 15.6, & 23.5 \\
14.3, & 15.6, & 55.8, & 45.6, & 33.6, & 28.9, & 20.8, & 19.2, & 24.6, & 21.6 \\
19.3, & 23.4, & 27.8, & 29.8, & 28.6, & 23.5, & 19.8, & 14.6, & 15.6, & 12.6
\end{array}$$

a) Use the appropriate statistical procedures for establishing a point and interval estimate of the mean work-in-process.

Hint: Are the observations independent? Can the data be combined to form two week or three week averages? How would this help?

9.11 Using the data in Table 9.8, with batch sizes of 2, then 3, then 4, then 6, use the sequential method to set point and confidence intervals on the mean inventory of the blood bank.

9.12 In Chapter 5 it was stated that $M/M/S$ queueing systems, which are series, act as independent processes if there is infinite storage between them. This is a surprising result since the output of one system is the input of the next system. Simulate a simple $M/M/1$ queueing system feeding its output to an $M/M/1$ queueing system. Let the arrival rate to the first system be 10.0 per hour and let the service time in both system 1 and system 2 be 7.5 minutes ($\rho = .80$).

a) Collect the appropriate statistics to test whether the two systems can be considered as independent systems.

b) Repeat this experiment but now let the customer arrival pattern be a constant 6.0 minutes between arrivals.

9.13 Consider the case of correlated random variables with

$$\text{Cov}\,(X_i, X_j) < 0.$$

a) How would this effect our confidence interval on $E(X)$ if we use

$$s^2 = \sum (\bar{X}_i - \bar{\bar{X}})^2 / (n-1)$$

as an estimate of the variance of $\bar{X}$?

b) Cite several examples of discrete-event systems where we would expect a negative covariance between successive observations of the measure of performance.

REFERENCES

1. Anderson, T.W., *The Statistical Analysis of Time Series*, Wiley, New York, 1971.

2. Crane, M.A. and A.J.Lemoine, *An Introduction to the Regenerative Method for Simulation Analysis*, Lecture Notes in Control and Information Systems, Springer-Verlag, New York, 1977.

3. Fishman, G. S., *Principles of Discrete Event Simulation*. Wiley, New York, 1978.

4. Law, A.M. and J.S. Carson, ''A Sequential Procedure for Determining the Length of a Steady State Simulation,'' *Oper. Res.* 27:1011-1025 (1979).

5. Lindgren, B.E., *Statistical Theory*, 3rd Edition, MacMillan Publishing Co., New York, 1976.

CHAPTER 10

MODEL EXPERIMENTATION AND OPTIMIZATION

Recent developments in user-friendly simulation languages which run on powerful microcomputers permit the functional expert, the person who really understands the intricacies of the problem, to build and experiment with a simulation model for alternative system designs. Adding graphical animation to observe the system in operation makes the results obtained even more impressive. However, as Jim Henriksen, a long-time simulation practitioner and simulation language designer cautions, "Watching cartoons on a screen is no substitute for good statistical work." Given the current state of the art of simulation languages, the sound statistical analysis must be provided by a human expert to ensure that valid conclusions are drawn from simulation results.

10.1 INTRODUCTION

The goal of any simulation analysis should be to provide the best possible system design given existing constraints on the decision variables. Since simulation models are descriptive rather than prescriptive, the quality of design achieved depends greatly on the skill of the analyst. No algorithms lead to guaranteed optimum solutions. In this chapter we present several approaches to evaluating alternative system designs, including some that seek, but do not guarantee, optimal solutions.

In evaluating any system design, we may be concerned with a single measure of performance or several measures. For example, we may wish to achieve an acceptable value for the single measures of performance, size of the inventory, or number of items backordered. But, in some instances we may wish to strive for both a small inventory and few backorders. The use of a single-performance measure is conceptually and methodologically simpler, and perhaps for those reasons, is the approach usually taken. We devote most of the chapter to single-performance measure techniques, including but one section to treat multiple measures.

We describe three techniques for evaluating system designs using a single measure of performance. To begin, we discuss the evaluation of a set of alternatives defined by varying one decision variable; for example, varying the number of checkout lanes open in a supermarket. Next, we present experimental design methods for varying several decision variables. System designs might be defined by varying both the number of checkout lanes open and the availability of baggers. Finally, we extend the notions of experimental design to permit systematic exploration of the solution space in an attempt to optimize the chosen measure of performance. For example, open checkout lanes and numbers of baggers might be varied in a fashion that leads to the best, or nearly the best, system design.

10.2 COMPARING GIVEN ALTERNATIVE SYSTEM DESIGNS

In this section we present ways of evaluating a set of alternative system designs defined by varying one decision variable. In so doing, we recognize that the best design in such a set may not be the optimal system design. This approach is defensible if the decision variables are constrained to a narrow range of values. We begin by comparing two alternative system designs and then extend these ideas to deal with several alternatives.

10.2.1   TWO SYSTEM DESIGNS

The comparison of two alternative system designs may arise in many settings: two levels of staffing for bank tellers, two possible queue disciplines, two re-order points for inventory replenishment, or two levels of investment in computer systems. In each case, we seek to determine if one design yields a better value for the selected performance measure than the other. Because simulation output is probabilistic in nature, this may not be immediately obvious. We must resort to statistical tests for significant differences to draw valid conclusions. It should be noted, however, that differences in system performance which are statistically significant may not be materially different.

If the statistical tests we use are to be valid, certain assumptions about the data to which we apply them must be satisfied. Perhaps the most important of these is statistical independence of the observations. The approaches to obtaining simulation output that satisfy these assumptions were discussed in Chapter 9. In all of the illustrative problems, it will be assumed that proper measures have been taken to obtain data appropriate for the chosen statistical analyses. We will focus in this chapter on the methods for system design comparisons.

If it is assumed that we have two sets of simulation output, one for each of the system designs to be evaluated, we may have three possible cases:

Case (1):   The two samples are independent and drawn from populations with equal variances

Case (2):   The samples are independent and drawn from populations with unequal variances

Case (3):   The samples are correlated and we analyze the differences between the two samples.

The first two cases require that the random number streams used in simulating the system designs be independent. But in the third case, the same stream of random numbers is used for both system designs.

To illustrate each of these approaches, we will return to the supermarket setting introduced in Chapter 2. Two system designs are considered: one provides an express checkout lane for customers with a small number of items, and one does not. Before providing the results of these evaluations, we will state the statistical analyses required in each of the three cases.

Independent Samples (Cases 1 and 2)   For the performance measure of interest, the simulation model output can provide two independent samples: $Y_{11}, Y_{21},...,Y_{n1}$ for design 1, and $Y_{12}, Y_{22},...,Y_{n2}$ for design 2. Each Y_{ij} represents the ith individual value of the performance measure for independent successive observations of the jth system design, or the ith value of some aggregate of the performance measure, say the mean, for independent successive replications of the jth system design. The samples are assumed to be the same size. To test the hypothesis that there is a significant difference between the two designs, we set a confidence interval on the difference in population means of the performance measures, $\mu_1 - \mu_2$. The confidence interval is calculated from differences in sample means, $\bar{Y}_1 - \bar{Y}_2$, as explained below.

Depending on the position of this confidence interval relative to zero, we may reach one of three possible conclusions:

1. the mean of population 1 is less than that of population 2
2. there is no significant difference between the means
3. the mean of population 1 is greater than that of population 2.

In Fig. 10.1 (a) the confidence interval is entirely to the left of zero. This shows substantial evidence for conclusion (1): $\mu_1 - \mu_2 < 0$, or equivalently, $\mu_1 < \mu_2$. Figure 10.1 (b) shows the confidence bracketing zero, which suggests conclusion (2): there is no strong statistical evidence μ_1 is different from μ_2. And in Figure 10.1 (c), the confidence interval appears entirely to the right of zero, which shows substantial evidence for conclusion (3): $\mu_1 - \mu_2 > 0$, or equivalently, $\mu_1 > \mu_2$.

To state the hypothesis test more formally:

$$H_0: \mu_1 - \mu_2 = 0$$

$$H_1: \mu_1 - \mu_2 \neq 0$$

The associated $(1 - \alpha)$ confidence interval is then:

$$\bar{Y}_{\cdot 1} - \bar{Y}_{\cdot 2} \pm t_{\alpha/2, v} s.d. (\bar{Y}_{\cdot 1} - \bar{Y}_{\cdot 2}) \tag{10.1}$$

where the sample means $\bar{Y}_{\cdot 1}$ and $\bar{Y}_{\cdot 2}$ are:

$$\bar{Y}_{\cdot 1} = 1/n \sum_{i=1}^{n} Y_{i1} \tag{10.2}$$

and

$$\bar{Y}_{\cdot 2} = 1/n \sum_{i=1}^{n} Y_{i2}$$

$s.d. (\bar{Y}_{\cdot 1} - \bar{Y}_{\cdot 2})$ is the standard deviation of the estimator of the difference in the parameters $\mu_1 - \mu_2$,

α is the level of significance of the test,

v is the degrees of freedom associated with the t distribution,

n is the sample size.

To calculate $s.d.(\bar{Y}_{\cdot 1} - \bar{Y}_{\cdot 2})$ we first observe that since these are two independent samples:

$$\text{Var} (\bar{Y}_{\cdot 1} - \bar{Y}_{\cdot 2}) = \text{Var} (\bar{Y}_{\cdot 1}) + \text{Var} (\bar{Y}_{\cdot 2}) \tag{10.3}$$

$$= \sigma_1^2/n + \sigma_2^2/n$$

Also, σ_j^2 can be estimated from the sample data as:

$$\hat{\sigma}_j^2 = s_j^2 = \sum_{i=1}^{n} (Y_{ij} - \bar{Y}_{\cdot j})^2/(n-1) \qquad j=1,2 \tag{10.4}$$

where s_j^2 is the sample variance.

Case 1: Samples with Equal Variances   If it can be reasonably assumed that $\sigma_1^2 = \sigma_2^2$, or if an appropriate F test confirms such a hypothesis, we can compute an estimate of $\sigma^2 = \sigma_1^2 = \sigma_2^2$ which pools the data from both samples as follows:

FIGURE 10.1   POSSIBLE CONFIDENCE INTERVAL OUTCOMES

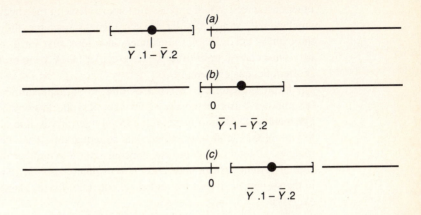

$$\hat{\sigma}^2 = s_p^2 = \frac{(n-1)s_1^2 + (n-1)s_2^2}{2n - 2} \tag{10.5}$$

which has $2n - 2$ degrees of freedom. Finally, rearranging equation (10.3) and substituting the pooled estimate, s_p^2, of the common σ_j^2, we have:

$$\text{Var } (\bar{Y}_{\cdot 1} - \bar{Y}_{\cdot 2}) = 2\sigma^2/n$$

$$= 2s_p^2/n \tag{10.6}$$

$$s.d.(\bar{Y}_{\cdot 1} - \bar{Y}_{\cdot 2}) = s_p \sqrt{2/n}$$

Case 2: Samples with Unequal Variances   If our assumption of equality of variances is not reasonable, or is explicitly rejected by a hypothesis test, then we cannot pool the sample variances to obtain a single estimate of σ^2. The appropriate calculation is then:

$$s.d.(\bar{Y}_{\cdot 1} - \bar{Y}_{\cdot 2}) = \sqrt{(s_1^2 + s_2^2)/n} \tag{10.7}$$

The degrees of freedom for the t distribution, as given by Natrella [15], are approximately:

$$v = \frac{((s_1^2 + s_2^2)/n)^2}{([s_1^2/n]^2 + [s_2^2/n]^2)/(n+1)} - 2 \tag{10.8}$$

The appropriate confidence interval is computed using equation (10.1) and this value of v.

ILLUSTRATIVE
PROBLEM
10.1

This example assesses the difference between two system designs by using the simulation model to generate independent samples for the performance measures.

    Two alternative checkout lane configurations are being considered for a small supermarket: all three checkout lanes available to all customers, or one checkout lane for express customers, those with six or fewer items, and the remaining two lanes for all other customers. When express customers arrive at the checkout lanes, they first look for any lane with an idle cashier. If such a lane is available, they use it. Otherwise they go to the express lane. Regular customers also look first for a lane with an idle cashier, but they must choose only from the two regular lanes. If no cashier is idle, the lane with the shorter queue is chosen.

Express customers arrive according to an exponential distribution with a mean of 0.8 minutes between successive arrivals. Regular customers also arrive according to an exponential distribution, but with a mean interrarival time of 3.1 minutes. Shoppers with few purchases tend to dominate this supermarket. The checkout time per item is 0.17 minutes, so total checkout time depends upon the number of purchases made. The measure of system performance chosen to evaluate these design alternatives is the total time in the system (waiting time and checkout time) for all classes of customers (regular and express).

Ten independent sample values for the mean total time in the system were obtained by producing replications of the simulation model for 10-hour days. An initialization period of 1 hour was used. The results of the runs appear in Table 10.1.

It is fairly clear from these results that an assumption of equal variance for the two populations would not be a good one. Therefore, we will use the procedure for unequal variance in the analysis.

To test the null hypothesis that there is no difference in the performance of the two designs, we must form the confidence interval of equation (10.1).

$\bar{Y}_{.1} - \bar{Y}_{.2}$ is easily calculated as: $14.86 - 9.16 = 5.7$.

The standard deviation of $\bar{Y}_{.1} - \bar{Y}_{.2}$ is calculated from equation (10.7) as:

$$s.d.(\bar{Y}_{.1} - \bar{Y}_{.2}) = \sqrt{(49.14 + 11.97)/10} = 2.47$$

The degrees of freedom for the associated t distribution given by equation (10.8) are:

$$v = \frac{[(49.14 + 11.97)/10]^2}{[(49.14/10)^2 + (11.97/10)^2]/11} - 2 = 14.09$$

Thus, the required confidence interval for $\alpha = .05$ and 14 degrees of freedom is:

$$5.7 \pm t_{(.025,14)}\, 2.47 = 5.7 \pm (2.145) \cdot (2.47) = 5.7 \pm 5.30$$

or

$$0.40 \text{ to } 11.00$$

Since the confidence interval does not include zero, we must reject the null hypothesis. Indeed, the entire confidence interval is to the right of zero which suggests that design 1 (no express lane) yields a significantly larger mean time spent in the system than design 2 (one express lane). Therefore, design 2 provides better service for all classes of customers.

Correlated Samples (Case 3)   The desirable effect of using positively, correlated samples is to reduce the variance of the difference, $Y_{.1} - Y_{.2}$. If this can be achieved, the

TABLE 10.1
COMPARATIVE RESULTS FOR TWO SUPERMARKET CHECKOUT
LANE DESIGNS USING INDEPENDENT SAMPLES

| | Mean Total Time in the System (Minutes) | |
| | Design 1: | Design 2: |
Replication	No Express Lane	One Express Lane
1	7.27	5.75
2	20.09	12.79
3	18.60	11.44
4	19.80	9.73
5	7.14	4.16
6	29.17	14.95
7	12.87	10.34
8	11.40	7.64
9	13.40	9.55
10	8.81	5.29
Sample Mean	14.86	9.16
Sample Variance	49.14	11.97
Sample S.D.	7.01	3.46

width of the associated confidence interval will also be reduced, thus providing a more sensitive hypothesis test. The correlation coefficient r_{12}, for Y_{i1} and Y_{i2}, which indicates the degree to which they behave similarly, is useful in this effort.

In general, the variance of the difference may be written as

$$\text{Var}\,(\bar{Y}_{\cdot1} - \bar{Y}_{\cdot2}) = \text{Var}\,(\bar{Y}_{\cdot1}) + \text{Var}\,(\bar{Y}_{\cdot2}) - 2 \cdot \text{Cov}(\bar{Y}_{\cdot1},\bar{Y}_{\cdot2}) \tag{10.9}$$

which may be expressed as

$$\text{Var}\,(\bar{Y}_{\cdot1} - \bar{Y}_{\cdot2}) = \frac{\sigma_1^2}{n} + \frac{\sigma_2^2}{n} - \frac{2r_{12}\sigma_1\sigma_2}{n} \tag{10.10}$$

since

$$r_{12} = \text{Cov}\,(Y_{i1},Y_{i2})/\sigma_1\sigma_2$$

and

$$\text{Cov}\,(\bar{Y}_{\cdot1},\bar{Y}_{\cdot2}) = \text{Cov}\,(Y_{i1},Y_{i2})/n$$

Compare the estimate of the variance of the difference in performance measures of equation (10.10) with that computed for independent samples in equation (10.3). We see that the variance for correlated samples must be smaller, if indeed we achieved the desired positive correlation between the two sets of output. To state this more concisely, let V_i be the variance of the difference for independent samples, and V_c the variance for correlated samples. Then

$$V_c = V_i - 2r_{12}\sigma_1\sigma_2/n \tag{10.11}$$

And, since $r_{12} > 0$

$$V_c < V_i \tag{10.12}$$

Thus we can obtain a more sensitive hypothesis test without the cost of additional model output.

To compute the confidence interval needed for the hypothesis test of differences between designs, we must define a new random variable,

$$D_i = Y_{i1} - Y_{i2}$$

where Y_{i1} and Y_{i2} are positively correlated, and D_i are independent random variables. The means of achieving this is described in the following paragraph. We may then calculate the required confidence interval as follows.

First, we compute the mean of the differences as:

$$\overline{D} = 1/n \sum_{i=1}^{n} D_i$$

or

$$\overline{D} = \overline{Y}_{\cdot 1} - \overline{Y}_{\cdot 2} \tag{10.13}$$

To compute the required standard deviation of $\overline{D}$, we first compute the variance and standard deviation of D_i as follows:

$$\text{Var}(D_i) = 1/(n-1) \sum_{i=1}^{n} (D_i - \overline{D})^2 \tag{10.14}$$

Then, the required variance and standard deviation for $\overline{D}$ are:

$$\text{Var}(\overline{D}) = \text{Var}(D_i)/n \tag{10.15}$$

and

$$s.d.(\overline{D}) = \sqrt{\text{Var}(D_i)/n} = \sqrt{1/(n-1)\sum_{i=1}^{n}(D_i - \overline{D})^2/n}$$

So, to test the hypothesis:

$$H_0: \mu_1 - \mu_2 = 0$$

$$H_1: \mu_1 - \mu_2 \neq 0$$

the required $(1 - \alpha)$ confidence interval with $n - 1$ degrees of freedom is:

$$\overline{D} \pm t_{\alpha/2,(n-1)} \; s.d.(\overline{D}) \tag{10.16}$$

One strategy to achieve positively correlated samples is to use identical streams of random numbers in the simulation of each of the system designs. If this is done, then Y_{11}, the value of the performance measure of the first replication of design 1, and Y_{12}, the value for the first replication of design 2, may no longer be independent, but may become correlated. If Y_{11} is a waiting time above the mean for system design 1, then Y_{12} should be above the mean for design 2. Similarly, all pairs of (Y_{i1}, Y_{i2}) are correlated. However, note that Y_{11} is correlated with only Y_{12} and independent of all other observations. This is similarly true for all Y_{ij}.

Unfortunately, the use of common random number streams alone does not guarantee the desired positive correlation between two model runs. Further, the implementation of common random numbers is model-dependent. However, some guidelines can be provided for the use of random number streams which will assist in synchronizing events, and thereby make positive correlation more likely. Useful hints from Banks and Carson [2] are summarized below.

- Devote a given random number stream to a specific purpose in the model, using as many streams as needed. For example, use a separate stream for each type of customer arriving and still another set for the service times of each type.

- Each entity arriving causes the random interval between it and the next arrival to be generated. And, all necessary random attributes for the entity are immediately generated and associated with it. For example, customers of three types arrive at a bank; each arrival causes the random interval until the next arrival to be computed. The customer type and service time are determined and affixed to the entity for use later in the model. Each customer type has dedicated random number streams for interarrival times and service times.

- Systems with entities performing in cyclic fashion should have a separate random number stream assigned to each such entity. Machines that alternate between an operating status and a down status are examples of this circumstance.

- When synchronization such as that described above is not possible for some part of the two model runs, independent streams of random numbers should be used for these variates.

ILLUSTRATIVE PROBLEM 10.2 In this problem, we revisit the setting of the previous example and conduct the same analysis using the simulation model to produce correlated samples of the performance measure.

Ten correlated sample values for the mean total time in the system were obtained from replications of the simulation model. A common random number stream was used for both system designs; all random events were generated from that stream. No particular attempt at synchronization such as those described above was made.

As in Illustrative Problem 10.1, ten replications using 10-hour days were produced, and an initialization period of 1 hour was used. The results of the runs appear in Table 10.2.

To test the hypothesis that there is no difference in the performance of the two designs, we form the confidence interval of equation (10.16).

The value of $\overline{D}$ is given in Table 10.2, and $s.d.(\overline{D})$ is calculated from equation (10.15) as: $\sqrt{25.60/10} = 1.60$. The required confidence interval for $\alpha = .05$ with 9 degrees of freedom is then:

$$6.29 \pm t_{(.025,9)}\ 1.60 = 6.29 \pm (2.262) \cdot (1.60) = 6.29 \pm 3.62$$

or

$$2.67 \text{ to } 9.91$$

Since the confidence interval lies entirely to the right of zero, we again conclude that design 1 (no express lane) has significantly greater customer time spent in the system than design 2 (one express lane). But notice that the width of the confidence interval is 7.24 compared with the interval width for the independent samples of 10.6. Thus we have a more precise estimate of our measure of performance. Or, we could have achieved the same level of precision as the independent sample analysis using fewer replications and correlated samples.

TABLE 10.2
COMPARATIVE RESULTS FOR TWO SUPERMARKET CHECKOUT LANE DESIGNS USING CORRELATED SAMPLES

Replication	Mean Total Time in the System (Minutes)		
	Design 1: No Express Lane	Design 2: One Express Lane	Time Differences
1	9.49	5.81	3.68
2	22.40	11.10	11.30
3	9.24	6.16	3.08
4	15.25	12.45	2.80
5	26.58	11.14	15.44
6	30.97	17.72	13.25
7	6.67	5.13	1.54
8	11.04	7.58	3.46
9	16.28	10.62	5.66
10	13.70	11.03	2.67
Sample Mean	16.16	9.87	6.29
Sample Variance	64.71	14.59	25.60
Sample S.D.	8.04	3.82	5.06

10.2.2   MANY SYSTEM DESIGNS

The extension of comparison of two system designs to comparison of many designs is made possible by relaxed constraints on the decision variables. For example, the analyst may now consider several levels of staffing for bank tellers, or many possible inventory re-order points. With this increased freedom to explore alternative system designs comes increased complexity.

A pair of system designs presents only one possible comparison, while four alternative designs yield six possible pairs to evaluate: a six-fold increase in comparisons for a doubling of alternatives. In general, N alternative designs require $N(N-1)/2$ comparisons. This not only adds to the number of simulation runs that must be made, but also presents some statistical complications as to the precision of parameter estimates. Consequently, we must choose our system design alternatives judiciously.

One way to reduce the number of comparisons required is to compare alternatives to some standard, such as the existing system. If this is done, the number of comparisons necessary increases only linearly: N alternative designs yields N comparisons. We will describe a method that works for pairwise comparisons in general, whether for all possible pairs or for pairs against a standard.

When we make multiple comparisons of system designs, we must test statistical hypotheses of the form:

$$H_0: \mu_i - \mu_j = 0,$$

where μ_i and μ_j are the population means of the performance measures for design i and j, respectively. The simultaneous testing of several hypotheses causes the overall level of significance for the tests to decrease as we increase the number of hypotheses tested.

Stated another way, the probability, α, of a Type *I* error (i.e., rejecting a true hypothesis) increases as the number of tests increases.

The Bonferroni inequality provides a way of estimating the overall significance of several simultaneous hypothesis tests [10]. We first develop the inequality for any set of simultaneous statements and then apply it to the test of hypotheses using confidence intervals.

Let there be m statements, $S_1, S_2, \dots S_m$, each with a Probability, α_i, of being incorrect. Then:

$$P(\text{one or more statements being incorrect}) \leq \sum_{i=1}^{m} \alpha_i \qquad (10.17)$$

If we define P (one or more statements being incorrect) to be α_E, the overall error probability, the Bonferroni inequality places an upper bound on α_E which may be stated as:

$$\alpha_E \leq \sum_{i=1}^{m} \alpha_i \qquad (10.18)$$

How is this conclusion justified? The case for two statements is first stated and then generalized to m statements. Consider the Venn diagram shown in Fig. 10.2 for two events, which may not be independent, where A_1 is the event S_1 is incorrect or false, and A_2 is the event S_2 is incorrect or false. The associated error probabilities are α_1 and α_2.
Then:

$$P(A_1 \cup A_2) = P(A_1) + P(A_2) - P(A_1 \cap A_2) \qquad (10.19)$$

If A_1 and A_2 are independent,

$$P(A_1 \cap A_2) = P(A_1) \cdot P(A_2)$$

and $P(A_1 \cup A_2)$ may be computed exactly. However, if the two events are not independent, we may state:

$$P(A_1 \cup A_2) \leq P(A_1) + P(A_2) \qquad (10.20)$$

$$\alpha_E \leq \alpha_1 + \alpha_2$$

FIGURE 10.2   TWO-EVENT VENN DIAGRAM

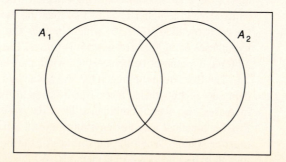

In general:

$$P(A_1 \cup A_2 \cup \cdots \cup A_m) \leq \sum_{i=1}^{m} P(A_i) \tag{10.21}$$

Since $P(A_i) = \alpha_i$ we conclude

$$P \text{ (one or more statements being incorrect)} \leq \sum_{i=1}^{m} \alpha_i \tag{10.22}$$

$$\alpha_E \leq \sum_{i=1}^{m} \alpha_i$$

Since we have seen that confidence intervals may be used to draw conclusions about hypothesis tests, we may interpret the Bonferroni inequality as:

$$P \text{ (One or more of } m \text{ confidence intervals does not include the hypothesized parameter value)} \leq \sum_{i=1}^{m} \alpha_i \tag{10.23}$$

or, the complementary statement

$$P \text{ (all } m \text{ confidence intervals include the hypothesized parameter value)} \geq 1 - \sum_{i=1}^{m} \alpha_i \tag{10.24}$$

As a specific example, consider three hypotheses:

$$H_1: \mu_1 - \mu_0 = 0$$
$$H_2: \mu_2 - \mu_0 = 0$$
$$H_3: \mu_3 - \mu_0 = 0$$

where μ_0 is a standard.

Suppose we desire an overall error, $\alpha_E \leq .10$. Then each α_i should be $.10/3 = .033$, and

$$P \text{ (one or more of the three confidence does not include the hypothesized parameter value of 0)} \leq .10$$

In this case, the hypothesized parameter value is actually a value for the difference between two parameters. This probability statement implies that the chances of at least one of the three hypotheses being rejected when it is true is 0.10 or less. Note that this tends to yield a higher level of risk than the more conventional $\alpha = \alpha$ .05. If .05 is used for each α_i, then $\alpha_E \leq .15$, which implies the probability of at least one of the three hypotheses being rejected when it is true is .15 or less, and conversely, the probability of all three hypotheses being accepted when they are true could be as low as .85.

The Bonferroni approach has the advantage of treating both independent and dependent sets of hypothesis tests. But it is readily seen that as the number of comparisons increases, the overall confidence level decreases dramatically, producing levels far too low for practical use. For anything beyond a handful of comparisons another approach must be sought. When the capabilities of the Bonferroni approach are exceeded, we can turn to experimental design methods. We discuss these in the next section, but first we provide an illustrative problem using the Bonferroni procedure.

<table>
<tr><td>**ILLUSTRATIVE**
PROBLEM
10.3</td></tr>
</table>

This problem extends the alternatives considered by Illustrative Problem 10.2 to include a third system design. In addition to designs with no express checkout lane and one express checkout lane, we now consider a system with two express lanes. Since the customers of this supermarket seem to be mostly "small order" shoppers, this would appear to be a reasonable additional alternative to assess.

The Bonferroni approach is used to compare each of the alternative designs in a pairwise fashion as follows. If we designate the no express lane alternative as design 1, the one express lane as design 2, and the two express lane as design 3, the pairwise comparisons of interest are: design 1 versus design 2, design 1 versus design 3, and design 2 versus design 3.

To perform this analysis we use the data of Illustrative Problem 10.2 for designs 1 and 2, and use the simulation model to produce ten replications of design 3, each replication being a 10-hour day. As before, we generate ten correlated sample values for the measure of performance, time in the system. The same random number stream was used for design 3 as for the other two designs. Table 10.3 shows both the results of the runs and the differences between them.

To determine whether there are pairwise differences among the designs we must test the following hypotheses:

$$H_1: \mu_{\bar{D}1} = 0$$
$$H_2: \mu_{\bar{D}2} = 0$$
$$H_3: \mu_{\bar{D}3} = 0$$

TABLE 10.3
RESULTS AND DIFFERENCES BETWEEN RESULTS FOR THREE SUPERMARKET CHECKOUT LANE DESIGNS USING CORRELATED SAMPLES

Rep No.	Mean Total Time in the System (Minutes)			Differences in Mean Total Time in the System		
	No Express Lane (0E)	One Express Lane (1E)	Two Express Lanes (2E)	0E-1E D_1	0E-2E D_2	1E-2E D_3
1	9.49	5.81	18.23	3.68	−8.74	−12.42
2	22.40	11.10	20.48	11.30	1.92	−9.38
3	9.24	6.16	24.47	3.08	−15.23	−18.31
4	15.25	12.45	22.88	2.80	−7.63	−10.43
5	26.58	11.14	20.60	15.44	5.98	−9.46
6	30.97	17.72	29.30	13.25	1.67	−11.58
7	6.67	5.13	24.27	1.54	−17.6	−19.14
8	11.04	7.58	21.29	3.46	−10.25	−13.71
9	16.28	10.62	23.93	5.66	−7.65	−13.31
10	13.70	11.03	22.07	2.67	−8.37	−11.04
Sample Mean	16.16	9.87	22.75	6.29	−6.59	−12.88
Sample Variance	64.71	14.59	10.18	25.60	63.84	12.96
Sample S.D.	8.04	3.82	3.19	5.06	7.99	3.6

where $\mu_{\bar{D}1}$, $\mu_{\bar{D}2}$, and $\mu_{\bar{D}3}$ are the mean differences in the performance measure for designs 1 and 2, 1 and 3, and 2 and 3, respectively. If we test each of the hypotheses at the 0.02 level, the overall error, $\alpha_E \le 0.06$, according to the Bonferroni inequality as expressed in equation (10.22). Notice that these are not independent hypotheses and yet the inequality still applies.

We will, as before, use confidence intervals to test these hypotheses. The required confidence intervals are defined by equation (10.16). The values of the D_i are given in Table 10.3, and the $s.d.(D_i)$ are calculated from equation (10.15) as follows.

$$s.d.(\bar{D}_1) = \sqrt{25.60/10} = 1.60$$

$$s.d.(\bar{D}_2) = \sqrt{63.84/10} = 2.53$$

$$s.d.(\bar{D}_3) = \sqrt{12.96/10} = 1.14$$

The confidence intervals for $\alpha = .02$ and with nine degrees of freedom are:

$$\mu_{\bar{D}1}: 6.29 \pm t_{(.01,9)} \, 1.6 = 6.29 \pm 2.821 \cdot 1.6$$
$$= 6.29 \pm 4.51$$
$$\text{or: } 2.67 \text{ to } 9.91$$

$$\mu_{\bar{D}2}: -6.59 \pm t_{(.01,9)} \, 2.53 = -6.59 \pm 2.821 \cdot 2.53$$
$$= -6.59 \pm 7.14$$
$$\text{or: } -13.73 \text{ to } 0.55$$

$$\mu_{\bar{D}3}: -12.88 \pm t_{(.01,9)} \, 1.14 = -12.88 \pm 2.821 \cdot 1.14$$
$$= -12.88 \pm 3.22$$
$$\text{or: } -16.1 \text{ to } -9.66$$

Since the confidence interval for $\mu_{\bar{D}2}$ includes zero, we cannot reject H_2. The other two confidence intervals do not include zero, and therefore we reject H_1 and H_3.

What does all this tell us about checkout lane design? As we already knew from the previous problem, design 2 (one express lane) is significantly better than design 1 (no express lanes) since it yields less total time in the system. But we now know that design 2 is also significantly better than design 3 (two express lanes) since it yields less time in the system than design 3. Finally, the evidence suggests that designs 1 and 3 are equally poor, since there is no significant difference between them.

Having examined all possibilities for this three-checkout supermarket, we can now conclude that the best design, using total time in the system as the performance measure, is one express lane and two regular lanes.

10.3   EXPLORING A RANGE OF ALTERNATIVE SYSTEM DESIGNS

Thus far we have considered ways to examine a relatively small number of alternative system designs defined by changing one decision variable. However, as constraints are relaxed, we may desire to explore a wider range of values for the decision variable or define system designs by changing more than one decision variable. Often, one explores a range of alternatives to gain insight into system behavior. To do this in a statistically valid way, we use experimental design and analysis constructs to permit the simultaneous testing of many hypotheses involving one or more decision variables. Note that we still are considering only one measure of system performance, and that the set of alternative designs examined does not necessarily include the optimum design.

10.3.1   SINGLE-FACTOR EXPERIMENTS

The simplest experimental design involves only a single factor or decision variable. It may be viewed as a natural extension of the multiple comparisons of the previous section, except the overall level of confidence does not decrease as we increase the number of alternative system designs. In our discussion of experimental designs, we will focus on the conclusions that can be drawn from the use of such designs to analyze simulation output. More complete coverage may be found in references such as [8] and [14].

We begin by considering a completely randomized, fixed-effects experiment with one factor, or decision variable, set at k levels. The statistical model for this experiment is:

$$Y_{ij} = \mu + \tau_j + e_{ij}$$

where: Y_{ij} is the ith observation of the performance measure for the jth factor level ($i=1,2,...,n$ and $j=1,2,...,k$), μ is the population mean of the performance measure, τ_j is the effect of the jth factor level, and e_{ij} is the random error present in the ith observation of the jth factor level. For single factor experiments τ_j is often referred to as the treatment effect. Each τ_j reflects a particular decision variable setting and defines a system design alternative.

The analysis of this experiment assumes that the e_{ij} are normally, independently distributed. Hence, each Y_{ij} represents the ith individual value of the performance measure for independent successive observations of the jth system design, or the ith value of some aggregate of the performance measure, say the mean, for independent successive replications of the jth system design.

The null and alternative hypotheses in this experiment are:

$$H_0: \tau_j = 0 \qquad \text{for } j = 1,2,...,n$$
$$H_1: \tau_j \neq 0 \qquad \text{for some } j$$

We test these hypotheses at a specified level of Type I error probability, α, usually $\alpha = .05$. If we cannot reject the null hypothesis, we conclude that there are no differences created in the measure of performance due to the changes in the particular decision variable. That is, all n system designs perform equally well within the limits of statistical tolerance selected. If we reject the null hypothesis, then there are statistically significant differences among the system designs.

To test our hypotheses, we use the quantities displayed in the Analysis of Variance (ANOVA) Table of Fig. 10.3 to compute a test statistic which follows the F distribution under the null hypothesis. The following auxiliary variables are defined to simplify the notation.

$$T.. = \sum_{i=1}^{n} \sum_{j=1}^{k} Y_{ij} \qquad T._j = \sum_{i=1}^{n} Y_{ij}$$

The required F statistic is computed using Mean Squares (MS) as follows: $F = MS_{\text{Between}} / MS_{\text{Error}}$ which is distributed according to the F distribution with $k - 1$

FIGURE 10.3   ANOVA TABLE FOR SINGLE-FACTOR EXPERIMENT

Source of Variation	Degrees of Freedom	Sum of Squares(SS)
Between Factor Levels	$k-1$	$\sum\limits_{j=1}^{k} \dfrac{T_{.j}^2}{n} - \dfrac{T_{..}^2}{nk}$
Within Factor Levels or Error	$k(n-1)$	$\sum\limits_{i=1}^{n}\sum\limits_{j=1}^{k} Y_{ij}^2 - \sum\limits_{j=1}^{k} \dfrac{T_{.j}^2}{n}$
Total	$kn-1$	$\sum\limits_{i=1}^{n}\sum\limits_{j=1}^{k} Y_{ij}^2 - \dfrac{T_{..}^2}{nk}$

and $k(n-1)$ degrees of freedom, where $MS_{\text{Between}} = SS_{\text{Between}}/(k-1)$ and $MS_{\text{Error}} = SS_{\text{Error}}/k(n-1)$.

If the value of this statistic exceeds the tabulated F, we reject the null hypothesis and conclude that there are statistically significant differences among the system designs. Then the relevant question is: Which design is the best of the set of n designs? Before dealing with this question, we consider a specific problem setting.

Returning to the supermarket checkout problem, suppose we have four alternative system designs defined by the number of staffed checkout lanes. This single factor then has four levels: level 1 is defined as one lane staffed, level 2 as two lanes staffed, level 3 as three lanes staffed, and level 4 as four lanes staffed. We decide to make three independent replications for each factor level. This defines a completely randomized, fixed effects experiment with $n = 3$, $k = 4$, and the total number of observations, $nk = 12$. It is completely randomized because there are no restrictions on the sequence in which the various cells (factor level observation combinations) of the experiment may be run. Fixed effects implies that we have considered all possible levels for the factor, as opposed to a random sample from a population of levels. We choose customer waiting time as our measure of performance. Suppose further that we construct the ANOVA Table, test the null hypothesis: $H_0: \tau_j = 0$ for all j, and reject it. The conclusion drawn is that these system designs yield significantly different values of customer waiting time. Now we must determine which of the four is best.

One approach is Duncan's Multiple Range Test. This test allows us to form homogeneous subgroups within which there are no significant differences, and among which, there are significant differences. In this way, we can possibly identify sets of system design alternatives which yield statistically the same level of the performance measure. The selection of the particular system design to implement could then be made based on other performance measures.

The general approach to Duncan's test is outlined here; a more complete description is available in Hicks [8]. Duncan's test relies upon a comparison of pairwise differences or ranges between means with critical values for such ranges derived from the t distribu-

tion. First, the treatment means are arranged in ascending order to compute all possible ranges: largest versus smallest, largest versus next smallest,..., second largest versus smallest, second largest versus next smallest,..., third largest versus smallest, etc. Then these actual values are compared to critical table values multiplied by the standard error, s_j, of each treatment mean,
where

$$s_j = \sqrt{MS_{Error}/n_j}$$

and nj is the number of observations for treatment j (all n_j have been considered equal for the model discussed above). We illustrate this technique as part of the following example problem.

ILLUSTRATIVE PROBLEM 10.4

In this problem, we use a single factor experiment to determine the proper number of mechanics to maintain a set of machines. Originally described by Emshoff and Sisson [5], the setting is four production lines of six identical automatic machines each of which randomly fail and require repair. The decision variable is the number of mechanics to be used, and the system performance measure is the total cost per hour for machine downtime and mechanics' salaries.

Since the four production lines are located close to one another, the possibility of sharing mechanics among the lines exists. To do this, one mechanic is assigned to a given production line and one or more mechanics rotate among the four lines. Also, since the production lines are comprised of identical machines, we can model only one of the lines and extend our conclusions to the others. The alternatives to be assessed are as follows:

System Design	Total No. of Mechanics	Rotating Mechanics	Rotation Time	Average No. of Mechanics per Line
1	4	0	None	1
2	5	1	15 minutes	1 1/4
3	6	2	30 minutes	1 1/2
4	7	3	45 minutes	1 3/4
5	8	0	None	2

For the cases of 4 and 8 mechanics, a fixed assignment of 1 and 2 mechanics per line, respectively, is used and there is no rotation. For the other cases, one mechanic has a fixed line assignment and the others move among the four lines at intervals indicated in the "Rotation Time" column. For example, with 6 mechanics, mechanics 1–4 are assigned to each of the four lines and the other two rotate among the lines at 30-minute intervals. One possible schedule would have mechanic #5 spend 30 minutes with line one and 30 minutes with line two, while mechanic #6 would divide his time between lines three and four. To implement this using our model of a single production line, we schedule mechanics so that two are present for 30 minutes of each hour and only one for the balance of the hour. Similar schedules exist for the other mechanics.

Turning to some of the details of the model, the time between machine failures may be described by an exponential distribution with a mean of 15 minutes. The repair time is also exponentially distributed, but with a mean of 5 minutes. Mechanics are paid a salary of $8.00 per hour. The cost of machine downtime per hour depends upon the number of machines down, as well as the duration of the downtime. It varies from pennies per minute with no machines down to $1.20 per minute with six machines down.

The total cost per hour for any number of mechanics is calculated as follows:

$$TC = ML + [\sum_{j=1}^{6} C_j D_j]/H$$

where:

M	= average number of mechanics per line
L	= hourly salary of mechanics ($8.00)
C_j	= machine downtime cost per hour when j machines are down
D_j	= number of hours with j machines down
H	= number of hours in each simulation run.

For each of the five alternative system designs defined above, eight replications were run; each replication processed 200 machine failures. Thus, we have a single-factor completely randomized, fixed-effect experiment with five levels of the factor and eight independent observations for each level. The mean total costs per hour for each of the system design alternatives are as follows:

System Design	Total No. of Mechanics	Mean Total Cost/Hour
1	4	19.47
2	5	17.87
3	6	17.82
4	7	18.04
5	8	19.00

The null hypothesis for this experiment is: $H_0: \tau_j = 0$, for $j=1,2,3,4,5$, where τ_j is the effect or difference due to alternative system design j. If accepted, the finding is that all five alternatives behave comparably in terms of total hourly cost. The Analysis of Variance (ANOVA) Table for this experiment is shown in Table 10.4. The results indicate a significant difference among the five alternative system designs. The F statistic, 3.01, is significant at the .05 level. The question now is which designs are different from which others? Duncan's Multiple Range test can help us to decide.

We begin by ordering the means in ascending order.

System Design	3	2	4	5	1
Means	17.82	17.87	18.04	19.00	19.47

TABLE 10.4
ANOVA TABLE FOR MECHANIC ASSIGNMENT

Source of Variation	Degrees of Freedom	Sum of Squares	Mean Square	F Statistic	$F_{.05}$
Between Factor Levels	4	17.959	4.989	3.01*	2.65
Error	35	52.227	1.492		
Total	39	70.186			

* Significant at the .05 level.

Next we compute the ranges between means, and the critical values for these ranges as shown in Table 10.5. The numbers in parentheses are the critical values, which were calculated by multiplying the tabled values for an α of .05 by

$$s_j = \sqrt{1.492/8} = 0.43.$$

The table values, obtained from Hicks [8,p.277] are:

No. of Intervening Means:	0	1	2	3
Critical Values:	2.88	3.03	3.11	3.18

For example, the critical value for design 3 versus design 5 is:

$$(3.11)\,(0.43) = 1.34,$$

since there are two intervening means in the ordered list (designs 2 and 4) between designs 3 and 5.

To help interpret the results of Duncan's test shown in Table 10.5, it is helpful to draw a line under sets of means, in the ordered list of means, which are not significantly different. For our results we have the following.

TABLE 10.5
DUNCAN'S MULTIPLE RANGE TEST RESULTS

System Design i	System Design j			
	2	4	5	1
3	.05 (1.24)	.22 (1.30)	1.18 (1.34)	1.65 (1.37)*
2		.17 (1.24)	1.13 (1.30)	1.60 (1.34)*
4			.96 (1.24)	1.43 (1.30)*
5				.47 (1.24)

* Significant at the .05 level.

System Design	3	2	4	5	1
Means	17.82	17.87	18.04	19.00	19.47

This display suggests that design 1 (1 mechanic per line) is fairly isolated, and similar only to design 5 (2 mechanics per line). These are the two most expensive designs. The other three alternatives are indistinguishable in terms of total hourly cost, and so the choice could be made by considering other factors, such as the need for skilled mechanics in other areas of the facility.

10.3.2   MULTIPLE FACTOR EXPERIMENTS

Thus far we have defined system design alternatives by changing the value of only one decision variable. A more varied set of system designs may be examined by changing the values of two or more decision variables. For example, we may wish to evaluate various inventory management policies defined by combinations of re-order levels and re-order quantities. Or, assess preventive maintenance policies defined by both the part replacement interval and the quality of the part. Is it less expensive to replace parts more often using inexpensive parts, or to replace less often with better quality, more expensive parts?

To accommodate the evaluation of system designs defined by changing two or more decision variables, we introduce the factorial experimental design. As in the single factor experiment, we will focus on the completely randomized, fixed-effects model. Although this approach can be extended to any number of factors, we will limit our discussion to two-factor experiments. Hicks [8] presents a clear exposition of extension to more than two factors.

The statistical model for the two-factor experiment is:

$$Y_{ijk} = \mu + A_i + B_j + AB_{ij} + e_{ijk}$$

where Y_{ijk} is the kth observation ($k=1,2,...,n$) with factor A set at level i ($i=1,2,...,a$) and factor B set at level j ($j=1,2,...,b$) [i.e., the kth observation in cell i,j], μ is the population mean of the performance measure, A_i is the effect of the ith level of factor A, B_j is the effect of the jth level of factor B, AB_{ij} is the interaction effect of factors A and B at levels i and j respectively, and e_{ijk} is random error present in the kth observation in cell i,j.

Considering two or more factors adds a complication to our model. No longer is it simply an additive model, $\mu + A_i + B_j$, but we may have a nonlinear effect of both factors in combination, AB_{ij}. Essentially this means that the effect of a change in the level of factor A on the performance measure depends upon the level at which factor B is set. For example, in inventory policy evaluation, we set the reorder point at two levels. At level 1, a change in the level of reorder quantity yields a reduction of $4000 in annual cost, while at level 2 the same change in re-order quantity provides only a $2000 reduction in annual cost. In this case, factors A and B are said to interact in changing the value of the performance measure. Illustrative Problem 10.5 discusses this further.

For the two-factor experiment there are three null hypotheses:

$H_1: A_i = 0$ for $i=1,2,...,a$
$H_{1a}: A_i \neq 0$ for some i

$H_2: B_j = 0$ for $j=1,2,...,b$
$H_{2a}: B_j \neq 0$ for some j

$H_3: AB_{ij} = 0$ for $i=1,2,...,a$; $j=1,2,...b$
$H_{3a}: AB_{ij} \neq 0$ for some i,j $i \neq j$

H_1 and H_2 test for the significance of main effects A and B, respectively, while H_3 tests the interaction effect, AB.

If the main effects and the interaction effect are found not to be statistically significant, we may treat all system designs defined by the factor, or factors, as essentially the same, and hence we are indifferent in choosing one over the other. However, if either or both factors test as being significant, we must determine which system designs are different from which others. Again, Duncan's Multiple Range Test may be used for this. If the interaction effect also proves to be significant, this implies that system designs defined by combinations of the factors are significant.

To test our hypotheses, we use the quantities displayed in the ANOVA Table of Fig. 10.4. The required F statistics and their associated degrees of freedom for the three hypotheses are:

For H_1, $F = MS_{(\text{Factor A})} / MS_{(\text{Error})}$ and $df = [a-1, ab(n-1)]$

For H_2, $F = MS_{(\text{Factor B})} / MS_{(\text{Error})}$ and $df = [b-1, ab(n-1)]$

For H_3, $F = MS_{(\text{Interaction } A \times B)} / MS_{(\text{Error})}$ and $df = [(a-1)(b-1), ab(n-1)]$

FIGURE 10.4   ANOVA TABLE FOR TWO-FACTOR EXPERIMENT

Source of Variation	Degrees of Freedom	Sum of Squares(SS)
Factor A	$a-1$	$\sum_{i=1}^{a} \dfrac{T_{i..}^2}{nb} - \dfrac{T_{...}^2}{nab}$
Factor B	$b-1$	$\sum_{j=1}^{b} \dfrac{T_{.j.}^2}{na} - \dfrac{T_{...}^2}{nab}$
AXB Interaction	$(a-1)(b-1)$	$\sum_{i=1}^{a}\sum_{j=1}^{b} \dfrac{T_{ij.}^2}{n} - \sum_{i=1}^{a} \dfrac{T_{i..}^2}{nb}$ $-\sum_{j=1}^{b} \dfrac{T_{.j.}^2}{na} + \dfrac{T_{...}^2}{nab}$
Error	$ab(n-1)$	$\sum_{i=1}^{a}\sum_{j=1}^{b}\sum_{k=1}^{n} Y_{ijk}^2 - \sum_{i=1}^{a}\sum_{j=1}^{b} \dfrac{T_{ij.}^2}{n}$
Total	$abn-1$	$\sum_{i=1}^{a}\sum_{j=1}^{b}\sum_{k=1}^{n} Y_{ijk}^2 - \dfrac{T_{...}^2}{nab}$

To make the foregoing discussion more concrete, we return again to the supermarket problem setting. Illustrative Problem 10.5 demonstrates how a two-factor experiment may be used to select the best of an expanded set of alternative system designs.

**ILLUSTRATIVE
PROBLEM
10.5**

Two decision variables are to be considered in this supermarket design problem: the number of checkout lanes to staff, and whether to use standard registers or bar-code readers. The measure of performance selected is the same as the one used in previous supermarket problems: the time spent by all types of customers waiting in line and checking out. The characteristics of the customer population in terms of arrival rates and size of orders are the same as those described in Illustrative Problem 10.1. The checkout time per item on the standard register remains the same, 0.17 minute, but a 25% reduction in this time is assumed for the bar-code reader. The number of checkout lanes staffed varies between three and five. No express lanes are provided for small-order shoppers.

We have described a situation which may be appropriately modeled as a two-factor experiment with interaction. Factor A designates the number of lanes staffed and has three levels: three, four, and five lanes. Factor B designates the type of equipment used and has two levels: standard register and bar-code reader. The data to analyze this experiment were obtained by running 10 replications of the simulation model for each of the six factor level combinations. As before, each replication was a 10-hour day with a 1-hour initialization period. The means for each of the experiment's cells appear in Table 10.6.

Visual inspection of these results suggests there should be differences attributable to one or both of the factors. Table 10.7 shows the ANOVA Table for the experiment which confirms these suspicions. We see that both main effects A and B are significant at the .05 level as is the interaction effect, AB. In fact, all effects are significant at much higher levels.

These results state that significant differences in the total time in the system are caused not only by the levels of the two factors (number of lanes staffed and type of equipment) but also by the particular combination of these levels. However, inspection of the individual cell means in Table 10.6 suggests that all means except the mean for

TABLE 10.6
TWO-FACTOR SUPERMARKET DESIGN EXPERIMENT RESULTS
TOTAL TIME IN THE SYSTEM (MINUTES)

Factor A: No. of Lanes Staffed	Factor B: Register Type		Overall Mean: Factor A
	Standard	*Bar-Code Reader*	
3	14.78	3.42	9.10
4	3.87	1.89	2.88
5	2.63	1.50	2.07
Overall Mean Factor B	7.09	2.27	

TABLE 10.7
ANOVA TABLE FOR TWO-FACTOR SUPERMARKET DESIGN EXPERIMENT

Source of Variation	Degrees of Freedom	Sum of Squares	Mean Square	F Statistic	$F_{.05}$
Factor A	2	592.73	296.37	34.30	3.15*
Factor B	1	349.31	349.31	40.43	4.00*
Interaction AB	2	322.34	161.22	18.66	3.15*
Error	54	466.70	8.64		
Total	59	1731.17			

* Significant at the .05 level.

three lanes and a standard register are closely clustered. Further analysis using multiple range tests such as Duncan's will fail to show any significant differences among the clustered means. This suggests that any design except that with three lanes and a standard register would perform about the same.

10.3.3   SCREENING EXPERIMENTS

When simulating complex systems, we often do not know which subset of many decision variables will have the most pronounced impact on a performance measure. If we are to explore alternative system designs which differ from one another in statistically significant and practically meaningful ways, an efficient means of identifying these relevant decision variables is needed. Variants of the factorial experiment discussed in the previous section provide the required means.

Full Factorial Experiments   If we set each decision variable at only two extreme values, a low value and a high value, experimental designs exist that test for the significance of main effects and interactions of main effects. Using comparatively few simulation runs, we can determine which decision variables cause significant changes in the performance measure, and therefore should be included in more detailed experimental designs. Since this procedure essentially screens out the less important decision variables, such experiments are referred to as screening experiments.

The simplest screening design is a completely randomized, 2^n factorial experiment with no replication, where 2^n refers to the number of observations in the experiment (n factors, each at 2 levels). For example, if we have three decision variables, $2^3 = 8$ simulation runs are required. But, if we have eight decision variables, $2^8 = 256$ simulation runs are required; and if we have 10 variables (not an unusually large number of variables for complex systems), $2^{10} = 1024$ runs are needed. It is apparent that the number of runs, and hence the amount of computer time, increases nonlinearly. Assuming a conservative estimate of 30 seconds of CPU time for each of the 1024 runs of the 10-variable experiment, we would use about 8.5 hours of computer time just for the screening experiment. Additional computer time would then be required for the detailed experiments involving the decision variables found to be of consequence.

To deal with this problem, screening experiments needing only a fraction of the runs required for a full factorial experiment have been devised. These so-called fractional factorial experiments reduce the number of observations required greatly, while diminishing the information provided by their analysis only modestly. We will begin by discussing the full 2^n experiment and then mention some fractional designs.

To be more specific, we will describe a 2^3 design and illustrate it with an example problem. Returning to the supermarket problem setting, we wish to examine the possible effect of three decision variables:

(1) number of checkout lanes staffed,

(2) whether standard register or bar code reader, and

(3) whether staffed with a bagger or not.

Which of these variables, if any, affects the performance measure customer waiting and checkout time? To answer this question, we will use a 2^3 experiment with a single replication of each factor set at high and low values. Thus we need a minimum of eight simulation runs.

Before we describe our 2^3 design, the construction of the simpler 2^2 design will be outlined. Hicks [8] discusses the construction of this and the general 2^n design in detail. To construct this design we first define the effect of any factor as the change in response (performance measure) produced by a change in that factor. Some simplifying notation will help in further explanation of effect. The response at the high level of a factor is designated by the presence of the lowercase letter name of that factor: for example "ab" indicates the response at high levels of factors A and B. The low level of a factor is designated by the absence of its letter name: for example "b" indicates the response with factor B at the high level and factor A at the low level. Both letter names absent is represented as "(1)" and indicates the response at low levels of both factors.

If we use "1" for the high level and "0" for the low level, then the proper expression for the response at a factor level combination is obtained by using the product of the factor letter names each raised to a power indicated by its level. Then "ab" is defined as a^1b^1, "b" as a^0b^1, etc.

So we denote the A effect at the low level of B as: $a - (1)$, and at the high level of B as: $ab - b$, as shown in the graph below. The responses associated with these factor level combinations could be represented in a third dimension rising out of the plane of this graph.

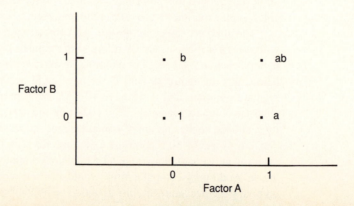

The average effect of A is then:

$$A = 1/2[(a - (1)) + (ab - b)]$$

$$A = 1/2[-(1) + a - b + ab]$$

which also may be rewritten as:

$$2A = -(1) + a - b + ab$$

Notice that the coefficients in the expression for $2A$ are always +1 when factor A is at the high level and -1 when A is at the low level. Also, this expression is defined as a contrast since the sum of the coefficients is zero. This fact is quite useful in determining the required sums of squares for the ANOVA Table. The contrast for the B effect is defined similarly as:

$$2B = -(1) - a + b + ab$$

To compute the interaction effect note that the A effect at the high level of factor B is: $ab - b$, and at the low level it is: $a - (1)$. If these two effects differ, we say there is interaction between A and B. So the interaction effect is the average difference between these two differences as:

$$AB = 1/2[(ab - b) - (a - (1))]$$

The contrast is:

$$2AB = (1) - a - b + ab$$

These ideas can be extended to three factors quite readily. The resulting eight-factor level combinations could be graphed as the vertices of a cube. We can summarize the coefficients needed to compute the contrasts for the 2^3 experiment in Fig. 10.5, where each column is a contrast. Note that all of these contrasts are orthogonal; that is, the sum of the products of corresponding rows for any two columns is zero. This makes it a simple matter to compute the necessary sums of squares for hypothesis testing.

The sum of squares for all main effects and interactions are calculated as follows:

$$SS_{\text{effect}} = (\text{contrast})^2 / 2^3$$

FIGURE 10.5   CONTRAST COEFFICIENTS FOR 2^3 EXPERIMENT

Factor Combination				Effect			
	A	**B**	**AB**	**C**	**AC**	**BC**	**ABC**
(1)	-	-	+	-	+	+	-
a	+	-	-	-	-	+	+
b	-	+	-	-	+	-	+
ab	+	+	+	-	-	-	-
c	-	-	+	+	-	-	+
ac	+	-	-	+	+	-	-
bc	-	+	-	+	-	+	-
abc	+	+	+	+	+	+	+

For example,

$$SS_A = (-(1) + a - b + ab - c + ac - bc + abc)^2/8.$$

The total degrees of freedom for this experiment is 7, 1 for each main effect and 1 for each interaction. This limits the hypothesis tests that can be conducted with any reasonable level of statistical power to only the three main effects. This problem could be alleviated by replicating observations in each of the eight cells. Even two replications per cell would yield 15 total degrees of freedom, permitting all main effects and interactions to be tested with reasonable power.

Since we did not replicate observations, we must assume that the 2-factor and 3-factor interactions are not significant, and use their associated sums of squares to estimate the error sum of squares used in the F test for the main effects A, B, and C. Thus, the hypothesis test for Factor A would be:.

$H_0: A_i = 0$ for all i No significant A effect

$H_1: A_i \neq 0$ for some i Significant A effect.

The appropriate F statistic is, $F = MS_A/MS_{\text{(all interactions)}}$, is distributed as F with (1,4) degrees of freedom, where:

$$MS_A = SS_A/1$$

$$MS_{\text{(all interactions)}} = (SS_{AB} + SS_{AC} + SS_{BC} + SS_{ABC})/4$$

The hypotheses for Factors B and C are conducted in an analogous fashion.

After conducting the hypothesis tests for each of the three main effects, we may be able to exclude one or more of them as not having any significant effect on the measure of performance. If no significance is revealed over the extreme range included in this experiment, we can drop the decision variable from further consideration. We would then conduct experiments with the remaining significant variables set at greater numbers of levels. Illustrative Problem 10.6 demonstrates some of these outcomes.

ILLUSTRATIVE PROBLEM 10.6

For this example we return to our ubiquitous supermarket. The experiment for this problem was mentioned in the discussion above; it involves three decision variables:

(1) number of checkout lanes staffed,

(2) equipment type, and

(3) whether staffed with a bagger or not.

Each decision variable is treated as a factor which is set at two levels. The number of lanes is set at 5 (high) and 3 (low), the equipment is either bar-code reader (high) or standard register (low), and baggers are either present (high) or not (low).

Customers arrive, on the average, every 3.2 minutes, with exponentially distributed interarrival intervals. Each customer purchases an average of 36 items. The average checkout time per item is 0.2 minutes, but this is reduced by 15% if a bar-code reader is used, and 5% if a bagger is present. So, a lane equipped with a bar-code reader and staffed with a bagger would experience a 20% reduction in checkout time per item.

Although the bar-code readers are faster, they are not as reliable as standard registers. While the standard registers experience negligible downtime, the time between

TABLE 10.8
RESULTS OF 2^3 SUPERMARKET EXPERIMENT
(TIME IN THE SYSTEM IN MINUTES)

	Factor B: Equipment Type			
	Bar-Code Reader		Standard Register	
Factor A:	Factor C: Baggers			
No. of Lanes	Present	Not Present	Present	Not Present
3	7.34	7.97	8.87	10.2
5	5.40	5.76	6.01	6.4

TABLE 10.9
ANOVA TABLE FOR 2^3 SUPERMARKET EXPERIMENT

Source of Variation	Degrees of Freedom	Sum of Squares	Mean Square	F Statistic	$F_{.05}$
A	1	14.61	14.61	53.11*	7.71
B	1	3.14	3.14	11.63*	7.71
C	1	0.92	.92	3.41	7.71
Error	4	1.09	.27		
Total	7	19.76			

*Significant at the .05 level.

failures for bar-code readers is exponentially distributed with a mean of 36 minutes. The repair time is also exponentially distributed and has a mean of 6 minutes.

As in the previous supermarket examples, a replication consists of a 10-hour day with 1-hour initialization period. One replication was run for each of the eight factor level combinations. Table 10.8 shows the output for the performance measure, customer time in the system.

In Table 10.9, the ANOVA Table for the experiment is presented. The sums of squares were calculated using the contrasts defined above for a 2^3 experiment. Comparing the calculated F statistics to the critical value, we see that both the number of checkout lanes staffed and the equipment type cause significant differences in our performance measure. Based on this finding, future experimentation should focus on a more detailed examination of these two factors. Experiments that set each factor at several different levels between the high and low levels of this experiment should be run. Also, replication of factor level combinations should be included to test for interaction effects.

Fractional Factorial Experiments In the preceding example, eight simulation runs is certainly not excessive to screen which decision variables are significant. But often, complex systems have many more decision variables, as in the case of a 10-variable experiment requiring 1024 simulation runs mentioned above. The use of fractional experiments offers some help. To illustrate this, consider a seven-variable screening experiment which requires $2^7 = 128$ simulation runs.

We will describe this experiment in terms of our supermarket problem by defining the following seven decision variables which are believed to affect the performance measure, customer waiting time. We seek to determine which, if any, really affect it.

1. Number of regular checkout lanes - cash only customers

2. Number of express checkout lanes - cash only customers

3. Initial number of regular checkout lanes - any customer

4. Length of longest waiting line required to open an additional regular checkout lane

5. Maximum number of items allowed for express lanes

6. Number of baggers per lane (maximum of one)

7. Standard register or bar-code reader

For even this modestly complex simulation model, the full experiment of 128 runs could require an excessive amount of computer time.

If we run only a fraction of the 128 cells defined in the 2^7 experiment, we may not be able to test some of the higher order interaction terms. But we may be willing to assume that many of these are insignificant. Even if significant, it is very difficult to attach useful interpretation to an interaction involving three or more factors. Consequently, we will lose little of value by the use of the fractional experiment and gain much in efficiency.

The conduct of fractional experiments results in aliases for main effects and interactions. That is, a particular sum of squares may estimate the effect of either a main effect or the interaction, but not both. We say that these effects are confounded. Exactly what do we lose by using such experiments? To answer this question we will examine a one-half and one-fourth replicate of a 2^7 experiment.

If we conduct a one-half replicate, we must make 64 simulation runs instead of 128. We choose our runs from two sets, or blocks, of 64 factor combinations which are aliases. The total of 63 degrees of freedom are distributed as shown in Fig. 10.6. This is a practical design. None of the main effects are confounded with each other, nor are any

FIGURE 10.6   ONE-HALF REPLICATE OF 2^7 EXPERIMENT

Source	Degrees of Freedom
Main effects $A, B,...,G$ (or six-factor interactions)	1 each for 7
Two-factor interactions $AB, AC,...$ (or five-factor interactions)	1 each for 21
Three-factor interactions $ABC,...$ (or four-factor interactions)	1 each for 35 [use as error]
Total	63

FIGURE 10.7   ONE-FOURTH REPLICATE OF 2^7 EXPERIMENT

Source	Degrees of Freedom
Main effects $A, B, ..., G$	1 each for 7
Two-factor interactions $AC, AD, ...$	1 each for 15
Two-factor interactions AB, AF, AG (or FG, BG, GF)	1 each for 3
Three-factor or higher interactions ABC, ABCD,...	1 each for 6
Total	31

of the two-factor interactions confounded with each other. We can test for the significance of both the main effects and the two-factor interactions. Assuming insignificance of the three or four-factor interactions, we have 35 degrees of freedom for the error term.

The use of a one-fourth replicate requires only 32 simulation runs to be made. We choose our runs from four blocks of 32 factor combinations which are aliases. What additional loss of information is incurred? A total of 31 degrees of freedom for this experiment are distributed, as shown in Fig. 10.7. Making only 32 runs, we can test all main effects, and all but three of the two-factor interactions. Using interactions involving three or more factors as the error, we have F tests with $(1, 6)$ degrees of freedom.

These two examples demonstrate well that fractional experiments offer great economies in screening decision variables. The savings thus achieved may then be applied to detailed examination of those variables that really matter. There are many more fractional experiments than suggested by the foregoing short discussion. For further discussion of their development and use see Cochran and Cox [4], Hicks [8], and Kleijnen [10].

10.4   OPTIMIZING SYSTEM DESIGNS

Experimental design techniques permit evaluating a wide range of alternative system designs as defined by combinations of decision variable settings. If the alternatives included in the experiment are judiciously chosen with some *a priori* knowledge of the system behavior, the system design ultimately selected may be optimal, or nearly so. However, this is not assured. In fact, there are no provably optimal algorithms for use with simulation models. So we can never define the truly optimal system design. Optimizing simulation models entails the use of effective heuristic algorithms in connection with appropriate statistical techniques. By iteration, these techniques allow one to define an increasingly better system design which may be a local optimum, or perhaps even a global optimum. Terms such as response-surface methodology and optimum-seeking are used to describe these approaches.

In this section, we define and illustrate the fundamental ideas of response-surface methodology and optimum-seeking techniques. In all cases we will be seeking optimum solutions with reference to but one performance measure.

10.4.1   RESPONSE-SURFACE METHODOLOGY CONCEPTS

A response surface is best described by analogy. Consider a three-dimensional model of a land mass which shows hills and depressions. The elevation of the terrain varies with rectangular coordinates, which represent latitude and longitude: that is, the elevation is a function of the latitude and longitude. The model may be reduced to two dimensions by using contour lines to represent the locus of points of equal elevation, as is typical on detailed topographical maps. Figure 10.8 shows some typical elevation patterns using contour lines, with latitude and longitude represented by X_1 and X_2.

By replacing latitude and longitude with two decision variables, and elevation with a system performance measure, we define a response surface for our system model. Thus, a response surface is the continuum of values for the performance measure determined by all feasible combinations of the two decision variables. For ease of analysis we usually assume a continuous surface. The appropriate equation for a two-dimensional response surface is: $R = f(X_1, X_2)$, over the feasible ranges of X_1 and X_2, where the function, f, is defined by the structure of the simulation model. For example, the time to checkout in a supermarket is affected by the average speed of the cashiers and the number of cashiers on duty.

Although the two-dimensional response surface is easiest to represent graphically and to apply optimum-seeking techniques to, surfaces may be extended to n dimensions

FIGURE 10.8   TYPICAL ELEVATION PATTERNS

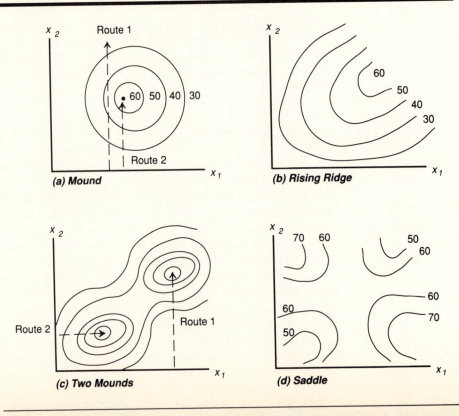

(a) Mound

(b) Rising Ridge

(c) Two Mounds

(d) Saddle

by including additional decision variables. We could certainly include variables such as the number of baggers, the number of express checkout lanes and the number of "cash only" checkout lanes in our supermarket model. However, the difficulty in optimization increases nonlinearly with the addition of variables.

Given such surfaces, we wish to determine the combination of decision variable values which are associated with either the "lowest" (minimum) or "highest" (maximum) point on the surface, depending on the performance measure being considered. There are many approaches to this problem, all of them fraught with pitfalls. Using our land mass analogy, we view the solution as either climbing to the highest point, or descending to the lowest point on the terrain. However, we must do this blindfolded, or at least in a dense fog, for in general we know very little about the shape of response surfaces. Also, we wish to achieve the summit gathering as little information as possible, since collecting such information from simulation runs is usually expensive.

To appreciate some of the problems in scaling a response surface, observe the response surfaces of Fig. 10.8. For surface (a) we could follow route 1 up one side of the hill and down the other, completely missing the summit, or, following the parallel route 2, we would arrive at the summit. For surface (c) we could follow route 1 and reach the lower of two summits (a local optimum), or route 2 and reach the highest point (the global optimum). Both the starting point and the route selected affect the likelihood of reaching the summit. Since the number of points to be explored is too large to permit total enumeration, and marching in a straight line offers little assurance of achieving the summit, we need effective strategies.

10.4.2 OPTIMUM-SEEKING TECHNIQUES

In this section we describe two strategies for finding optimum values of response surfaces which are fundamentally different. The first strategy proceeds methodically from one solution to a better one without attempting to estimate the shape of the surface beforehand, while the second continuously assesses the likely benefit due to decision variable changes before making them.

A Direct Search Approach   A conceptually simple approach to finding the minimum or maximum of a response surface is the one-at-a-time method [18]. Using this method, only one variable at a time is altered in seeking the optimum system design. We will confine our discussion to two decision variables. For a response surface which is a function of two variables, say $R(x_1, x_2)$, we would hold x_2 constant and optimize over x_1. Then fix x_1 at the value that produced the optimal response surface and optimize over x_2. Repeat this procedure, alternately varying x_1 and x_2 until there is no change in the response surface. This procedure will terminate when

$$R(x_1, x_2^*) \leq R(x_1^*, x_2^*) \geq R(x_1^*, x_2)$$

for all values of x_1 and x_2. Thus, x_1^* and x_2^* are the values of the decision variables which yield the optimal system design.

The success of this approach depends upon the starting values of x_1 and x_2 and the increments for changes in these values. Figure 10.9 illustrates some possible outcomes. In climbing surface (a) the summit is achieved fairly quickly, while in (b) it requires many iterations. However, in (c) we stop well down the side of the hill, and in (d) only a local optimum is achieved. The global optimum could be found for (c) if a different

FIGURE 10.9   CLIMBING RESPONSE SURFACES WITH THE ONE-AT-A-TIME METHOD

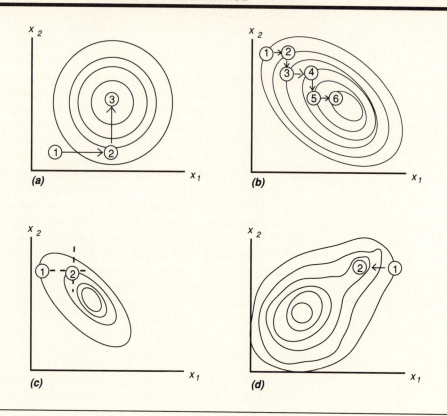

starting point for the search was used, as shown in Figure 10.10 (a). Similarly, if a different starting point were used for (d), the optimum would be found as shown in Figure 10.10 (b).

FIGURE 10.10   EFFECT OF STARTING POINT ON ONE-AT-A-TIME METHOD

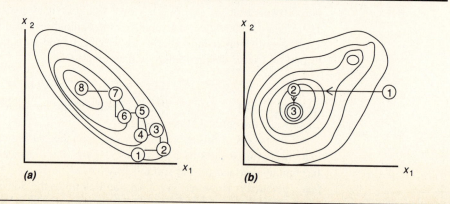

To alleviate this sensitivity to search starting point, multiple random starting points could be used. We demonstrate this in the following example by applying the one-at-a-time method to a response surface which has totally known characteristics.

ILLUSTRATIVE PROBLEM 10.7

To illustrate the one-at-a-time approach we will first fully develop the response surface for a machine repair problem. A set of 18 automatic machines randomly fail at intervals of 12 minutes; two classes of mechanics are available to repair them: expert mechanics and apprentice mechanics. Expert mechanics are paid more than apprentice mechanics, but they can repair a machine much faster. Machine repair time for an expert mechanic is 4 minutes, on the average, distributed normally with a standard deviation of 2 minutes, while that for an apprentice mechanic is 5 minutes distributed normally with a standard deviation of 3 minutes. Apprentice mechanics are paid $10.00 per hour and the higher skill level of expert mechanics is recognized by a rate of $30.00 per hour. Downtime cost for the machines are estimated to be $50.00 per hour per machine.

The measure of performance is total hourly cost. The two decision variables are the number of expert mechanics and apprentice mechanics assigned to keep the machines running.

Total hourly cost for this example may be expressed as:

$$TC = M_a S_a + M_e S_e + C \sum_{j=1}^{N} D_j$$

where:

M_a	=	Number of apprentice mechanics assigned
S_a	=	Hourly salary of apprentice mechanics
M_e	=	Number of expert mechanics assigned
S_e	=	Hourly salary of expert mechanics
C	=	Cost per machine-hour of downtime
D_j	=	Number of machine-hours of downtime during hour j of the replication
N	=	Number of hours in a replication.

To construct the response surface, the number of expert and apprentice mechanics were varied from 0 to 5 to yield 35 discrete points (the 0,0 combination was not run). The model was replicated five times for each combination of mechanics. The length of a replication was one 8-hour day. Thus there were 175 simulation runs in all. Approximate contour lines developed from these runs are plotted at intervals of $50 of hourly cost in Fig. 10.11. The contours were obtained by interpolating between the mean total hourly cost for the 35 points shown in Table 10.10. The fractional assignment of mechanics which may result from a solution lying on one of these contour lines may be rationalized by considering the unused portion of a mechanics time to be spent on other duties or, as was the case for Illustrative Problem 10.4, by considering this set of machines to be one of several identical ones which are maintained by the assigned mechanics.

We will apply the one-at-a-time method twice by selecting two random starting points and compare the results. For the first application we use an incremental change in the decision variables of .5 mechanics, and the second a change of 1 mechanic. For the

FIGURE 10.11 RESPONSE SURFACE FOR TWO-MECHANIC CLASS MACHINE REPAIR PROBLEM (MEAN TOTAL HOURLY COST)

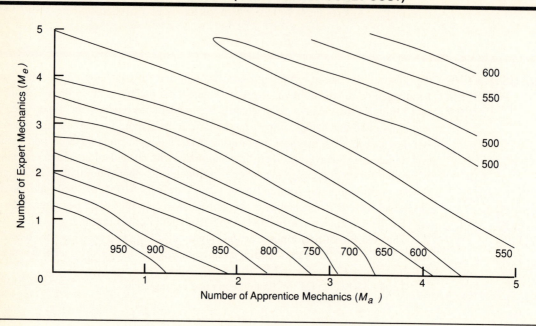

first application we begin by setting apprentice mechanics, M_a, to a randomly selected value of 4, and varying expert mechanics, M_e, over the range 0 to 5 in increments of .5 to find the lowest mean total hourly cost.

Since we normally know nothing of the shape of the response surface, we must vary the decision variable for which we are optimizing over its entire range. At least one simulation run would be required to evaluate the response surface at each point. But we have these results already in Table 10.10 and Fig. 10.11.

TABLE 10.10
TOTAL COSTS FOR TWO-MECHANIC CLASS MACHINE REPAIR PROBLEM
(MEAN TOTAL HOURLY COST ROUNDED TO NEAREST $10)

No. of Expert Mechanics	Number of Apprentice Mechanics					
	0	*1*	*2*	*3*	*4*	*5*
0		980	900	780	660	560
1	990	890	770	650	560	520
2	850	740	630	550	530	530
3	720	620	550	540	540	560
4	600	550	540	560	570	590
5	550	550	570	590	610	630

Interpolating between the values in Table 10.10, we find the lowest mean cost to be $535 with $M_e = 2.5$. We now fix M_e at this value and vary M_a over its range from 0 to 5. We find the lowest cost, $535, to be at $M_a = 4$. Since we began with a value of four apprentice mechanics, further evaluation would be cyclical. Thus we have satisfied the conditions for optimality described for the method. Namely,

$$R(M_a, M_e = 2.5) \leq R(M_a = 4, M_e = 2.5) \geq R(M_a = 4, M_e)$$

for all values of M_a and M_e. Since we know the shape of the entire response surface, we can state that this application of the method produced a global optimum.

For the second attempt we use a randomly chosen value of $M_a = 0$, and vary M_e over the range 1 to 5 in increments of 1 to find the lowest mean cost. Referring to Table 10.10, we see that the lowest mean cost, $550, occurs at $M_e = 5$. Fixing M_e at this value, we vary M_a in increments of 1 to find the minimum cost of $550 with $M_a = 0$ and $M_a = 1$, since $M_a = 0$ was our starting value. This application produced a lowest cost just $15 more than the first.

It would appear that the one-at-a-time method is particularly robust when applied to our response surface. Other starting points will yield similar results. If we examine Fig. 10.11 and Table 10.10, we see that the terrain drops precipitously from a cost of $980 at $M_a = 1$, $M_e = 0$, or (1,0) to $560 at (2.5,2.5). This valley ultimately drops to a low of $500 and then the terrain slowly climbs to a level of $630 at (5,5). The conclusion is that for response surfaces with such dramatic and regular contours, this method will work well. Unfortunately, not all response surfaces are like this.

One final word about the application of the one-at-a-time method to response surfaces generated by simulation models. Note that the function $R(M_a, M_e)$ was treated deterministically by using mean values. It is in fact a probabilistic function. If one includes the effect of the probability distribution of the costs, the optimal selection may change. The method considered below takes a probabilistic approach to the problem.

Response Surface Methodology   The second optimum-seeking approach we discuss is really a family of approaches called response-surface methodology. Taking advantage of an assumption that the response surface is continuous, these methods begin by estimating the shape of the surface in the immediate neighborhood. Then the most promising direction in which to proceed to reach a maximum or minimum is selected. The various methods use different experimental designs to estimate the shape of the surface, make different assumptions about the nature of the shape, and use diverse rules to determine how to alter the decision variable values and thus move in a particular direction. For example, some approaches assume a planar surface, while others use a curvilinear surface. Descriptions of these various methods may be found in Biles and Swain [3], and Wilde [20].

To illustrate this family of approaches we employ repeated use of a 2^2 experimental design to fit a planar surface to the response surface and choose a direction in which to move. This approach may be referred to as the gradient or steepest ascent (descent) method. We use the setting of Illustrative Problem 10.7 to explain this approach.

The plane to be fitted to our data can be described by the equation:

$$T = b_0 + b_1 M_a + b_2 M_e$$

FIGURE 10.12 2^2 DESIGN CENTERED ON (0,0)

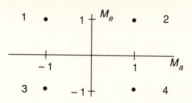

As described in Hicks [8], we can greatly simplify the required regression equations if we code M_a and M_e such that each 2^2 experiment is centered at the origin of the M_a, M_e grid with the four experimental points located at (-1,1), (1,1), (-1,-1), and (1,-1). This design is shown in Fig. 10.12.

Because of the resulting orthogonality of the independent variables, M_a and M_e, the values of the coefficients b_i may be computed as:

$$b_0 = \Sigma T / 4$$
$$b_1 = \Sigma TM_a / \Sigma M_a^2$$
$$b_2 = \Sigma TM_e / \Sigma M_e^2$$

where the summations are over the four design points in all cases.

Since the data from our simulation model is available for discrete values of the decision variables, we consider a surface defined only at these points. Our problem is one of cost minimization, and therefore we are looking for direction in which the fitted plane tilts downward. First, we use T values for each point in the experiment determined by the simulation model and compute the b_i. For each of the four points, we calculate a predicted T value using the b_i, and then the difference in elevation, or T, as:

$$D_i = T_0 - T_i \qquad i=1,2,3,4$$

where T_i is the total cost for the ith point, and T_0 is the total cost at the origin. The steepest descent is max (D_i) and the direction of steepest descent is then the vector from (0,0) to the coordinates of the point in the experiment yielding max (D_i).

The approach taken to moving downward on the surface is an unsophisticated but fairly effective one. The coordinates of the lowest point in the current experiment become coordinates for the complementary point in the next experiment. For example, if the Northwest (NW) corner of the current experiment were the lowest corner of the plane, it would be the Southeast (SE) corner of the next experiment; the NE corner would become the SW corner, etc. We proceed in this way through a series of 2^2 experiments, each centered at a "relative" origin.

The procedure stops when either of two following conditions occur: (1) the next experiment would define points beyond the range of the decision variables, or (2) the direction of steepest descent points back toward a previous experimental point. In either case, the optimal solution is defined as the decision variable values of the current experiment which yield the minimum T. Figure 10.13 shows a search procedure for two decision variables, X_1 and X_2, which terminate after eight experiments due to condition (2).

**FIGURE 10.13   SEQUENCE OF EXPERIMENTS FOR RESPONSE
SURFACE SEARCH**

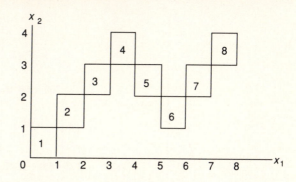

The optimal solution is then defined by the decision variable values which yield the minimum response surface in experiment number 8.

To make this method more concrete, we now apply it to the data of Illustrative Problem 10.7, and compare the resulting solution with that obtained using the one-at-a-time method.

**ILLUSTRATIVE
PROBLEM
10.8**

To gain some insight into the robustness of our approach, we will conduct two searches: one beginning with an experiment centered at $M_a = 1.5$, $M_e = .5$ [or more simply $(1.5,.5)$] and one centered at $(4.5,4.5)$. In the first case, the absolute coordinates for the first 2^2 experiment are: 1:(1,1), 2:(2,1), 3:(1,0), and 4:(2,0) where, as before, point 1 is the NW corner, point 2, the NE, point 3 the SW, and point 4 the SE. The coordinates for the second experiment are: 1:(4,5), 2:(5,5), 3:(4,4), and 4:(5,4). As we proceed through the series of necessary experiments, we consider each to be centered at (0,0), but these relative coordinates must be converted to absolute ones to interpret the final solution.

Each of the searches was conducted using the data of Illustrative Problem 10.7 shown in Table 10.10. Figure 10.14 shows the sequence of experiments for the first search including the absolute coordinates and response surface values for each experimental point. After a search using three experiments we achieve an optimal solution of 3 apprentices and 2 experts with a total cost of $544. The first experiment pointed to a steepest descent of $117 (i.e., the maximum D_i is

$$D_2 = T_0 - T_2 = \$893 - \$776 = \$117$$

occurring at the (2,1) corner of the plane. The second experiment pointed to (3,2) with steepest descent value of $106, and the third pointed back to (3,2) with steepest descent of $78. Thus, the best solution found has a cost of $544 using 3 apprentice and 2 expert mechanics.

Figure 10.15 shows the sequence of experiments for the second search. Three experiments produce an optimal solution of 3 apprentices and 3 experts with a total cost

FIGURE 10.14   EXPERIMENTAL RESULTS FOR FIRST SEARCH

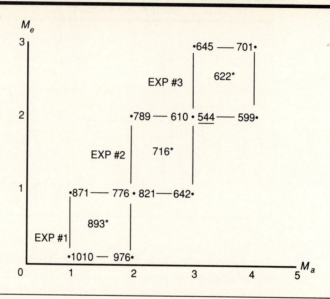

FIGURE 10.15   EXPERIMENTAL RESULTS FOR SECOND SEARCH

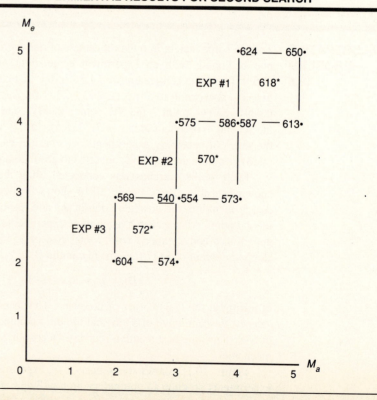

of $540. The first experiment pointed to a steepest descent of $31 occurring at the (4,4) corner of the plane. The second experiment pointed to (3,3) with a steepest descent value of $16, and the third pointed back to (3,3).

Each of the two searches produced similar results, with optimal costs differing by only $4 ($544 vs. $540) and the staffing differing by only one mechanic (6 vs. 5). Each of the two applications of the one-at-a-time method also produced comparable results: 6.5 mechanics with a total cost of $535, and 5 mechanics at $550. (The higher cost of the latter solution is due to the use of more expert mechanics.)

Although the results are similar, the effort to achieve them varied markedly. The first application of the one-at-a-time method required 22 runs of the simulation model, and the second, 10. Each of the searches for the gradient method only required 10 runs. Thus, taking advantage of knowledge about the shape of the response surface gained using the gradient method provides significant savings in model execution time.

The problems considered thus far have been essentially unconstrained in character. That is, the decision variables were permitted to take on any value from a large set of feasible values. There were, in a sense, implicit constraints, since some real numbers were excluded from consideration in our attempt to obtain an optimum system design. For example, in staffing checkout lanes in the supermarket problem, the number of cashiers could not exceed the number of lanes. However, constraints involving both decision variables were not addressed. In general, when constraints involve two or more decision variables, the complexity of the optimization is greatly increased. See Biles and Swain [3] for a discussion of this complication.

The previous examples certainly demonstrate that optimum-seeking techniques require many simulation runs. But it is also apparent that the whole optimization process would be much more efficient if the simulation model could be embedded in an interactive computer program that contained the optimum-seeking technique and any required statistical procedures. This cannot be done conveniently with existing software. One compromise currently possible would be a SIMAN model embedded in a FORTRAN program which implements the optimum-seeking technique and calls any required statistical routines.

10.5   DEALING WITH MULTIPLE MEASURES OF PERFORMANCE

The experimental structure and models needed to deal with multiple measures of performance are more complex than anything discussed thus far. In fact, detailed consideration of appropriate methodologies are beyond the scope of this book. In this section we will sketch broadly some approaches which may be used, and provide references for further reading.

As in the case of single measures of performance, we may wish to examine predetermined system designs by specifying decision variable values, or we may seek the set of values for the decision variables which defines an optimum system design. To assist us in these efforts there are analogous multivariate procedures for experimental design and system optimization. We consider first an experimental design technique, and then several optimization approaches.

10.5.1 EXPERIMENTAL DESIGN APPROACH

The experimental design procedure that treats more than one measure of performance is multivariate analysis of variance, known as MANOVA. This procedure is analogous to ANOVA, which treats only one measure of performance. In each case, we seek to identify possible differences in performance of a set of system designs. As one-way ANOVA for the univariate case is an extension of a two-sample t test to many samples, so MANOVA is an extension of a t test (Hotelling's T^2 test) to many samples for the multivariate test. It is helpful to begin the description of MANOVA at the fundamental level of two samples.

In the univariate case, the null hypothesis is: $H_0: \mu_1 = \mu_2$, where μ_1 and μ_2 are the mean values for the selected performance measure for each of two specified system designs. The appropriate t statistic is computed from the sample data and compared with a tabled t value with appropriate degrees of freedom to test H_0.

In the multivariate case, the null hypothesis involves a vector of μ's, one for each of k measures of performance for the two system designs, as:

$$H_0: \quad \begin{vmatrix} \mu_{11} \\ \cdot \\ \cdot \\ \cdot \\ \mu_{1k} \end{vmatrix} = \begin{vmatrix} \mu_{21} \\ \cdot \\ \cdot \\ \cdot \\ \mu_{2k} \end{vmatrix}$$

For example, consider a job shop for which we may wish to know if two performance measures of interest ($k = 2$) are affected by the rule used to select jobs from machine queues. Hotelling's T^2 test applies here since we have multiple measures of performance, and only one decision variable, job selection rule, being altered to define two different system designs. The measures of performance are: average job lateness in completion and average cost of job lateness. The first measure arises from a concern with customer satisfaction, and the second is due to penalty costs for tardiness which vary from job to job. Hotelling's T^2 test will determine if the two rules perform equally well in terms of the selected measures.

In order to conduct the actual t test, each vector must be reduced to a single number by applying weighting factors, which are a function of the sample data, to the μ_{ij}. Hotelling's T^2 statistic is then computed from the sample data and compared with a tabled F value with the appropriate degrees of freedom to test H_0. If $\mu_{1j} \neq \mu_{2j}$ for any j, then H_0 is rejected. The exact method for conducting the test is contained in multivariate statistical analysis texts such as Anderson [1] or Harris [7].

In the univariate case, extending the analysis from two samples to many yields the familiar one-way ANOVA procedure with the null hypothesis:

$$H_0: \mu_1 = \mu_2 = ... \mu_n,$$

where the μ_i are the means of the selected performance measure for n system designs. A test statistic is computed from a ratio of variances and compared with a tabled F value to test H_0. For one-way MANOVA, the null hypothesis involves vectors of means as:

$$H_0: \quad \begin{vmatrix} \mu_{11} \\ \cdot \\ \cdot \\ \cdot \\ \mu_{1k} \end{vmatrix} = \begin{vmatrix} \mu_{21} \\ \cdot \\ \cdot \\ \cdot \\ \mu_{2k} \end{vmatrix} \cdots = \begin{vmatrix} \mu_{n1} \\ \cdot \\ \cdot \\ \cdot \\ \mu_{nk} \end{vmatrix}$$

Extending our job shop example, we may wish to know if there is any difference in the two ($k = 2$) performance measures of interest (average job lateness, and average cost of job lateness) due to a set of four ($n = 4$) selection rules. One-way MANOVA is required here since we have multiple measures of performance and one decision variable, job selection rule, being altered to define several, rather than just two, system designs. If we were to reject a null hypothesis stating there is no difference among the rules, it would mean any of the four rules is as effective as another.

Again, in order to conduct the hypothesis test we must reduce the vectors to scaler quantities and compute an F statistic using the sample data to compare to a tabled F value. The null hypothesis is rejected unless

$$\mu_{1i} = \mu_{2i} = ... = \mu_{ni}, \quad \text{for } i = 1, 2, ..., k.$$

The calculation of the necessary test statistic is explained in multivariate statistics texts such as Anderson [1] or Harris [7].

10.5.2   OPTIMUM-SEEKING STRATEGIES

There are several possible approaches to the optimization problem with several performance measures. We consider four techniques:

(1) Optimization of all performance measures independently

(2) Optimization of a selected performance measure while constraining the remaining measures

(3) Optimization of a linear function of the performance measures

(4) Optimization through goal programming algorithms.

Each of these techniques is best suited to solving deterministic problems and their application to stochastic settings such as simulation models has not been fully resolved. Our description is in a deterministic framework, with reference to the complications caused by stochastic models. Again, the goal is to furnish insight into the concepts of these methods, not a detailed tutorial on how to use them. References to further reading are provided for that purpose.

To illustrate the four techniques we use the now familiar supermarket example. We are interested in two performance measures: average customer waiting time and salary cost per hour. Two decision variables are to be manipulated to define alternative system designs: the number of cashiers and the number of baggers assigned to checkout lanes. There are some constraints placed on the decision variables. First, we require at least one cashier, but the number of cashiers may not exceed the number of checkout lanes, taken to be eight. Also, the number of baggers may not exceed the number of cashiers.

The problem statement may be summarized as follows.

Minimize:

$$Z_1(X_1\ X_2)$$
$$Z_2(X_1\ X_2)$$

(10.25)

Subject to:

$$X_1 \geq 1$$
$$X_1 \leq 8$$
$$X_2 \leq X_1$$
$$X_2 \geq 0$$

(10.26)

where, X_1 and X_2 are the number of cashiers and baggers, respectively, and $Z_1(X_1,X_2)$, and $Z_2(X_1,X_2)$ are functions that define the average customer waiting time and the salary cost per hour, respectively. The Z_1 function is defined by operating characteristics of the simulation model, while $Z_2 = 4X_1 + 2X_2$. The minimization specified is ambiguous, but it will be defined explicitly for each of the four optimization techniques. Figure 10.16 shows the feasible solution space for this problem.

Independent Optimization of Performance Measures The first technique optimizes all of the performance measures independently. In general, we would use one of the optimum-seeking techniques described in Section 10.4 to search the response surfaces

FIGURE 10.16 FEASIBLE SOLUTION SPACE FOR CASHIER AND BAGGER STAFFING PROBLEM

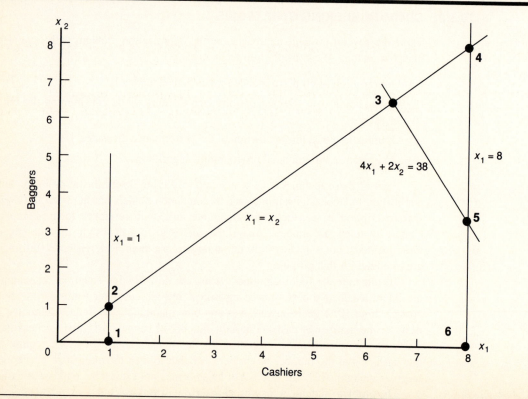

Z_1 and Z_2 independently, and find the optimum system design with respect to each of the performance measures. For illustrative purposes we make an approximation which permits examination of points in the solution space without running a simulation model. Based on knowledge of similar supermarkets, we will estimate $Z_1(X_1 + X_2) = 100/(4X_1 + X_2)$. This equation defines average waiting time as a nonlinearly decreasing function, with cashiers being four times as effective as baggers in reducing waiting time. Now both response surfaces are either monotonically increasing or decreasing functions of X_1 and X_2.

With both response surfaces regular and well-defined, we need examine the values of Z_1 and Z_2 only at extreme points 1, 2, 4, and 6 (see Fig. 10.16) to determine the optimal system designs to be:

$$Z^*_1 = Z_1(8,8) = 100/40 = 2.5 \qquad \text{at point 4}$$

$$Z^*_2 = Z_2(1,0) = 4 \qquad \text{at point 1}$$

The success of this method relies on the ability to find one solution which will dominate all others. That is, the optimal solution with respect to one of the performance measures will also be optimal with respect to all the other measures. In our supermarket example, two quite different optimal systems emerge depending upon the performance measure used: one system design with eight cashiers, and one with only the minimum of one. This is not surprising, since the goals of minimizing salary cost and waiting time are diametrically opposed. In most complex models where there are trade-offs to be made, such as salary cost for waiting time in this example, this method is of limited usefulness.

Optimization of a Selected Performance Measure   The second technique converts a multiple performance measure problem to one involving only a single performance measure by optimizing one measure while constraining all the others. In this example we choose to focus upon the service level, as measured by customer waiting time Z_1, so salary cost will be constrained not to exceed a budgeted amount of \$38 per hour. The additional constraint required is: $4X_1 + 2X_2 \leq 38$.

The problem may now be stated as:

Minimize:

$$Z_1(X_1, X_2) = 100/(4X_1 + X_2) \qquad (10.27)$$

Subject to:

$$\begin{aligned} X_1 &\geq 1 \qquad\qquad (10.28)\\ X_1 &\leq 8 \\ X_2 &\leq X_1 \\ 4X_1 + 2X_2 &\leq 38 \\ X_2 &\geq 0 \end{aligned}$$

We will again use the approximation for waiting time, rather than searching the response surface, to illustrate this technique, since then we need only examine extreme points of the solution space. Examining the values of Z_1 and Z_2 at extreme points 1, 2, 3, 5, and 6, we find the optimum solution to be:

$$Z^*_1 = Z_1(8,3) = 100/35 = 2.86 \text{ at extreme point 5.}$$

Thus, we have a third "optimal" solution. The optimal waiting time for this solution does not differ greatly from that of the previous formulation (2.86 vs. 2.5), but the salary cost $[Z_2 (8,3) = 38]$ is far greater than the optimal value of Z_2 $[Z_2(1,0) = 4]$. In fact, the cost is at its upper limit.

The waiting time versus salary cost trade-off may be examined using this method by relaxing the budget constraint gradually (i.e., increasing the upper limit) and observing the improvement in waiting time. The question that must then be answered by the decision maker is: How many dollars of hourly salary am I willing to expend to achieve reduction in waiting time of one minute? So, the inconsistency in dimensions for our performance measures is treated implicitly, rather than explicitly, as in the optimizing technique described next.

Optimization of a Linear Function of Performance Measures   The third technique again reduces multiple performance measures to a single one, but still optimizes, in a sense, all of the measures. We achieve this by assigning a weighting factor to each of the performance measures based upon the decision maker's perception of their relative importance. The inconsistency in dimensions is resolved by the decision maker, but now by very conscious judgment.

For our supermarket example the problem becomes:

Minimize:

$$Z(X_1,X_2) = W_1 Z_1(X_1,X_2) + W_2 Z_2(X_1,X_2) \tag{10.29}$$

Subject to:

$$
\begin{aligned}
X_1 &\geq 1 \\
X_1 &\leq 8 \\
X_2 &\leq X_1 \\
X_2 &\geq 0
\end{aligned}
\tag{10.30}
$$

To obtain the optimal value of Z, we would in general search the new response surface defined by the weighted objective function, but to illustrate this method we continue to use the approximation for waiting time.

To explore the sensitivity of the solution to the weighting factors, we evaluate the objection function, Z, using three sets of W_i: one set with equal weights, one with waiting time (Z_1) heavily weighted, and one with salary cost (Z_2) heavily weighted. To determine the optimal solution for each case, all X_1, X_2 combinations in the feasible solution space are evaluated (44 points in all). The values of Z, Z_1, and Z_2 for selected points are shown in Table 10.11. For the weighting scheme used, a factor of 10 indicates the highest level of relative importance, while 1 indicates the lowest level. Thus in the unequally weighted cases, one performance measure is perceived to be about 2.33 times as important as the other.

The solutions obtained using the varying set of weights are quite different, but not counterintuitive. When a heavy weight is applied to waiting time, the optimum number of cashiers is four, while a heavy weight applied to salary cost yields an optimum number of cashiers of two. This simple comparison considers only one aspect of sensitivity: the relative weights applied to performance measures. In addition, the ratio of the weights has significant impact. For example, if the ratio $W_1/W_2 = 10$ instead of 2.33, the results would be quite different.

TABLE 10.11
SELECTED VALUES FOR RESPONSE SURFACE

				Z		
X_1	X_2	Z_1	Z_2	$W_1 = 5$ $W_2 = 5$	$W_1 = 7$ $W_2 = 3$	$W_1 = 3$ $W_2 = 7$
1	0	25.0	4	145	187	103
1	1	20.0	6	130	158	102
2	0	12.5	8	103*	112	94*
2	2	10.0	12	110	106	114
3	0	8.3	12	102	94	109
3	3	6.7	18	123	101	146
4	0	6.3	16	111	92*	131
4	4	5.0	24	145	107	183
5	0	5.0	20	125	95	155
5	5	4.0	30	170	118	222
6	0	4.2	24	141	101	181
6	6	3.3	36	197	131	262
7	0	3.6	28	158	109	207
7	7	2.9	42	224	146	303
8	0	3.1	32	176	118	234
8	8	2.5	48	253	162	344

* Indicates optimal value of Z.

Optimization Using Goal Programming   The last technique to be covered is a form of linear programming, namely, goal programming. The solutions obtained for all deterministic problems are provably optimum. We describe this technique conceptually, but space does not permit a full explanation of the goal programming approach applied to our example problem. For fuller treatment reference is made to operations research texts such as Hillier and Lieberman [9] and Goicoechea [6].

The use of goal programming permits progress toward a number of goals simultaneously. Goals may be of three types: upper bound, lower bound, or specific numeric. Upper bound goals reflect a desire to keep a measure of performance from exceeding a specified value, while lower bound goals are minimum values which should be exceeded. Specific numeric goals are explicit targets, deviation above or below which is undesirable. In our supermarket example we might state the following goals:

$Z_1(X_1, X_2) \leq 5$ Upper bound goal for waiting time

$Z_2(X_1, X_2) \leq 38$ Upper bound goal for salary cost.

In the goal-programming algorithm, upper bound goals have penalty values associated with them if they are exceeded. Similarly, lower bound goals are assigned penalty values associated with them if they are not exceeded. A specific numeric goal incurs a penalty if it deviates in either direction from the stated goal value.

In framing the problem for solution we define the auxiliary variables Y^+ as the amount by which a stated goal is exceeded and Y^- as the amount by which the performance measure falls short of the goal. Upper bound goals have Y^+ variables associated with them, lower bound goals have Y^- variables associated with them, and specific numeric goals require both types of auxiliary variables. The auxiliary variables appear in both the constraint set and the objective function of this programming formulation.

To pursue all of the goals at once, an objective function is formed which consists of all of the Y_i^+ and Y_i^-. The coefficients used are penalty weights, assigned by the decision maker, for failing to achieve the goals. In our example we might define the following objective function:

$$Z = 4Y_1^+ + Y_2^+$$

This implies that it is four times worse to exceed the waiting time goal than to exceed the salary cost goal.

A multiple performance measure formulated in this way is amenable to solution using standard linear programming algorithms. In a sense, this technique is the extension of the weighting factor approach discussed above to cases where the number of feasible solutions is too large to enumerate in finding the optimal solution.

In all of the optimizing techniques discussed in this section, we have dealt with a deterministic problem formulation and a well-behaved response surface. Most simulations are not deterministic. Applying these techniques to simulation model output is more complex. For example, finding the optimal value of performance measures requires irregular response surfaces to be searched. Also, determining if a probabilistic constraint is satisfied may involve the testing of a statistical hypothesis. This issue is dealt with in connection with a large simulation model by Perry [19]. Further, goal programming algorithms do not exist to completely deal with the complications introduced by probabilistic constraints and objective functions. Thus our ability to deal with the optimization of multiple performance measures is currently quite limited.

10.6   CONCLUSION

It is evident from the discussion of this chapter that the specific approach to model experimentation depends heavily on the aims of the simulation study and the setting in which it is performed. In our exploration, should we examine a few specified system designs, or a broad range of alternatives? If options are limited by real-world constraints, it makes sense to just explore the set of alternatives that are feasible. We should compare the merits of a few system designs, as discussed in Section 10.2.

On the other hand, if the aim of the simulation study is to gain insight into system behavior, or if there are many degrees of freedom in the real-world setting (e.g., a large budget, enthusiastic managers, etc.), then many more alternative system designs should be explored. The experimental design and optimizing techniques of Sections 10.3 and 10.4 are applicable here. Finally, if there are several measures of performance which must be considered in selecting a system design, the multivariate statistical and optimizing techniques of Section 10.5 are useful.

EXERCISES

10.1 Two equipment maintenance policies being considered for implementation were modeled using simulation. Ten replications of each policy were evaluated, where each replication consists of machine failures occurring over a one-month period. All replications are independent of one another. The measure of performance used is total monthly cost, including machine downtime and repair personnel.

Given the monthly cost data below, which of the two policies is better?

TOTAL MONTHLY MAINTENANCE COST

POLICY 1	POLICY 2
$955	$695
1014	670
982	684
983	618
989	681
879	625
946	571
878	554
911	522
915	575

10.2 Based on further analysis of available data, a third maintenance policy is devised. The monthly cost data derived from running the simulation model for 10 replications is shown below.

POLICY 3

$587
680
569
684
554
559
670
520
695
617

a) Using the Bonferroni approach, which policy should be chosen?

b) Using a single-factor experiment and Duncan's Multiple Range test, which policy is preferred?

c) Are the results different? If so, in which method would you place more credence? Why?

10.3 Refer to Exercise 4.1 in Chapter 4.

a) Suggest an explicit procedure or experimental approach to assess the impact of the supply of shopping carts on the total number of customers who balk (refuse to wait for an available cart).

b) Replicate the simulation model five times for each alternative system design defined, conduct the analysis proposed in part (a), and make a recommendation regarding the number of carts to maintain.

10.4 Refer to Exercise 4.7 part (b), of Chapter 4.

   a) Based on the discussion of this chapter (Chapter 10), propose an explicit experiment to aid in deciding how many car wash stalls and how much car waiting space to provide. For your experiment state the number of replications for each experimental point.

   b) Comment on the level of confidence to be placed in the experimental results of part (a). Relate your answer to the number of observations for each system design alternative. Can your experiment treat any possible interaction effect?

   c) For each system design proposed in part (a), conduct at least three model replications, and perform the analysis. Which design is ''best''? Why?

10.5 In Exercise 10.4 it is desired to find the optimum combination of car stalls and car waiting space. Consider a range of stalls from 4 to 8, and a range of queue space of from 3 to 8.

   a) Apply the one-at-a-time method to find the optimal system design. Use the method twice with two randomly chosen starting values for number of stalls.

10.6 Repeat Exercise 10.5 using the gradient response-surface search algorithm. Conduct at least a 2^2 experiment to determine direction of steepest gradient at each iteration. Conduct two searches starting at two randomly chosen center points for the initial experiment.

10.7 Compare the results of Exercises 10.5 and 10.6. Are the optimal solutions in agreement? If not, what might be responsible?

10.8 Refer to Exercise 4.12 of Chapter 4. Define completely an experiment to assess the merits of the six communication systems determined by varying transmission mode and speed. Recommend the number of observations for each experimental point as well as the total number of observations.

10.9 Expand the solution space of Illustrative Problem 10.6 to include the use of express lanes. There are now four decision variables: (1) number of express lanes, (2) number of regular lanes, (3) baggers present or not, and (4) bar-code reader or standard register. Add any necessary specifics, such as what constitutes an express customer, so that a model may be built and executed.

   a) Define a 2^n screening experiment to determine which, if any of the decision variables have an impact on the performance measure time in the system.

   b) Run the experiment of part (a) and comment on which decision variables are of concern. If your experimental design permits, comment on any interaction effect.

REFERENCES

1. Anderson, T. W., *Introduction to Multivariate Statistical Analysis*, New York: John Wiley & Sons, Inc., 1958.

2. Banks, J., and Carson, J., *Discrete-Event System Simulation*, Englewood Cliffs, New Jersey: Prentice-Hall, Inc., 1984.

3. Biles, W., and Swain, J., *Optimization and Industrial Experimentation*, New York: John Wiley & Sons, 1980.

4. Cochran, W., and Cox, G., *Experimental Designs*, New York: John Wiley & Sons, 1957.

5. Emshoff, J. and Sisson, R., *Design and Use of Computer Simulation Models*, New York: Macmillan Publishing Co., 1970.

6. Goicoechea, A., et al., *Multiobjective Decision Analysis with Engineering and Business Applications*, New York: John Wiley & Sons, 1982.

7. Harris, R. J., *A Primer of Multivariate Statistics*, New York: Academic Press, 1975.

8. Hicks, C., *Fundamental Concepts in the Design of Experiments*, New York: Holt, Rinehart and Winston, 1964.

9. Hillier, F. S., and Lieberman, G. J., *Introduction to Operations Research*, 3rd Edition, San Francisco: Holden-Day, Inc., 1980.

10. Kleijnen, J., *Statistical Techniques in Simulation*, New York: Marcel Dekker, Inc., 1974.

11. Law, A., and Kelton, W., *Simulation Modeling and Analysis*, New York: McGraw-Hill Book Co., 1982.

12. Meier, R., Newell, W., and Pazer, H., *Simulation in Business and Economics*, Englewood Cliffs, New Jersey: Prentice-Hall, 1969.

13. Mirham, G., *Simulation: Statistical Foundations and Methodology*, New York: Academic Press, 1972.

14. Montgomery, D. C., *Design and Analysis of Experiments*, New York: John Wiley & Sons, 1976.

15. Natrella, M. G., *Experimental Statistics*, Washington, D.C.: National Bureau Standards Handbook 91, 1966.

16. Naylor, T., Editor, *The Design of Computer Simulation Experiments*, Durham, North Carolina: Duke University Press, 1969.

17. Naylor, T., Editor, *Computer Simulation Experiments with Models of Economic Systems*, New York: John Wiley & Sons, 1971.

18. Nemhauser, G., *Introduction to Dynamic Programming*, New York: John Wiley & Sons, 1966.

19. Perry, R. F., "Resource Allocation and Scheduling for a Radiology Department," in *Cost Control in Hospitals*, Ann Arbor, Michigan: Health Administration Press, 1976.

20. Wilde, D., *Optimum Seeking Methods*, Englewood Cliffs, New Jersey: Prentice-Hall, Inc., 1964.

CHAPTER 11

IMPLEMENTATION OF SIMULATION RESULTS

Increasingly complex technology and competition in world markets demand more effective solutions to today's manufacturing problems. Implementation of simulation analysis results can provide these solutions. The use of a graphically animated simulation recently allowed Northern Research and Engineering Corporation to save $750,000 when designing a complicated assembly line for a client. Further, a senior engineer for the firm states that savings of several million dollars are not uncommon from such analyses. But the value of even the most promising simulation result lies in its implementation; without implementation, all the money and effort expended on the study are for naught.

11.1 INTRODUCTION

Implementation is the last step in the simulation analysis procedure described in Chapter 2; it is last, but by no means least. Although this step appears at the end of any sequential list of elements in a simulation analysis, it will become clear from the discussion of this chapter that the actions necessary to assure full and successful implementation must begin long before the conclusion of any study. In fact, they should commence at the problem formulation stage of the simulation analysis.

In this chapter, we describe what is required to implement the results of a simulation analysis, and make suggestions for improving the likelihood of successful implementation. We begin with a description of the process of implementation in Section 11.2. Next, we present the experience of practitioners in implementing results, as distilled from the literature. Finally, in Section 11.4, we consider the issues which must be addressed to ensure successful implementation.

11.2 THE IMPLEMENTATION PROCESS

A recent study revealed that implementation of simulation results may include any or all of the following [5]:

- Providing the user with the computer code for the simulation model.
- Establishing the simulation model in the user's environment, including installing the computer code on the user's computer and training in the use of the model.
- Converting simulation results into decisions that affect organizational performance.

We prefer the last definition of implementation, since it is the only one that could truly justify the cost of the simulation study. To achieve such implementation requires a complex process involving members of the organization with differing backgrounds, expertise, and goals. Specifically, persons with management, modeling, and computer programming skills must interact with the ultimate users who will make the necessary decisions.

In any organization, two major categories of decisions exist: (1) one-time or very infrequent decisions, and (2) recurring decisions. Examples falling into the first category include: plant relocation, computer system selection, and new product or business venture assessment. Second category examples include: inventory management, machine scheduling, and staffing decisions.

The actions necessary to implement simulation results for decisions in each category are quite different. The one-time or infrequent decision simply requires that the study results be followed. The implementation of this type of study finding typically involves fewer people in the organization than is required for recurring decisions (although it may affect great numbers of people, as in plant relocations). Also, it is the authors' experience that users of this type of study finding are usually middle or top management.

To implement results for recurring decisions, one must provide a mechanism to make them an integral part of day-to-day decision making. For example, inventory management policies must become part of any manual or computer-based re-ordering procedure. The data on demand and inventory levels required for the policy must be provided in a timely way. This type of implementation is inherently more difficult for three reasons:

(1) It typically involves large numbers of people in the organization.

(2) It requires the establishment of an ongoing information system.

(3) It is necessary to monitor the real system for changes which should be reflected in the simulation model and alterations made as needed.

In an attempt to contrast the two categories of implementation, Table 11.1 lists some tasks necessary to achieve implementation and their relative importance for each category.

Oversimplifying somewhat, the one-time decision implementation process involves a relatively small number of people, highly placed in the organization. The effort is focused on explaining the model and study results to this group. The worth of such results will be assessed totally by the end-user managers. By contrast, the recurring decision implementation process requires interacting with a large number of people to explain the results, convince them of their value, and provide detailed assistance so the end user can apply the results effectively. The development of the supporting information system may or may not involve the simulation analysts.

TABLE 11.1
IMPLEMENTATION TASKS

Task	Importance for:*	
	One-Time Decisions	Recurring Decisions
End user training	NR	E
User manuals	NR	H to E
Develop supporting information system	NR	E
Install model at multiple sites	NR	H to E
Explain and justify study results	E	E
Convince end user of study value	H	E
Deal with many organization members	NR	H to E

*E: Essential
 H: Helpful
NR: Not Required

Based upon this analysis of the implementation process, it is apparent that one skill is unquestionably necessary to success in this endeavor: communications. The implementers must be able to explain technical material to potential users in terms that will be both comprehensible and significant. This is true whether the users are a relatively small homogeneous group, as is typical for a one-time decision implementation, or the larger more diverse group commonly associated with a recurring decision implementation. There are, however, additional skills needed to address other problems associated with implementation, as discussed in later sections.

11.3   CURRENT STATUS OF IMPLEMENTATION EFFORTS

Implementation of operations research study results has been a difficult task. Two recent surveys of the practice of management science explored the reasons for this. One study found the three most pressing problems in implementing operations research results in general to be: selling management science methods to management, lack of quantitative education of middle and top managers, and lack of good data [7]. A second more recent study confirmed these findings for simulation analyses in particular [1].

The findings of the second study are shown in Table 11.2. The respondents were 90 nonacademic members of the Operations Research Society of America and The Institute of Management Science who were simulation users. They were asked to cite major problems in the implementation of simulation analyses.

The results of this survey confirm the need for good communications skills as cited above. The two most frequently cited problems could be alleviated by an improved ability to communicate and explain the workings of the simulation model and the value of the model to the particular decision. Also, items 5, 6, and 7 in Table 11.2 could benefit from better communications.

TABLE 11.2
IMPLEMENTATION PROBLEMS

Implementation Problem	Percent Citing Problem
1. Lack of quantitative education of top and middle managers	40
2. Lack of end user education	30
3. Lack of time	29
4. Lack of good data	25
5. Individuals feel threatened by MS/OR professionals	19
6. Selling management science methods to management	16
7. Poor reputation of management scientists as problem solvers	16
8. Payoff of unsophisticated method is good enough	6
9. Hard to define and model problems	2
10. Personnel shortage	2

Communications in this context implies more than simply clear exposition of ideas by simulation analysts for users. It implies that analysts develop a clear understanding of users' problems and have a commitment to solving them which takes priority over other considerations, such as preference for a particular solution or simulation technique. Conversely, communications implies that the users be willing to become better educated and informed about the simulation analysis techniques used to solve their problems. However, this is not a meeting on middle ground. The analysts must realize and accept the notion that their value lies totally in the ability to improve the operation of the business, and all other considerations in problem solving are secondary.

The respondents to the survey of reference [1] were also asked to make recommendations for improving the use of simulation. These results are shown in Table 11.3.

These findings correlate somewhat with the assessment of the problems shown in Table 11.2. The top ranking recommendation, improve knowledge of simulation techniques, corresponds to the top ranking problem, lack of quantitative education of managers. Better communications is recommended, but only by a very small number of respondents. However, communications is apparently perceived much more narrowly than in our definition above, since in Table 11.3 it is singled out as item 4, distinct from the education issue mentioned as item 1. Interestingly, success in implementation is not explicitly cited as a recommendation.

A great deal of importance is attached to technology as a means to improve the use of simulation analysis. Items 2, 3, and 5 of Table 11.3 suggest computer software and hardware hold the key to better simulation analysis. Also, these items might be construed to mean that users desire to reduce or eliminate the interfacing role of the simulation analyst. In light of the considerable concern expressed about education of users, such efforts should proceed with extreme caution.

Despite the acknowledged difficulties surrounding implementation, there is a paucity of research and development effort in this area. The most recent bibliography

TABLE 11.3
RECOMMENDATIONS TO IMPROVE SIMULATION ANALYSIS

Recommendation	Percent Making Recommendation
1. Improve knowledge of simulation techniques by end users and older managers	28
2. Develop easier to use, less expensive software	26
3. Provide more accessible, larger, better quality data bases	20
4. Develop better communication between analysts and users	8
5. Develop easier interfaces with data bases; integrated models	6
6. Improve understanding of the technique and its philosophy by modelers	5
7. Better hardware	4
8. Lower costs	3

cataloged some 300 papers from the operations research literature dealing with implementation research [8]. The evidence suggests that concern for this problem is recent, since the overwhelming majority of such papers have appeared during the last decade.

The importance of implementation of study results is underscored by the College on the Practice of Management Science of The Institute of Management Sciences. In an annual contest, the college makes sizable cash awards for papers which report the implementation of study results that yield demonstrable savings. It is interesting to note that simulation studies are often among the winning papers.

The obvious conclusion to be drawn from the foregoing discussion is that implementation is not a task that follows automatically from a technically well-executed study. Rather, implementation strategies must be formulated. This conclusion was reached some years ago in the kindred discipline of information systems, and subsequent changes in the development process for such systems has improved the implementation success rate. In the next section we consider the use of implementation strategies for simulation study results.

11.4 ACHIEVING SUCCESSFUL IMPLEMENTATION

11.4.1 IMPLEMENTATION AS A CHANGE PROCESS

The act of implementing the results of a simulation study may alter the way people in the organization accomplish their jobs and the way decisions are made. Hence, it is referred to as a change process. The person responsible for bringing about the change is designated a change agent. In the case of simulation studies, the analyst is usually viewed as the change agent, even though it may require management action to adopt the analyst's recommendations. The simulation analyst works with the user to help diagnose and solve problems; the relationship is that of a consultant and client.

Even changes that appear to bring great benefit to all are often resisted by some members of the organization. This resistance is usually based upon something other than an assessment of the merits of the proposed change. Typically, it arises because of a lack of coincidence of personal and organizational goals. For example, a productivity improvement change which disrupts social work groups may be resisted. Overcoming such resistance is the key to a successful change.

To appreciate the relative merits of alternative strategies for overcoming resistance to change, we need a brief digression into the field of social psychology. Particular models of organizational behavior underlay such strategies.

One of the earliest models is that of Rational Economic Man [6]. It assumes an organization member is motivated solely by economic incentives. On the basis of this model, the strategy of choice is formal authority; either the worker performs as directed or he is shown the exit.

More enlightened models of organizational behavior include: Theory X, Social Man and Self Actualizing Man [6]. These models envision a more complex set of motivations than simply economic gain. They assume an organization member derives satisfaction from less tangible things such as recognition and a feeling of achievement from contributing to some common goal; he internalizes many of the organization's goals. These models suggest a wide variety of strategies for overcoming resistance to change, or more positively, motivating an organization member to be an active participant in the change.

11.4.2   ELEMENTS OF A CHANGE PLAN

Many activities in organizations may be viewed as change processes. The installation of computer-based information systems, for example, has received considerable study in an attempt to link the manner in which change, or implementation, is accomplished to the ultimate success of the information system [3,4]. Many of the findings from the study of this problem may be applied to implementation of simulation results.

As suggested above, active participation is essential to successful implementation. But why is participation so important? Some of the more compelling reasons include: ego enhancement, intrinsic satisfaction, control over organizational destiny, a greater commitment to the change, and better solutions through use of end-user knowledge. So, the task at hand is to devise a plan for the design, development, and implementation of simulation study results that promotes constructive participation by the end users, that is, a change plan.

Lucas [3,4] suggests an extensive set of elements for a change plan for computer-based information systems. The following list presents those items that cover issues germane to simulation study implementation.

1. Use a system design team consisting of computer specialists and representative group of users.
2. Let the user initiate the request for a system, if possible; this enhances commitment to the effort.
3. Let the user design the system, if possible; the information system specialist should serve as a catalyst.
4. Form a high-level management steering committee to demonstrate support and resolve resource allocation problems.
5. Stress development of favorable attitudes during the design phase.
6. Plan carefully for implementation, considering the impact of the system in advance.
7. Plan for essential implementation tasks, such as training and development of user manuals.

These guidelines suggest that the user should be involved in the development of a computer-based information systems from its very inception. With the possible exception of item 3, these recommendations can serve as a model for developing a change plan to implement simulation study results.

Given the level of technical expertise required to develop simulation models, the user will require considerable assistance in the technical details of simulation model development. But the role of the end user is still far from trivial. The user is an invaluable source of information upon which to base the simulation model.

Early efforts in modeling were highly structured, omitting elements of reality in favor of easily constructed and optimized models. As user tolerance for this approach diminished, more of the user experience was included, and models were made more user-interactive so that users could approach a solution iteratively. Today, models tend toward generalizing and applying user experience rather than embodying some all-explaining structure. The vehicle for doing this is the so-called expert system, which contains decision making rules distilled from user experience. Emshoff provides an excellent summary of this model evolution [2].

We see that the end user is a most important participant in implementing any simulation study result. Not only is he/she a valuable source of information to facilitate the modeling process, but also the one who will determine the ultimate worth of the study results to the organization. If the user does not understand the model or results achieved, or does not find them convenient to apply, all of the simulation study effort will have been for naught. This underscores the need to pay special heed to three of the items cited in the change plan guidelines above: (1) development of favorable attitudes (item 5), (2) anticipation of the impact of system implementation (item 6), and (3) planning for training and development of user documentation (item 7).

The goals of all three guidelines can be greatly facilitated by improved communications between analysts and end users, where communications is used in the broad sense introduced in Section 11.3. A concerted effort should be made by analysts to make clear to users the workings of the simulation model and how the results follow from the model manipulation. This may require *ad hoc* meetings to deal with the particular project, as well as periodic general meetings or seminars to explore the methods of simulation analysis and how they relate to the users' problems.

Finally, to institutionalize the results of some simulation studies requires significant change or addition to the organization's infrastructure. For example, if large numbers of users are involved, extensive training programs may be needed. If much detailed data are required for model use, a new computer-based information system may need to be developed. As the study progresses, these issues are typical of those the high-level management steering committee should resolve. This committee should ensure the necessary resources are available for such needs.

11.4.3   THE IMPACT OF TECHNOLOGY ON IMPLEMENTATION

Among the major problems confronting simulation users are poor communications between users and analysts, and lack of familiarity on the part of the users with simulation techniques. Technology may be used to alleviate both of these problems.

With the advent of powerful microcomputers and user-oriented software, it is now possible for nontechnical users to readily apply the computer to the solution of their problems. As mentioned in Chapter 4, the number of simulation languages available for microcomputers is growing rapidly. Many of these languages permit the functional specialist, who understands the problem to be solved but knows nothing of simulation or its languages, to create and experiment with simulation models. The use of graphical input/output and animations of the progress of the simulation using meaningful icons to represent real system entities are major features of such languages. Thus the functional specialist can better understand his problem and evaluate trial system designs using a simulation model.

This microcomputer-based technology not only reduces the need for the user to learn many technical details of simulation, but also greatly enhances communication, in the broadest sense, between users and analysts. In fact, many organizations cite increased ability to explain and sell simulation-derived solutions to management as the primary reason for purchasing expensive, color-graphics animation hardware and software.

All of this points to increased involvement of users in simulation analysis, which is certainly to be encouraged. But some caveats to totally eliminating the simulation analyst from the process must be raised. The subtleties and nuances of model validation and output analysis have not yet been reduced to such a level of rote that they can be completely embodied in computer software. The user may draw incorrect inferences from his model. Forming appropriate conclusions from simulation model output relies heavily on a solid understanding of statistics, as was discussed in Chapters 9 and 10. Imparting this sort of intelligence to the computer software may yet occur, but it awaits major advances in the field of artificial intelligence.

How does this new technology alter the role of the simulation analyst? To the degree that easy-to-use simulation software improves the understanding by users of the workings of simulation models and promotes participation in their construction, it is most desirable. However, it is not yet in the end user's best interest for the simulation analyst to withdraw, leaving the user with only the software, even complete with computerized tutorial, and his/her own devices.

11.5   CONCLUSION

Implementation of simulation results provides the return on the investment of resources in the simulation analysis. Consequently, it is most important that we do all things reasonable to ensure successful implementation. First, we must define implementation and the tasks necessary to achieve it. Then, it is instructive to consider the users' perceptions of problems in implementation and their recommendations for improvement. The most pervasive problem identified is lack of communications between the end user and the simulation analyst. Communications is used here in a very broad sense referring not only to a particular simulation project, but also to an understanding of simulation techniques by the end user and an appreciation of the results-oriented perspective of the end user by the analyst.

With this background, the question of how to increase the chances of successful implementation can be addressed. Viewing the implementation of simulation results as a change process provides useful insights for achieving this goal. Any change in an organization has associated with it resistance by those it will affect. Consequently, one must devise an implementation strategy to actively deal with this phenomenon. The similar change process of computer-based information system development provides a useful model for simulation implementation.

Experience in this field suggests the importance of carefully planning all aspects of change of this great a magnitude. Adapting from the information systems arena, a change plan for simulation should include the following elements:

- A design team consisting of users and analysts
- An active role for users in the modeling process
- User-initiated simulation study requests
- Support of high level management
- Development of favorable attitudes toward study goals
- Careful planning for implementation from the outset
- Appropriate attention to training and user manuals.

Finally, advances in computer hardware and software for simulation potentially alter the traditional role of the simulation analyst. The newly found ease with which models can be constructed and experiments run may cause users to draw statistically-unwarranted conclusions. The software as yet does not embody the statistical "intelligence" to dispense with the analyst. Until this occurs, effective use of simulation models will require even better communications, in the broadest sense, between end users and analysts.

EXERCISES

11.1 Search the simulation literature for papers which have as their main topic implementation of simulation results. Journals and proceedings to search include: *Simulation, Winter Simulation Conference, Industrial Engineering, Management Science, IIE Transactions,* and *Interfaces.* Based upon frequency of occurrence of such articles, make an inference as to the importance of implementation in simulation studies today. Compare the content of these papers with the approach of Chapter 11.

11.2 Examine several other general texts on simulation analysis for material dealing with implementation of results. Contrast what is said with Chapter 11.

11.3 Search the simulation literature for several reports of implemented simulation studies and read them carefully. From your reading, what are the main problems encountered in implementation?

11.4 Based on a reading of some of the papers identified in exercises 11.1 and 11.3, state at least two definitions given to implementation: for example, giving the model code to the users, or installing the code on the users' computer. If discussed in the papers, indicate how these definitions were developed.

11.5 Based upon a thorough reading of some of the papers found in the searches of exercises 11.1 and 11.3, identify at least two different approaches taken to implement simulation results. If discussed in the papers, comment on the effectiveness of these approaches.

11.6 Reread Section 11.4.3 which discusses the impact of developing technology on implementation of simulation results. Using specific examples of the technology (e.g., model animation using personal computers), describe how these will alleviate the communications gap between users and analysts. Discuss any problems you foresee in the use of the technology.

11.7 You have been assigned to lead a group conducting a simulation analysis of a production line for a new product. The product is currently in the final design stages but the management and line workers are currently performing other tasks and would be available for comments. Indicate in some detail the design for a change plan for this simulation.

REFERENCES

1. Christy, D., & Watson, H., "The Application of Simulation: A Survey of Industry Practice," *Interfaces*, Vol. 13, No. 5 (1983).

2. Emshoff, J. R., "Experience-Generalized Decision Making: The Next Generation of Managerial Models," *Interfaces*, Vol. 8, No. 4 (1978).

3. Lucas, H. C., *Toward Creative Systems Design*, New York: Columbia University Press, 1974.

4. Lucas, H. C., *Why Information Systems Fail*, New York: Columbia University Press, 1975.

5. Perry, R., Hoover, S., & Zelasky, B., ''Implementation of Simulation Results: An Assessment,'' paper presented at TIMS XXVII International Meeting, Gold Coast City, Australia, July, 1986.

6. Schein, E., *Organizational Psychology*, Englewood Cliffs, New Jersey: Prentice-Hall, 1965.

7. Watson, H., & Marett, P., ''A Survey of Management Science Implementation Problems,'' *Interfaces*, Vol. 9, No. 4 (1979).

8. Wysocki, R., ''OR/MS Implementation Research: A Bibliography,'' *Interfaces*, Vol. 9, No. 2 (1979).

APPENDIX **A**

GPSS PRIMER

APPENDIX A   GPSS PRIMER

OUTLINE

1.0 INTRODUCTION

The goal of this primer is to provide sufficient knowledge of the GPSS language to permit the programming of reasonably complex and realistic simulation models without recourse to detailed reference manuals. The approach taken is to develop GPSS concepts and language elements and then immediately illustrate their use with example problems. Also included are some hints and caveats to permit one to take maximum advantage of the properties of the language. In this way, the student very quickly develops a feel for the modeling process using GPSS.

GPSS, or more fully, General Purpose Simulation System, is a special-purpose programming language designed to facilitate coding of simulation models. It was developed by Geoffrey Gordon (Gordon,1961) in the late 1950's, and as hardware and software capabilities have improved, it has evolved into an extremely powerful and easily learned language. The version described here is GPSS V. Although GPSS V is supported by many different computer models, its structure and syntax is relatively standard across all of them. The language is described here in a computer-free context, but some statements specific to the particular GPSS implementation or operating system are necessary to execute programs.

The GPSS language may be described as being process interaction (Fishman,1973) or transaction-flow oriented. This approach focuses on a particular entity or transaction in the system being modeled, say a customer in a supermarket, and tracks this entity through the system noting all significant happenings, such as waiting, service, and departure. The system components are represented by blocks whose shapes identify their functions. These are then logically interconnected, and each block type is directly converted into a program statement. This property of the language makes it extremely isomorphic to the real system, thus increasing the ease and speed with which models may be constructed. If more complicated logic than that permitted by the use of blocks is required, the ability to interface the GPSS program with subroutines in general purpose languages, such as FORTRAN or PASCAL, exists in many implementations of GPSS.

The organization of this primer is designed to facilitate programming of increasingly complex models with the introduction of minimum sets of new concepts at each stage. To do this the primer is organized as follows. In Section 2.0, an overview of the GPSS language is presented. In Section 3.0, basic modeling concepts and a fundamental set of blocks are introduced, and some simple GPSS programs are constructed. Section 4.0 treats the mechanism by which GPSS controls the flow of transactions through models. Although this is transparent to the user for most simple models, it is extremely important as more complex situations are considered. In Section 5.0, intermediate modeling concepts are discussed and more blocks are presented. Also, GPSS functions and variables are introduced. The illustrative problems in this section treat more realistic and complex systems. Section 6.0 deals with advanced modeling concepts where the analyst intervenes significantly in controlling the flow of transactions. The illustrative problems included here demonstrate the ability of GPSS to model quite intricate real world systems. Section 7.0 treats control statements and miscellaneous topics. Control statements are used to manipulate some things which are unique to simulation runs, such as the initialization period, statistics collection, and seeding of random-number generators.

The last two sections are designed primarily for reference once the language has been mastered. Section 8.0 lists all of the GPSS blocks discussed and their operands, and Section 9.0 contains a list of the standard numerical attributes (SNA) and standard logical attributes (SLA) associated with the various blocks. Finally, in the references and bibliography, books and program reference manuals are included for the reader who seeks more detailed treatment of the intricacies of the language, or more complex and varied models.

2.0 OVERVIEW OF THE GPSS LANGUAGE

2.1 GPSS Entities

Most of the GPSS language structure can be described by considering entities or elemental model abstractions. An entity models objects flowing through the system, a component of the system, or something which supports the logic flow of the system, such as a computational or statistics collection mechanism.

There are fourteen entities in GPSS, which may be grouped into six categories as follows:

    I. Basic Entities
        Blocks
        Transactions
   II. Equipment Entities
        Facilities
        Storages
        Logic Switches
  III. Statistical Entities
        Queues
        Distribution Tables
  IV. Computational Entities
        Arithmetic Variables
        Boolean Variables
        Functions
   V. Reference Entities
        Savevalues
        Matrices
  VI. Chain Entities
        System Chains
        User Chains

Each entity has associated with it one or more standard numerical attributes (SNA) which are used to define its nature or current status, or to collect cumulative statistics about its operation. In addition, there are system-wide SNAs not associated with any particular entity. Most notable of these is the simulation clock (described in Section 4.0) which is instrumental in advancing the model through time. The fourteen entities and their uses are briefly described in the following paragraphs.

Basic Entities   There are two basic entities: blocks and transactions. These entities are fundamental to GPSS, since they define components of the system being modeled and the flow route through the system, and trigger the collection of relevant statistics. Block entities consist of distinct block types uniquely associated with one of the fourteen entities, as will be discussed later. Transaction entities represent the objects flowing through the model. They may represent such varied units as messages in a computer system, manufactured parts in a factory, people in a bank, or cargo ships in a harbor.

Each transaction can have a large number of parameters associated with it. Parameters are one of several SNAs associated with transactions and are used to describe characteristics of the transaction. For example, they may designate a class of customer, a type of ship, the unloading time for a ship, or the dimensions of an object.

Equipment Entities   This category of entities comprises facilities, storages, and logic switches. Facilities represent equipment that can accommodate only one transaction at a time. A bank teller, a machine that can hold only one part, or a vehicle that can only carry one part or person could be represented using a facility. Some of the block types associated with facilities are SEIZE, RELEASE, and GATE. The first two blocks take and relinquish control of the facility, while the third can be used to control the flow to a facility by testing for availability.

Storages are essentially multiple-capacity facilities; they can accommodate more than one transaction simultaneously. Storages can be used to model warehouses (an obvious analogy), several servers which are identical in nature, or an 8-bit wide communications bus. Some block types associated with storages are: ENTER, LEAVE, and GATE. The first two block types behave analogously to the SEIZE and RELEASE blocks, and the GATE block controls flow into the storage.

Logic switches are commonly used to control the flow of the transactions through the model. Logic switches exist in one of two states: set or reset.

Statistical Entities   This category of entities consists of queues and distribution tables. Queues are used to gather statistics at any point in the model where blocking and delays can occur. Transactions may be routed to QUEUE blocks when they are blocked, which increases the contents of a queue. They may enter a DEPART block when the blockage ceases, and the queue contents are decreased. Delays occur at blocks such as SEIZE, ENTER, and GATE. Statistics about SNAs such as the current number of transactions in the queue, the average queue length, and the average time spent in the queue are collected automatically by GPSS.

If more detailed information about a model variable than that provided by simple statistics like the mean is desired, distribution tables provide frequency distributions for any specified SNA. TABLE statements and TABULATE blocks are used to collect these data. SNAs for which a frequency distribution might be of interest include time spent in a queue, time spent in a facility or storage, or the number of transactions in a queue.

Computational Entities   The entities included in this category are: arithmetic variables, Boolean variables, and functions. Arithmetic variables permit an arithmetic combination of SNAs to be calculated. Arithmetic variables may be used to direct the flow of transactions, or to provide a value used by the model, such as a service time defined by a combination of transaction parameter values.

Boolean variables permit decisions on routing through the model logic based on the status or value of a wide variety of entities. The value of a Boolean variable, which is itself an SNA, is 1 if the conditions tested are true and 0 if the conditions are false. For example, a transaction may refuse to join a queue if it exceeds a certain length. This is implemented by a Boolean expression involving queue length.

Functions permit continuous or discrete functional relationships to be defined using SNAs as arguments. A common use of functions in simulation models is the definition of a random arrival interval or service time using a uniform random number as the argument of a function.

Reference Entities   Savevalues and matrices make up this category of entities. Savevalues may contain only one value at a time. They are initialized through an INITIAL statement and may be altered during a GPSS run by the SAVEVALUE block. Savevalues are typically used to contain values that change over time and which must be referenced by more than one transaction at a time, for example, a counter that tallies the number of transactions passing through a particular segment of the model.

Matrices are two-dimensional analogs to savevalues which contain arrays of values. Their dimensions and initial values are specified by MATRIX and INITIAL statements, respectively. Values may be modified during execution by using an MSAVEVALUE block. Matrices are useful in specifying information common to classes of transactions. For example, in a job shop model, a matrix could contain the machine routing and processing times for each of several types of jobs.

Chain Entities   A chain is the terminology used by GPSS to refer to what is more commonly known as a linked list. GPSS uses two types of chains, system chains (those controlled by the system logic) and user chains (those controlled by the user). The system chains, which will be described in detail in Section 4.0, are the means used to control the flow of transactions through the model and the advance of time.

User chains permit user-defined set membership and deviation from the normal rules governing transaction flow. Through the use of the LINK and UNLINK blocks, transactions may be removed from consideration by GPSS system logic until explicitly retrieved by the user. An application where this would be useful is a complicated queue discipline, such as selecting the next part to work on from a queue of parts for a machine based on the shortest processing time for that machine.

2.2   An Example GPSS Model

A GPSS model of a simple system is described in this section to provide the flavor of the language. The use of some of the GPSS blocks will be immediately obvious. The constructions which are not, will become clear after reading Section 3.0, Basic Modeling Concepts.

Example Problem   The system modeled here is a single-server queue. The setting for such a system could vary widely; examples include a bank, a small store, a gas station, or a post office. For concreteness we will consider our queueing system to be a small bank. The time between successive customer arrivals is distributed uniformly over the interval 5 ± 3 minutes. Customers queue up, and are served on a first-in-first-out (FIFO) basis. The time for a customer to transact his/her bank business is uniformly distributed over the interval 4±2 minutes. Upon completion of service, customers leave the bank. We wish to represent the servicing of 100 customers in our model.

The GPSS flow chart for this model appears in Figure 2.1, and the GPSS code is shown in Figure 2.2.

2.3   GPSS Coding Conventions

In this section we define the GPSS statement format and certain other coding conventions which must be known before a GPSS model may be coded. These conventions are fairly universal across all GPSS implementations, but the requirements of the specific version of GPSS being used should be reviewed before attempting to run a program. Any system-specific bias contained in the discussion is that associated with the VAX/VMS version of GPSS.

FIGURE 2.1   EXAMPLE PROBLEM FLOW CHART

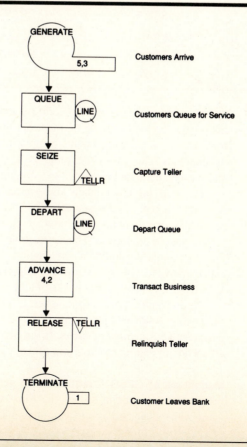

FIGURE 2.2   EXAMPLE PROBLEM CODE

```
        SIMULATE
* SMALLTOWN BANK
        GENERATE        5,3             CUSTOMERS ARRIVE
        QUEUE           LINE            CUSTOMERS QUEUE FOR SERVICE
        SEIZE           TELLR           CAPTURE TELLER
        DEPART          LINE            DEPART QUEUE
        ADVANCE         4,2             TRANSACT BUSINESS
        RELEASE         TELLR           RELINQUISH TELLER
        TERMINATE       1               CUSTOMER LEAVES BANK
        START           100             NO. OF CUSTOMERS TO PROCESS
        END
```

Statement Format   GPSS statements contain four fields: block location or label (optional), block name or operation, operand, and comments (optional). Each of these field definitions must appear in the columns designated below, or alternatively, they may be separated by blanks or tabs.

COL. 1–6	COL. 8–18	COL. 19–71	
BLOCK LABEL	BLOCK NAME	OPERAND A,B,C,..	COMMENTS
BLOC1	SEIZE	SHIP	CAPTURE SHIP
2	SEIZE	1;CAPTURE FACILITY 1	
	ENTER	MACH;CAPTURE 1 UNIT OF CAPACITY	
BLOC3	ENTER	XH$MACH	
	SEIZE	V$2	

Operands are separated by commas and must contain no embedded blanks. In many instances, operands may be omitted, but their associated commas must still be present: for example, A,C,D. Comments begin with the first semi-colon, blank, or tab following the operands. This varies according to the dictates of the particular version of GPSS. An entire statement may be devoted to a comment by placing an "*" in column 1.

In specifying block labels and operands, symbolic or numeric designations may be used, and in general, operands may be specified using SNAs or constants. The symbolic references may contain from three to five alphanumeric characters, the first three of which must be alphabetic. This is illustrated in the chart above. The last two examples in the chart require additional explanation. XH$MACH specifies a halfword savevalue called MACH, which contains the number of a STORAGE to be utilized. Similarly, VARIABLE number 2 contains the number of a facility to be used.

Note that the proper form when using symbolic references for SNAs is the SNA designation followed by the "$" and an SNA number or a properly formed three to five character SNA symbol or name. If the SNA is referred to by number, some versions of GPSS do not require the insertion of the "$".

Magnitude of GPSS Quantities   In general GPSS does not deal well with high-precision floating-point arithmetic. Most variables and constants in GPSS models are appropriately handled as integers, including the system numerical attributes, relative and absolute clock times. Since GPSS models can consume large amounts of computer memory, one should not squander memory on unnecessary floating-point quantities. To facilitate memory conservation GPSS allows some entities to be specified as either half-word or fullword quantities; for example, the halfword and fullword parameters and savevalues referred to above.

Control Statements   The execution of GPSS programs is directed by many control statements. We will discuss these in the following sections as they are required to operate the GPSS models which are developed. Most notable among them are SIMU-LATE, END, and START.

The SIMULATE statement signals the GPSS assembler that the program is to be assembled and executed. Without this statement, programs are only evaluated for syntax errors. The END statement signals the conclusion of the GPSS program. The START statement initializes a counter which may then be used to control the length of the run.

3.0   BASIC MODELING CONCEPTS

The coding of a GPSS program is greatly facilitated by the close correspondence of block types to program statements. Further, each GPSS block type has a unique shape which identifies its function, and aids in the ready comprehension of the program flow chart. Thus once a logically correct flow chart is constructed using the GPSS block symbols, the program code is essentially determined.

In general, the operands for all blocks may be specified as any of the following Standard Numerical Attributes (SNA) types.

1. K   Integer constant
2. sn   Symbolic name (e.g., SHIP, MACH)
3. SNA   Family name of a Standard Numerical Attribute (e.g., Q, S, R, or XH)
4. SNA$j   Family name of a Standard Numerical Attribute followed by a dollar sign ($) and a numerical entity name (e.g., Q$1, S$3, R$4, or XH$1)
5. SNA$sn   Family name of a Standard Numerical Attribute followed by a dollar sign ($) and a symbolic entity name (e.g., Q$LINE, S$STORE, or XH$SAVE)
6. SNA*Px$j   Family name of a Standard Numerical Attribute followed by an asterisk (*) and the designation of a halfword (x = H) or fullword (x = F) parameter whose value is a numeric entity name (i.e., an indirect address such as, Q*PH$1, MX*PF$3, or XH*PF$2)

Exceptions to the general use of these operand specifications will be noted for specific blocks and operands as they are discussed. A complete list of the GPSS blocks covered in this Primer and the allowable operands appears in Section 8.0.

In Section 3.1, the minimum set of GPSS blocks and control statements necessary to build a GPSS model is described. Then, in Section 3.2, we illustrate their use by developing flow charts and GPSS code for some simple models.

3.1   A Fundamental Set of GPSS Blocks

GENERATE   This block creates the transactions which flow through the model. In GPSS flow charts, the GENERATE block is represented by the following block shape.

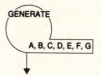

Its operands have the following definitions:

OPERAND	DESCRIPTION	DEFAULT
A*	Interval between creation of transactions	0
B**	Spread time or function modifier	0
C	Offset interval	No offset
D	Maximum number of transactions to be created	Infinite
E	Transaction priority	0
F	Number of transaction parameters associated with each transaction	***
G	Fullword or halfword parameter specification [For H]	***

* SNA types 1, 4, or 5 may be used for operands A–F, and they are further restricted to: K, and the SNAs FN, V, XH, XF, RN, N, and C1.
** For the spread time of operand B, FN may not be used. For the function modifier, only FN may be used.
*** Machine dependent.

Transactions are created at the rate specified by the A operand unless the block immediately following can block the flow of transactions, such as a SEIZE block. Since this would alter the creation pattern of transactions, it is not advisable to do this. If the A operand is left blank, transactions are created at a rate that will quickly exhaust memory.

Random variation may be introduced into the creation rate in two ways: by using a spread time or a GPSS function. In the first case the B operand specifies the limits for a uniformly distributed random variable, and the creation interval will vary over the range $A \pm B$ time units. Care should be taken to assure that $B \leq A/2$, since negative intervals will result otherwise. A valid set of values for the A and B operands would be $A = 10$, $B = 3$. This would yield creation intervals of 7,8,9,10,11,12, and 13 with equal probability, since the GPSS clock variable can deal only with integers.

The second use of the B operand is to specify a function whose value is multiplied by the A operand to yield creation intervals. In this way probability distributions other than the uniform may be used. If a constant interval between creations is desired, this operand may be left blank.

The offset interval specified by operand C permits a GENERATE block to be dormant for a period of time before creating its first transaction. Subsequent transactions are created according to the values of the A and B operands. The value of the C operand has no relationship to that of the A operand. If no offset is desired the C operand may be left blank.

Operand D specifies a creation limit for the GENERATE block. When the designated number of transactions has been created, the GENERATE block no longer plays a role in the operation of the model. If no limit is desired, this operand may be left blank.

The E operand specifies the priority to be associated with the transaction, which may range from 0 to 127. If left blank, a value of 0 is assumed. A higher priority entitles a transaction to service before a transaction with a lower priority. Transactions of equal priority are handled on a first-come-first-served basis.

The number of parameters associated with a transaction is specified by operand F. Since parameters consume memory, it is desirable to limit them to the minimum required. A common default value is 12, but this is far too great for all but the most complex of models.

The G operand permits specification of halfword or fullword parameters. Again, for reasons of memory conservation, one should use only as large a parameter as is dictated by the specific model needs. A halfword parameter is usually indicated by ''H,'' and a fullword by ''F''. Halfword parameters are referred to by the prefix ''PH'' before the parameter number, and fullword parameters use ''PF''. The usual default for this operand is halfword.

In specifying operands, embedded blank operands may be indicated using commas, as follows. The statement:

GENERATE   10,2,,,4

will create transactions at intervals of 8,9,10,11, and 12 with equal probability. Creation will start immediately with no offset interval, and will continue without limit as long as the model runs. Transactions will have a priority value of 4. They will have the default values of 12 parameters which are halfword.

The following GENERATE block will create transactions with a mean inter-creation time specified by a fullword savevalue named MEAN, which will first be multiplied by the value of a function named EXP to obtain a particular creation interval.

GENERATE   X$MEAN,FN$EXP

If the function EXP defined an appropriately adjusted CDF for the exponential probability distribution, the transactions created could represent random arrivals to the model.

TERMINATE   This block is the simplest of all GPSS blocks. Upon completion of flow through the model, it removes a transaction from the model logic.

The flow chart symbol for the TERMINATE block is as follows.

The single operand for TERMINATE is:

OPERAND	DESCRIPTION	DEFAULT
A*	Number of units by which the simulation start count is to be decremented	0

* SNA types 1, 4, 5, or 6 may be used.

Using the count value specified by the START control statement, the TERMINATE block can end a simulation run after the specified number of transactions have passed through it. The use of this block in controlling run length is illustrated in the following section.

SEIZE   This block allows the entering transaction to obtain control of a facility designated by the block's single operand. It will refuse entry to a transaction if the facility is already in use. A transaction may occupy more than one facility at a time.

The flow chart symbol for the SEIZE block is:

The single operand of the SEIZE block is:

OPERAND	DESCRIPTION	DEFAULT
A*	Facility name or number	None

* SNA types 1, 2, 4, 5, or 6 may be used

Valid SEIZE statements include the following:

SEIZE   1
SEIZE   CAR
SEIZE   PH$1

The last statement permits a transaction to take control of a facility whose number is contained in halfword parameter number 1.

RELEASE   The RELEASE block is complementary in function to the SEIZE block. GPSS contains many such complementary pairs of blocks. In this case, the block yields control of the facility by causing the transaction currently using it to leave. If there were any transactions waiting to use the facility, one of these may now gain control of it.

The flow chart symbol for this block is:

Again, there is only one operand for this block.

OPERAND	DESCRIPTION	DEFAULT
A*	Facility name or number	None

* SNA types 1, 2, 4, 5, or 6 may be used.

The SEIZE and RELEASE blocks influence the status of the SNAs associated with facilities as transactions flow through the blocks. These SNAs include: F_j, in-use facility status for facility j (1= in use, 0 otherwise); FC_j, total number of transactions to use facility j; and FT_j, average utilization time for facility j.

ENTER This block allows a transaction to occupy one or more units of the equipment entity, storage. Storages may be viewed as facilities which can accommodate more than one transaction simultaneously. This block will refuse entry if the storage is filled to capacity. A transaction may occupy an unlimited number of storages. The operands are:
The flow chart symbol for the ENTER block is:

Its operands are as follows:

OPERAND	DESCRIPTION	DEFAULT
A*	Storage name or number	None
B**	Number of units of capacity to be utilized	1

* SNA types 1, 2, 4, 5, or 6 may be used.
** SNA types 1, 4, 5, or 6 may be used.

The usual case is that a transaction will occupy only one unit of a storage, and this is assumed if the B operand is omitted.
Valid ENTER statements include:

ENTER   1

ENTER   SHIP

ENTER   PH$3,4

In the last statement the transaction would enter a storage designated by the value of halfword parameter number 3, and occupy 4 units of capacity.
If the capacity of a storage is not specified, the default value is "infinite" (i.e., limited only by computer memory). Storage capacity is defined using a storage definition statement as follows:

Block Label	Block Name	Operands
	STORAGE	S$SHIP,100/S$1,20/S2-S4,30

where STORAGE is placed in the Block Name field, and the definitions are in the Operand field. This statement defines the storage named SHIP to have a capacity of 100, storage number 1 a capacity of 20, and storages number 2 through 4 a capacity of 30.

LEAVE The LEAVE block is complementary in function to the ENTER block. It releases one or more units of capacity of the storage.

The flow chart symbol for the LEAVE block is:

Its operands are:

OPERAND	DESCRIPTION	DEFAULT
A*	Storage name or number	None
B**	Number of units of capacity freed	1

* SNA types 1, 2, 4, 5, or 6 may be used.
** SNA types 1, 4, 5, or 6 may be used.

Some examples of LEAVE statements are:

LEAVE   1

LEAVE   SHIP,3

LEAVE   PH$4

When using the LEAVE block, one must be careful not to cause more units of capacity to be freed than were occupied. Doing so could result in negative storage contents, which is intuitively unappealing and distresses the GPSS assembler.

SNAs influenced by action of the ENTER and LEAVE blocks include: S_j, current contents of the storage; R_j, remaining capacity of the storage; and SM_j, the maximum contents of the storage.

ADVANCE   This block will delay the progress of a transaction through the model logic. It is used to represent some purposeful delay, such as service to a bank customer, or processing of a part in a machine. It uses the A and B operands in the same fashion as the GENERATE block.

The flow chart symbol for the ADVANCE block is:

Its operands are:

OPERAND	DESCRIPTION	DEFAULT
A*	Mean delay time for a transaction	0
B**	Spread time or function modifier	0

* SNA types 1, 4, 5, or 6 may be used.
** For spread time, SNA types 1, 4, 5, or 6 may be used, except FN. For function modifier, only FN may be used.

The mean delay time may assume any integer value, including zero. If the delay is zero, the transaction will attempt to enter the next sequential block during the same clock time. The mean delay time may be altered by specifying a spread or a function. Specification of a spread value causes the delay time to be uniformly distributed over the interval $A \pm B$, while use of a function causes the mean delay to be multiplied by the function value to determine a particular delay time.

The following are examples of valid ADVANCE statement constructions.

ADVANCE

ADVANCE   12,4

ADVANCE   XH*PH$1,FN$EXP

To evaluate the delay time for the last statement, GPSS must first obtain the value of halfword parameter 1 from the current transaction, determine the value of the halfword savevalue designated by that number, and then multiply it by the value of the function named EXP.

QUEUE   The QUEUE block, and the complementary DEPART block, are statistical entities whose sole function in a model is to collect information on delays caused by blocks such as the SEIZE and ENTER blocks, which can refuse transactions entry. When a transaction enters a QUEUE block, one or more units are added to a queue for purposes of accumulating statistics on waiting time and queue length. A QUEUE block will not refuse a transaction entry. A transaction may occupy as many as five queues simultaneously.

The flow chart symbol for a QUEUE block is as follows.

The QUEUE block operands are:

OPERAND	DESCRIPTION	DEFAULT
A*	Name or number of the queue to which units are to be added	None
B**	Number of units to be added to the queue	1

* SNA types 1, 2, 4, 5, or 6 may be used.
** SNA types 1, 4, 5, or 6 may be used.

Normally transactions are added to a queue one at a time, and if the B operand is omitted, it is assumed to be 1. However, in situations where queue space is limited and different types of transactions may occupy differing amounts of space, such as in discrete parts manufacturing, the B operand can be used.

The following are examples of legitimate QUEUE statement constructions.

```
QUEUE      1
QUEUE      PH$2
QUEUE      LINE
QUEUE      MX$LINE(PH$1,3)
```

The last statement designates a QUEUE whose number is contained in the fullword matrix savevalue called LINE. To obtain the QUEUE number, GPSS determines the value of halfword parameter number 1 of the current transaction, and then refers to column 3 of the row thus defined.

DEPART   The DEPART block reduces the contents of a queue by one or more units. Its operands are as follows.

The flowchart symbol for the DEPART block is:

The DEPART operands are:

OPERAND	DESCRIPTION	DEFAULT
A*	Name or number of the queue from which units are to be removed	None
B**	Number of units to be removed from the queue	1

* SNA types 1, 2, 4, 5, or 6 may be used.
** SNA types 1, 4, 5, or 6 may be used.

Two cautions in using QUEUE/DEPART blocks are: the number of units removed from a queue may not exceed the current contents, and the same transaction that increments the queue should also decrement it to avoid confusing GPSS.

Some of the SNAs affected by these two blocks are: Q_j, current contents of queue j; QM_j, maximum contents of queue j; QA_j, average number of units in queue j; and QT_j the average time a unit spends in queue j.

We have now described sufficient block types to build a simple model with GPSS, but we must also have available some control statements to direct the execution of the model. We will need the control statements END, SIMULATE, and START. The format for these statements uses the Block Name field for the control statement.

END   This is the simplest of control statements. Its function is to return control to the operating system after a GPSS model has completed its run. It must be the last statement in a GPSS program. It has no operands.

SIMULATE   This statement indicates that the model is to be executed following assembly. Without this statement the run will terminate, indicating any syntactical errors found in the coding. Some GPSS implementations allow an optional maximum run time to be specified in operand A. SIMULATE is generally the first statement in a GPSS program.

START   The START statement is used to initiate and control the length of a run by decrementing a pre-set termination counter. The START statement initializes this counter, and the TERMINATE block decrements it as transactions enter it. When the counter has been decremented to zero, the run is terminated, and a standard GPSS report is printed. The START operands are:

OPERAND	DESCRIPTION	DEFAULT
A*	Run termination count	None
B	Output report suppression [NP or blank]	Report printed
C	Snap interval	Infinite

* Operands A and C must be type 1.

If operand B contains "NP," a report is not printed at the end of the run. This is often desirable at the end of an initialization run used to achieve steady-state, or typical system behavior, before collecting statistics. Operand C can be used to specify reports to be produced at regular intervals, referred to as "snap intervals," throughout the run. The START statement must be the last statement related to a particular model definition. Usually this means just before the END statement.

The following are illustrations of valid START statements.

```
START     100
START     100,NP
START     500,,100
```

The last statement will produce reports at intervals of 100 terminations, that is at termination 100, 200, 300, 400, and 500.

3.2   Illustrative Problem Set I

With the foregoing block and control statement definitions established, we may now examine some simple systems coded in GPSS. A most prevalent problem structure for real-world situations is that of a waiting line or queue for a limited resource. In this problem set we begin with the simplest of all queueing formulations, a single server with a single queue. The second example adds the complication of customers with different priorities, and the third extends the model to include many servers with a single queue.

PROBLEM I.1   The setting for this problem is a single-physician medical clinic. Patients arriving at this clinic are of two types: those who have visited the clinic before, and those who are visiting for the first time. The mean interval between arrivals for "old" patients is 40 minutes, while that for "new" patients is 60 minutes. The interarrival times for both classes of patients are uniformly distributed over a range defined as the mean interval ±10 minutes. Examination and treatment for either class requires 20±5 minutes, uniformly distributed. In addition, the taking of a medical history for "new" patients requires 10 ± 3 minutes. Upon completion of their treatment, patients immediately leave the clinic. The GPSS flow chart for this problem is shown in Fig. 3.1, and the GPSS code is listed in Fig. 3.2.

As defined thus far, and coded in the first two model segments, the clinic would continue without ever closing. We need a method of defining the run duration. Two basic approaches are available: close the clinic when a specified number of patients have been treated, or close it after a specified amount of time has elapsed. We take the latter approach here. In the third model segment, a transaction is created every 480 minutes, or 8 hours, and it flows immediately through a terminate block which decrements the run counter by one. If we wish to run the model for one day, we initialize the counter at the value 1 using the START control statement, for two days, initialize it at 2, etc. This will stop the model run and produce output reports after the desired number of days of operation has been simulated. Consideration of the issue of clinic status at closing time (people waiting, being treated, etc.) is postponed until a later section.

FIGURE 3.1   PROBLEM I.1 FLOW CHART

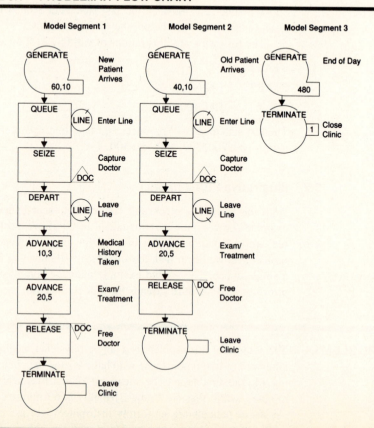

FIGURE 3.2   PROBLEM I.1 CODE

```
LINE    BLOCK   BLOCK   BLOCK NAME              `COMMENTS
NO.     NO.     LOC.
  1                     SIMULATE
  2             *       MODEL SEGMENT 1 - NEW PATIENTS
  3       1             GENERATE        60,10   ARRIVAL TIME - MINUTES
  4       2             QUEUE           LINE    ENTER LINE
  5       3             SEIZE           DOC     CAPTURE PHYSICIAN
  6       4             DEPART          LINE    LEAVE LINE
  7       5             ADVANCE         10,3    TAKE MEDICAL HISTORY
  8       6             ADVANCE         20,5    EXAMINE/TREAT
  9       7             RELEASE         DOC     FREE PHYSICIAN
 10       8             TERMINATE
 11             *       MODEL SEGMENT 2 - OLD PATIENTS
 12       9             GENERATE        40,10   ARRIVAL TIME - MINUTES
 13      10             QUEUE           LINE    ENTER LINE
 14      11             SEIZE           DOC     CAPTURE PHYSICIAN
 15      12             DEPART          LINE    LEAVE LINE
 16      13             ADVANCE         20,5    EXAMINE/TREAT
 17      14             RELEASE         DOC     FREE PHYSICIAN
 18      15             TERMINATE
 19             *       MODEL SEGMRNT 3 - RUN LENGTH CONTROL
 20      16             GENERATE        480     END OF CLINIC DAY
 21      17             TERMINATE       1       CLOSE CLINIC
 22                     START           20
```

Some observations are in order concerning the model logic. First, there are three GENERATE blocks. GPSS permits an unlimited number of GENERATE blocks. Two separate streams of transactions are directed to the same QUEUE and DEPART blocks and they compete for the same facility. This can be accommodated by GPSS. Finally, the sequence of the model segments in the coding is for the convenience of the user, not GPSS. The assembler could handle any permutation of these three segments.

The GPSS output report for this model is shown in Fig. 3.3. The first section contains a listing of the GPSS code indicating both line numbers and block numbers. The next section begins with the relative and absolute clock values that indicate the length of the run. These values will be the same, unless a RESET or CLEAR control statement has been included in the model. The balance of the section displays for each block the SNAs which contain the current number of transactions in the block, and the total number of transactions which passed through the block during the model run. This information is useful in debugging a model, since an excessive accumulation of transactions in a block, or no transaction flow in a block, often indicates a logic error.

The balance of the report is grouped by entity type, beginning with QUEUES, and continuing with FACILITIES, and STORAGES, etc. For each entity type, SNAs that reflect aggregate performance of the entity are displayed. For example, the QUEUE report includes for each queue the average waiting time (average time/transaction), average queue contents, and maximum queue contents. A less than obvious designation is the column heading "$AVERAGE TIME/TRANS". This column contains the average waiting time for the set of transactions that were required to wait. That is, it excludes all transactions with zero waiting time.

FIGURE 3.3   PROBLEM I.1 OUTPUT

```
RELATIVE CLOCK 9600      ABSOLUTE CLOCK 9600


  BLOCK  CURRENT   TOTAL     BLOCK  CURRENT   TOTAL
   1    1       161      11     0      239
   2    1       160      12     0      239
   3    0       159      13     1      239
   4    0       159      14     0      238
   5    0       159      15     0      238
   6    0       159      16     0       20
   7    0       159      17     0       20
   8    0       159
   9    1       241
  10    1       240
```

QUEUE	MAXIMUM CONTENTS	AVERAGE CONTENTS	TOTAL ENTRIES	ZERO ENTRIES	PERCENT ZEROS	AVERAGE TIME/TRANS	$AVERAGE TIME/TRANS	TABLE NUMBER	CURRENT CONTENTS
LINE	6	2.500	400	5	1.250	59.995	60.754		2

FACILITY	AVERAGE UTILIZATION	NUMBER ENTRIES	AVERAGE TIME/TRANS	SEIZING TRANS. NO.	PREEMPTING TRANS. NO.
DOC	0.994	398	23.965	9	

Turning now to the substance of the output, we see that average waiting time for a patient of either class is approximately 60 minutes and the doctor has a utilization of approximately 99%. These statistics are based on a run of 20 8-hour, or 480-minute, days. It appears that this clinic has little room to accommodate any increased patient load. Also, an average wait of 60 minutes may cause one to question the adequacy of the level of service provided. How could the clinic operate in a manner more responsive to patient needs without increased resources?

Observe that "new" patients require an additional 10 minutes to have their medical history taken, and that "old" patients arrive with greater frequency than "new" patients. If the patients requiring a shorter service time could be given a higher priority, thereby being processed before those requiring a longer time, it might be possible to reduce the average waiting time for all patients. This possibility is explored in the following problem.

PROBLEM I.2   This example deals with two streams of arrivals with different priorities, "old" patients and "new" patients, competing for the same facility. The setting is the same medical clinic as that in the previous problem. If both classes of patients are waiting, those with appointments are treated first. This is accomplished in GPSS by assigning the "old" patients a higher priority using the GENERATE block which creates them.

FIGURE 3.4 PROBLEM I.2 FLOW CHART

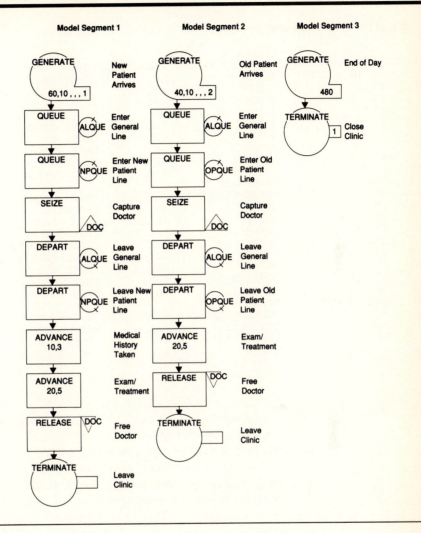

The flow chart and coding for this model are very similar to the previous one. The flow chart is shown in Fig. 3.4, and the GPSS code in Fig. 3.5. The major differences are the use of priority 1 and 2 for "new" and "old" patients, respectively, and the addition of patient class QUEUE blocks. Both classes of patients flow through a QUEUE named ALQUE, and in addition, "new" patients flow through the QUEUE, NPQUE, and "old" patients through OPQUE. In this way we can collect statistics on the aggregate experiences of all patients as well as those of the separate classes.

The output for a run of 20 days of 480 minutes, or 8 hours, each is shown in Fig. 3.6. The single physician is still as harried as he was under the original clinic operation, being utilized approximately 99% fully. But the average waiting time for all patients has been reduced to 42 minutes from 60, and the average number of patients waiting has

FIGURE 3.5   PROBLEM I.2 CODE

```
LINE   BLOCK   BLOCK    BLOCK NAME                      COMMENTS
NO.    NO.     LOC.
1                       SIMULATE
2              *        MODEL SEGMENT 1 - NEW PATIENTS
3      1                GENERATE        60,10,,,1 ARRIVALS
4      2                QUEUE           ALQUE     JOIN GENERAL QUEUE
5      3                QUEUE           NPQUE     JOIN NEW PAT QUEUE
6      4                SEIZE           DOC       CAPTURE PHYSICIAN
7      5                DEPART          ALQUE     LEAVE GENERAL QUEUE
8      6                DEPART          NPQUE     LEAVE NEW PAT QUEUE
9      7                ADVANCE         10,3      TAKE MEDICAL HISTORY
10     8                ADVANCE         20,5      EXAMINE/TREAT
11     9                RELEASE         DOC       FREE PHYSICIAN
12     10               TERMINATE
13             *        MODEL SEGMENT 2 - OLD PATIENTS
14     11               GENERATE        40,10,,,2 ARRIVALS
15     12               QUEUE           ALQUE     JOIN GENERAL QUEUE
16     13               QUEUE           OPQUE     JOIN OLD PAT QUEUE
17     14               SEIZE           DOC       CAPTURE PHYSICIAN
18     15               DEPART          ALQUE     LEAVE GENERAL QUEUE
19     16               DEPART          OPQUE     LEAVE OLD PAT QUEUE
20     17               ADVANCE         20,5      EXAMINE/TREAT
21     18               RELEASE         DOC       FREE PHYSICIAN
22     19               TERMINATE
23             *        MODEL SEGMENT 3 - RUN LENGTH CONTROL
24     20               GENERATE        480       END OF CLINIC DAY
25     21               TERMINATE       1         CLOSE CLINIC
26                      START           20
```

declined to approximately 1.7 from 2.5. Thus the overall experience of a patient in this clinic has been greatly improved.

The explanation of this apparent prestidigitation lies, of course, in the disparity in waiting times for the two classes of patients. ''New'' patients wait about six times as long, on the average, as ''old'' patients. So, the assessment of the quality of clinic performance depends on one's vantage point.

FIGURE 3.6   PROBLEM I.2 OUTPUT

RELATIVE CLOCK 9600   ABSOLUTE CLOCK 9600

QUEUE	MAXIMUM CONTENTS	AVERAGE CONTENTS	TOTAL ENTRIES	ZERO ENTRIES	PERCENT ZEROS	AVERAGE TIME/TRANS	$AVERAGE TIME/TRANS	TABLE NUMBER	CURRENT CONTENTS
ALQUE	5	1.747	397	19	4.786	42.244	44.368		0
NPQUE	4	1.388	159	9	5.660	83.818	88.847		0
OPQUE	2	0.359	238	10	4.202	14.471	15.105		0

FACILITY	AVERAGE UTILIZATION	NUMBER ENTRIES	AVERAGE TIME/TRANS	SEIZING TRANS. NO.	PREEMPTING TRANS. NO.
DOC	0.987	397	23.874	1	

PROBLEM I.3 In an attempt to improve patient service, the clinic modeled in the previous problem is considering adding another physician to the staff. Before seeking the necessary budget increase, the clinic wishes to assess the impact of these additional resources on service. To accomplish this we must now represent the physician part of the model as a storage with a capacity of 2. With the added physician it is felt that old patients will no longer require priority attention, so we return to the single priority model of Problem I.1. The flow chart for this configuration is shown in Fig. 3.7 and the GPSS code in Fig. 3.8.

The results of these changes can be observed from the model output of Fig. 3.9. Patient service has improved dramatically as seen in the QUEUE statistics. No patient is ever required to wait. However, this is accomplished at the expense of an extremely low physician utilization of 50%, shown in the statistics of the storage DOC. It would appear that this clinic could not justify an additional full-time physician. Perhaps a half-time physician would be a cost effective way to improve clinic service. A somewhat more complicated GPSS model could be used to evaluate this option.

FIGURE 3.7 PROBLEM I.3 FLOW CHART

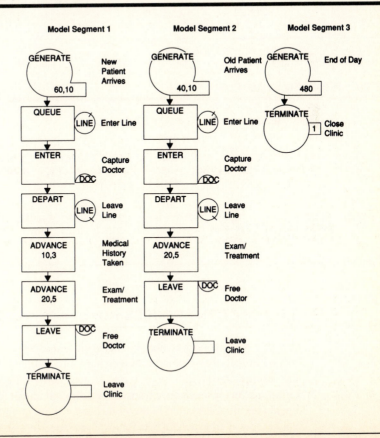

FIGURE 3.8   PROBLEM I.3 CODE

```
LINE   BLOCK   BLOCK   BLOCK NAME                    COMMENTS
NO.    NO.     LOC.

1                      SIMULATE
2              *       MODEL SEGMENT 1 - NEW PATIENTS
3                      STORAGE          S$DOC,2
4      1               GENERATE         60,10       ARRIVALS
5      2               QUEUE            LINE        JOIN LINE
6      3               ENTER            DOC         CAPTURE A PHYSICIAN
7      4               DEPART           LINE        LEAVE LINE
8      5               ADVANCE          10,3        TAKE MEDICAL HISTORY
9      6               ADVANCE          20,5        EXAMINE/TREAT
10     7               LEAVE            DOC         FREE A PHYSICIAN
11     8               TERMINATE
12             *       MODEL SEGMENT 2 - OLD PATIENTS
13     9               GENERATE         40,10       ARRIVALS
14     10              QUEUE            LINE        JOIN LINE
15     11              ENTER            DOC         CAPTURE A PHYSICIAN
16     12              DEPART           LINE        LEAVE LINE
17     13              ADVANCE          20,5        EXAMINE/TREAT
18     14              LEAVE            DOC         FREE A PHYSICIAN
19     15              TERMINATE
20             *       MODEL SEGMRNT 3 - RUN LENGTH CONTROL
21     16              GENERATE         480         END OF CLINIC DAY
22     17              TERMINATE        1           CLOSE CLINIC
23                     START            20
```

FIGURE 3.9   PROBLEM I.3 OUTPUT

```
RELATIVE CLOCK 9600    ABSOLUTE CLOCK 9600
```

QUEUE	MAXIMUM CONTENTS	AVERAGE CONTENTS	TOTAL ENTRIES	ZERO ENTRIES	PERCENT ZEROS	AVERAGE TIME/TRANS	$AVERAGE TIME/TRANS	TABLE NUMBER	CURRENT CONTENTS
LINE	1	0.000	399	399	100.000	0.000	0.000		0

STORAGE	CAPACITY	AVERAGE CONTENTS	TOTAL ENTRIES	AVERAGE TIME/TRANS	AVERAGE UTILIZ.	AVAIL. UTILIZ.	UNAVAIL. UTILIZ.	CURRENT STATUS	FRACTION AVAIL.	CURRENT CONTENTS	MAXIMUM CONTENTS
DOC	2	0.997	399	23.995	0.499			A	1.000	0	2

4.0 TRANSACTION PROCESSING

A GPSS transaction has thus far been viewed as residing in a particular block of the model. In fact, the situation is somewhat more complex. In this section we digress from the description of GPSS block types, to consider the file structure and logic used by the GPSS assembler to advance transactions through model blocks. For simple models these operations are transparent to the user, but for more complex ones, a lack of understanding of the way in which GPSS "thinks" may lead to some very confusing results.

4.1   GPSS Chains

At the beginning of a model run, the GPSS assembler creates a fixed number of transactions. Initially all of these transactions are in what is referred to as the latent pool. As transactions are created in GENERATE blocks, they are removed from the latent pool and placed in the active pool, and conversely, when transactions pass through a TERMINATE block at the end of their flow through the model, they are replaced in the latent pool. Transactions in the active pool are associated with a particular block in the model, but in addition they are also on one of the GPSS chains.

There are six types of GPSS system chains:

1. Current Events Chain (CEC)
2. Future Events Chain (FEC)
3. Delay Chains
4. Interrupt Chains
5. Matching Chains
6. User Chains

The first two chain types are fundamental to the way in which GPSS controls the flow of transactions and will be considered in some detail. The role of the next three types contribute to the efficiency of model execution and complexity of model structure. They will be mentioned in summary fashion. User chains permit the user to intervene in transaction-flow control. Discussion of user chains is deferred to Section 6.0, Advanced Modeling Concepts.

The CEC contains transactions which are scheduled to move through one or more blocks at the current instant in simulated time, or as soon as possible (e.g., a transaction to be created by a GENERATE block at this instant, or a transaction waiting to gain entry to a presently occupied facility). The FEC holds transactions that are not scheduled to move through one or more blocks until some future time. This can arise in two ways: a transaction in an ADVANCE block not scheduled to attempt a move to the next block until a later time, or a transaction in a GENERATE block not due to be created until some later time. Using the logic described in the following section, GPSS moves transactions between these two chains and thus executes the coded model.

4.2   Transaction Flow

In moving transactions through the model, there are two major logic sequences: a scan phase, which attempts to move transactions on the CEC through as many blocks as possible at a particular instant of time; and the update phase, which advances the clock to the next imminent event and transfers all transactions due to attempt a move at that time from the FEC to the CEC.

Before considering chain transfer logic in detail, it is necessary to describe the ordering of transactions on the FEC and FEC. Transactions are placed on the CEC by priority, the highest priority being at the head of the chain. Within a given priority, transactions are ordered by their arrival time at the chain, that is a first-come-first-served (FCFS) discipline. Transactions on the FEC are ordered first by their move time, then by priority, and finally by arrival time at the chain. Figure 4.1 depicts transactions on the CEC and FEC ordered in the proper manner.

FIGURE 4.1   ORGANIZATION OF TRANSACTIONS ON CEC AND FEC

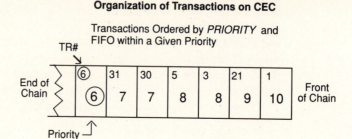

Organization of Transactions on CEC

Transactions Ordered by *PRIORITY* and FIFO within a Given Priority

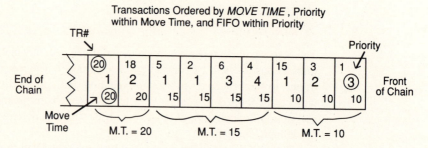

Organization of Transactions on FEC

Transactions Ordered by *MOVE TIME*, Priority within Move Time, and FIFO within Priority

To explain the chain transfer logic-reference will be made to the scan phase logic of Fig. 4.2, and the clock update phase logic of Fig. 4.3. We begin with the scan phase. The transaction at the head of the CEC is moved through the model blocks until one of the following three conditions occurs: (1) the transaction enters an ADVANCE block, (2) a blocking condition occurs preventing the transaction from entering a block (e.g., an attempt to enter the SEIZE block of a facility which is occupied), or (3) the transaction enters a TERMINATE block. If condition 1 is encountered, the transaction is transferred to the FEC with a move time equal to the current time plus the delay time of the ADVANCE block. If condition 2 is the case, the transaction remains on the CEC and makes no further progress in the model. Condition 3 causes the transaction to be removed from the active pool and placed in the latent pool. These actions are shown in blocks 1 – 3 of Fig. 4.2.

Depending on the blocks moved through by a given transaction, GPSS may restart the scanning of the CEC at the head of the chain, or it may seek the next transaction on the chain to attempt to move. The scan is restarted only if certain blocks, such as the RELEASE block, have been traversed by the transaction which has just come to rest. In this case, a transaction closer to the head of the chain may be waiting to occupy the facility which was released by the transaction just processed. If a restart were not accomplished, the waiting transaction would be delayed unnecessarily. If the restart conditions are not met, GPSS seeks the next transaction on the CEC and attempts to move it

FIGURE 4.2   GPSS SCAN PHASE

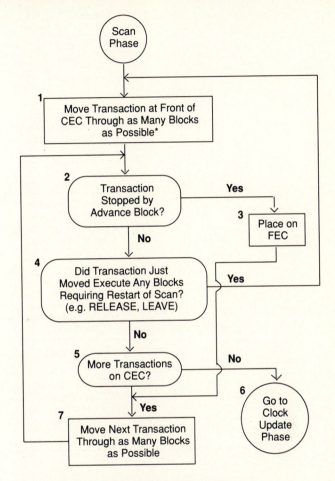

* May Be Blocked by SEIZE, ENTER, TEST, etc.

through as many blocks as possible. If there are no more transactions on the CEC, control is transferred to the clock update scan. This logic is depicted in blocks 4–7 of Fig. 4.2.

Turning now to the clock update phase, the first action is to advance the clock to the move time (MT) of the first transaction on the FEC. This transaction is removed from the FEC and placed on the CEC as the last member of its priority class. This is shown in blocks 1–2 of Fig. 4.3. GPSS next checks the MT of the next transaction on the FEC to see if it equals the current clock value. If it does, this transaction is also removed and placed on the CEC. This process continues until a transaction is encountered which has an MT greater than the current clock value. At this point control is transferred to the scan phase to attempt to move the transferred transactions through model blocks, thus completing one CEC–FEC–CEC cycle. This logic is shown in blocks 3–5 of Fig. 4.3.

FIGURE 4.3   GPSS CLOCK UPDATE PHASE

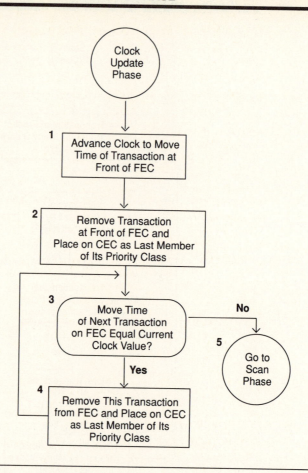

In describing the scan phase logic, we made a simplification that does not reflect GPSS's approach with total accuracy. Specifically, when a transaction is blocked, for example by an occupied facility, it is not left on the CEC to be fruitlessly scanned at each clock update. Rather, GPSS places the transaction on a delay chain until the blocking condition ceases, and then replaces it on the CEC for normal processing.

The remaining two system chain types also deserve brief explanations. The interrupt chains are used in handling preemption. A transaction being served in a facility may be interrupted or preempted by a transaction of a higher priority. When this happens, the preempted transaction is placed on an interrupt chain until service of the interrupting transaction is completed. Then the original transaction is returned for the balance of its service, or until interrupted again.

Matching chains are used to synchronize the flow of a pair of transactions through some portion of the model. The one of the pair that arrives first at a particular block is removed from the overall flow and held on a matching chain until the second of the pair arrives, at which time they proceed together. Matching chains and interrupt chains are discussed further in Section 7.

5.0 INTERMEDIATE MODELING CONCEPTS

In this section we continue to develop the repertoire of GPSS block types begun in Section 3. First, sets of blocks which are used to modify transaction attributes and flow are described and illustrated with several example problems. These permit logically more complicated real systems to be modeled. Then some useful statistical entities are presented. These allow detailed portrayal of the statistics collected by GPSS, and may greatly facilitate decision making using the model. Finally, we discuss computational and reference entities.

5.1 Some Blocks That Modify Transaction Attributes and Flow Logic

ASSIGN This block replaces, increments, or decrements the current contents of a transaction parameter. Optionally, the replacement or increment/decrement amount may be first multiplied by a FUNCTION value. This is similar to the way in which the B operands of the GENERATE and ADVANCE blocks are used. The ASSIGN block never refuses entry to a transaction. This block is useful in ascribing attributes to a transaction which distinguish it from others for model flow and processing purposes.

The flow chart symbol for the ASSIGN block is:

The operands for this block are:

OPERAND	DESCRIPTION	DEFAULT
A*	Parameter number, followed by "+" for increment and "−" for decrement	None
B	The value to replace the current value, be added to it, or subtracted from it	None
C	Function modifier name or number	None

* SNA types 1, 4, 5, or 6 may be used for operands A–C.

Examples of valid ASSIGN statements include:

```
ASSIGN    1,3
ASSIGN    2+,PH$4
ASSIGN    4-,V$3,EXP
```

The first statement replaces the current value of parameter number 1 with the value 3, and the second increments the current value of parameter number 2 by the current value of halfword parameter number 4. The last statement decrements the current value of parameter number 4 by the value of variable 3 multiplied by the function named EXP.

MARK The MARK block makes it possible to measure the elapsed time for a transaction's progress from creation to some point in a model, or between any two points in a model by capturing the time that a transaction passes a particular point in the model.

The flow chart symbol for the MARK block is:

The MARK block then has just the one optional operand:

OPERAND	DESCRIPTION	DEFAULT
A*	Parameter number to retain clock value	None

* SNA types 1, 4, 5, or 6 may be used.

Initially, each transaction carries with it the absolute clock time it entered the model, but the MARK block can change this value to the current absolute clock time. The transaction SNA M1, transaction transit time, is computed as the current absolute clock time minus the mark time currently recorded on the transaction. Thus if a transaction passes through no MARK blocks, M1 is the time from creation; if it passes through one or more MARK blocks, M1 is the time elapsed from the most recent MARK block until the current time.

If one wishes to preserve the original creation time and still note intermediate transit times, the optional A operand can be used to specify a transaction parameter to retain the clock value when passing through a MARK block. The transaction SNA MPj will contain the elapsed time from the last MARK block until the current time. Thus, if the A operand is 5, MP\$5 contains the most recent intermediate transit time.

TEST   This block controls the flow of transactions through a logical relationship involving two SNAs. Determination of the next block for a transaction is based on the truth of the relationship. The TEST block operates in two modes: transactions are blocked until the relationship is true, or transactions are directed to an alternate next block if the relationship is not true. Transactions are never refused entry to this block.

The flow chart symbol for the TEST block is:

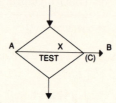

The operands for the TEST block are:

OPERAND	DESCRIPTION	DEFAULT
A*	First SNA to be compared	None
B	Second SNA to be compared	None
C**	Next block if relationship is false	None

* SNA types 1, 4, 5, or 6 may be used for operands A and B.
** SNA types 1, 2, 4, 5, or 6 may be used.

The following relational operators may be used in expressions for the TEST block, and appear as part of the block name field.

L   less than: if the A operand SNA is less than the B operand, the relationship is true.

LE   less than or equal to: if the A operand SNA is less than or equal to the B operand SNA, the relationship is true.

E   equal to: if the A operand SNA is equal to the B operand SNA, the relationship is true.

NE   not equal to: the relationship is true if the two SNAs are unequal.

G   greater than: if the A operand SNA is greater than the B operand SNA, the relationship is true.

GE   greater than or equal to: if the A operand SNA is greater than or equal to the B operand SNA, the relationship is true.

Some sample TEST statements are:

TEST GE	R$SHIP,10
TEST LE	Q$LINE,5,QUIT
TEST E	N$START,N$END

In the first statement, the TEST block will detain transactions when the remaining capacity in the storage SHIP is less than 10 units. All transactions will wait at this block until the remaining capacity increases. The second statement prevents transactions from joining a QUEUE if the current contents exceeds 5 units. Such transactions will go to the block location END, which could be a TERMINATE block. The last statement compares the number of transactions that pass through a block location START to that which pass through END. Such a comparison could be used to determine if a model were emptied of transactions.

When the TEST block is used without a C operand next block, the operation of the model can be slowed considerably since the number of transactions on the current events chain which must be checked at each clock update may become quite large. Consequently, use of many TEST blocks in this mode is to be discouraged.

GATE   The GATE block is similar in function to the TEST block. However, it uses the truth of logical attributes associated with particular entities, rather than a more general logical relationships to determine the flow of transactions. Like the TEST block, the GATE block operates in two modes: preventing transactions from progressing until the logical attribute is true, or directing transactions to an alternate block location if the logical attribute is not true. Transactions are never refused entry to this block.

The flow chart symbol for the GATE block is:

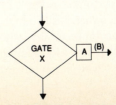

The operands for this block are:

OPERAND	DESCRIPTION	DEFAULT
A*	Name or number of entity	None
B	Next block if logical attribute is false	None

* SNA types 1, 2, 4, 5, or 6 may be used for operands A and B.

The following are some of the logical attributes which can be used with the GATE block. They appear as part of the Block Name field. A complete list of logical attributes may be found in Section 9.

FACILITY LOGICAL ATTRIBUTES

NU   Facility specified by operand A is not in use.

U   Facility specified by operand A is in use.

STORAGE LOGICAL ATTRIBUTES

SE   Storage specified by operand A is empty.

SNE   Storage specified by operand A is not empty.

SNF   Storage specified by operand A is not full.

SF   Storage specified by operand A is full.

LOGIC SWITCH ATTRIBUTES

LS   Logic switch specified by operand A is in the set condition.

LR   Logic switch specified by operand A is in the reset condition.

The following are valid GATE block statements.

GATE SNF   SHIP,OTHER

GATE LR   1

GATE NU   TELLR

The first statement permits a transaction into the GATE block if the storage called SHIP is not full, otherwise the transaction is directed to block location OTHER. In the next statement, transactions are prevented from entering the GATE block until logic switch number 1 is in the reset condition. A logic switch is a binary device which will be discussed as the next block. In the last statement, transactions are detained until a facility named TELLR is not occupied.

LOGIC   This block establishes a logical condition at one location in a model which may be tested from another. The LOGIC switch block will never refuse a transaction entry. Each switch has two logical attributes: LR_j for LOGIC switch j reset and LS_j for LOGIC switch j set. If the switch is reset, LR_j is true, and LS_j is false. If the switch is set, LS_j is true and LR_j is false. Initially all LOGIC switches are in the reset state. The LOGIC switch block can be used to set, reset, or invert the state of the switch.

The flow chart symbol for the LOGIC switch block is:

The operands associated with a LOGIC switch block are:

OPERAND	DESCRIPTION	DEFAULT
A*	Name or number of logic switch	None

* SNA types 1, 2, 4, 5, or 6 may be used.

In addition, three auxiliary operators, which appear as part of the Block Name field, are used to alter the state of a LOGIC switch.

S   Places the logic switch in the set state.

R   Places the logic switch in the reset state.

I   Inverts the state of the logic switch; that is, if set it is reset, if reset it is set.

The following sample LOGIC switch statements are self-explanatory.

LOGIC R   SWCH1

LOGIC I   2

LOGIC S   3

A common application of the LOGIC switch is in conjunction with a GATE block, as illustrated above, and in the following example. The following series of blocks can be used to send transactions alternately to two queues.

BLOC   LOGIC I   LSW1
BLOC1   GATE LS   LSW1,ALT
BLOC2   QUEUE   QUE1
  .   .   .
  .   .   .
  .   .   .
ALT   QUEUE   QUE2

Initially, LOGIC switch LSW1 is reset; the first transaction inverts the state to set, which makes LS true and directs it through the GATE block to QUE1 at block location BLOC2. The next transaction inverts the state again to reset, thus causing LS to be false and directing the transaction to QUE2 at block location ALT.

TRANSFER   The TRANSFER block directs transactions to specific block locations in a model either deterministically or probabilistically using several different modes. The operands for this block are similar for each mode of operation, but are given special interpretations by mode, as explained below. Even though some modes are described in terms of block numbers, blocks may have alphanumeric labels, provided the numbers by which GPSS internally references blocks satisfy the stated relationships. Transactions are never refused entry to a TRANSFER block.

The flow chart symbol for the TRANSFER block is:

The operands for the TRANSFER block are:

OPERAND	DESCRIPTION	DEFAULT
A*	Mode of operation	None
B**	First next block	Depends on mode
C	Second next block	None
D	Indexing factor	None

* Allowable values specified below.
** SNA types 1, 2, 4, 5, or 6 may be used.

UNCONDITIONAL MODE   When operating in this mode an unconditional transfer is made to the block specified by operand B. Operand A, which is omitted, is replaced by a comma, as:

TRANSFER   ,NEXT.

FRACTIONAL MODE   This mode effects a probabilistic transfer based on the value of the A operand. The A operand is decimal ranging from .000 to .999. Transfer to the C operand block occurs with the probability specified in operand A, and transfer to the B operand block with the complementary probability. If the B operand is omitted, transfer is to the next sequential block.

For example:

```
TRANSFER     .600,,NEXT
TRANSFER     .6,NEXT1,NEXT.
```

In each case, transfer to block location NEXT occurs 60% of the time, on the average. For 40% of the transfers, transactions are directed to the next sequential block in the first case, and to block NEXT1 in the second.

BOTH MODE   If operand A is specified as BOTH, transactions are first directed to the B operand block, and if entry is refused (such as might happen for SEIZE or ENTER, TEST, or GATE blocks), the C operand block is tried. If this block also refuses entry, the transaction waits in the TRANSFER block until one of the two choices is available, and is scanned at each clock update. For example:

TRANSFER BOTH,NEXT,NEXT1.

ALL MODE   This is a generalization of the BOTH mode to more than two choices. The B operand block is tried first; if it refuses entry, a block location specified by the sum of the B and D operands (block B+D) is tried. If this fails, block B+2D is tried. This continues until a block is entered, or until the block designated by the C operand is tried. If all trials fail, the transaction waits in the TRANSFER block until one block is available, being scanned at each clock update.

In using this mode, the difference between the operand B and C block numbers must be an exact multiple of operand D. Also, care must be taken to place the alternative blocks appropriately.

For example:

TRANSFER   ALL,NEXT,NEXT+6,1

Blocks NEXT through NEXT+6 will be tried sequentially.

PICK MODE   This mode permits a random selection of a next block. A block is selected with equal probability from those specified by operand B through operand C, that is, blocks B, B+1,...B+C.

For example:

TRANSFER   PICK,NEXT,NEXT+6

A next block will be selected using a random number RN1 from the blocks NEXT through NEXT+6. RN1 is a number in the range .000 to .999 selected from a uniform probability distribution. Further discussion of GPSS random-number generators is contained in Section 5.7 in connection with the description of FUNCTIONS.

FUNCTION MODE   If the A operand contains FN, then the B operand is taken to be the number of a FUNCTION. This FUNCTION is evaluated and added to the C operand to determine a transfer block location. FUNCTIONS are fully described in Section 5.7.

For example, TRANSFER FN,3,PH3 will evaluate FUNCTION 3 and add the value of halfword parameter 3 to it to determine the transfer block number.

SUBROUTINE MODE   If the A operand contains SBR, then the TRANSFER block operates in the following manner. The current transaction is directed to the block specified in the B operand and the number of the TRANSFER block is stored in a parameter designated by the C operand. This mode is useful for routing a transaction through the same set of blocks (or subroutine) from different locations in the model and then returning to the block transferred from, as explained below. This mode operates as a subroutine call does in general-purpose computer languages. For example, TRANSFER SBR,SUB1,4 will direct a transaction to block SUB1 and retain the block number of the TRANSFER block in parameter 4.

PARAMETER MODE   If the A operand contains PH or PF, the TRANSFER block operates in the parameter mode. Operand B is a parameter number, the value of which is added to the C operand to determine the block number for transfer. When placed at the end of a ''subroutine'' set of blocks, transfer to the block immediately following the ''calling'' block can be effected.

For example:

HERE	TRANSFER SBR,THERE,4
HERE1	[main program continues]

.

.

THERE	[first block of subroutine]

.

.

[last block of subroutine]

TRANSFER PH,4,1

This sequence of blocks will direct transactions to block THERE, retaining the block number of block HERE in halfword parameter 4. The TRANSFER block at the end of the subroutine will direct transactions to the block immediately following HERE (HERE plus the C operand value of 1). Thus we have effected a subroutine call/return sequence.

LOOP   In general-purpose programming languages the function of loops is to execute a sequence of instructions repeatedly. In GPSS the purpose of the LOOP block is much the same, namely to pass a transaction through a series of blocks several times. In specifying a loop, both the range of blocks to be traversed and the number of iterations must be stated.

The flow chart symbol for the LOOP block is:

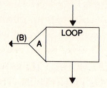

The two required operands are:

OPERAND	DESCRIPTION	DEFAULT
A*	Parameter number which contains count for loop iterations	None
B**	Next block if parameter specified by operand A is not zero	None

* SNA types 1, 4, 5, or 6 may be used.
** SNA types 1, 2, 4, 5, or 6 may be used.

The LOOP block is placed at the end of the series of blocks to be traversed and operates as follows. The A operand parameter contains the number of times the blocks are to be traversed, and upon each iteration it is decremented by one. If this parameter has a nonzero value when the transaction passes through the LOOP block, it returns to the B operand next block, which should be the first block in the series. When this parameter reaches zero, the required number of iterations have been accomplished and the transaction passes into the next sequential block. For example:

```
             ASSIGN    3,10
BEGIN        [first block of series]
                  .

             [last block of series]
             LOOP      3,BEGIN
```

This construction would cause the series of blocks beginning with block BEGIN to be traversed 10 times before exiting.

5.2   Illustrative Problem Set II

In this problem set we model some real systems which permit the use of the blocks just described. We begin with a multiple-server model with two classes of customers: those with a short service time, and those with a much longer time for service. In this example we highlight the use of the TRANSFER, GATE, and LOGIC switch blocks. The second problem considers a simple assembly line with limited queue space between work stations. The ASSIGN and LOOP blocks and indirect addressing are illustrated in this problem. In the final problem of this set we construct a simplified model of a multiprogrammed computer system which demonstrates the use of the TEST, and MARK blocks.

PROBLEM II.1   To facilitate customers with only check cashing needs, a certain bank has assigned one teller to perform only this service. About 40% of arriving customers are of this nature. The remaining 60% have additional transactions to process and must use one of the other four tellers in the bank. Customers arrive at intervals described by a uniform distribution with a mean of 66 seconds and a range of ±10 seconds, and either join the check-cashing teller line or the single line for the other four tellers. Check cashing requires 120±30 seconds, and all other bank business takes 360±120 seconds per customer. The run length is controlled by a separate GENERATE block which creates a transaction at the end of a 7-hour banking day to terminate the run. The flow chart and GPSS code for this problem appear in Figs. 5.1 and 5.2.

In this problem we will be concerned, for the first time, with the state of the model when the run ceases. In previous examples we have possibly had customers remaining in the modeled facility when it closed. Using the LOGIC switch and GATE blocks we can easily accomplish this. The LOGIC switch named LOCK is initially in the reset state, so all arriving transactions pass through the GATE LR block immediately following the GENERATE block. When the terminating transaction is created at the end of the day, it places the LOGIC switch in the set state, thus making GATE LR false and preventing any more transactions from entering the model.

To be certain that the bank is empty before closing it, we compare the block count SNAs, N, for the QUEUE LINE1 block and the LEAVE TELRS block, and for the QUEUE LINE2 block and the RELEASE CHECK block. When N\$LINE1 and N\$END are equal, the number of customers who have entered the queue and the number who have left the storage TELRS will be equal. Similarly, when N\$BEGIN and N\$QUIT

FIGURE 5.1   PROBLEM II.1 FLOW CHART

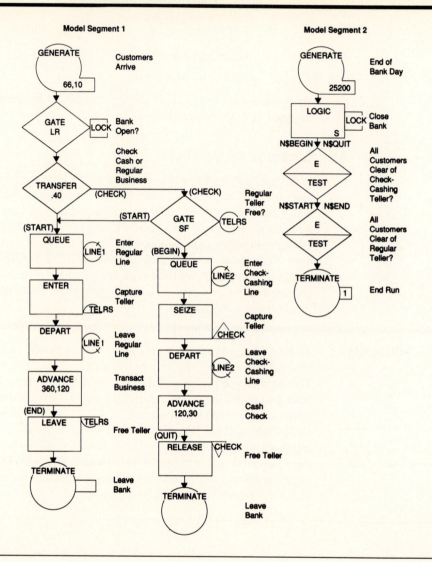

are equal, the number of customers who have entered the queue and the number who have left the facility CHECK will be the same. If both of these relationships are satisfied, the bank will be empty, and the TEST blocks will permit the run-terminating transaction to pass.

One other portion of the model logic requires comment. When a check-cashing customer is routed to the dedicated teller, he first ascertains if one of the regular tellers is available before joining the check-cashing line. This is accomplished using the GATE SNF logical test; if the storage TELRS is not full, then the customer will be transferred to QUEUE LINE1 and pass through into the storage for service.

We turn now to decisions to be aided by this model and the GPSS output. The model output is shown in Fig. 5.3. A dedicated teller is a helpful service for check-

FIGURE 5.2   PROBLEM II.1 CODE

```
LINE    BLOCK    BLOCK    BLOCK NAME                    COMMENTS
NO.     NO.      LOC.
 1               *BANK TELLER ASSIGNMENT MODEL
 2                        SIMULATE
 3               *MODEL SEGMENT 1 - REGULAR BANK BUSINESS
 4                        STORAGE       S$TELRS,4      4 REGULAR TELLERS
 5      1                 GENERATE      66,10          INTERARRIVAL TIME, SECONDS
 6      2                 GATE LR       LOCK           TEST IF BANK CLOSED
 7      3                 TRANSFER      .40,,CHECK     CHECK-CASHING LINE?
 8      4       START     QUEUE         LINE1          ENTER REGULAR LINE
 9      5                 ENTER         TELRS          ENGAGE A TELLER
10      6                 DEPART        LINE1          LEAVE REGULAR LINE
11      7                 ADVANCE       360,120        TRANSACT BUSINESS
12      8       END       LEAVE         TELRS          DISENGAGE TELLER
13      9                 TERMINATE
14               *MODEL SEGMENT 2 - CHECK CASHING ONLY
15      10       CHECK     GATE SF       TELRS,START    CHECK REGULAR TELLER FREE?
16      11       BEGIN     QUEUE         LINE2          ENTER CHK CASHING LINE
17      12                 SEIZE         CHECK          ENGAGE CHK-CASHING TELLER
18      13                 DEPART        LINE2          LEAVE CHK CASHING LINE
19      14                 ADVANCE       120,30         CASH CHECK
20      15       QUIT      RELEASE       CHECK          DISENGAGE CHK-CASHING TELR
21      16                 TERMINATE
22               *MODEL SEGMENT 3 - RUN LENGTH CONTROL
23      17                 GENERATE      25200          END OF 7-HOUR BANK DAY
24      18                 LOGIC S       LOCK           CLOSE BANK
25      19                 TEST E        N$BEGIN,N$QUIT  CUSTOMERS IN CHK
26               *                                      CASHING LINE?
27      20                 TEST E        N$START,N$END  ANY CUSTOMERS IN OTHER
28               *                                      LINE?
29      21                 TERMINATE     1
30                         START         1
```

FIGURE 5.3   PROBLEM II.1 OUTPUT

```
RELATIVE CLOCK 25647    ABSOLUTE CLOCK 25647
```

QUEUE	MAXIMUM CONTENTS	AVERAGE CONTENTS	TOTAL ENTRIES	ZERO ENTRIES	PERCENT ZEROS	AVERAGE TIME/TRANS	$AVERAGE TIME/TRANS	TABLE NUMBER	CURRENT CONTENTS
LINE1	4	0.546	269	108	40.149	52.063	86.988		0
LINE2	2	0.084	112	74	66.071	19.188	56.553		0

FACILITY	AVERAGE UTILIZATION	NUMBER ENTRIES	AVERAGE TIME/TRANS	SEIZING TRANS. NO.	PREEMPTING TRANS. NO.
CHECK	0.516	112	118.116		

STORAGE	CAPACITY	AVERAGE CONTENTS	TOTAL ENTRIES	AVERAGE TIME/TRANS	AVERAGE UTILIZ.	AVAIL. UTILIZ.	UNAVAIL. UTILIZ.	CURRENT STATUS	FRACTION AVAIL.	CURRENT CONTENTS	MAXIMUM CONTENTS
TELRS	4	3.810	269	363.264	0.953			A	1.000	0	4

```
"SET" LOGIC SWITCHES

   LOCK
```

cashing customers, but is this teller kept sufficiently occupied? To answer this question we examine the utilization of the facility CHECK. What about the service provided the other bank customers? Are the waiting times too long, and could the dedicated teller be used more generally to provide better service to all categories of customers? The output provided by the QUEUE named LINE1 can provide information to aid in deciding this.

The waiting times for both classes of customers seem to be inconsequential; check-cashing customers wait an average of 19 seconds, and regular customers, an average of 52 seconds. This is accomplished at the expense of an under-utilized check-cashing teller, who is idle 49% of the time. A better use of the teller resources might be to use all five tellers to serve the entire customer population. This alternative could easily be evaluated using the model.

PROBLEM II.2   We turn to a manufacturing setting in this problem. The model is a progressive assembly line for large products requiring expensive conveyors to move them from one work station to another, and to store them between stations. The assembly line has three work stations with conveyor buffer space intervening. Subassemblies arrive at the first work station every 410 seconds. The assembly times at the three stations have been balanced to be 400 ± 300 seconds at each station.

The LOOP block is a convenient and efficient way to model this assembly line. Because the LOOP parameter is decremented with iterations, beginning in this case with the value 3, another transaction parameter is initialized at 1 and incremented at each iteration to designate the work station number.

The way the run is terminated is different from the approach taken previously. As each completed assembly flows through the terminate block, it decrements the start count by one. By using the START statement to initialize the count at some desired output, the number of assemblies completed then determines the run length. The flow chart and GPSS code for this model are shown in Figs. 5.4 and 5.5.

Since conveyors are expensive, we seek to minimize the amount of buffer space between work stations, while not requiring work to be placed on the floor due to lack of conveyor space. This buffer space may be viewed as a queue. In addition, to observe the utilization that buffer spaces of varying amounts would receive, we include storages between the work stations. To vary the buffer space, we simply redefine the storage capacities. Notice that the queue tallies transactions from leaving the previous work station to seizing the next work station. Part of this time is spent in the storage, and part of it may be spent waiting to gain access to the storage. The excess time spent in the queue reflects the number of units which would be placed on the floor using conveyor space of the specified capacity.

From the GPSS output, which appears in Fig. 5.6, we see that a storage capacity of 3 for work station buffers yields a utilization of 52%, 72%, and 59% for work stations 1, 2, and 3, respectively. But, these numbers are misleading. The maximum contents of each storage is 3 and, even more telling, the maximum contents of the work stations queues are 7, 15, and 13. Even the average contents of the queues for work stations 2 and 3 exceed the buffer storage capacity. It would seem there is much product placed on the floor.

FIGURE 5.4   PROBLEM II.2 FLOW CHART

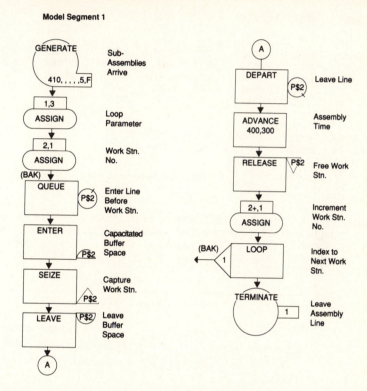

Model Segment 1

FIGURE 5.5   PROBLEM II.2 CODE

```
LINE   BLOCK   BLOCK   BLOCK NAME                      COMMENTS
NO.    NO.     LOC.
 1             *PROGRESSIVE ASSEMBLY LINE
 2                     SIMULATE
 3             *MODEL SEGMENT 1 - ASSEMBLY LINE LOGIC
 4                     STORAGE         S$1-S$3,3     INTER WORK STN QUEUE
 5             *                                     CAPACITY
 6      1              GENERATE        410,,,,,5,F   ARRIVING SUBASSEMBLIES -
 7             *                                     seconds
 8      2              ASSIGN          1,3           LOOP PARAMETER
 9      3              ASSIGN          2,1           WORK STN NO.
10      4      BAK     QUEUE           P$2           QUEUE BEFORE BUFFER SPACES
11      5              ENTER           P$2           CAPACITY ON QUEUE
12      7              SEIZE           P$2           SEIZE WORK STN
13      8              LEAVE           P$2
14      6              DEPART          P$2           LEAVE BUFFER SPACE
15      9              ADVANCE         400,300       ASSEMBLE
16     10              RELEASE         P$2           FREE WORK STATION
17     11              ASSIGN          2+,1          INCREMENT WORK STN NO.
18     12              LOOP            1,BAK         INDEX TO NEXT WORK STN
19     13              TERMINATE       1
20                     START           1000          PRODUCE 1000 PARTS
```

FIGURE 5.6   PROBLEM II.2 OUTPUT

RELATIVE CLOCK 412875   ABSOLUTE CLOCK 412875

QUEUE	MAXIMUM CONTENTS	AVERAGE CONTENTS	TOTAL ENTRIES	ZERO ENTRIES	PERCENT ZEROS	AVERAGE TIME/TRANS	$AVERAGE TIME/TRANS	TABLE NUMBER	CURRENT CONTENTS
1	4	0.231	1007	771	76.564	94.756	404.318		0
2	12	2.100	1005	499	49.652	862.791	1713.646		0
3	10	1.254	1001	592	59.141	517.087	1265.535		0

FACILITY	AVERAGE UTILIZATION	NUMBER ENTRIES	AVERAGE TIME/TRANS	SEIZING TRANS. NO.	PREEMPTING TRANS. NO.
1	0.973	1006	399.499	13	
2	0.974	1002	401.399	11	
3	0.948	1000	391.388		

STORAGE	CAPACITY	AVERAGE CONTENTS	TOTAL ENTRIES	AVERAGE TIME/TRANS	AVERAGE UTILIZ.	AVAIL. UTILIZ.	UNAVAIL. UTILIZ.	CURRENT STATUS	FRACTION AVAIL.	CURRENT CONTENTS	MAXIMUM CONTENTS
1	3	1.587	1007	650.769	0.529			A	1.000	1	3
2	3	2.168	1005	890.632	0.723			A	1.000	3	3
3	3	1.779	1001	733.646	0.593			A	1.000	1	3

To alleviate this situation, we could increase the storage capacities of the conveyor, but what is really needed to make an effective decision is an estimate of the fraction of the time the buffer capacity is exceeded. We deal with this in Problem IV.2 of Section 5.6.

PROBLEM II.3 In the design of a multiprogrammed computer system, the size and speed of the CPU, and the scheduling algorithm for jobs are major considerations. This example provides a simple model of such a system which permits evaluation of alternative designs and schedules. Jobs arrive every 6±3 seconds. The job stream consists of 30% long jobs (25 seconds) and 70% short jobs (17 seconds). The CPU can accommodate four jobs for concurrent execution. Each job is allotted 8 seconds in the CPU, but because of I/O interrupts, a job typically spends an average of 6 seconds uniformly distributed over the range 6±5 seconds. Jobs are recycled through the CPU until completed. Upon completion, jobs queue at the printer where each job requires 5±2 seconds for printing. The flow chart and GPSS code for this example are shown in Figs. 5.7 and 5.8, respectively.

Features you should notice about the model logic are the following. The MARK block is used in this model to compute the elapsed time spent by a job at each turn in the CPU. The cumulative CPU time is accumulated in transaction parameter 2, and when it equals or exceeds the assigned job execution time, the job exits to the printer. A queue named QSYS is used to tally the time from first entering the CPU to final departure.

With this model we can address questions about the size of the CPU (affects the number of jobs executed concurrently), the time slice allotted each job, and the speed of

FIGURE 5.7   PROBLEM II.3 FLOW CHART

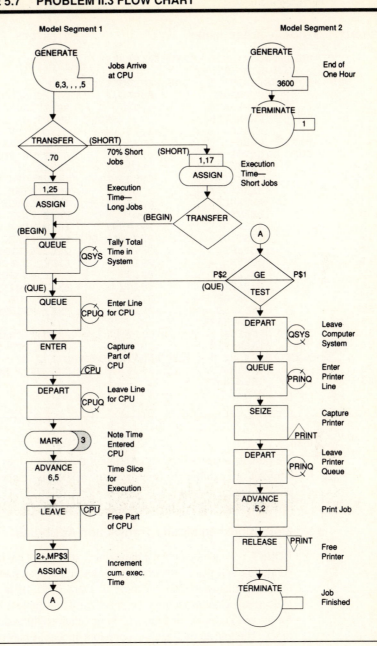

the printer. All of these factors influence the job processing time, and hence user service. Based on the output of Fig. 5.9, the adequacy of all these may be assessed.

The CPU utilization of 96% does not appear to delay jobs excessively. The average time to complete a job is 33 seconds, which is about 14 seconds more than the average job execution time. The average wait for a turn in the CPU is about 3 seconds, and for

FIGURE 5.8   PROBLEM II.3 CODE

```
LINE   BLOCK   BLOCK    BLOCK NAME                    COMMENTS
NO.    NO.     LOC.
 1             *MULTIPROGRAMMED COMPUTER SYSTEM
 2                      SIMULATE
 3             *MODEL SEGMENT 1 - JOB SCHEDULING LOGIC
 4                      STORAGE       S$CPU,4         NO. CONCURRENT JOBS IN CPU
 5      1               GENERATE      6,3,,,,5        ARRIVING JOBS (SEC.)
 6      2               TRANSFER      .70,,SHORT      SHORT OR LING JOB?
 7      3               ASSIGN        1,25            EXECUTION TIME, LONG JOBS
 8      4       BEGIN   QUEUE         QSYS            TALLY ELAPSED EXEC. TIME
 9      5       QUE     QUEUE         CPUQ            LINE UP FOR CPU
10      6               ENTER         CPU             ENTER CPU
11      7               DEPART        CPUQ            LEAVE CPU QUEUE
12      8               MARK          3               NOTE TIME JOB ENTERED CPU
13      9               ADVANCE       6,5             TIME SLICE FOR EXECUTION
14     10               LEAVE         CPU             FREE PART OF CPU
15     11               ASSIGN        2+,MP$3         INCREMENT CUM EXEC. TIME
16     12               TEST GE       P$2,P$1,QUE     TOTAL EXEC. TIME ELAPSED?
17     13               DEPART        QSYS            TALLYS ELAPSED EXEC TIME
18     14               QUEUE         PRINQ           LINE UP FOR PRINTER
19     15               SEIZE         PRINT           CAPTURE PRINTER
20     16               DEPART        PRINQ           LEAVE PRINTER LINE
21     17               ADVANCE       5,2             PRINT JOB
22     18               RELEASE       PRINT           FREE PRINTER
23     19               TERMINATE
24     20      SHORT    ASSIGN        1,17            EXECUTION FOR SHORT JOBS
25     21               TRANSFER      ,BEGIN          GO TO CPU QUEUE
26             *MODEL SEGMENT 2 - RUN LENGTH CONTROL
27     22               GENERATE      3600            END OF 1 HOUR
28     23               TERMINATE     1
29                      START         1
```

the printer, about 3 seconds. Although the system does not seem overly congested, we could easily explore the impact of an inexpensive policy change, such as a larger time slice, using the model.

5.3   More Blocks to Modify Transaction Attributes

COUNT   This block counts the number of entities having an SNA that meets a specific condition, and places the count in a designated parameter. For example, the number of queues with fewer than 3 people in them ($Qj \leq 3$), or the number of empty storages ($SE = true$). Conditions may be specified using logical attributes, such as those defined for the GATE block, or using algebraic relationships, such as those defined for the TEST block. The logical or algebraic operators appear as part of the Block Name field.

The flow chart symbol for the COUNT block is:

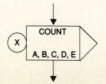

FIGURE 5.9   PROBLEM II.3 OUTPUT

RELATIVE CLOCK 3600   ABSOLUTE CLOCK 3600

QUEUE	MAXIMUM CONTENTS	AVERAGE CONTENTS	TOTAL ENTRIES	ZERO ENTRIES	PERCENT ZEROS	AVERAGE TIME/TRANS	$AVERAGE TIME/TRANS	TABLE NUMBER	CURRENT CONTENTS
CPUQ	9	1.911	2329	1863	79.991	2.954	14.762		1
PRINQ	3	0.533	607	191	31.466	3.161	4.613		0
QSYS	13	5.758	612	0	0.000	33.869	33.869		5

FACILITY	AVERAGE UTILIZATION	NUMBER ENTRIES	AVERAGE TIME/TRANS	SEIZING TRANS. NO.	PREEMPTING TRANS. NO.
PRINT	0.854	607	5.066	11	

STORAGE	CAPACITY	AVERAGE CONTENTS	TOTAL ENTRIES	AVERAGE TIME/TRANS	AVERAGE UTILIZ.	AVAIL. UTILIZ.	UNAVAIL. UTILIZ.	CURRENT STATUS	FRACTION AVAIL.	CURRENT CONTENTS	MAXIMUM CONTENTS
CPU	4	3.847	2328	5.949	0.962			A	1.000	4	4

The COUNT block operands are:

OPERAND	DESCRIPTION	DEFAULT
A*	Parameter in which to place the count	None
B**	Lower limit of entity examined	None
C	Upper limit of entity examined	None
D	Comparison value for algebraic expressions	None
E***	Symbol of SNA to be counted	None

* SNA types 1, 4, 5, or 6 may be used.
** SNA types 1, 2, 4, 5, or 6 may be used for operands B, C, and D.
*** May be any SNA except MX or MH.

The following are examples of valid count statements.

COUNT LE   1,1,6,10,Q
COUNT NU   1,1,5
COUNT E   1,P$1,P$2,XH$CHECK,Q

The first statement counts the number of queues in the range 1 through 6 with no more than 10 transactions in them, and places the count in parameter number 1. The second statement counts the number of facilities in the range 1 through 5 that are not currently in use, and places the count in parameter number 1. The operands A through D may be specified using SNAs rather than constants, as in the last statement.

SELECT   The SELECT block is quite similar in function to the COUNT block. This block selects the first entity in the specified range with an SNA value or state that meets the prescribed condition, and places the number of the entity in a designated parameter.

For example, find the first storage that is not full (SNF = true). SELECT has two additional operators: MIN and MAX, which will find the minimum and maximum SNA values.

The flow chart symbol for the SELECT block is:

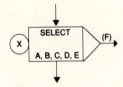

The operands for this block are as follows:

OPERAND	DESCRIPTION	DEFAULT
A*	Parameter in which to place entity number	None
B**	Lower limit of entity examined	None
C	Upper limit of entity examined	None
D	Comparison value for algebraic expressions	None
E***	Symbol of SNA to be examined	None
F	Alternate block if condition not satisfied	Next block

* SNA types 1, 4, 5, or 6 may be used.
** SNA types 1, 2, 4, 5, or 6 may be used for operands B, C, D, and F.
*** May be any SNA except MX or MH.

The SELECT block may be used as follows:

SELECT LE   1,1,5,4,Q,QUIT
SELECT MIN   1,1,5,,Q
SELECT SNF   1,P$2,P$3

The first statement selects the first queue in the range 1 through 5 which contains 5 or fewer transactions, and places the number of the queue in parameter 1. If no queues meet this condition, the transaction is directed to block location QUIT, which could be a TERMINATE block. The second statement finds the minimum queue in the range 1 through 5. The last statement selects the first storage in the range P$2 to P$3 which is not full.

PRIORITY   The PRIORITY block changes a transaction's priority from that which was assigned when created. This is desirable when one wants to influence the order in which transactions on the current events chain are processed, as in the case of simultaneous happenings which must be properly sequenced. An example of this appears in the following Illustrative Problem Set. The PRIORITY block also has a buffer option designed to force a restart of the current events chain scan after changing a transaction's priority. The use of the word BUFFER as the B operand accomplishes this.

The flow chart symbol for this block is:

The operands for this block are:

OPERAND	DESCRIPTION	DEFAULT
A*	Priority to be assigned	None
B	Buffer option [BUFFER]	None

* SNA types 1, 4, 5, or 6 may be used for operand A.

The PRIORITY block may appear as:

PRIORITY   2

PRIORITY   P$3,BUFFER

BUFFER   The function of the BUFFER block is to immediately stop the processing of the current transaction and reinitiate the scan of the current events chain at its beginning. It behaves in the same manner as a PRIORITY block with the BUFFER option, except it does not alter the priority of the transaction. Like the PRIORITY block, this block is useful in controlling the sequence of complicated simultaneous events.

The flow chart symbol for the BUFFER block is:

The BUFFER block has no operands.

5.4   Illustrative Problem Set III

We illustrate here the use of the SELECT and PRIORITY blocks for choosing among several alternative queues to join. Also, the role of the PRIORITY block in controlling simultaneous events is portrayed.

PROBLEM III.1   In this problem we explore a situation that permits each resource to have its own queue. The setting used is a bank, although this arrangement is equally common in many other settings such as car washes, toll booths, and supermarkets.

Customers arrive at the bank every 33 ± 10 seconds during a peak period. Before entering, we check to see if the bank is open using the GATE block, as illustrated previously in Problem II.1. Customers choose the shortest line from one of six lines and tellers. If the shortest queue exceeds two, the customer balks and leaves the bank. Once a line is selected, a customer will not change lines (unlike the jockeying of most real-life situations).

FIGURE 5.10   PROBLEM III.1 FLOW CHART

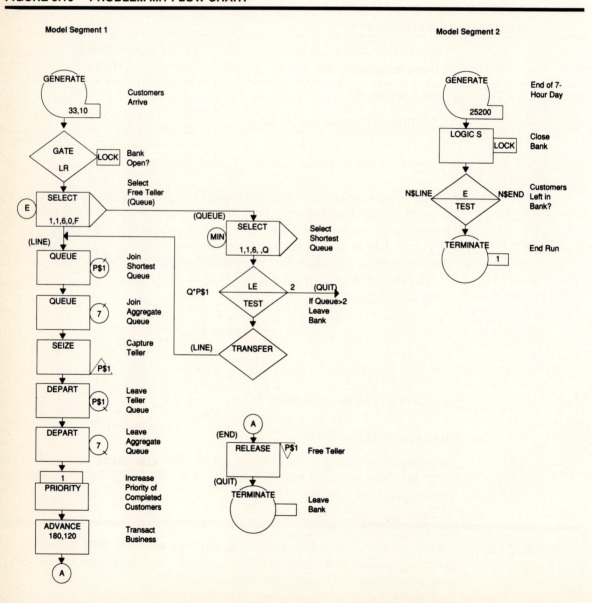

The logic of the model highlights the function of the SELECT block. A SELECT block is first used to check for an idle teller, and if one cannot be found, a second SELECT block finds the minimum queue. Before customers begin to transact their business in the ADVANCE block, their priority is increased using a PRIORITY block. In this way, service completions will be accomplished by GPSS before arrivals are processed. Thus, an arriving customer will stop momentarily and wait for customers leaving at the same instant before making a decision on which line, if any, to join. In addition to QUEUE blocks for each of the six individual lines, there is a seventh QUEUE block that tallies aggregate customer waiting time. The flow chart and GPSS code for this model are shown in Figs. 5.10 and 5.11. From the output of Fig. 5.12, we observe a large variance in the average waiting times for the six tellers, ranging from 0 to 107 seconds, while the average waiting time for all customers is 43 seconds. In general, the waiting times and the facility utilizations decrease as the teller number increases. This is so because the SELECT block picks the first facility or queue that satisfies the specified condition. The level of service in this bank is exemplary. Perhaps fewer tellers are required during this peak period. Also, perhaps a single line for all tellers would be perceived as more fair since it would reduce the variance in individual waiting times.

FIGURE 5.11   PROBLEM III.1 CODE

```
LINE   BLOCK   BLOCK   BLOCK NAME                         COMMENTS
NO.    NO.     LOC.
 1             *BANK TELLER PROBLEM REVISITED- SINGLE QUEUE FOR ALL TELLERS
 2                     SIMULATE
 3             *MODEL SEGMENT 1 - TELLER SELECTION LOGIC
 4      1              GENERATE      33,10                INTERARRIVAL TIME
 5             *                                          (SECONDS)
 6      2              GATE LR       LOCK                 TEST IF BANK CLOSED
 7      3              SELECT E      1,1,6,0,F,QUEUP      SELECT AVAILABLE TELR
 8      4      LINE    QUEUE         P$1                  JOIN SHORTEST QUEUE
 9      5              QUEUE         7                    AGGREGATE QUEUE
10      6              SEIZE         P$1                  ENGAGE TELLER
11      7              DEPART        P$1                  LEAVE SHORTEST QUEUE
12      8              DEPART        7                    LEAVE AGGREGATE QUEUE
13      9              PRIORITY      1                    INCREASE PRIORITY OF
14             *                                          SERVED CUSTOMER
15     10              ADVANCE       180,120              TRANSACT BUSINESS
16     11      END     RELEASE       P$1                  FREE TELLER
17     12      QUIT    TERMINATE
18     13      QUEUP   SELECT MIN    1,1,6,,Q             SELECT MIN QUEUE
19     14              TEST LE       Q*P$1,2,QUIT         IF QUEUE GREATER THAN
20             *                                          2, LEAVE
21     15              TRANSFER      ,LINE                GO TO SHORTEST QUEUE
22             *MODEL SEGMENT 2 - RUN LRNGTH CONTROL
23     16              GENERATE      25200                END OF 7-HOUR BANK DAY
24     17              LOGIC S       LOCK                 CLOSE BANK
25     18              TEST E        N$LINE,N$END         ANY CUSTOMERS LEFT IN
26             *                                          BANK?
27     19              TERMINATE     1
28                     START         1
```

FIGURE 5.12   PROBLEM III.1 OUTPUT

RELATIVE CLOCK 25538   ABSOLUTE CLOCK 25538

QUEUE	MAXIMUM CONTENTS	AVERAGE CONTENTS	TOTAL ENTRIES	ZERO ENTRIES	PERCENT ZEROS	AVERAGE TIME/TRANS	$AVERAGE TIME/TRANS	TABLE NUMBER	CURRENT CONTENTS
1	1	0.581	139	26	18.705	106.777	131.345		0
2	1	0.406	128	45	35.156	81.016	124.940		0
3	1	0.203	131	82	62.595	39.649	106.000		0
4	1	0.081	128	107	83.594	16.109	98.190		0
5	1	0.015	123	117	95.122	3.179	65.167		0
6	1	0.000	113	113	100.000	0.000	0.000		0
7	6	1.287	762	490	64.304	43.122	120.805		0

FACILITY	AVERAGE UTILIZATION	NUMBER ENTRIES	AVERAGE TIME/TRANS	SEIZING TRANS. NO.	PREEMPTING TRANS. NO.
1	0.984	139	180.770		
2	0.961	128	191.758		
3	0.928	131	180.855		
4	0.875	128	174.609		
5	0.847	123	175.886		
6	0.769	113	173.841		

"SET" LOGIC SWITCHES

    LOCK

5.5   Some Statistical Entities

Statistical entities include queues and distribution tables. We have already discussed how queues can be implemented in a model using the QUEUE and DEPART blocks, and the output they provide. Often we need to know more than the average and maximum values supplied as queue output. Distribution tables are the means of providing this information. These tables provide the mean, standard deviation, relative frequency, percentage, cumulative percentage, and more for any designated argument. With this kind of information one can be more precise in defining performance measures such as level of service. Instead of striving simply for an acceptable average waiting time, one could specify that no more than 5% of the customers should wait longer than 10 minutes.

Distribution tables are implemented using a table definition statement, and TABULATE and QTABLE blocks as explained below.

TABLE   This statement defines the argument of the table, the number of cells, and the cell boundaries. Tables must be given a name or number in the block location field.

The operands are as follows:

OPERAND	DESCRIPTION	DEFAULT
A*	Table argument	None
B**	Upper limit of lowest frequency cell	None
C	Frequency cell size	None
D	Number of frequency cells	None

* Must be SNA type 3.
** Operands B – D must be SNA type 1.

All operands except the table argument must be constants. The table argument may be almost any SNA.

Some valid table statements are:

TAB1 TABLE   Q$LINE,10,5,10

TAB2 TABLE   P$1,10,5,10

The first table will provide information on the length of a queue named LINE. The upper limit of the first cell is 10 minutes, and the cell size for all other cells is 5 minutes. Thus the first cell includes 0 to 10 minutes, the second cell 11 to 15, the third 16 to 20, etc., up to the tenth cell, which includes 51 to the largest number the computer being used can accommodate. The second table tabulates P$1, which could be a service time. The table would then provide a frequency distribution of the service times.

TABULATE   This block causes the argument in the specified table to be tabulated. It is placed in the GPSS program at the point where the data are to be tabulated. For the first example above the TABULATE block should be placed in the model to sample the status of the queue at regular intervals, say every two minutes. This will require a separate GENERATE block. For the second example, the TABULATE block would be placed immediately after an ADVANCE block.

The flow chart symbol for the TABULATE block is:

The operand for the TABULATE block is:

OPERAND	DESCRIPTION	DEFAULT
A*	Table number or name for tabulation	None

* SNA types 1, 2, 4, 5, or 6 may be used.

TABULATE blocks take the following form:

TABULATE   TAB1.

QTABLE   Since waiting time is of considerable importance in judging the performance of a system, a special table is defined to tabulate the delay times in queues. If a QTABLE is defined for a queue, the waiting time is automatically tabulated whenever a transaction passes through a DEPART block.

The operands for this statement are similar to those for the TABLE definition statement.

OPERAND	DESCRIPTION	DEFAULT
A*	The number or name of queue for which waiting time is to be tabulated	None
B**	Upper limit of lowest frequency cell	None
C	Frequency cell size	None
D	Number of frequency cells	None

* SNA types 1 or 2 must be used.
** SNA type 1 must be used for operands B–D.

The QTABLE statement takes the form:

QTABLE   LINE,5,5,10.

To illustrate the efficiency of this statement, we present an alternative way of collecting waiting times using the TABLE definition statement and TABULATE block, which is then contrasted with the QTABLE method.

```
        MARK        2
        QUEUE       LINE
        SEIZE       1
        DEPART      LINE
        TABULATE    TAB1
TAB1    TABLE       MP$2,0,5,40
```

An equivalent way of obtaining waiting times using the QTABLE is:

```
        QUEUE       LINE
        SEIZE       1
        DEPART      LINE
TAB1    QTABLE      LINE,0,5,40
```

5.6   Illustrative Problem Set IV

In this problem set we revisit some previous examples to show how TABLE, QTABLE, and TABULATE can provide more detailed information for decision making.

PROBLEM IV.1   In Problem II.1 of Section 5.2, we made judgments on customer service based upon the average waiting times for two categories of customer: check cashing, and regular bank business. A more informed decision could be made if we knew what fraction of customers waited longer than some specified time. Service level could be more precisely stated if we could say, for example, that 95% of check-cashing customers waited 2 minutes or less. A simple way to obtain this information is the use of the QTABLE statement. Figure 5.13 shows the GPSS code for Problem II.1 with the addition of QTABLE statements for each of the two queues.

The summary output for tables includes: the number of entries, the mean, and the standard deviation. For each frequency cell defined for a table, the information provided includes: the upper limit of the cell, the observed frequency, percent of total, and cumulative percentage.

FIGURE 5.13 PROBLEM IV.1 CODE

```
LINE   BLOCK   BLOCK   BLOCK NAME                          COMMENTS
NO.    NO.     LOC.
 1             *BANK TELLER ASSIGNMENT MODEL: PROBLEM II.1 WITH TABLES
 2                     SIMULATE
 3             *MODEL SEGMENT 1 - REGULAR BANK BUSINESS
 4                     STORAGE         S$TELRS,4           4 REGULAR TELLERS
 5      1              GENERATE        66,10               INTERARRIVAL TIME
 6             *                                           (SECONDS)
 7      2              GATE LR         LOCK                TEST IF BANK CLOSED
 8      3              TRANSFER        .40,,CHECK          CHECK CASH ONLY?
 9      4      START   QUEUE           LINE1               ENTER REGULAR LINE
10      5              ENTER           TELRS               ENGAGE A TELLER
11      6              DEPART          LINE1               LEAVE REGULAR LINE
12      TAB1           QTABLE          LINE1,0,15,15       TABULATE WAITING
13             *                                           TIMES- LINE1
14      7              ADVANCE         360,120             TRANSACT BUSINESS
15      8      END     LEAVE           TELRS               DISENGAGE TELLER
16      9              TERMINATE
17             *MODEL SEGMENT 2 - CHECK CASHING ONLY
18     10      CHECK   GATE SF         TELRS,START         CHECK FOR REGULAR
19             *                                           TELLER FREE
20     11      BEGIN   QUEUE           LINE2               ENTER CHK CASH LINE
21     12              SEIZE           CHECK               ENGAGE CHK-CASHING
22             *                                           TELLER
23     13              DEPART          LINE2               LEAVE CHK CASHING LINE
24      TAB2           QTABLE          LINE2,0,15,15       TABULATE WAITING
25             *                                           TIMES- LINE2
26     14              ADVANCE         120,30              CASH CHECK
27     15      QUIT    RELEASE         CHECK               DISENGAGE CHK-CASHING
28             *                                           TELLER
29     16              TERMINATE
30             *MODEL SEGMENT 3 - RUN LENGTH CONTROL
31     17              GENERATE        25200               END OF 7-HOUR BANK DAY
32     18              LOGIC S         LOCK                CLOSE BANK
33     19              TEST E          N$BEGIN,N$QUIT      ANY CUSTOMERS IN CHECK
34             *                                           CASHING LINE?
35     20              TEST E          N$START,N$END       ANY CUSTOMERS IN OTHER
36             *                                           LINE?
37     21              TERMINATE       1
38                     START           1
```

FIGURE 5.14   PROBLEM IV.1 OUTPUT

RELATIVE CLOCK 25647   ABSOLUTE CLOCK 25647

QUEUE	MAXIMUM CONTENTS	AVERAGE CONTENTS	TOTAL ENTRIES	ZERO ENTRIES	PERCENT ZEROS	AVERAGE TIME/TRANS	$AVERAGE TIME/TRANS	TABLE NUMBER	CURRENT CONTENTS
LINE1	4	0.546	269	108	40.149	52.063	86.988	1	0
LINE2	2	0.084	112	74	66.071	19.188	56.553	2	0

FACILITY	AVERAGE UTILIZATION	NUMBER ENTRIES	AVERAGE TIME/TRANS	SEIZING TRANS. NO.	PREEMPTING TRANS. NO.
CHECK	0.516	112	118.116		

STORAGE	CAPACITY	AVERAGE CONTENTS	TOTAL ENTRIES	AVERAGE TIME/TRANS	AVERAGE UTILIZ.	AVAIL. UTILIZ.	UNAVAIL. UTILIZ.	CURRENT STATUS	FRACTION AVAIL.	CURRENT CONTENTS	MAXIMUM CONTENTS
TELRS	4	3.810	269	363.264	0.953			A	1.000	0	4

"SET" LOGIC SWITCHES

    LOCK

TABLE ENTRIES	TAB1 MEAN ARGUMENT	STANDARD DEVIATION	SUM OF ARGUMENTS	
269	52.063	65.726	14005.000	NON-WEIGHTED

UPPER LIMIT	OBSERVED FREQUENCY	PER CENT OF TOTAL	CUMULATIVE PERCENTAGE	CUMULATIVE REMAINDER	MULTIPLE OF MEAN	DEVIATION FROM MEAN
0	108	40.15	40.15	59.85	0.000	-0.792
15	20	7.43	47.58	52.42	0.288	-0.564
30	14	5.20	52.79	47.21	0.576	-0.336
45	16	5.95	58.74	41.26	0.864	-0.107
60	21	7.81	66.54	33.46	1.152	0.121
75	8	2.97	69.52	30.48	1.441	0.349
90	16	5.95	75.46	24.54	1.729	0.577
105	8	2.97	78.44	21.56	2.017	0.805
120	14	5.20	83.64	16.36	2.305	1.034
135	12	4.46	88.10	11.90	2.593	1.262
150	6	2.23	90.33	9.67	2.881	1.490
165	7	2.60	92.94	7.06	3.169	1.718
180	3	1.12	94.05	5.95	3.457	1.947
195	5	1.86	95.91	4.09	3.745	2.175

AVERAGE VALUE OF THE 11 OVERFLOW ITEMS IS   236.545

TABLE ENTRIES	TAB2 MEAN ARGUMENT	STANDARD DEVIATION	SUM OF ARGUMENTS	
112	19.188	31.449	2149.000	NON-WEIGHTED

UPPER LIMIT	OBSERVED FREQUENCY	PER CENT OF TOTAL	CUMULATIVE PERCENTAGE	CUMULATIVE REMAINDER	MULTIPLE OF MEAN	DEVIATION FROM MEAN
0	74	66.07	66.07	33.93	0.000	-0.610
15	2	1.79	67.86	32.14	0.782	-0.133
30	2	1.79	69.64	30.36	1.564	0.344
45	13	11.61	81.25	18.75	2.345	0.821
60	7	6.25	87.50	12.50	3.127	1.298
75	6	5.36	92.86	7.14	3.909	1.775
90	3	2.68	95.54	4.46	4.691	2.252
105	2	1.79	97.32	2.68	5.472	2.729
120	1	0.89	98.21	1.79	6.254	3.206
135	2	1.79	100.00	0.00	7.036	3.683

From the output in Fig. 5.14 we see that although the average waiting time for check-cashing customers is 19 seconds, about 12% of such customers waited longer than a minute. Similarly, for regular customers the average wait is 52 seconds, while fully 33% waited longer than a minute, and 16% waited longer than 2 minutes. Thus we obtain a very different assessment of service level from this additional information.

PROBLEM IV.2   Problem II.2 of Section 5.2 modeled an assembly line with conveyor buffer space between work stations. A main concern was the length of conveyor required. The model output provided information on average and maximum number of units waiting between work stations. Since the number of waiting units has a large variance, this information is likely to lead to a poor decision. The use of a TABULATE block will be of great value in deciding on buffer space requirements.

Figure 5.15 shows the GPSS code for Problem II.2 with tables added to tabulate the length of the queues between the work stations. In Model Segment 2, we sample the

FIGURE 5.15   PROBLEM IV.2 CODE

```
LINE   BLOCK   BLOCK   BLOCK NAME                  COMMENTS
NO.    NO.     LOC.
 1             *PROGRESSIVE ASSEMBLY LINE: PROBLEM II.2 WITH TABLES
 2                     SIMULATE
 3             *MODEL SEGMENT 1 - ASSEMBLY LINE LOGIC
 4                     STORAGE       S$1-S$3,3    INTER WORK STN QUEUE
 5             *                                  CAPACITY
 6             1        TABLE        MP$3,1500,500,20
 7             TAB1     TABLE        Q$1,1,1,10   TABLE DEFN FOR QUEUE 1
 8             TAB2     TABLE        Q$2,1,1,10   "    "    "    "   2
 9             TAB3     TABLE        Q$3,1,1,10   "    "    "    "   3
10     1                GENERATE     410,,,,,5,F  ARRIVING SUBASSEMBLIES
11             *                                  (seconds)
12     2                ASSIGN       1,3          LOOP PARAMETER
13     3                ASSIGN       2,1          WORK STN NO.
14     4                MARK         3            RECORD ARRIVAL TIME
15     5       BAK      QUEUE        P$2          QUEUE BEFORE BUFFER SPACES
16     6                ENTER        P$2          CAPACITY ON QUEUE
17     7                SEIZE        P$2          SEIZE WORK STN
18     8                LEAVE        P$2
19     9                DEPART       P$2          LEAVE BUFFER SPACE
20     10               ADVANCE      400,300      ASSEMBLE
21     11               RELEASE      P$2          FREE WORK STATION
22     12               ASSIGN       2+,1         INCREMENT WORK STN NO.
23     13               LOOP         1,BAK        INDEX TO NEXT WORK STN
24     14               TABULATE     1            TABULATE TOTAL ASSB. TIME
25     15               TERMINATE    1
26             *MODEL SEGMENT 2 - TABULATE NO. IN QUEUES
27     16               GENERATE     500          TR TO SAMPLE QUEUE STATUS
28     17               TABULATE     TAB1         TABULATE NO. IN QUEUE 1
29     18               TABULATE     TAB2         "              "   2
30     19               TABULATE     TAB3         "              "   3
31     20               TERMINATE
32                      START        1000         PRODUCE 1000 PARTS
```

state of the system every 500 seconds and record the number of units in the queue in front of each work station. In the table definition statements, we specify the arguments to be tabulated as the SNAs Q$1, Q$2, and Q$3. In addition, we use the MARK block to note the time a unit begins processing, and compute the total elapsed time for a unit to traverse the assembly line as MP$3, which is also tabulated.

In Fig. 5.16 the table output shows that although the average number of units in front of work stations is under the designated storage capacity, the number of units present at a particular time may be as great as 10. Again, the question to be answered is what fraction of the time should the conveyor space suffice? For work station 1, a

FIGURE 5.16   PROBLEM IV.2 OUTPUT

RELATIVE CLOCK 415811   ABSOLUTE CLOCK 415811

QUEUE	MAXIMUM CONTENTS	AVERAGE CONTENTS	TOTAL ENTRIES	ZERO ENTRIES	PERCENT ZEROS	AVERAGE TIME/TRANS	$AVERAGE TIME/TRANS	TABLE NUMBER	CURRENT CONTENTS
1	5	1.408	1014	139	13.708	577.358	669.075		2
2	10	2.628	1011	77	7.616	1080.935	1170.048		0
3	13	2.572	1010	95	9.406	1059.018	1168.970		10

FACILITY	AVERAGE UTILIZATION	NUMBER ENTRIES	AVERAGE TIME/TRANS	SEIZING TRANS. NO.	PREEMPTING TRANS. NO.
1	0.960	1012	394.340	1	
2	0.964	1011	396.581	2	
3	0.959	1000	398.895		

STORAGE	CAPACITY	AVERAGE CONTENTS	TOTAL ENTRIES	AVERAGE TIME/TRANS	AVERAGE UTILIZ.	AVAIL. UTILIZ.	UNAVAIL. UTILIZ.	CURRENT STATUS	FRACTION AVAIL.	CURRENT CONTENTS	MAXIMUM CONTENTS
1	3	1.367	1014	560.405	0.456			A	1.000	2	3
2	3	1.978	1011	813.524	0.659			A	1.000	0	3
3	3	1.813	1003	751.543	0.604			A	1.000	3	3

TABLE	1			
ENTRIES	MEAN ARGUMENT	STANDARD DEVIATION	SUM OF ARGUMENTS	
1000	3908.480	971.212	3908480.000	NON-WEIGHTED

UPPER LIMIT	OBSERVED FREQUENCY	PER CENT OF TOTAL	CUMULATIVE PERCENTAGE	CUMULATIVE REMAINDER	MULTIPLE OF MEAN	DEVIATION FROM MEAN
1500	2	0.20	0.20	99.80	0.384	-2.480
2000	8	0.80	1.00	99.00	0.512	-1.965
2500	55	5.50	6.50	93.50	0.640	-1.450
3000	112	11.20	17.70	82.30	0.768	-0.935
3500	154	15.40	33.10	66.90	0.895	-0.421
4000	242	24.20	57.30	42.70	1.023	0.094
4500	202	20.20	77.50	22.50	1.151	0.609
5000	115	11.50	89.00	11.00	1.279	1.124
5500	33	3.30	92.30	7.70	1.407	1.639
6000	31	3.10	95.40	4.60	1.535	2.154
6500	36	3.60	99.00	1.00	1.663	2.668
7000	10	1.00	100.00	0.00	1.791	3.183

REMAINING FREQUENCIES ARE ALL ZERO

TABLE	TAB1					
ENTRIES	MEAN ARGUMENT		STANDARD DEVIATION		SUM OF ARGUMENTS	
831	1.394		1.141		1158.000	NON-WEIGHTED

UPPER LIMIT	OBSERVED FREQUENCY	PER CENT OF TOTAL	CUMULATIVE PERCENTAGE	CUMULATIVE REMAINDER	MULTIPLE OF MEAN	DEVIATION FROM MEAN
1	465	55.96	55.96	44.04	0.718	-0.345
2	215	25.87	81.83	18.17	1.435	0.532
3	119	14.32	96.15	3.85	2.153	1.408
4	31	3.73	99.88	0.12	2.870	2.285
5	1	0.12	100.00	0.00	3.588	3.161

REMAINING FREQUENCIES ARE ALL ZERO

TABLE	TAB2					
ENTRIES	MEAN ARGUMENT		STANDARD DEVIATION		SUM OF ARGUMENTS	
831	2.625		2.021		2181.000	NON-WEIGHTED

UPPER LIMIT	OBSERVED FREQUENCY	PER CENT OF TOTAL	CUMULATIVE PERCENTAGE	CUMULATIVE REMAINDER	MULTIPLE OF MEAN	DEVIATION FROM MEAN
1	280	33.69	33.69	66.31	0.381	-0.804
2	161	19.37	53.07	46.93	0.762	-0.309
3	131	15.76	68.83	31.17	1.143	0.186
4	100	12.03	80.87	19.13	1.524	0.681
5	78	9.39	90.25	9.75	1.905	1.175
6	47	5.66	95.91	4.09	2.286	1.670
7	20	2.41	98.32	1.68	2.667	2.165
8	12	1.44	99.76	0.24	3.048	2.659
9	2	0.24	100.00	0.00	3.429	3.154

TABLE	TAB3					
ENTRIES	MEAN ARGUMENT		STANDARD DEVIATION		SUM OF ARGUMENTS	
831	2.594		2.495		2156.000	NON-WEIGHTED

UPPER LIMIT	OBSERVED FREQUENCY	PER CENT OF TOTAL	CUMULATIVE PERCENTAGE	CUMULATIVE REMAINDER	MULTIPLE OF MEAN	DEVIATION FROM MEAN
1	320	38.51	38.51	61.49	0.385	-0.639
2	168	20.22	58.72	41.28	0.771	-0.238
3	132	15.88	74.61	25.39	1.156	0.163
4	68	8.18	82.79	17.21	1.542	0.563
5	54	6.50	89.29	10.71	1.927	0.964
6	24	2.89	92.18	7.82	2.313	1.365
7	6	0.72	92.90	7.10	2.698	1.766
8	20	2.41	95.31	4.69	3.083	2.167
9	16	1.93	97.23	2.77	3.469	2.567

AVERAGE VALUE OF THE 23 OVERFLOW ITEMS IS   10.565

---

storage capacity of 3 will be sufficient 96% of the time, for work station 2, 68% of the time, and for work station 3, 74% of the time. This suggests that we should evaluate larger capacities using the model.

Finally, we observe from Table 1 in Fig. 5.16 that the average time to traverse the assembly line is 3908 seconds, but a small number take as long as 7000 seconds. Since the total elapsed time is the sum of three independent random variables, we would expect the frequency distribution to approximate the normal probability distribution, according to the central limit theorem. The frequencies portrayed in the table do appear to be tending in this direction.

5.7   Computational Entities

GPSS has two computational entities: variables and functions. Variables may be either arithmetic or Boolean, and arithmetic variables are further classified as integer or floating-point, based on the approach taken to value truncation. GPSS recognizes five function types, but we shall describe only the two most common: continuous numerical valued and discrete numerical valued.

Arithmetic Variables–Integer   Arithmetic variables permit the algebraic combination of values of SNAs, including other variables. Variables themselves are SNAs. Their definitions resemble FORTRAN statements.

Five arithmetic operators are allowed:

+   algebraic addition

-     algebraic subtraction

*   algebraic multiplication

/   algebraic division, quotient retained

@   modulo division, remainder retained.

The precedence of operation for ungrouped terms is division, including modulo division, and multiplication first, followed by addition and subtraction. Terms may be grouped using parentheses to alter the operation precedence.

Each variable must be defined in the following way. The Block Location field contains the name or number of the VARIABLE, the Block Name field contains "VARIABLE," and the Operand field holds the algebraic expression for the variables. For, example:

BLOCK LOCATION	BLOCK NAME	OPERANDS
VAR1	VARIABLE	P$1*Q$LINE/3
2	VARIABLE	P$1*(V$VAR1+4)
VAR2	VARIABLE	(C1 – 1)@480+1
3	VARIABLE	10*(11/3)

The third variable demonstrates a useful application of the modulo division operator. VAR2 will provide the number of minutes into an 8-hour day. C1 is the SNA, relative clock, and 480 is the number of minutes in an 8-hour day.

When an integer variable is evaluated, all SNAs in the variable expression are truncated before computation. Also, interim quotients as well as the final value are truncated. This can be seen in the last variable definition where 11/3 is first evaluated as 3, and then multiplied by 10 to yield a value of 30 for the variable. If one wants to retain decimal portions of variables, floating-point variables must be used.

Arithmetic Variables–Floating-Point   Floating-point variables are defined similarly to integer variables, the only differences are that the Block Name field contains "FVARIABLE," and the modulo division operator, @, may not be used.

Floating-point variables are evaluated differently from integer variables. The SNAs in the variable expression are not truncated before computation, and interim quotients are also not truncated. The final value, however, is truncated, unless it is to be placed in a floating-point SNA such as a SAVEVALUE or MSAVEVALUE.

Floating-point variables may be defined as:

BLOCK LOCATION	BLOCK NAME	OPERANDS
FVAR1	FVARIABLE	V$VAR*(P$1+3)/6
2	FVARIABLE	10*(11/3)

The second example illustrates the difference in the way floating-point variables are evaluated. First, 11/3 is computed as 3.67, and then the final value is computed as 36.7, and truncated to 36.

Boolean Variables   Boolean variables allow the combination of SNAs, and logical attributes, including other Boolean variables. Boolean variables are themselves SNAs. In this way, the model logic may be affected by the status of several entities. Boolean variables may have only two values: 1 if true, and 0 if false. They are defined in the same way as arithmetic variables, except that the Block Name field contains "BVARIABLE".

The relational operators used in defining Boolean expressions are the same as those already defined for the TEST and SELECT blocks. They include: G, GE, L, and LE. Examples of logical attributes that may be used include, SF, and SE, which were previously defined to describe the full or empty status of a storage. In addition, Boolean operators for logical "and," denoted by a "*," and logical "or," denoted by a "+," may be used to form more complicated variable expressions.

The following examples illustrate how Boolean variables can be used.

BLOCK LOCATION	BLOCK NAME	OPERANDS
VAR1	BVARIABLE	BV$V4*(Q$LINE'L'5+Q$LINE2'L'5)
2	BVARIABLE	SNF1+SNF2

In order for Boolean variable VAR1 to be true, Boolean variable V4 must be true, and either queue LINE or queue LINE2 must have fewer than 5 transactions in it. Otherwise it will be evaluated as false, or 0. If Boolean variable 2 is true, either storage 1 or storage 2 is not full, otherwise it is false.

Functions–Continuous Numerical Valued   Functions are used to describe variable interrelationships. For example, the checkout time in a supermarket may depend on the number of items purchased. The number of items is the independent variable or argument, and the checkout time is computed as the value of the function. The argument of the function may be any SNA, and the value of the function is itself an SNA.

One very common application of functions is the generation of random variates from a particular probability distribution. The argument is a random number, RN, such that $0 \le RN \le 1$, which represents a probability, and the function value is a particular value of the random variable. Such function values may be used for service times or interarrival times.

Functions are described to GPSS by providing pairs of points, each pair containing one point for the argument, and one for the associated function value. For values of the function between specified points, GPSS performs linear interpolation. If a sufficient number of points is provided, the error introduced by this method is tolerable.

Continuous numerical valued functions are defined in a function definition statement as follows. The Block Location field contains the function name or number; the Block Name field contains "FUNCTION"; and the Operand field holds the argument, function type, and number of points used to define the function. Immediately following the definition are sufficient function follower statements to contain the pairs of argument points, X, and function value points, Y. The pairs of points are listed in the order X,Y, with a "," to separate X from Y, and a "/" to delimit pairs of points. Values may be placed in columns 1 through 71, and must be listed in ascending order of the X.

The following is an example of a continuous numerical valued function.

BLOCK LOCATION	BLOCK NAME	OPERANDS
FUN1	FUNCTION	RN1,C5
0.,2./.4,3.5/.7,4.6/.8,8./1.,10.5		

The function named FUN1 has an argument RN1, which is a random number between 0 and 1, and is a continuous numerical valued function with five pairs of points defining it, as indicated by C5. Notice that both the argument and function values may be noninteger. This function defines values of random variables ranging from 2 to 10.5 with the probability specified by the function values.

In evaluating continuous numerical valued functions GPSS observes the following conventions, which are illustrated in Fig. 5.17. For all argument values equal to or less than X_1, the function has the value Y_1, and similarly, for all argument values equal to or greater than X_n, the function has the value Y_n. For argument values between two specified points, linear interpolation is performed and truncation of the result occurs such that if $X_i \le$ argument value $< X_{i+1}$, the function value $= y_i$, where y_i are interpolated integer values of the function. Thus in the example above the possible function values are 2 through 10. Function values are not truncated when the precision of floating point is required, as in the case of the function modifiers of GENERATE and ASSIGN blocks.

Functions–Discrete Numerical Valued   This type of function will produce only integer values. It is defined in the same manner as a continuous numerical valued function, but is evaluated differently. The function definition statement identifies this type of function by "Dn" in the Operand field, where n is the number of pairs of points used in the function follower statements.

FIGURE 5.17   EVALUATION OF CONTINUOUS NUMERICAL VALUED FUNCTIONS

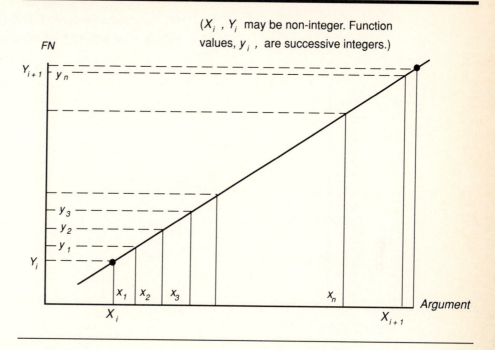

$(X_i$, Y_i may be non-integer. Function values, y_i , are successive integers.)

An example of a discrete numerical valued function is:

BLOCK LOCATION	BLOCK NAME	OPERANDS
FUN2	FUNCTION	RN2,D4
0.,4/.3,8/.8,12/1.,16		

The function FUN2 has an argument RN2, and is defined by 4 pairs of points. It will yield as values of a random variable the integers in the range from 4 to 16.

The evaluation of a discrete numerical valued function is accomplished in the following way, as illustrated in Fig. 5.18. For all argument values equal to or less than X_1, the function has the value Y_1, and similarly, for all argument values equal to or greater than X_n, the function has the value Y_n. For argument values between two specified points, no linear interpolation is performed, and the function is evaluated such that if $X_{i-1} <$ argument value $\leq X_i$, function value $= Y_i$, where Y_i are integer values supplied in defining the function. Thus, in the example above, the possible function values are 4, 8, 12, and 16.

5.8   Reference Entities

Reference entities permit retention of SNA values for subsequent use, and access to the same model attribute by different transactions. They are of two types: SAVEVALUES

FIGURE 5.18   EVALUATION OF DISCRETE NUMERICAL VALUED FUNCTIONS

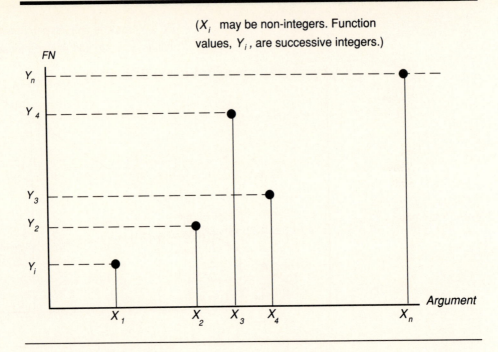

(X_i may be non-integers. Function values, Y_i, are successive integers.)

and MSAVEVALUES. The former can retain only a single value, while the latter may contain a large matrix of values.

SAVEVALUES   Initially, GPSS sets all SAVEVALUES to the value of 0, but the SAVEVALUE block may be used to alter the initial value. Also, the INITIAL statement discussed later may be used to select a nonzero starting value.

The flow chart symbol for the SAVEVALUE block is:

The operands of the SAVEVALUE block are:

OPERAND	DESCRIPTION	DEFAULT
A*	Savevalue name or number, followed by "+" for increment or "−" for decrement	None
B**	SNA value used as increment, decrement, or replacement	
C	Savevalue type [H or blank]	***

* SNA types 1, 2, 4, 5, or 6 may be used.
** SNA types 1, 4, 5, or 6 may be used.
*** Machine dependent.

SAVEVALUE blocks operate in the same way as ASSIGN blocks in that they may increment, decrement, or replace the current value of the savevalue. There are several types of savevalue including full and halfword. The primary motivation for using halfword savevalue is to conserve memory. The contents of halfword savevalues are denoted XH$NAME, and fullword savevalues as X$NAME. The contents are SNAs.

The following are examples of SAVEVALUE blocks.

```
SAVEVALUE      SAVE+,Q$LINE,H
SAVEVALUE      10,3,F
```

The first example increments the halfword savevalue named SAVE by the contents of the queue LINE, Q$LINE. The second block replaces the contents of fullword savevalue 10 with the value 3.

MSAVEVALUES   By using a matrix savevalue, an array of values may be retained and altered by the GPSS program, unlike the SAVEVALUE block which deals with a single value.

The flow chart symbol for the MSAVEVALUE block is:

The operands of the MSAVEVALUE block are:

OPERAND	DESCRIPTION	DEFAULT
A*	Matrix name or number, followed by "+" for increment or "−" for decrement	None
B**	Row of the matrix to be altered	None
C	Column of the matrix to be altered	None
D	SNA value used as increment, decrement, or replacement	None
E	Msavevalue type [H or blank]	***

* SNA types 1, 2, 4, 5, or 6 may be used.
** SNA types 1, 4, 5, or 6 may be used for operands B–D.
*** Machine dependent.

Before referencing a matrix savevalue in an MSAVEVALUE block, the size of the matrix to be used must be specified in a matrix definition statement. The Block Location field of the statement contains the name or number of the matrix, the Block Name field contains "MATRIX," and the Operand field has the matrix type, number of rows, and number of columns in the matrix. Several types of matrices may be defined, including full and halfword.

Some example matrix definition statements are:

BLOCK LOCATION	BLOCK NAME	OPERANDS
MAT1	MATRIX	MX,3,10
2	MATRIX	MH,4,7

The first statement defines a fullword matrix named MAT1 which has 3 rows and 10 columns. The second statement defines a halfword matrix number 2 which has 4 rows and 7 columns.

All matrices are initialized with zeroes by GPSS, but can be given other starting values using the INITIAL statement. As a model run progresses, the matrix values may be altered using the MSAVEVALUE block.

The MSAVEVALUE block operates exactly the same as the SAVEVALUE block once the row and column to be altered have been specified. Again, to conserve memory one would choose a halfword msavevalue. The contents of msavevalues are denoted as MH$NAME(1,3) for a halfword msavevalue, and MX$NAME(P$1,P$3) for a fullword msavevalue, where the SNAs enclosed in parentheses designate the row and column of the msavevalue. The contents of msavevalues are SNAs.

Some properly specified MSAVEVALUE blocks are:

MSAVEVALUE   MAT1+,1,3,40,MX

MSAVEVALUE   MAT2,P$1,P$2,XH$SAVE,MH

The first example increments the 1,3 element (row 1, column 3) of a fullword msavevalue named MAT1 by 40. In the second block, a halfword msavevalue named MAT2 has the element defined by P$1 and P$2 replaced with the current value of a halfword savevalue named SAVE.

INITIAL   This statement is used to insert starting values in savevalues and msavevalues. The Block Name field of the statement contains "INITIAL," and the Operand field contains the savevalue or msavevalue name and the starting value to be inserted. In the case of an msavevalue, a complete designation must include the element or elements to be initialized. If more than one value is initialized in a statement, "/" should be used to delimit the values. The INITIAL statement is best illustrated by example.

The following examples of INITIAL statements indicate how individual savevalues or msavevalues as well as ranges of them may be initialized.

BLOCK LOCATION	BLOCK NAME	OPERANDS
	INITIAL	X$1,30/XH$3-XH$10,5/MX$20(1,3),89
	INITIAL	MH$MAT1(1-2,1-4),6/MH$MAT1(3-5,5),8

The first statement sets fullword savevalue 1 to 30, halfword savevalues 3 through 10 to 5, and element 1,3 of fullword msavevalue 20 to 89. Notice that both savevalues

and msavevalues may be included on the same INITIAL statement. The second statement sets elements 1,2 through 2,4 (8 elements in total) of a halfword msavevalue
named MAT1 to 6, and elements 3,5 through 5,5 (3 elements in total) of the same
msavevalue to 8.

5.9   Illustrative Problem Set V

The goal of the problems in this set is to illustrate uses of functions, variables,
savevalues, and matrix savevalues. These entities permit us to model an inventory system, and a fairly complex job shop.

PROBLEM V.1   The system modeled in this problem manages an inventory on a daily basis. The model
will assist in determining values for order quantity and re-order level.

The daily demand is sampled from an empirical distribution. Each day the amount
demanded is compared to the stock on hand. If it exceeds the stock, the balance
demanded is a lost sale and a penalty cost of $1.00 per unit not supplied is incurred.
Next, the quantity on hand is compared to the re-order level. If it is below this level, an
order for a specified number of units is placed. The order is placed at a fixed cost of
$5.00, and it arrives at the end of five days. There is a carrying charge of $0.40 per unit
per day for all inventory. The total cost of the inventory system is the sum of the order,
penalty, and carrying charges.

The GPSS flow chart and code are shown in Figs. 5.19 and 5.20. Savevalues are
used to define stock on hand, stock on hand plus on order, re-order level, order quantity,
and cumulative inventory. Variables are used to compute the penalty cost and total cost.
To facilitate displaying the total cost of the inventory policy, a savevalue is equated to
the total cost variable at the end of the run. The major outputs of interest are the total
cost and a tabulation of inventory. Initially, the re-order level is set at six units, and the
order quantity at 25. The model can be used to seek to optimize the total cost by altering
these.

The GPSS output of Fig. 5.21 indicates a total cost of $1508 for nine months in
savevalue TCOST, and tabulates the stock on hand in Table TAB1. According to this
table, the average inventory level is 13 units, the maximum level is 30 units and the
inventory was at the zero level, after accounting for goods received, only 5% of the
time. Possible additional model experiments would include increasing the order quantity
and/or increasing the re-order level. Both of these changes would have the affect of
reducing the penalty cost for stockouts, while increasing the inventory carrying charge.

PROBLEM V.2   A job shop is a collection of processing centers through which jobs are routed in different sequences depending on the characteristics of the particular job. It is a common
method of grouping resources for producing small lots with widely varying processing
requirements.

FIGURE 5.19   PROBLEM V.1 FLOW CHART

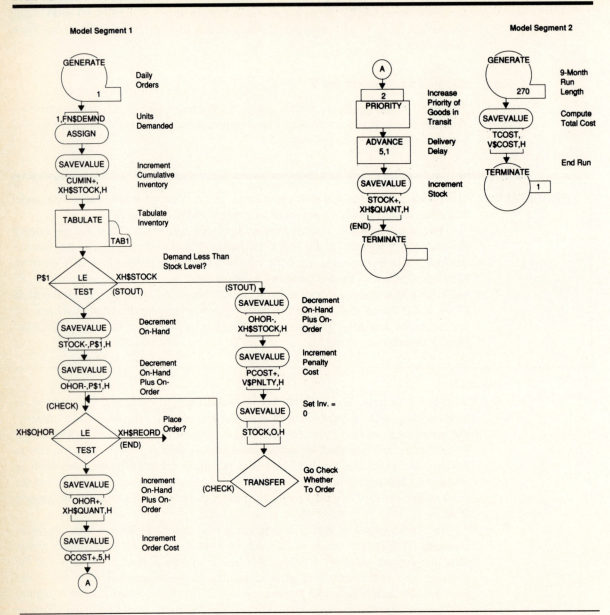

FIGURE 5.20   PROBLEM V.1 CODE

LINE NO.	BLOCK NO.	BLOCK LOC.	BLOCK NAME		COMMENTS
1			*INVENTORY PROBLEM		
2			SIMULATE		
3			*MODEL SEGMENT 1 - MODEL LOGIC		
4			*INITIALIZE ITEMS: ONHAND (XH$STOCK), ORDER QUANTITY		
5			*(XH$QUANT), REORDER POINT (XH$REORD), ITEMS ONHAND-		
6			*PLUS-ONORDER (XH$OHOR), CUMULATIVE INVENTORY (XH$CUMIN)		
7			INITIAL	XH$STOCK,20/XH$QUANT,25/XH$REORD,6	
8			INITIAL	XH$OHOR,20/XH$CUMIN,0	
9		TAB1	TABLE	XH$STOCK,0,5,12 TABLE FOR STK ON HAND	
10		DEMND	FUNCTION	RN1,D6	DEMAND FUNCTION
11			.14,0/.41,1/.68,2/.86,3/.95,4/1.,5		
12		PNLTY	VARIABLE	(P$1-XH$STOCK)*1 PENALTY COST	
13		TCOST	FVARIABLE	XH$OCOST+XH$PCOST+XH$CUMIN*40/100	
14		*			TOTAL COST
15	1		GENERATE	1	DAILY ORDERS
16	2		ASSIGN	1,FN$DEMND	DAILY DEMAND
17	3		SAVEVALUE	CUMIN+,XH$STOCK,H	INCREMENT CUM
18		*			INVENTORY
19	4		TABULATE	TAB1	TABULATE STK ON HAND
20	5		TEST LE	P$1,XH$STOCK,STOUT DEMAND LESS	
21		*			THAN ONHAND?
22	6		SAVEVALUE	STOCK-,P$1,H	DECREMENT ONHAND
23	7		SAVEVALUE	OHOR-,P$1,H	DECREMENT ONHAND-PLUS-
24		*			ONORDER
25	8	CHECK	TEST LE	XH$OHOR,XH$REORD,END	PLACE ORDER?
26	9		SAVEVALUE	OHOR+,XH$QUANT,H	INCREMENT BY ORDER
27		*			QUANTITY
28	10		SAVEVALUE	OCOST+,5,H	ORDER COST
29	11		PRIORITY	2	ARRIVING GOODS HAVE
30		*			PRIORITY
31	12		ADVANCE	5,1	DELIVERY TIME
32	13		SAVEVALUE	STOCK+,XH$QUANT,H	ORDER ARRIVES
33	14	END	TERMINATE		
34	15	STOUT	SAVEVALUE	OHOR-,XH$STOCK,H	DECREMENT ONHAND-
35		*			PLUS-ONORDER
36	16		SAVEVALUE	PCOST+,V$PNLTY,H	STOCKOUT PENALTY
37		*			COST
38	17		SAVEVALUE	STOCK,0,H	SET ONHAND=0
39	18		TRANSFER	,CHECK	GO TO CHECK IF REORDER
40		*			NEEDED
41			*MODEL SEGMENT 2 - RUN LENGTH CONTROL		
42	19		GENERATE	270	9 MONTH RUN LENGTH
43	20		SAVEVALUE	TCOST,V$TCOST,H	TOTAL INV COST
44	21		TERMINATE	1	
45			START	1	

In this problem, the shop consists of four machines through which five types of jobs are routed. All jobs go to all machines, but with different routings. The data for job routings and processing times are contained in a halfword matrix savevalue named JOB. Each row of the matrix provides information for a given job type; the first four columns contain the machine numbers in the order to be visited, and the last four columns, the processing times at each of these machines. By extensive use of transaction parameters and the LOOP block, the logic for the four processing centers can be described very concisely. The flow chart and GPSS code are shown in Figs. 5.22 and 5.23.

A measure of performance for job shops is the tardiness of completed jobs: that is, the number of hours beyond a specified due time that the job is completed. An early completion would yield a negative value of job tardiness. An important variable which has been found to influence this measure is the order in which jobs are selected from the queue in front of a machine for processing. In this model a simple first-come-first-served (FCFS) rule is used, but in Problem VI.2 we will explore a more complicated rule: shortest processing time (SPT). In the model we calculate job tardiness using a variable called TARDY, and tabulate the tardiness in Table TAB1. To simplify matters, due times are calculated as 10% longer than the sum of a job's total processing time. The GPSS output is shown in Fig. 5.24. From Table TAB1 we observe that the mean tardiness is 96.5 minutes, and that 98% of the jobs are completed no later than one day (500 minutes) beyond the due time. We will compare these results with those of Problem VI.2 in the following section.

FIGURE 5.21   PROBLEM V.1 OUTPUT

RELATIVE CLOCK 270   ABSOLUTE CLOCK 270

NON-ZERO HALFWORD SAVEVALUES

SAVEX	VALUE	SAVEX	VALUE	SAVEX	VALUE	SAVEX	VALUE
CUMIN	3429	OCOST	95	OHOR	16	PCOST	42
QUANT	25	REORD	6	STOCK	16	TCOST	1508

TABLE	TAB1			
ENTRIES	MEAN ARGUMENT	STANDARD DEVIATION	SUM OF ARGUMENTS	
269	12.747	7.850	3429.000	NON-WEIGHTED

UPPER LIMIT	OBSERVED FREQUENCY	PER CENT OF TOTAL	CUMULATIVE PERCENTAGE	CUMULATIVE REMAINDER	MULTIPLE OF MEAN	DEVIATION FROM MEAN
0	14	5.20	5.20	94.80	0.000	-1.624
5	44	16.36	21.56	78.44	0.392	-0.987
10	58	21.56	43.12	56.88	0.784	-0.350
15	47	17.47	60.59	39.41	1.177	0.287
20	47	17.47	78.07	21.93	1.569	0.924
25	55	20.45	98.51	1.49	1.961	1.561
30	4	1.49	100.00	0.00	2.353	2.198

FIGURE 5.22   PROBLEM V.2 FLOW CHART

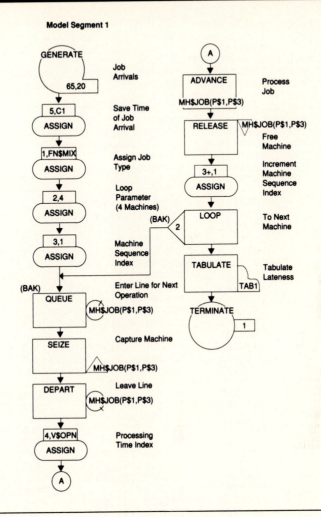

Model Segment 1

GENERATE — 65,20 — Job Arrivals

ASSIGN — 5,C1 — Save Time of Job Arrival

ASSIGN — 1,FN$MIX — Assign Job Type

ASSIGN — 2,4 — Loop Parameter (4 Machines)

ASSIGN — 3,1 — Machine Sequence Index

(BAK)

QUEUE — MH$JOB(P$1,P$3) — Enter Line for Next Operation

SEIZE — MH$JOB(P$1,P$3) — Capture Machine

DEPART — MH$JOB(P$1,P$3) — Leave Line

ASSIGN — 4,V$OPN — Processing Time Index

A

A

ADVANCE — MH$JOB(P$1,P$3) — Process Job

RELEASE — MH$JOB(P$1,P$3) — Free Machine

ASSIGN — 3+,1 — Increment Machine Sequence Index

LOOP — (BAK) 2 — To Next Machine

TABULATE — TAB1 — Tabulate Lateness

TERMINATE — 1

FIGURE 5.23   PROBLEM V.2 CODE

```
LINE BLOCK BLOCK  BLOCK NAME                          COMMENTS
NO.  NO.   LOC.
1                  SIMULATE
2          *JOB SHOP MODEL- FCFS RULE
3           TAB1   TABLE       V$TARDY,50,50,20        TABULATE JOB LATENESS
4           MIX    FUNCTION    RN1,D5                  JOB TYPE MIX
5          .1,1/.5,2/.7,3/.85,4/1,5
6          *VARIABLES: DDATE=DUE DATE FOR JOB; OPN=COL NO. FOR JOB PROC.
7          *TIME; TARDY=JOB LATENESS
8           TVAR1  VARIABLE    MH$JOB(P$1,5)+MH$JOB(P$1,6)+MH$JOB(P$1,7)
9           DDATE  FVARIABLE   1.1*(V$TVAR1+MH$JOB(P$1,8)+P$5)
10          OPN    VARIABLE    P$3+4
11          TARDY  VARIABLE    C1-V$DDATE
12          JOB    MATRIX      MH,5,8                  MACH SEQUENCE AND
13          *                                          PROC. TIMES
14                 INITIAL     MH$JOB(1,1),2/MH$JOB(1,2),4/MH$JOB(1,3),1
15                 INITIAL     MH$JOB(1,4),3/MH$JOB(1,5),45/MH$JOB(1,6),60
16                 INITIAL     MH$JOB(1,7),75/MH$JOB(1,8),60
17                 INITIAL     MH$JOB(2,1),1/MH$JOB(2,2),2/MH$JOB(2,3),4
18                 INITIAL     MH$JOB(2,4),3/MH$JOB(2,5),70/MH$JOB(2,6),70
19                 INITIAL     MH$JOB(2,7),50/MH$JOB(2,8),50A
20                 INITIAL     MH$JOB(3,1),3/MH$JOB(3,2),4/MH$JOB(3,3),2
21                 INITIAL     MH$JOB(3,4),1/MH$JOB(3,5),50/MH$JOB(3,6),60
22                 INITIAL     MH$JOB(3,7),60/MH$JOB(3,8),70
23                 INITIAL     MH$JOB(4,1),4/MH$JOB(4,2),2/MH$JOB(4,3),3
24                 INITIAL     MH$JOB(4,4),1/MH$JOB(4,5),80/MH$JOB(4,6),40
25                 INITIAL     MH$JOB(4,7),80/MH$JOB(4,8),40
26                 INITIAL     MH$JOB(5,1),3/MH$JOB(5,2),4/MH$JOB(5,3),1
27                 INITIAL     MH$JOB(5,4),2/MH$JOB(5,5),70/MH$JOB(5,6),50
28                 INITIAL     MH$JOB(5,7),40/MH$JOB(5,8),80
29         *MODEL SEGMENT 1 - MODEL LOGIC
30    1            GENERATE    60,10                   GENERATE JOBS (min.)
31    2            ASSIGN      5,C1                    SAVE TIME JOB ARRIVED
32    3            ASSIGN      1,FN$MIX                 ASSIGN JOB TYPE
33    4            ASSIGN      2,4                     LOOP PARAMETER
34    5            ASSIGN      3,1                     NEXT MACH. IN SEQUENCE
35    6     BAK    QUEUE       MH$JOB(P$1,P$3)         QUEUE FOR NEXT OPN.
36    7            SEIZE       MH$JOB(P$1,P$3)         SEIZE MACH. NEXT OPN.
37    8            DEPART      MH$JOB(P$1,P$3)         LEAVE MACH QUEUE
38    9            ASSIGN      4,V$OPN                 PROCESSING TIME INDEX
39   10            ADVANCE     MH$JOB(P$1,P$4)         PROCESS JOB
40   11            RELEASE     MH$JOB(P$1,P$3)         FREE MACHINE
41   12            ASSIGN      3+,1                    INCREMENT MACH NO
42   13            LOOP        2,BAK                   TO NEXT MACHINE
43   14            TABULATE    TAB1                    TABULATE LATENESS
44   15            TERMINATE   1
45                 START       200
```

FIGURE 5.24   PROBLEM V.2 OUTPUT

REMAINING FREQUENCIES ARE ALL ZERO

RELATIVE CLOCK 13253   ABSOLUTE CLOCK 13253

QUEUE	MAXIMUM CONTENTS	AVERAGE CONTENTS	TOTAL ENTRIES	ZERO ENTRIES	PERCENT ZEROS	AVERAGE TIME/TRANS	$AVERAGE TIME/TRANS	TABLE NUMBER	CURRENT CONTENTS
1	10	3.638	211	7	3.318	228.479	236.319		5
2	8	3.508	210	12	5.714	221.419	234.838		2
3	11	3.196	218	18	8.257	194.294	211.780		10
4	6	1.461	214	33	15.421	90.505	107.006		2

FACILITY	AVERAGE UTILIZATION	NUMBER ENTRIES	AVERAGE TIME/TRANS	SEIZING TRANS. NO.	PREEMPTING TRANS. NO.
1	0.971	206	62.451		
2	0.973	208	62.019	18	
3	0.906	208	57.740	8	
4	0.916	212	57.288	10	

TABLE	TAB1			
ENTRIES	MEAN ARGUMENT	STANDARD DEVIATION	SUM OF ARGUMENTS	
200	96.505	190.853	19301.000	NON-WEIGHTED

UPPER LIMIT	OBSERVED FREQUENCY	PER CENT OF TOTAL	CUMULATIVE PERCENTAGE	CUMULATIVE REMAINDER	MULTIPLE OF MEAN	DEVIATION FROM MEAN
50	72	36.00	36.00	64.00	0.518	-0.244
100	25	12.50	48.50	51.50	1.036	0.018
150	26	13.00	61.50	38.50	1.554	0.280
200	19	9.50	71.00	29.00	2.072	0.542
250	19	9.50	80.50	19.50	2.591	0.804
300	13	6.50	87.00	13.00	3.109	1.066
350	4	2.00	89.00	11.00	3.627	1.328
400	13	6.50	95.50	4.50	4.145	1.590
450	3	1.50	97.00	3.00	4.663	1.852
500	2	1.00	98.00	2.00	5.181	2.114
550	2	1.00	99.00	1.00	5.699	2.376
600	2	1.00	100.00	0.00	6.217	2.638

REMAINING FREQUENCIES ARE ALL ZERO

HALFWORD MATRIX SAVEVALUE   JOB

ROW/COL	1	2	3	4	5	6	7	8
1	2	4	1	3	45	60	75	60
2	1	2	4	3	70	70	50	50
3	3	4	2	1	50	60	60	70
4	4	2	3	1	80	40	80	40
5	3	4	1	2	70	50	40	80

6.0 ADVANCED MODELING CONCEPTS

6.1 Sophisticated Transaction Routing and Processing

Thus far, we have modeled systems that could be described by a single stream of transactions: patients in a clinic or parts on an assembly line. In more complicated systems it
is often necessary to have two or more streams of transactions to represent simultaneous
activities, for example, operation of a machine while its spare part is being repaired.
Also, in the models considered, it has been sufficient to allow GPSS to process transactions in accordance with the conventions described in Section 4. In many instances it
is necessary to implement different rules of transaction processing to accurately model
the real-word situation. In this section we describe the use of the SPLIT block for simultaneous activities and LINK and UNLINK blocks to invoke a different method of transaction processing.

SPLIT   This block creates copies of the transaction entering it, including parameter
values. The original transaction is often referred to as the parent and the copies as
offspring.

The flow chart symbol for the SPLIT block is:

The operands for the SPLIT block are:

OPERAND	DESCRIPTION	DEFAULT
A*	Number of copies to be created	None
B**	Next block for the copies	None
C	Parameter number for serializing copies	No serializing
D	Number of parameters for copies	Same as parent

* SNA types 1, 4, 5, or 6 may be used for operands A, C, and D.
** SNA types 1, 2, 4, 5, or 6 may be used.

All copies are directed to the block location specified by operand B. For some modeling
situations, it is to useful to attach a unique serial number to each copy, which can be
done using operand C. Depending on its function in the model, a copy may require
fewer parameters than the original transaction. To save memory, we can limit the
number of parameters assigned to the copies using operand D.

The SPLIT block may take the following forms:

```
SPLIT    20,NEXT,,1
SPLIT    P$2,NEXT
```

LINK   The LINK block permits transactions to be removed from the current-events chain and placed temporarily in an inactive state on a user chain. In this way, transactions are totally controlled by the user and not further addressed by GPSS until explicitly removed from the chain using the UNLINK block. Using such chains, one can implement transaction processing rules other than the priority-based first-come-first-served scheme normally followed by GPSS.

The flow chart symbol for the LINK block is:

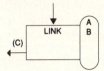

The operands for the LINK block are:

OPERAND	DESCRIPTION	DEFAULT
A*	User chain name or number	None
B**	Ordering of transactions on the user chain	None
C	Alternate block exit	Trans. always linked

* SNA types 1, 2, 4, 5, or 6 may be used for operands A and C.
** LIFO, FIFO, PH$j, or PF$j.

The allowable options for operand B are: "LIFO," join the front of chain; "FIFO," join the end of the chain; or a parameter number. If a parameter is used, transactions are merged onto the chain in ascending order of the parameter value.

Operand C specifies an alternate exit if the transaction does not join the chain. The decision to join or not is made in the following way. When a transaction moves into a LINK block, if it finds the link indicator for the associated chain in the "off" state, it sets the indicator to the "on" state and moves to the operand C next block. When a transaction enters the LINK block and finds the indicator in the "on" state, it does not alter the state, but it joins the user chain. This is useful when a user chain is to serve as a QUEUE block. The first transaction to enter the LINK block can capture the desired resource (facility or storage), and subsequent transactions will be queued on the user chain. When a transaction relinquishes the resource, it is used in connection with the UNLINK block to set the link indicator to the "off" state, if the user chain is empty. Exactly how this is accomplished is explained in the discussion of the UNLINK block.

Some example LINK block specifications are:

LINK   QUE,FIFO

LINK   1,P$2

UNLINK   This block removes transactions from a user chain according to the specifications of the operands. The destinations of both the unlinking transaction and the unlinked transactions are designated by the operand values. Unlinked transactions again come under the control of the GPSS scan.

The flow chart symbol for the UNLINK block is:

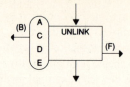

The operands for the UNLINK block are:

OPERAND	DESCRIPTION	DEFAULT
A*	User chain name or number	None
B	Next block for transactions being unlinked	None
C**	Number of transactions to be unlinked	None
D	Selection of transactions to be removed [BACK]	Unlink
E	Match argument used in selecting transactions for removal	from front
F	Next block for the unlinking transaction when the chain is empty	Next block in sequence

* SNA types 1, 2, 4, 5, or 6 may be used for operands A, B, and F.
** SNA types 1, 4, 5, or 6 may be used for operands C, D, and E.

Operand C may be "ALL," in which case all transactions are unlinked from the chain, or it may be an SNA indicating how many transactions to remove. Operand D may be "BACK," which causes transactions to be removed from the end of the chain, or it may be a parameter number which is used in conjunction with the E operand in determining which transactions to remove. If the E operand is omitted, the value of the specified parameter of the unlinking transaction is matched with the same parameter of transactions on the chain. If the E operand is specified, the value of the specified parameter of the transactions on the user chain is matched with the E operand. In matching values, the relational operators described for the TEST block are used (G, L, E, etc.). If both the D and E operands are omitted, transactions are removed from the front of the chain. If the user chain is empty, the F operand may be used to indicate an alternate next block for the unlinking transaction. Normally it would be directed to the next sequential block.

The following are representative of UNLINK block specifications:

```
UNLINK       QUE,NEXT,ALL
UNLINK GE    QUE,NEXT,1,P$2,3,BAK
```

The second example attempts to unlink one transaction from the chain QUE. The chain is searched from the front for a transaction which has a parameter 2 value greater than or equal to 3. If such a transaction is found, it is routed to the block location NEXT. The unlinking transaction proceeds to the next sequential block, unless the user chain is found to be empty.

The following sequence of blocks illustrates the use of the link indicator mentioned above.

```
              QUEUE        LINE
              LINK         QUE,FIFO,BAK
   BAK        SEIZE        MACH
              DEPART       LINE
              ADVANCE      10
              RELEASE      MACH
              UNLINK       QUE,BAK,1
```

When the first transaction arrives, it finds the link indicator in the "off" state; it places the indicator in the "on" state and then goes to block location BAK to occupy the facility MACH. Subsequent transactions arrive to find the link indicator in the "on" state and join the user chain QUE. Note that the time spent waiting for the facility is tallied in the QUEUE block LINE. As the facility MACH is relinquished, the departing transaction passes through the UNLINK block, removes one transaction from the front of the chain, and directs it to block location BAK where it can SEIZE the facility. The unlinking transaction passes to the next sequential block. The link indicator will remain in the "on" state until a transaction moves into an UNLINK block to find the chain empty. Then the link indicator will be set to "off." Thus if the queue LINE is empty and the facility MACH is unoccupied, transactions will not join the chain; otherwise they will.

6.2   Illustrative Problem Set VI

In this problem set we illustrate the use of the SPLIT block, and the LINK and UNLINK blocks. These blocks permit the user to alter significantly the way in which GPSS selects and processes transactions. With this capability one has much greater flexibility to model more complex systems. Two problems are treated: a spare parts inventory and an alternative design for the job shop of Problem V.2.

PROBLEM VI.1   Five radar units used to give early warning of air attack have an expensive component subject to frequent failure. In an attempt to keep all units operational, spare components are kept on hand. When a radar fails, a spare part is installed, if available, and the failed part is sent for repair, which takes 15 days. The time between successive failures may be described by the exponential probability distribution. The model provides the ability to observe the impact of the number of spares kept on hand on the distribution of the number of radar units which are operating.

The key to implementing the necessary logic is the SPLIT block. Upon each failure, the inventory is checked for spares using a TEST block and the savevalue ONHAND. If a spare is not available, the radar becomes inoperative pending the arrival of a repaired part; if a spare is available it is installed, and the failed part sent to be repaired. The latter action is accomplished by using the SPLIT block to send the original transaction for repair, while one copy is returned to an ADVANCE block to generate the next failure. In this case, the copy could have been used to send the unit for repair with the same results. The flow chart and GPSS code for this model are shown in Figs. 6.1 and 6.2.

FIGURE 6.1   PROBLEM VI.1 FLOW CHART

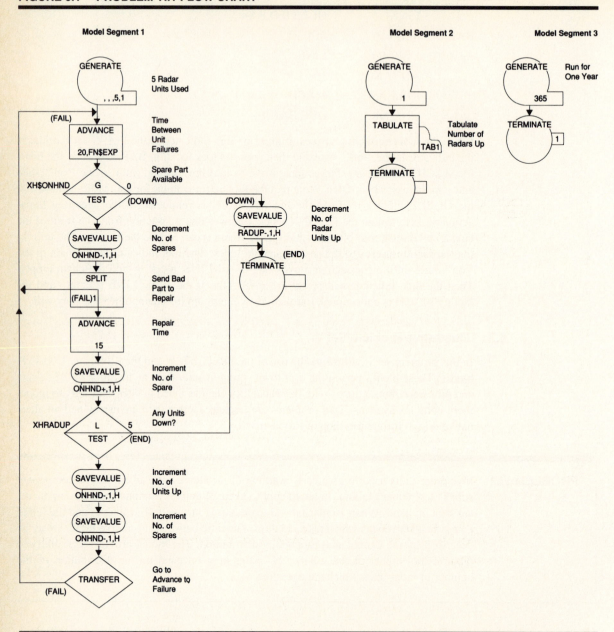

For the model run conducted, the number of spare parts used, XH$ONHAND, was five. In the output for this run, Fig. 6.3, the number of operational radar units, XH$RADUP, is tabulated in Table TAB1. From the cumulative remainder column, it can be seen that for 78% of the time there are one or more units operational, leaving 22% of the time with no radar coverage. Perhaps some additional investment in spare parts would improve security.

FIGURE 6.2   PROBLEM VI.1 CODE

```
LINE   BLOCK   BLOCK   BLOCK NAME                      COMMENTS
NO.    NO.     LOC.
 1             *SPARE PARTS PROBLEM
 2                     SIMULATE
 3             *MODEL SEGMENT 1 - MODEL LOGIC
 4             EXP     FUNCTION      RN1,C24           TIME BETWEEN FAILURES
 5             0,0/.1,.104/.2,.222/.3,.335/.4,.509/.5,.69/.6,.915
 6             .7,1.2/.75,1.38/.8,1.6/.84,1.83/.88,2.12/.9,2.3
 7             .92,2.52/.94,2.81/.95,2.99/.96,3.2/.97,3.5
 8             .98,3.9/.99,4.6/.995,5.3/.998,6.2/.999,7/.9997,8
 9             *INITIALIZE ONHAND SPARES AND NO. OF RADARS UP
10                     INITIAL       XH$ONHND,5/XH$RADUP,5
11             TAB1    TABLE         XH$RADUP,0,1,7    TABLE FOR RADARS UP
12      1              GENERATE      ,,,5,1            FIVE UNITS USED
13             *PRIORITY 1 TO INSURE UPDATE BEFORE TABULATE
14      2      FAIL    ADVANCE       20,FN$EXP         TIME BETWEEN FAILURES
15             *                                       (DAYS)
16      3              TEST G        XH$ONHND,0,DOWN   SPARES ON HAND?
17      4              SAVEVALUE     ONHND-,1,H        DECREMENT NO. SPARES
18      5              SPLIT         1,FAIL            RETURN TO FAIL, COPY
19             *                                       TO REPAIR
20      6              ADVANCE       15                REPAIR TIME
21      7              SAVEVALUE     ONHND+,1,H        INCREMENT NO. SPARES
22      8              TEST L        XH$RADUP,5,END    ANY RADARS DOWN?
23      9              SAVEVALUE     RADUP+,1,H        INCRMNT NO. RADARS UP
24      10             SAVEVALUE     ONHND-,1,H        DECREMENT NO. SPARES
25      11             TRANSFER      ,FAIL             TRANSFER TO FAIL
26      12     DOWN    SAVEVALUE     RADUP-,1,H        DECREMENT RADARS UP
27      13     END     TERMINATE
28             *MODEL SEGMENT 2 - TABULATE NO. OF RADARS UP
29      14             GENERATE      1
30      15             TABULATE      TAB1              TABULATE AT DAY'S END
31      16             TERMINATE
32             *MODEL SEGMENT 3 - RUN LENGTH CONTROL
33      17             GENERATE      365               RUN FOR 1 YEAR
34      18             TERMINATE     1
35                     START         1
```

FIGURE 6.3   PROBLEM VI.1 OUTPUT

```
RELATIVE CLOCK 365     ABSOLUTE CLOCK 365
```

TABLE	TAB1					
ENTRIES	MEAN ARGUMENT	STANDARD DEVIATION		SUM OF ARGUMENTS		
364	3.530	2.166		1285.000		NON-WEIGHTED

UPPER LIMIT	OBSERVED FREQUENCY	PER CENT OF TOTAL	CUMULATIVE PERCENTAGE	CUMULATIVE REMAINDER	MULTIPLE OF MEAN	DEVIATION FROM MEAN
0	79	21.70	21.70	78.30	0.000	-1.630
1	29	7.97	29.67	70.33	0.283	-1.168
2	4	1.10	30.77	69.23	0.567	-0.707
3	1	0.27	31.04	68.96	0.850	-0.245
4	10	2.75	33.79	66.21	1.133	0.217
5	241	66.21	100.00	0.00	1.416	0.679

PROBLEM VI.2   In this final illustrative problem we revisit the job shop of Problem V.2. All characteristics of the model remain the same, except the rule for selecting the next job from a machine queue for processing. The rule used here is; the next job to be processed is the one in the queue with the shortest processing time on that machine. This rule is usually referred to as the shortest processing time (SPT) rule.

To implement this rule we use the LINK and UNLINK blocks. Normally GPSS would select the next transaction based on its arrival time to a block and its priority, which is to be ignored by our rule. When a job reaches a machine, it will immediately seize the machine if the machine is free, otherwise it will go to a LINK block to join a user chain associated with that machine. It is placed on the chain according to its processing time, shorter processing times at the front of the chain. When a job leaves a machine, it passes through an UNLINK block and removes the transaction at the front of the chain, the one with the shortest processing time, and sends it to a SEIZE block to be processed. It should be noted that this approach is equivalent to the use of the link indicator discussed above, but the transaction processing relative to the user chains is more obvious. Figures 6.4 and 6.5 show the flow chart and GPSS code for the model.

The output for the model is in Fig. 6.6. We may contrast job tardiness tabulated in Table TAB1 with that found in Problem V.2. We observe that the mean tardiness is −.835 minutes, which indicates that jobs are, on the average, completed ahead of schedule. However, one day (500 minutes) beyond the due time, we find only 88% of the jobs completed, as compared with the FCFS rule of Problem V.2 which resulted in 98% of the jobs being completed by this time. In general, the SPT rule provides better average tardiness than the FCFS rule, but has a much higher variance. This may be seen by comparing the tables TAB1 of the two models.

FIGURE 6.4   PROBLEM VI.2 FLOW CHART

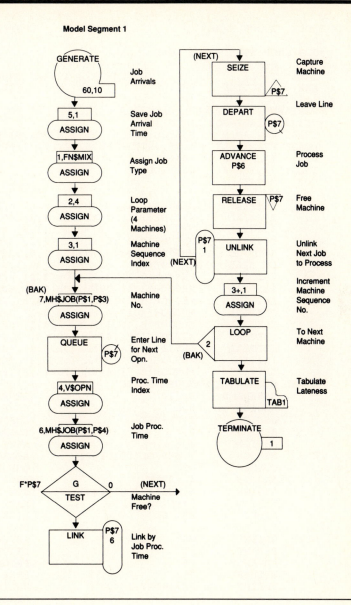

Model Segment 1

FIGURE 6.5   PROBLEM VI.2 CODE

```
LINE BLOCK BLOCK  BLOCK NAME                            COMMENTS
NO.  NO.   LOC.
1           *JOB SHOP MODEL- SOT RULE
2                  SIMULATE
3            TAB1  TABLE        V$TARDY,0,100,20 TABULATE JOB LATENESS
4            MIX   FUNCTION     RN1,D5                  JOB TYPE MIX
5           .1,1/.5,2/.7,3/.85,4/1,5
6           *VARIABLES: DDATE=DUE DATE FOR JOB; OPN=COL NO. FOR JOB PROC.
7           * TIME; TARDY=JOB LATENESS
8            TVAR1 VARIABLE     MH$JOB(P$1,5)+MH$JOB(P$1,6)+MH$JOB(P$1,7)
9            DDATE FVARIABLE    1.1*(V$TVAR1+MH$JOB(P$1,8)+P$5)
10           OPN   VARIABLE     P$3+4
11           TARDY VARIABLE     C1-V$DDATE
12           JOB   MATRIX           MH,5,8            MACH SEQUENCE AND
13          *                                         PROC. TIMES
14                 INITIAL      MH$JOB(1,1),2/MH$JOB(1,2),4/MH$JOB(1,3),1
15                 INITIAL      MH$JOB(1,4),3/MH$JOB(1,5),45/MH$JOB(1,6),60
16                 INITIAL      MH$JOB(1,7),75/MH$JOB(1,8),60
17                 INITIAL      MH$JOB(2,1),1/MH$JOB(2,2),2/MH$JOB(2,3),4
18                 INITIAL      MH$JOB(2,4),3/MH$JOB(2,5),70/MH$JOB(2,6),70
19                 INITIAL      MH$JOB(2,7),50/MH$JOB(2,8),50
20                 INITIAL      MH$JOB(3,1),3/MH$JOB(3,2),4/MH$JOB(3,3),2
21                 INITIAL      MH$JOB(3,4),1/MH$JOB(3,5),50/MH$JOB(3,6),60
22                 INITIAL      MH$JOB(3,7),60/MH$JOB(3,8),70
23                 INITIAL      MH$JOB(4,1),4/MH$JOB(4,2),2/MH$JOB(4,3),3
24                 INITIAL      MH$JOB(4,4),1/MH$JOB(4,5),80/MH$JOB(4,6),40
25                 INITIAL      MH$JOB(4,7),80/MH$JOB(4,8),40
26                 INITIAL      MH$JOB(5,1),3/MH$JOB(5,2),4/MH$JOB(5,3),1
27                 INITIAL      MH$JOB(5,4),2/MH$JOB(5,5),70/MH$JOB(5,6),50
28                 INITIAL      MH$JOB(5,7),40/MH$JOB(5,8),80
29          *MODEL SEGMENT 1 - MODEL LOGIC
30   1             GENERATE     60,10                   GENERATE JOBS
31   2             ASSIGN       5,C1                    SAVE TIME JOB ARRIVED
32   3             ASSIGN       1,FN$MIX                ASSIGN JOB TYPE
33   4             ASSIGN       2,4                     LOOP PARAMETER
34   5             ASSIGN       3,1                     NEXT MACH. IN SEQUENCE
35   6     BAK     ASSIGN       7,MH$JOB(P$1,P$3)       ASSIGN MACHINE NO.
36   7             QUEUE        P$7                     QUEUE FOR NEXT OPN.
37   8             ASSIGN       4,V$OPN                 PROCESSING TIME INDEX
38   9             ASSIGN       6,MH$JOB(P$1,P$4)       JOB PROC TIME
39   10            TEST G       F*P$7,0,NEXT            MACHINE FREE?
40   11            LINK         P$7,6                   LINK ACCORDING TO
41          *                                           PROCESSING TIME
42   12    NEXT    SEIZE        P$7                     SEIZE MACH. NEXT OPN.
43   13            DEPART       P$7                     LEAVE MACHINE QUEUE
44   14            ADVANCE      P$6                     PROCESS JOB
45   15            RELEASE      P$7                     FREE MACHINE
46   16            UNLINK       P$7,NEXT,1              UNLINK JOB TO PROCESS
47          *                                           NEXT
48   17            ASSIGN       3+,1                    INCREMENT MACH
49          *                                           SEQUENCE NO.
50   18            LOOP         2,BAK                   TO NEXT MACHINE
51   19            TABULATE     TAB1                    TABULATE LATENESS
52   20            TERMINATE    1
53                 START        200                     PROCESS 200 JOBS
```

FIGURE 6.6   PROBLEM VI.2 OUTPUT

RELATIVE CLOCK 13225   ABSOLUTE CLOCK 13225

QUEUE	MAXIMUM CONTENTS	AVERAGE CONTENTS	TOTAL ENTRIES	ZERO ENTRIES	PERCENT ZEROS	AVERAGE TIME/TRANS	$AVERAGE TIME/TRANS	TABLE NUMBER	CURRENT CONTENTS
1	9	3.729	210	4	1.905	234.848	239.408		2
2	10	3.620	219	9	4.110	218.621	227.990		9
3	5	1.769	215	23	10.698	108.809	121.844		4
4	5	1.497	219	30	13.699	90.379	104.725		3

FACILITY	AVERAGE UTILIZATION	NUMBER ENTRIES	AVERAGE TIME/TRANS	SEIZING TRANS. NO.	PREEMPTING TRANS. NO.
1	0.978	208	62.154	14	
2	0.979	210	61.667	2	
3	0.914	211	57.299		
4	0.937	216	57.347	17	

USER CHAIN	TOTAL ENTRIES	AVERAGE TIME/TRANS	CURRENT CONTENTS	AVERAGE CONTENTS	MAXIMUM CONTENTS
1	206	228.631	2	3.561	9
2	210	178.990	8	2.842	9
3	192	114.240	3	1.659	5
4	192	80.172	3	1.164	5

TABLE	TAB1			
ENTRIES	MEAN ARGUMENT	STANDARD DEVIATION	SUM OF ARGUMENTS	
200	-0.835	576.937	-167.000	NON-WEIGHTED

UPPER LIMIT	OBSERVED FREQUENCY	PER CENT OF TOTAL	CUMULATIVE PERCENTAGE	CUMULATIVE REMAINDER	MULTIPLE OF MEAN	DEVIATION FROM MEAN
0	108	54.00	54.00	46.00	0.000	0.001
100	35	17.50	71.50	28.50	-119.760	0.175
200	14	7.00	78.50	21.50	-239.521	0.348
300	11	5.50	84.00	16.00	-359.281	0.521
400	7	3.50	87.50	12.50	-479.042	0.695
500	1	0.50	88.00	12.00	-598.802	0.868
600	2	1.00	89.00	11.00	-718.563	1.041
700	3	1.50	90.50	9.50	-838.323	1.215
800	2	1.00	91.50	8.50	-958.084	1.388
900	1	0.50	92.00	8.00	-1077.844	1.561
1000	1	0.50	92.50	7.50	-1197.605	1.735
1100	1	0.50	93.00	7.00	-1317.365	1.908
1200	2	1.00	94.00	6.00	-1437.126	2.081
1300	0	0.00	94.00	6.00	-1556.886	2.255
1400	3	1.50	95.50	4.50	-1676.647	2.428
1500	2	1.00	96.50	3.50	-1796.407	2.601
1600	0	0.00	96.50	3.50	-1916.168	2.775
1700	1	0.50	97.00	3.00	-2035.928	2.948
1800	2	1.00	98.00	2.00	-2155.689	3.121

AVERAGE VALUE OF THE 4 OVERFLOW ITEMS IS   2020.750

7.0 CONTROL STATEMENTS AND MISCELLANEOUS BLOCKS

7.1 Control Statements and Their Uses

In Section 3.0 we described a rudimentary set of control statements to permit GPSS model execution. There are many more such statements that facilitate execution of more complex models and model experiments. We shall cover only the most useful of these statements, and when operands are optional, we shall not complicate the discussion by mentioning them.

RESET This statement resets selected entity statistics and system attributes. The relative clock is set to zero, while the absolute clock remains unchanged. Entities affected include blocks, queues, facilities, storages, and distribution tables. This statement is useful when one wishes to examine steady-state behavior of the model. The model is run for a warm-up, or initialization period, and then the statistics are reset to zero while the number and location of transactions in the system remain unchanged. Statistics are then collected for operations from this point in time to the end of the model run.

The RESET statement would be included in a model as follows:

```
SIMULATE
GENERATE      1
      .
      .
TERMINATE     1
START         200
RESET
START         1000
END
```

In this model, 200 transactions would be used during the initialization period, then the RESET statement would reset statistics, and 1000 more transactions would be allowed to flow through the model.

CLEAR This statement resets all entity statistics, and clears the model of entity contents and transactions. The relative and absolute clock values are also reset to zero. The net affect of the CLEAR statement is to restore system status to the same condition as prevailed at the start of the run. This statement is useful in running several model alternatives sequentially.

The CLEAR statement is included in a model as follows:

```
SIMULATE
STORAGE       S$1,50/S$2,100
GENERATE
      .
      .
TERMINATE     1
START         500
```

```
STORAGE          S$1,100/S$2,200
CLEAR
START            500
END
```

Storages number 1 and 2 are initially defined with capacities of 50, and 100, respectively, and 500 transactions are allowed to flow through the model. The storage capacities are then doubled, and a new model run is made for 500 transactions.

JOB   Although initially used to separate multiple runs submitted as one batch job, this statement has evolved in most GPSS implementations to control allocation of memory to entities and to provide a title for the output. If used, it must appear as the first statement in the model. The JOB statement generally has two operands, as follows:

OPERAND	DEFINITION
A	Entity options - insert A, B, or C
B	String of text to be use as first line of output for each page

The number of each of the entities permitted by the A, B, and C options may vary with the particular installation of GPSS, but the following table is representative for major classes of entities.

ENTITY TYPE	MNEMONIC	ENTITY OPTIONS		
		A	B	C
Transaction	XAC	100	500	1200
Block	BLO	80	500	1000
Storage	STO	20	150	300
Facility	FAC	20	150	300
Queue	QUE	35	150	300
Function	FUN	20	50	200
Variable	VAR	20	50	200
Table	TAB	15	30	100
Savevalue				
Fullword	FSV	100	400	1000
Halfword	HSV	50	200	500
Matrix savevalue				
Fullword	FMS	5	10	25
Halfword	HMS	5	10	25
Logic switches	LOG	100	400	1000
User chain	CHA	20	40	100

REALLOCATE   This statement reapportions the number of entity types permitted in a model to suit the needs of a particular modeling situation. If the entity options available through the JOB statement are not suitable, particular allocations my be made as follows using the mnemonics of the previous table.

REALLOCATE   FAC,5000,QUE,1000,TAB,0

RMULT   This statement permits the analyst to use eight separate random number strings. In complex models, this feature is of value in improving the accuracy of estimates of system performance measures.

The eight operands of the RMULT statement specify initial seed values for each of the strings, as follows:

RMULT   13667,2399,13

No operand may exceed five digits in length.

7.2   Miscellaneous GPSS Blocks and Statements

In a primer of this length it is not possible to cover all the features of the GPSS language. In this section, we briefly describe some blocks that implement the more sophisticated features of GPSS. If any of these blocks appear to be useful for a particular modeling situation, the reader is referred to the sources cited in the Bibliography for more details.

EQU   This statement assigns a specified number to a symbol used for reference to one or more entities. For example, the statement: CPU EQU 1,F,Q,S, will associate the symbol CPU with facility 1, queue 1, and storage 1. A unique set of mnemonics is used to designate entities in the EQU statement.

PREEMPT   This block allows a transaction currently in a facility to be replaced by another transaction for a period of time. For example, PREEMPT FAC.

RETURN   The reverse of preemption is effected by this block. It causes a preempting transaction to relinquish control of a facility, as: RETURN FAC.

FAVAIL   This block causes specified facilities which were previously unavailable, to now become available for use. For example, FAVAIL 2−6, causes the facilities numbered 2 through 6 to now be available for use. Used in conjunction with the FUNAVAIL block, one can take facilities out of service, say, for repair, and subsequently return them to service.

FUNAVAIL   This block causes a facility, or facilities, to be unavailable until returned to service by a FAVAIL block, as, FUNAVAIL 2−6.

SAVAIL/SUNAVAIL   This conjugate pair of blocks operates to accomplish the same affect as the FAVAIL/FUNAVAIL pair, except for storages. It has the form: SAVAIL STO1 and SUNAVAIL STO1.

MATCH   In some applications, a transaction will pass through a SPLIT block creating a copy which must be synchronized with the original at a point downstream in the model logic. This can be accomplished using a pair of MATCH blocks, one for each transaction stream. The MATCH block takes the following form:

	Stream 1			**Stream 2**	
13	MATCH	22	22	MATCH	13

In effect, each block points to the other.

TRACE/UNTRACE   This block is helpful in debugging complex models. It causes the paths of transactions to be recorded until these transactions subsequently enter an UNTRACE block. The TRACE block provides information on each transaction such as: transaction number, previous block number, next block, clock time, current run termination count, and priority.

PRINT   The PRINT block is also helpful in debugging code. It permits statistics for specified SNAs to be printed at the point in the code where the block is inserted. Operand C indicates the family name of the SNA (e.g., Q, XH, or F), and operands A and B specify the lower and upper limits, respectively, of the SNAs.

MACROS   GPSS macros provide a convenient way of generating the same sequence of blocks many times within a model, thus reducing the amount of coding and input errors.

Two control statements are required to define each macro: STARTMACRO and ENDMACRO. The Block Location field in the STARTMACRO statement is used to specify the name of the macro. In the GPSS blocks contained in the macro, arguments may be specified as #A, #B,...,#J. If the sequence of blocks SEIZE, ADVANCE, RELEASE were common in a model, the following macro could be defined.

```
EASY STARTMACRO
        SEIZE           #A
        ADVANCE         #B
        RELEASE         #A
        ENDMACRO
```

This macro would be called by a MACRO statement as follows:

```
        GENERATE        30,10
           .
           .
EASY MACRO              4,30
           .
           .
EASY MACRO              5,20
```

These statements would generate the following GPSS code:

```
        GENERATE        30,10
           .
           .
        SEIZE           4
        ADVANCE         30
        RELEASE         4
           .
           .
        SEIZE           5
        ADVANCE         20
        RELEASE         5
```

HELP   GPSS permits the user to write subroutines in FORTRAN which can be compiled and assimilated into the GPSS code. This is accomplished using the HELP block. Of the types of HELP block interfaces available, perhaps the most useful is the HELPB block. This block allows two-way passing of information between a FORTRAN subroutine and certain GPSS SNAs.

For example, the following GPSS statements

```
1 MATRIX      MH,3,3
  HELPB       MATRIX,MH1(1,1),P$3,P$5
```

might call the subroutine defined by:

```
SUBROUTINE MATRIX(MX,PAR3,PAR5)
INTEGER MX(3,3),PAR3,PAR5
      .
      .
      .

RETURN
END
```

To integrate this subroutine into the GPSS code, one must first compile it to yield an object file. The use of HELP blocks depends heavily on the particular computer system supporting GPSS, and therefore one must check the GPSS system-specific documentation carefully.

7.3   Some GPSS Addressing and Memory Allocation Conventions

Relative Addressing   It is often necessary to refer to specific block locations in GPSS model logic. This may be done by reference to a specific block number or symbolic name, or relative to a block already specified. For example, we may transfer to a particular block as follows:

```
TRANSFER      ,BLOC1
TRANSFER      ,BLOC1+1
TRANSFER      ,*+3
```

In the first example, transfer is made to a block location specified symbolically as BLOC1, while in the second, transfer is to the block following BLOC1. The last example illustrates a block location specified relative to the current block. That is, transfer is to the third block following the TRANSFER block.

Indirect Addressing   The simplest way to refer to a GPSS entity is directly by name or number. Often one does not know what entity, say a facility, will be used by a particular transaction until the transaction arrives. The choice may be based on the status of the system at that time; for instance, the facility with the shortest queue in front of it may be selected. This level of indirect addressing may be achieved as follows:

```
SEIZE     PH$2
```

where PH$2 designates halfword parameter number 2. Thus the facility whose number is contained in this parameter will be used. If PH$2 contains the number of the facility with the shortest queue, the desired effect is achieved.

A further level of indirect addressing can be obtained as follows. The statement:

$$MX*PH\$1(1,PH\$2)$$

specifies an element of a fullword matrix savevalue. The number of the matrix savevalue is contained in halfword parameter 1, the row designation is row 1, and the column is specified in halfword parameter 2. The "*" indicates that the matrix savevalue is indirectly addressed. This construction would be useful in specifying a series of facilities through which a transaction must traverse according to its type. The transaction type is contained in PH$1, thus defining a different matrix for each transaction type, and the series of facilities is stated by the columns of each one-row matrix.

Indirect addressing constructions can become quite complicated, for example: $MX*V\$2(FN*PH\$4,2)$, where, not only the matrix savevalue, but also the row number is indirectly specified. Before attempting such complicated constructions, one should review the documentation of the particular GPSS version being used to see if they are supported.

Magnitude of GPSS Quantities   In general GPSS does not deal well with high-precision floating-point arithmetic. Most variables and constants in GPSS models are appropriately handled as integers, including the system numerical attributes, relative and absolute clock times. Since GPSS models can consume large amounts of computer memory, one should not squander memory on unnecessary floating-point quantities. If needed, GPSS can deal with precise floating-point values in entities such as FVARI-ABLE, and floating-point matrix savevalues.

To facilitate memory conservation, GPSS allows some entities to be specified as either halfword or fullword quantities; for example, the halfword and fullword parameters and savevalues referred to above. In general, the following three specifications are possible: signed fullword integer, which allows values ranging from -2^{31} to $+2^{31}$; signed halfword integer, which allows values from -2^{15} to $+2^{15}$; and signed floating point, which allows magnitudes from approximately 10^{-38} to 10^{38}. These specifications may be applied to parameters, savevalues, and matrix savevalues. The ranges of values cited assume the use of a computer with a 32-bit word length.

8.0   LIST OF GPSS BLOCKS AND THEIR OPERANDS

The following conventions and notation are used in summarizing the GPSS blocks. First, the block and its associated operands are listed. A brief description is provided for each operand followed by allowable values placed within { }, and the default value placed within [ ]. Allowable operands are specified as one of six types of SNAs, as described in Section 3.0 and repeated here for convenience.

1. K   Integer constant

2. sn   Symbolic name (e.g., SHIP, MACH)

3. SNA   Family name of a Standard Numerical Attribute (e.g., Q, S, R, or XH)

4. SNA$j   Family name of a Standard Numerical Attribute followed by a dollar sign ($) and a numerical entity name (e.g., Q$1, S$3, R$4, or XH$1)

5. SNA$sn   Family name of a Standard Numerical Attribute followed by a dollar sign ($) and a symbolic entity name (e.g., Q$LINE, S$STORE, or XH$SAVE)

6. SNA*Px$j   Family name of a Standard Numerical Attribute followed by an asterisk (*) and the designation of a halfword (x = H) or fullword (x = F) parameter whose value is a numeric entity name (i.e., an indirect address such as, Q*PH$1, MX*PF$3, or XH*PF$2)

The page reference for the block description appears next to the right margin as: page 000.

ADVANCE

A,B   page A-14

A   Mean time {SNA types 1, 4, 5, or 6} [0]

B   Spread modifier {SNA types 1, 4, 5, or 6, except FN} [0], or function modifier {FN$j, FN$sn, or FN*P$j} [0]

ASSIGN

A,B,C   page A-29

A   Parameter No. {± SNA types 1, 4, 5, or 6} [None]

B   Value to be assigned {SNA types 1, 4, 5, or 6} [None]

C   No. of function modifier {SNA types 1, 4, 5, or 6} [None]

BUFFER

No operands   page A-47

COUNT

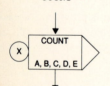

{ Logical relational } A,B,C,D,E   page A-44

A   Parameter in which to place the count {SNA types 1, 4, 5, or 6} [None]

B   Lower limit of entity examined {SNA types 1, 2, 4, 5, or 6} [None]

C   Upper limit of entity examined {SNA types 1, 2, 4, 5, or 6} [None]

D   Comparison value for use with relational operators {SNA types 1, 2, 4, 5, or 6} [None]

E   Name of SNA to be counted {Any SNA except MX or MH} [None]

DEPART

A,B

page A-16

A   Queue name {SNA types 1, 2, 4, 5, or 6} [None]

B   No. of units {SNA types 1, 4, 5, or 6} [1]

ENTER

A,B

page A-13

A   Storage name {SNA type 1, 2, 4, 5, or 6} [None]

B   No. of units {SNA types 1, 4, 5, or 6} [1]

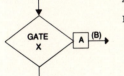

GATE

{Logical Attribute} A,B

page A-31

A   Logic switch, facility or storage name {SNA types 1, 2, 4, 5, or 6} [None]

B   Next block if condition false {SNA types 1, 2, 4, 5, or 6} [None]

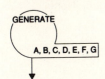

GENERATE

A,B,C,D,E,F,G,

page A-10

A   Mean time {SNA types 1, 4, or 5} [0]

B   Spread modifier {SNA types 1, 4, or 5, except FN} [0] or function modifier {FN$j or FN$sn} [None]

C   Offset interval {SNA types 1, 4, or 5} [No offset]

D   Limit count {SNA types 1, 4, or 5} [Infinite]

E   Priority level {SNA types 1, 4, or 5} [0]

F   No. of parameters {SNA types 1, 4, or 5} [Machine dependent]

G   Type of parameter {H or F} [Machine dependent]

Note: Operands A through F are restricted to K (integer constant),
     and the following specific SNAs: FN, V, X, XH, RN, N, and C1.

LEAVE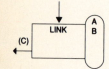

A,B

A   Storage name {SNA types 1, 2, 4, 5, or 6} [None]

B   No. of units {SNA types 1, 4, 5, or 6} [1]

page A-13

LINK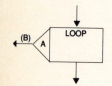

A,B,C

A   User chain name {SNA types 1, 2, 4, 5, or 6} [None]

B   Ordering of transactions on chain {LIFO, FIFO, or P$j} [None]

C   Alternate block exit {SNA types 1, 2, 4, 5, or 6} [Always link to chain]

page A-73

LOGIC

A

A   Logic switch name {SNA types 1, 2, 4, 5, or 6} [None]

page A-32

LOOP

A,B

A   Parameter {SNA types 1, 4, 5, or 6} [None]

B   Next block if parameter not equal to zero {SNA types 1, 2, 4, 5, or 6} [None]

page A-36

MARK

A

A   Parameter no. {SNA types 1, 4, 5, or 6} [None]

page A-29

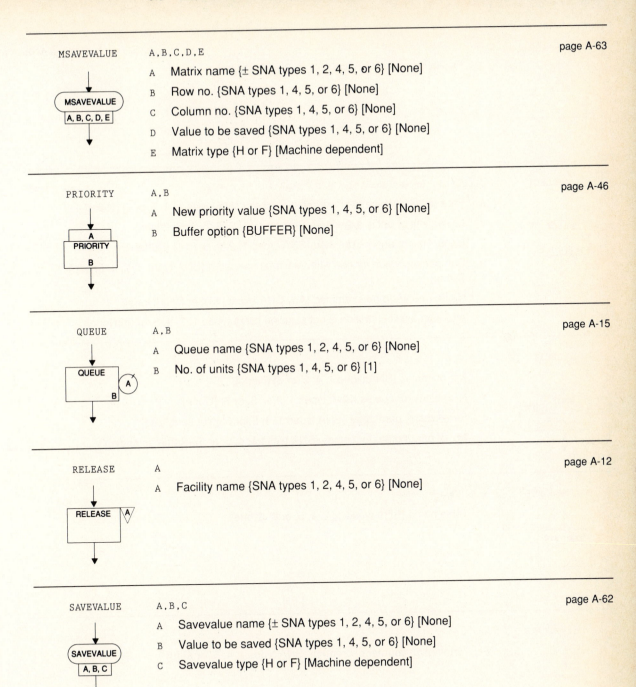

MSAVEVALUE   A,B,C,D,E   page A-63

A   Matrix name {± SNA types 1, 2, 4, 5, or 6} [None]

B   Row no. {SNA types 1, 4, 5, or 6} [None]

C   Column no. {SNA types 1, 4, 5, or 6} [None]

D   Value to be saved {SNA types 1, 4, 5, or 6} [None]

E   Matrix type {H or F} [Machine dependent]

PRIORITY   A,B   page A-46

A   New priority value {SNA types 1, 4, 5, or 6} [None]

B   Buffer option {BUFFER} [None]

QUEUE   A,B   page A-15

A   Queue name {SNA types 1, 2, 4, 5, or 6} [None]

B   No. of units {SNA types 1, 4, 5, or 6} [1]

RELEASE   A   page A-12

A   Facility name {SNA types 1, 2, 4, 5, or 6} [None]

SAVEVALUE   A,B,C   page A-62

A   Savevalue name {± SNA types 1, 2, 4, 5, or 6} [None]

B   Value to be saved {SNA types 1, 4, 5, or 6} [None]

C   Savevalue type {H or F} [Machine dependent]

SEIZE

A

A   Facility name {SNA types 1, 2, 4, 5, or 6} [None]

page A-12

SELECT

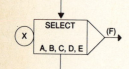

{Logical, Relational, or MIN, MAX} A,B,C,D,E,F

A   Parameter in which to place entity number {SNA types 1, 4, 5, or 6} [None]

B   Lower limit of entity examined {SNA types 1, 2, 4, 5, or 6} [None]

C   Upper limit of entity examined {SNA types 1, 2, 4, 5, or 6} [None]

D   Comparison value for use with relational operators {SNA types 1, 2, 4, 5, or 6} [None]

E   Name of SNA to be examined {Any SNA except MX or MH} [None]

F   Alternate exit if condition is not satisfied {SNA types 1, 2, 4, 5, or 6} [None]

page A-45

SPLIT

A,B,C,D

A   No. of copies {SNA types 1, 4, 5, or 6} [None]

B   Next block for copies {SNA types 1, 2, 4, 5, or 6} [None]

C   Serialization parameter {SNA types 1, 4, 5, or 6} [Not serialized]

D   No. of parameters for copies {SNA types 1, 4, 5, or 6} [Same as original]

page A-72

TABULATE

A

A   Table name {SNA types 1, 2, 4, 5, or 6} [None]

page A-51

TERMINATE

A

A   Termination counter decrement {SNA types 1, 4, 5, or 6} [0]

page A-11

TEST

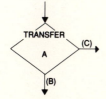

{Relational Operator} A,B,C   page A-30

A   First value to be compared {SNA types 1, 4, 5, or 6} [None]

B   Second value to be compared {SNA types 1, 4, 5, or 6} [None]

C   Next block if relationship is false {SNA types 1, 2, 4, 5, or 6} [None]

TRANSFER

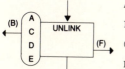

A,B,C   page A-33

A   Mode of operation {Both=BOTH, Unconditional=blank, Fractional=0.xxx, All=ALL, Pick=PICK, Function=FN$j, Subroutine=SBR, and Parameter=PF or PH} [None]

B   First next block {SNA types 1, 2, 4, 5, or 6} [Mode dependent]

C   Second next block {SNA types 1, 2, 4, 5, or 6, not used with unconditional mode} [None]

UNLINK

A,B,C,D,E,F   page A-73

A   User chain name {SNA types 1, 2, 4, 5, or 6} [None]

B   Next block for unlinked transactions {SNA types 1, 2, 4, 5, or 6} [None]

C   No. of transactions to unlink {SNA types 1, 4, 5, or 6, or ALL} [None]

D   Selection of transaction to be removed {SNA types 1, 4, 5, or 6} [Unlink from front of chain]

E   Match argument {SNA types 1, 4, 5, or 6} [Unlink from front of chain]

F   Alternate exit when chain is empty {SNA types 1, 2, 4, 5, or 6} [Next sequential block]

9.0   LIST OF STANDARD NUMERICAL AND LOGICAL ATTRIBUTES

Standard Numerical Attributes

In the following list of SNAs, j may be any of the following: integer constant, symbolic name, or parameter number.

ENTITY	SNA	DEFINITION
Blocks	N_j	Total number of transactions to enter block j
	W_j	Current number of transactions in block j
Facilities	F_j	Use status: 1, if facility j in use, 0, otherwise
	FR_j	Utilization of facility j
	FC_j	Total number of transactions to use facility j
	FT_j	Average time per transaction in facility j
Functions	FN_j	Computed value of function j

Msavevalues	MX_j (a,b)	Current contents of the (a,b) element of fullword msavevalue j
	$MH_j(a,b)$	Current contents of the (a,b) element of halfword savevalue j
Queues	Q_j	Current number of units in queue j
	QA_j	Average number of units in queue j
	QM_j	Maximum number of units of queue j
	QC_j	Total number of units to enter queue j
	QZ_j	Number of units spending zero time in queue j
	QT_j	Average time spent in queue j (including transactions that wait zero time)
	QX_j	Average time spent in queue j (excluding transactions that wait zero time)
Savevalues	X_j	Current contents of fullword savevalue j
	XH_j	Current contents of halfword savevalue j
Storages	S_j	Current contents of storage j
	R_j	Number of units of capacity remaining in storage j
	SR_j	Utilization of Storage j
	SA_j	Average contents of storage j
	SM_j	Maximum contents of storage j
	SC_j	Total number of units to enter storage j
	ST_j	Average time per transaction in storage j
System Attributes	RN_j	Computed random number
	C1	Current value of the relative clock
	AC1	Current value of the absolute clock
Transactions	PF_j	Current value of fullword parameter j
	PH_j	Current value of halfword parameter j
	M1	Time in the model (from creation or most recent MARK block)
	PR	Priority
User Chains	CH_j	Current number of units on user chain j
	CA_j	Average number of units on user chain j
	CM_j	Maximum number of units on user chain j
	CC_j	Total number of units which have been linked to user chain j
	CT_j	Average time spent on the user chain
Variables	V_j	Computed value of variable j
	BV_j	Computed value of Boolean variable j

Standard Logical Attributes

In the following list of Standard Logical Attributes (SLAs), j may be any of the following: integer constant, symbolic name, or parameter number.

ENTITY	SLA	DEFINITION
Logic Switches	LR_j	True if logic switch j is reset
	LS_j	True if logic switch j is set

Facilities	U_j	True if facility j is seized or preempted
	NU_j	True if facility j is neither seized nor preempted
	I_j	True if facility j is preempted
	NI_j	True if facility j is not preempted
	FV_j	True if facility j is in available status
	FNV_j	True if facility j is in unavailable status
Storages	SE_j	True if storage j is empty ($S_j = 0$)
	SNE_j	True if storage j is not empty ($S_j > 0$)
	SF_j	True if storage j is full ($R_j = 0$)
	SNF_j	True if storage j is not full ($R_j > 0$)
	SV_j	True if storage j is in available status
	SNV_j	True if storage j is in unavailable status

REFERENCES

Fishman, G., *Concepts and Methods in Discrete Event Digital Simulation*, New York: John Wiley, and Sons, 1973.

Gordon, G., *A General Purpose Systems Simulation Program*, Proceedings of the EJCC, Washington, D.C., New York: Macmillan Publishing, Inc., 1961.

SELECTED BIBLIOGRAPHY

Bobillier, P., Kahan, B., Probst, A., *Simulation with GPSS and GPSS V*, Englewood Cliffs, N. J.: Prentice-Hall, Inc., 1976.

Fishman, G., *Principles of Discrete Event Simulation*, New York: John Wiley, and Sons, 1978.

General Purpose Simulation System V User's Manual, Third Edition, New York: International Business Machines, Inc., 1977.

Gordon, G., *System Simulation*, Second Edition, Englewood Cliffs, N.J.: Prentice-Hall, Inc., 1978.

Gordon, G., *The Application of GPSS V to Discrete System*, Englewood Cliffs, N.J.: Prentice-Hall, Inc., 1975.

Schriber, T., *Simulation Using GPSS*, New York: John Wiley, and Sons, 1974.

SIMAN PRIMER

APPENDIX B   SIMAN PRIMER

OUTLINE

1.0   INTRODUCTION

The objective of this primer is to provide sufficient knowledge of the SIMAN (SIMulation ANalysis) language to permit the programming of reasonably complex and realistic simulation models. However, this primer does not treat all of the modeling options of SIMAN. For these, the reader is referred to the reference manual by SIMAN's creator (Pegden,1986). In the presentation, the descriptions of SIMAN language concepts and elements are closely followed by example problems which illustrate their use. In this way the student can quickly develop a feel for the modeling process using SIMAN.

SIMAN is a simulation language suitable for modeling discrete-event, continuous, and combined continuous/discrete-event systems. In this primer, however, coverage is limited to discrete-event modeling using SIMAN block diagrams. This approach may be described as process interaction (Fishman,1973) or entity-flow oriented. The model focuses on one entity at a time, say a customer in a bank or a part in a manufacturing process, and tracks it through the model, noting all significant happenings, such as waits, services, and departure from the system. A unique and valuable feature of SIMAN is the ability to separate the model definition from experiments with the model.

SIMAN is a FORTRAN-based language which may be run on microcomputers or larger machines without alteration to the source statements. Although SIMAN is supported on a wide variety of computers, its structure and syntax are the same for all machines. For the aspects of language described in this primer, only minimal familiarity with the host computer operating system is necessary.

The organization of this primer is designed to facilitate programming of increasingly complex models with the introduction of small sets of new concepts in stages. This is accomplished by the following organization. In Section 2.0 an overview of the SIMAN language is presented. Section 3.0 basic modeling concepts and a fundamental set of SIMAN language elements are introduced, and some rudimentary SIMAN programs are constructed. In Section 4.0 intermediate modeling concepts are discussed and more language elements are presented. Section 5.0 treats the advanced modeling concepts embodied in the use of stations and submodels. In Section 6.0 a set of language elements designed expressly to deal with material handling systems modeling is presented. Finally, in Section 7.0, SIMAN elements that facilitate display and analysis of simulation output are covered.

The last three sections are summaries of SIMAN language elements treated in the primer, and assembled there for easy reference. Section 8.0 summarizes SIMAN blocks and their operands, Section 9.0 experimental elements, and Section 10.0 output display and analysis elements.

2.0   OVERVIEW OF SIMAN

SIMAN has the capability to model very complex systems, and consequently it requires detailed model specification. Even limiting consideration to discrete-event models using block diagrams, as this primer does, one must assimilate a reasonably large set of concepts and language conventions. Before delving into the language proper, we take an overview of SIMAN in this section. We consider the world view of SIMAN, and how it defines and executes models, and analyzes their results. Also, preparatory to dealing with the details of the language, the means of defining blocks and their coding conventions are discussed.

2.1   SIMAN Software Structure

SIMAN explicitly recognizes and separates three major phases of simulation analysis: model definition, model experimentation, and output analysis. The advantages in doing this include the ability to run several experiments without altering the model, and to perform several output analyses using the same model results data files.

To accomplish this segmentation, the SIMAN software comprises five individual processors which interact through four data files as described below and illustrated in Fig. 2.1.

1. The MODEL PROCESSOR is used to construct a block diagram model of the system. The resulting data file is the MODEL FILE.

2. The EXPERIMENT PROCESSOR is used to define the experiments to be run with the model, or the experimental frame. The resulting data file is the EXPERIMENT FILE.

3. The LINK PROCESSOR combines the MODEL FILE and the EXPERIMENT FILE to produce an executable PROGRAM FILE.

FIGURE 2.1   SIMAN SOFTWARE STRUCTURE

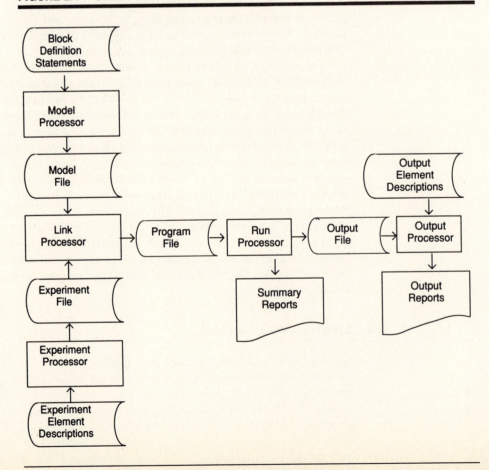

4. The PROGRAM FILE is input to the RUN PROCESSOR which executes the simulation model and writes results on the OUTPUT FILE.

5. The OUTPUT PROCESSOR is used to analyze, format, and display the results contained in the OUTPUT FILE.

The SIMAN statements that define the model are referred to as the model frame, and those that define the experiments as the experimental frame. The output provided by the output processor is an augmentation of output statistics obtained using experimental frame elements.

2.2   SIMAN Model Frame

To describe a discrete-event model, SIMAN uses a directed block diagram consisting of several block types, each of which has a unique function. The world view taken by SIMAN is that of entities flowing through the blocks that define system components. The blocks may alter the nature or the flow of entities, or both. Entities may represent a wide variety of animate and inanimate objects: for example, patients in a clinic, customers in a bank, cars in a toll booth queue, manufactured parts in a production facility, or parts in an inventory system.

The SIMAN block diagram repertoire consists of the block types shown in Table 2.1. Most of the blocks are of three types: OPERATION, TRANSFER, and HOLD. The OPERATION blocks are used to model a wide range of entity transformations, including creation of entities (CREATE), delays representing processing of entities (DELAY), or modification of one or more characteristics of an entity (ASSIGN). The TRANSFER blocks effect movement between specific physical locations in the system and are designed primarily for modeling material-handling systems. The HOLD blocks are used to model delays caused by system status, for example, entities attempting to seize a machine that is busy (SEIZE). The remaining blocks cover functions such as queueing for a resource (QUEUE), selecting from among several queues (PICKQ), defining physical locations in the model (STATION), and entity flow control (BRANCH).

The STATION block plays a particularly important role in SIMAN modeling. Not only is it associated with a specified physical location in the model, but it also defines the beginning of a submodel, or series of blocks, which represents logic to be replicated in more than one place in the model. For example, one might send entities to one of a series of supermarket checkout stations which are identical in processing logic. The STATION block affords economy in coding, since identical model structures need not be repeated.

To model certain phenomenon it is often necessary to "do" something to an entity, and then subsequently "undo" it, as in gaining control of a resource and then releasing that resource after processing. The complementary SIMAN blocks for accomplishing this are the SEIZE and RELEASE blocks. There are many such complementary pairs of blocks in SIMAN: for example, GROUP-SPLIT, which combine and ultimately separate entities; and REQUEST-FREE, and ACTIVATE-HALT, which deal with the status of material-handling resources.

The last two block pairs illustrate a special type of SIMAN block: the material-handling block. Such blocks are designed to reproduce faithfully the action of broad classes of material-handling equipment which are represented by SIMAN as conveyors and transporters. The material-handling blocks greatly facilitate the modeling of

TABLE 2.1
BASIC BLOCK TYPES

Name	Symbol	Function
OPERATION		Models a wide range of activities, such as processing delays, and attribute assignments (DELAY, ASSIGN, COUNT, TALLY)
TRANSFER		Models transfers between stations via material-handling systems (ROUTE, CONVEY)
HOLD		Models situations in which entity movement is delayed by system status, such as waiting for busy resources (SEIZE, PREEMPT, WAIT)
QUEUE		Provides waiting space for entities delayed in movement
STATION		Defines physical locations in the model, as are used in material-handling systems
BRANCH		Models branching in the flow of entities in the model
PICKQ		Selects a QUEUE block from a set of following QUEUE blocks for an entity to join
SELECT		Selects a resource from a set of following OPERATION blocks for an entity to occupy
QPICK		Selects a QUEUE block from a set of preceding QUEUE blocks from which to remove an entity
MATCH		Delays entities in a set of preceding QUEUE blocks until entities with the same value of a specified attribute reside in each QUEUE

complex automated material-handling systems, such as automated guided vehicle systems and automated storage/retrieval systems.

The use of SIMAN blocks provides a convenient and efficient way to model complex systems, since there is a high degree of isomorphism between the blocks and the system components. Also, as can be seen from Table 2.1, the unique shape of the block for each function improves the understanding of the model derived from the block diagram.

2.3   SIMAN Experimental Frame and Output Analysis Elements

The block diagram, or model frame, describes the structure and dynamics of model operation, but leaves unspecified many specific quantities necessary to conduct experiments using the model. Detailed analysis and display of results are also left unspecified in the model frame. These two sets of tasks are treated by the experimental frame and output analysis elements, respectively. Although both of these topics are covered in later sections of the primer, it is deemed insightful to provide brief examples here.

Some elements of the experimental frame are associated with specific blocks, others pervade the definition of the entire model. In general, the experimental frame expressly defines items such as the model's physical dimensions, dynamic behavior, statistics collection, length of runs, and initial conditions. For example, the experimental frame element, DISCRETE, defines limits such as the maximum number of entities and the maximum number of queueing facilities in the model. The element RESOURCES specifies the capacity of resources. The element PARAMETERS is primarily used to define parameters associated with probability distributions, but also provides a convenient way to enter large arrays of data. This element is often used to determine arrival patterns, or processing times for entities. TALLIES collects statistics such as the mean, standard deviation, maximum value, and minimum value on a designated output variable. REPLICATE defines values such as the number of runs to conduct, the maximum length of the run, and the initial conditions for the run. The elements of the experimental frame are discussed in detail in conjunction with the blocks described in Sections 3.0 through 6.0.

The output analysis element may be included in the experimental frame either separately or as part of another experimental frame element. The effect of either approach is to cause data on a variable of interest to be collected and stored for subsequent analysis, while the simulation model is running. Once the output files have been created, they serve as input for the several output analysis and display elements of the output processor. Many different analyses may be performed using the same output file.

The following are representative of the output analysis elements which are discussed fully in Section 7.0. The element PLOT generates a graph of one or more variables plotted against time. HISTOGRAM creates a frequency distribution graph for a specified variable. To set confidence intervals on a variable, use the element INTERVAL.

2.4   An Example SIMAN Model

In this section we present a SIMAN model of a simple system intended to provide the flavor of the language. The use of some of the SIMAN blocks and experimental frame elements will be immediately obvious. That which is not, will become clear after reading Section 3.0, Basic Modeling Concepts.

FIGURE 2.2   EXAMPLE PROBLEM

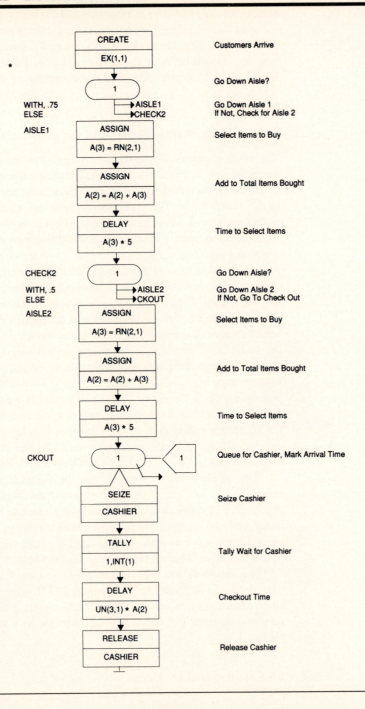

Example Problem The system modeled is a small grocery store consisting of two aisles and a cashier. The customer arrival pattern is described by an exponential probability distribution. Once inside the store, customers may choose to shop in one, two, or none of the aisles. The probability of shopping aisle one is 0.75, and of shopping aisle two is 0.5. The number of items selected in each aisle is described by a normal distribution, and the time that these careful shoppers require to select an item is 5 minutes. When all desired items have been selected, customers queue up at the cashier to pay for them. The time to check out is a uniformly distributed random variable which depends on the number of items purchased. The model provides statistics on the waiting time of customers and the utilization of the cashier.

The SIMAN flow chart for this model appears in Fig. 2.2. The model and experimental frames are shown in Figs. 2.3 and 2.4, respectively.

FIGURE 2.3   MODEL FRAME

```
BEGIN;
;SMALL GROCERY STORE
        CREATE:EX(1,1);                   CUSTOMERS ARRIVE
        BRANCH,1:
          WITH,.75,AISLE1:                !GO DOWN AISLE 1?
          ELSE,CHECK2;                    IF NOT, CHECK FOR AISLE 2
AISLE1  ASSIGN:A(3)=RN(2,1);              SELECT ITEMS TO BUY
        ASSIGN:A(2)=A(2)+A(3);            ADD TO TOTAL ITEMS BOUGHT
        DELAY:A(3)*5;                     TIME TO SELECT ITEMS
CHECK2          BRANCH,1:
          WITH,.5,AISLE2:                 !GO DOWN AISLE 2?
          ELSE,CKOUT;                     IF NOT, GO TO CHECK OUT
AISLE2  ASSIGN:A(3)=RN(2,1);              SELECT ITEMS TO BUY
        ASSIGN:A(2)=A(2)+A(3);            ADD TO TOTAL ITEMS BOUGHT
        DELAY:A(3)*5;                     TIME TO SELECT ITEMS
CKOUT   QUEUE,1:MARK(1);                  QUEUE FOR CASHIER,
;                                         NOTE ARRIVAL TIME
        SEIZE:CASHIER;                    CAPTURE CASHIER
        TALLY:1,INT(1);                   TALLY WAIT FOR CASHIER
        DELAY:UN(3,1)*A(2);               CHECKOUT TIME
        RELEASE:CASHIER:DISPOSE;          RELEASE CASHIER, LEAVE
END;
```

FIGURE 2.4   EXPERIMENTAL FRAME

```
BEGIN;
PROJECT,SMALL GROC STORE,PERRY,3/16/85;
DISCRETE,50,3,1;                  DEFINE MODEL SIZE
RESOURCES:1,CASHIER;              DEFINE RESOURCE CAPACITY
PARAMETERS:1,18:                  !DEFINE INTERARRIVAL TIME (MIN)
         2,15,5:                  !DEFINE NO. ITEMS SELECTED
         3,.1,1.1;                DEFINE CHECKOUT TIME PER ITEM
DSTAT:1,NR(1),CASHIER UTIL;       CASHIER UTILIZATION
TALLIES:1,WAIT FOR CASHIER;       TIME WAITING FOR CASHIER
REPLICATE,1,0,480;                RUN LENGTH= 8 HOURS
END;
```

TABLE 2.2
SIMAN ATTRIBUTES AND VARIABLES

Attributes

A(N)*	Real valued attribute N of an entity
M	Attribute of an entity denoting current station number
NS	Number of the sequence set defined by the SEQUENCES element that an entity is following
IS**	Index indicating how far into the sequence an entity has progressed

User-Assignable Variables

X(N)	Real valued global system variable N
J	Integer system index variable
P(IP,IS)**	The value of parameter number IS in parameter set IP
VT(N)	Velocity of transporter N
VC(N)	Velocity of conveyor N

SIMAN System Variables

TNOW	Current time in simulation run
NE(N)	Number of entities enroute to station N
NQ(N)	Number of entities residing in QUEUE N
NC(N)	Current value of COUNT N
NR(N)	Number of busy units of resource N
MR(N)	Number of units of capacity of resource N
NT(N)	Number of busy units of transporter N
LC(N)	Length of occupied cells on conveyor N
MT(N)	Number of units of capacity of transporter N
IT(N,NU)*	The status of unit NU of transporter N
LT(N,NU)	The current station location or destination of unit NU of transporter N

* N or NU denotes A(I), X(I), or I, where the subindex I can be M±K, or J±K, or K, where K is an integer.
** IP and IS denote A(K) or K, where K is an integer.

2.5 SIMAN Block Diagrams and Model Definition

2.5.1 Entities, Attributes, and Variables As mentioned earlier, the world view of SIMAN is that of entities flowing through a block diagram. The functions performed by the individual blocks contribute much to the definition of the model structure and dynamics. To make the model definition more explicit, attributes, and variables are used. Table 2.2 presents a complete list of attributes and variables used in SIMAN block models.

Attributes refer to characteristics of a specific entity, for example, the type of job in a shop, or the class of a patient in a clinic. They take the form of a one-dimensional

TABLE 2.2
SIMAN ATTRIBUTES AND VARIABLES (Cont'd)

SIMAN Random
Variables

Each of the following probability distributions are defined using parameter set IP and random-number stream IS**.

BE(IP,IS)*	Beta
CP(IP,IS)	Continuous (user-defined)
DP(IP,IS)	Discrete (user-defined)
ER(IP,IS)	Erlang
EX(IP,IS)	Exponential
GA(IP,IS)	Gamma
NP(IP,IS)	Poisson
RL(IP,IS)	Lognormal
RN(IP,IS)	Normal
TR(IP,IS)	Triangular
UN(IP,IS)	Uniform
WE(IP,IS)	Weibull
RA(IS)	Uniform distribution over the interval $0-1$
CO(IP)	Constant
ED(N)**	Experimental distribution, assigned in experimental frame

Table Lookup
Variable

TF(N,VAR)	A real value from table number N, corresponding to the value of the independent variable given by VAR. The independent may be any SIMAN variable listed above.

* IP and IS denote A(K) or K, where K is an integer.
** N denotes A(I), X(I), or I, where the subindex I can be $M\pm K$, or $J\pm K$, or K, where K is an integer.

array, designated A(N). In addition to these general purpose attributes, each entity has an attribute called station number, M, which refers to a specific physical location, and is most useful in modeling material-handling systems.

In contrast to attributes, variables refer to characteristics of the system that are global, and are not related to any specific entity. SIMAN defines three types of variables: user-assigned variables, SIMAN system variables, and SIMAN random variables. The user-assigned variables of interest in defining block diagram models are: X(N), an array of real-valued variables; J, an integer system index variable useful for indirect referencing; and P(IP,IS), sets of real-valued parameters where IS and IP are used to refer to the ISth parameter in the IPth set.

The subscripts used in the arrays above and also in those of the following paragraphs, must be integers, but they may reflect the values of the station number attribute, M, or the system index variable, J, or an attribute, A(I), as explained in Table 2.2.

SIMAN system variables describe the current state of the system. They include TNOW, the current time in the run; NQ(I), the number of entities currently in queue I;

and NR(I), the number of occupied units of resource I. Table 2.2 contains a complete list of SIMAN system variables.

SIMAN random variables provide many of the common probability distributions used to describe arrival patterns or processing delays. These include the uniform UN(IP,IS), exponential EX(IP,IS), gamma GA(IP,IS), and normal RN(IP,IS). In addition, a user-defined discrete probability distribution, DP(IP,IS), is permitted; and the assignment of one of SIMAN's probability distributions in the experimental frame using ED(N) is possible. This latter capability allows the use of varied probability distributions without changing the model. See Table 2.2 for a complete list of distributions.

In the designation of a probability distribution, IP and IS are integers that refer to a parameter set number and a random-number stream, respectively. Either of these indexes may be set equal to A(I). Particular values for the indicated parameter set and the random number stream are provided in the experimental frame. SIMAN offers 10 separate streams of random numbers.

2.5.2 Model Frame Format   To define a SIMAN model one must define each block in the block diagram in terms of function, and in terms of the operands that quantify that function. For example, the CREATE block, which introduces entities into the model, has the form:

CREATE,NB,TF:TBC,MC:MARK(2);

The operands for this block are: NB, the number of entities in an arriving batch; TF, the time from the beginning of the simulation run at which the create block is activated (usually time zero); TBC, the time between batches of arrivals; MC, the maximum number of batches to be created by that block; and MARK(2), which indicates that A(2) will be marked with the arrival time of the entity. The types of operands which may be used in block definition statements will be described after statement syntax is explained.

The syntax of block definition statements can be explained by considering the following general form:

LABEL BLOCKNAME,OP(1,1)..OP(1,N):...:OP(M,1)..OP(M,N):MODIFIERS;

The optional LABEL or name is used for reference by other blocks, in branching, for example. It must begin with an alphabetic character and not exceed eight characters in length. The BLOCKNAME is one of the SIMAN blocks. It is separated from the operands by a comma (,) or colon (:). The operands are divided into groups: group 1: OP(1,1)...OP(1,N); group 2 OP(2,1)...OP(2,N); ... group M: OP(M,1)...OP(M,N). A block need not have an operand in each group, and need not have equal numbers in each group. The groups are separated by a colon (:), and each operand within a group is separated by a comma (,). Some operands are optional or have default values.

MODIFIERS are used optionally with blocks to alter the way in which they function. They are separated from the last operand group by a colon (:), and from each other by commas (,). Some modifiers are block-specific, but most may be used with all blocks. The modifiers DISPOSE, MARK(MA), and NEXT(LABEL) are common to all blocks. The DISPOSE modifier indicates that entities leaving that block will be destroyed. MARK(MA) is used to mark the time an entity passed through a block. MA is the attribute number used to save the information. NEXT(LABEL) is used to transfer unconditionally to the block named LABEL. Whether modifiers are present or not, the block definition statement must end with a semicolon (;).

The specific format requirements for the block definition statements in the model frame are as follows. The block Label is placed in columns 1 through 8; the blockname, operand groups, and modifier begin in column 10, or later, and are separated as described above. All blanks within a statement are ignored except for embedded blanks in label or name fields. The statement must end with a semicolon (;), after which comments not to be processed by SIMAN may be included. Comments may be embedded in a statement by preceding them with an exclamation point (!). If an entire line in the model frame is to be a comment, it must begin with a semicolon (;).

Each block definition statement is restricted to columns 1 through 74, and in addition, an operand may not be split between two lines. However, operand groups may be placed on separate lines, each line ending with a colon (:), and the last line of the statement ending with a semicolon (;). Indeed, such an arrangement may enhance the clarity of the program.

The following examples illustrate the application of these conventions.

COL. 1–8	COL. 10–74	
LABEL	**BLOCKNAME,OPERANDS:MODIFIERS;**	**COMMENTS**
	CREATE:2,100:MARK(1);	GENERATE ENTITIES
DRILL	DELAY:EX(1,1);	DRILL HOLE
;THIS IS A COMMENT LINE		
	CREATE,5:14,12:	!CREATE TYPE ONE JOBS
	MARK(2);	MARK ARRIVAL TIME

The first statement introduces entities into the model every two time units in batches of 1, up to a maximum of 100 batches, and marks their arrival time in A(1). The second statement defines a processing delay at a block DRILL; the third is a comment; and the fourth is simply another CREATE block using a two-line entry format.

Turning now to the types of operands that may be used in block definition statements, Table 2.3 lists the eight allowable types. Although all operand fields require one of these eight operand types, three specific substitutions are permitted: an integer constant may be substituted for a real constant; an integer or a real constant may be substituted for a variable; and an integer or real constant, or a variable, may be substituted for an expression.

Some of the operand types require further elaboration. Keyword refers to allowable entries for modifiers. Expression and condition operand types involve SIMAN attributes and variables. In evaluating these, the following operator priorities are used:

FIRST   Evaluation within parentheses (innermost first)

SECOND   Arithmetic operators in the following order:
  a) exponentiation (**)
  b) multiplication and division (*,/)
  c) addition and subtraction (+,−)

THIRD   Relational operators (.EQ.,.LE.,.GE.,.LT.,.GT.,.NE.)

FOURTH   Logical operators
  a) .AND.
  b) .OR.

TABLE 2.3
BLOCK OPERAND TYPES

Operand Type	Description	Examples
Integer constant	A whole number	34 or −1
Real constant	A rational real number with decimal point (F or E type format in FORTRAN)	6.78 or 2.3E+1
Label or string	Alphanumeric string of characters, beginning with an alphabetic character	LOOP (block label) or MACHINE (resource name)
Keyword	Alphabetic string having a specific meaning in SIMAN	DISPOSE or MARK
Variable or attribute	SIMAN variable or attribute from Table 2.2	NQ(2), X(3) or A(1)
Expression	Arithmetic expression computed from SIMAN variables using the operators: +,−,*,/, and **, and parentheses	A(1)*X(3)+6.5
Condition	Logical statement evaluated using SIMAN expressions and the operators .OR.,.AND.,.EQ..,.LE., .GE.,.LT.,.GT.,and .NE. with grouping by parentheses	(A(1)+X(4)) .GT.6
Built-in functions	Common functions useful to define entity characteristics or routing	SQRT(A(I))

Most common functions:*

SQRT(a)	Square root of a
ABS(a)	Absolute value of a
AINT(a)	Round a to nearest integer
MOD(a_1,a_2)	Integer remainder when a_1 is divided by a_2 (real arguments truncated before division)
AMOD(a_1,a_2)	Real remainder when a_1 is divided by a_2
MX(a_1,a_2,...)	Maximum value of a_1, a_2,...
MN(a_1,a_2,...)	Minimum value of a_1, a_2,...

where a,a_1,a_2, are function arguments

* See (Pegden, 1986) for the complete set.

In forming expressions, no two operators may appear in succession, but must be separated by parentheses, as in FORTRAN. For example, A(1)/–3 becomes A(1)/(–3).

A set of built-in functions is provided in SIMAN to assist in defining the characteristics and routing of entities. Many of the common FORTRAN functions are included and referenced by the same name, for example, SQRT, MOD, and ABS. Function arguments may be any valid SIMAN expression, possibly involving other built-in functions. Some of the more common built-in functions and their arguments appear in Table 2.3.

2.5.3 Experimental Frame Format   As noted previously, the elements of the experimental frame make the model defined in the model frame more explicit, and quantify all aspects of it. The syntax for experimental frame elements is similar to that for the model frame. The general form of an experimental element definition statement is:

ELEMENTNAME,1,OP(1,1)..OP(1,N):...:M,OP(M,1)..OP(M,N);

The ELEMENTNAME must be one of the experimental frame elements defined by SIMAN. The operands are separated from ELEMENTNAME by a comma (,) or colon (:). Operands are divided into groups, each group being separated from the next by a colon (:), and operands within groups being separated by commas (,). When optional operands are omitted, commas are required to separate missing operands within a group. With very few exceptions, the first entry of each operand group is a sequential indexing integer, which may have a particular use for a given element, or may just serve to number repeating groups of operands. The statement must end with a semicolon (;), after which, comments not to be processed by SIMAN may be included. A comment may be embedded in a statement by preceding it with an explanation point (!).

A statement may be placed on more than one line, provided each line terminates with a colon (:), or in the case of the last operand group, a semicolon (;). Readability of the overall program may indeed be improved by doing this. The types of operands allowed depend on the particular experimental frame element, but, in general, operands tend to be string, integer constants, or real constants.

The specific format requirements are as follows. An experimental element definition statement must be placed in columns 1 through 74. All blanks except those embedded in user-provided names are ignored, and thus may be used to improve readability. Finally, within a given experiment, each experimental element may be entered at most once.

The following examples illustrate these rules.

COL. 1–74

ELEMENTNAME,OPERANDS:MODIFIERS;	COMMENTS

PROJECT, HEALTH CLINIC MODEL, S. JONES, OCT 1983;
RESOURCES:
    1,DRILL,3:   !DRILL CAPACITY
    2,LATHE,4;   LATHE CAPACITY
  PARAMETERS:
    1, .1,2, .2,3, .8,4 1.0,5;

The first statement is used to assign a title to the model output report, the second defines capacities for two resources, and the third defines the cumulative distribution function for a discrete probability distribution with a random variable taking values of 2, 3, 4, or 5.

3.0   BASIC MODELING CONCEPTS

In this section we cover a group of SIMAN blocks and experimental frame elements sufficient to construct and execute some simple SIMAN models. Section 3.1 defines the blocks, and Section 3.2 the associated experimental frame elements. Section 3.3 describes some general experimental frame elements required for the execution of any model, and Section 3.4 covers the procedure for linking and running SIMAN models. We then include these constructs in some illustrative problems in Section 3.5.

3.1   A Fundamental Set of SIMAN Blocks

CREATE   This block is an operation block which introduces entities into the model. The CREATE block has the form:

CREATE,NB,TF:TBC,MC:MODIFIERS;

The block diagram symbol used for the CREATE block is:

Its operands are defined as follows:

OPERAND	OPERAND GROUP	DESCRIPTION	ALLOWABLE VALUES	DEFAULT
NB	1	Number of entities in each batch	X(N)* or integer constant	1
TF	1	Offset time for activation of CREATE block	X(N), real constant, or random variable	0.0
TBC	2	Time between entity batch creations	expression	Infinite
MC	2	Maximum number of batches to be created	X(N) or integer constant	Infinite

* N denotes A(I), X(I), or I, where the subindex I can be M±K, J±K, or K, where K is an integer.

The MC operand may be used to control the model run length. After the CREATE block stops generating arrivals, SIMAN processes those currently in the system and terminates the run. If the MC operand is omitted, the CREATE block will continue to introduce entities into the model without limit, and thus some other means of terminating the model run must be used. Other methods for terminating the run are discussed in the following sections.

Some examples of CREATE blocks follow.

CREATE:EX(1,1);
CREATE,4,10:DP(2,1),100;
CREATE:UN(3,2):MARK(2);

The first statement generates arrivals in batches of size 1 according to an exponential distribution defined by parameter set 1, and using random number stream 1. The second, creates a maximum of 100 batches of entities with a batch size of 4, according to a user-defined discrete probability distribution specified by parameter set 2 and random-number stream 1. However, this block does not begin creating entities until time 10. The third block generates arrivals from a uniform distribution defined by parameter set 3 and random-number stream 2, and marks their arrival time in A(2). Parameter sets are defined in the experimental frame as described in Section 3.2.

ASSIGN   This block is an operation block which assigns specific values to attributes or variables.

The ASSIGN block has the form:

ASSIGN:VAR = VALUE:MODIFIERS;

The block diagram symbol for the ASSIGN block is:

ASSIGN
VAR=VALUE

Its operands are defined as:

OPERAND	OPERAND GROUP	DESCRIPTION	ALLOWABLE VALUES	DEFAULT
VAR	2	Attributes or variables	A(N),X(N), P(IP,IS),J M, VC(N), VT(N), NS, or IS*	None
VALUE	2	Expression to be assigned to attribute or variable	Expression	None

* N denotes A(I), X(I), or I, where the subindex I can be M±K, J±K, or K, and IP and IS denote A(K) or K where K is an integer.

Examples of the ASSIGN block are:

ASSIGN:A(1) = 3:NEXT(TYPE1);
ASSIGN:X(1) = EX(3,1)/2;
ASSIGN:A(1) = CP(A(2),2);

The first block assigns the integer constant 3 to A(1) and sends the entity to a block labeled TYPE1; and the second assigns the value obtained by dividing an exponential variate (defined by parameter set 3 and random number stream 1) by 2 to X(1). In the final block, the value of a random variable from a continuous probability distribution (defined by parameter set A(2) and random number stream 2) is assigned to A(1). Notice that there is a second level of indirect reference used to define the probability distribution.

DELAY   The DELAY block is an operation block that models the processing of entities as an expression involving SIMAN variables. By using SIMAN random variables, one can introduce probabilistic delay into the model. The DELAY block defines a definite delay, as opposed to an indefinite delay, which is terminated by some particular event. The indefinite delay is discussed in Section 4.0.

The DELAY block takes the form:

DELAY:DURATION:MODIFIERS;

The block diagram symbol for the DELAY block is:

```
┌──────────┐
│  DELAY   │
├──────────┤
│ DURATION │
└──────────┘
```

Its single operand is:

OPERAND	OPERAND GROUP	DESCRIPTION	ALLOWABLE VALUES	DEFAULT
DURATION	2	The length of the delay	Expression	0.0

Examples of valid DELAY blocks are:

DELAY:EX(2,1);
DELAY:3.*DP(1,2);

The first block defines an exponential delay, where the probability distribution is described by parameter set 2 and random number stream 1. The delay in the second block is determined by the product of the real constant 3, and a user-defined probability distribution described by parameter set 1, and random number stream 2.

QUEUE   As entities move through a model they will encounter delays resulting from the status of the system: for example, a busy machine. To process entities in an orderly fashion, SIMAN uses a QUEUE block.

The QUEUE block has the following form:

QUEUE,IFL,QC,LBALK:MODIFIERS;

The block diagram symbol for QUEUE is:

```
   ╭──────────╮
  (   IFL,QC   )
   ╰─────╲────╯
          ╲──→ LBALK
```

Its operands are:

OPERAND	OPERAND GROUP	DESCRIPTION	ALLOWABLE VALUES	DEFAULT
IFL	1	File (queue) number	K, M±K	None
QC	1	Capacity of the queue	A(N),X(N) or N*	Infinite
LBALK	1	Label of block where balking entities are routed	Label	Destroy the entity

* N denotes A(I), X(I), or I, where the subindex I can be M±K, J±K, or K, where K is an integer.

The associated experimental frame element is RANKINGS, which is used to assign a queue discipline. The associated SIMAN system variable is NQ(I), the current number of entities in the QUEUE.

The operand IFL denotes a reference file number for the queue, and QC the capacity of the queue. If the QUEUE is full when an entity attempts to enter it, the entity is either destroyed or routed to the block labeled LBALK. The queue discipline is assumed to be FIFO (first-in-first-out) unless defined to be otherwise by the RANKINGS element of the experimental frame.

The QUEUE block has a modifier unique to it: DETACH. The function of DETACH is to disassociate a QUEUE block from its immediate successor block. One application of DETACH allows entities to be selected from one of several queues for processing, another permits entities to wait indefinitely until explicitly released from the QUEUE by an event occurring somewhere else in the system. This is in contrast to waiting for available units of capacity of a resource associated with a particular QUEUE. The use of the DETACH modifier is discussed in detail in Section 4.1.

Valid QUEUE block examples include:

```
QUEUE,1,3,QUIT;
QUEUE,1;
QUEUE,1,X(2),BALK:DETACH
```

The first block queues entities in QUEUE 1, which has a capacity of 3. If the queue cannot accommodate an arriving entity, it is routed to a block labeled QUIT. The second QUEUE block is labeled 1, and has infinite capacity. In the third statement, QUEUE 1 has a capacity defined by the value of $X(2)$, and routes entities to a block named BALK when the queue is full. Also, QUEUE 1 is associated with an indefinite delay, since the DETACH modifier is present.

SEIZE This block is a hold block which captures a stated number of units of capacity from a resource, such as machine or server. When an entity arrives at a QUEUE-SEIZE block combination, it attempts to seize the required number of units of capacity. If it cannot, it waits in the QUEUE block until the units become available.

The SEIZE block has the form:

```
SEIZE,PR:RNAME,NR:MODIFIERS;
```

The block diagram symbol for the SEIZE block is:

Its operands are defined as follows:

OPERAND	OPERAND GROUP	DESCRIPTION	ALLOWABLE VALUES	DEFAULT
PR	1	Integer priority number	A(N), X(N), or N*	1
RNAME	2	Name of resource to be seized	String	None
NR	2	Integer number of resource units to be seized	A(N), X(N), or N	1

* N denotes A(I), X(I), or I, where the subindex I can be M±K, J±K, or K, where K is an integer.

The associated experimental frame element for the SEIZE block is RESOURCES, and the associated SIMAN system variables are NR(I), the number of busy units of resource I, and MR(I), the capacity of resource I.

The PR operand deals with entities in QUEUE blocks waiting for the same resource at more than one SEIZE block. When resource units become available, they are allocated based on the PR priority, with preference being given to low values of priority.

RNAME may be either a simple name or an indexed name. In the latter case the resource name looks much a FORTRAN array: for example, MACHINE(1) and MACHINE(2) are two different machines, possibly with different capacities. The index may be expressed as an integer constant or as M±K, or J±K, where K is an integer. The use of indexed resources is illustrated in Section 5.0. NR defines the number of resource units occupied by the entity entering the SEIZE block. The capacity of a resource is defined in the experimental frame, as described in Section 3.2.

Valid examples of SEIZE blocks are:

```
SEIZE:WORKER;
SEIZE,1:MACHINE(M),2;
SEIZE,2:SERVER,1:DISPOSE;
```

The first statement defines a block wherein entities attempt to seize a resource named WORKER. The priority and required resource units assume the default values of 1. In the second block, entities attempt to seize two units of the resource MACHINE(M) with a priority of 1, where M is the station number attribute. In the last block, entities attempt to seize one unit of SERVER with a priority of 2. Entities leaving this block are destroyed.

Whenever a block can create a queue, it must be preceded by at least one QUEUE block. Since blocks of a hold type, such as the SEIZE block, create queues in SIMAN, these blocks must always be preceded by at least one QUEUE block. The modeling of several queues of entities, and hence several QUEUE blocks, competing for the same resource is accomplished using the QPICK block discussed in Section 4.1.

Examples of QUEUE-SEIZE pairings are:

QUEUE,1;
SEIZE:MACHINE;

QUEUE,1,3,QUIT;
SEIZE,A(2):CONVEYOR,2;

The first pair of blocks models entities waiting in QUEUE 1, which has infinite capacity, for a single unit of capacity of the resource MACHINE. In the second case, entities wait in QUEUE 1, which has a capacity of 3, for two units of a resource named CON-VEYOR. When there is competition for CONVEYOR, entities attempting to seize it using this SEIZE block have a priority indicated by A(2). Entities finding the queue full, are routed to a block named QUIT.

The block diagrams for these QUEUE-SEIZE pairings are as follows:

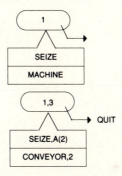

RELEASE The RELEASE block is an operation block which returns a specified number of units of capacity to the available state.

RELEASE has the form:

RELEASE:RNAME,NR:MODIFIERS;

The block diagram symbol for RELEASE is:

| RELEASE |
| RNAME,NR |

Its operands are:

OPERAND	OPERAND GROUP	DESCRIPTION	ALLOWABLE VALUES	DEFAULT
RNAME	2	Name of resource to be released	String	None
NR	2	Integer number of resource units to be released	A(N), X(N), or N*	1

* N denotes A(I), X(I), or I, where the subindex I can be M±K, J±K, or K, where K is an integer.

Two examples of the RELEASE block are:

RELEASE:MACHINE,3;
RELEASE:CASHIER,X(2);

The first block releases 3 units of capacity of the resource MACHINE, and the second releases X(2) units of capacity of the resource CASHIER.

QUEUE-SEIZE-DELAY-RELEASE   This sequence of blocks is a very common one, used to model entities waiting for a resource, capturing it, using the resource, and then leaving it. The following group of blocks represents such a sequence with customers in a bank waiting for a teller.

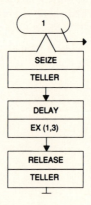

The corresponding SIMAN statements are:

QUEUE,1;

SEIZE:TELLER;

DELAY:EX(1,3);

RELEASE:TELLER:DISPOSE;

Customers wait in QUEUE 1, which has unlimited capacity (a questionable assumption), until the resource TELLER has a single unit of capacity available. Processing time by the teller is exponentially distributed as defined by parameter set 1, and random-number stream 3. When processing is finished, the customer relinquishes one unit of TELLER capacity and the customer entity is destroyed. If TELLER is defined to have a capacity greater than one in the experimental frame, this block sequence would represent a bank with a single waiting line and several identical tellers.

BRANCH   This block is one of several SIMAN blocks that can be used to direct entities to blocks other than the next sequential block in the model. In the BRANCH block, copies of the entering entity are created and transferred to other blocks in the model; the original entity becomes the primary entity while the copies are secondary entities. The primary and secondary entities are identical, having the same attribute values and station value. But, only the primary entity is assigned the resources of the original entity.

The format of the BRANCH block is:

BRANCH,MAXTAKE:CRITERION,LABEL:Repeats through group M:

The block diagram symbol for the BRANCH block is:

Its operands are:

OPERAND	OPERAND GROUP	DESCRIPTION	ALLOWABLE VALUES	DEFAULT
MAXTAKE	1	The maximum number of copies that will be branched	Integer	Infinite
CRITERION	2-M	The condition or probability that determines branch selection (C = condition, and P = probability)	IF, C; WITH, P; ALWAYS; or ELSE	None
LABEL	2-M	The label of the block to which the entity copy is routed	String	None

The CRITERION,LABEL operands may be repeated as many times as necessary.

Up to MAXTAKE copies of the original entity will be made, and branched to blocks in the model. The branching criteria are evaluated in the order listed and if none of the criteria are met, no copies of the entity will be made. Once MAXTAKE copies are made, no further criteria will be evaluated and the simulation continues.

When the IF, C criterion is selected, the logical expression is evaluated, and if the expression is true the branch is taken. When WITH, P is used, the branch will be taken with probability P. The probability of taking the branch, P, may be a constant, or an expression, but must be between 0 and 1.0. Also, the sum of the probabilities for all WITH, P branches must not exceed 1.0.

A deterministic branch is denoted by ELSE or ALWAYS, and the branch will be taken if the number of branches previously selected is less than MAXTAKE. If the Kth branch is deterministic and K is equal to or less than MAXTAKE, then ALWAYS should be used; if K exceeds MAXTAKE, then ELSE should be used.

Examples of the BRANCH block are:

```
BRANCH,1:
    IF,A(1).LT.5,LINE1:
    IF,A(2).LT.5,LINE2;

BRANCH,2:
    WITH,0.500,OPER1:
    WITH,A(2),OPER2:
    ELSE,OPER3;

BRANCH,2:
    ALWAYS,STAT1:
    ALWAYS,STAT2;
```

In the first example, the original entity will be sent to block LINE1 if attribute A(1) is less than 5, or to block LINE2 if A(2) is less than 5, or be destroyed if neither statement is true. In the second example, up to two copies of the original entity will be made and sent independently to blocks OPER1 and OPER2 with probabilities of .500 and A(2), respectively. If fewer than two copies are branched to OPER1 and OPER2, then a copy will be branched to OPER3. In the third example, two copies of the original entity will be branched to blocks STAT1 and STAT2. The entity branched to STAT1 is the primary entity.

TALLY   This block is an operation block that records the value of a specified variable at each entity arrival to the block. The TALLY block computes the mean, standard deviation, minimum and maximum values of the specified variable and displays them in the SIMAN Summary Report.
The TALLY block has the form:

TALLY:N,VAR:MODIFIERS;

The block diagram symbol for TALLY is:

TALLY
N,VAR

Its operands are:

OPERAND	OPERAND GROUP	DESCRIPTION	ALLOWABLE VALUES	DEFAULT
N	2	Identifying tally number	A(N),X(N), or N*	None
VAR	2	Value to be tallied	Expression or INT(K) or BET(K)	None

* N denotes A(I), X(I), or I, where the subindex I can be M±K, J±K, or K, where K is an integer.

The associated experimental frame element is TALLIES.
The operand N identifies the TALLY for the output report, and VAR specifies the variable or expression to be tallied. The operands INT(K) and BET(K) permit statistics to be collected on the time to travel between particular points in the model, or on interarrival times. The INT(K) tallies the interval TNOW−A(K), where A(K) contains the arrival time at some preceding block, placed there using the MARK modifier. Thus, INT(K) records the time for an entity to move between two specified blocks in the model. The BET(K) tallies the interval TNOW−X(K), where X(K) is automatically maintained as the time of the last arrival to the TALLY block. So in this case, BET(K) provides the time between successive arrivals at the TALLY block.
Some examples of TALLY blocks are:

TALLY:1,INT(1);
TALLY:A(1),BET(2);
TALLY:2,A(1)+A(2);

The first block tallies the time for an entity to move from a block where the time was noted in A(1) using the MARK modifier, to the TALLY block. The second block records the time between arrivals to the TALLY block using X(2) to maintain the time of the last arrival to the TALLY block. This tally is identified with the value contained in A(1). In the last statement, the sum of the attributes A(1) and A(2) are recorded in tally number 2.

COUNT   The COUNT block is an operation block that increments a counter by a specified amount at each entity arrival.
The form of the COUNT block is:

COUNT:N,INC:MODIFIERS;

The block diagram symbol for the COUNT block is:

The operands are:

OPERAND	OPERAND GROUP	DESCRIPTION	ALLOWABLE VALUES	DEFAULT
N	2	Identifying counter number	A(N),X(N), or N*	None
INC	2	Counter increment	A(N),X(N), or N*	1

* N denotes A(I), X(I), or I, where the subindex I can be M±K, J±K, or K, where K is an integer.

The associated experimental frame element is COUNTERS, and the associated SIMAN system variable is NC(I), the current value of the counter.
The operand N identifies the COUNTER for the output report, and INC is the amount by which the counter is incremented each time an entity enters the block. Each time the counter is incremented, it is compared to a count limit for counter N, which is defined in the experimental frame. If the current value of counter N exceeds the limit, the simulation run is ended and the output report is displayed. This is a second way to terminate the simulation run, in addition to limiting the creation of entities which was discussed previously.
Valid examples of the COUNT block are:

COUNT:1,1;
COUNT:A(1),2;

In the first statement, counter number 1 is incremented by 1 every time an entity moves into the block. The second block increments counter number A(1) by 2 for each entering entity.

3.2   Associated Experimental Frame Elements

We now discuss the experimental frame elements associated with the SIMAN blocks described in the previous section. The experimental frame elements underpin and make more specific the block diagram of the model frame, but have no logic flow relationship as do the SIMAN blocks. Consequently, they only appear in the experimental frame as statements, and have no block diagram symbols.

PARAMETERS   The PARAMETERS element defines the parameters associated with SIMAN random variables, and is also used to make arrays of data accessible to a model.
The PARAMETERS element has the form:

PARAMETERS:N,P(N,1),..P(N,J):..Repeats through group M;

Its operands are defined as follows:

OPERAND	OPERAND GROUP	DESCRIPTION	ALLOWABLE VALUES	DEFAULT
N	2-M	Parameter set number	Integer constant	None
P(N,J)*	2-M	Value of the Jth parameter in the Nth set	Real constant	None

*N, J denote A(K), or K, where K is an integer.

When used to define a probability distribution, the number of parameters required and their meaning depends on the specific distribution. Table 3.1 shows the assignment of parameters for SIMAN probability distributions. In the case of continuous probability distributions, linear interpolation is used to obtain the probability for values of the random variable which lie between two specified values.

TABLE 3.1
PARAMETER ASSIGNMENTS FOR RANDOM VARIABLES

Distribution (SIMAN Name)	P(1)	P(2)	P(3)
Beta(BE)	Alpha	Beta	
Constant(CO)	Constant value		
Empirical discrete(DP)	P(K), K = 1,3,5,...	Associated cumulative probability	
Empirical continuous(CP)	P(K), K = 2,4,6,...	Values of the random variable	
Erlang(ER)	Exponential mean	K	
Exponential(EX)	Mean		
Gamma(GA)	Beta	Alpha	
Lognormal(RL)	Mean	Standard deviation	
Normal(RN)	Mean	Standard deviation	
Poisson(NP)	Mean		
Triangular(TR)	Minimum	Mode	Maximum
Uniform(UN,RA)	Minimum	Maximum	
Weibull(WE)	Beta	Alpha	

The following examples illustrate the use of the PARAMETERS element.

PARAMETERS:1,3.0:
          2,.2,1, .5,2, 1.0,3;

Parameter set 1 could represent the mean of an exponential, or Poisson probability distribution. Parameter set 2 is a user-defined probability distribution in which the value of the random variable is specified in parameters 2, 4, and 6, and the cumulative probability in parameters 1, 3, and 5.

RANKINGS   The RANKINGS element is used to assign a queue discipline, or ranking rule, other than FIFO. The allowable ranking rules for ordering entities in a queue file are shown in Table 3.2.

The RANKINGS element has the form:

RANKINGS:N,MRANK:..Repeats through group M;

Its operands are defined as:

OPERAND	OPERAND GROUP	DESCRIPTION	ALLOWABLE VALUES	DEFAULT
N	2-M	Queue number or range of queue numbers to which the ranking rule applies	Integer constant	None
MRANK	2-M	Ranking rule	See Table 3.2	None

A valid use of the RANKINGS element is:

RANKINGS:1–3,HVF(1):4,LIFO;

QUEUES 1 through 3 are ordered in the queue file according to the value of attribute 1, high values toward the head of the queue. QUEUE 4 is governed by a last-in-first-out queue discipline.

TABLE 3.2
RANKING RULES FOR QUEUE DISCIPLINE

Rule	Definition
FIFO	Entities ranked according to time of insertion into the queue file, early insertion given priority (first-in, first-out).
LIFO	Entities ranked according to time of insertion into the queue file, late insertion given priority (last-in, first-out).
LVF(K)	Entities are ranked low value first, based on the value of attribute K of the entity.
HVF(K)	Entities are ranked high value first, based on the value of attribute K of the entity.

RESOURCES   This element defines the names and capacities of resources used in the model.

It has the form:

RESOURCES:N,RNAME,NCAP:...Repeats through group M;

The operands are defined as:

OPERAND	OPERAND GROUP	DESCRIPTION	ALLOWABLE VALUES	DEFAULT
N or N1 – N2	2-M	Resource number or range (N1 – N2) of resource numbers for indexed resources	Integer constant	None
RNAME	2-M	Resource name	String	None
NCAP or NCAP1, NCAP2,..	2-M	Initial capacity of the resource or list of capacities for indexed resources	Integer constant, or SCHED(K)*	1

* SCHED(K) defines a schedule of resource capacities for the simulation run length. See Section 4.3.

The operand NCAP defines the capacity of the resource at the beginning of the model. As explained in Section 4.1, resource capacities can be altered during a run.

An illustration of the use of RESOURCES is:

RESOURCES:1,TELLERS,4:2,OFFICER;
RESOURCES:2-3,MACHINE,2,4;

In the first example, a certain bank has four tellers (resource 1), and one bank officer (resource 2). The second statement defines an indexed resource named MACHINE. Resource 2 is named MACHINE(1) and has a capacity of 2; resource 3 is named MACHINE(2) and has a capacity of 4. Indexed resources are useful in describing resources that are essentially the same, but differ in capacity or some other significant characteristic.

TALLIES   This element provides a title for use in the SIMAN Summary Output, and other identifying information for variables recorded by a TALLY block.

The TALLIES element has the following form:

TALLIES:N,ID,NUNIT:...Repeats through group M;

Its operands are defined as:

OPERAND	OPERAND GROUP	DESCRIPTION	ALLOWABLE VALUES	DEFAULT
N	2-M	Tally number	Integer constant	None
ID	2-M	Report identifier for labelling on Summary Report	String (max of 16 characters)	Blank
NUNIT	2-M	Output unit to save individual observations	Integer constant	Obs. not saved

The operands N and ID appear on the SIMAN Summary Report to identify the summary statistics (mean, standard deviation, etc.) displayed for the variable with the same tally number specified in the TALLY block. In addition, individual observations of the variable are saved for subsequent analysis using the output processor if NUNIT is specified. NUNIT should be equal to or greater than 11, because in some implementations SIMAN uses input/output units 5 – 10 in manipulating files to produce the executable SIMAN program.

An example of the TALLIES element is:

```
TALLIES:1,TIME IN SYSTEM,12:
       2,TIME BET ARRVALS;
```

The first example identifies statistics for the time to progress between two blocks, which were obtained using the INT(K) operand of a TALLY block. Individual observations are saved for subsequent analysis by the output processor in unit 12. The second, identifies statistics for interarrival times at a given block, which were recorded using the BET(K) operand of a TALLY block. The corresponding TALLY blocks for these example elements would be:

```
TALLY:1,INT(2);
TALLY:2,BET(1);
```

COUNTERS   This element specifies the Summary Report identifier and count limit for a COUNT block.

The COUNTERS element has the form:

COUNTERS:N,ID,LIMIT:..Repeats through group M;

Operands for this element are:

OPERAND	OPERAND GROUP	DESCRIPTION	ALLOWABLE VALUES	DEFAULT
N	2-M	Counter number	Integer constant	None
ID	2-M	Report identifier for labelling on Summary Report	String (max of 16 characters	Blank
LIMIT	2-M	Counter limit	Integer constant	Infinity

The operands N and ID appear on the SIMAN Summary Report to identify the particular COUNT block. When the count exceeds the value of LIMIT, the simulation run is terminated.

Examples of COUNTERS are the following:

```
COUNTERS:1,PATIENTS EXAMINED,1000;
COUNTERS:1,PATIENT TYPE 1:
         2,PATIENT TYPE 2;
```

In the first example, the simulation is ended when the value of COUNT block 1 is 1000, indicating that 1000 patients have been examined. The second example simply counts the number of patients of type 1 and 2 which are examined, using COUNT blocks 1 and 2, respectively. The length of the simulation run is controlled by another means.

The associated COUNT blocks could appear as:

COUNT:1,1;   for the first example

COUNT:1,1;   } for the second example
COUNT:2,1;

3.3   General Experimental Frame Elements

In this section we discuss some experimental frame elements that impact the definition of the entire model, as opposed to being associated with a particular SIMAN block, as are the elements covered in the previous section.

PROJECT   This element is used to label the SIMAN Summary Report. This report is automatically generated by the run processor at the conclusion of a simulation run. The PROJECT element must be included in the experimental frame.

PROJECT has the following form:

PROJECT,TITLE,ANALYST,MO/DAY/YEAR;

Its operands are defined as follows:

OPERAND	OPERAND GROUP	DESCRIPTION	ALLOWABLE VALUES	DEFAULT
TITLE	1	Project title	String (max of 20 characters	Blank
ANALYST	1	Name of analyst	String (max of 20 characters)	Blank
MON/DAY/ YEAR	1	Date (month/day/year)	Three integer constants	1/1/2000

PROJECT may be illustrated with the following example:

PROJECT,HEALTH CLINIC I,J. SMITH,10/30/83

DISCRETE   This element defines quantities that affect the size and other characteristics of the block diagram model.

It has the form:

DISCRETE,MENT,MATB,NFIL,NSTA;

The operands are defined as:

OPERAND	OPERAND GROUP	DESCRIPTION	ALLOWABLE VALUES	DEFAULT
MENT	1	Maximum number of entities allowed in the model	Integer constant	0
MATB	1	The number of attributes associated with an entity	Integer constant	0
NFIL	1	The largest file number (QUEUES) in the model	Integer constant	0
NSTA	1	The largest station number in the model	Integer constant	0

The default values for all operands is 0. Thus if the user does not include a DISCRETE element in the experimental frame, **the model will not execute**. One should give careful consideration to the number of entities that will be present in the model concurrently. If MENT is exceeded, the run is ended with an error message. Similarly, the number of attributes referenced in the model must not exceed MATB.

The following is a valid use of DISCRETE:

DISCRETE,100,2,4;

The model will accommodate 100 entities simultaneously, two attributes per entity, four QUEUE files and zero stations.

REPLICATE   This element is used to define characteristics of simulation runs, such as starting time of run, length of run, and initial conditions.

It takes the form:

REPLICATE,NRUNS,TBEG,DTRUN,ISYS,ISTAT,DTCLR;

Its operands are as follows:

OPERAND	OPERAND GROUP	DESCRIPTION	ALLOWABLE VALUES	DEFAULT
NRUNS	1	Number of runs to execute	Integer constant	1
TBEG	1	Starting time for the first run	Real constant	0.0
DTRUN	1	Maximum length of each run	Real constant	Infinite
ISYS	1	Initialization of system	YES or NO	YES
ISTAT	1	Discard previous observations between runs	YES or NO	YES
DTCLR	1	Offset time from beginning of run when summary statistics are cleared	Real constant	0.0

The REPLICATE element provides still another way to control run length, using the DTRUN operand. The two previously described methods are: (1) the limiting of entity generation by the CREATE block, and (2) the use of the COUNT block. It should be noted that the run may not be as long as specified by DTRUN if one of these other two limits is reached first.

The first binary operand of this element, ISYS, permits the user to elect whether or not the system is reset to its original conditions at the start of each run. If YES is selected, all system variables and queue files are reset; if NO is the choice, the ending conditions for run N are the initial conditions for run N + 1. The second binary operand, ISTAT, determines whether statistics collected are for individual runs or cumulative over all runs. The YES option provides statistics in the Summary Report based on a given run, while the NO option yields aggregate statistics in the Summary Report based on all runs thus far.

The operand DTCLR permits all summary statistics collected prior to the specified time to be discarded without altering the state of the system. In this way, runs can be conveniently brought to steady-state behavior, and more meaningful statistics collected.

The REPLICATE element can be illustrated by the following examples.

```
REPLICATE,1,0,540,,,60;
REPLICATE,4,0,100,NO;
REPLICATE,4,0,100,NO,NO;
```

In the first example, one simulation run is made beginning at time zero, and its duration is 540 minutes. The system is brought to steady state during the first 60 minutes, and the summary statistics up to that time are discarded. Thus, the collected statistics reflect a run of 480 minutes, or one 8-hour shift. The second REPLICATE element dictates that four runs be made beginning at time zero, and each having a maximum duration of 100 time units. The second run begins at time 100, the third at time 200, and the fourth at time 300. The system is not initialized between runs, so ending conditions for a given run are the initial conditions for the next. Statistics are gathered for the four runs individually and will be displayed in Summary Reports for four runs of 100 time units each. The last example is the same as the previous one, except that the statistics are aggregated for runs, reflecting the total set of observations thus far, and ultimately the data from all four runs.

DSTAT   This element is used to obtain statistics about any SIMAN or user-defined system variable. The statistics collected are the mean, standard deviation, maximum value, and minimum value of the designated variable.

The DSTAT element has the form:

DSTAT:N,DVAR,ID,NUNIT:..Repeats through group M;

Its operands are defined as follows:

OPERAND	OPERAND GROUP	DESCRIPTION	ALLOWABLE VALUES	DEFAULT
N	2-M	DSTAT number	Integer constant	None
DVAR	2-M	System variable for which statistics are collected	User or SIMAN system variable*	None
				(cont'd)

OPERAND	OPERAND GROUP	DESCRIPTION	ALLOWABLE VALUES	DEFAULT
ID	2-M	Identifier for labelling on Summary Report	String (max of 16 characters)	Blank
NUNIT	2-M	Output unit to save individual observations	Integer constant	Observation not saved

* Listed and defined in Table 2.2.

The operands N and ID appear on the Summary Report to identify the collected statistics; DVAR specifies the system variable for which statistics are gathered; and NUNIT permits the saving of individual observations for subsequent analysis by the output processor, as described in Section 7.

The following examples illustrate the use of DSTAT.

```
DSTAT:1,NQ(1),QUEUE:
      2,NR(2),DRILL;
DSTAT:1,NQ(2),PATIENT WAIT,11;
```

The first example collects statistics on queue 1 and resource 2, which are labelled QUEUE and DRILL, respectively. The second use of DSTAT records data about queue 2 and labels it as PATIENT WAIT. In addition, the individual observations are saved on output unit 11 for analysis by the output processor.

TRACE   This element reports the details on movement through blocks of the SIMAN block diagram. It describes entity processing such as creation of entities, seizing and releasing of resources, and variable assignments.

The TRACE element has the following form:

TRACE,DTBT,DTFT,TC,VAR1,VAR2,VAR3,VAR4;

Its operands are:

OPERAND	OPERAND GROUP	DESCRIPTION	ALLOWABLE VALUES	DEFAULT
DTBT	1	Time at which trace begins	Real constant	0
DTFT	1	Time at which trace ends	Real constant	Infinite
TC	1	Trace condition	Condition	Trace all
VAR1.. VAR4	1	Variable or attribute to be displayed by trace (maximum of 4)	Attribute, system, or user variable*	No values displayed

* Listed and defined in Table 2.2.

The operand TC allows a trace switch to be turned on and off according to the truth of the specified condition, so that tracing can be confined to periods when the system has a particular status. For example, if TC is NQ(1).GT.3, the trace switch is on whenever

QUEUE 1 contains more than three entities, and off otherwise. It should be noted that the trace switch changes value only at a time advance. In this example, if QUEUE 1 decreases to 3, the trace switch will not be turned off until the next time advance.

The TRACE element is illustrated by the following examples.

```
TRACE;
TRACE,,,,NQ(2);
TRACE,10,1000,NC(1).GT.100,A(1),NQ(2);
```

The first example is the standard TRACE for the entire run length with no variables displayed, while the second traces the value of QUEUE 2, also for the entire run. Note the commas denoting missing operands. The third TRACE element begins the trace at time 10 and ends it at time 1000. Attribute 1 and QUEUE 2 are traced only if COUNT 1 is greater than 100, where COUNT 1 is used to record the total number of entities that have arrived thus far.

OUTPUT   The element permits collection of values of response variables at the end of each replication. These data may then be used as input to the Output Processor as described in Section 7.0.

The OUTPUT element has the following form:

OUTPUT:N,VAR,NU:..Repeats through group M;

Its operands are:

OPERAND	OPERAND GROUP	DESCRIPTION	ALLOWABLE VALUES	DEFAULT
N	2-M	Output variable number	Integer	None
VAR	2-M	Output variable for which data are to be collected	Any SIMAN variable	None
NU	2-M	Output data set number	Integer	None

The following example illustrates the use of OUTPUT.

OUTPUT:1,TAVG(1),11:2,DMAX(1),12;

Two output variables are defined: output variable 1 is the average of TALLY variable 1 (collected as data set 11), and output variable 2 is the maximum of DSTAT variable 1 (collected as data set 12).

3.4   Running SIMAN Models

The block diagram of the model frame and the experimental frame described above fully define the system to be simulated and the experiments to be run. However, to execute the simulation using SIMAN, a model and experiment file must be entered and combined into an executable program, as explained in Section 2.1. In this section, we describe the procedure used to accomplish this. There are four steps in the procedure:

1. Create a MODEL FILE using the MODEL PROCESSOR and block diagram definition statements.

2. Create an EXPERIMENT FILE using the EXPERIMENT PROCESSOR and experimental frame elements description.

3. Combine the MODEL and EXPERIMENT FILES into a PROGRAM FILE using the LINK PROCESSOR.

4. Execute the PROGRAM FILE using the RUN PROCESSOR.

3.4.1 Creating the Model File   To create a model file, the model processor requires the block diagram definition statements and, in addition, two control statements: BEGIN and END. There is also an optional control statement, SYNONYMS, which allows the use of character strings to improve program readability. These statements are described below.

The BEGIN statement has the following form and operands. The END statement has no operands.

BEGIN,BSEQ,ISEQ,ILIST;

OPERAND	OPERAND GROUP	DESCRIPTION	ALLOWABLE VALUES	DEFAULT
BSEQ	1	Sequence number of first statement in the model	Integer constant	10
ISEQ	1	Increment used in assigning statement numbers	Integer constant	10
ILIST	1	Generate a model listing	YES or NO	YES

Each set of input to the model processor must begin with a BEGIN statement and end with an END statement. Both statements begin in column 1 and are terminated by a semicolon (;).

The SYNONYMS statement allows the assignment of a user-defined character string to any SIMAN character string in the model frame. Such assignments include: attributes and variables, such as A(N) and X(N); commonly used expressions; and even SIMAN block names. The SYNONYMS statement has the following form and operands.

SYNONYMS:character string = associated original string:..repeats through group M;

OPERAND	OPERAND GROUP	DESCRIPTION	ALLOWABLE VALUES	DEFAULT
Character string	2-M	Any alphanumeric string	String	None
Associated original string	2-M	SIMAN attribute, variable, or block name	String	None

The SYNONYMS statement must be placed before the first reference to its character strings, therefore, immediately after the BEGIN statement is a safe placement. The SYNONYMS statement starts in column 1, just as the BEGIN statement does. The character string to be substituted for the SIMAN characters must appear in single quotes (' ') in the model frame.

An example of the use of this statement is:

```
BEGIN;
SYNONYMS:JOB TYPE = A(1):GENERATE = CREATE;
          'GENERATE':EX(1,1);
          ASSIGN:'JOB TYPE' = DP(2,1);
                       .
                       .
                       .
```

The string GENERATE is substituted for the SIMAN block CREATE, perhaps by a GPSS language veteran. Also, JOB TYPE replaces the attribute A(1).

Using the block diagram model description in conjunction with control statements, the model file is created by the model processor, which is a SIMAN program named MODEL. It is one of the files required by the link processor to produce the executable program. MODEL checks for correct syntax, and if errors are found, an error message is entered in the model listing immediately following the offending block.

There is an alternative method to create the model file. Using the SIMAN program BLOCKS, and a microcomputer with graphics capability, one can display the block diagram symbols and interconnect them to form a complete block diagram. This program does not permit inclusion of blocks that are syntactically incorrect, thus the completed model will contain no errors.

3.4.2 Creating the Experiment File

Each set of experimental frame element descriptions must also start and conclude with BEGIN and END statements. The order of element description statements is arbitrary, with one exception. The DISCRETE element may be preceded only by the PROJECT element. Practically, this means that the PROJECT element should come first, followed immediately by the DISCRETE element. Also, within a given experiment, each element may be entered, at most, once. Thus, all information for the element should be linked to its single occurrence using the colon (:), as illustrated in previous sections.

The experiment file is created by the experiment processor, a SIMAN program named EXPMT, using the experimental frame element descriptions as the input. It is the second file required by the link processor to produce the executable program. Syntax error checking is performed by EXPMT and errors are noted in the listing immediately following the incorrect element.

3.4.3 Combining the Model and Experiment Files

When the model and experiment files are created, they are submitted to the link processor, a SIMAN program named LINKER, to produce the executable program. If errors are detected during linking, error messages are displayed and no executable program is created. If there are no errors, LINKER writes the message "Link Completed," and generates an executable program.

3.4.4 Executing the Program File

The final step needed to run a SIMAN simulation is the execution of the program file. This is accomplished by the run processor, a SIMAN program named SIMAN. This program accepts the program file as input, and generates SIMAN Summary Reports and data files for subsequent analysis by the output processor, if requested.

SIMAN also provides dynamic, graphical output displays using the SIMAN program CINEMA. Using a microcomputer with graphics capability, CINEMA will display dynamically the status of the system during the simulation execution.

3.5   Illustrative Problem Set I

This problem set employs the basic modeling concepts and SIMAN blocks described in the previous sections to model some commonly encountered systems. The first problem treats a health clinic where two types of patients visit a single physician. The remaining two problems deal with production environments: a flow shop with two machines that process four types of jobs, and two processes in tandem with blocking. These problems illustrate both simple straight line flow of entities and some simple branching.

PROBLEM I.1   The setting for this problem is a single-physician medical clinic. Patients arriving at this clinic are of two types: those who have visited the clinic before, and those who are visiting for the first time. The mean interval between arrivals for ''old'' patients is 40 minutes, while that for ''new'' patients is 63 minutes. The interarrival times for both classes of patients are uniformly distributed over a range defined as the mean interval ±10 minutes. Examination and treatment for either class requires 20±5 minutes, uniformly distributed. In addition, the taking of a medical history for ''new'' patients requires 10±3 minutes. Upon completion of their treatment, patients immediately leave the clinic. The SIMAN flow chart for this problem is shown in Fig. 3.1, and the SIMAN statements for the model and experimental frames are listed in Fig. 3.2.

Some observations concerning the logic of the model frame are in order. Two independent streams of entities are created: one for ''new'' patients, and one for ''old'' patients. As each patient entity arrives, it is marked with the arrival time so that waiting times may be tallied. Also, ''new'' patients are assigned a time for taking medical history. Both patient types then proceed to QUEUE 1, where they await the physician. When available, the physician takes the medical history (for new patients only) and examines the patients. Patients leave the clinic immediately following the examination.

The experimental frame defines specific model characteristics, such as TALLY table names; DISCRETE table names; RESOURCE capacities; PARAMETERS specification; and the maximum number of concurrent entities, attributes, and queues permitted. In this example, the REPLICATE element is used to control the run length, which begins at time zero and ends after 60 days of 480-minute duration have been simulated.

The SIMAN summary report for this model is shown in Fig. 3.3. The report first lists run identification information: run number, project title, analyst, date, and the value of simulated time at the end of the run. Then the tally variables appear, followed by the discrete change variables, and finally the execution time for the run. For both tally and discrete variables, the average, standard deviation, minimum value, and maximum value are provided.

Turning now to the substance of the output, we see that average waiting time for a patient of either class (PAT WAIT) is approximately 21.5 minutes, and the average

FIGURE 3.1   PROBLEM I.1 FLOW CHART

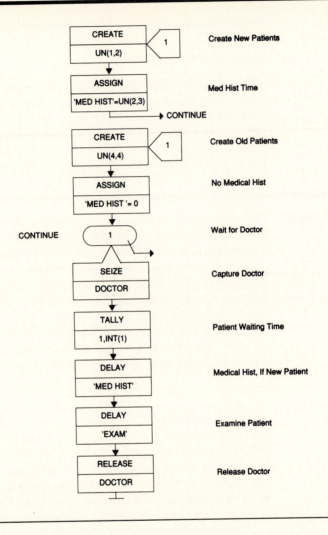

length of the queue (PAT QUEUE) is less than one patient. The doctor has a utilization (DOC UTIL) of approximately 98%. It appears that this clinic has little room to accommodate any increased patient load. Also, an average wait of 21.5 minutes may cause one to consider whether the level of service provided could be improved. How could the clinic operate in a manner more responsive to patient needs without increased resources?

Observe that "new" patients require an additional 10 minutes to have their medical history taken, and that "old" patients arrive with greater frequency than "new" patients. If the patients requiring a shorter service time could be given a higher priority, thereby being processed before those requiring a longer time, it might be possible to reduce the average waiting time for all patients.

In exploring this possibility, we would like to compare the relative waiting times of "old" and "new" patients. To do this, the single stream of patient entities must branch to one of two separate TALLY blocks after seizing the physician. This is accomplished

FIGURE 3.2   PROBLEM I.1 CODE

```
BEGIN;
;HEALTH CLINIC WITH OLD AND NEW PATIENTS
;
SYNONYMS:MED HIST=A(2):EXAM=UN(3,1);
         CREATE:UN(1,2):MARK(1);                    NEW PATS
         ASSIGN:'MED HIST'=UN(2,3):NEXT(CONTINUE);  MED HIST TIME
         CREATE:UN(4,4):MARK(1);                    OLD PATS
         ASSIGN:'MED HIST'=0;                        NO MED HISTORY
CONTINUE QUEUE,1;                                    WAIT FOR DOC
         SEIZE:DOCTOR;                               CAPTURE DOC
         TALLY:1,INT(1);                             PAT WAIT TIME
         DELAY:'MED HIST';                           MED HIST IF NEW PAT
         DELAY:'EXAM';                               EXAMINE PAT
         RELEASE:DOCTOR:DISPOSE;                     RELEASE DOC
END;



BEGIN;
PROJECT,HEALTH CLINIC,PERRY,9/13/84;
DISCRETE,90,2,1;              90 ENTITIES,2 ATTRIBUTES, 1 QUEUE
TALLIES:1,PAT WAIT;           TALLY PAT WAIT
DSTAT:1,NR(1),DOC UTIL:       !PHYSICIAN UTILIZATION
      2,NQ(1),PAT QUEUE;      NO. OF PAT IN QUEUE
RESOURCES:1,DOCTOR;           PYSICIAN CAPACITY =1
PARAMETERS:1,53,73:           !NEW PAT ARRIVAL PROCESS
           2,7,13:            !MED HIST PROB DIST
           3,15,25:           !PAT EXAM TIME PROB DIST
           4,30,50;           OLD PAT ARRIVAL PROCESS
REPLICATE,1,0,28800;          1 RUN BEG AT TIME 0 FOR 60 480 MIN DAYS
END;
```

in the model frame by assigning a 1 to A(3) of the "new" patient entities, and a 2 to A(3) of the "old" patient entities, and branching to the appropriate TALLY block based on the value of A(3). Figures 3.4 and 3.5 show the block diagram, model frame, and experimental frame statements that implement this change from the original formulation.

To give the "old" patients priority using a SIMAN model, we must alter the order in which patients join the QUEUE. This can be accomplished by using the RANKINGS element in the experimental frame. The value of A(3) assigned for branching is also used to order the entities properly in the queue using the HVF (high value first) ranking rule. Since the "old" higher priority patients have the higher value of A(3), they will be inserted in the queue ahead of "new" patients.

The output for a run of 60 days of 480 minutes duration is shown in Fig. 3.6. The single physician is still as harried as he was under the original clinic operation, since he is busy approximately 98% of the time. But the average waiting time for all patients has been reduced to 19.5 minutes from 21.5. Thus the overall experience of a patient in this clinic has been improved.

The explanation of this apparent prestidigitation lies, of course, in the disparity in waiting times for the two classes of patients. "New" patients wait about twice as long, on the average, as "old" patients. So, the assessment of the quality of clinic performance depends on one's vantage point.

FIGURE 3.3   PROBLEM I.1 OUTPUT

SIMAN Summary Report

Run Number   1 of   1

Project: HEALTH CLINIC
Analyst: PERRY
Date   :   9/13/1984

Run ended at time :   .2880E+05

Tally Variables

Number	Identifier	Average	Standard Deviation	Minimum Value	Maximum Value	Number of Obs.
1	PAT WAIT	21.47149	16.60606	.00000	89.40137	1178

Discrete Change Variables

Number	Identifier	Average	Standard Deviation	Minimum Value	Maximum Value	Time Period
1	DOC UTIL	.98	.14	.00	1.00	28800.00
2	PAT QUEUE	.88	.77	.00	4.00	28800.00

Run Time : 2 minute(s) and 11 Second(s)

PROBLEM I.2   In this example, we model a small flow shop which has two machines and processes four different job types. Each job requires time on both machines. They arrive singly at machine 1 with exponentially distributed interarrival times with a mean of 30 minutes, and are processed by machines 1 and 2 in sequence.

The processing time on each of the machines and the relative fraction of each of four job types is as follows:

JOB	PROCESSING TIME ON MACHINE 1	PROCESSING TIME ON MACHINE 2	PERCENT OF TOTAL JOBS
A	20 minutes	15 minutes	10%
B	5	25	30
C	25	20	45
D	10	5	15

FIGURE 3.4   PROBLEM I.1a FLOW CHART

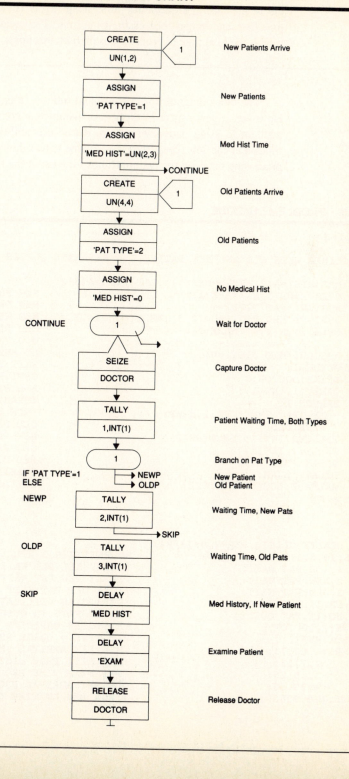

We wish to evaluate the following queue disciplines to be used in selecting the next job in the machine queue for processing: FIFO (first-in-first-out), shortest processing time first, and longest processing time first. The measure of system performance to be used is the total time to process jobs on both machines.

The block diagram for this problem follows straight line flow, as shown in Fig. 3.7. However, a new aspect in the use of parameters complicates the model somewhat. In addition to using parameter sets to define probability distributions for the job arrival times and the job types, they also define a two-dimensional array which specifies the processing times on the two machines for each of the four job types. Four parameter sets

FIGURE 3.5   PROBLEM I.1a CODE

```
BEGIN;
;HEALTH CLINIC WITH OLD AND NEW PATIENTS - SEPARATE QUEUES
;
SYNONYMS:MED HIST=A(2):EXAM=UN(3,1):PAT TYPE=A(3);
         CREATE:UN(1,2):MARK(1);                      NEW PATS ARRIVE
         ASSIGN:'PAT TYPE'=1;                         NEW PAT
         ASSIGN:'MED HIST'=UN(2,3):NEXT(CONTINUE);    MED HIST TIME
         CREATE:UN(4,4):MARK(1);                      OLD PATS ARRIVE
         ASSIGN:'PAT TYPE'=2;                         OLD PAT
         ASSIGN:'MED HIST'=0;                         NO MED HISTORY
CONTINUE QUEUE,1;                                     WAIT FOR DOC
         SEIZE:DOCTOR;                                CAPTURE DOC
         TALLY:1,INT(1);                              ALL PAT WAIT
         BRANCH,1:                                    !BRANCH ON PAT TYPE
            IF,'PAT TYPE'.EQ.1,NEWP:                  !NEW PAT
            ELSE,OLDP;                                OLD PAT
NEWP     TALLY:2,INT(1):NEXT(SKIP);                   NEW PATS WAIT
OLDP     TALLY:3,INT(1);                              OLD PAT WAIT
SKIP     DELAY:'MED HIST';                            MED HIST IF NEW PAT
         DELAY:'EXAM';                                EXAMINE PAT
         RELEASE:DOCTOR:DISPOSE;                      RELEASE DOC
END;


BEGIN;
PROJECT,HEALTH CLINIC,PERRY,9/13/84;
DISCRETE,90,3,1;                      90 ENTITIES,3 ATTRIBUTES,1 QUEUE
TALLIES:1,ALL PAT WAIT:               !TALLY ALL PAT WAIT
        2,NEW PAT WAIT:               !TALLY NEW PAT WAIT
        3,OLD PAT WAIT;               TALLY OLD PAT WAIT
DSTAT:1,NR(1),DOC UTIL:               !PHYSICIAN UTILIZATION
      2,NQ(1),PAT QUEUE;              NO. OF PATS IN QUEUE
RESOURCES:1,DOCTOR;                   PHYSICIAN CAPACITY =1
RANKINGS:1,HVF(3);                    PAT TYPE = QUEUE PRIORITY
PARAMETERS:1,53,73:                   !NEW PAT ARRIVAL PROCESS
           2,7,13:                    !MED HIST PROB DIST
           3,15,25:                   !PAT EXAM TIME PROB DIST
           4,30,50;                   OLD PAT ARRIVAL PROCESS
REPLICATE,1,0,28800;                  1 RUN BEG AT TIME 0 FOR 60 480 MIN DAYS

END;
```

FIGURE 3.6   PROBLEM I.1a OUTPUT

SIMAN Summary Report

Run Number   1 of   1

Project: HEALTH CLINIC
Analyst: PERRY
Date   :   9/13/1984

Run ended at time :   .2880E+05

Tally Variables

Number	Identifier	Average	Standard Deviation	Minimum Value	Maximum Value	Number of Obs.
1	ALL PAT WAIT	19.51003	20.73678	.00000	143.23440	1178
2	NEW PAT WAIT	28.87926	28.75545	.00000	143.23440	456
3	OLD PAT WAIT	13.59262	9.46475	.00000	36.36914	722

Discrete Change Variables

Number	Identifier	Average	Standard Deviation	Minimum Value	Maximum Value	Time Period
1	DOC UTIL	.98	.14	.00	1.00	28800.00
2	PAT QUEUE	.80	.71	.00	3.00	28800.00

Run Time :   2 Minute(s) and 35 Second(s)

---

are used, one for each of the job types. The first member of a parameter set is the processing time on machine 1, and the second member is the processing time on machine 2. The particular parameter set to use is determined by sampling a job type from a user-defined probability distribution which is assigned to A(2). Thus, the processing time on machine 1 (designated PROC 1, where PROC 1 = A(3) in the model frame) is P(A(2),1), and that on machine 2 (PROC 2 = A(4)) is P(A(2),2). Figure 3.8 lists the model and experimental frame statements required to define this flow shop.

The three queue disciplines are included in the model using the RANKINGS element to determine the order in the queue. To assess the first-in-first-out policy, the FIFO ranking rule is used. The shortest and longest processing time rules are evaluated by using the LVF (lowest value first) and HVF (highest value first) ranking rules, where the attribute ranked reflects the processing time [A(3) for machine 1 and A(4) for machine 2].

The REPLICATE element is not present in the experimental frame. How is run length controlled? This is accomplished using the COUNT block and associated COUNTERS element of the experimental frame. COUNTERS is set at 500, the desired

FIGURE 3.7   PROBLEM I.2 FLOW CHART

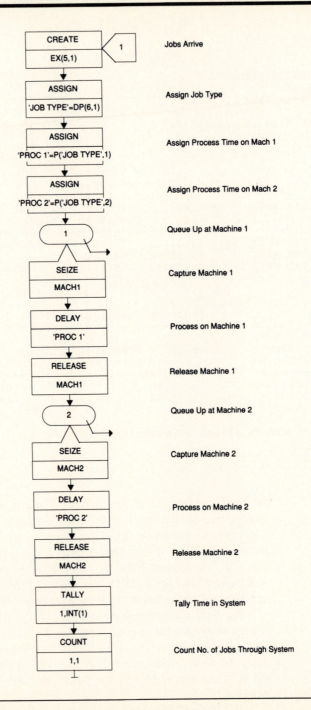

CREATE / EX(5,1)	Jobs Arrive
ASSIGN / 'JOB TYPE'=DP(6,1)	Assign Job Type
ASSIGN / 'PROC 1'=P('JOB TYPE',1)	Assign Process Time on Mach 1
ASSIGN / 'PROC 2'=P('JOB TYPE',2)	Assign Process Time on Mach 2
1	Queue Up at Machine 1
SEIZE / MACH1	Capture Machine 1
DELAY / 'PROC 1'	Process on Machine 1
RELEASE / MACH1	Release Machine 1
2	Queue Up at Machine 2
SEIZE / MACH2	Capture Machine 2
DELAY / 'PROC 2'	Process on Machine 2
RELEASE / MACH2	Release Machine 2
TALLY / 1,INT(1)	Tally Time in System
COUNT / 1,1	Count No. of Jobs Through System

FIGURE 3.8   PROBLEM I.2 CODE

```
BEGIN;
;TWO MACHINES IN TANDEM
;
SYNONYMS:JOB TYPE=A(2):PROC 1=A(3):PROC 2=A(4);
         CREATE:EX(5,1):MARK(1);              JOBS ARRIVE
         ASSIGN:'JOB TYPE'=DP(6,1);           ASSIGN JOB TYPE
         ASSIGN:'PROC 1'=P('JOB TYPE',1);     ASSIGN PROC TIME MACH 1
         ASSIGN:'PROC 2'=P('JOB TYPE',2);     ASSIGN PROC TIME MACH 2
         QUEUE,1;                             QUEUE AT MACH 1
         SEIZE:MACH1;                         SEIZE MACHINE 1
         DELAY:'PROC 1';                      PROCESS ON MACHINE 1
         RELEASE:MACH1;                       RELEASE MACHINE 1
         QUEUE,2;                             QUEUE FOR MACHINE 2
         SEIZE:MACH2;                         SEIZE MACHINE 2
         DELAY:'PROC 2';                      PROCESS ON MACHINE 2
         RELEASE:MACH2;                       RELEASE MACHINE 2
         TALLY:1,INT(1);                      TALLY TIME IN SYSTEM
         COUNT:1,1:DISPOSE;                   COUNT NO OF JOBS THRU SYS
END;



BEGIN;
PROJECT,QUEUE DISC EVAL,PERRY,9/10/84;
DISCRETE,50,5,2;                         50 ENTITIES, 5 ATTRIBUTES, 2 QUEUES
PARAMETERS:1,20.,15.:                    !PROC TIME JOB A MACH 1 AND 2
           2,5.,25.:                     !PROC TIME JOB B MACH 1 AND 2
           3,25.,20.:                    !PROC TIME JOB C MACH 1 AND 2
           4,10.,5.:                     !PROC TIME JOB D MACH 1 AND 2
           5,30.:                        !MEAN TIME BETWEEN JOB ARRIVALS
           6,.1,1,.4,2,.85,3,1.,4;       PROB DIST OF JOB TYPES
RESOURCES:1,MACH1:2,MACH2;               MACHINE CAPACITIES
COUNTERS:1,NO. OF JOBS,500;              COUNTS NUMBER OF JOBS THROUGH SHOP
TALLIES:1,TIME IN SYS;                   TALLY TIME IN SHOP
RANKINGS:1,FIFO:2,FIFO;            PRIORITY IN MACH QUEUES
END;
```

number of jobs to complete. When the COUNT block has been incremented to that value, the run ceases.

A representative SIMAN summary report for this model is shown in Fig. 3.9. The results for the three queue disciplines may be summarized as follows:

QUEUE DISCIPLINE	AVERAGE TIME IN THE SHOP
FIFO	62.0
LVF	57.9
HVF	70.0

Thus the LVF ranking rule, which represents a shortest-processing-time first-queue discipline, is superior to the other two disciplines. This finding is consistent with that of the flow and job shop literature.

FIGURE 3.9   PROBLEM I.2 OUTPUT

```
                          SIMAN Summary Report

                          Run Number    1 of  1

Project:   QUEUE DISC EVAL
Analyst:   PERRY
Date    :    9/10/1984

Run ended at time :    .1531E+05
```

```
                          Tally Variables
                          ---------------

Number Identifier      Average    Standard  Minimum   Maximum   Number
                                  Deviation Value     Value     of Obs.
-------------------------------------------------------------------------
   1   TIME IN SYS     62.04828   32.26839  15.00000  184.54640   500
```

```
                          Counters
                          --------

Number Identifier      Count    Limit
-------------------------------------------
   1   NO. OF JOBS      500      500
```

```
Run Time : 1 Minute(s) and 4 Second(s)
```

PROBLEM I.3   This example is taken from a SIMAN workshop by Pegden. It treats a situation that can often occur when two or more processes are arranged such that the output of the previous process moves directly to the next. In such situations, the condition known as blocking can result from an imbalance in the processing rates and insufficient buffer space between processes. When a unit is blocked, it may not leave the current process due to lack of space at the next. If buffer space is expensive, for example, when using conveyors, it is desirable to minimize its use. But, the reduced production rate caused by blocking may be more expensive. Hence, the interest in modeling such problems.

In this illustration, parts arrive at a production line which consists of two processes every three minutes. The processes are insertion and welding. Before the parts can leave insertion for welding, there must be room in the queue preceding the weld operation. The weld queue capacity is three units. Insertion and welding are each staffed with one worker. The processing time at insertion is triangular with a minimum value of 1 minute, a maximum of 5 minutes, and a mode of 2 minutes. Processing time at welding is uniformly distributed over the range 3 to 6 minutes. The measure of system performance is the waiting time in the queues before each process.

The blocking condition is implemented in the SIMAN model by using a pseudo resource: the welding queue space. Before a unit can RELEASE the inserter, it must be possible for it to SEIZE the weld queue space. When a unit of weld queue space is seized, the unit then enters the actual QUEUE in front of the weld operation. The block diagram, model, and experimental frame are shown in Figs. 3.10 and 3.11. The SIMAN summary report appears in Fig. 3.12. Note that the parts in QUEUE 2 are those that are blocked due to insufficient welder queue space.

FIGURE 3.10   PROBLEM I.3 FLOW CHART

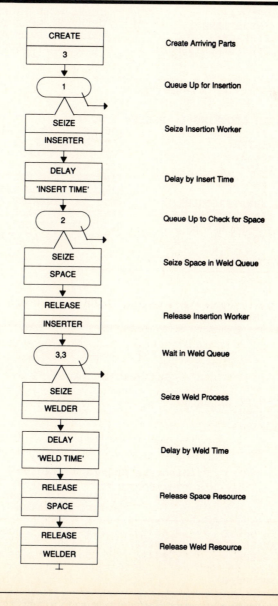

FIGURE 3.11   PROBLEM I.3 CODE

```
BEGIN;
;PRODUCTION LINE WITH BLOCKING
;
SYNONYMS:INSERT TIME=TR(1,1):WELD TIME=UN(2,1);
        CREATE:3;                       CREATE ARRIVING PARTS
        QUEUE,1;                        QUEUE UP FOR INSERTION
        SEIZE:INSERTER;                 SEIZE INSERTION WORKER
        DELAY:'INSERT TIME';            DELAY BY INSERT TIME
        QUEUE,2;                        QUEUE UP TO CHECK FOR SPACE
        SEIZE:SPACE;                    SEIZE SPACE IN WELD QUEUE
        RELEASE:INSERTER;               RELEASE INSERTION WORKER
        QUEUE,3,3;                      WAIT IN WELD QUEUE
        SEIZE:WELDER;                   SEIZE WELD PROCESS
        DELAY:'WELD TIME';              DELAY BY WELD TIME
        RELEASE:SPACE;                  RELEASE SPACE RESOURCE
        RELEASE:WELDER:DISPOSE;         FREE WELD RESOURCE
END;



BEGIN;
PROJECT,LINE WITH BLOCKING,L. PEGDEN,8/22/84;
DISCRETE,100,0,3;                  100 ENTITIES, 0 ATTRIBUTES, 3 QUEUES
RESOURCES:1,INSERTER:              !INSERTER CAP =1
          2,SPACE,3:               !WELD QUEUE CAP =3
          3,WELDER;                WELD CAP =1
PARAMETERS:1,1,2,5:                !INSERT TIME PROB DIST
           2,3,6;                  WELD TIME PROB DIST
DSTAT:1,NQ(1),INSERTER QUEUE:      !NO. IN INSERTER QUEUE
      2,NQ(2),SPACE AVAILABLE?:    !CHECK FOR SPACE IN WELDER QUEUE
      3,NQ(3),WELDER QUEUE;        QUEUE FOR WELDER
REPLICATE,1,0,240;                 1 RUN BEGIN AT TIME 0 FOR 240 MIN
END;
```

FIGURE 3.12   PROBLEM I.3 OUTPUT

```
                        SIMAN Summary Report

                        Run Number    1 of  1

Project:  LINE WITH BLOCKING
Analyst:  L. PEGDEN
Date   :   8/22/1984

Run ended at time :   .2400E+03
```

Discrete Change Variables

Number	Identifier	Average	Standard Deviation	Minimum Value	Maximum Value	Time Period
1	INSERTER QUEUE	9.65325	7.45330	.00000	24.00000	240.00
2	SPACE AVAILABLE?	.39238	.48828	.00000	1.00000	240.00
3	WELDER QUEUE	1.83496	.50516	.00000	2.00000	240.00

```
Run time:  5 Second(s)
```

4.0   INTERMEDIATE MODELING CONCEPTS

In this section we will present SIMAN blocks which will allow us to build more complex models than possible with the blocks described in the previous section. We also consider experimental frame elements which will give us greater control and flexibility in our simulation experiments.

4.1   Intermediate SIMAN Blocks

Parallel Queues and Resources: (PICKQ, QPICK and SELECT)   It is common in entity flow systems to have parallel queues such that an entity must select from one of several queues, and similarly, when a resource becomes available, the next seizing entity may be drawn from one of several queues. Figure 4.1 shows a set of parallel queues and the decisions that must be made at each end of the queues.

PICKQ   This block is used to allow an entity to select one of several different queues while the QPICK is used to allow one of several queues to be selected for the next entering entity.
     The format of PICKQ is:

PICKQ,QSR,BALK:LABEL:LABEL:...:LABEL;

The block diagram symbol is:

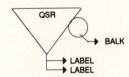

FIGURE 4.1   PARALLEL QUEUES

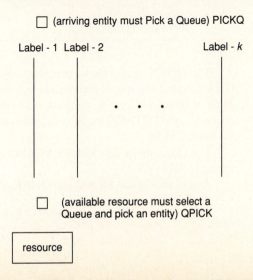

Its operands are defined as:

OPERAND	OPERAND GROUP	DESCRIPTION	ALLOWABLE VALUES	DEFAULT
QSR	1	Queue Selection Rule	See Table 4.1	POR
BALK	1	Label of destination if all queues are full	Label	Entity destroyed
LABEL	2	Labels of parallel queues	Label	None

When an entity enters the PICKQ block the specified Queue Selection Rule, QSR, will be used to determine which of the labeled queues will be selected for entity filing.

QPICK   This block is complementary to the PICKQ block. The format of the QPICK block is:

QPICK,QSR:LABEL:LABEL:...:LABEL;

The block diagram symbol is:

Its operands are defined as:

OPERAND	OPERAND GROUP	DESCRIPTION	ALLOWABLE VALUES	DEFAULT
QSR	1	Queue Selection Rule	See Table 4.1	POR
LABEL	2	Labels of preceding queues for selecting next entity	Label	None

The QPICK immediately precedes a block of the Hold type and is used by this block to select the queue file from which the next entity will be selected. Because the entity will not proceed to the next sequential block when removed from the chosen queue file, the DETACH modifier must be used with the labeled QUEUE blocks listed in the QPICK block.

The Queue Selection Rules (QSR) which the PICKQ and QPICK blocks use are shown in Table 4.1

An example of the PICKQ and QPICK blocks is:

```
              PICKQ,RAN:QUEUE1:QUEUE2;
QUEUE1        QUEUE,10:DETACH;
QUEUE2        QUEUE,20:DETACH;
              QPICK,LNQ:QUEUE1,QUEUE2;
              SEIZE:SERVER;
```

TABLE 4.1
QUEUE SELECTION RULE

Queue Selection Rule	Description
CYC	Cyclic Priority. Select the first available QUEUE block starting with the successor of the last QUEUE block selected.
RAN	Random Priority. Select randomly from the available QUEUE blocks.
POR	Preferred Order Rule. Select the first available Queue block, checking for availability in the preferred order.
LNQ	Largest Number in Queue. Select the QUEUE block with currently the largest number of entities. Break ties using POR.
SNQ	Smallest Number in Queue. Select the QUEUE block with currently the smallest number of entities. Break ties using POR.
LRC	Largest Remaining Capacity. Select the QUEUE block with the current largest remaining capacity. Break ties using POR.
SRC	Smallest Remaining Capacity.Select the QUEUE block with the current smallest remaining capacity. Break ties using POR.
UR(K)	User Rule. Select the URth queue block where UR is computed in a FORTRAN function.
ER(N)	Experimental Rule. Select QUEUE block based on rule N defined in the RULES element of the experimental frame.

In this example, entities randomly choose between QUEUE 10 and QUEUE 20. Because the entities will be removed from QUEUE 10 and QUEUE 20 using a QPICK, the entity must be detached to allow it to flow to some block other than the next sequential block. The choice of queue for removing an entity is based upon the length of QUEUE 10 and QUEUE 20. An entity from the queue with the largest number of entities filed is selected for seizing the resource SERVER.

As a second example of using the PICKQ block, consider the problem of modeling a bank where customers line up at separate queues at a teller's window. Assume that the customers do not jockey between lines and there are three different tellers. The code to represent such a process might be:

```
        PICKQ,SNQ:LINE1:LINE2:LINE3;
LINE1   QUEUE,1;
        SEIZE:TELLER1;
        DELAY:EX(1,1);
        RELEASE:TELLER1:DISPOSE;
LINE2   QUEUE,2;
        SEIZE:TELLER2;
        DELAY:EX(1,1);
        RELEASE:TELLER2:DISPOSE;
LINE3   QUEUE,3;
        SEIZE:TELLER3;
        DELAY:EX(1,1);
        RELEASE:TELLER3:DISPOSE;
```

In this example, an arriving entity selects the teller with the smallest queue, waits until the teller is available and then seizes the teller for an exponentially distributed time, using parameter set 1, and then releases the teller. After releasing the teller, the entity is destroyed.

SELECT   This block is similar to the PICKQ block, except that when an entity encounters the SELECT block, a selection is made over a number of Hold blocks, rather than QUEUE blocks. Because an entity may be delayed in entering the selected Hold block, the SELECT block must be preceded by a QUEUE block.

The format of the SELECT block is

SELECT,RSR:LABEL:LABEL:...:LABEL;

The block diagram symbol is:

Its operands are defined as:

OPERAND	OPERAND GROUP	DESCRIPTION	ALLOWABLE VALUES	DEFAULT
RSR	1	Resource Selection Rule	See Table 4.2	POR
LABEL	2-M	Labels of HOLD blocks for selection	Label	None

The Resource Selection Rules are shown in Table 4.2.

An application of the SELECT block is:

```
        QUEUE, 1;
        SELECT, POR:TELLR1,TELLR2;
TELLR1 SEIZE: TELLR1;
        .
        .
        .
TELLR2 SEIZE: TELLR2;
        .
        .
```

This sequence models the now-familiar "quick line" used by most banks. Customers join a common queue and use the first teller who becomes available. SELECT with the POR rule sends the entity to the first SEIZE block for which the required resources are available. If TELLR1 and TELLR2 each have a capacity of one, this is equivalent to accessing the first available teller.

Indefinite Time Delays: (WAIT, SIGNAL and SCAN)   In SIMAN, entities can be delayed for an indefinite time, waiting for an event to occur somewhere else in the model. When

TABLE 4.2
RESOURCE SELECTION RULES

Resource Selection Rule	Description
CYC	Cyclic Priority. Select the first available resource beginning with the successor of the last SEIZE or PREEMPT block.
RAN	Random Priority. Select randomly from the SEIZE or PREEMPT blocks for which the required resource units are available.
POR	Preferred Order Rule. Select the first SEIZE or PREEMPT block for which the required number of resource units are available.
LNB	Largest Number Busy. Select the SEIZE or PREEMPT block which has the largest number of resource units busy. Break ties by POR.
SNB	Smallest Number Busy. Select the SEIZE or PREEMPT block which has the smallest number of resource units busy. Break ties by POR.
LRC	Largest Remaining Capacity. Select the SEIZE or PREEMPT block which has the largest remaining resource capacity. Break ties by POR.
SRC	Smallest Remaining Capacity. Select the SEIZE or PREEMPT block which has the smallest remaining resource capacity. Break ties by POR.
UR(K)	User Rule. Select the URth SEIZE or PREEMPT block where UR is computed in a FORTRAN function.
ER(N)	Experimental Rule. Select the SEIZE or PREEMPT block based on rule N defined in the experimental frame.

an entity encounters a WAIT block it must remain in the preceding queue until an appropriate SIGNAL is issued by another entity.

WAIT   The format of the WAIT block is:

WAIT:NSIG:MODIFIERS;

The block diagram symbol is:

Its operand is defined as:

OPERAND	OPERAND GROUP	DESCRIPTION	ALLOWABLE VALUES	DEFAULT
NSIG	2	An integer signal code.	A(N),X(N),N*	None

*N denotes A(I), X(I), I, where the subindex I can be M±K, J±K, or K, where K is an integer.

SIGNAL   The format of the SIGNAL block is:

SIGNAL:NSIG:MODIFIERS;

The block diagram symbol is:

```
┌──────────────┐
│    SIGNAL    │
├──────────────┤
│    NSIG      │
└──────────────┘
```

and its operand is defined as:

OPERAND	OPERAND GROUP	DESCRIPTION	ALLOWABLE VALUES	DEFAULT
NSIG	2	An integer signal code	A(N),X(N),N*	None

*N denotes A(I), X(I), I, where the subindex I can be M±K, J±K, or K, where K is an integer.

Since the WAIT block is a Hold type block, it must be preceded by a QUEUE block to accommodate entities waiting for a signal. As an example of the WAIT and SIGNAL blocks, consider a process in which orders arrive and are processed by a clerk. The orders arrive randomly but the clerk only picks up arriving orders every hour on the hour. The SIMAN blocks necessary to model such a system would be:

```
CREATE:EX(1,1);            ORDERS ARRIVE
QUEUE,1;                   QUEUE UP WAITING FOR CLERK
WAIT:1;                    WAIT FOR HOURLY SIGNAL TO OCCUR
QUEUE,2;                   QUEUE FOR CLERK
SEIZE:CLERK;               OBTAIN CLERKS SERVICES
DELAY:EX(2,1);             PROCESSING TIME
RELEASE:CLERK:DISPOSE;     ORDER IS FINISHED
CREATE:1;                  EVERY HOUR CLERK COLLECTS ORDERS
SIGNAL:1:DISPOSE;          SEND SIGNAL TO ORDERS TO PROCEED
;                          TO CLERK
```

SCAN   SIMAN provides the SCAN block which can delay entities in a queue file until a specific condition arises. This scanning for conditions occurs just prior to the next advancement of time, and every entity being held in the queue file is checked to determine if the condition for further advancement through the model is satisfied. If the scan indicates that an entity can advance, it is moved through the model until it encounters a delay or is destroyed. The scan continues for each waiting entity and ends when every waiting entity has been checked. Because of the exhaustive nature of such an entity by entity scan, and associated increased model running time, it is recommended that scans be avoided if other SIMAN Hold type blocks can be used to control an entity's movement.

The format of the SCAN block is:

SCAN,ML – MU:CONDITION:MODIFIERS;

The block diagram symbol is:

Its operands are defined as:

OPERAND	OPERAND GROUP	DESCRIPTION	ALLOWABLE VALUES	DEFAULT
ML – MU	1	The range of the station numbers used in the scan	Integer	No ranging
CONDITION	2	The logical condition for an entity to be removed from the queue file	Logical statement	None

When the range of station number is used, the scan occurs for each value of M and therefore a separate queue file must exist for entities at each station. To facilitate the specification of queue files for scanning across stations, queue files can be identified using the station index M.

Examples of the SCAN block are:

```
QUEUE,10;
SCAN:NQ(10).GT.5;

QUEUE,1;
SCAN:(NR(1).LT.MR(1)).AND.
      NR(2).LT.MR(2));          RESOURCE 1 AND 2 BOTH
;                               AVAILABLE
QUEUE,2;
SEIZE:OPERATOR;                 OBTAIN OPERATOR
QUEUE,3;
SEIZE:MACHINE;                  OBTAIN MACHINE
DELAY:10;                       OPERATION TIME
RELEASE:OPERATOR;               RELEASE OPERATOR
RELEASE:MACHINE;                RELEASE MACHINE
```

In the first example, entities are held in Queue 10 until five or more entities have built up, and then entities will be removed until the queue is lower than five. In the second example, a check is made to insure that an operator and a machine are available before the entity moves out of the queue file.

ALTER   In SIMAN it is possible, during a simulation, to either increase or decrease the capacity of a resource by using the ALTER block.

The format of the ALTER block is:

```
ALTER:RNAME,CC:MODIFIERS;
```

The block diagram symbol for the ALTER block is:

ALTER
RNAME,CC

Its operands are defined as:

OPERAND	OPERAND GROUP	DESCRIPTION	ALLOWABLE VALUES	DEFAULT
RNAME	2	The name of the Resource which is to have its capacity altered	String	None
CC	2	The capacity change in RNAME	A(N),X(N),N*	None

*N denotes A(I), X(I), I, where the subindex I can be M±K, J±K, or K, where K is an integer.

When the capacity change is negative and there are less than CC available resource units, the number of remaining resource units are eliminated and the rest of the CC units are removed as they become available. This is to prevent the illogical conditions of removing resources that are currently being seized by entities in the model. If CC is prefaced by a ''-'' and is greater than the total resource units, the capacity of the resource is set of zero; it cannot become negative. Any further reduction in the resource is disregarded.

Examples of the ALTER block are:

ALTER:SERVER,+2;
ALTER:MACHINE,–A(3);

In the first example, the number of units of the resource SERVER is immediately increased by two, while in the second example the number of units of the resource MACHINE is decreased by the current value of attribute A(3). This reduction may occur immediately, or may be delayed if less than A(3) units of the MACHINE are currently available. If the total units of MACHINE are A(3) or less, the resource will eventually be eliminated.

PREEMPT   This block is used to allow an entity to seize a resource which is currently controlled by another entity. A preempting entity always preempts the last entity that gained control of the resource through a SEIZE block, regardless of the priorities of the two competing entities. Only one unit of resource capacity may be preempted, even if the number of units of capacity occupied by the preempted entity was greater than one.

Once an entity gains control of a resource by preemption, it can lose control only if it is preempted by an entity of higher priority. When an entity at a SEIZE or PREEMPT block is preempted, it is refiled in the front of the QUEUE immediately preceding the SEIZE block, or it may be routed to another block with its remaining processing time stored in an attribute. Also, when an entity is preempted, the remaining time the entity was scheduled to control the resource is saved. Upon release of the resource by the preempting entity, through a release block, the preempted entity is returned to the resource to continue processing.

The format of the PREEMPT block is:

PREEMPT,PR:RNAME,NA,LSEND:MODIFIERS;

The block diagram symbol is:

```
        /\
       /  \
      /____\
  | PREEMPT,PR     |
  | RNAME,NA,LSEND |
```

Its operands are defined as:

OPERAND	OPERAND GROUP	DESCRIPTION	ALLOWABLE VALUES	DEFAULT
PR	1	The priority of the preempting entity	A(N),X(N),N*	1
RNAME	2	The name of the resource to be preempted	String	None
NA	2	The attribute number for storing the remaining delay	N	None
LSEND	2	The label of the block to which the preempted entity is to be sent	Label	QUEUE of previous SEIZE or PREEMPT block where resource was allocated

*N denotes A(I), X(I), I, where the subindex I can be M±K, J±K, or K, where K is an integer.

Examples of the PREEMPT block are:

QUEUE,10;
PREEMPT:DRILL;
DELAY:EX(1,1);
RELEASE:DRILL;

QUEUE,15,5;
PREEMPT,5:DOCK,1,DOCK2;

In the first example, a preempting entity has the default priority of 1 and will preempt any entity controlling DRILL through a SEIZE block. Entities at a SEIZE block are refiled in the QUEUE preceding the seize (not shown). After an exponential delay, which could represent downtime, the DRILL is released by the preempting entity.

In the second example, entities that are preempted are sent to block DOCK2 and their remaining processing times are stored in A(1). In this example, there cannot be more than five entities waiting to preempt since a capacity of five was placed on the queue file preceding the PREEMPT block.

MATCH   SIMAN provides a mechanism for coordinating the movement of entities through the model with the MATCH block. The entities whose movement is to be controlled are identified by a common "class code." This class code must be stored in an entity attribute and entities having the same attribute value can be considered as being in the same class.

When an entity enters a MATCH block, a set of QUEUE blocks are examined for entities with the specified class code, and if matching entities are found at each queue file, they are moved on through the model or destroyed. The QUEUE blocks to be examined must have the modifier DETACH, since the entities will not move to the next sequential Hold type block. If no destination block is given for an entity when a match occurs, the entity is destroyed.

The format of the MATCH block is:

MATCH,MA:QLBL,LABEL:...:QLBL,LABEL;

The block diagram symbol is:

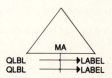

Its operands are defined as:

OPERAND	OPERAND GROUP	DESCRIPTION	ALLOWABLE VALUES	DEFAULT
MA	1	The number of the attribute containing the class code	Integer	None
QLBL	2-M	The label of the preceding queue blocks to be examined	Label	None
LABEL	2-M	The destination of the entity at queue block QLBL	Label	Destroy the entity

As an example of the MATCH block, consider a shop in which three subassemblies are brought together into one single part and then processed as a single unit. The SIMAN blocks to model such a process would be:

```
;PARTS FROM CENTER 1
CENTR1    QUEUE,1:DETACH;        ENTER INTO FIRST QUEUE
;PARTS FROM CENTER 2;
CENTR2    QUEUE,2:DETACH;        ENTER INTO SECOND QUEUE
;PARTS FROM CENTER 3;
CENTR3    QUEUE,3:DETACH;        ENTER INTO THIRD QUEUE
:
:
;MATCHING OF PARTS FROM CENTERS 1,2 AND 3
          MATCH,3:CENTR1,FNLASSM:CENTR2:CENTR3;
FNLASSM   QUEUE,4;               QUEUE FOR FINAL ASSEMBLY
```

In this example it is assumed that in another part of the model the parts were assigned a class code in A(3), and after each subassembly was completed it was transferred to the appropriate QUEUE block. The entity in queue file 1 is moved into the queue file 4, while the entities in queue file 2 and 3 are destroyed after being removed.

SEARCH   SIMAN provides a mechanism for searching queue files and then either removing an entity from the file or making a copy of an entity in the file. Before an entity can be removed or copied from a file, however, its rank in the file must be determined, using the SEARCH block. The location of the entity found in the search is stored in the system index variable J and if the search is unsuccessful, J is set to 0.

The format of the SEARCH block is:

SEARCH,IFL,J1,J2:CONDITION:MODIFIERS;

The block diagram symbol is:

```
SEARCH,IFL,J1,J2
CONDITION
```

Its operands are defined as:

OPERAND	OPERAND GROUP	DESCRIPTION	ALLOWABLE VALUES	DEFAULT
IFL	1	The number of the queue file to be searched	A(N),X(N),N*	None
J1	1	The starting rank for the search	A(N),X(N),N or NQ	1
J2	1	The ending rank for the search	A(N),X(N),N or NQ	NQ
CONDITION	2	The search condition	Expression, MIN(expression) MAX(expression)	None

*N denotes A(I), X(I), I, where the subindex I can be M±K, J±K, or K, where K is an integer.

When MIN or MAX is used the expression must involve one or more attributes of the entity being searched.

Once an entity has been located in a queue file, it can be removed and sent to another block using the REMOVE block, or duplicated and the copy sent to another block using the COPY block.

REMOVE   The REMOVE block is used to extract entities from a queue file and send them to another block.

The REMOVE block has the form:

REMOVE:NR,IFL,LABEL:MODIFIERS;

The block diagram symbol is:

```
REMOVE
NR,IFL,LABEL
```

Its operands are defined as:

OPERAND	OPERAND GROUP	DESCRIPTION	ALLOWABLE VALUES	DEFAULT
NR	2	The rank of the entity removed	A(N),X(N),N* NQ or J	1
IFL	2	The queue file from which the entity is to be removed	A(N),X(N),N or J	None
LABEL	2	The label of the block to which the removed entity is sent	Label	None

*N denotes A(I), X(I), I, where the subindex I can be M±K, J±K, or K, where K is an integer.

COPY   The COPY block is used to duplicate an entity and send the duplicate to a specified block.

The format of the COPY block is:

COPY:NR,IFL,LABEL:MODIFIERS;

The block diagram symbol is:

```
┌─────────────────┐
│      COPY        │
├─────────────────┤
│  NR,IFL,LABEL    │
└─────────────────┘
```

Its operands are defined as:

OPERAND	OPERAND GROUP	DESCRIPTION	ALLOWABLE VALUES	DEFAULT
NR	2	The rank of the entity to be copied	A(N),X(N),N* NQ or J	None
IFL	2	The queue file number from which the entity is to be copied	A(N),X(N),N or J	None
LABEL	2	The label of the block to which the copied entity is to be sent	Label	None

*N denotes A(I), X(I), I, where the subindex I can be M±K, J±K, or K, where K is an integer.

As an example of the SEARCH and REMOVE blocks, consider a system in which a queue is to be searched for entities that have a value of A(1) which is less than five, and all such entities are sent to a separate queue. The SIMAN blocks needed to accomplish this are:

SEARCH	BRANCH,1: IF,NQ(1).GT.0,NEXTSRCH: ELSE,STOPSRCH;	IS QUEUE 1 NOT EMPTY?
NEXTSRCH	SEARCH,1,1,NQ:A(1).LT.5; BRANCH,1: IF,J.EQ.0,STOPSRCH: ELSE,REMOVE;	REPEAT SEARCH DID SEARCH FAIL?
REMOVE	REMOVE:J,1,QUEUEA; BRANCH,1: ALWAYS,SEARCH;	CONTINUE SEARCH
STOPSRCH ;	ASSIGN:A(1)=0:DISPOSE;	DESTROY ENTITY USED FOR SEARCH
QUEUEA ;	QUEUE,2;	PLACE ENTITY INTO QUEUE FILE 2

In this example, the IF branch condition was used to loop through the entire set of entities in queue file 1, removing an entity once it was located. The looping could have been made more efficient by using the search statement

SEARCH,1,J,NQ:A(1).LT.5

since J will be the location of the last element located. This avoids searching through the queue file, checking entities already tested.

FINDJ   To search across entity attributes or across system variables, the FINDJ block is used. The FINDJ block requires the range of the index for the search and either the logical condition needed to end the search, or a MIN or MAX operation. At the completion of the search, the system index J is set equal to the index of the variable, satisfying the search. If an unsuccessful search is made, J is set to 0.

The format of the FINDJ block is:

FINDJ,J1,J2:CONDITION:MODIFIERS;

The block diagram symbol is:

```
FINDJ,J1,J2
CONDITION
```

Its operands are defined as:

OPERAND	OPERAND GROUP	DESCRIPTION	ALLOWABLE VALUES	DEFAULT
J1	1	The initial value of search range	A(N),X(N),N*	None
J2	1	The final value of search range	A(N),X(N),N	None
CONDITION	2	The search condition (must use the index J)	Logical Statement MIN(),MAX()	None

*N denotes A(I), X(I), I, where the subindex I can be M±K, J±K, or K, where K is an integer.

As an example of the FINDJ block, consider the case of locating the index of the attribute with the largest value, which will determine the duration of a delay:

FINDJ,1,4:MAX(A(J));
DELAY:EX(1,1)*A(J);

In this example a search will be made of A(1) through A(4), and after the search, J will be the index of the largest valued attribute. The delay time will then be found by multiplying an exponentially distributed random variable by the largest attribute. Notice that there cannot be a delay between the location of J and the use of J in an expression, since J is a system variable and could change. That is, the following statements:

FINDJ,1,4:MAX(A(J));
QUEUE,1;
SEIZE:OPERATOR;
DELAY:EX(1,1)*A(J);

could involve a delay between QUEUE and SEIZE, allowing J to change. To avoid this problem, the resource should be seized before the FINDJ search is done.

Temporary and Permanent Sets: (GROUP,SPLIT,COMBINE)

Temporary or permanent sets of entities can be formed in SIMAN using the GROUP or COMBINE blocks. The GROUP block forms temporary sets of entities which can later be SPLIT back into the individual member entities while the COMBINE block forms a permanent set in which the individual entities lose their identity.

GROUP   The GROUP block is a Hold-type block that will collect a group of entities and then create a new entity that acts as a single representative entity. The entities in the group move passively through the model attached to the representative entity. If the representative entity passes through a BRANCH block, the group is then associated with the primary (the first branch) entity, and the secondary copies of the representative entity cannot be split at a later time. Groups can subsequently be grouped and then later be split back into the original subgroups.

When a group is formed, the attributes of the representative entity can be assigned as the value of the FIRST entity, the LAST entity, or the SUM or PRODUCT of corresponding attributes of the entities in the set.

An example of the use of groups would be a transportation system in which a group of passengers fill a bus and are transported to a destination and then each passenger splits off to his/her next destination. The buses may themselves be grouped into convoys, etc.

The format of the GROUP block is:

GROUP:N,SAVE:MODIFIERS;

The block diagram symbol is:

Its operands are defined as:

OPERAND	OPERAND GROUP	DESCRIPTION	ALLOWABLE VALUES	DEFAULT
N	2	The size of the set to be grouped	A(N),X(N),N*	1
SAVE	2	The criterion for assigning representative attributes	FIRST, LAST,SUM, PRODUCT	LAST

*N denotes A(I), X(I), I, where the subindex I can be M±K, J±K, or K, where K is an integer.

SPLIT   Entities in a temporary group can be separated out using the SPLIT block. When entities are split out, the representative entity is destroyed.

The SPLIT block has no operands. Its form is simply:

SPLIT:MODIFIERS;

The block diagram symbol for the SPLIT block is:

COMBINE   Permanent sets can be formed using the COMBINE block in the same way that temporary sets are formed, except that the member entities are destroyed when the permanent set is formed.

The format of the COMBINE block is:

COMBINE:N,SAVE:MODIFIERS;

The block diagram symbol is:

Its operands are defined as:

OPERAND	OPERAND GROUP	DESCRIPTION	ALLOWABLE VALUES	DEFAULT
S	2	The size of the set to be combined	A(N),X(N),N*	1
SAVE	2	The criterion for assigning representative attributes	FIRST, LAST,SUM, PRODUCT	LAST

*N denotes A(I), X(I), I, where the subindex I can be M±K, J±K, or K, where K is an integer.

Examples of the GROUP, COMBINE and SPLIT blocks are:

```
QUEUE,1;
GROUP:3;
QUEUE,2;
SEIZE:OPERATOR;
DELAY:UN(1,1);
RELEASE:OPERATOR;
SPLIT;
QUEUE,3;

QUEUE,1;
COMBINE:3;
QUEUE,2;
SEIZE:OPERATOR;
DELAY:UN(1,1);
QUEUE,3;
```

In the first example, entities are temporarily grouped into sets of three, through the set representative placed in queue file 2 and then processed as a single entity. After processing, the group is split back into individual entities and placed in queue file 3. In the second example, the entities in queue file 1 are combined permanently into a single entity and processed, but it cannot be split. One single entity is placed into queue file 3.

4.2 Associated Experimental Frame Elements

In this section, we discuss the experimental frame elements associated with the SIMAN blocks described in the preceding section.

RULES, DISTRIBUTIONS   In a simulation experiment it is often desirable to examine the effect of changing the operating rules and distributions of the model. SIMAN provides a method of changing the rules used in PICKQ, QPICK and SELECT in the RULES element. Random variable distributions may be changed using the DISTRIBUTIONS experimental element. By using the experimental frame for declaration of Rules and Distributions, the experiments become more explicit and changes can be made without changing the simulation model.

RULES   The format of this experimental element is:

RULES:N,RULE:...Repeats through group M;

Its operands are defined as:

OPERAND	OPERAND GROUP	DESCRIPTION	ALLOWABLE VALUES	DEFAULT
N	2-M	The rule number or range of rule numbers	Integer	None
RULE	2-M	The queue or resource selection rule	Rules shown in Tables 4.1 and 4.2	None

An example of the RULES element is:

RULES:1,LRC:2-5,SNQ;

In this example, experimental rule 1 is defined as selecting the resource with the largest remaining capacity when a resource is to be selected. Rules 2-5 state that entities should pick queues, or queues should be picked, using the smallest number in the queue as the criterion.

DISTRIBUTIONS   The format of this experimental element is:

DISTRIBUTIONS:N,TYPE:...Repeats through group M;

Its operands are defined as:

OPERAND	OPERAND GROUP	DESCRIPTION	ALLOWABLE VALUES	DEFAULT
N	2-M	The distribution number, range of distribution numbers	Integer	None
TYPE	2-M	The distribution type [type ED(N) not allowed]	Distributions shown in Table 3.1	None

An example of the DISTRIBUTIONS element is:

DISTRIBUTIONS:1,RN(1,1):2-5,EX(1,2);

In this example, experimental distribution 1 is a normal distribution, using parameter set 1. Random-number generator 1 and experimental distributions 2 through 5 are exponential distributions using parameter set 1 and random-number generator 2.

4.3   General Experimental Frame Elements

In this section we describe some additional experimental frame elements which impact the entire model. These elements permit greater control of a simulation experiment and allow for more complex experiments.

SEEDS   Any of SIMAN's ten random-number generators can be seeded in the experimental frame using the SEEDS element. For each of the random-number generators, the user can specify the initial seed. The user can further specify whether, at the end of each simulation run, the seed should: (1) be reset to its initial value, (2) on even number runs be reset to the previous initial value and the antithetic values used, or (3) the seed should be initialized to its value at the beginning of the previous run plus 100,000. If a random-number generator is not given an explicit seed, a default seed is used.

The format of the SEEDS element is:

SEEDS:IS,ISEED,RI:...Repeats through group M;

Its operands are defined as:

OPERAND	OPERAND GROUP	DESCRIPTION	ALLOWABLE VALUES	DEFAULT
IS	2-M	The stream number to be initialized	1 to 10	None
ISEED	2-M	The initial seed value	Integer	Machine dependent
RI	2-M	Reinitialization on repeat runs of the model	YES,NO, A,C*	NO

*A: Use antithetic methods between even and odd runs. C: Reinitialize to 100,000 beyond current value at end of last run.

An example of the SEEDS element is:

SEEDS:2,11771,YES:3,111137,A;

In this example all the random-number generators except generators 2 and 3 are seeded with the default seeds. Generator 2 is seeded with 11771 and will be reinitialized to this value on each replication. For generator 3 the initial seed is 111137, and on even-numbered runs, the antithetic method of generating random numbers is used. Generator 3 uses the same starting seeds for runs (1,2), (3,4), etc., and the starting seed for run $i + 2$ is the same as the ending seed for run i.

INITIALIZE   Just as random-number seeds can be initialized before the model is executed, SIMAN system variables can be initialized using the INITIALIZE element. If a system is not initialized, it is by default set to 0.
  The form of the INITIALIZE element is:

INITIALIZE,VAR=VALUE,...Repeats;

Its operands are defined as:

OPERAND	OPERAND GROUP	DESCRIPTION	ALLOWABLE VALUES	DEFAULT
VAR	1	The system variable to be initialized	J or X(K)	None
VALUE	1	The value to be assigned to the variable	Real or integer constant	None

An example of the INITIALIZE element is:

INITIALIZE,X(1)=1,J=5;

In this example, the system variable X(1) and the system index J are initialized to 1.0 and 5, respectively.

SCHEDULES   This element, used in conjunction with the RESOURCES element, provides the means to periodically alter the available capacities of resources. Reasons for doing this include scheduled breaks or maintenance, and unscheduled downtime. SCHEDULES is an alternative to using the ALTER block to establish varying resource capacities. Like the ALTER block, SCHEDULES cannot claim resource capacity that is occupied, and resource capacity can never be made negative.

The form of the SCHEDULES element is:

SCHEDULES:N,NCAP*DUR,...:Repeats through M;

Its operands are defined as:

OPERAND	OPERAND GROUP	DESCRIPTION	ALLOWABLE VALUES	DEFAULT
N	2-M	The schedule number	Integer constant	None
NCAP	2-M	The resource capacity	Integer constant	None
DUR	2-M	The corresponding capacity duration	Real constant, or SIMAN random var.	Infinite

An example of the SCHEDULES element is:

RESOURCES:1,WORKER,SCHED(1):2-3,MACHINE,SCHED(2),SCHED(2);

SCHEDULES:1,3*8,1*16,2,:2,1*EX(1,1),0*UN(2,1);

In this example, WORKER is a resource whose capacity is defined by schedule number 1, and resources 2 and 3 are indexed resources, MACHINE(1) and MACHINE(2) with capacities defined by schedule 2. Schedule 1 initializes the capacity of WORKER at 3. After 8 hours (one shift), the capacity is changed to 1 for a period of 16 hours (two shifts), and then it is set at 2 for the remainder of the simulation.

According to Schedule 2, MACHINE(1) and MACHINE(2) begin with a capacity of 1 and remain at that level for durations that are separate samples from an exponential distribution, perhaps corresponding to intervals between failures. The two machines' capacities are eventually decreased to 0 for periods of time that are separate samples from a uniform distribution, perhaps representing repair time. This cycle is repeated until the end of the simulation run.

If the sum of the capacity durations specified should be less than the simulation run length, the sequence of schedules is repeated, beginning with the first capacity duration combination.

TABLES   The SIMAN user can create special functions that are straight-line segments between pairs of points using the TABLES element. This is particularly useful when building empirical distributions or functions into a model. Each empirical function is given a function number, along with the number of points of the function, the low and incremental values of the independent variable and the values of the dependent variable. The format of TABLES element is:

TABLES:N,XLOW,XINC,Y(1),Y(2),...Y(p):Repeats through group M;

Its operands are defined as:

OPERAND	OPERAND GROUP	DESCRIPTION	ALLOWABLE VALUES	DEFAULT
N	2-M	The table number	Integer	None
XLOW	2-M	The low value of the independent variable	Constant	None
XINC	2-M	The increment between successive values of the independent variable	Constant	None
Y(i)	2-M	The values of the dependent variable (1=1,2,...p)	Constant	None

As an example of using the TABLES element consider a system in which the mean time between entity creations (arrivals) is a function of the time of day as shown in Fig. 4.2.

FIGURE 4.2   TIME VARYING INTERARRIVAL TIMES

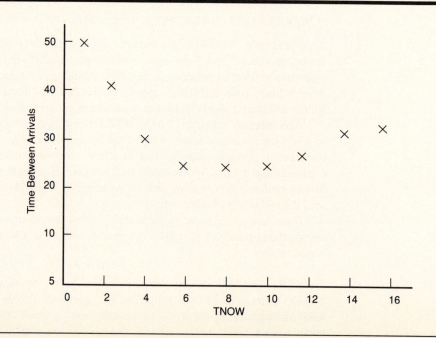

The function can be declared using the TABLES element:

TABLES:1,0.0,2.0,50.,40.,25.,20.,20.,20.,25.,30.,30.;

and the function can then be referenced in a block such as:

CREATE:EX(1,1)*TF(1,TNOW);

which will create entities with a mean time between creation equal to the product of an exponentially distributed random variable and the table function TF whose value changes with TNOW. TF is computed using linear interpolation within the range of the independent variable.

ARRIVALS   This experimental element allows scheduling of entity arrivals at specific times in simulation. When scheduled entities arrive, they must be directed to a QUEUE, or STATION block.

The format of the ARRIVALS element is:

ARRIVALS:N,TYPE,DT,NB,A1,A2..:Repeats through group M;

Its operands are defined as:

OPERAND	OPERAND GROUP	DESCRIPTION	ALLOWABLE VALUES	DEFAULT
N	2-M	The arrival number	Integer	None
TYPE	2-M	The entry type	STATION(K) or QUEUE(K)*	None
DT	2-M	The time of arrival	Real Constant	0.0
NB	2-M	The batch size	Integer	1
A1,A2..	2-M	The attribute values of the entity	Constant	0.0

* K is integer.

An example of the ARRIVALS element is:

ARRIVALS:1,QUEUE(3),10.0,2,1.0,5.0,0.0,6.0;

In this example, after the simulation has executed for 10 time units, two entities arrive at QUEUE 3. For both of the entities the values of A(1) through A(4) are 1.0, 5.0,0.0, and 6.0, respectively. All other entity attributes are 0.0.

4.4   Illustrative Problem Set II

This problem set consists of two examples which illustrate the use of some of the blocks and elements discussed in the previous three sections. The first problem models a system where rush and regular jobs vie for two available machines. In the second problem, we model two machines in parallel, in tandem with a single machine that represents an assembly process.

PROBLEM II.1   This problem is adapted from one of the SIMAN workshops offered by Pegden and others. A department assembles electrical connectors using a fully automatic or semiautomatic machine. Jobs arrive in batches of 5, and are classified as either regular (80%) or rush (20%). Rush orders are processed before regular orders. Processing time on the automatic machine ranges from 10 to 30 minutes, uniformly distributed, and from 40 to 60 minutes, uniformly distributed, on the semiautomatic machine.

The SIMAN model and experimental frames for this system are shown in Fig. 4.3, and the SIMAN Summary Report appears in Fig. 4.4.

In this example, we use a discrete user-defined probability function to determine whether a job is regular or rush. Rush jobs are placed in QUEUE 1 ahead of regular jobs using the RANKINGS element, and thus given priority. The SELECT block uses the preferred order rule (POR) to try first to use the automatic machine, and if it is busy, then the semiautomatic machine.

FIGURE 4.3   PROBLEM II.1 CODE

```
BEGIN;
          CREATE,5:240:MARK(2);       CREATE ARRIVING BATCHES
          ASSIGN:A(1)=DP(1,1);        REGULAR OR RUSH JOB
          QUEUE,1;                    WAIT FOR ASSEMBLY
          SELECT,POR:AUTO:SEMI;       SELECT A MACHINE
AUTO      SEIZE:AUTO;                 CAPTURE AUTOMATIC MACH
          DELAY:UN(2,1);              ASSEMBLE PARTS
          RELEASE:AUTO:NEXT(TALLY);   RELEASE MACHINE
SEMI      SEIZE:SEMI;                 CAPTURE SEMIAUTOMTIC MACH
          DELAY:UN(3,1);              ASSEMBLE PARTS
          RELEASE:SEMI;               RELEASE MACHINE
TALLY     TALLY:A(1),INT(2):DISPOSE; TALLY TIME IN SYS BY TYPE
END;



BEGIN;
PROJECT,PARTS ASSEMBLY,MEDEIROS,6/12/84;
DISCRETE,50,2,1;
PARAMETERS:1,.2,1,1.0,2:
           2,10,30:
           3,40,60;
RANKINGS:1,LVF(1);
REPLICATE,1,0,600;
RESOURCES:1,AUTO:
          2,SEMI;
TALLIES:1,RUSH JOB TIME:
        2,REGULAR TIME;
END;
```

FIGURE 4.4   PROBLEM II.1 OUTPUT

```
                        SIMAN Summary Report

                      Run Number    1 of  1

Project:   PARTS ASSEMBLY
Analyst:   MEDEIROS
Date   :    6/12/1984

Run ended at time :    .6000E+03


                        Tally Variables
                        ----------------

Number Identifier       Average    Standard   Minimum    Maximum    Number
                                   Deviation  Value      Value      of Obs.
-----------------------------------------------------------------------------
  1  RUSH JOB TIME      31.39215   16.86946   11.94928   53.56219      7
  2  REGULAR TIME       62.86142   23.59335   26.30167   93.88644      8


Run Time :   1 Second(s)
```

PROBLEM II.2 Jobs arrive at two identical machines according to an exponential distribution with a mean interarrival time of 12 minutes. The first available machine is selected. Processing on either machine is normally distributed with a mean of 10 minutes and a standard deviation of 3 minutes. Upon completion, jobs are sent to a third machine where they queue up for assembly, which requires 5 minutes, normally distributed with a standard deviation of 2 minutes. Jobs are selected from the queue for assembly based on the estimated assembly time. Completed jobs then leave the system.

The assembly machine is unreliable. It fails at intervals which may be described by an exponential distribution with a mean of 50 minutes. Repair time is uniformly distributed over the range 5 to 15 minutes. Also, parts in the assembly machine may be preempted by high-priority jobs which arrive according to a uniform distribution over the range of 1 to 50 minutes. Assembly time for these jobs is the same as that for regular jobs.

The SIMAN model and experimental frames for this system are shown in Fig. 4.5, and the SIMAN Summary Report appears in Fig. 4.6

The SELECT block is used in this example to choose the next available machine to process the parts. Once processed, the parts are sent to two separate QUEUE blocks (labeled QUEUE2 and QUEUE3) which have the DETACH modifier appended. This is required because the entities are not proceeding to the next sequential block, but rather are being extracted from the QUEUE blocks by a MATCH block. The MATCH block takes entities from QUEUE 2 and QUEUE 3 which are coded in A(2), routes the entities

FIGURE 4.5   PROBLEM II.2 CODE

```
BEGIN;
;MACHINES IN TANDEM
          CREATE:EX(1,1):MARK(1);            JOBS ARRIVE
          QUEUE,1;                            WAIT BEFORE MACH1 AND MACH2
          SELECT,SNB:MACH1:MACH2;             SELECT FIRST MACH AVAIL.
MACH1     SEIZE:MACHINE(1);                   CAPTURE MACHINE
          TALLY:1,INT(1);                     TALLY WAIT TIME
          DELAY:RN(2,1);                      PROCESS ON MACH1
          ASSIGN:A(2)=1;                      ASSIGN MATCHING CODE
          RELEASE:MACHINE(1):NEXT(QUEUE2);    RELEASE MACH1
MACH2     SEIZE:MACHINE(2);                   CAPTURE MACHINE
          TALLY:1,INT(1);                     TALLY WAIT TIME
          DELAY:RN(2,1);                      PROCESS ON MACH2
          ASSIGN:A(2)=1;                      ASSIGN MATCHING CODE
          RELEASE:MACHINE(2):NEXT(QUEUE3);    RELEASE MACH2
QUEUE2    QUEUE,2:DETACH;                     QUEUE FOR FINAL ASSB.
QUEUE3    QUEUE,3:DETACH;                     QUEUE FOR FINAL ASSB.
          MATCH,2:QUEUE2,FINAL:QUEUE3;        DESTROY ONE COPY OF ENTITY
FINAL     ASSIGN:A(3)=RN(3,1);                ASSIGN ASSB. TIME
          QUEUE,4:MARK(4);                    QUEUE IN ORDER OF OPN. TIME
          SEIZE:MACHINE(3);                   CAPTURE MACH3
          TALLY:2,INT(4);                     TALLY WAIT TIME
          DELAY:A(3);                         ASSB. ON MACH3
          RELEASE:MACHINE(3);                 RELEASE MACH3
          TALLY:3,INT(1):DISPOSE;             TALLY TIME IN SYSTEM
;HIGH PRIORITY JOBS WHICH PREEMPT MACHINE(3)
          CREATE:UN(4,1);                     HI PRIORITY JOB ARRIVES
          QUEUE,5;
          PREEMPT:MACHINE(3);                 PREEMPTS JOB ON MACHINE
          DELAY:RN(3,1);                      PROCESS OM MACH3
          RELEASE:MACHINE(3);                 RELEASE MACH3
          COUNT:1:DISPOSE;                    COUNT NO. OF PREEMPTS
;MACHINE DOWNTIME SEGMENT
          CREATE:EX(5,1),1:MARK(5);           CREATE MACHINE FAILURE ENTITY
BACK      ALTER:MACHINE(3),-1:MARK(5);        MACH FAILS, REDUCE CAP. TO 0
          DELAY:UN(6,1);                      REPAIR TIME
          ALTER:MACHINE(3),+1;                MACHINE REPRD, INCREASE CAP TO 1
          TALLY:4,INT(5);                     TALLY DOWNTIME
          DELAY:EX(5,1):NEXT(BACK);           TIME TO NEXT FAILURE
END;


BEGIN;
PROJECT,MACHINES IN TANDEM,PERRY,3/16/85;
DISCRETE,60,8,5;
RESOURCES:1-3,MACHINE;
PARAMETERS:1,12:
           2,10,3:
           3,5,2:
           4,1,50:
           5,50:
           6,5,15;
RANKINGS:4,LVF(3);
DSTAT:1,NR(1),MACHINE 1 UTIL:
      2,NR(2),MACHINE 2 UTIL:
      3,NR(3),MACHINE 3 UTIL;
COUNTERS:1,NO. OF PREEMPTS;
TALLIES:1,WAIT FOR MACH 1,12:
        2,WAIT FOR MACH 3:
        3,TIME IN SYSTEM:
        4,MACH 3 DOWNTIME;
REPLICATE,1,0,480;
END;
```

FIGURE 4.6   PROBLEM II.2 OUTPUT

```
                        SIMAN Summary Report

                        Run Number   1 of  1

Project:   MACHINES IN TANDEM
Analyst:   PERRY
Date   :    3/16/1985

Run ended at time :   .4800E+03



                        Tally Variables
                        ---------------

Number Identifier       Average    Standard   Minimum    Maximum    Number
                                   Deviation  Value      Value      of Obs.
-------------------------------------------------------------------------------
  1   WAIT FOR MACH 1    .40102    1.14171     .00000    4.90187      37
  2   WAIT FOR MACH 3   2.85909    5.87872     .00000   20.51425      12
  3   TIME IN SYSTEM  150.98220   44.90519   79.28545  219.15580      12
  4   MACH 3 DOWNTIME    9.58356   3.21673    5.85799   14.10291       7


                    Discrete Change Variables
                    -------------------------

Number Identifier       Average    Standard   Minimum    Maximum    Time
                                   Deviation  Value      Value      Period
-------------------------------------------------------------------------------
  1   MACHINE 1 UTIL     .44808     .49730     .00000    1.00000     480.00
  2   MACHINE 2 UTIL     .23120     .42160     .00000    1.00000     480.00
  3   MACHINE 3 UTIL     .31786     .46564     .00000    1.00000     480.00


                              Counters
                              --------
Number Identifier        Count     Limit
-------------------------------------------------
  1  NO. OF PREEMPTS      19    Infinite


Run Time :   6 Second(s)
```

from QUEUE 2 to a block labeled FINAL, and destroys the entities from QUEUE 3. In this way we can represent the assembly of the two parts. Parts to be assembled are selected from QUEUE 4 based on the lowest estimated assembly time, accomplished using the RANKINGS element.

There are two additional model segments: one to implement high-priority jobs preempting the regular jobs, and one to represent the machine failure-repair cycle. The first segment uses the PREEMPT block to capture resource units from lower priority entities, while the second uses the ALTER block to change the number of resource units available in response to machine failures and repairs.

5.0 ADVANCED MODELING CONCEPTS: STATIONS AND SUBMODELS

A powerful modeling concept in SIMAN is that of a station, which allows the modeler to build submodels and then route entities through these submodels. A submodel can also be used to model a number of similar operations in a system. For example, a job shop or assembly line may consist of many stations, with each station differing only in parameters such as the number of machines, and processing times. If the operating rules within each station are similar, all the stations can be represented through a single submodel.

5.1 Station and Submodel Blocks and Experimental Frame Elements

To facilitate the use of submodels, each entity has in addition to an array of attributes, A(N), a station index M, a sequence set number NS, and a sequence index IS. The entity variables M, NS, and IS are used to control the flow of entities through stations and submodels.

Initially an entity's station index M is 0 and can be changed using the ASSIGN block. In addition, whenever an entity is moved to a new station or submodel using a transfer block such as ROUTE, or the material-handling blocks discussed in the following section (TRANSPORT or CONVEY), the station index M is automatically updated to the new station number. The station attribute M can be used as part of an arithmetic or logical expression, used in the SCAN block to establish the scan range, or in the QUEUE block as an offset.

STATION   The STATION block is used to define a submodel in SIMAN denoting the beginning of one or more stations. The format of the STATION block is:

STATION,N1 – N2:MODIFIERS;

The block diagram symbol is:

N1–N2

Its operands are defined as:

OPERAND	OPERAND GROUP	DESCRIPTION	ALLOWABLE VALUES	DEFAULT
N1 – N2	1	The range of stations that begin at this block	Integer	None

Examples of the STATION blocks are:

STATION,1;
STATION,3 – 7;

In the first example, the block represents the beginning of a single station, Station 1. In the second example the block marks the beginning to stations 3 through 7. Notice that the station range must be expressed using integer constants and cannot be an expression.

ROUTE   An entity can be transferred to a submodel, starting with the STATION block by the ROUTE, TRANSFER, or CONVEY block. Here we will only consider the ROUTE block, and in the next section the TRANSFER and CONVEY blocks will be described.

The format of the ROUTE block is:

ROUTE:DURATION,NS:MODIFIERS;

The block diagram symbol is:

Its operands are:

OPERAND	OPERAND GROUP	DESCRIPTION	ALLOWABLE VALUES	DEFAULT
DURATION	2	The duration of the routing delay	Expression	0.0
NS	2	The station number to which the entity is to be sent	A(N),X(N), N* or SEQ	None

*N denotes A(I), X(I), or I, where the subindex I, can be M±K, J±K, or K, where K is an integer.

SEQUENCES   When the experimental frame element, SEQ, is used to route an entity to a station, the entity's sequence index, IS, is incremented by one and the entity is routed to the ISth station listed in sequence set NS. The sequence sets are defined in the experimental frame using the SEQUENCES element described below.

The format of the SEQUENCES element is:

SEQUENCES:N,NSTA1, a_1, a_2../NSTA2, a_1, a_2..:Repeats through group M;

OPERAND	OPERAND GROUP	DESCRIPTION	ALLOWABLE VALUES	DEFAULT
N	2-M	The sequence set number	Integer	None
NSTA	2-M	A sequential station number	Integer	None
a_1, a_2..	2-M	The assigned value of attributes when entity is routed to station NSTA	Real constant, SIMAN random variable	Current value

When an entity is transferred to a station using the SEQ option, the entity's attributes are assigned the values a_1, a_2..., unless no value for a_i is given, in which case it remains unchanged.

5.2   Queues and Scans Within Submodels

To facilitate the use of submodels, SIMAN allows for queue files and scan ranges to be specified using an entity's current station number.

The form of the QUEUE using the station attribute is:

QUEUE,I±M;

and for the SCAN block the form using the station attribute M is:

SCAN,ML–MU:CONDITION;

When the SCAN block uses a range of stations, it must be preceded by a QUEUE block with a queue file specified as a function of M, and the station number of entities must be within the scan range ML–MU. The scan condition is tested for each station number in the range and can lead to long running times. An example of QUEUE and SCAN blocks using the station number M is:

```
CREATE:EX(1,1);
ROUTE:0,1;
STATION,1-5;
QUEUE, M+5;
SCAN,1–5:NQ(M+5).GT.3;
QUEUE,M;
SEIZE:OPER(M);
DELAY:EX(M,2);
RELEASE:OPER(M);
ROUTE:0,M+1;
STATION,6:DISPOSE;
```

In this example we have two submodels, the first representing the processing at stations 1–5 and a second submodel, representing the processing at station 6. As the entity passes through the submodels we use its station attribute M to control: the queue files it joins, the scan condition for leaving the queue file, the resources it seizes, and the parameter sets it uses for delay times.

The entities are created and immediately routed to station 1. Upon being routed to the STATION block, the entity's station number M is changed to 1. The entity is filed in QUEUE M+5 (initially QUEUE file 6). Using the SCAN block the entity is delayed until the queue file builds up to 4 and then the entity moves to QUEUE M and attempts to seize the resource OPER(M). After seizing OPER(M), a delay occurs, using parameter set M and upon releasing OPER(M), the entity's station attribute, M, is incremented and the process is repeated. When the station attribute is incremented to 6, the entity transfers to station 6 where it is disposed. Without the SIMAN station facility the above model would have required a number of tests and branches, and would have been much less structured.

5.3   Illustrative Problem Set III

In this section we present two examples of models of systems that use the station capabilities of SIMAN. The first example deals with small appliance assembly, and the second with printed-circuit board assembly.

PROBLEM III.1   In the first example, small appliances are assembled in four stages. After each assembly step, the appliance is inspected or tested and if a defect is found, it must be corrected and then checked again. The assemblies arrive at a constant rate of 1 assembly per minute, and times to assembly, test, and correct defects are normally distributed. The mean and standard deviation of the time to assemble, inspect, and correct defects, as well as the likelihood of an assembly error are shown in the following table. If an assembly is found defective, the defect is corrected, and it is inspected again. After a defect is corrected, the likelihood of another defect being found is the same as during the first inspection. We assume, in this model, that an assembly defect is eventually corrected and then it is passed on to the next station.

	Assembly Time		Inspect. Time			Correct. Time	
Center	Mean	Std. Dev.	Mean	Std. Dev.	P(error)	Mean	Std. Dev.
1	.70	.20	.20	.05	.10	.20	.05
2	.75	.25	.20	.05	.05	.15	.04
3	.80	.15	.15	.03	.03	.10	.02
4	.85	.20	.10	.03	.10	.25	.06

The SIMAN model and experimental frame for this example are shown in Fig. 5.1. A SIMAN Summary Report is shown in Fig. 5.2. We see that all four assembly stations

FIGURE 5.1   PROBLEM III.1 CODE

```
BEGIN;
        CREATE:1;                          ASSEMBLIES ARRIVE 1 PER MINUTE
        ASSIGN:M=1;                        INITIALIZE STATION TO 1
;
        STATION,1-4;                       ASSEMBLY SUB-MODEL
        ASSIGN:A(2)=M+12;                  STORE IN A(2) INDEX P(FAIL TEST)
        QUEUE,M;                           WAIT IN STATION QUEUE
        SEIZE:OPER(M);                     SEIZE OPERATOR AT STATION M
        ASSIGN:A(1)=M;                     SET A(1) TO CURRENT STATION
        DELAY:RN(A(1),1);                  ASSEMBLY TIME
        ASSIGN:A(1)=M+4;                   INDEX A(1) TO PAR. SET M+4
TEST    DELAY:RN(A(1),1);                  INSPECTION OR TEST TIME
        BRANCH,1:
            WITH,P(A(2),1),REPROC:         !PART DEFECTIVE?
            ELSE,NEXTSTA;                   PART GOOD, GO TO NEXT STN.          (Continued)
```

```
REPROC     ASSIGN:A(3)=M+8;             INDEX A(3) TO M+8
           DELAY:RN(A(3),1):NEXT(TEST); CORRECT ASSEM. PROBLEM
NEXTSTA    RELEASE:OPER(M);             RELEASE OPERATOR
           ROUTE:,M+1;                  TRANSFER TO NEXT STATION
;
           STATION,5-5;                 ASSEMBLY COMPLETED
           COUNT:1,1:DISPOSE;           DESTROY ENTITY
END;


BEGIN;
PROJECT,FOUR STATION ASSEMBLY,S.V.HOOVER,10/26/84;
DISCRETE,100,3,8,5;
RESOURCES:1-4,OPER;
PARAMETERS:1,.70,.20:2,.75,.25:3,.80,.15:4,.85,.20:
   5,.20,.05:6,.20,.05:7,.15,.03:8,.10,.03:
   9,.20,.05:10,.15,.04:11,.10,.02:12,.25,.06:
   13,.10:14,.05:15,.03:16,.10;
REPLICATE,1,0,200;
DSTAT:1,NQ(1),QUEUE 1:
     2,NQ(2),QUEUE 2:
     3,NQ(3),QUEUE 3:
     4,NQ(4),QUEUE 4:
     5,NR(1),UTIL. OPER1:
     6,NR(2),UTIL. OPER2:
     7,NR(3),UTIL. OPER3:
     8,NR(4),UTIL. OPER4;
COUNTERS:1,TOTAL ASSM.;
END;
```

FIGURE 5.2   PROBLEM III.1 OUTPUT

```
                        SIMAN Summary Report

                        Run Number   1 of  1

Project:  FOUR STATION ASSEMBL
Analyst:  S.V.HOOVER
Date   :  10/26/1984

Run ended at time :   .2000E+03

                    Discrete Change Variables
                    -------------------------

                                    Standard  Minimum   Maximum   Time
Number Identifier       Average     Deviation Value     Value     Period
------------------------------------------------------------------------
   1   QUEUE 1           .38495      .57308   .00000    3.00000   200.00
   2   QUEUE 2           .82023      .78105   .00000    3.00000   200.00
   3   QUEUE 3           .62341      .77197   .00000    3.00000   200.00
   4   QUEUE 4          1.37409     1.22876   .00000    4.00000   200.00
   5   UTIL. OPER1       .93279      .25039   .00000    1.00000   200.00
   6   UTIL. OPER2       .94321      .23145   .00000    1.00000   200.00
   7   UTIL. OPER3       .93533      .24594   .00000    1.00000   200.00
   8   UTIL. OPER4       .95893      .19846   .00000    1.00000   200.00

                            Counters
                            --------

Number Identifier     Count    Limit
--------------------------------------------
   1   TOTAL ASSM.      191    Infinite

Run Time : 47 Second(s)
```

can be represented with one submodel, using the station attribute M to assign a value to A(1), A(2) and A(3) for arguments in DELAY and BRANCH blocks. Using submodels we have made the size of the model much smaller and also more structured.

PROBLEM III.2   The second example using submodels is a SIMAN model of an electronics assembly operation, in which there are three different printed-circuit boards to be assembled. Each board is routed through four assembly areas and the routing order is different for each of the boards. Further, the number of stations in each assembly area is different, and the times to assemble a board depends upon the board type and the operation. The model is intended to determine the time to complete 50 boards of each type. The assembly times per board are exponentially distributed with the mean times shown below.

Board A		Board B		Board C	
Area	*Mean Time*	*Area*	*Mean Time*	*Area*	*Mean Time*
1	10.0	2	5.0	3	12.0
2	12.0	4	6.0	2	14.0
4	15.0	3	8.0	3	15.0
		1	4.0	1	8.0
				4	7.0

The model and experimental frame for this system are shown in Fig. 5.3. The SIMAN Summary Report is shown in Fig. 5.4.

In this model, additional boards can be introduced by adding additional SEQUENCES elements in the experimental frame and adding another CREATE, ASSIGN, ROUTE at the beginning of the model. This example shows how models of very complex systems can be reduced to a simple form in SIMAN using its submodel capability. In the next section, we discuss the use of stations to model material-handling systems, such as transporters and conveyors.

FIGURE 5.3   PROBLEM III.2 CODE

```
BEGIN;
            CREATE,50:0,1;      CREATE BATCH OF 50 BOARD A
            ASSIGN:NS=1;        ASSIGN TO SEQUENCE 1
            ROUTE:,SEQ;         START THROUGH SEQUENCE
            CREATE,50:0,1;      CREATE BATCH OF 50 BOARD B
            ASSIGN:NS=2;        ASSIGN TO SEQUENCE 2
            ROUTE:,SEQ;         START THROUGH SEQUENCE
            CREATE,50:0,1;      CREATE BATCH OF 50 BOARD C
            ASSIGN:NS=3;        ASSIGN TO SEQUENCE 3
            ROUTE:,SEQ;         START THROUGH SEQUENCE
;
            STATION,1-4;
            QUEUE,M;            QUEUE FOR OPERATOR
            SEIZE:OPER(M);      SEIZE OPERATOR
            DELAY:A(1)*EX(1,1); PROCESS TIME
            RELEASE:OPER(M);    FREE OPERATOR
            ROUTE:,SEQ;         GO TO NEXT STATION
;
            STATION,5:DISPOSE;  DESTROY ENTITY
END;


BEGIN;
PROJECT,BOARD ASSEMBLY,S.V.HOOVER,10/26/84;
DISCRETE,200,1,4,5;
RESOURCES:1-4,OPER;
PARAMETERS:1,1;
SEQUENCES:1,1,10.0/2,12.0/4,15.0/5:
          2,2,5.0/4,6.0/3,8.0/1,4.0/5:
          3,3,12.0/2,14.0/3,15.0/1,8.0/4,7.0/5;
REPLICATE,1;
DSTAT:1,NQ(1),QUEUE 1:
      2,NQ(2),QUEUE 2:
      3,NQ(3),QUEUE 3:
      4,NQ(4),QUEUE 4;
END;
```

FIGURE 5.4   PROBLEM III.2 OUTPUT

```
                      SIMAN Summary Report

                      Run Number    1 of  1

Project:   BOARD ASSEMBLY
Analyst:   S.V.HOOVER
Date   :   10/26/1984

Run ended at time :   .1672E+04
```

Discrete Change Variables

Number	Identifier	Average	Standard Deviation	Minimum Value	Maximum Value	Time Period
1	QUEUE 1	9.90	13.52	.00	49.00	1671.78
2	QUEUE 2	33.76	22.47	.00	67.00	1671.78
3	QUEUE 3	34.35	24.34	.00	75.00	1671.78
4	QUEUE 4	4.71	4.38	.00	16.00	1671.78

Run Time : 10 Second(s)

6.0   ADVANCED MODELING CONCEPTS: MATERIAL HANDLING SYSTEMS

One of the most unique and powerful capabilities of SIMAN is direct incorporation of material-handling processes. The SIMAN material-handling capabilities include both variable-path TRANSPORTERS and fixed-path CONVEYORS. The path that transporters or conveyors take is defined by stations and the distance between stations. The transporters and conveyors are also characterized by their capacity and velocity.

6.1   Transporter Blocks

REQUEST   To gain control of a transporter, an entity must REQUEST a transporter, very much like an entity would seize a resource. Like the SEIZE block, a priority rule is required. The major difference between the SEIZE block and the REQUEST block is that an entity may experience two delays waiting for the transporter. An initial delay may occur if the requested transporter is not available, in which case the entity is held in a preceding QUEUE block. A REQUEST block must be immediately preceded by a QUEUE block. When the transporter becomes available, a second delay may occur if the transporter must move from its current station to the station of the requesting entity. The entity leaves the REQUEST block when the transporter arrives at the station of the requesting entity.

The format of the REQUEST block is:

REQUEST,PR:TUNIT(TSR,NA):MODIFIERS;

The block diagram symbol block is:

Its operands are:

OPERAND	OPERAND GROUP	DESCRIPTION	ALLOWABLE VALUES	DEFAULT
PR	1	The priority of the request	A(N),X(N) or N*	1
TUNIT(TSR,NA)	2	The transporter name	String	None
		TSR is request rule	See Table 6.1	None
or		NA is the index of an attribute which will be assigned as the transporter index	A(N),X(N) or N	None
TUNIT(T)	2	The transporter name with an integer index	String and K or M±K	None

*N denotes A(I), X(I), or I, where the subindex I, can be M±K, J±K, or K, where K is integer.

The Transporter Selection Rules are shown in Table 6.1.

TABLE 6.1
TRANSPORTER SELECTION RULES

Transporter Selection Rule	Description
CYC	Cyclic Priority. Select the first available transporter unit beginning with the successor of the last unit selected.
RAN	Random Priority. Select randomly from the available transporter units.
POR	Preferred Order Rule. Select the available transporter unit which has the lowest index.
SDS	Smallest Distance to Station. Select the available transporter nearest the requesting station.
LSD	Largest Distance to Station. Select the available transporter farthest from the requesting station.
UR(K)	User Rule. Select the transporter index UR, where UR is computed in a FORTRAN function.
ER(N)	Experimental Rule. Select the transporter unit based on rule number N, specified in the experimental frame.

Examples of the REQUEST block are:

```
QUEUE,1;
REQUEST,4:TRUCK(SDS,2);

QUEUE,2;
REQUEST:HOIST(RAN,1);
```

In the first example, a transporter TRUCK is requested with a priority of 4. The nearest available truck is assigned to the requesting entity. If no TRUCK is available, the entity is placed in a queue file according to its priority. When the entity's REQUEST is honored, the index of the assigned TRUCK will be stored in A(2).

In the second example, a transporter, HOIST, is requested with a priority of 1. One of the available HOISTs is randomly selected and the index of the selected HOIST is stored in A(1) of the entity. If no HOIST is available the entity is filed in the preceding queue and will, based upon priority, be assigned the first available HOIST.

ALLOCATE and MOVE

The process of requesting a transporter can be divided into two steps: first the transporter is allocated to a requesting entity, and then the transporter is moved to the station of the requesting entity. In some applications it is desirable to divide the REQUEST of a transporter into these two separate steps using the ALLOCATE, and MOVE blocks.

ALLOCATE   The ALLOCATE block is a Hold type block and must be preceded by a QUEUE block.

The format of the ALLOCATE block is:

```
ALLOCATE,PR:TUNIT(TSR,NA):MODIFIERS;
```

The block diagram symbol is:

It has the following operands:

OPERAND	OPERAND GROUP	DESCRIPTION	ALLOWABLE VALUES	DEFAULT
PR	1	The priority of the request	A(N),X(N) or N*	1
TUNIT(TSR,NA)	2	The transporter name	String	None
		TSR is the request rule	See Table 6.1	None
or		N is the index of an attribute which will be assigned as the transporter index	A(N),X(N) or N	None
TUNIT(T)	2	The transporter name with an integer index	String and K or M±K	None

*N denotes A(I), X(I), or I, where the subindex I can be M±K, J±K, or K, where K is integer.

MOVE   After an entity has been allocated a transporter, the delay until the transporter arrives at the entity's station is modeled using the operation block MOVE.

The form of the MOVE block is:

MOVE:TUNIT(NA),NS,VEL:MODIFIERS;

The block diagram symbol is:

MOVE
TUNIT,NS,VEL

The operands of the MOVE block are:

OPERAND	OPERAND GROUP	DESCRIPTION	ALLOWABLE VALUES	DEFAULT
TUNIT(NA)	2	The indexed transporter unit	String and A(N),X(N) or N*	None
NS	2	The destination station of the transporter being moved	A(N),X(N) or N	None
VEL	2	The velocity of the transporter as it moves to its destination station	Expression	VT(N)

*N denotes A(I), X(I), or I, where the subindex I, can be M±K, J±K, or K, where K is integer.

The ALLOCATE-MOVE can be used to model transporters that travel at different speeds when unloaded or when the transporter must obtain control of resources, such as a pathway, before it can move to a new station.

Examples of the ALLOCATE-MOVE are

```
QUEUE,M+5;
ALLOCATE,3:TRUCK((SDS,A(3));
MOVE:TRUCK((A(3)),M,VT(2)*1.5;

QUEUE,M+5;
ALLOCATE,3:TRUCK(2);
QUEUE,M+10;
SEIZE:PATHWAY(M);
MOVE:TRUCK(2),M;
RELEASE:PATHWAY(M)
```

In the first example, entities allocate the transporter using the Shortest Distance to Station rule, storing the index of the allocated transporter in A(3). The request has a priority value of 3. While an entity waits for a transporter it is filed in Queue M+5. Once the transporter has been allocated, it moves to the entity's current station M, at one and a half times the normal velocity.

In the second example, entities allocate TRUCK(2), waiting in Queue M+5 until TRUCK(2) is available. Before the transporter can move to station M it must first obtain control of an indexed resource PATHWAY(M). Once the entity has been allocated the transporter and obtained the resource, the transporter moves at its currently defined velocity, to the current station M, and upon arrival, releases the resource PATHWAY(M).

TRANSPORT   After an entity has gained control of a transporter, through either a REQUEST or ALLOCATE-MOVE, it may use the transporter to transfer to a STATION block in the model using the TRANSPORT block. The TRANSPORT block requires an index of the transporter being used by the entity and a destination station. When the entity arrives at the specified STATION block, its station number, M, is changed to the new station. The duration of the transport is determined by the experimental elements TRANSPORTERS and DISTANCES, which are defined in the next section.

The format of the TRANSPORT block is:

TRANSPORT:TUNIT(NA),NS:MODIFIERS;

The block diagram symbol is:

Its operands are as follows:

OPERAND	OPERAND GROUP	DESCRIPTION	ALLOWABLE VALUES	DEFAULT
TUNIT(NA)	2	The transporter expressed as an indexed name	String and A(N), X(N), N, or SEQ*	None
				(cont'd)

OPERAND	OPERAND GROUP	DESCRIPTION	ALLOWABLE VALUES	DEFAULT
NS	2	The destination station number	A(N),X(N), or N	None
VEL	2	The transporter velocity	Expression	VT(N)

*N denotes A(I), X(I), or I, where the subindex I, can be M±K, J±K, or K, where K is integer.

An example of the TRANSPORT block is

TRANSPORT:TRUCK(A(2)),A(1),1.5*VT(A(2));

In this example, the entity is transported to the station specified by the contents of A(1), using the TRUCK specified by A(2), at velocity of 150% of the standard velocity VT.

FREE   Transporters are relinquished by an entity using the FREE block, just as entities relinquish resources using the RELEASE block. The format of the FREE block is:

FREE:TUNIT(NA):MODIFIERS;

The block diagram symbol is:

```
┌─────────────┐
│    FREE     │
├─────────────┤
│    TUNIT    │
└─────────────┘
```

Its operands are as follows:

OPERAND	OPERAND GROUP	DESCRIPTION	ALLOWABLE VALUES	DEFAULT
TUNIT(NA)	2	The transporter expressed as an indexed name	String and A(N), X(N), or N*	None

*N denotes A(I), X(I), or I, where the subindex I, can be M±K, J±K, or K, where K is integer.

An example of the FREE block is:

FREE:TRUCK(A(2));

which will make the truck with index A(2) available for another requesting entity.

HALT and ACTIVATE

SIMAN provides a mechanism for making transporters inactive or active through the HALT and ACTIVATE blocks. This is a useful way of including in the model, shifts where the transporter is not being operated and equipment failures. If a transporter is being controlled by an entity (through an honored REQUEST) it does not become inactive until the controlling entity has made it available through a FREE block.

HALT   The HALT block causes the status of a transporter to be set to inactive. The format of the HALT block is:

HALT:TUNIT(NA):MODIFIERS;

The block diagram symbol is:

HALT
TUNIT

It has the following operands:

OPERAND	OPERAND GROUP	DESCRIPTION	ALLOWABLE VALUES	DEFAULT
TUNIT(NA)	2	The transporter expressed as an indexed name	String and A(N), X(N), or N*	None

*N denotes A(I), X(I), or I, where the subindex I, can be M±K, J±K, or K, where K is integer.

ACTIVATE   This block causes the status of the transporter to be set to active.
The format of the ACTIVATE block is:

ACTIVATE:TUNIT(NA):MODIFIERS;

The block diagram symbol is:

ACTIVATE
TUNIT

Its operands are:

OPERAND	OPERAND GROUP	DESCRIPTION	ALLOWABLE VALUES	DEFAULT
TUNIT(NA)	2	The transporter expressed as an indexed name	String and A(N), X(N), or N*	None

*N denotes A(I), X(I), or I, where the subindex I, can be M±K, J±K, or K, where K is integer.

As an example of the HALT and ACTIVATE blocks, consider a system with a single crane which fails at random times and the repair time is a random variable. In this example only the process of the crane failing and being repaired is shown. It is assumed there is only one crane.

```
        CREATE:0.0,1;            GENERATE A SINGLE ENTITY FOR FAILURES
LOOP    DELAY:EX(1,1);           WAIT UNTIL FAILURE TIME
        HALT:CRANE(1);           CRANE IS HALTED (FAILURE)
        DELAY:UN(1,2);           DELAY TIME FOR CRANE TO BE REPAIRED
        ACTIVATE:CRANE(1);       CRANE IS REPAIRED;
        BRANCH,1
        ALWAYS,LOOP;             REPEAT FAILURE CYCLE
```

The time until failure will not be exactly exponentially distributed with a mean from parameter set 1, since at times the crane will be busy when the HALT block is executed.

6.2   Transporter Experimental Frame Elements

In order to include a transporter in a SIMAN model, one must first define certain characteristics of the transporter and the distance between the work stations serviced by it. This is done in the experimental frame using the TRANSPORTERS and DISTANCES elements.

DISTANCES   SIMAN assumes that the distance between two stations does not depend upon the direction of movement. That is, the distance (and correspondingly the time) from station 1 to station 2 is the same as the distance from 2 back to 1. It is also assumed the intrastation distance is 0.0, implying it takes no time to move from station 1 to station 1. By these assumptions the distance between stations can be described using a sparse matrix with no elements on the diagonal such as

		To		
From	*1*	*2*	*3*	*4*
1	—	10	20	15
2		—	25	16
3			—	10
4				—

In general, the distances between N stations requires only $N(N - 1)/2$ values. There can be more than one set of distances defined for a pair of stations, accommodating different paths between stations.

The format of the DISTANCES element is:

DISTANCES:N,ML – MU,D_{ij}../..:..Repeats through group M;

Its operands are:

OPERAND	OPERAND GROUP	DESCRIPTION	ALLOWABLE VALUES	DEFAULT
N	2-M	The distance set number	Integer	None
ML	2-M	The lower range of station numbers in distance matrix	Integer	None
MU	2-M	The upper range of station numbers in distance matrix	Integer	None
D_{ij}	2-M	The set of station distances	Constants	None

An example of the distance element is:

DISTANCES:1,1 – 4,10.,20.,15./25.,16/10.;

In this example, distance set 1 is defined for stations 1 thru 4 using the values from the matrix above. Note the use of ''/'' to separate the rows of the matrix.

TRANSPORTERS   This element assigns a transporter a number, name, capacity, distance set number, velocity, initial position, and initial status (active or operational, or, inactive or failed).

The format of the TRANSPORTERS element is:

TRANSPORTERS:N,TNAME,TCAP,NDS,VT,(P-S)$_i$ ...:...

Repeats through group M;

It has the following operands:

OPERAND	OPERAND GROUP	DESCRIPTION	ALLOWABLE VALUES	DEFAULT
N	2-M	The transporter number	Integer	None
TNAME	2-M	The transporter name	String	None
TCAP	2-M	The number of transporter units	Integer	1
NDS	2-M	The number of the distance set transporter uses	Integer	1
VT	2-M	The standard velocity of the transporter*	Constant	1.0
(P – S)$_i$	2-M	The position and status of transporter i	Station-A, or Station-I	**

* The standard velocity of the transporter can be redefined using an ASSIGN block during execution by assigning a new value to VT(N) where N is the transporter number.
** The position can be any station in the distance set and the status is Active (A) or Inactive (I). If (P – S)$_i$ is not given, it defaults to first station in the distance set and active or the last (P – S)$_i$ given.

An example (using the previously defined DISTANCES element) of the TRANSPORTERS element is:

TRANSPORTERS:1,TRUCK,2,1,10.0,1-A,4-A:2,CRANE,1,2,5.0;

In this example, the first transporter, named TRUCK, uses distance set 1 (implying it can move between stations 1 through 4) with a velocity of 10.0. There are two TRUCK units and both are initially active, with TRUCK(1) placed at station 1 and TRUCK(2), placed at station 4. There also is a single transporter named CRANE which uses distance set 2 (moves between stations 1 and 2), has a velocity of 5.0 and is, by default, active and placed at station 1.

6.3   Conveyor Blocks

In SIMAN, a conveyor is viewed as a fixed path connecting a set of stations. The portion of the conveyor connecting any two stations is a segment. Any segment of a conveyor consists of a finite number of cells, each cell capable of containing one SIMAN entity. Similar to a transporter, in order for an entity to be moved by the conveyor, it must first obtain control of an available cell. Once an entity occupies a cell, the cell is unavailable until the occupying entity departs the cell.

In order for an entity to gain control of a cell it must be at a station that the conveyor services. When an entity needs one or more cells of a conveyor, it must first ACCESS the conveyor, much like an entity REQUESTed a transporter. The ACCESS block is a Hold type block and must be preceded by a QUEUE block to file entities waiting for sufficient available cells to pass by its current station.

When the last conveyor cell has been accessed, the conveyor stops moving (is disengaged) and the status of the just accessed cells becomes "occupied." The conveyor begins moving again through the CONVEY block and will continue moving until it is again disengaged by an entity. The time to move to the next STATION block is determined by the experimental elements CONVEYORS and SEGMENTS associated with the conveyor. These are described in the following section. When the entity arrives at the destination station, its station attribute, M, is changed to the new station number.

ACCESS   This block disengages a conveyor and provides for the transition of entities from a queue to cells of a conveyor.

The format of the ACCESS block is:

ACCESS:CNAME,NC:MODIFIERS;

The block diagram symbol is:

Its operands are:

OPERAND	OPERAND GROUP	DESCRIPTION	ALLOWABLE VALUES	DEFAULT
CNAME	2	The name of the conveyor to be accessed	String	None
NC	2	The number of consecutive cells being requested	A(N),X(N), or N*	1

*N denotes A(I), X(I), or I, where the subindex I, can be M±K, J±K, or K, where K is integer.

CONVEY   This block causes the conveyor, which was disengaged by an ACCESS block, to be re-engaged and begin moving the entities toward the desired station.

The format of the CONVEY block is:

CONVEY:CNAME,NS:MODIFIERS;

The block diagram symbol is:

Its operands are:

OPERAND	OPERAND GROUP	DESCRIPTION	ALLOWABLE VALUES	DEFAULT
CNAME	2	The name of the conveyor to be engaged	String	None
NS	2	The destination station number	A(N),X(N), N, or SEQ*	1 SEQ

*N denotes A(I), X(I), or I, where the subindex I, can be M±K, J±K, or K, where K is integer.

EXIT   When an entity arrives by conveyor at its destination, the conveyor is again disengaged and the entity enters its destination STATION block. The conveyor will not start moving again until the entity releases the occupied cells through the EXIT block.

The format of the EXIT block is:

EXIT:CNAME,NC:MODIFIERS;

The block diagram symbol is:

```
┌─────────────┐
│    EXIT     │
├─────────────┤
│  CNAME,NC   │
└─────────────┘
```

Its operands are:

OPERAND	OPERAND GROUP	DESCRIPTION	ALLOWABLE VALUES	DEFAULT
CNAME	2	The name of the conveyor being exited	String	None
NC	2	The number of consecutive cells being released	A(N),X(N), or N*	1

*N denotes A(I), X(I), or I, where the subindex I, can be M±K, J±K, or K, where K is integer.

A Simple Conveyor Model

Associated with each conveyor is a system variable, LC, which contains the current number of cells occupied on a conveyor. As cells are occupied and released the variable LC is automatically updated.

As example of modeling with conveyors is:

```
STATION,1-4;                    BEGINNING OF STATIONS 1-4
EXIT:BELT,3;                     LEAVE CONVEYOR
QUEUE,M+5;                       ENTER QUEUE AT STATION
SEIZE:MACHINE(M);               OBTAIN MACHINE
DELAY:100;                       PROCESSING TIME;
RELEASE:MACHINE(M):DISPOSE;      END OF PROCESSING;
..
..
```

```
CREATE:EX(1,1);              JOBS ARRIVE
ASSIGN:A(1)=DP(1,1);         ASSIGN A DESTINATION STATION
QUEUE,1;                     WAIT FOR AVAIL. CELL
ACCESS:BELT,3;               OBTAIN 3 CONSECUTIVE CELLS
CONVEY:BELT,A(1);            MOVE TO STATION A(1)
```

In this example, entities are created and assigned a destination station in A(1), using discrete probability function 1 and a random number. The entities are placed in queue file 1 and wait for three consecutive unoccupied conveyor cells to pass by.(The characteristics and segments of the conveyor are not shown.) The entities then move to station 1, 2, 3, or 4 and exit the conveyor, entering a queue file until the machine at the station is available. After the entity is processed it is disposed.

STOP   Similar to transporters, the status of conveyors can alternate between active and inactive using the blocks STOP and START. The STOP block places the conveyor in inactive status.

The format of the STOP block is:

STOP:CNAME:MODIFIERS;

The block diagram symbol is:

```
┌─────────────┐
│    STOP     │
├─────────────┤
│    CNAME    │
└─────────────┘
```

Its operands are:

OPERAND	OPERAND GROUP	DESCRIPTION	ALLOWABLE VALUES	DEFAULT
CNAME	2	The name of the conveyor to be made inactive	String	None

START   This block places the conveyor in active status.
The form of the START block is:

START:CNAME:MODIFIERS;

The block diagram symbol is:

```
┌─────────────┐
│    START    │
├─────────────┤
│    CNAME    │
└─────────────┘
```

Its operands are:

OPERAND	OPERAND GROUP	DESCRIPTION	ALLOWABLE VALUES	DEFAULT
CNAME	2	The name of the conveyor to be made active	String	None

As an example of the START and STOP blocks, consider a conveyor system which, every 1000 time units, is halted and quality control examines (but does not remove) a part on the conveyor. Assume it takes 10 time units for quality control to inspect the entity.

```
CREATE:1000;            GENERATE A QC INSPECTOR
STOP:BELT;              STOP MOVEMENT OF CONVEYOR
DELAY:10;               TIME TO INSPECT
START:BELT:DISPOSE;     RESTART BELT QC LEAVES SYSTEM
```

6.4 Conveyor Experimental Frame Elements

Conveyor characteristics are defined using the CONVEYORS and SEGMENTS experimental frame elements. The path of the conveyor is defined in the SEGMENTS element, and in the CONVEYORS element the conveyor is further defined in terms of speed and size.

CONVEYORS   This element has the following format:

CONVEYORS:N,CNAME,NSS,VEL,CL,S:..Repeats through group M;

Its operands are:

OPERAND	OPERAND GROUP	DESCRIPTION	ALLOWABLE VALUES	DEFAULT
N	2-M	The conveyor number	Integer	None
CNAME	2-M	The conveyor name	String (max of 8 alpha characters)	None
NSS	2-M	The segment set number	Integer	1
VEL	2-M	The conveyor velocity*	Constant	1.0
CL	2-M	The length of a conveyor* cell	Integer	1
S	2-M	The initial status of the conveyor	A or I	A

* The time for the conveyor to move an element one cell length is CL/VEL (dimensions of CL and VEL must agree).

An example of the CONVEYORS element is:

CONVEYORS:3,LINKBELT,3,2.5,1,A;

In this example, conveyor number 3 is named LINKBELT, uses the segment set 3 for defining its length and path, has a velocity of 2.5 distance-unit per time-unit (e.g., ft/s), the cell length is 1 distance-unit and the conveyor is initially active. It follows that the time for the conveyor to move one cell length is then 0.40 time-units.

SEGMENTS   The path of the conveyor is defined using the SEGMENTS element, which identifies the stations the conveyor connects and the conveyor distance between connecting stations. The format of the SEGMENTS element is:

FIGURE 6.1   LOOP CONVEYOR

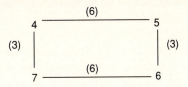

SEGMENTS:N,KB,(K − D)$_i$..:Repeats through group M;

It has the following operands:

OPERAND	OPERAND GROUP	DESCRIPTION	ALLOWABLE VALUES	DEFAULT
N	2-M	The segment set number	Integer	None
KB	2-M	The station beginning the first segment of the conveyor*	Integer	None
(K − D)$_i$	2-M	The station/distance pair for each sequential segment **	Integer	None

* If the ending station number in the set (K − D)$_i$ is KB, then the conveyor is a continuous loop.
** (K − D)$_i$ is the distance from the preceding station to the current one.

An example of the SEGMENTS element is:

SEGMENTS:1,4,5 − 6,6 − 3,7 − 6,4 − 3;

This element describes a conveyor connecting station 4,5,6, and 7 and then back to station 4, completing the loop. The conveyor is shown in Fig. 6.1.

6.5   Illustrative Problem Set IV

PROBLEM IV.1   This example is a material-handling system which incorporates both a transporter and conveyor. Printed-circuit boards arrive randomly from the preparation department. The boards are moved in sets of five by a handtruck to the component assembly department where the board components are manually assembled. There are five identical assembly stations connected by a loop conveyor.

When boards are placed onto the conveyor, they are directed to the assembly station with the least number of boards waiting to be processed. After the components are assembled onto the board, they are set aside and removed for inspection at the end of the shift. The time between boards arriving from preparation is exponentially distributed with a mean of 5 seconds. The hand truck moves at a velocity of 5 feet per second and the conveyor moves at a velocity of 2 feet per second. The conveyor is 100 feet long and the length of a cell on the conveyor is 4 feet. No more than 20 boards can be placed on the belt at any one time, leaving at least five cells open.

At each assembly station no more than two boards can be waiting for assembly. If a board arrives at an assembly station and there is no room for the board (there are already two boards waiting) the board goes around the conveyor for another time and again tries to enter the station. The assembly time is normally distributed with a mean of 35 seconds and standard deviation of 8 seconds. The assembly stations are uniformly distributed around the belt, and boards are placed onto the belt 4 feet before the first station. After all five boards are placed onto the belt, the handtruck waits until five boards have arrived from the the preparation area before returning for another set of boards. The model and experimental frames for this example are shown in Fig. 6.2.

FIGURE 6.2   PROBLEM IV.1 CODE

```
BEGIN;
        CREATE:EX(1,1);                          PREPARE NEW KIT
        STATION,7;                               BEGINNING OF STATION
        QUEUE,10,5;                              QUEUE FOR MATCH
        GROUP:5,FIRST;                           GROUP  5 KITS
        QUEUE,9;                                 QUEUE FOR FREE TRUCK
        SCAN:(NQ(6)+NQ(7).EQ.0).AND.(NT(1).EQ.0);
;                                                IS TRUCK EMPTY?
        QUEUE,8;                                 WAIT FOR TRUCK
        REQUEST:TRUCK(1);                        REQUEST TRUCK
        TRANSPORT:TRUCK(1),6;                    MOVE 5 KITS TO CONVEYOR
        STATION,6-6;                             UNLOADING STATION
        FREE:TRUCK(1);                           FREE TRUCK
        SPLIT;                                   SPLIT BACK INTO 5 UNITS
        QUEUE,7;
        SEIZE:BLTSPACE;                          IS THERE SPACE ON BELT?
        ASSIGN:M=1;                              PLACE JUST BEYOND STATION 1
        QUEUE,6;
        ACCESS:BELT;                             GET ONTO BELT
        FINDJ,1,5:MIN(NQ(J));                    LOCATE STATION WITH MIN BUFFER
        ASSIGN:A(1)=J;                           SET DESTINATION
        CONVEY:BELT,A(1);                        MOVE TO DESTINATION
        STATION,1-5;                             ASSEMBLY STATIONS
        BRANCH,1:
          IF,NQ(M).LT.2,OFFBELT:
          ELSE,CONTINUE;                         ROOM AT THE BUFFER
CONTINUE  CONVEY:BELT,8;                         RECYCLE
OFFBELT   RELEASE:BLTSPACE;                      FREE SPACE ON BELT
        EXIT:BELT;                               GET OFF BELT
```

```
          QUEUE,M;                          QUEUE UP IN BUFFER
          SEIZE:OPER(M);                    SEIZE STATION OPERATOR
          DELAY:RN(2,2);                    ASSEMBLY TIME
          RELEASE:OPER(M);                  REALEASE ASSEMBLY OPERATOR
          COUNT:M;                          ACCUM.ASSEMB. AT STATION M
          COUNT:6,1:DISPOSE;                END OF PROCESSING
          STATION,8;                        DUMMY STATION
          CONVEY:BELT,A(1);                 SEND TO DESTINATION
END;


BEGIN;
PROJECT,BELT_CONVEYOR,HOOVER__PERRY,10/12/84;
DISCRETE,150,1,10,8;
RESOURCES:1-5,OPER,1:6,BLTSPACE,20;
PARAMETERS:1,5:2,35,8;
REPLICATE,1,0;
COUNTER:1,STAT1 ASSEMBLIES:
        2,STAT2 ASSEMBLIES:
        3,STAT3 ASSEMBLIES:
        4,STAT4 ASSEMBLIES:
        5,STAT5 ASSEMBLIES:
        6,TOTAL ASSEMBLIES,100;
DSTAT:1,NT(1),UTIL. OF TRUCK:
      2,LC(1),UTIL. OF CONVEYOR:
      3,NR(1),UTIL OF OPER1:
      4,NR(2),UTIL OF OPER2:
      5,NR(3),UTIL OF OPER3:
      6,NR(4),UTIL OF OPER4:
      7,NR(5),UTIL OF OPER5:
      8,NQ(10),AVE QUEUE 10:
      9,NQ(6),AVE QUEUE 6:
      10,NQ(7),AVE QUEUE 7:
      11,NQ(9),AVE QUEUE 9:
      12,NQ(8),AVE QUEUE 8:
      13,NQ(2),AVE AT BUFFER2;
DISTANCES:1,6-7,100;
TRANSPORTERS:1,TRUCK,1,1,5,7-A;
CONVEYORS:1,BELT,1,2,4,A;
SEGMENTS:1,1,2-20,3-20,4-20,5-20,8-4,1-16;
END;
```

In this model, a SCAN block is used to control the movement of the handtruck between the conveyor and the preparation area. The truck cannot be requested unless all the parts are off the truck and placed onto the conveyor, and there are five parts waiting to be transported to the conveyor. The system is simulated until 100 boards have been assembled. Counter 6 is used to keep track of the number of boards assembled. Figure 6.3 shows a SIMAN Summary Report of this model.

FIGURE 6.3   PROBLEM IV.1 OUTPUT

```
                        SIMAN Summary Report

                        Run Number   1 of  1

Project:  BELT_CONVEYOR
Analyst:  HOOVER  PERRY
Date   :  10/12/1984

Run ended at time :   .1199E+04

                       Discrete Change Variables
                       -------------------------
Number Identifier       Average    Standard   Minimum   Maximum   Time
                                   Deviation  Value     Value     Period
-----------------------------------------------------------------------------
    1  UTIL. OF TRUCK      .74       .44       .00       1.00     1199.38
    2  UTIL. OF CONVEYO   4.65      1.66       .00       9.00     1199.38
    3  UTIL OF OPER1       .78       .42       .00       1.00     1199.38
    4  UTIL OF OPER2       .90       .30       .00       1.00     1199.38
    5  UTIL OF OPER3       .69       .46       .00       1.00     1199.38
    6  UTIL OF OPER4       .41       .49       .00       1.00     1199.38
    7  UTIL OF OPER5       .18       .39       .00       1.00     1199.38
    8  AVE QUEUE 10       2.14      1.43       .00       5.00     1199.38
    9  AVE QUEUE 6         .57      1.18       .00       5.00     1199.38
   10  AVE QUEUE 7         .00       .00       .00        .00     1199.38
   11  AVE QUEUE 9        9.18      6.59       .00      21.00     1199.38
   12  AVE QUEUE 8         .00       .00       .00        .00     1199.38
   13  AVE AT BUFFER2      .99       .73       .00       2.00     1199.38

                             Counters
                             --------
Number Identifier       Count     Limit
------------------------------------------
    1  STAT1 ASSEMBLIES    27    Infinite
    2  STAT2 ASSEMBLIES    30    Infinite
    3  STAT3 ASSEMBLIES    24    Infinite
    4  STAT4 ASSEMBLIES    13    Infinite
    5  STAT5 ASSEMBLIES     6    Infinite
    6  TOTAL ASSEMBLIES   100       100

Run Time : 23 Second(s)
```

7.0   OUTPUT ANALYSIS

Certain experimental frame elements have the ability to record a history of data as the simulation is running, as in the case of the DSTAT and TALLIES elements described in Section 3.0. These histories of data can be analyzed and displayed in a number of different ways using the Output Processor of SIMAN. The OUTPUT experimental frame element is a generalization of this capability to include any SIMAN variable. The operands for the OUTPUT element were described in Section 3.3. In this section, we describe some of the ways in which these history files may be analyzed and displayed using SIMAN's Output Processor.

7.1   Output Processor Elements

PLOT   This element produces a plot of a maximum of six SIMAN variables using simulated time as the independent variable. The plot uses an 80-column format and standard characters.

The PLOT element has the form:

PLOT,TITLE,INDLABEL,TBEG,TEND,DTPLOT:
        NUI,DEPLABEL,SYMBOL,LOWORD,HIGHORD:...Repeats through group M;

Its operands are defined as follows:

OPERAND	OPERAND GROUP	DESCRIPTION	ALLOWABLE VALUES	DEFAULT
TITLE	1	Plot title	String (max of 20 chars.)	None
INDLABEL	1	Time axis label	String (max of 20 chars.)	None
TBEG	1	Beginning time for plot	Constant	None
TEND	1	Ending time for plot	Constant	None
DTPLOT	1	Time increment between plot points	Constant	None
NUI	2-M	Data set number containing data to be plotted	Constant	None
DEPLABEL	2-M	Label of SIMAN variable to be plotted	String (max of 8 chars.)	None
SYMBOL	2-M	Symbol use to plot SIMAN variable	Single alpha character	None
LOWORD	2-M	Low ordinate value for SIMAN variable	MIN or MIN(RND)*	MIN
HIGHORD	2-M	High ordinate value for SIMAN variable	MAX or MAX(RND)*	MAX

* MIN, MAX, and RND are constants. MIN and MAX are the minimum and maximum values of the data set. MIN(RND) is the value of MIN rounded down to the nearest RND. MAX(RND) is the value of MAX rounded up to the nearest RND.

A valid example of PLOT is:

PLOT,WAITING TIME,MINUTES,0,1000,1:
        11,TYPE 1,A:
        12,TYPE 2,B:
        13,TYPE 3,C;

This element plots the waiting time in minutes for three classes of customers, beginning at time zero and ending a time 1000, at intervals of one minute. The history files for customers labeled TYPE 1, TYPE 2, and TYPE 3 are contained in data sets 11, 12, and 13, respectively, and they are plotted using the symbols A, B, and C.

BARCHART   This element produces a bar chart for a designated SIMAN variable. The bars are printed horizontally using the asterisk (*) character in an 80-column format.

Positive values are shown by bars to the right of the zero ordinate position, and negative values by bars to the left of the zero ordinate position.

The BARCHART element has the following form:

BARCHART,TITLE,INDLABEL,DEPLABEL,XBEG,XEND,NUI,LOWORD,HIGHORD;

Its operands are:

OPERAND	OPERAND GROUP	DESCRIPTION	ALLOWABLE VALUES	DEFAULT
TITLE	1	Barchart title	String (max of 20 chars.)	None
INDLABEL	1	Label for vertical axis (observation number)	String (max of 8 chars.)	None
DEPLABEL	1	Label for horizontal axis (SIMAN variable name)	String (max of 8 chars.)	None
XBEG	1	Beginning observation number	Constant	None
XEND	1	Ending observation number	Constant	None
NUI	1	Data set number containing data to be charted	Constant	None
LOWORD	1	Low ordinate for SIMAN variable	Non-positive constant	None
HIGHORD	1	High ordinate for SIMAN variable	Constant > LOWORD	None

An example of the BARCHART element is:

BARCHART,SERVICE TIME,CUST NO.,1,100,12,0,10

This bar chart will display 100 service-time observations which have been recorded in data set 12. The bar chart is labeled SERVICE TIME, and the observation number is labelled CUST NO. The smallest service time represented is 0, and the largest is 10.

HISTOGRAM   This element produces a histogram for a specified SIMAN variable. The cell and cumulative frequencies are displayed in both tabular and histogram form.

The HISTOGRAM element has the following form:

HISTOGRAM,TITLE,NCELLS,HLOW,HWIDTH,NUI,NUCELLF,NUCUMF;

It operands are:

OPERAND	OPERAND GROUP	DESCRIPTION	ALLOWABLE VALUES	DEFAULT
TITLE	1	Histogram title	String (max of 20 chars.)	None
NCELLS	1	Number of interior cells	Constant	None

(cont'd)

OPERAND	OPERAND GROUP	DESCRIPTION	ALLOWABLE VALUES	DEFAULT
HLOW	1	Lower cell limit of first interior cell	Constant	None
HWIDTH	1	Width of each interior cell	Constant	None
NUI	1	Data set number containing data for the histogram	Constant	None
NUCELLF	1	Data set number to save relative cell frequencies	Constant	No Saving
NUCUMF	1	Data set number to save cumulative cell frequencies	Constant	No Saving

In addition to the interior cells defined by the operands, an open cell is appended to each end of the histogram to tabulate those observations that do not fall within the interior cells. Cell 0 ranges from minus infinity to HLOW, and cell NCELLS+1 ranges from HLOW+NCELLS×HWIDTH to plus infinity. If it is desired to save the relative cell frequencies or cumulative cell frequencies as a data file for further analysis or plotting, the data set numbers are specified by NUCELLF and NUCUMF.

An example of a valid HISTOGRAM element is:

HISTOGRAM,TIME IN BANK,50,5,1,11;

This histogram has 52 cells in all, the first interior cell beginning with the value of 5 minutes. Each of the interior cells has a width of 1 minute.

INTERVALS   This element generates 95% confidence intervals for a designated set of SIMAN variables. It is assumed that observations are from identically distributed, independent, normal samples. A maximum of 10 SIMAN variables can be specified in each INTERVALS element.

The INTERVALS element has the form:

INTERVALS,TITLE:NUI,LABEL:..Repeats through group M;

Its operands are:

OPERAND	OPERAND GROUP	DESCRIPTION	ALLOWABLE VALUES	DEFAULT
TITLE	1	Title of intervals table	String (max of 20 chars.)	None
NUI	2-M	Data set number containing the observations	Constant	None
LABEL	2-M	Label assigned to the SIMAN variable	String (max of 10 chars.)	None

An example of the INTERVALS element is:

INTERVALS,BANK OPERATIONS:11,WAITIME;

This INTERVALS element computes a confidence interval for the data in data set 11, which are customer waiting times in a bank. The table produced will display the mean, standard deviation, minimum and maximum values, 95% confidence interval half width, and the number of observations in the data set.

7.2 Running the Output Processor

The output processor is a SIMAN program named OUTPT. It accepts the history files collected during the simulation run and analyzes and displays them in different fashions.

The microcomputer version of SIMAN executes the output processor in an interactive manner. Entering the command OUTPT produces the response: "SIMAN Output Processor Release x.x," and a prompt. At this point one may enter any of the output elements described previously, and the results are displayed on the screen.

The mainframe versions of SIMAN require some knowledge of the operating system and the job control language to manipulate the required files to generate output displays and analyses.

8.0 LIST OF SIMAN BLOCKS AND THEIR OPERANDS

The following conventions and notation are used in summarizing the SIMAN blocks. First, the block and its operands are stated in proper syntactical form. A brief description is provided for each operand, followed by allowable values placed within { }, and the default value placed within []. Subscript, attribute, and variable notation used is as follows: N denotes A(I), X(I), or I, where the index, I, can be M±K, J±K, or K; and IP and IS denote A(K) or K, where K is an integer.

The page reference for the block description appears next to the right margin as: page 000.

```
ACCESS:CNAME,NC:MODIFIERS;
```
page B-89

CNAME	Name of the conveyor to be accessed {String} [None]
NC	Number of consecutive cells being requested {A(N),X(N) or N} [1]

ACCESS
CNAME,NS

```
ACTIVATE:TUNIT(NA):MODIFIERS;
```
page B-86

ACTIVATE
TUNIT

TUNIT   Transporter expressed as an indexed name {String and A(N), X(N), or N} [None]

`ALLOCATE,PR:TUNIT(TSR,NA):MODIFIERS;`   page B-83

ALLOCATE,PR / TUNIT	PR	Priority of the request {A(N), X(N), or N} [1]
	TUNIT(TSR,NA)	Transporter name {String, request rule (Table 6.1) and A(N), X(N), or N} [None]
	or	
	TUNIT(T)	Transporter expressed as an indexed name {String and K or M±K} [None]

`ALTER:RNAME,CC:MODIFIERS;`   page B-55

ALTER / RNAME,CC	RNAME	Name of the resource which is to have its capacity altered {String} [None]
	CC	Capacity change in RNAME {A(N), X(N), or N} [None]

`ASSIGN:VAR=VALUE:MODIFIERS;`   page B-17

ASSIGN / VAR=VALUE	VAR	Attributes or variables {A(N), X(N), P(IP,IS), J, M, VC(N), VT(N), NS or IS} [None]
	VALUE	Expression to be assigned to attribute or variable {Expression} [None]

`BEGIN,BSEQ,ISEQ,ILIST;`   page B-35

BSEQ	Sequence number of first statement in the model {Integer constant} [10]
ISEQ	Increment used in assigning statement numbers {Integer constant} [10]
ILIST	Generate a model listing {YES or NO} [YES]

`BRANCH,MAXTAKE:CRITERION,LABEL:..Repeats ...;`   page B-22

MAXTAKE / IF,C → LABEL / WITH,P → LABEL / ELSE or ALWAYS → LABEL	MAXTAKE	Maximum number of copies that will be branched {Integer} [Infinite]
	CRITERION	Condition or probability which determines branch selection (C = condition, and P = probability) {IF, C; WITH, P; ALWAYS; or ELSE} [None]
	LABEL	Label of the block to which entity copy is routed{String} [None]

`COMBINE:N,SAVE:MODIFIERS;`   page B-63

COMBINE / N,SAVE	N	Size of the set to be combined { A(N),X(N),N} [1]
	SAVE	Criterion for assigning representative attributes {FIRST, LAST, SUM, or PRODUCT} [LAST]

`CONVEY:CNAME,NS:MODIFIERS;` page B-89

CONVEY		
CNAME,NS		

	CNAME	Name of the conveyor to be engaged {String} [None]
	NS	Destination station number {A(N), X(N), N,or SEQ} [SEQ]

`COPY:NR,IFL,LABEL:MODIFIERS;` page B-60

COPY	
NR,IFL,LABEL	

NR	Rank of the entity to be copied {A(N), X(N), N, NQ, or J} [None]
IFL	Queue file number from which the entity is to be copied {A(N), X(N), N, or J} [None]
LABEL	Label of the block to which the copied entity is to be sent {Label} [None]

`COUNT:N,INC:MODIFIERS;` page B-25

COUNT	
N,INC	

N	Identifying counter number {A(N), X(N), or N} [None]
INC	Counter increment {A(N), X(N), or N} [1]

`CREATE,NB,TF:TBC,MC:MODIFIERS;` page B-16

CREATE,NB,TF	
TBC,MC	

NB	Number of entities in each batch {X(N) or integer constant} [1]
TF	Offset time for activation of CREATE block {X(N), constant, or random variable} [0.0]
TBC	Time between entity batch creations {Expression} [Infinite]
MC	Maximum number of batches {X(N) or integer constant} [Infinite]

`DELAY:DURATION:MODIFIERS;` page B-18

DELAY	
DURATION	

DURATION	Length of the delay {Expression} [0.0]

`EXIT:CNAME,NC:MODIFIERS;` page B-90

EXIT	
CNAME,NC	

CNAME	Name of the conveyor being exited {String} [None]
NC	Number of consecutive cells being released {A(N), X(N), or N} [1]

```
FINDJ,J1,J1:CONDITION:MODIFIERS;
```
page B-61

	J1	Initial value of search range {A(N), X(N), or N} [None]
FINDJ,J1,J2	J2	Final value of search range {A(N), X(N), or N} [None]
CONDITION	CONDITION	Search condition {Logical statement using the index J, MIN (), or MAX()} [None]

```
FREE:TUNIT:MODIFIERS;
```
page B-85

	TUNIT(NA)	Transporter expressed as an indexed name {String and A(N), X(N), or N} [None]
FREE		
TUNIT		

```
GROUP:N,SAVE:MODIFIERS;
```
page B-62

	N	Size of the set to be grouped {A(N), X(N), or N} [1]
GROUP	SAVE	Criterion for assigning representative attributes {FIRST, LAST, SUM, or PRODUCT} [LAST]
N,SAVE		

```
HALT:TUNIT(NA):MODIFIERS;
```
page B-85

	TUNIT(NA)	Transporter expressed as an indexed name {String and A(N), X(N), or N} [None]
HALT		
TUNIT		

```
MATCH,MA:QLBL,LABEL:...:QLBL,LABEL;
```
page B-58

	MA	Number of the attribute containing the class code {Integer} [None]
MA	QLBL	Label of the preceding queue blocks to be examined {Label} [None]
QLBL →LABEL QLBL →LABEL	LABEL	Destination of the entity at queue block QLBL {Label} [Destroy the entity]

```
MOVE:TUNIT(NA),NS,VEL:MODIFIERS;
```
page B-83

	TUNIT(NA)	Indexed transporter unit {String and A(N), X(N), or N} [None]
MOVE	NS	Destination station of the transporter being moved {A(N), X(N), or N} [None]
TUNIT,NS,VEL	VEL	Velocity of the transporter as it moves to its destination station {Expression} [VT(N)]

---

page B-49

`PICKQ,QSR,LBALK:LABEL:LABEL:...:LABEL;`

	QSR	Queue Selection Rule {see Table 4.1} [POR]
	BALK	Label of destination if all queues are full {Label} [Entity destroyed]
	LABEL	Labels of following parallel queues {Label} [None]

---

page B-56

`PREEMPT,PR:RNAME,NA,LSEND:MODIFIERS;`

	PR	Priority of the preempting entity {A(N), X(N), or N} [1]
	RNAME	Name of the resource to be preempted {String} [None]
	NA	Attribute number for storing the remaining delay {N} [None]
	LSEND	Label of the block to which the preempted entity is to be sent {Label} [QUEUE of previous SEIZE or PREEMPT block where resource was allocated]

---

page B-50

`QPICK,QSR:LABEL:LABEL:...:LABEL;`

	QSR	Queue Selection Rule {see Table 4.1} [POR]
	LABEL	Labels of preceding queues for selecting next entity {Label} [None]

---

page B-18

`QUEUE,IFL,QC,LBALK:MODIFIERS;`

	IFL	File (queue) number {K, M±K} [None]
	QC	Capacity of the queue {A(N), X(N), or N} [Infinite]
	LBALK	Label of block where balking entities are routed {Label} [Destroy the entity]

---

page B-21

`RELEASE:RNAME,NR:MODIFIERS;`

	RNAME	Name of resource to be released {String} [None]
	NR	Integer number of resource units to be released {A(N), X(N), or N} [1]

---

page B-59

`REMOVE:NR,IFL,LABEL:MODIFIERS;`

	NR	Rank of the entity removed {A(N), X(N), N, NQ, or J} [1]
	IFL	Queue file from which the entity is to be removed {A(N), X(N), N, or J} [None]
	LABEL	Label of the block to which the removed entity is sent {Label} [None]

`REQUEST,PR:TUNIT(TSR,NA):MODIFIERS;`   page B-81

	PR	Priority of the request {A(N), X(N), or N} [1]
REQUEST,PR / TUNIT	TUNIT(TSR,NA)	Transporter name {String, request rule, and A(N), X(N), or N} [None]
	or	
	TUNIT(T)	Transporter expressed as an indexed name {String and K or M±K} [None]

`ROUTE:DURATION,NS:MODIFIERS;`   page B-75

	DURATION	Duration of the routing delay {Expression} [0.0]
ROUTE / DURATION,NS	NS	Station number to which the entity is to be sent {A(N), X(N), N. or SEQ} [None]

`SCAN,ML-MU:CONDITION:MODIFIERS;`   page B-55

	ML-MU	Range of the station numbers used in the scan {Integer} [No ranging]
SCAN,ML-MU / CONDITION	CONDITION	Logical condition for an entity to be removed from the queue file {Logical statement} [None]

`SEARCH,IFL,J1,J2:CONDITION:MODIFIERS;`   page B-59

	IFL	Number of the queue file to be searched {A(N), X(N), or N} [None]
SEARCH,IFL,J1,J2 / CONDITION	J1	Starting rank for the search {A(N), X(N), N, or NQ} [1]
	J2	Ending rank for the search {A(N), X(N), N, or NQ} [NQ]
	CONDITION	Search condition {Expression, MIN(expression), MAX(expression)} [None]

`SEIZE,PR:RNAME,NR:MODIFIERS;`   page B-19

	PR	Integer priority number {A(N), X(N), or N} [1]
SEIZE,PR / RNAME,NR	RNAME	Name of resource to be seized {String} [None]
	NR	Integer number of resource units to be seized {A(N), X(N), or N} [1]

`SELECT,RSR:LABEL:LABEL:...:LABEL;`   page B-52

RSR   Resource Selection Rule {see Table 4.2} [POR]

LABEL   Labels of following Hold blocks for selection {Label} [None]

`SIGNAL:NSIG:MODIFIERS;`   page B-54

NSIG   An integer signal code {A(N), X(N), or N} [None]

`SPLIT:MODIFIERS;`   page B-63

`SPLIT` has no operands.

`START:CNAME:MODIFIERS;`   page B-91

CNAME   Name of the conveyor to be made active {String} [None]

`STATION,N1-N2:MODIFIERS;`   page B-74

N1-N2   Range of stations which begin at this block {Integer} [None]

`STOP:CNAME:MODIFIERS;`   page B-91

CNAME   Name of the conveyor to be made inactive {String} [None]

`SYNONYMS: character string=associated original string: repeats ...;`   page B-35

character string   Any alphanumeric string {String} [None]

Associated original string   SIMAN attribute, variable, or block name {String} [None]

```
TALLY:N,VAR:MODIFIERS;
```
page B-24

TALLY	N	Identifying tally number {A(N), X(N), or N} [None]
N,VAR	VAR	Value to be tallied {Expression, INT(K), or BET(K)} [None]

```
TRANSPORT:TUNIT(NA),NS:MODIFIERS;
```
page B-84

TRANSPORT	TUNIT(NA)	Transporter expressed as an indexed name {String and A(N), X(N), N, or SEQ} [None]
TUNIT,NS,VEL	NS	Destination station number {A(N), X(N), or N} [None]
	VEL	Transporter velocity {Expression} [VT(N)]

```
WAIT:NSIG:MODIFIERS;
```
page B-53

WAIT	NSIG	An integer signal code {A(N), X(N), or N} [None]
NSIG		

9.0   LIST OF SIMAN EXPERIMENTAL FRAME ELEMENTS AND THEIR OPERANDS

The following conventions and notation are used in summarizing the SIMAN experimental frame elements. First, the element and its operands are stated in proper syntactical form. A brief description is provided for each operand, followed by allowable values placed within { }, and the default value placed within [ ]. The subscript, K, denotes a constant.

Unless otherwise noted, string variables are limited to 8 alphanumeric characters.

The page reference for the experimental frame element description appears next to the right margin as: page 000.

```
ARRIVALS:N,TYPE,DT,NB,A1,A2..:Repeats ...;
```
page B-69

N	Arrival number {Integer} [None]
TYPE	Entry type {STATION(K), QUEUE(K), or EVENT(K) } [None]
DT	Time of arrival {Real constant} [0.0]
NB	Batch size {Integer} [1]
A1,A2..	Attribute values of the entity {Constant} [0.0]

```
CONVEYORS:N,CNAME,NSS,VEL,CL,S:..Repeats ...;
```
page B-92

N	Conveyor number {Integer} [None]
CNAME	Conveyor name {String, max of 8 alphanumeric characters} [None]
NSS	Segment set number {Integer} [1]
VEL	Conveyor velocity {Constant} [1.0]
CL	Length of a conveyor cell {Integer} [1]
S	Initial status of the conveyor {A or I} [A]

```
COUNTERS:N,ID,LIMIT:..Repeats ...;
```
page B-29

N	Counter number {Integer constant} [None]
ID	Report identifier for labeling on Summary Report {String, max of 16 characters} [Blank]
LIMIT	Counter limit {Integer constant} [Infinity]

```
DISCRETE,MENT,MATB,NFIL,NSTA;
```
page B-30

MENT	Maximum number of entities allowed in the model {Integer constant} [0]
MATB	Maximum number of attributes associated with an entity {Integer constant} [0]
NFIL	Maximum number of files (QUEUES) allowed in the model {Integer constant} [0]
NSTA	Maximum number of stations allowed in the model {Integer constant} [0]

```
DISTANCES:N,ML-MU,D_{ij}...:..Repeats ...;
```
page B-87

N	Distance set number {Integer} [None]
ML	Lower range of station numbers in distance matrix {Integer} [None]
MU	Upper range of station numbers in distance matrix {Integer} [None]
D_{ij}	Set of station distances {Constants} [None]

```
DISTRIBUTIONS:N,TYPE:..Repeats...;
```
page B-65

N	Distribution number, or range of distribution numbers {Integer} [None]
TYPE	Distribution type (type ED(N) not allowed) {Distributions shown in Table 3.1} [None]

```
DSTAT:N,DVAR,ID,NUNIT:..Repeats ...;
```
page B-32

N	DSTAT number {Integer constant} [None]
DVAR	Discrete change variable for which statistics are collected {X(K), NE(K), NQ(K), NR(K), NT(K), LC(K), MR(K) or MT(K)} [None]
ID	Identifier for labeling on Summary Report {String, max of 16 characters} [Blank]
NUNIT	Output unit to save individual observations {Integer constant} [Observations not saved]

```
INITIALIZE,VAR=VALUE,...Repeats...;
```
page B-66

VAR	System variable to be initialized {J, or X(K)} [None]
VALUE	Value to be assigned to the variable {Real or integer constant} [None]

```
OUTPUT:N,VAR,NU:..Repeats...;
```
page B-34

N	Output variable number {Integer} [None]
VAR	Output variable for which data is to be collected {Any SIMAN variable} [None]
NU	Output data set number {Integer} [None]

```
PARAMETERS:N,P(N,1)...P(N,J)..:..Repeats...;
```
page B-26

N	Parameter set number {Integer constant} [None]
P(N,J)	Value of the Jth parameter in the Nth set {real constant} [None]

```
PROJECT,TITLE,ANALYST,MO/DAY/YEAR;
```
page B-30

TITLE	Project title {String, max of 20 characters} [Blank]
ANALYST	Name of analyst {String, max of 20 characters} [Blank]
MON/DAY/YEAR	Date (month/day/year) {Three integer constants} [1/1/2000]

```
RANKINGS:N,MRANK:..Repeats...;
```
page B-27

N	Queue number or range of queue numbers to which the ranking rule applies {integer constant} [None]
MRANK	Ranking rule {See Table 3.2} [None]

```
REPLICATE,NRUNS,TBEG,DTRUN,ISYS,ISTAT,DTCLR;
```
page B-31

NRUNS	Number of runs to execute {Integer constant} [1]
TBEG	Starting time for the first run {Real constant} [0.0]
DTRUN	Maximum length of each run {Real constant} [Infinite]
ISYS	Initialization of system {YES or NO} [YES]
ISTAT	Discard previous observations between runs {YES or NO} [YES]
DTCLR	Offset time from beginning of run when summary statistics are cleared {Real constant} [0.0]

```
RESOURCES:N,RNAME,NCAP:..Repeats...;
```
page B-28

N or ·N1−N2	Resource number or range (N1 − N2) of resource numbers for indexed resources {Integer constant} [None]
RNAME	Resource name {String} [None]
NCAP or NCAP1, NCAP2...	Initial capacity of the resource or list of resource capacities for indexed resources {Integer constant, or SCHED(K)} [1, or last specified]

```
RULES:N,RULE:..Repeats through group M;
```
page B-64

N	Rule number or range of rule numbers {Integer} [None]
RULE	Queue or resource selection rule {Rules shown in Tables 4.1 and 4.1} [None]

```
SCHEDULES:N,NCAP*DUR,..Repeats...;.
```
page B-67

N	Schedule number {Integer constant} [None]
NCAP	Resource capacity {Integer constant} [None]
DUR	Corresponding capacity duration {Real constant or SIMAN random variable} [Infinite]

```
SEEDS:IS,ISEED,RI:..Repeats...;
```
page B-65

IS	Stream number to be initialized {1 to 10} [None]
ISEED	Initial seed value {Integer} [Machine dependent]
RI	Reinitialization on repeat runs of the model {YES, NO, A, or C} [NO]

SEGMENTS:N,KB,(K-D)$_i$..:Repeats...;   page B-92

N	Segment set number {Integer} [None]	
KB	Station beginning the first segment of the conveyor {Integer} [None]	
(K-D)$_i$	Station/distance pair for each sequential segment {Integer-integer} [None]	

SEQUENCES:N,NSTA$_1$,a$_1$,a$_2$../NSTA$_2$,a$_1$,a$_2$..:..Repeats...;   page B-75

N	Sequence set number {Integer} [None]
NSTA$_i$	Sequential station number {Integer} [None]
a$_1$,a$_2$..	Assigned value of attributes when entity is routed to station NSTA {Real or SIMAN random variable} [Current]

TABLES:N,XLOW,XINC,Y(1),Y(2),...,Y(n):..Repeats..;   page B-67

N	Table number {Integer} [None]
XLOW	Low value of the independent variable {Constant} [None]
XINC	Increment between successive values of the independent variable {Constant} [None]
Y(i)	Values of the dependent variable {Constant} [None]

TALLIES:N,ID,NUNIT:..Repeats...;   page B-28

N	Tally number {Integer constant} [None]
ID	Report identifier for labeling on Summary Report {String, max of 16 characters} [Blank]
NUNIT	Output unit to save individual observations {Integer constant} [Observations not saved]

TRACE,DTBT,DTFT,TC,VAR1,VAR2,VAR3,VAR4;   page B-33

DTBT	Time at which trace begins {Real constant} [0]
DTFT	Time at which trace ends {Real constant} [Infinite]
TC	Trace condition {Condition} [Trace]
VAR1.. VAR4	Variable or attribute to be displayed by trace (maximum of 4) {Attribute, system, or user variable} [No values displayed]

```
TRANSPORTERS:N,TNAME,TCAP,NDS,VT,(P-S) ;..Repeats...;                          page B-88
                                    i
```

N	Transporter number {Integer} [None]
TNAME	Transporter name {String} [None]
TCAP	Number of transporter units {Integer} [1]
NDS	Number of the distance set used by transporter {Integer} [1]
VT	Standard velocity of transporter {Constant} [1.0]
$(P-S)_i$	Position and status of transporter i {Station-A, or Station-I} [1-A or most recent P-S entry]

10.0 LIST OF SIMAN OUTPUT PROCESSOR ELEMENTS AND THEIR OPERANDS

The following conventions and notation are used in summarizing the SIMAN output processor elements. First, the element and its operands are stated in proper syntactical form. A brief description is provided for each operand, followed by allowable values placed within { }, and the default value placed within [ ].

The page reference for the output processor element description appears next to the right margin as: page 000.

```
BARCHART,TITLE,INDLABEL,DEPLABEL,XBEG,XEND,NUI,LOWORD,HIGHORD;               page B-97
```

TITLE	Bar chart title {String, max of 20 characters} [None]
INDLABEL	Label for vertical axis (observation number) {String, max of 8 characters} [None]
DEPLABEL	Label for horizontal axis (SIMAN variable name) {String, max of 8 characters} [None]
XBEG	Beginning observation number {Constant} [None]
XEND	Ending observation number {Constant} [None]
NUI	Data set number containing data to be charted {Constant} [None]
LOWORD	Low ordinate for SIMAN variable {Non-positive constant} [None]
HIGHORD	High ordinate for SIMAN variable {Constant > LOWORD} [None]

```
HISTOGRAM,TITLE,NCELLS,HLOW,HWIDTH,NUI,NUCELLF,NUCUMF;
```
page B-98

TITLE	Histogram title {String, max of 20 characters} [None]
NCELLS	Number of interior cells {Constant} [None]
HLOW	Lower cell limit of first interior cell {Constant} [None]
HWIDTH	Width of each interior cell {Constant} [None]
NUI	Data set number containing data for the histogram {Constant} [None]
NUCELLF	Data set number to save relative cell frequencies {Constant} [No saving]
NUCUMF	Data set number to save cumulative cell frequencies {Constant} [No saving]

```
INTERVALS,TITLE:NUI,LABEL:..Repeats...;
```
page B-99

TITLE	Title of intervals table {String, max of 20 characters} [None]
NUI	Data set number containing the observations {Constant} [None]
LABEL	Label assigned to the SIMAN variable {String, max of 10 characters} [None]

```
PLOT,TITLE,INDLABEL,TBEG,TEND,DTPLOT:
NUI,DEPLABEL,SYMBOL,LOWORD,HIGHORD:..Repeats...;
```
page B-97

TITLE	Plot title {String, max of 20 characters} [None]
INDLABEL	Time axis label {String, max of 20 characters} [None]
TBEG	Beginning time for plot {Constant} [None]
TEND	Ending time for plot {Constant} [None]
DTPLOT	Time increment between plot points {Constant} [None]
NUI	Data set number containing data to be plotted {Constant} [None]
DEPLABEL	Label of SIMAN variable {String, max of 8 characters} [None]
SYMBOL	Symbol use to plot SIMAN variable {Single alphabetic character} [None]
LOWORD	Low ordinate value {MIN or MIN(RND) } [MIN]
HIGHORD	High ordinate value {MAX or MAX(RND) } [MAX]

REFERENCES

Fishman, G., *Concepts and Methods in Discrete Event Digital Simulation*, New York: John Wiley and Sons, 1973.

Pegden, C. D., *Introduction to SIMAN*, State College, Pennsylvania: Systems Modeling Corp., 1986.

SIMSCRIPT II.5 PRIMER

OUTLINE

1.0   INTRODUCTION

SIMSCRIPT is a very rich and complex programming language incorporating features not found in older programming languages such as FORTRAN, COBOL, or BASIC. SIMSCRIPT is probably not the best choice for one's first programming language, and in this primer it is assumed that the reader has written programs in some other general purpose programming language such as FORTRAN, BASIC, Pascal, C, COBOL, etc.

SIMSCRIPT provides the user with a rich choice of data structures, a large library of functions particularly suitable for simulation models and language features such as dynamic allocation, pointer variables, and recursion. SIMSCRIPT is viewed by many in the simulation community as the most stable, powerful, and flexible simulation language available. It is a proprietary language available only from CACI of Los Angeles, California. CACI makes the language available to educational institutions for a nominal price. As of 1984, SIMSCRIPT has been implemented on the IBM/360, Honeywell, PDP-11/70, VAX-11/780, CDC, Univac, and PRIME computers. A PC-DOS version of SIMSCRIPT is also available. Additional features are constantly being implemented and each release of SIMSCRIPT is upward compatible to older releases.

SIMSCRIPT has its origins in the RAND Corporation, when in 1962, under the guidance of H. M. Markowitz, the language was developed for implementation on the IBM 7090 series. In 1964, SIMSCRIPT I.5 was developed by CACI and marketed for a broader class of computers. In 1968, RAND developed SIMSCRIPT II for the IBM/360 and, in 1971, CACI developed SIMSCRIPT II.5 and has since been the only source of the language. In 1979, the modeling concepts of resources and processes were added to the language and these two concepts are now a central part of modeling in SIMSCRIPT II.5. In this primer we will refer to SIMSCRIPT II.5 simply as SIMSCRIPT.

In this primer we cannot cover every aspect and detail of SIMSCRIPT , for it is a much more complex and extensive language than FORTRAN, PASCAL, or most general-purpose programming languages. Upon completing this primer, however, one should be able to build relatively sophisticated SIMSCRIPT models and, as the need for additional features or understanding of SIMSCRIPT arises, this primer can serve as a springboard to the more detailed and technical documents available from CACI. A particularly fine treatment of modeling in SIMSCRIPT is Russell [1] and CACI [2]. Although the error diagnostics in SIMSCRIPT are very good it is also recommended that one have access to a user's manual for the specific implementation on which models will be run, including a listing of compiler and run-time error messages.

We will first, in Section 2, describe the general purpose programming features of SIMSCRIPT. Then in Section 3 the basic concepts and features of SIMSCRIPT as a simulation language are presented. In Sections 4 and 5 the intermediate and advanced features of SIMSCRIPT are described. Finally, in Section 6, a brief overview of the internal organization of SIMSCRIPT is presented. Throughout each section, the SIMSCRIPT features and concepts being presented are illustrated using examples appropriate to a simulation audience.

2.0   SIMSCRIPT: A GENERAL-PURPOSE PROGRAMMING LANGUAGE

Although SIMSCRIPT is not marketed as a general-purpose programming language, it has all the capabilities of most popular programming languages. The overall structure of a SIMSCRIPT program is:

PREAMBLE section
MAIN program
ROUTINES

The PREAMBLE section of a SIMSCRIPT program defines all global variables as well as establishing the default mode of undeclared variables. It must always be the first section in a SIMSCRIPT program. MAIN is the section at which execution is begun but from MAIN, control can be passed to other routines which either return control back to MAIN, pass control onto additional routines, or bring the execution of the program to a halt.

As an example of a SIMSCRIPT program listed below is a program which will prompt for two numbers and then print out their sum. Although we have not yet presented the syntax of SIMSCRIPT the logic of the program is somewhat self-evident. A particular strength of SIMSCRIPT is the clarity of the code:

```
PREAMBLE
DEFINE 1ST.NUMBER, 2ND.NUMBER AND SUM AS REAL VARIABLES
END

MAIN
PRINT 1 LINE THUS
INPUT TWO REAL NUMBERS TO FIND THEIR SUM
READ 1ST.NUMBER AND 2ND.NUMBER
LET SUM = 1ST.NUMBER + 2ND.NUMBER
PRINT 1 LINE WITH 1ST.NUMBER,2ND.NUMBER AND SUM THUS
THE ANSWER IS:     ***.** + ***.** = ***.**
END
```

In this first, and very simple program we could dispense with the preamble and define all variables in the MAIN program, since the program consists of only a MAIN module.

2.1   Statement Structure

When describing the syntax of SIMSCRIPT statements the following conventions and notation will be used:

All keywords will be capitalized.

All identifiers will be lower case.

Braces, { }, indicate a choice must be made.

Brackets, [ ], indicate an optional choice.

* indicates the argument or phrase can be repeated.

SIMSCRIPT has no reserved words, but has a large vocabulary of keywords and keyword qualifiers. A statement can begin at any location of any line of the program. A single statement may carry over to several lines or a single line may contain several SIMSCRIPT statements. SIMSCRIPT processes statements starting from left to right and continues building up the statement until the statement is syntactically complete, at which point the processing of a new statement begins. Every SIMSCRIPT statement begins with a keyword but keywords are not reserved words. Comments are included on a line of code by preceding the comment with two single quote marks. The following are examples of SIMSCRIPT statements:

```
LET A = B + C   "ADD B AND C AND STORE IN A
LET LET = LET + 2*LET   "A POOR CHOICE OF VARIABLE NAMES
LET A
   = B
   +
                C      "5 LINES USED FOR LET A=B+C
```

Although we find the last two examples confusing at first glance, they conform to the syntax rules of SIMSCRIPT and will be compiled without error. In SIMSCRIPT the statement:

A = B + C

is syntactically incorrect because it does not begin with a key word.

2.2   Identifiers and Variable Types

Identifiers, or variable names, in SIMSCRIPT can begin with and contain any upper or lowercase letter, a number, or a period. However, an identifier must contain at least one character so that it can be distinguished from a number. Identifiers can be up to 80 characters in length but the first 30 characters must be unique. Examples of SIMSCRIPT identifiers are:

SUM
1ST
AAAXXXBBBYYYCCCZZZAAAJLLKMPNQUUDODODOZZZ122000116678AAA
HOURS.PER.DAY

Notice how, in the last example, the ".'' was used to make the meaning of the identifier clearer.

SIMSCRIPT has four types of variables:

INTEGER
REAL
ALPHA
TEXT

With the exception of the SIMSCRIPT implementation on the CDC computer, all INTEGER and REAL variables are identically represented on all target machines. This implies that except for the CDC version of SIMSCRIPT, the results of a program will be identical when run on any computer.

TEXT variables are designated by being enclosed in quotation marks such as:

"THIS IS A 36 CHARACTER TEXT VARIABLE"

The length of ALPHA variables depended upon the implementation but it is commonly four characters.

2.3   Arithmetic and Logical Expressions

The arithmetic operators in order of hierarchy are:

**   exponentiation

/,*   division, multiplication

+,−   addition, subtraction.

The result of performing these operations on two arguments A and B are:

		A	
		Integer	*Real*
B	*Integer*	+,−,* →INTEGER /,** →REAL	+,−,*,/,** →REAL
	Real	+,−,*,/,** →REAL	+,−,*,/,** →REAL

Parentheses can be used to form subexpressions that will be evaluated starting with the innermost set of parentheses, working outward. All expressions are evaluated from left to right, following the above hierarchy. Unlike most other general-purpose languages, when real expressions are stored as integers, the REAL is first rounded to the nearest integer.

Logical expressions are formed by the logical operators AND, NOT, and OR, using the relational operators shown in Table 2.1

TABLE 2.1
RELATIONAL OPERATORS

Relational Oper.	SIMSCRIPT Notation
=	=, EQ, EQUALS, EQUAL TO
≠	NE, NOT EQUAL TO
<	<, LT, LS, LESS THAN
≤	<=, LE, NOT GREATER THAN
>	>,GT, GR, GREATER THAN
≥	>=, GE, NOT LESS THAN

A logical expression will be either TRUE or FALSE. If an expression contains more than one logical operator, parentheses can be used to control the order of evaluation. Within an expression, the AND operator is first performed and then evaluation is from left to right. We strongly suggest the use of parentheses to set the order of evaluation. Examples of logical expressions are:

A = B
A >= B
(A + B > C) AND (C > 0)
A NE (C + D)

If the modes of the arithmetic arguments are not the same, all integer expressions are converted to REAL before evaluation.

SIMSCRIPT includes, as part of its system library, all of the arithmetic functions that one would expect to find in a general-purpose language. These functions are listed in Table 7.1. SIMSCRIPT also has a number of useful constants defined as part of the language. These constants are listed in Table 7.2.

2.4   PREAMBLE Section

The first section of a SIMSCRIPT program is always the PREAMBLE which serves as a section for the definitions and declarations necessary for compilation of the MAIN program and routines. In Section 3, when we consider SIMSCRIPT as a simulation language, the PREAMBLE will be taken up again. During compilation the compiler has a ''background condition'' which acts as the default type for any variable whose type is not explicitly declared. The default mode can be set through the statement

NORMALLY MODE IS mode

where mode can be INTEGER, REAL, DOUBLE, ALPHA, TEXT or UNDEFINED. We strongly recommend that the first statement in the Preamble be:

NORMALLY MODE IS UNDEFINED

thereby forcing the explicit declaration of all global and local variables.

The mode of variables can be defined using the statement:

$$\text{DEFINE \{list of identifiers\} AS [A]} \left\{ \begin{array}{l} \text{REAL} \\ \text{INTEGER} \\ \text{TEXT} \\ \text{ALPHA} \end{array} \right\} \text{VARIABLE[S]}$$

Example of the DEFINE statement are:

DEFINE X,Y,Z AS REAL VARIABLES
DEFINE 10.OCTAL AND 20.OCTAL AS INTEGER VARIABLES
DEFINE NAME AS A TEXT VARIABLE

The dimensions of an array variable can be defined using the DEFINE statement of the form:

$$\text{DEFINE identifier AS [A]} \left\{ \begin{array}{l} \text{REAL} \\ \text{INTEGER} \\ \text{TEXT} \\ \text{ALPHA} \end{array} \right\} \text{k-DIM[ENSIONAL] VARIABLE}$$

For example

DEFINE DATA AS A REAL 2-DIMENSIONAL VARIABLE

The dimensions of arrays are declared in the PREAMBLE but the length of each dimension is set during execution using the RESERVE statement which has the format:

RESERVE identifier(*,*..,*) as k_1 BY k_2...BY k_n

where k_i can be a constant, variable or expression. For the previous example, the array DATA could be reserved by:

RESERVE DATA(*,*) AS 5 BY N.COLUMNS.

During execution, the length of each dimension of an array can be redefined using the RESERVE statement.

The DEFINE statement can also be used to define string substitutions during compilation. The form of the DEFINE statement is then:

DEFINE string$_1$ TO MEAN string$_2$

For example

DEFINE A + B TO MEAN 10

would cause the complier to interpret LET C = A + B as LET C = 10, or

DEFINE PI.3DIGITS TO MEAN 3.142

would interpret

LET CIRCUM = DIAMETER*PI.3DIGITS as:
LET CIRCUM = DIAMETER*3.142.

Other examples of the DEFINE statement are

DEFINE NOT.FULL TO MEAN N < CAPACITY
DEFINE WRONG TO MEAN FALSE
DEFINE ASSIGN TO MEAN LET.

The NORMALLY and DEFINE statements can appear anywhere in the PREAMBLE, the MAIN program, or ROUTINES. Except when placed in the PREAMBLE, the NORMALLY statement changes the background only for the section in which it occurs.

2.5 Assignment Statements

In SIMSCRIPT the form of the assignment statement is

LET identifier = expression

where the expression is evaluated as described in Section 2.3. Before a SIMSCRIPT program is executed all variables are initialized to zero. To improve the ease of reading a program, SIMSCRIPT provides the two assignment statements:

ADD variable TO variable

SUBTRACT variable FROM variable

making the statement

LET X = X + Y equivalent to ADD Y TO X.

2.6 Conditional Statements

SIMSCRIPT provides the conditional statements IF and IF–ELSE. Every IF statement has an accompanying ALWAYS statement which defines the scope of the conditional statement. The IF statement has the form

IF logical expression
   {statements}
ALWAYS

If the logical expression is true, the statements between IF and ALWAYS are executed.

(Notice that no ''THEN'' phrase is used in the IF statement.) As an example of the IF statement, consider the code below. In this example, an accumulator and a counter are incremented when the variable X is positive.

```
IF X > 0.0
   ADD X TO POS.SUM
   ADD 1 TO N.POS
ALWAYS
ADD X TO X.SUM
```

In this example, the two assignment statements following IF will be executed only if X is greater than 0.0, while the assignment following ALWAYS will be executed regardless the value of X.

The form of the IF – ELSE statement is

```
IF expression
   {statement set 1}
ELSE
   {statement set 2}
ALWAYS
```

If the logical expression is true, then the first set of statements is executed, otherwise the second set of statements is executed. For example:

```
IF X > 0.0
   ADD X TO POS.SUM
   ADD 1 TO N.POS
ELSE
   ADD X TO NOT.POS.SUM
   ADD 1 TO N.NOT.POS
ALWAYS
ADD X TO X.SUM
ADD 1 TO N
```

IF statements can be nested, but each IF statement requires its own ALWAYS statement. For example to test if a number is between 0 and 10.0 we could use:

```
IF X >= 0.0
   IF X <= 10.0
      ADD X TO SUM.0.TO.10
      ADD 1 TO N.0.TO.10
   ALWAYS
ALWAYS
```

2.7   Iterative Statements

SIMSCRIPT has three forms of iteration (looping): FOR, WHILE, and UNTIL. In all three forms, the condition for iteration is tested before beginning the scope of the iterative statement. If the scope of iteration is more than a single statement, it must be defined by a DO and LOOP pair.

SIMSCRIPT has several forms of the FOR statement, some of which we consider in Section 3. The basic form of the FOR statement is:

FOR identifier $\left\{ \begin{array}{l} = \\ \text{BACK FROM} \end{array} \right\}$ initial value TO final value [BY increment].

If the increment is not specified, it defaults to 1. As an example of the FOR statement

```
FOR X = 0 TO 10 BY 0.5
DO
    ADD X TO X.SUM
    ADD X*X TO X.SQR
LOOP
```

The form of the WHILE statement is

WHILE expression

Iteration will continue as long as the expression is true. As an example of the WHILE statement, consider:

```
WHILE X <= 10.0
DO
    ADD X TO X.SUM
    ADD X*X TO S.SQR
    ADD 1 TO X
LOOP
```

The form of the UNTIL statement is

UNTIL expression

Iteration ends when the expression is true. The previous example can be equivalently coded using the UNTIL statement as:

```
UNTIL X > 10.0
DO
    ADD X TO X.SUM
    ADD X*X TO X.SQR
    ADD 1 TO X
LOOP
```

The FOR statement can be further modified using a WITH, WHILE, or UNTIL qualifier. When the WITH qualifier is used, the current iteration is skipped unless the WITH expression is true. Iteration is terminated when the WHILE expression is false, or when the UNTIL expression is true. As examples

```
FOR I = 1 TO 10, WITH X(I) > 0
    LET X.SUM = X.SUM + X(I)

FOR I = 1 TO 10, WHILE X(I) > 0
    LET X.SUM = X.SUM + X(I)

FOR I = 1 TO 10, UNTIL X(I) <= 0
    LET X.SUM = X.SUM + X(I)
```

In the first example all positive X(I) will be summed but in the second and third examples iteration stops when the first nonpositive value of X(I) is encountered.

2.8   Input/output

SIMSCRIPT provides several different mechanisms for I/O but here we will consider
only the READ, PRINT, and LIST statements. The READ statement has the form

$$\text{READ variable list [USING} \left\{ \begin{array}{l} \text{TAPE} \\ \text{UNIT} \end{array} \right\} \{k\}]$$

If the qualifier USING TAPE UNIT is not included, the input defaults to the user's terminal, or the card reader in a batch environment. Input is considered to be a continuous
stream and a ''skip to next record'' does not occur at either the beginning or the end of a
READ statement. Each element of data read must be separated by at least one blank
character. ALPHA and TEXT variables cannot have embedded blanks, as input ends
upon encountering a blank character. To skip to the next record (line or card), a SKIP
statement is provided with the form

$$\text{SKIP expression} \left\{ \begin{array}{l} \text{LINE[S]} \\ \text{CARD[S]} \end{array} \right\}$$

where LINES or CARDS imply the standard input device. Examples of the READ statement are

READ X,Y

FOR I = 1 TO N
READ X(I)

READ X
IF X < 0
SKIP 2 CARDS
READ Y

Output in SIMSCRIPT is accomplished through the PRINT and LIST statements.
The LIST statement is intended to be used only for debugging and temporary unformat-
ted output.

The form of the PRINT statement is

PRINT integer_constant LINES WITH {variable list} THUS
integer_constant lines showing format of output

In the lines that show the format of the output, strings without quotes and field
specifications using * and . are used. Examples of print statements are

PRINT 1 LINE WITH X AND Y THUS
THE VALUE OF X IS ***.* AND THE VALUE OF Y IS .***

FOR I = 1 TO 10
PRINT 1 LINE WITH I AND X(I) THUS
X(**) = ***.**

PRINT 3 LINES WITH A,B,C THUS
THE VALUES OF A,B,C
A = **.**, B = **.** AND C = ***.*
IF YOU WANT TO CHANGE A,B AND C TYPE IN ''CHANGE''

The form of the LIST statement is

LIST variable list [USING TAPE integer_value]

If the USING phrase is omitted, the listing occurs on the default output device, typically the user's terminal or the printer. The LIST statement outputs both the name of the identifier and the value of the identifier. Examples of the LIST statement are

LIST A,B,C

FOR I = 1 TO N.ROWS
FOR I = 1 TO N.COL
LIST I,J,X(I,J) USING TAPE 6

In the first example, if A = 2, B = 5, and C = 1 SIMSCRIPT would output:

A = 2.00, B = 5.00, C = 1.00

2.9 Subprograms: Routines and Functions

Like most general-purpose languages, subprograms can be written in SIMSCRIPT and then "called" or executed by the Main program or other subprograms. Subprograms may be part of the current program or may be compiled separately and linked to the program prior to execution. SIMSCRIPT has two types of subprograms: routines and functions.

In the Preamble, routines are defined using the statement:

DEFINE routine-name AS [A] ROUTINE
[GIVEN integer ARGUMENT[S]] [YIELDING integer ARGUMENT[S]]

and functions are defined by

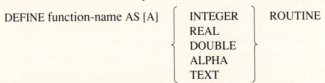

```
DEFINE function-name AS [A]  ⎧ INTEGER ⎫  ROUTINE
                             ⎪ REAL    ⎪
                             ⎨ DOUBLE  ⎬
                             ⎪ ALPHA   ⎪
                             ⎩ TEXT    ⎭
```

[GIVEN integer ARGUMENT[S]]

It is not strictly necessary for routines to be defined in the Preamble but functions must be declared in order to distinguish a reference to a function from an array reference. If the number of GIVEN and YIELDING arguments is omitted, the definition is complete but the SIMSCRIPT compiler cannot check if references to the routines and functions are made using the correct number of arguments. It is strongly recommended that the GIVEN and YIELDING arguments be included in the Preamble definition of routines and functions.

The body of routines and functions start with the statement

```
⎧ ROUTINE  ⎫  name [GIVEN variable list] [YIELDING variable list]
⎩ FUNCTION ⎭
```

and ends with the END statement.

Subprograms must include at least one RETURN statement which returns control back to the statement that follows the call to the subprogram. The form of the RETURN statement is

RETURN [[WITH] quantity].

If the subprogram is a function, the RETURN WITH quantity must be used and the mode of the quantity returned will be coerced to agree with the mode of the function.

Routines are executed through the CALL statement which has the form

CALL routine_name [GIVEN list] [YIELDING list]

while functions are executed by direct reference to the function in an expression.

As shown in Fig. 2.1, we can think of a routine as a subprogram that accepts constants and variables as input and returns one or more variables as output. The GIVEN phrase defines the input, and the YIELDING phrase defines the output of the subprogram.

Routines and functions can reference and change the global variables defined in the PREAMBLE, and can have locally defined variables which are defined only within the scope of the subprogram.

We will demonstrate the use of routines and functions through variations on a subprogram which forms the sum of two real numbers. In practice, of course, subprograms are used to execute much more complex logic and the task of adding two numbers together would be too simple to justify a separate subprogram.

In the examples that follow, assume the PREAMBLE contains the definition statement

DEFINE A,B,C AS REAL VARIABLES

In the first example we will add the global variables A and B and store the sum in C
In the PREAMBLE the routine is defined by

DEFINE ADD2 AS A ROUTINE

```
ROUTINE ADD2
LET C = A + B
RETURN
END
```

The routine is called using the statement

CALL ADD2

In order for the routine to add variables, other than those named A and B, and to store the sum in a location other than C, we can use arguments that serve as the mecha-

FIGURE 2.1   SUBPROGRAM

nism for exchange of data between the calling routine and the routine itself. To add together A, B, and C, we could have the routine ADD2 defined in the PREAMBLE as

DEFINE ADD2 AS A ROUTINE GIVEN 2 ARGUMENTS YIELDING 1 ARGUMENT

```
ROUTINE ADD2 GIVEN X AND Y, YIELDING Z
DEFINE X,Y,Z AS REAL VARIABLES
LET Z = X + Y
RETURN
END
```

and the routine can be called using a statement such as

CALL ADD2 GIVEN 3.0 AND B YIELDING C

In the routine ADD2, the local variables X and Y are given the values of 3.0 and B, and upon completion, the variable C is given the value of Z. There should be a one-to-one matching between the GIVEN variables and the YIELDING variables for the CALL statement and the ROUTINE statement. The variables should match in number and in type. In our example, if a text or integer variable was passed to the routine, the results would be undefined, and possibly result in a fatal execution error. A variable can appear more than once in the CALL statement. For example, if we wanted to double the variable A and store it in the current location of A, we could invoke the routine as

CALL ADD2 GIVEN A,A YIELDING A

The ADD2 routine could be changed to a function using the definition

DEFINE ADD2 AS A REAL FUNCTION GIVEN 2 ARGUMENTS

and the body of ADD2 would be changed to

```
FUNCTION ADD2 GIVEN X,Y
DEFINE X,Y AS REAL VARIABLES
RETURN X + Y
END
```

and the function could be referenced in a statement such as:

C = ADD2(A,B)

SIMSCRIPT routines are recursive, allowing a routine to reference itself. The routine's local variables are initially zero upon entry, with the GIVEN arguments being supplied by the calling routine. When a routine transfers control to another routine through a CALL or function reference, the values of the local variables in the referenced subprogram are preserved using a stack. The variables listed as GIVEN arguments are passed by value, resulting in the assignment of local variables to the passed values, while the variables listed as YIELDING arguments are passed through pointer or reference variables.

When arrays are passed as arguments they are always passed by pointer rather than values, and the array must be defined in the called routine using the DEFINE statement

DEFINE array_name AS A variable_type k – DIMENSIONAL ARRAY

When the array is passed, its dimensionality must be shown in the CALL statement using (*,*) notation. The actual dimensions of the array may be passed or determined in the called routine. SIMSCRIPT provides a function DIM.F which will return the dimensions of an array. As an example of using the DIM.F function, assume A is a 2 dimensional array. Then

LET N.ROWS = DIM.F(A(*,*))
LET N.COLS = DIM.F(A(N.ROWS,*))

will set the variables N.ROWS and N.COLS to the number of rows and columns of the matrix A.

One of the real strengths of SIMSCRIPT is its library of functions which includes standard arithmetic functions, string functions, and random variable functions. Table 7.1 of this primer lists these functions along with their arguments and mode.

2.10   Examples of SIMSCRIPT Programs

In this section we demonstrate SIMSCRIPT as a general-purpose language using two example programs. The first program is a bubble sort and the second program is a simulation of a popular dice game.

Example 1   This program will read in a list of names and associated scores. The list will then be sorted using the simple "bubble sort" which exchanges adjacent elements if they are out of order. The list will be sorted in descending order of scores and then printed out. Listing 1 is an annotated listing of the program.

(1) By declaring the mode is undefined we force the explicit definition of every variable in the program. Without this statement all undefined variables would default to REAL.

(2) Space is set aside in memory to hold a text array of length LIST.LENGTH. The variable NAME is a pointer to the first element of the array.

(3) Since NAME is TEXT we must input solid text ending with a space, and the next field is accepted as a value for SCORE.

(4) Arrays NAME and SCORE are passed off to the routine SORT, with the number of dimensions of each array indicated by (*). The length of the arrays was passed but could have been determined using the function DIM.F(NAME(*)).

(5) Routine SORT equates the pointers to the arrays NAME and SCORE as the pointers to A and B, respectively. Notice that the routine yields no arguments. Although this is allowed in most cases, routines usually yield arguments to the calling routine.

(6) Although the arrays being sorted are created outside the routine, the "dummy arrays" A and B must still be declared using the DEFINE statement.

Example 2   A popular dice game, sometimes referred to as "Craps," involves the tossing of two dice. The player tossing the dice wins or loses depending on the sum of the two dice. To start the game the player tosses the dice and immediately wins if the sum is 7 or 11, and loses if the sum is 2, 3, or 12. If the sum is 4,5,6,8,9, or 10 the player has established a number called the "point" and continues tossing the dice until either the point comes up again, resulting in a win, or until the sum of the dice is 7, resulting in a loss. The SIMSCRIPT program shown in Listing 2 simulates the game an arbitrary number of times. The program makes use of several functions in the SIMSCRIPT library as well as a user-written function which determines the sum of the two dice.

(1) DICE.F is a user-written function that calls the SIMSCRIPT library function RANDI.F. An integer value between 1 and 12 is returned from DICE.F.

LISTING 1   A SORT PROGRAM IN SIMSCRIPT

CODE FOR A SORT PROGRAM

```
PREAMBLE
''THIS PROGRAM READS IN A LIST OF NAMES AND ASSOCIATED SCORES
''AND THEN SORTS THEM USING A BUBBLE SORT
''AFTER THE LIST IS SORTED BY SCORE, IN DESCENDING ORDER THE
''LIST IS PRINTED OUT
NORMALLY MODE IS UNDEFINED[1]
DEFINE SORT AS A ROUTINE GIVEN 3 ARGUMENTS YIELDING 0 ARGUMENTS
DEFINE NAME AS A TEXT 1-DIMENSIONAL ARRAY
DEFINE SCORE AS AN INTEGER 1-DIMENSIONAL ARRAY
DEFINE LIST.LENGTH AS AN INTEGER VARIABLE
DEFINE I AS AN INTEGER VARIABLE
END

MAIN
PRINT 1 LINE THUS
INPUT LENGTH OF LIST
READ LIST.LENGTH
RESERVE NAME(*) AS LIST.LENGTH[2]
RESERVE SCORE(*) AS LIST.LENGTH
FOR I=1 TO LIST.LENGTH
READ NAME(I),SCORE(I)[3]
CALL SORT GIVING NAME(*),SCORE(*),LIST.LENGTH[4]
PRINT 1 LINE THUS
I    NAME                   SCORE
FOR I=1 TO LIST.LENGTH
PRINT 1 LINE WITH I,NAME(I),SCORE(I) THUS
**   ********************** *****
END

ROUTINE SORT GIVEN A,B,N[5]
DEFINE N AS AN INTEGER VARIABLE
DEFINE A AS A TEXT 1-DIMENSIONAL VARIABLE[6]
DEFINE B AS AN INTEGER 1-DIMENSIONAL VARIABLE
DEFINE A.TEMP AS TEXT VARIABLE
DEFINE SCORE.TEMP AS INTEGER VARIABLE
DEFINE B.TEMP AS AN INTEGER VARIABLE
DEFINE I,J AS INTEGER VARIABLES
FOR I=1 TO N-1
FOR J=1 TO N-I
DO
IF B(J) <=B(J+1)
LET B.TEMP=B(J)
LET B(J)=B(J+1)
LET B(J+1)=B.TEMP
LET A.TEMP=A(J)
LET A(J)=A(J+1)
LET A(J+1)=A.TEMP
ALWAYS
LOOP
RETURN
END
```

LISTING 2 DICE GAME IN SIMSCRIPT

```
                        CODE FOR A DICE GAME

PREAMBLE
 NORMALLY MODE IS UNDEFINED
 DEFINE 1ST.TOSS,NEXT.TOSS,N.WIN AND N.LOSE AS INTEGER VARIABLES
 DEFINE DICE.F AS AN INTEGER FUNCTION
 DEFINE GAME,N.GAMES AND SEED AS INTEGER VARIABLES
 DEFINE PROB.WIN AND PROB.LOSE AS REAL VARIABLES
END

MAIN
PRINT 3 LINES THUS
THIS IS A SIMULATION OF A CRAPS GAME WHICH ESTIMATES THE PROBABILITY
OF WINNING. PLEASE ENTER THE NUMBER OF GAMES TO BE SIMULATED AND AN
INTEGER SEED
READ N.GAMES,SEED.V(1)
FOR GAME= 1 TO N.GAMES DO
 LET 1ST.TOSS=DICE.F(1)¹
 IF 1ST.TOSS=2 OR
    1ST.TOSS=3 OR
    1ST.TOSS=12
  LET N.LOSS=N.LOSS+1
 ELSE
  IF 1ST.TOSS=7 OR
     1ST.TOSS=11
   LET N.WIN=N.WIN+1
  ELSE
   LET NEXT.TOSS=DICE.F(1)
   UNTIL NEXT.TOSS=1ST.TOSS
      OR NEXT.TOSS=7
   LET NEXT.TOSS=DICE.F(1)
   IF NEXT.TOSS=7
    ADD 1 TO N.LOSS
    ELSE
    ADD 1 TO N.WIN
   ALWAYS           ''SCOPE OF IF N.TOSS=7
  ALWAYS            ''SCOPE OF IF 1ST.TOSS=7,11
 ALWAYS             ''SCOPE OF IF 1ST.TOSS=2,3,12
LOOP                ''SCOPE OF FOR GAME=1 TO N.GAMES
PRINT 3 LINES WITH N.GAMES,REAL.F(N.WIN)/N.GAMES
               AND REAL.F(N.LOSS)/N.GAMES THUS
BASED ON ***** GAMES
THE PROBABILITY OF WINNING IS *.***   AND
THE PROBABILITY OF LOSING  IS *.***
END

ROUTINE DICE.F GIVEN SEED.INDEX
DEFINE SEED.INDEX AS AN INTEGER VARIABLE
RETURN WITH RANDI.F(1,6,SEED.INDEX)+RANDI.F(1,6,SEED.INDEX)
END
```

3.0 SIMSCRIPT AS A SIMULATION LANGUAGE: BASIC CONCEPTS

Although SIMSCRIPT is a powerful general-purpose programming language, it is primarily used to program discrete-event simulation models. As a simulation language, SIMSCRIPT has its own particular world view which is implemented in statements whose general syntax follows the same rules as statements described in the previous section. Rather than systematically present each and every facet of SIMSCRIPT's simulation capabilities, we will first present the more basic simulation components of the language and then in later sections present its more advanced features. After completing this section, however, the reader will be able to develop SIMSCRIPT models of many complex systems.

In its most primitive form SIMSCRIPT views the world as consisting of: Events, Entities, and Sets. There are, however, two special cases of events and entities: Processes and Resources, which we will initially consider. In SIMSCRIPT an Event occurs in an instant of time and the simulation clock cannot be advanced until the Event logic is completed. In contrast, SIMSCRIPT Processes can occur over time and the simulation clock can be advanced many times before the process is completed. SIMSCRIPT Resources are special entities that have finite capacity, and when unavailable to a requesting process, can cause the process to be delayed.

Processes and Resources were not initially part of SIMSCRIPT and the language was strictly event-oriented. With the addition of Processes and Resources, SIMSCRIPT became both event-oriented and process-interaction oriented, which accounts for much of its power and ease of modeling.

At this first level we will develop models of discrete-event systems using only Processes and Resources, and in subsequent sections we will go onto the more advanced features of the language.

3.1 Representation of Time in SIMSCRIPT

In SIMSCRIPT, time is represented by a real global variable, TIME.V. Time is, by default, measured in DAYS, and subdivided into hours and minutes using the system variables HOURS.V and MINUTES.V. By default, the relationships between these time units are:

HOURS.V = 24 (HOURS)
MINUTES.V = 60 (MINUTES)

but these relationships can be changed to allow for a different time scale. For example, if the units of time within a model are seconds, milliseconds, and microseconds we can make the assignments

LET HOURS.V = 1000
LET MINUTES.V = 1000.

We could further clarify the meaning of these time units by placing in the Preamble the definitions

DEFINE SECONDS TO MEAN DAYS
DEFINE MILLISECONDS TO MEAN HOURS
DEFINE MICROSECONDS TO MEAN MINUTES

(The DEFINE statement will be explained in detail in the section ahead.)

In SIMSCRIPT, time expressions are formed by combining arithmetic expressions with units of time. Time expressions are used as part of the following statements:

WORK
WAIT
ACTIVATE
SCHEDULE

The units of time can be DAYS, HOURS, or MINUTES and must be specified in a time expression. We will take these statements up in detail in the sections ahead, but examples of using time expressions are

WAIT 30 MINUTES
WORK UNIFORM.F(10.0,20.0,1) HOURS
SCHEDULE A CUSTOMER IN 10 MINUTES
ACTIVATE AN ORDER NOW

In the last example the keyword NOW is equivalent to TIME.V + 0.0 DAYS.

3.2 Random Numbers and Random Variables

SIMSCRIPT defaults to 10 random-number streams, each stream starting with a different seed value, SEED.V( ). Except for the CDC version of SIMSCRIPT, the default initial seeds are:

SEED.V(1) = 2,116,429,302   SEED.V(6) = 1,157,240,309
SEED.V(2) =   683,743,814   SEED.V(7) =   17,726,055
SEED.V(3) =   964,393,174   SEED.V(8) =   48,108,509
SEED.V(4) = 1,217,426,631   SEED.V(9) = 1,797,920,909
SEED.V(5) =   618,433,579   SEED.V(10) =   477,424,540

The user can, however, change the number of streams using the RESERVE statement. For example,

RESERVE SEED.V(*) AS 20

will allow for 20 random-number streams, but the user must initialize the extra 10 random numbers.

To change the initial seeds for the random-number streams only requires changing the array SEED.V. For the above example, initializing the 20 random-number streams could be accomplished by:

RELEASE SEED.V "GET RID OF STANDARD ARRAY
RESERVE SEED.V AS 20 "DEFINE A NEW ARRAY OF 20
FOR I = 1 TO 20
READ SEED.V(I)

Since SEED.V is a global variable, initialization can occur anywhere in our model.

SIMSCRIPT provides a number of library functions for generating random variables. Whenever a random variable function is called, the user must provide parameter to be used for generating the random variable and an integer argument for the random number stream to be used for generating the random variable. Table 7.4 lists the random variable functions included in the SIMSCRIPT system library.

Antithetic random numbers are random numbers found by subtracting a random number from 1.0. That is, if U is a random number then the associated antithetic random number is $(1 - U)$. Antithetic random numbers are often used as a technique for reducing the variance of simulation experiments. Antithetic random numbers can be generated in SIMSCRIPT by specifying the random-number stream with a negative integer. For example,

EXPONENTIAL.F(MEAN,−1)

3.3   Empirical Distributions

Although the SIMSCRIPT library includes functions for sampling from the more commonly used theoretic distributions, it is sometimes necessary to sample from distributions that are based on empirical data. In SIMSCRIPT we can easily define and sample from empirical distributions. To define an empirical distribution we use the statement

$$\left\{ \begin{matrix} \text{THE SYSTEM} \\ \text{EVERY ENTITY} \end{matrix} \right\} \text{ HAS A identifier RANDOM } \left\{ \begin{matrix} \text{STEP} \\ \text{LINEAR} \end{matrix} \right\} \text{ VARIABLE}$$

and to define the mode and random-number stream associated with the random variable we use

$$\text{DEFINE identifier AS A } \left\{ \begin{matrix} \text{REAL} \\ \text{INTEGER} \end{matrix} \right\} \text{ STREAM integer VARIABLE}$$

where the integer following STREAM specifies the random-number stream to be used. If no stream is listed the default stream is 1.

When the STEP qualifier is used, the random variable is discrete, if the LINEAR qualifier is used, the variable is continuous.

Examples of empirically defined random variables are

THE SYSTEM HAS A DAILY.DEMAND RANDOM STEP VARIABLE
DEFINE DAILY.DEMAND AS AN INTEGER STREAM 3 VARIABLE

EVERY JOB.CENTER HAS A PROCESS.TIME RANDOM LINEAR VARIABLE
DEFINE PROCESS.TIME AS A REAL STREAM 2 VARIABLE

In the first example, a global integer random variable DAILY.DEMAND is defined which uses random number stream 3. In the second example, each entity JOB.CENTER has an attribute PROCESS.TIME which is a real random variable, using random-number stream 2.

The READ statement is used to read pairs of data which define an empirical distribution. For continuous random variables the data is read in as pairs (F,x) where F is the cumulative distribution at x. F must be increasing. Discrete random variables can be read in similarly, or in pairs (f,x) where f is the probability the random variable equals x. The sum of the f's must be 1.0. The terminator * should follow the last pair of (F,x) or (f,x).

As an example of a user-defined random variable, consider the distribution of the number of units ordered each day in an inventory simulation model.

Order	f(order)	F(Order)
0	0.10	0.10
1	0.30	0.40
2	0.20	0.60
3	0.15	0.75
4	0.10	0.85
5	0.10	0.95
6	0.05	1.00

The SIMSCRIPT random variable corresponding to this distribution would be declared as

THE SYSTEM HAS AN ORDER.F RANDOM STEP VARIABLE
DEFINE ORDER.F AS AN INTEGER STREAM 2 VARIABLE

The pairs of data that would be read in using this statement is

READ ORDER.F

and the data values to be read in would be

.1 0 .4 1 .6 2 .75 3 .85 4 .95 5 1.0 6

or as

.1 0 .3 1 .2 2 .15 3 .10 4 .10 5   .05 6

If the second set of pairs is read in, SIMSCRIPT calculates the cumulative distribution for the user.

If the random variable is defined as a continuous random variable through the LINEAR qualifier, it should be declared as a REAL variable in the DEFINE statement. For a linear random variable SIMSCRIPT linearly interpolates between pairs of (F,x) to generate a random sample for F(x)

3.4   Processes

In SIMSCRIPT, a process is used to represent an activity that occurs over time. An example of a process would be the activity of a customer at the supermarket checkout. During this process of being checked out, suspensions of activities and delays may occur. When the customer first joins the queue at the checkout, no further processing will occur until the customer reaches the head of the queue. While the customer is waiting in line for the checkout clerk, its processing is suspended. When the customer gets to the checkout clerk it is again activated, but now there is a delay in the process while the customer's purchases are counted by the checkout clerk. After this delay the process is completed and the customer exits the supermarket and is no longer part of the simulation. There can be many such processes being carried out simultaneously, either in the suspended, delayed or active state.

A process is similar in many ways to a SIMSCRIPT routine, except that a routine cannot be suspended or delayed. In SIMSCRIPT, all processes must be declared in the Preamble using the statement

PROCESSES INCLUDE process_names

or

PROCESSES
EVERY process_name HAS attribute list

The second form will be discussed later when we take up process attributes.

The logic of the process is contained in the set of code starting with

PROCESS process_name

and terminated by the END statement, as in any other SIMSCRIPT module.

A process is initiated or scheduled using the ACTIVATE statement which has the form:

ACTIVATE process_name IN time expression.

For example,

ACTIVATE A NEW.CUSTOMER IN EXPONENTIAL.F(2.0,1) HOURS.

Many images of a process can be active at the same time. For example, one could include as part of a model the code:

FOR I = 1 TO 10
ACTIVATE A NEW.CUSTOMER NOW

which would cause 10 processes called NEW.CUSTOMER to be activated immediately.

The effect of the ACTIVATE statement is to file in the list of pending events a notice of the process, along with the time it is to become active. When TIME.V is advanced to the time associated with the pending process, the process is removed from the pending list, and the process logic is executed. During the execution of the process logic, the process may be suspended or encounter a delay any number of times. When a suspension or delay occurs, the attributes, local variables, and the address of the next executable statement are filed in either a pending or suspended list, thus allowing many images of the same process to exist at the same time.

After a process has begun, it can be explicitly delayed using the WAIT/WORK statement which has the form:

$$\left\{ \begin{array}{l} \text{WAIT} \\ \text{WORK.} \end{array} \right\} \quad \{\text{time expression}\}$$

For example,

WAIT EXPONENTIAL.F(10.0,1) HOURS

will place the process on the pending list for a random time, sampled from an exponential distribution with a mean of 10.0.

3.5 Starting and Ending a Simulation in SIMSCRIPT

A SIMSCRIPT simulation is, in essence, the execution of the processes and events on the pending list, sometimes called the future event list. During the simulation, the size of the list will grow and shrink but the process or event to be executed is always based on the first element of the list.

The execution of a SIMSCRIPT simulation model is started using the statement:

START SIMULATION

which is placed in the Main program. Prior to starting the simulation we must place at least one process or event on the pending list. The START SIMULATION statement passes control to the first element (a process or event) on the pending list. The simulation ends when either the pending list becomes empty or a STOP statement is encountered. A STOP statement may occur in any part of the simulation model, except the Preamble. If the pending list becomes empty, control returns to the statement immediately following the START SIMULATION statement. If a STOP statement is executed, the program immediately terminates execution.

As an example of a very simple SIMSCRIPT simulation, consider a model of a system in which particles arrive every 2 minutes, experience a delay which is exponentially distributed with a mean of 2 minutes, and then exit the system. The program shown in Listing 3 simulates this system for 1000 minutes.

This simulation will run for approximately 1000 minutes ending when there are no longer any processes on the pending list. Notice also that the program produces no output. Unlike many simulation languages, SIMSCRIPT does not automatically produce statistics or reports. It is, however, very easy to collect and print model statistics in SIMSCRIPT, as shown in the next section.

3.6   Collecting and Reporting Statistics

Statistics can be collected during a SIMSCRIPT simulation using the ACCUMULATE or TALLY statement. The form of these statements are:

LISTING 3   SIMSCRIPT SIMULATION OF PARTICLES ARRIVING AND DEPARTING
_____

```
                        CODE FOR PARTICLE SIMULATION

PREAMBLE
'' THIS IS A SIMULATION OF A SYSTEM IN WHICH PARTICLES ARRIVE EVERY
'' 2 MINUTES, DELAYED ACCORDING TO AN EXPONENTIAL DISTRIBUTION WITH
'' A MEAN OF 2 MINUTES AND THEN LEAVE THE SYSTEM.
PROCESSES INCLUDE ARRIVAL
END

MAIN
ACTIVATE AN ARRIVAL NOW
START SIMULATION
END

PROCESS ARRIVAL
IF TIME.V < 1000/(24*60)          ''1000 MINUTES EXPRESSED IN DAYS
ACTIVATE AN ARRIVAL IN 2 MINUTES
WAIT EXPONENTIAL.F(2.0,1) MINUTES
ALWAYS
END
```

$$\left\{ \begin{array}{l} \text{ACCUMULATE} \\ \text{TALLY} \end{array} \right\} \quad \begin{array}{l} \text{variable name AS [THE qualifier-name]} \\ \text{statistical measure OF variable} \end{array}$$

where the statistical measures shown in Table 7.5 and the variable can be any

> System variable
>
> Global variable
>
> Entity attribute.

The use of a qualifier-name is discussed in Section 5.3. Examples of the statement are

ACCUMULATE AVE.INVENTORY AS THE AVERAGE OF INVENTORY

TALLY AVE.TIME AS MEAN OF TIME.V

ACCUMULATE BIGGEST.INVENTORY AS MAXIMUM OF INVENTORY

The value of the statistic being collected can be used as part of any arithmetic expression or printed at any time during the simulation. For example

PRINT 1 LINE WITH AVE.INVENTORY THUS
THE AVERAGE INVENTORY WAS ***.**

If the keyword ACCUMULATE is used, the statistic is collected as a time integral, while if TALLY is used, the statistic is based on an equal weighting of each value. To see the difference between ACCUMULATE and TALLY, consider a variable X whose value over time is shown in Figure 3.1.

If the statement

ACCUMULATE X.MEAN AS MEAN OF X

was used, we would calculate X.MEAN as

$$\text{X.MEAN} = \frac{1(5-0) + 0(7-5) + 2(10-7) + 1(12-10)}{12} = 13/12$$

If the statement

TALLY X.MEAN AS THE MEAN OF X

was used, we would calculate X.MEAN as

$$\text{X.MEAN} = \frac{1+0+2+1}{4} = 4/4$$

SIMSCRIPT can also accumulate or tally histograms through the ACCUMULATE and TALLY statement:

$$\left\{ \begin{array}{l} \text{ACCUMULATE} \\ \text{TALLY} \end{array} \right\} \quad \text{variable\_name (lower\_limit TO upper\_limit BY width)}$$

AS THE [qualifier-name] HISTOGRAM OF variable

A histogram of the values of the variable will be accumulated, recording data in the array variable_name. The length of the array will be (upper_limit − lower_limit)/ width + 1, with the first cell of the histogram used for all values of the variable that fall

FIGURE 3.1 X vs TIME

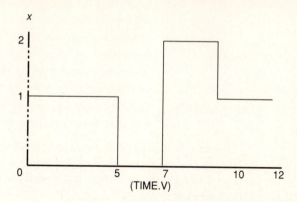

below the lower limit, and the last cell being used for values of the variable that fall at or above the upper limit. If the keyword ACCUMULATE is used, the cells of the histogram contain the time the variable was in a cell's range, while if TALLY is used, the cells of the histogram contain the frequency the variable was in a cell's range. It is up to the user to label the cells of the histogram when printing histogram data. Examples of histogram definitions are

ACCUMULATE INVENTORY.GRAPH(0 TO 250 BY 10) AS THE HISTOGRAM OF INVENTORY
TALLY AGE.HISTO (0 TO 100 BY 5) AS THE HISTOGRAM OF AGE

In the first example, INVENTORY.GRAPH will be the proportion of time the variable INVENTORY is below 10 (cell 1), between 10 and 250 (cells 2 through 25), and 250 or more (cell 26). In the second example, the AGE.HISTO will be the number of times AGE was below 5 (cell 1), 5 to 100 (cell 2 through 20), and 100 or more (cell 21).

We will finish this section with an example of a complete SIMSCRIPT simulation model including input of data and the printing of a simulation report.

PROBLEM III.1 We simulate a simple inventory system in which orders are received daily. The daily demand is Poisson distributed and the mean daily demand is read in as data. When inventory falls below a pre-established re-order point, the item is re-ordered from the supplier. The quantity to be re-ordered and the re-order point are read in as data. If on any day there is not enough inventory on hand to meet that day's demand, the unfilled demand is backordered, and when the replenishment order arrives all backorders are filled. During the simulation we will collect statistics on the average inventory, the average backorders, the total number of orders and the number of days that demand was backordered.

In this model we will have three processes:

RE-ORDER   Represents the process of a replenishment order being placed, wait-
                  ing for the replenishment to arrive, filling backorders and updating
                  inventory.

DEMAND   Represents the process of daily orders being received, reducing
                  inventory or backordering, and placing an order when on-hand and
                  on-order inventory is below the re-order point.

PRINT.REPORT   This process prints out the summary statistics and halts the simula-
                  tion after the required number of days have been simulated.

Because SIMSCRIPT is a well structured language and we have complete freedom
in naming variables, the program is nearly self documenting. The program is shown in
Listing 4 along with the SIMSCRIPT prompts for input and the output of the process
PRINT.REPORT.

LISTING 4   SIMSCRIPT MODEL OF AN INVENTORY SYSTEM

```
                    CODE FOR INVENTORY SIMULATION

PREAMBLE

'' THIS IS A SIMULATION MODEL OF AN INVENTORY SYSTEM.
'' THE AVERAGE DAILY DEMAND FOR THE ITEM BEING INVENTORIED IS READ IN
'' AND IS ASSUMED POISSON DISTRIBUTED. WHEN A REPLACEMENT ORDER IS
'' PLACED IT WILL TAKE UNIFORMLY 5 TO 8 DAYS FOR THE ORDER
'' TO ARRIVE.  THE USER MUST SPECIFY THE RE-ORDER QUANTITY AND THE
'' THE REORDER POINT.  THE MODEL ALLOWS FOR BACKORDERING DEMAND

NORMALLY  MODE IS UNDEFINED
PROCESSES INCLUDE REORDER, DEMAND AND PRINT.REPORT
DEFINE INVENTORY, BACKORDER, ORDER.QUANTITY, REORDER.PT, NO.ORDERS,
       ON.ORDER, NO.BACKORDERS, N.DAYS.SIMULATE AS INTEGER VARIABLES
DEFINE AVE.DAILY.DEMAND AS A REAL VARIABLE
ACCUMULATE AVE.INVENTORY AS THE AVERAGE OF INVENTORY
ACCUMULATE AVE.BACKORDER AS THE AVERAGE OF BACKORDER
ACCUMULATE MAX.BACKORDER AS THE MAXIMUM OF BACKORDER
END

MAIN
PRINT 1 LINE THUS
INPUT ORDER QUANTITY AND REORDER POINT
READ ORDER.QUANTITY,REORDER.PT
PRINT 1 LINE THUS
INPUT AVERAGE DAILY DEMAND
READ AVE.DAILY.DEMAND
PRINT 1 LINE THUS
INPUT THE INITIAL INVENTORY
READ INVENTORY
PRINT 1 LINE THUS
INPUT THE NO. OF DAYS TO SIMULATE THE INVENTORY SYSTEM
READ N.DAYS.SIMULATE
ACTIVATE A DEMAND NOW
ACTIVATE A PRINT.REPORT IN N.DAYS.SIMULATE DAYS
START SIMULATION
END
```

```
PROCESS REORDER
WAIT RANDI.F(5,8,1) DAYS
ADD ORDER.QUANTITY TO INVENTORY
SUBTRACT ORDER.QUANTITY FROM ON.ORDER
IF INVENTORY>BACKORDER
   SUBTRACT BACKORDER FROM INVENTORY
   LET BACKORDER=0
ELSE
   SUBTRACT INVENTORY FROM BACKORDER
   LET INVENTORY=0
ALWAYS
END

PROCESS DEMAND
DEFINE DAILY.DEMAND AS AN INTEGER VARIABLE
WHILE TIME.V<N.DAYS.SIMULATE
DO
 LET DAILY.DEMAND=POISSON.F(AVE.DAILY.DEMAND,2)
 IF INVENTORY>DAILY.DEMAND
  SUBTRACT DAILY.DEMAND FROM INVENTORY
 ELSE
  ADD 1 TO NO.BACKORDERS
  ADD DAILY.DEMAND-INVENTORY TO BACKORDER
  LET INVENTORY=0
 ALWAYS
 IF (INVENTORY + ON.ORDER) - BACKORDER < REORDER.PT
  ADD 1 TO NO.ORDERS
  ADD ORDER.QUANTITY TO ON.ORDER
  ACTIVATE A REORDER NOW
 ALWAYS
 WAIT 1 DAY
LOOP
END

PROCESS PRINT.REPORT
DEFINE N.YEARS AS A REAL VARIABLE
LET N.YEARS=N.DAYS.SIMULATE/365
PRINT 9 LINES WITH N.DAYS.SIMULATE, AVE.DAILY.DEMAND, ORDER.QUANTITY,
          REORDER.PT, AVE.INVENTORY, AVE.BACKORDER,MAX.BACKORDER,
          NO.ORDERS/N.YEARS, NO.BACKORDERS/N.DAYS.SIMULATE THUS
BASED ON A **** DAY SIMULATION
WHEN THE AVERAGE DAILY DEMAND IS ***.** PER DAY
     THE REORDER QUANTITY IS ****, AND THE REORDER POINT IS ***

THE AVERAGE INVENTORY IS ****.**
THE AVERAGE BACKORDER IS ****.**
THE MAXIMUM BACKORDER IS *****
THE AVERAGE NO. OF ORDERS/YEAR IS ***.**
THE PROBABILITY OF A BACKORDER ON ANY GIVEN DAY IS *.***
STOP
END
```

PROMPTS AND INPUT DATA

```
INPUT ORDER QUANTITY AND REORDER POINT
II.5> 200 20
INPUT AVERAGE DAILY DEMAND
II.5> 4.5
INPUT THE INITIAL INVENTORY
II.5> 200
INPUT THE NO. OF DAYS TO SIMULATE THE INVENTORY SYSTEM
II.5> 4000
```
                                                            (Continued)

OUTPUT

```
BASED ON A 4000 DAY SIMULATION
WHEN THE AVERAGE DAILY DEMAND IS   4.50 PER DAY
    THE REORDER QUANTITY IS  200, AND THE REORDER POINT IS   20

THE AVERAGE INVENTORY IS    90.65
THE AVERAGE BACKORDER IS     .43
THE MAXIMUM BACKORDER IS     25
THE AVERAGE NO. OF ORDERS/YEAR IS    8.21
THE PROBABILITY OF A BACKORDER ON ANY GIVEN DAY IS   .057
```

3.7   Resources

Resources in SIMSCRIPT provide a mechanism for including in a simulation model, elements whose capacity or number are finite. Examples of resources are: main memory in a computer system, space on a conveyor belt, tables in a restaurant, and physicians in a health clinic.

In the SIMSCRIPT world view, processes request and relinquish units of a resource, and if there are insufficient units of the requested resource available, the process is suspended until the requested number of resource units becomes available. There can be more than one resource within a general resource class, each resource distinguished by its resource index. Generically, resources are arrays with the columns of the array corresponding to the index of the resource and the rows of the resource being resource attributes.

All resource classes, along with any user-defined attributes, must be declared in the Preamble section of the model using the statement

RESOURCES INCLUDE resource_class

or

RESOURCES
    EVERY resource_class HAS list of attributes

The global variable N.resource_class is the number of resources within a resource class and acts as an upper limit for indexing across resources in the same class. A resource does not exist in the model until it has been created using the statement

CREATE EACH resource_class

or

CREATE EACH resource_class (integer expression)

If the first form is used N.resource_class must be previously initialized, while if the second form is used, N.resource_class is assigned the value of the integer expression. Synonyms for EACH are EVERY and ALL. Examples of CREATE are:

CREATE EVERY TELLER(5)

READ N.DOCTOR
CREATE EACH DOCTOR

In the first example, five resources with indices 1 through 5 are created and the value of N.TELLER becomes 5. In the second example the number of doctors, N.DOCTOR, is first read and then used to set the number of DOCTOR resources created.

When a resource is created the number of units of the resource is initialized to 0. For example

CREATE CONVEYOR(1)

creates a single resource called CONVEYOR(1), as well as sets N.CONVEYOR to 1 and U.CONVEYOR(1) to 0. The CREATE statement should be followed by a statement such as

U.CONVEYOR(1) = 10.

A process requests a resource through the statement:

REQUEST integer_value [UNIT[S] OF] resource[index]
            [WITH priority integer_value]

If the number of requested units of the resource are available the process gains control of these units of the resource; the process then continues. If the number of requested resource units are not available, the process is suspended and placed, according to the priority of the request, in a set of processes requesting the resource. When the requested number of resources becomes available the process is resumed.

A process releases resources using the statement:

RELINQUISH integer_value [UNIT[S] OF] resource[index]

When a process releases a resource, processes which are waiting for the released resource may be resumed. The statements REQUEST and RELINQUISH can only appear in process routines. Examples of REQUEST and RELINQUISH are:

REQUEST 1 UNIT OF DOCTOR(MY.DOCTOR)
WAIT 20 MINUTES
RELINQUISH 1 UNIT OF DOCTOR(MY.DOCTOR)

REQUEST 2 MEMORY(1) WITH PRIORITY 10
WAIT 3 SECONDS
RELINQUISH 1 UNIT OF MEMORY(1)
WAIT 2 SECONDS
RELINQUISH 1 UNIT OF MEMORY(1)

In the first example, one unit of the resource DOCTOR(MY.DOCTOR) is requested and, if available, the process will have control of the resource for 20 minutes. If one unit of DOCTOR(MY.DOCTOR) is not available the process is suspended until a unit of the resource is available. After controlling the resource for 20 minutes, the process releases one unit of DOCTOR(MY.DOCTOR), and if another process is waiting for the resource, it can be resumed.

In the second example, two units of resource MEMORY are requested, but with a priority of 10. Any other processes requesting MEMORY, but with a lower priority, would be passed over in favor of this process. The process also releases the resource in two phases, first releasing one unit and then, after a 2-second delay, releasing the second unit.

Each resource within a resource class has three attributes that describe its capacity and utilization:

U.resource   The number of available resource units

N.X.resource   The number of processes currently using the resource

N.Q.resource   The number of processes waiting for the resource.

A resource can be thought of as the array

	1	2 . . .	N.resource
U.resource			
N.X.resource			
N.Q.resource			
{additional system defined attributes}			
{user defined attributes}			

Statistics on resource attributes can be collected by including an ACCUMULATE or TALLY statement in the Preamble. For example

```
RESOURCES INCLUDE MACHINE
ACCUMULATE MACH.QUEUE AS THE AVERAGE OF N.Q.MACHINE
ACCUMULATE MACH.UTIL AS THE AVERAGE OF N.X.MACHINE
```

During the simulation, statistics will be collected on N.Q.MACHINE and N.X.MACHINE for MACHINE(1) to MACHINE(N.MACHINE). At the end of the simulation these statistics can be printed out using the print statement

```
FOR I = 1 TO N.MACHINE
DO
PRINT 1 LINE WITH I.MACH.QUEUE(I) AND MACH.UTIL(I) THUS
MACHINE **     AVERAGE QUEUE = ***.**     UTILIZATION = *.**
LOOP
```

We will conclude this section with an example of a simulation which includes both processes and resources.

PROBLEM III.2   No simulation text is complete without at least one simulation model of the classic barber shop. We will assume that the shop opens each day with no customers in the shop and during the day the number of barbers available remains constant. The barber shop has a limited number of seats for waiting customers and if a potential customer arrives and finds all the seats occupied he or she does not enter the shop. If a seat is available the customers wait until a barber is available. The time between customer arrivals is exponentially distributed and the time to cut a customer's hair is lognormal distributed. At the end of the day the shop closes and no further customers may enter. Those customers already in the shop will, however, be serviced. The model we develop will allow the user to input the number of hours the shop is open, the number of barbers, the number of seats for waiting customers, the mean time between arrivals, and the mean and standard deviation of the time to cut a customer's hair. At the end of the simulation, we will print out the number of hours the shop operated, the number of customers arriving, the number of customers lost because no seats were available, the average number of customers waiting, the mean time a customer waited, and the utilization of the barbers.

In this model we will have two processes: CUSTOMER.GENERATOR, which will randomly generate customers, and CUSTOMER, which describes the passage of the customer through the shop. There will be just one resource, BARBER(1), but the number of units (barbers) of this resource is read as data in the Main section. This model will simulate only one day, but in a later section we will describe methods of repeating a simulation in order to build up more accurate statistics. Again, notice that SIMSCRIPT models can be nearly self documenting and little explanation of the model is necessary. Because SIMSCRIPT is a general-purpose language we do not have to resort to subtle and arcane uses of the elements of language. The SIMSCRIPT program for this model is shown in Listing 5 along with the input to the model, as SIMSCRIPT would prompt for input, and a listing of the output of the model for the given set of inputs.

3.8   Multiple Resources

In the previous example, the number of resources in the resource class, BARBER, was 1, but in many models we need to have more than one resource within the same resource class. For example, at a turnpike toll plaza there may be several toll booths, each with its own queue and mean processing time. Other examples of the use of multiple resources include disk drives in a computer system, physicians in a health clinic, and machine centers in a manufacturing facility. Very often, in a simulation model, it is necessary to scan across all the resources in a resource class, identifying a resource with a particular attribute. A driver, upon approaching the toll plaza, will look for the toll booth with the shortest line. A patient, coming into a clinic, may need a particular type of physician, or a job may need to go to a particular machine center. To facilitate searching across resources within the same class or elements of an array, SIMSCRIPT provides a FIND statement which is used together with the FOR statement. There are several forms of the FOR . . . FIND construction, but we will only consider here the forms which are particularly useful in simulation models. The general form of the FIND statement is:

LISTING 5   BARBER SHOP MODELED IN SIMSCRIPT

```
                        CODE FOR BARBER SHOP MODEL

PREAMBLE

''THIS IS A SIMULATION MODEL OF A BARBER SHOP WITH LIMITED SEATING
''CAPACITY.  AN ARRIVING  CUSTOMER, WHO FINDS ALL THE SEATS OCCUPIED,
''LEAVES. AT CLOSING TIME NO MORE CUSTOMERS ARE ACCEPTED INTO THE SHOP
''BUT ANY CUSTOMERS STILL IN THE SHOP ARE SERVED.  AS INPUT THE USER
''PROVIDES THE NUMBER OF BARBERS, NUMBER OF SEATS, HOURS OPEN, MEAN
''TIME BETWEEN ARRIVALS AND THE MEAN AND STD. DEV. OF THE TIME TO
''CUT A CUSTOMER'S HAIR.

NORMALLY MODE IS UNDEFINED
PROCESSES INCLUDE CUSTOMER.GENERATOR AND CUSTOMER
RESOURCES INCLUDE BARBER
DEFINE N.CHAIRS,N.ARRIVALS,N.REFUSE,N.NO.WAIT,N.CHAIRS.OCCUPIED,
    N.ENTER AS INTEGER VARIABLES
DEFINE MEAN.ARRIVAL.TIME, WAIT.TIME, MEAN.CUT.TIME, STD.DEV.CUT,
    HOURS, CLOSE.TIME AS REAL VARIABLES
DEFINE SHOP.NOT.FULL TO MEAN N.CHAIRS.OCCUPIED<N.CHAIRS
ACCUMULATE UTIL.BARBER AS THE AVERAGE OF N.X.BARBER
ACCUMULATE QUEUE.BARBER AS THE AVERAGE OF N.Q.BARBER
TALLY MEAN.WAIT AS THE AVERAGE OF WAIT.TIME
END


MAIN
CREATE EVERY BARBER(1)
PRINT 3 LINES THUS
INPUT NUMBER OF BARBERS, NUMBER OF CHAIRS, NUMBER HOURS OPEN
  MEAN TIME BETWEEN ARRIVALS (IN MINUTES),
  MEAN AND STD.DEV. OF TIME TO CUT HAIR
READ U.BARBER, N.CHAIRS, HOURS, MEAN.ARRIVAL.TIME, MEAN.CUT.TIME,
  STD.DEV.CUT
LET CLOSE.TIME=HOURS/24
SCHEDULE A CUSTOMER.GENERATOR NOW
START SIMULATION
PRINT 6 LINES WITH TIME.V*24, N.ARRIVALS, N.ENTER, N.REFUSE,
    N.REFUSE/N.ARRIVALS*100, U.BARBER(1),UTIL.BARBER(1)/U.BARBER(1),
    QUEUE.BARBER(1), N.NO.WAIT*100/N.ENTER ,MEAN.WAIT*60*24   THUS
THE SHOP CLOSED AFTER **.** HOURS, WITH *** ARRIVALS
*** ARRIVALS ENTERED THE SHOP AND *** WERE REFUSED (**.*%)
THE UTILIZATION OF THE ** BARBERS WAS *.**
THE MEAN NUMBER OF CUSTOMERS WAITING WAS ***.**
THE PERCENT OF CUSTOMERS WHO DID NOT WAIT FOR A BARBER WAS **.*%
IF A CUSTOMER DID WAIT THE AVERAGE WAIT WAS ***.** MINUTE
END


PROCESS CUSTOMER.GENERATOR
WHILE TIME.V < CLOSE.TIME
DO
  ACTIVATE A CUSTOMER NOW
  WAIT EXPONENTIAL.F(MEAN.ARRIVAL.TIME,1) MINUTES
LOOP
END
```

```
PROCESS CUSTOMER
DEFINE ARRIVE.TIME AS A REAL VARIABLE
ADD 1 TO N.ARRIVALS
IF SHOP.NOT.FULL
 ADD 1 TO N.ENTER
 LET ARRIVE.TIME=TIME.V
 ADD 1 TO N.CHAIRS.OCCUPIED
 REQUEST 1 BARBER(1)
 SUBTRACT 1 FROM N.CHAIRS.OCCUPIED
 IF ARRIVE.TIME=TIME.V
   ADD 1 TO N.NO.WAIT
 ELSE
   LET WAIT.TIME=TIME.V-ARRIVE.TIME
 ALWAYS
 WAIT LOG.NORMAL.F(MEAN.CUT.TIME,STD.DEV.CUT,2) MINUTES
 RELINQUISH 1 BARBER
ELSE
 ADD 1 TO N.REFUSE
ALWAYS
END
```

PROMPTS AND INPUT DATA


```
INPUT NUMBER OF BARBERS, NUMBER OF CHAIRS, NUMBER HOURS OPEN
  MEAN TIME BETWEEN ARRIVALS (IN MINUTES),
  MEAN AND STD.DEV. OF TIME TO CUT HAIR

II.5> 4 15 8 5 20 5
```

OUTPUT


```
THE SHOP CLOSED AFTER  9.52 HOURS, WITH 109 ARRIVALS
104 ARRIVALS ENTERED THE SHOP AND   5 WERE REFUSED ( 4.6%)
THE UTILIZATION OF THE          4 BARBERS WAS  .97
THE MEAN NUMBER OF CUSTOMERS WAITING WAS   9.99
THE PERCENT OF CUSTOMERS WHO DID NOT WAIT FOR A BARBER WAS  5.8%
IF A CUSTOMER DID WAIT THE AVERAGE WAIT WAS  58.22 MINUTE
```

FOR index control [WITH expression]

FIND THE FIRST CASE, [IF $\left\{ \begin{array}{c} \text{FOUND} \\ \text{NONE} \end{array} \right\}$]

or

FOR index control [WITH expression]
FIND variable = THE FIRST expression, IF $\left\{ \begin{array}{c} \text{FOUND} \\ \text{NONE} \end{array} \right\}$

Iteration will continue until the FOR looping is completed or the WITH expression is true. When an IF statement is included as part of the FIND, it will be executed according to whether the search was successful (FOUND) or unsuccessful (NONE). If the FIND operation is successful, the index of the resource or array element will be equal to the index of the FOR statement. An additional and very useful form of the FOR statement is:

FOR EACH resource class

which is equivalent to indexing across each of the resources in the class.

Examples of FOR . . . FIND statement are:

```
FOR I = 1 TO 10 WITH X(I) < 0.0
   FIND THE FIRST CASE,
      IF FOUND
      LIST X(I)
      ELSE
      LIST 'NO ELEMENT FOUND < 0'
      ALWAYS

FOR EACH TOLL_BOOTH WITH N.X.TOLL_BOOTH(TOLL_BOOTH) = 0
   FIND THE FIRST CASE,
      IF FOUND
         LET CHOICE = TOLL_BOOTH
      ELSE
         .
         .
         .
      ALWAYS
```

In the first example, a search was made across the first 10 elements of the array X. If a negative element is found, its value is printed out, otherwise a message that no element is less than zero is printed. In the second example, each resource within the resource class TOLL_BOOTH is examined until N.X (the number of processes utilizing the resource) is zero. If a resource is found that satisfies the WITH condition, the variable CHOICE is assigned the value of the resource index; otherwise the logic following the ELSE is executed. The FOR . . . FIND structure allows a process to search across a number of resources in the same class, looking for a resource currently available.

In addition to the FIND statement, SIMSCRIPT has a COMPUTE statement that provides for indexing across an array, resource or permanent entity class or set, calculating any of the statistical_quantities listed in Table 7.5. The COMPUTE statement is used with the FOR statement and has the form:

```
FOR index control [WITH expression]
   COMPUTE variable AS THE statistical_quantity OF variable
```

Examples of the FOR . . COMPUTE statement are

```
FOR I = 1 TO N WITH X(I) > 0
   COMPUTE POS.TOTAL AS THE SUM OF X(I)

FOR EACH TOLL.BOOTH WITH N.Q.TOLL.BOOTH(TOLL.BOOTH) > 0
   COMPUTE SHORT.LINE AS
   THE MINIMUM OF N.Q.TOLL.BOOTH(TOLL.BOOTH)

FOR EACH DOCTOR
   COMPUTE CHOICE AS THE MINIMUM(DOCTOR) OF
   N.Q.DOCTOR(DOCTOR)
```

In the first example, POS.TOTAL becomes the sum of the positive elements of the array X. In the second example, each resource, TOLL.BOOTH, with a queue of requests, is checked and the length of the minimum queue is stored in the variable SHORT.LINE. In the third example, the variable CHOICE is set to the index of the resource DOCTOR with the shortest queue. Notice the difference between the expression MINIMUM and MINIMUM(resource class). In the first case a statistical quantity is returned, while in the second case the index of the entity with the statistical quantity is returned.

3.9   Resource and Process Attributes

SIMSCRIPT resources and processes may have user-defined attributes. In the Preamble, when resources and processes are declared, we may also declare that they have attributes. Attributes can be any mode variable but, if undeclared in a define statement, they will default to the background mode. If the mode is UNDEFINED, we must declare mode for all attributes. Examples of attribute declarations are

```
RESOURCES
    EVERY TOLL.BOOTH HAS A TYPE
DEFINE TYPE AS AN INTEGER VARIABLE
```

```
RESOURCES INCLUDE NURSE
    EVERY DOCTOR HAS A SPECIALTY AND MEAN.TIME
DEFINE SPECIALTY AS A TEXT VARIABLE
DEFINE MEAN.TIME AS A REAL VARIABLE
PROCESSES
    EVERY PATIENT HAS A COMPLAINT AND ASSIGNED.DOCTOR
DEFINE COMPLAINT AS TEXT VARIABLE
DEFINE ASSIGNED.DOCTOR AS AN INTEGER VARIABLE
```

In the first example, the resource TOLL.BOOTH is declared and given the attribute TYPE, which can be used to assign it a particular class, such as "exact change," "cars only," or "any vehicle." In the second example, the resource NURSE has no user-defined attributes, while DOCTOR has a TEXT and a REAL attribute. The process PATIENT has two attributes, which can be used to indicate the patient's complaint and the physician to which the patient is assigned.

Attributes of resources and processes can be read in or assigned using a LET statement. In addition, attributes of processes can be passed as parameters of the ACTIVATE statement using the form:

ACTIVATE A process GIVEN argument list IN time expression.

The matching of arguments to the attributes of the process follows in the order the attributes are listed in the Preamble section.

For example, using the above declaration of the process PATIENT:

ACTIVATE A PATIENT GIVEN "INTERNAL" IN 10 MINUTES

assigns the attribute called COMPLAINT the TEXT value INTERNAL.

We conclude this section with a simulation model of a walk-in health clinic. The model we develop includes both resources and processes with attributes.

PROBLEM III.3 An inner-city health clinic provides health care on a walk-in basis. The clinic is staffed by nurses and physicians. The physicians are specialized and will treat patients according to the patient's complaint. When a patient enters the health clinic, a nurse decides if the patient's complaint requires the service of an internal, surgical, or orthopedic physician. Patients wait until a physician appropriate for their complaint is available. A patient arrives at the clinic on the average every 5 minutes, with the time between arrivals, exponentially distributed. It takes the nurse between 5 and 10 minutes (uniformly distributed) to get the necessary information from a patient and the patient is then assigned to a physician. If more than one physician is available within a specialty, the nurse assigns the patient to the physician with the least number of patients waiting. The distribution of diagnoses and associated treatment times are

Diagnosis	Percent of Patients	Mean Treatment Time
Internal	50%	20 minutes
Surgical	30%	30 minutes
Orthopedic	20%	35 minutes

The time to treat any single patient is normally distributed with a standard deviation equal to 20% of the mean time. The model of the system along with sample input and output is shown in Listing 6.

LISTING 6   SIMSCRIPT MODEL OF WALK-IN HEALTH CLINIC

```
                    CODE FOR WALK-IN HEALTH CLINIC


PREAMBLE
NORMALLY MODE IS UNDEFINED
PROCESSES INCLUDE PATIENT.GENERATOR, STOP.SIMULATION
   EVERY PATIENT HAS A COMPLAINT
RESOURCES INCLUDE NURSE
   EVERY PHYSICIAN HAS A SPECIALTY AND A MEAN.TIME
DEFINE COMPLAINT AND SPECIALTY AS TEXT VARIABLES
DEFINE MEAN.TIME AS A REAL VARIABLE
TALLY AVE.WAIT AS THE AVERAGE OF WAITING.TIME
TALLY N.PATIENTS AS THE NUMBER OF WAITING.TIME
ACCUMULATE NURSE.UTIL AS THE AVERAGE OF N.X.NURSE
ACCUMULATE PATIENTS.WAIT.NRS AS THE AVERAGE OF N.Q.NURSE
ACCUMULATE PHYSICIAN.UTIL AS THE AVERAGE OF N.X.PHYSICIAN
ACCUMULATE PATIENTS.WAIT.PHYSICIAN AS THE AVERAGE OF N.Q.PHYSICIAN
DEFINE WAITING.TIME AS A REAL VARIABLE
DEFINE T.END AS A REAL VARIABLE
END
```

```
MAIN
LET N.NURSE=1
CREATE EVERY NURSE
PRINT 1 LINE THUS
INPUT NUMBER OF NURSES
FOR EACH NURSE
READ U.NURSE(NURSE)
PRINT 1 LINE THUS
INPUT NUMBER OF PHYSICIANS
READ N.PHYSICIAN
CREATE EVERY PHYSICIAN
FOR EACH PHYSICIAN
DO
PRINT 1 LINE THUS
INPUT SPECIALTY AND AVERAGE VISIT TIME
LET U.PHYSICIAN(PHYSICIAN)=1
READ SPECIALTY(PHYSICIAN)
READ MEAN.TIME(PHYSICIAN)
LOOP
PRINT 1 LINE THUS
INPUT LENGTH OF SIMULATION IN DAYS
READ T.END
ACTIVATE A PATIENT.GENERATOR NOW
ACTIVATE A STOP.SIMULATION IN T.END DAYS
START SIMULATION
END

PROCESS STOP.SIMULATION
PRINT 1 LINE WITH T.END, N.PATIENTS AND AVE.WAIT*1440 THUS
AFTER **.* DAYS THE AVE. WAIT FOR **** PATIENTS WAS ***.* MINUTES
PRINT 1 LINE THUS
STAFF    UTILIZATION    AVERAGE NO. PATIENTS WAITING
FOR EACH NURSE
PRINT 1 LINE WITH NURSE.UTIL(1)/(U.NURSE(1)+N.X.NURSE(1)),
     PATIENTS.WAIT.NRS(1) THUS
NURSE          *.**              **.**
FOR EACH PHYSICIAN
PRINT 1 LINE WITH SPECIALTY(PHYSICIAN),PHYSICIAN.UTIL(PHYSICIAN)
 AND PATIENTS.WAIT.PHYSICIAN(PHYSICIAN) THUS
**********    *.**           **.**
STOP
END
PROCESS PATIENT.GENERATOR
DEFINE X AS A REAL VARIABLE
DEFINE THIS.COMPLAINT AS A TEXT VARIABLE
WHILE TIME.V GE 0.0    ''THIS PUTS PATIENT.GENERATOR IN AN INFINITE LOOP
DO
 LET X=RANDOM.F(1)
 IF X LT 0.50
  LET THIS.COMPLAINT="INTERNIST"
 ELSE
  IF X LT 0.70
   LET THIS.COMPLAINT="SURGEON"
  ELSE
   LET THIS.COMPLAINT="ORTHOPEDIC"
  ALWAYS
 ALWAYS
 ACTIVATE A PATIENT GIVING THIS.COMPLAINT NOW
 WAIT EXPONENTIAL.F(5.0,2) MINUTES
LOOP
END
```

(Continued)

```
PROCESS PATIENT
DEFINE ARRIVE.TIME AS AN REAL VARIABLE
DEFINE CHOICE AS AN INTEGER VARIABLE
LET ARRIVE.TIME = TIME.V
REQUEST 1 NURSE(1)
WAIT UNIFORM.F(5.0,10.0,3) MINUTES
RELINQUISH 1 NURSE(1)
FOR EACH PHYSICIAN WITH
     COMPLAINT(PATIENT) EQ SPECIALTY(PHYSICIAN)
COMPUTE CHOICE=MINIMUM(PHYSICIAN) OF N.Q.PHYSICIAN(PHYSICIAN)
REQUEST 1 PHYSICIAN(CHOICE)
WAIT NORMAL.F(MEAN.TIME(CHOICE),.20*MEAN.TIME(CHOICE),3) MINUTES
RELINQUISH 1 PHYSICIAN(CHOICE)
LET WAITING.TIME=TIME.V-ARRIVE.TIME
END
```

PROMPTS AND INPUT DATA

```
INPUT NUMBER OF NURSES
II.5> 2
INPUT NUMBER OF PHYSICIANS
II.5> 7
INPUT SPECIALTY AND AVERAGE VISIT TIME
II.5> INTERNIST 20
INPUT SPECIALTY AND AVERAGE VISIT TIME
II.5> INTERNIST 20
INPUT SPECIALTY AND AVERAGE VISIT TIME
II.5> INTERNIST 20
INPUT SPECIALTY AND AVERAGE VISIT TIME
II.5> SURGEON 30
INPUT SPECIALTY AND AVERAGE VISIT TIME
II.5> SURGEON 30
INPUT SPECIALTY AND AVERAGE VISIT TIME
II.5> ORTHOPEDIC 35
INPUT SPECIALTY AND AVERAGE VISIT TIME
II.5> ORTHOPEDIC 35
INPUT LENGTH OF SIMULATION IN DAYS
II.5> 5
```

OUTPUT

```
AFTER  5.  DAYS THE AVE. WAIT FOR 1430 PATIENTS WAS  78.1 MINUTES
STAFF     UTILIZATION   AVERAGE NO. PATIENTS WAITING
NURSE          .75              1.28
INTERNIST      .36               .14
INTERNIST      .75               .37
INTERNIST      .95               .66
SURGEON        .40               .16
SURGEON        .82               .47
ORTHOPEDIC     .97              2.67
ORTHOPEDIC    1.00              3.17
```

4.0   INTERMEDIATE SIMSCRIPT CONCEPTS

In this section we present two new concepts in SIMSCRIPT: sets, and temporary and permanent entities. Using sets and temporary and permanent entities we can build simulation models of more complex systems. We first describe sets and their properties, and then show how sets can be used to build models of systems, including models that have process interaction, allowing processes to be suspended, interrupted and resumed. We will then describe temporary and permanent entities and show how they are used in building SIMSCRIPT models.

4.1   Sets

In SIMSCRIPT, a set is defined as an ordered collection of entities. All the entities in the set must be the same entity type. Sets, along with their ownership and membership, are defined in the Preamble, using the form

DEFINE set-name AS A $\begin{bmatrix} \text{FIFO} \\ \text{LIFO} \end{bmatrix}$ SET

$\begin{bmatrix} \text{RANKED BY} \begin{Bmatrix} \text{HIGH attribute} \\ \text{LOW} \end{Bmatrix} \end{bmatrix}$

$\begin{bmatrix} \text{THEN BY} \begin{Bmatrix} \text{HIGH attribute} \\ \text{LOW} \end{Bmatrix} \end{bmatrix}$*

The FIFO (first-in-first-out) or LIFO (last-in-first-out) clause is optional, but if used, organizes the entities in the set according to the time of entry into the set. The RANKED clause is also optional and can be repeated any number of times to give rules for ranking by more than one attribute. Ties on attribute ranking are broken using FIFO. Examples of set definition are:

DEFINE FLIGHT.LIST AS A SET RANKED BY HIGH CLASS

DEFINE ORDERS AS A LIFO SET

DEFINE JOB.SET AS A SET RANKED BY HIGH PRIORITY THEN BY
      LOW CUMULATIVE.CPU.TIME THEN BY LOW MEMORY

DEFINE PRINT.QUEUE AS A SET

In the first example, the set FLIGHT.LIST is organized in descending order of the entity's attribute, CLASS. If two entities have the same value for the attribute CLASS, the first entity filed in the set will be first in order. In the second example, the set ORDERS is organized in LIFO order, providing for entities to be removed from the set in the reverse order they were filed into the set.

In the third example, entities are filed in the set JOBS first by descending value of the attribute PRIORITY, with ties in PRIORITY broken using the attribute CUMULATIVE.CPU.TIME, giving the entity with the lowest value the first ranking in the set. Finally, if ties occur on both PRIORITY and CUMULATIVE.CPU.TIME, then the entity with the smallest value of attribute MEMORY is filed first. In the case of a tie on all three attributes, the order is FIFO. In the fourth example, the set PRINT.QUEUE is a general set, defaulting to FIFO ordering.

Set membership and ownership is declared in the Preamble using the OWNS and BELONGS TO phrase in the EVERY statement.

EVERY entity $\left\{ \begin{array}{l} \text{OWNS} \\ \text{BELONGS TO} \end{array} \right\}$ A set-name . . .

The OWNS and BELONGS TO phrase can be repeated any number of times and the phrase MAY or CAN is optionally used to add clarity. Examples of set membership and ownership declarations are

EVERY FLIGHT OWNS A FLIGHT.LIST
EVERY PASSENGER BELONGS TO A FLIGHT.LIST

EVERY CPU OWNS A JOB.SET AND A WAITING.SET
EVERY JOB MAY BELONG TO A JOB.SET,
        MAY BELONG TO A WAITING.SET
        AND OWNS A TASK.LIST

THE SYSTEM OWNS THE ORDERS
EVERY REQUISITION BELONGS TO ORDERS

In the first example, each entity, FLIGHT, owns a set of type FLIGHT.LIST. The elements in the set FLIGHT.LIST are entities of type PASSENGER.

In the second example, the CPU entity owns (points to) two sets: JOB.SET and WAITING.SET. The entities JOBS are eligible members of two sets JOB.SET and WAITING.SET and may belong to one, both, or neither of the two sets.

In the first two examples, access to the entities in the sets must be made through the owners of the sets. Sets can, however, be made global by declaring the SYSTEM as the owner. In the third example, the set ORDERS is owned by the system and can be globally referenced. The entities REQUISITION belong to the global set ORDERS.

4.2 Filing and Removing Elements from a Set

Entities are not automatically included in a set but must be added to and removed from sets using the FILE and REMOVE statements. The form of the FILE statement is

FILE entity-identifier $\left[\begin{array}{l} \text{FIRST} \\ \text{LAST} \\ \text{BEFORE entity} \\ \text{AFTER entity} \end{array} \right]$ IN set-identifier

When a BEFORE or AFTER phrase is used, the referenced entity must be in the set.
    The form of the REMOVE statement is

REMOVE $\left[\begin{array}{l} \text{FIRST} \\ \text{LAST} \\ \text{THIS} \end{array} \right]$ entity-identifier FROM set-identifier

Upon removal from the set, the order of the entities remaining in the set reflects the absence of the element just removed and the entity-identifier points to the entity removed.

The phrase THIS is used in conjunction with a FIND or COMPUTE operation on the set.

Examples of the FILE statement are:

FILE THE PASSENGER IN THE FLIGHT.LIST

FILE THE REQUISITION FIRST IN ORDERS

FILE JOB LAST IN PRINT.QUEUE

In the first example, the entity PASSENGER is filed in the set FLIGHT.LIST using the ordering declared in the Preamble. In the second example, the entity REQUISITION is filed as the first element in the set ORDERS. In the third example, the entity job is filed at the end of the set PRINT.QUEUE.

Examples of the REMOVE statement are:

REMOVE THE LAST PASSENGER FROM THE FLIGHT.LIST

REMOVE THE FIRST REQUISITION FROM ORDERS

In the first example, the identifier PASSENGER points to the entity which was at the end of the set FLIGHT.LIST. In the second example, REQUISITION points to the entity which was at the start of the set ORDERS.

Like multiple resources, sets can be examined element by element and searched for an entity meeting a desired condition, using a FOR ... FIND or FOR ... COMPUTE loop. For example:

FOR EACH JOB OF JOB.SET WITH MEMORY(JOB) LT 1000
FIND THE FIRST CASE, IF FOUND
REMOVE THIS JOB FROM JOB.SET

FOR EACH REQUISITION OF ORDERS
COMPUTE HOT.ORDER AS MIN(REQUISITION) OF
    DUE.DATE(REQUISITION)
REMOVE HOT.ORDER FROM ORDERS

In the first example, the attribute, MEMORY, of the entities in the set, JOB.SET, is checked for being less than 1000, and the FOR loop ends upon the first such occurrence. If the search was successful (FOUND is true) the entity (which is pointed to by the identifier JOB) is removed from the set. In the second example, all the entities, REQUISITIONS, in the set ORDERS are searched to determine the entity with minimum attribute DUE.DATE. After the search is completed, the identifier HOT.ORDER points to the entity with the minimum attribute DUE.DATE. This entity is then removed from the set.

4.3   Suspending, Interrupting and Resuming Processes

In SIMSCRIPT models, a process can be suspended or interrupted and then resumed at a later time. A process can suspend itself and can be interrupted by another process. Once a process has become inactive by being suspended or interrupted, it can be resumed by another process or an event. Often a suspended or interrupted process is made a member of a set, thereby allowing other processes to examine the set and reactivate one or more inactive processes. The SUSPEND statement is used to make inactive a process in progress. The INTERRUPT statement is used to halt a process that is in the WORK or WAIT state. When a process has been interrupted, the time remaining to WORK or WAIT is stored in the process attribute TIME.A which can be referenced when the process is resumed.

The form of the SUSPEND statement is:

SUSPEND

The form of the interrupt statement is:

INTERRUPT THE process [CALLED process-identifier]

Examples of the INTERRUPT statement are:

INTERRUPT THE ORDER.GENERATOR

INTERRUPT THE JOB CALLED CURRENT.JOB

In the first example, the process ORDER.GENERATOR is halted. It becomes inactive but the time remaining for the completion of the WORK or WAIT statement is stored in TIME.A(ORDER.GENERATOR). In the second example, the process JOB pointed to by CURRENT.JOB is made inactive and the time remaining to be WORKed or WAITed is stored in TIME.A(CURRENT.JOB).

Processes are reactivated by the RESUME statement which has the form

RESUME THE process [CALLED process-identifier]

If the process being resumed was in a suspended state, upon resumption it starts at the statement following the SUSPEND statement. If the process was interrupted, it continues in the WORK or WAIT state for TIME.A.

Examples of the RESUME statement are:

RESUME THE ORDER.GENERATOR

RESUME THE JOB CALLED CURRENT.JOB

4.4 More on Sets

In the Preamble, the ownership of sets is declared. If the owner of the set is an entity, the set must be referenced through that entity. For example, we could use sets to represent the queues of jobs in a job shop, with the machine centers being resources and the jobs being processes waiting for a machine to become available. We will consider a job shop example in the next section, but for now, only the set, process, and resource declarations are shown. To establish the relationship between the resources and processes the Preamble would include:

```
PREAMBLE
RESOURCES
    EVERY MACHINE.CENTER HAS A MEAN.TIME AND OWNS A JOB.QUEUE
PROCESSES
    EVERY JOB HAS A PROCESS.TIME AND MAY BELONG TO A JOB.QUEUE
DEFINE JOB.QUEUE AS A FIFO SET
```

To file a JOB in the set of JOBs waiting at a MACHINE.CENTER we reference the set by:

FILE JOB IN JOB.QUEUE(MACHINE.CENTER)

letting MACHINE.CENTER act as an index to the appropriate set.

In SIMSCRIPT we can test if a set is empty using the phrase

set IS EMPTY

or

set IS NOT EMPTY

In the job shop example, to test if a machine center has jobs waiting, we could use:

IF JOB.QUEUE(MACHINE.CENTER) IS NOT EMPTY
FILE JOB IN JOB.QUEUE(MACHINE.ENTER)

In SIMSCRIPT, the first and last elements in a set can be referenced by F.set and L.set, respectively. To remove the last element in a set we can use REMOVE L.set(index or pointer). For example, to reference the last job in the queue at a machine center we could use

LET THIS.JOB = L.JOB.QUEUE(MACHINE.CENTER)

We complete this section with a simulation model of a job shop.

PROBLEM IV.1   In this example, jobs arrive at random times and then proceed to any of N machine centers or out of the job shop when processing is completed. The likelihood of a job being completed after being processed at any machine center is $1/(N+1)$. If the job is not completed, it will proceed with equal likelihood to any of the centers. In this example, the job could immediately return back to the center in which it currently resides. At each center there can be more than one identical machine for processing jobs, allowing more than one job to be concurrently processed in the same center. Each center has a mean processing time for a job at the center, and each job has a processing time for the next operation, a due date, and a priority. The simulation model to be developed can evaluate various rules for scheduling the next job at a machine center. The measure of effectiveness of a scheduling rule will be the mean job lateness, with a job being late if the completion time in the job shop exceeds the due date. In our simulation model we will schedule jobs for processing at a center based on due date.

Listing 7 shows the SIMSCRIPT model, sample input, and sample output. In this model, the rule for selecting the next job was first-come-first-serve but a new scheduling rule can be implemented by changing the ranking of the set JOB.QUEUE. For example, if jobs were to be selected based on the due date, we would define the set as

DEFINE JOB.QUEUE AS A SET RANKED BY LOW DUE.DATE

and then jobs would be selected according to nearest due date. In this simulation we assume that a job arrives every 20 minutes and the mean processing time at each center is 20 minutes. Jobs are due, on the average, 48 hours after they have arrived in the shop.

In this model, when a job arrives and all the machines in a center are busy [U.MACHINE.ENTER(NEXT.CENTER)=0], it is filed in a set of jobs waiting and the process is suspended. When a job's processing is finished, the job checks whether the set of waiting jobs is empty. If any jobs are waiting, the first job in the set is removed, and processing is resumed.

LISTING 7   SIMSCRIPT MODEL OF A JOB SHOP

```
                           CODE FOR JOBSHOP


PREAMBLE
NORMALLY MODE IS UNDEFINED
PROCESSES INCLUDE JOB.GENERATOR AND END.SIM
  EVERY JOB HAS A PRIORITY, A PROCESS.TIME AND A DUE.DATE
  AND MAY BELONG TO A JOB.QUEUE
RESOURCES
  EVERY MACHINE.CENTER HAS A MEAN.PROCESS.TIME,
  A TOTAL.JOBS.PROCESSED AND OWNS A JOB.QUEUE
DEFINE JOB.QUEUE AS A SET RANKED BY DUE.DATE
DEFINE PRIORITY, DUE.DATE, PROCESS.TIME, MEAN.PROCESS.TIME,
    TIME.IN.SHOP AND LATENESS AS REAL VARIABLES
DEFINE T.MAX AS A REAL VARIABLE
DEFINE TOTAL.JOBS.DONE AND TOTAL.JOBS.PROCESSED AS INTEGER VARIABLES
ACCUMULATE AVE.QUEUE AS THE AVERAGE OF N.JOB.QUEUE
ACCUMULATE N.JOB.LATE AS THE NUMBER OF LATENESS
ACCUMULATE AVE.LATENESS AS THE AVERAGE OF LATENESS
ACCUMULATE AVE.TIME.IN.SHOP AS THE AVERAGE OF TIME.IN.SHOP
ACCUMULATE UTIL AS THE AVERAGE OF N.X.MACHINE.CENTER
END

MAIN
PRINT 1 LINE THUS
INPUT NUMBER OF MACHINE CENTERS AND LENGTH OF SIMULATION IN DAYS
READ N.MACHINE.CENTER AND T.MAX
CREATE EVERY MACHINE.CENTER
FOR EACH MACHINE.CENTER
DO
PRINT 1 LINE WITH MACHINE.CENTER THUS
INPUT NUMBER OF MACNINES FOR MACHINE CENTER **
READ U.MACHINE.CENTER(MACHINE.CENTER)
LOOP
SCHEDULE AN END.SIM IN T.MAX DAYS
SCHEDULE A JOB.GENERATOR NOW
START SIMULATION
END

PROCESS JOB.GENERATOR
WHILE TIME.V < T.MAX
DO
SCHEDULE A JOB NOW
WAIT 20 MINUTES
LOOP
END
```

```
PROCESS JOB
DEFINE ARRIVE.TIME AS A REAL VARIABLE
DEFINE NEXT.CENTER AS AN INTEGER VARIABLE
DEFINE NEXT.JOB AS AN INTEGER VARIABLE
LET DUE.DATE(JOB)=TIME.V+EXPONENTIAL.F(48.0,2)/HOURS.V          ''HOURS
LET NEXT.CENTER=RANDI.F(1,N.MACHINE.CENTER,3)
LET ARRIVE.TIME=TIME.V
WHILE NEXT.CENTER <=N.MACHINE.CENTER
DO
 LET PROCESS.TIME(JOB)=EXPONENTIAL.F(20.0,4)
 IF U.MACHINE.CENTER(NEXT.CENTER)=0
  FILE THIS JOB IN JOB.QUEUE(NEXT.CENTER)
  SUSPEND
 ALWAYS
 REQUEST 1 UNIT MACHINE.CENTER(NEXT.CENTER)
 WAIT PROCESS.TIME(JOB) MINUTES
 ADD 1 TO TOTAL.JOBS.PROCESSED(NEXT.CENTER)
 RELINQUISH 1 UNIT OF MACHINE.CENTER(NEXT.CENTER)
 IF JOB.QUEUE(NEXT.CENTER) IS NOT EMPTY,
  REMOVE THE FIRST NEXT.JOB FROM JOB.QUEUE(NEXT.CENTER)
  REACTIVATE THE JOB CALLED NEXT.JOB NOW
 ALWAYS
 LET NEXT.CENTER=RANDI.F(1,N.MACHINE.CENTER+1,4)
LOOP
END
```

PROMPTS AND INPUT DATA

```
INPUT NUMBER OF MACHINE CENTERS AND LENGTH OF SIMULATION IN DAYS
II.5> 4 10
INPUT NUMBER OF MACHINES FOR MACHINE CENTER  1
II.5> 1
INPUT NUMBER OF MACHINES FOR MACHINE CENTER  2
II.5> 2
INPUT NUMBER OF MACHINES FOR MACHINE CENTER  3
II.5> 1
INPUT NUMBER OF MACHINES FOR MACHINE CENTER  4
II.5> 2
```

OUTPUT

```
AFTER 10.  DAYS   32 JOBS OUT OF   533 WERE LATE
THE AVERAGE TIME IN THE SHOP WAS     .23 DAYS
THE AVERAGE LATENESS WAS     .22 DAYS
```

CENTER	AVERAGE QUEUE	UTILIZATION	JOBS PROCESSED
1	35.37	.980	691
2	.32	.550	810
3	61.82	.994	668
4	.33	.510	759

4.5   Permanent Entities

The SIMSCRIPT world view includes entities, which can be used to represent passive elements in the simulation model. Entities can be created and destroyed, formed into sets, given unique names and assigned attributes. Like resources and processes, SIM-SCRIPT entities, along with any of their attributes and set properties, must be declared in the Preamble of the model.

Permanent entities are defined and processed very similarly to SIMSCRIPT resources. In fact, resources are SIMSCRIPT extensions of permanent entities. Permanent entities that do not have any attributes are declared in the Preamble using the statement:

PERMANENT ENTITIES INCLUDE [list]

Entities with attributes are declared using the EVERY qualifier in the form:

PERMANENT ENTITIES
    EVERY entity class HAS A attribute list
        [AND OWNS A set]
        [AND BELONGS TO A set]

For each permanent entity class there is a system variable, N.entity_class, which is equal to the number of entities within the entity class. The value of N.entity_class is established before or at the time of the creation of the permanent entity.

Examples of the PERMANENT ENTITIES statement are

PERMANENT ENTITIES INCLUDE CUSTOMER

PERMANENT ENTITIES
    EVERY TEACHER HAS A SUBJECT, A SALARY, AND A YEARS_OF_SERVICE
    AND OWNS A CLASS
    AND BELONGS TO A TENURED_GROUP

In the first example, the entity class CUSTOMER is declared and given no attributes, while in the second example, the entity TEACHER is declared as having the three attributes, SUBJECT, SALARY, and YEARS_OF_SERVICE, owns a set called CLASS, and may belong to a set called TENURED_GROUP. Every entity of class TEACHER may or may not belong to the set called TENURED_GROUP, but the BELONGS qualifier makes such membership a possibility. For clarity, the BELONGS phrase could be replaced by the phrase MAY BELONG. Like every other SIMSCRIPT variable, the attributes of entities must be typed using either a DEFINE statement or default to the background mode. In the above example, we could declare the attributes of TEACHER using DEFINE statements:

DEFINE SALARY AS A REAL VARIABLE
DEFINE YEARS_OF_SERVICE AS AN INTEGER VARIABLE
DEFINE CLASS AS A TEXT VARIABLE

Permanent entities come into existence in a SIMSCRIPT model through the statement

CREATE EVERY permanent entity class [integer number of entities]

If the system variable N.entity_class has not been specified, the number of entities to be created must be included as part of the CREATE statement. After the CREATE statement is executed the number of entities is defined by either the value used in the CREATE statement or from a previous assignment statement. Examples of the CREATE statement are

CREATE EVERY CUSTOMER(3)

CREATE EVERY CUSTOMER(RANDI.F(1,10,2))

LET N.TEACHER = 15
CREATE EVERY TEACHER

In the first example, three permanent entities are created and N.CUSTOMER is assigned the value of 3. In the second example, the SIMSCRIPT library function RANDI.F is used to select a random number between 1 and 10 which is used to determine the number of CUSTOMERs created. The variable N.CUSTOMER is assigned the value of RANDI.F. In the third example, N.TEACHER is first specified to be 15 and then used as the default value for the number of entities to be created.

Like resources, the attributes of a permanent entity are referenced using an index identifier. Permanent entities can be sequentially processed using a FOR loop or individually processed using the appropriate index. Examples of entity references are:

LET TOTAL_YEARS_SERVICE = 0
FOR EACH TEACHER DO
    READ YEARS_SERVICE(TEACHER)
    ADD YEARS_SERVICE(TEACHER) TO TOTAL_YEARS_SERVICE
LOOP

READ SUBJECT(1)

In the first example, the YEARS_SERVICE attribute for all the permanent entities TEACHER are assigned a value. In this example the variable TEACHER serves as an index variable, indexing from 1 to N.TEACHER. In the second example, only the first permanent entity TEACHER is assigned a value.

Permanent entities cannot individually be removed from the model but can, as an entire group, be removed from the model using the statement

DESTROY EACH entity_class

which frees the memory space allocated to the entity. Once destroyed, the permanent entities cannot be referenced unless they are brought back into the model using the CREATE statement.

To demonstrate the use of permanent entities we will present a model of the spread of an infectious disease in a fixed size population.

PROBLEM IV.2 Any person in the population will either be susceptible to the disease, infected with the disease or, after having the disease, be immune. It will be assumed that when a person is infected, the disease remains active for a period of time and then the infected person becomes immune, and can no longer spread the disease. The likelihood, on any given day, of a susceptible person contracting the disease is proportional to the number of persons in the population with the disease. For example, if a population consists of 1000 persons and 100 of them currently have the disease, then on any given day, the probability that a susceptible person will contract the disease is 100/1000 = 0.10. The disease will stop spreading in the population when there are no persons with the disease. To model this process we will use a permanent entity PERSON and three sets: SUSCEPTIBLE.GROUP, ACTIVE.GROUP, and IMMUNE.GROUP. Each PERSON has two attributes: ACTIVE.TIME, which is the time an infected person is in the ACTIVE.GROUP, and NEXT.STATE which is an indicator of whether a PERSON in the SUSCEPTIBLE.GROUP will move to the ACTIVE.GROUP. In this model TIME.V will be stepped day by day, each day removing and filing PERSONs across the three groups. The SIMSCRIPT model, along with a sample output is shown in Listing 8.

LISTING 8   SIMSCRIPT MODEL OF THE SPREAD OF AN INFECTIOUS DISEASE

CODE FOR SPREAD OF INFECTIOUS DISEASE MODEL

```
PREAMBLE
NORMALLY MODE IS UNDEFINED
PERMANENT ENTITIES
     EVERY PERSON HAS AN ACTIVE.TIME AND A NEXT.STATE,
     MAY BELONG TO A SUSCEPTIBLE.GROUP,
     AN INFECTED.GROUP, AND AN IMMUNE.GROUP
THE SYSTEM OWNS A SUSCEPTIBLE.GROUP, AN INFECTED.GROUP,
     AND AN IMMUNE.GROUP
DEFINE SUSCEPTIBLE.GROUP,INFECTED.GROUP AND IMMUNE.GROUP
     AS SETS
DEFINE ACTIVE.TIME AS A REAL VARIABLE
DEFINE NEXT.STATE AS AN INTEGER VARIABLE
DEFINE INFECTED TO MEAN 1
DEFINE INITIAL.INFECTED AS AN INTEGER VARIABLE

PROCESSES INCLUDE
    SPREAD.OF.DISEASE

TALLY MAX.INFECTED AS THE MAXIMUM OF N.INFECTED.GROUP
END

MAIN
DEFINE I AS AN INTEGER VARIABLE
PRINT 1 LINE THUS
INPUT NUMBER OF PERSONS IN POPULATION
READ N.PERSON
CREATE EVERY PERSON
PRINT 1 LINE THUS
INPUT NUMBER OF PERSONS INITIALLY INFECTED
READ INITIAL.INFECTED
FOR EACH PERSON
FILE THIS PERSON IN SUSCEPTIBLE.GROUP
FOR I=1 TO INITIAL.INFECTED  DO            ''SET UP INFECTED SET
REMOVE THE FIRST PERSON FROM SUSCEPTIBLE.GROUP
LET ACTIVE.TIME(PERSON)=GAMMA.F(4.0,2.0,1)
FILE THIS PERSON IN INFECTED.GROUP
LOOP
SCHEDULE A SPREAD.OF.DISEASE NOW
START SIMULATION
PRINT 4 LINES WITH N.PERSON, INITIAL.INFECTED,
    TIME.V, MAX.INFECTED AND
    N.IMMUNE.GROUP/N.PERSON*100 THUS
FOR A POPULATION OF **** PERSONS, WITH **** INITIALLY INFECTED
THE MAXIMUM NUMBER OF INFECTED WAS ****
THE DISEASE SPREAD FOR ***.* DAYS
***.* % OF THE POPULATION BECAME INFECTED WITH THE DISEASE
END
```

```
PROCESS SPREAD.OF.DISEASE
WHILE N.INFECTED.GROUP IS NOT EMPTY DO
WAIT 1 DAY
FOR EACH PERSON IN SUSCEPTIBLE.GROUP DO
    IF RANDOM.F(2) < REAL.F(N.INFECTED.GROUP)/N.PERSON
      LET NEXT.STATE(PERSON)=INFECTED
    ALWAYS
LOOP  ''FOR EACH PERSON

FOR EACH PERSON IN INFECTED.GROUP  DO
    IF ACTIVE.TIME(PERSON)<=TIME.V
     REMOVE THIS PERSON FROM INFECTED.GROUP
     FILE THIS PERSON IN IMMUNE.GROUP
    ALWAYS
LOOP  ''FOR EACH PERSON

FOR EACH PERSON IN SUSCEPTIBLE.GROUP DO
    IF NEXT.STATE(PERSON)=INFECTED
     REMOVE THIS PERSON FROM SUSCEPTIBLE.GROUP
     FILE THIS PERSON IN INFECTED.GROUP
     LET ACTIVE.TIME(PERSON)=TIME.V+GAMMA.F(4.0,2.0,1)
    ALWAYS
LOOP  ''FOR EACH PERSON
LOOP  ''WHILE N.SUSCEPTIBLE.GROUP IS NOT EMPTY
END
```

PROMPTS AND INPUT DATA

```
INPUT NUMBER OF PERSONS IN POPULATION
II.5> 1000
INPUT NUMBER OF PERSONS INITIALLY INFECTED
II.5> 10
```

OUTPUT

```
FOR A POPULATION OF 1000 PERSONS, WITH          10 INITIALLY INFECTED
THE MAXIMUM NUMBER OF INFECTED WAS   26
THE DISEASE SPREAD FOR 604.  DAYS
 99.9 % OF THE POPULATION BECAME INFECTED WITH THE DISEASE
```

4.6   Temporary Entities

Temporary entities are used to model objects that have a limited life in a simulation or that vary in number during the simulation. Temporary entities are declared, along with their attributes and set relationships in the Preamble section. The rules for declaring temporary entities are identical to rules for declaring permanent entities except that the declaration begins with

TEMPORARY ENTITIES

An example of declaring a temporary entity is

TEMPORARY ENTITIES
    EVERY ORDER HAS AN ORDER.QUANTITY

Temporary entities are introduced into the model individually, in contrast to permanent entities which are created simultaneously. Likewise, temporary entities can be removed from the model individually. A new temporary entity is brought into the model using the statement:

CREATE A temporary_entity [CALLED pointer variable].

When a temporary entity is created, memory space for containing the entity and its attributes is allocated, and unlike permanent entities, temporary entities are not placed sequentially in memory. The entity identifier acts as a pointer to the temporary entity and an optional pointer variable can be used to provide a path to the temporary entity. If temporary entities need to be accessed sequentially, an array of pointer variables can be used. Examples of the CREATE statement are

CREATE AN ORDER

CREATE AN ORDER CALLED EXPRESS

```
RESERVE X AS 10
FOR I = 1 TO 10
    CREATE AN ORDER CALLED X(I)
FOR I = 1 TO 10
    READ ORDER.QUANTITY(X(I))
```

In the first example a single temporary entity is created and is accessed through the pointer ORDER. In the second example a single temporary entity is created but can be accessed only through the pointer EXPRESS. In the third example the 10 elements in the array X are used to store pointers to the 10 temporary entities created, and then used to access the entities in the order they were created.

Unlike permanent entities, temporary entities can be individually removed from the simulation, releasing memory space, with the statement

DESTROY THE temporary entity [CALLED pointer variable]

Examples of the DESTROY statement are

DESTROY THE ORDER

DESTROY THE ORDER CALLED EXPRESS

```
FOR I = 1 TO 10 DO
DESTROY THE ORDER CALLED X(I)
LOOP
```

To demonstrate the use of temporary entities, we present a simulation model of a blood bank.

PROBLEM IV.3   In this model it is assumed that donors to the blood bank arrive randomly at the mean rate of two per day. Each donor gives exactly one unit of blood. Requests for blood occur at the mean rate of one per day. Blood recipients request at least one unit of blood. The number of units of blood requested after the first unit is Poisson distributed with a mean of 1.0. Blood has a limited storage life and any blood that is older than 21 days cannot be used. A SIMSCRIPT model of the blood bank along with the results of a 1000 day simulation is shown in Listing 9.

LISTING 9   SIMSCRIPT MODEL OF A BLOODBANK

CODE FOR BLOODBANK MODEL

```
PREAMBLE
NORMALLY MODE IS UNDEFINED
PROCESSES INCLUDE
    DONOR,RECIPIENT, AND STOP.SIM
TEMPORARY ENTITIES
    EVERY BLOOD.UNIT HAS A LIFE
      AND MAY BELONG TO        A BLOODBANK
THE SYSTEM OWNS THE BLOODBANK
DEFINE FALSE TO MEAN 1
DEFINE TRUE TO MEAN 0
DEFINE BLOODBANK AS A FIFO SET
DEFINE LIFE AS AN INTEGER VARIABLE
DEFINE STARTING.UNITS AS AN INTEGER VARIABLE
DEFINE T.END AS REAL VARIABLE
DEFINE UNITS.SHORT AS AN INTEGER VARIABLE
DEFINE UNITS.ISSUED AS AN INTEGER VARIABLE
DEFINE UNITS.OUTDATED AS AN INTEGER VARIABLE
DEFINE TOTAL.UNITS.REQUESTED AS AN INTEGER VARIABLE
DEFINE TOTAL.UNITS.DONATED AS AN INTEGER VARIABLE
ACCUMULATE AVE.UNITS AS THE AVERAGE OF N.BLOODBANK
END


MAIN
SCHEDULE A DONOR NOW
SCHEDULE A RECIPIENT NOW
PRINT 1 LINE THUS
INPUT NUMBER OF DAYS TO SIMULATE BLOODBANK, AND INITIAL INVENTORY
READ T.END, STARTING.UNITS
SCHEDULE A STOP.SIM IN T.END DAYS
START SIMULATION
END


PROCESS DONOR
DEFINE I AS AN INTEGER VARIABLE
DEFINE UNITS.NEEDED AS AN INTEGER VARIABLE
FOR I = 1 TO STARTING.UNITS              ''INITIALIZE BLOODBANK
DO
  CREATE A BLOOD.UNIT
  LET LIFE(BLOOD.UNIT)=TIME.V+ 21 ''DAYS
  FILE THIS BLOOD.UNIT IN BLOODBANK
LOOP
WHILE TIME.V <T.END                      ''LOOP FOR GENERATING
DO                                       ''DONORS
  WAIT EXPONENTIAL.F(0.50,1) DAYS
  CREATE A BLOOD.UNIT
  LET LIFE(BLOOD.UNIT)=TIME.V + 21        ''SET LIFE AT 21 DAYS
  ADD 1 TO TOTAL.UNITS.DONATED
  FILE THIS BLOOD.UNIT IN BLOODBANK
LOOP
END
```

(Continued)

```
PROCESS RECIPIENT
DEFINE SEARCHING.SET AS AN INTEGER VARIABLE
DEFINE UNITS.NEEDED AS AN INTEGER VARIABLE
WHILE TIME.V < T.END
DO
WAIT EXPONENTIAL.F(1.0,2) DAYS                    ''TIME BETWEEN REQUESTS
LET UNITS.NEEDED=1+POISSON.F(1.0,3)        ''NUMBER UNITS NEEDED
ADD UNITS.NEEDED TO TOTAL.UNITS.REQUESTED
LET SEARCHING.SET = TRUE
  WHILE SEARCHING.SET = TRUE
  DO
    IF N.BLOODBANK=0
       ADD UNITS.NEEDED TO UNITS.SHORT
       LET SEARCHING.SET = FALSE
    ELSE
       REMOVE FIRST BLOOD.UNIT FROM BLOODBANK
       IF LIFE(BLOOD.UNIT) > TIME.V
        ADD 1 TO UNITS.ISSUED
        SUBTRACT 1 FROM UNITS.NEEDED
        IF UNITS.NEEDED = 0
          LET SEARCHING.SET = FALSE
        ALWAYS
       ELSE
        ADD 1 TO UNITS.OUTDATED
       ALWAYS
       DESTROY THIS BLOOD.UNIT
    ALWAYS
  LOOP            ''WHILE SEARCHING.SET
LOOP     ''WHILE TIME.V
END

PROCESS STOP.SIM
PRINT 3 LINES WITH T.END, TOTAL.UNITS.REQUESTED,TOTAL.UNITS.DONATED,
    UNITS.ISSUED,UNITS.ISSUED/TOTAL.UNITS.REQUESTED*100,
    UNITS.OUTDATED,UNITS.OUTDATED/TOTAL.UNITS.DONATED*100 THUS
AFTER ***.*  DAYS  **** UNITS WERE REQUESTED AND **** UNITS DONATED
   **** UNITS OR **.** % OF REQUESTS MET
   **** UNITS OR **.** % OF BLOOD UNITS OUTDATED
STOP
END
```

PROMPTS AND INPUT DATA

```
INPUT NUMBER OF DAYS TO SIMULATE BLOODBANK, AND INITIAL INVENTORY

II.5> 1000 10
```

OUTPUT

```
AFTER1000.   DAYS  1959 UNITS WERE REQUESTED AND 2005 UNITS DONATED
   1913 UNITS OR 97.65 % OF REQUESTS MET
     98 UNITS OR  4.89 % OF BLOOD UNITS OUTDATED
```

5.0   ADVANCED SIMSCRIPT CONCEPTS

In this section we take up several advanced concepts in SIMSCRIPT including events and control of experiments in SIMSCRIPT. In its earlier versions, SIMSCRIPT models consisted only of events. To facilitate process interaction modeling the language was extended to include processes and resources. Events can, however, be put to good advantage in SIMSCRIPT models and will be described in this section.

When a simulation model is developed, the experimenter must consider the tactics of using the model, including the length of a single simulation run, the number of runs, and resetting of statistics. In this section we present the mechanisms SIMSCRIPT provides for performing simulation experiments.

5.1   SIMSCRIPT Events

In discrete-event models an event is an occurrence that happens in an instant of time, as opposed to a process that occurs over a period of time. The effect of an occurrence of an event is the instantaneous change in state variables of the simulation model. In SIMSCRIPT, events are modeled through event routines which are similar to general-purpose routines as described in Section 2.9 with the following exceptions:

1. Through event notices, events can be scheduled to occur in the future.

2. Event routines can receive input arguments.

3. Event routines cannot return output arguments.

4. Event notices can be given unique names.

5. Event notices can be cancelled.

Like processes, events must be declared in the Preamble of the SIMSCRIPT model using the statement

EVENT NOTICES INCLUDE event notice list

and if events are passed a set of arguments to be used when the event is executed, the event is declared using the EVERY statement

EVENT NOTICES
EVERY event notice HAS A list of event notice attributes.

Examples of event declarations are

EVENT NOTICES INCLUDE ARRIVAL

EVENT NOTICES
    EVERY ARRIVAL HAS A SERVICE.TIME AND A PRIORITY
DEFINE SERVICE TIME AS A REAL VARIABLE
DEFINE PRIORITY AS AN INTEGER VARIABLE

The event routine begins with the statement

EVENT name [(list of input arguments)]

or

EVENT name [GIVEN list of input arguments]

Examples of the EVENT statement are

EVENT END.SIMULATION

EVENT NEWJOB(JOB.PRIORITY)

EVENT PLACE.ORDER GIVEN ORDER.QUANTITY,SUPPLIER.

In the first example, the event routine is defined as having no arguments while in the second and third examples, the event routines have, respectively, one and two input arguments.

Within the event routine, the event logic is expressed through SIMSCRIPT statements. A RETURN statement is required to pass control back to the event management logic of SIMSCRIPT, and an END statement defines the end of the event logic. An event routine cannot, however, contain a WAIT or WORK statement since an event occurs at an instant in time, as opposed to a process, which occurs over an interval of time.

Unlike regular routines, event routines cannot be called by other subprograms but must be scheduled through the statement

SCHEDULE A {event notice} [CALLED pointer variable]

$$[\text{GIVEN argument list}] \left\{ \begin{array}{l} \text{AT quantity} \\ \text{NOW} \\ \text{IN quantity DAYS} \\ \qquad\qquad \text{HOURS} \\ \qquad\qquad \text{MINUTES} \end{array} \right\}$$

Examples of the SCHEDULE statement are

SCHEDULE AN END.SIMULATION IN SIMULATION.LEN DAYS

SCHEDULE AN EXPRESS.ORDER GIVEN 100 AND REGULAR.SUPPLIER NOW

SCHEDULE AN ARRIVAL CALLED SPECIAL GIVEN ARRVL.PRIORITY
                              IN EXPONENTIAL.F(10.0,3) HOURS

In the first example, an event is scheduled with no arguments being passed, while in the second example, two arguments are passed to the event routine. In the third example, the pointer variable SPECIAL is used to identify the event notice of class ARRIVAL.

Once an event is scheduled it can later by cancelled using the statement

CANCEL event notice [CALLED pointer variable]

If no pointer variable is supplied, the global variable having the same name as the event_notice is used to point to the event. Examples of the CANCEL statement are

CANCEL THE ARRIVAL CALLED SPECIAL

CANCEL EXPRESS.ORDER

In the first example, the scheduled event called SPECIAL is cancelled. In the second example, the last referenced event called EXPRESS.ORDER is cancelled. A fatal event occurs if an event that has not been scheduled is cancelled and the SIMSCRIPT simulation ends.

PROBLEM V.1 In Section 3.7 a model of a barber shop was developed using SIMSCRIPT resources and processes. We will now model the barber shop using SIMSCRIPT events. In this model there will be two events: ARRIVAL and SERVICE.COMPLETION. The model will also include a temporary entity class, CUSTOMER.WAITING, which forms a set called WAITING.GROUP. An ARRIVAL event is scheduled in the Main program and the simulation is then started. In the ARRIVAL event, if there is an unoccupied chair in the shop, the number of available chairs is reduced by one. If a barber is available, a SERVICE.COMPLETION event is scheduled and the number of available barbers is reduced by one. If a barber is not available, a temporary entity, CUSTOMER.WAITING, is created and filed in the set WAITING.GROUP. The arrival of the next customer is also scheduled in the event ARRIVAL. In the event SER-VICE.COMPLETION, a check is first made whether there are any customers waiting, and if so, one CUSTOMER.WAITING entity is removed from the set WAITING.GROUP, a new SERVICE.COMPLETION event is scheduled, and the temporary entity is destroyed. If no customers are waiting, the number of busy barbers is decreased by one. The simulation continues until no future events are scheduled and control returns to the Main program. In the Main program, statistics that were being accumulated and tallied during the simulation are output. Listing 10 shows the model, input to the program, and program output.

LISTING 10   SIMSCRIPT MODEL OF A BARBER SHOP USING EVENTS

CODE FOR BARBER SHOP MODEL USING EVENT ROUTINES

```
PREAMBLE

''   THIS IS A SIMULATION MODEL OF A BARBER SHOP WITH LIMITED SEATING
''   CAPACITY.  AN ARRIVING  CUSTOMER, WHO FINDS ALL THE SEATS OCCUPIED,
''   LEAVES. AT CLOSING TIME NO MORE CUSTOMERS ARE ACCEPTED INTO THE SHOP
''   BUT ANY CUSTOMERS STILL IN THE SHOP ARE SERVED.  AS INPUT THE USER
''   PROVIDES THE NUMBER OF BARBERS, NUMBER OF SEATS, HOURS OPEN, MEAN
''   TIME BETWEEN ARRIVALS AND THE MEAN AND STD. DEV. OF THE TIME TO
''   CUT A CUSTOMER'S HAIR.
NORMALLY MODE IS UNDEFINED
EVENT NOTICES INCLUDE ARRIVAL AND SERVICE.COMPLETION
TEMPORARY ENTITIES
    EVERY CUSTOMER.WAITING HAS AN ARRIVAL.TIME
        AND MAY BELONG TO A WAITING.GROUP
THE SYSTEM OWNS THE WAITING.GROUP
DEFINE N.CHAIRS,N.ARRIVALS,N.REFUSE,N.NO.WAIT,N.CHAIRS.OCCUPIED,
    N.BARBERS,N.BARBERS.BUSY,N.ENTER AS INTEGER VARIABLES
DEFINE MEAN.ARRIVAL.TIME, WAIT.TIME, MEAN.CUT.TIME, STD.DEV.CUT,
    ARRIVAL.TIME, HOURS, CLOSE.TIME AS REAL VARIABLES
DEFINE SHOP.NOT.FULL TO MEAN N.CHAIRS.OCCUPIED<N.CHAIRS
ACCUMULATE UTIL.BARBER AS THE AVERAGE OF N.BARBERS.BUSY
ACCUMULATE QUEUE.BARBER AS THE AVERAGE OF N.WAITING.GROUP
TALLY MEAN.WAIT AS THE AVERAGE OF WAIT.TIME
END
```

(Continued)

```
MAIN
PRINT 3 LINES THUS
INPUT NUMBER OF BARBERS, NUMBER OF CHAIRS, NUMBER HOURS OPEN
  MEAN TIME BETWEEN ARRIVALS (IN MINUTES),
  MEAN AND STD.DEV. OF TIME TO CUT HAIR
READ N.BARBERS, N.CHAIRS, HOURS, MEAN.ARRIVAL.TIME, MEAN.CUT.TIME,
  STD.DEV.CUT
LET CLOSE.TIME=HOURS/24
SCHEDULE AN ARRIVAL NOW
START SIMULATION
PRINT 6 LINES WITH TIME.V*24, N.ARRIVALS, N.ENTER, N.REFUSE,
  N.REFUSE/N.ARRIVALS*100, N.BARBERS,UTIL.BARBER/N.BARBERS,
  QUEUE.BARBER, N.NO.WAIT*100/N.ENTER ,MEAN.WAIT*60*24   THUS
THE SHOP CLOSED AFTER **.** HOURS, WITH *** ARRIVALS
*** ARRIVALS ENTERED THE SHOP AND *** WERE REFUSED (**.*%)
THE UTILIZATION OF THE ** BARBERS WAS *.**
THE MEAN NUMBER OF CUSTOMERS WAITING WAS ***.**
THE PERCENT OF CUSTOMERS WHO DID NOT WAIT FOR A BARBER WAS **.*%
IF A CUSTOMER DID WAIT THE AVERAGE WAIT WAS ***.** MINUTE
END


EVENT ARRIVAL
IF  TIME.V < CLOSE.TIME
  SCHEDULE AN ARRIVAL IN EXPONENTIAL.F(MEAN.ARRIVAL.TIME,1) MINUTES
  ADD 1 TO N.ARRIVALS
  IF SHOP.NOT.FULL
    ADD 1 TO N.ENTER
    IF N.BARBERS.BUSY < N.BARBERS
      SCHEDULE A SERVICE.COMPLETION
      IN LOG.NORMAL.F(MEAN.CUT.TIME,STD.DEV.CUT,2) MINUTES
      ADD 1 TO N.BARBERS.BUSY
      ADD 1 TO N.NO.WAIT
    ELSE
      CREATE A CUSTOMER.WAITING
      ADD 1 TO N.CHAIRS.OCCUPIED
      LET ARRIVAL.TIME(CUSTOMER.WAITING)=TIME.V
      FILE CUSTOMER.WAITING IN WAITING.GROUP
    ALWAYS      ''IF N.BARBERS,BUSY < N.BARBERS
  ELSE
    ADD 1 TO N.REFUSE
  ALWAYS          '' IF SHOP.NOT.FULL
ALWAYS              ''IF TIME.V < CLOSE TIME
RETURN
END


EVENT SERVICE.COMPLETION
IF N.WAITING.GROUP IS NOT EMPTY
  REMOVE FIRST CUSTOMER.WAITING FROM WAITING.GROUP
  LET WAIT.TIME=TIME.V - ARRIVAL.TIME(CUSTOMER.WAITING)
  SUBTRACT 1 FROM N.CHAIRS.OCCUPIED
  DESTROY THIS CUSTOMER.WAITING
  SCHEDULE A SERVICE.COMPLETION
      IN LOG.NORMAL.F(MEAN.CUT.TIME,STD.DEV.CUT,2) MINUTES
ELSE
  SUBTRACT 1 FROM N.BARBERS.BUSY
ALWAYS
RETURN
END
```

(Continued)

PROMPTS AND INPUT DATA

```
INPUT NUMBER OF BARBERS, NUMBER OF CHAIRS, NUMBER HOURS OPEN
  MEAN TIME BETWEEN ARRIVALS (IN MINUTES),
  MEAN AND STD.DEV. OF TIME TO CUT HAIR
II.5> 4 15 8 5 20 5
```

OUTPUT

```
THE SHOP CLOSED AFTER  9.52 HOURS, WITH 109 ARRIVALS
104 ARRIVALS ENTERED THE SHOP AND   5 WERE REFUSED ( 4.6%)
THE UTILIZATION OF THE          4 BARBERS WAS  .97
THE MEAN NUMBER OF CUSTOMERS WAITING WAS   9.99
THE PERCENT OF CUSTOMERS WHO DID NOT WAIT FOR A BARBER WAS 5.8%
IF A CUSTOMER DID WAIT THE AVERAGE WAIT WAS  58.22 MINUTE
```

5.2   Printing Intermediate Statistics

In order to perform simulation experiments it is desirable that the analyst be able to:

a) Print intermediate statistics during a simulation run

b) Reset statistical counters and accumulators

c) Make multiple runs of the model.

In this section we will show the mechanisms SIMSCRIPT provides to accomplish each of the above.

In this section and the two to follow we will illustrate the mechanisms SIMSCRIPT provides for the accumulation and resetting of statistics in a simulation model. The concepts presented will be illustrated using a SIMSCRIPT model of a multiserver queue. As the model is written, the user can specify the number of days to be simulated as well as the length of a day. The user can also specify the number of servers and the mean arrival rate and service times. For our discussion, however, we will simulate a queueing system with only one server, for 10 8-hour days. The mean number of arrivals per hour will be 10.0 and the mean service time per arrival will be .08 hours.

For printing intermediate statistics in SIMSCRIPT, an event routine can be included in the model that will print out the statistics being accumulated and tallied. By scheduling this event the current values of the statistics being collected can be printed at the desired points in time. To illustrate the use of statistical event routines, consider the model of the single queueing system shown in Listing 11, along with the output of the simulation.

In this model, statistics on the utilization of the servers and the length of the queue are printed out daily. The values printed out do not, however, show the day-to-day variation in the statistics, but are the cumulative values of the statistics. In the next section, the SIMSCRIPT method of resetting statistics will be presented.

5.3   Resetting Statistical Variables

Statistics that are being accumulated or tallied can be reset in SIMSCRIPT using the RESET statement. The form of the RESET statement is

LISTING 11   SIMSCRIPT MODEL OF A QUEUING SYSTEM WITH INTERMEDIATE OUTPUT

```
                CODE FOR A QUEUEING SYSTEM WITH DAILY OUTPUT

''THIS IS A SIMSCRIPT MODEL OF A MULTI-SERVER QUEUEING SYSTEM
''EACH DAY CUMULATIVE STATISTICS ON THE  QUEUE AND SERVER
''UTILIZATION ARE PRINTED OUT
PREAMBLE
NORMALLY MODE IS UNDEFINED
EVENT NOTICES INCLUDE PRINT.STATS
PROCESSES INCLUDE CUSTOMER
RESOURCES INCLUDE SERVER
ACCUMULATE UTIL.SERVER AS THE AVERAGE OF N.X.SERVER
ACCUMULATE AVE.QUEUE.LENGTH AS THE AVERAGE OF N.Q.SERVER
ACCUMULATE MAX.QUEUE.LENGTH AS THE MAXIMUM OF N.Q.SERVER
DEFINE N.DAYS,NO.OF.ARRIVALS AND
        NO.OF.SERVERS AS INTEGER VARIABLES
DEFINE LENGTH.DAY, ARRIVAL.RATE AND
        MEAN.SERVICE.TIME AS REAL VARIABLES
END

MAIN
PRINT 1 LINE THUS
INPUT NUMBER OF DAYS TO BE SIMULATED AND LENGTH OF EACH DAY
READ N.DAYS AND LENGTH.DAY
PRINT 1 LINE THUS
INPUT THE NO. OF SERVERS, MEAN ARRIVALS/HR AND MEAN SERVICE TIME IN HOURS
READ NO.OF.SERVERS, ARRIVAL.RATE, MEAN.SERVICE.TIME
CREATE EVERY SERVER(1)
LET U.SERVER(1)=NO.OF.SERVERS
PRINT 3 LINE WITH U.SERVER(1), ARRIVAL.RATE*MEAN.SERVICE.TIME THUS
NO. OF SERVERS = *** AND THE TRAFFIC INTENSITY = *.***

DAY  NO. ARRIVALS    UTILIZATION   AVERAGE QUEUE     MAXIMUM QUEUE
SCHEDULE A PRINT.STATS IN LENGTH.DAY HOURS
ACTIVATE A CUSTOMER IN EXPONENTIAL.F(1/ARRIVAL.RATE,1) HOURS
START SIMULATION
END

EVENT PRINT.STATS
PRINT 1 LINE  WITH 24*TIME.V/LENGTH.DAY, NO.OF.ARRIVALS,
 UTIL.SERVER(1)/NO.OF.SERVERS, AVE.QUEUE.LENGTH(1),
 AND MAX.QUEUE.LENGTH(1) THUS
 ***.    ****          *.***        ***.**            ****
IF TIME.V < (LENGTH.DAY/24)*N.DAYS
SCHEDULE A PRINT.STATS IN LENGTH.DAY HOURS
ELSE
STOP
ALWAYS
END

PROCESS CUSTOMER
ADD 1 TO NO.OF.ARRIVALS
ACTIVATE A CUSTOMER IN EXPONENTIAL.F(1/ARRIVAL.RATE,1) HOURS
REQUEST 1 UNIT OF SERVER(1)
WORK EXPONENTIAL.F(MEAN.SERVICE.TIME,2) HOURS
RELINQUISH 1 UNIT OF SERVER(1)
END
```

PROMPTS AND INPUT DATA

```
INPUT NUMBER OF DAYS TO BE SIMULATED AND LENGTH OF EACH DAY
II.5> 10 8
INPUT THE NO. OF SERVERS,MEAN ARRIVALS/HR AND MEAN SERVICE TIME IN HOURS
II.5> 1 10 .08
NO. OF SERVERS =   1 AND THE TRAFFIC INTENSITY =  .800
```

OUTPUT

DAY NO.	ARRIVALS	UTILIZATION	AVERAGE QUEUE	MAXIMUM QUEUE
1.	91	.769	1.18	6
2.	167	.817	2.33	10
3.	252	.856	3.12	11
4.	331	.863	3.48	12
5.	412	.833	3.00	12
6.	484	.806	2.71	12
7.	561	.800	2.56	12
8.	641	.797	2.53	12
9.	720	.785	2.44	12
10.	807	.797	2.63	12

RESET THE [name] TOTAL[S] OF variable

where [name] is an optional reference to a qualifier name for the variable listed in an ACCUMULATE or TALLY statement. If no qualifier name is used, all the statistical totals of the variable are reset.

For example, if the Preamble included the statement

ACCUMULATE DAILY.QUEUE AS THE DAILY AVERAGE
        AND WEEKLY.QUEUE AS THE WEEKLY AVERAGE OF
            N.Q.SERVER

then, during execution of the simulation model, we could reset the statistical counters for DAILY.QUEUE by

FOR EACH SERVER
   RESET THE DAILY TOTALS OF N.Q.SERVER(SERVER)

Alternatively if the RESET statement was

FOR EACH SERVER
   RESET THE TOTALS OF N.Q.SERVER(SERVER)

the statistical counters for both DAILY.QUEUE and WEEKLY.QUEUE would have been reset. In these two examples, the qualifiers DAILY and WEEKLY are not SIM-SCRIPT keywords but selected to describe the interval between successive statistical resets.

To illustrate the use of RESET, the previous simulation model of a multiserver is modified so that daily, weekly, and overall statistics are printed out on the utilization of the server and length of the queue. The program and the associated output is shown in Listing 12.

LISTING 12   SIMSCRIPT MODEL OF A QUEUEING SYSTEM WITH DAILY AND WEEKLY STATISTICS

```
            CODE FOR A QUEUEING SYSTEM WITH DAILY AND WEEKLY STATISTICS


''THIS IS A SIMSCRIPT MODEL OF A SINGLE SERVER QUEUE SYSTEM
''AT THE END OF EACH DAY AND EACH WEEK SUMMARY STATISTICS
''ON THE QUEUE AND SERVER UTILIZATION ARE PRINTED AND THEN RESET
PREAMBLE
NORMALLY MODE IS UNDEFINED
EVENT NOTICES INCLUDE DAILY.PRINT.STATS, WEEKLY.PRINT.STATS AND
    FINAL.PRINT.STATS
PROCESSES INCLUDE CUSTOMER
RESOURCES INCLUDE SERVER
ACCUMULATE
    DAILY.UTIL.SERVER AS THE DAILY AVERAGE,
    WEEKLY.UTIL.SERVER AS THE WEEKLY AVERAGE AND
    OVERALL.UTIL.SERVER AS THE OVERALL AVERAGE OF N.X.SERVER
ACCUMULATE
    DAILY.QUEUE.LENGTH AS THE DAILY AVERAGE,
    WEEKLY.QUEUE.LENGTH AS THE WEEKLY AVERAGE AND
    OVERALL.QUEUE.LENGTH AS THE          OVERALL AVERAGE OF N.Q.SERVER
ACCUMULATE
    DAILY.MAX.QUEUE.LENGTH AS THE DAILY MAXIMUM,
    WEEKLY.MAX.QUEUE.LENGTH AS THE WEEKLY MAXIMUM AND
    OVERALL.MAX.QUEUE.LENGTH AS THE OVERALL MAXIMUM OF N.Q.SERVER
DEFINE N.DAYS,NO.OF.ARRIVALS, NO.DAILY.ARRIVALS,
    NO.WEEKLY.ARRIVALS AND NO.OF.SERVERS AS INTEGER VARIABLES
DEFINE LENGTH.DAY, ARRIVAL.RATE AND MEAN.SERVICE.TIME AS REAL VARIABLES
END

MAIN
PRINT 1 LINE THUS
INPUT NUMBER OF DAYS TO BE SIMULATED AND LENGTH OF EACH DAY
READ N.DAYS AND LENGTH.DAY
PRINT 1 LINE THUS
INPUT THE NO. OF SERVERS, MEAN ARRIVALS/HR AND MEAN SERVICE TIME IN HOURS
READ NO.OF.SERVERS, ARRIVAL.RATE, MEAN.SERVICE.TIME
CREATE EVERY SERVER(1)
LET U.SERVER(1)=NO.OF.SERVERS
PRINT 3 LINE WITH U.SERVER(1), ARRIVAL.RATE*MEAN.SERVICE.TIME THUS
NO. OF SERVERS = *** AND THE TRAFFIC INTENSITY = *.***

DAY NO. ARRIVALS    UTILIZATION    AVERAGE QUEUE       MAXIMUM QUEUE
SCHEDULE A DAILY.PRINT.STATS IN LENGTH.DAY HOURS
SCHEDULE A WEEKLY.PRINT.STATS IN 5*LENGTH.DAY HOURS
SCHEDULE A FINAL.PRINT.STATS IN N.DAYS*LENGTH.DAY HOURS
ACTIVATE A CUSTOMER IN EXPONENTIAL.F(1/ARRIVAL.RATE,1) HOURS
START SIMULATION
END

EVENT DAILY.PRINT.STATS
PRINT 1 LINE   WITH TIME.V*24/LENGTH.DAY, NO.DAILY.ARRIVALS,
 DAILY.UTIL.SERVER(1)/NO.OF.SERVERS, DAILY.QUEUE.LENGTH(1),
 AND DAILY.MAX.QUEUE.LENGTH(1) THUS
 ***.*          ****            *.***          ***.**                ****
SCHEDULE A DAILY.PRINT.STATS IN LENGTH.DAY HOURS
RESET THE DAILY TOTALS OF N.X.SERVER(1)
RESET THE DAILY TOTALS OF N.Q.SERVER(1)
LET NO.DAILY.ARRIVALS =0
END
```

```
EVENT WEEKLY.PRINT.STATS
PRINT 1 LINE  WITH TIME.V*24/LENGTH.DAY, NO.WEEKLY.ARRIVALS,
 WEEKLY.UTIL.SERVER(1)/NO.OF.SERVERS, WEEKLY.QUEUE.LENGTH(1),
 AND WEEKLY.MAX.QUEUE.LENGTH(1) THUS
 ***.*         ****        *.***         ***.**          **** (WEEKLY)
SKIP 1 LINE
SCHEDULE A WEEKLY.PRINT.STATS IN 5*LENGTH.DAY HOURS
RESET THE WEEKLY TOTALS OF N.X.SERVER(1)
RESET THE WEEKLY TOTALS OF N.Q.SERVER(1)
LET NO.WEEKLY.ARRIVALS=0
END

EVENT FINAL.PRINT.STATS
PRINT 1 LINE  WITH TIME.V*24/LENGTH.DAY, NO.OF.ARRIVALS,
 OVERALL.UTIL.SERVER(1)/NO.OF.SERVERS, OVERALL.QUEUE.LENGTH(1),
 AND OVERALL.MAX.QUEUE.LENGTH(1) THUS
 ***.*         ****        *.***         ***.**          **** (FINAL)
STOP
END

PROCESS CUSTOMER
ADD 1 TO NO.OF.ARRIVALS
ADD 1 TO NO.DAILY.ARRIVALS
ADD 1 TO NO.WEEKLY.ARRIVALS
ACTIVATE A CUSTOMER IN EXPONENTIAL.F(1/ARRIVAL.RATE,1) HOURS
REQUEST 1 UNIT OF SERVER(1)
WORK EXPONENTIAL.F(MEAN.SERVICE.TIME,2) HOURS
RELINQUISH 1 UNIT OF SERVER(1)
END
```

PROMPTS AND INPUT DATA

```
INPUT NUMBER OF DAYS TO BE SIMULATED AND LENGTH OF EACH DAY
II.5> 10 8
INPUT THE NO. OF SERVERS,MEAN ARRIVALS/HR AND MEAN SERVICE TIME IN HOURS
II.5> 1 10 .08

NO. OF SERVERS =   1 AND THE TRAFFIC INTENSITY =  .800
```

OUTPUT

DAY NO.	ARRIVALS	UTILIZATION	AVERAGE QUEUE	MAXIMUM QUEUE	
1.	91	.769	1.18	6	
2.	76	.865	3.48	10	
3.	85	.933	4.70	11	
4.	79	.886	4.56	12	
5.	412	.833	3.00	12	(WEEKLY)
5.	81	.711	1.06	7	
6.	72	.671	1.25	7	
7.	77	.768	1.70	8	
8.	80	.774	2.27	9	
9.	79	.691	1.77	8	
10.	87	.907	4.37	10	
10.	395	.762	2.27	10	(WEEKLY)
10.	807	.797	2.63	12	(FINAL)

5.4 Making Multiple Runs of a Simulation in SIMSCRIPT

In the last two models the multiserver queue was simulated once for 10 days. During the 10 days the system was simulated, statistics were accumulated, reset, and printed out, but the ending conditions on any day were the starting conditions on the next day. In many systems we would like to model, the system terminates operating after some time. For example, in the barber shop model, after 8 hours the shop closed and the simulation ended when the customers remaining in the shop were serviced.

Multiple runs of a simulation model can be made in SIMSCRIPT by restarting the simulation model in the Main program. Typically this is done using an iterative statement such as

```
FOR I = 1 TO N.RUNS DO
SCHEDULE A initial event or process NOW
START SIMULATION

{print statements}

LOOP
```

To illustrate how multiple runs of a simulation model can be made in SIMSCRIPT, the multiserver queueing model is modified so that the totals of all statistics are reset at the start of each simulation. Statistics are printed out at the end of each day but the daily simulation of the system continues until no more processes or events are scheduled. The model and the output of the simulation are shown in Listing 13.

LISTING 13   SIMSCRIPT MODEL OF A QUEUEING SYSTEM WITH MULTIPLE RUNS OF MODEL

```
            CODE FOR A QUEUEING SYSTEM WITH MULTIPLE MODEL RUNS


''THIS IS A SIMSCRIPT MODEL OF A MULTISERVER QUEUEING SYSTEM
''THE MODEL IS RUN FOR MULTIPLE DAYS, EACH DAY STARTING
''WITH NO CUSTOMERS IN THE SYSTEM
PREAMBLE
NORMALLY MODE IS UNDEFINED
EVENT NOTICES INCLUDE PRINT.STATS
PROCESSES INCLUDE CUSTOMER
RESOURCES INCLUDE SERVER
ACCUMULATE UTIL.SERVER AS THE AVERAGE OF N.X.SERVER
ACCUMULATE AVE.QUEUE.LENGTH AS THE AVERAGE OF N.Q.SERVER
ACCUMULATE MAX.QUEUE.LENGTH AS THE MAXIMUM OF N.Q.SERVER
DEFINE DAY.INDEX, N.DAYS, NO.OF.ARRIVALS AND
                NO.OF.SERVERS AS INTEGER VARIABLES
DEFINE LENGTH.DAY, ARRIVAL.RATE, END.DAY AND
                MEAN.SERVICE.TIME AS REAL VARIABLES
END
```

```
MAIN
PRINT 1 LINE THUS
INPUT LENGTH OF EACH DAY IN HOURS AND NO. DAYS TO BE SIMULATED
READ LENGTH.DAY AND N.DAYS
PRINT 1 LINE THUS
INPUT THE NO. OF SERVERS, MEAN ARRIVALS/HR AND MEAN SERVICE TIME IN HOURS
READ NO.OF.SERVERS, ARRIVAL.RATE, MEAN.SERVICE.TIME
CREATE EVERY SERVER(1)
LET U.SERVER(1)=NO.OF.SERVERS
PRINT 1 LINE THUS
DAY  NO. ARRIVALS    UTILIZATION   AVERAGE QUEUE     MAXIMUM QUEUE

FOR DAY.INDEX = 1 TO N.DAYS DO
SCHEDULE A PRINT.STATS IN   LENGTH.DAY HOURS
ACTIVATE A CUSTOMER IN EXPONENTIAL.F(1/ARRIVAL.RATE,1) HOURS
LET END.DAY=TIME.V+LENGTH.DAY/24 ''HOURS
START SIMULATION
RESET TOTALS OF N.X.SERVER(1)
RESET TOTALS OF N.Q.SERVER(1)
LET NO.OF.ARRIVALS=0
LOOP
END

EVENT PRINT.STATS
PRINT 1 LINE  WITH DAY.INDEX, NO.OF.ARRIVALS,
 UTIL.SERVER(1)/NO.OF.SERVERS, AVE.QUEUE.LENGTH(1),
 AND MAX.QUEUE.LENGTH(1) THUS
 ***.*          ****          *.***         ***.**            ****
END

PROCESS CUSTOMER
IF TIME.V < END.DAY
ADD 1 TO NO.OF.ARRIVALS
ACTIVATE A CUSTOMER IN EXPONENTIAL.F(1/ARRIVAL.RATE,1) HOURS
REQUEST 1 UNIT OF SERVER(1)
WORK EXPONENTIAL.F(MEAN.SERVICE.TIME,2) HOURS
RELINQUISH 1 UNIT OF SERVER(1)
ALWAYS
END
```

PROMPTS AND INPUT DATA

```
INPUT LENGTH OF EACH DAY IN HOURS AND NO. DAYS TO BE SIMULATED
II .5> 8 10
INPUT THE NO. OF SERVERS, MEAN ARRIVALS/HR AND MEAN SERVICE TIME IN HOURS
II.5> 1 10 .08
```

OUTPUT

DAY NO.	ARRIVALS	UTILIZATION	AVERAGE QUEUE	MAXIMUM QUEUE
1.	91	.769	1.18	6
2.	76	.765	1.35	6
3.	83	.929	3.93	11
4.	79	.814	2.56	9
5.	81	.717	1.06	5
6.	73	.670	1.89	9
7.	74	.721	1.35	6
8.	81	.795	1.44	8
9.	82	.670	1.41	8
10.	80	.791	2.79	11

6.0 SIMSCRIPT INTERNAL ORGANIZATION

It is often helpful, when building a SIMSCRIPT model, to have some understanding of how a SIMSCRIPT simulation is internally organized. In this section we will give a brief overview of the internal organization of SIMSCRIPT entities, sets, events, and processes. For a more complete description of the SIMSCRIPT language, the reader should refer to the CACI references at the end of this primer.

6.1 SIMSCRIPT Entities

In SIMSCRIPT, entities can be either permanent or temporary. The distinction between permanent and temporary entities lies in how they are allocated space in memory and how they are accessed.

Permanent entities of the same class are all created at the same time and located contiguously in memory. Because they are contiguously located in memory they can be referenced using an entity index. Because permanent entities are all created at the same time, the user must provide SIMSCRIPT with a count of the number of entities to be created. Temporary entities, on the other hand are created one at a time and their location in memory is stored in a pointer variable. This pointer variable provides a path to the temporary entity for modification of the attributes of the entity, inclusion in sets, and destroying the entity. Because temporary entities are not located contiguously in memory, they can only be accessed using a pointer, unlike permanent entities which can be accessed using their index.

A block of memory representing an entity contains all the attributes of the entity as well as pointers and counters for any sets the entity may own or belong to. When the entity is destroyed, the pointers are lost but the sets the entity owns are not destroyed.

To illustrate the differences between permanent and temporary entities, consider the definitions and create statements:

```
PERMANENT ENTITIES
    EVERY CAR HAS A PLATE.NUMBER
TEMPORARY ENTITIES
    EVERY DRIVER HAS A LICENCE.NUMBER


MAIN
LET N.CAR=2
CREATE EVERY CAR(N.CAR)
CREATE A DRIVER CALLED FRED
LET LICENCE.NUMBER(FRED)=8754381
CREATE A DRIVER CALLED DICK
LET LICENCE.NUMBER(FRED)=8792180
```

Figure 6.1 shows the layout in memory of these entities.

Notice that the amount of memory allocated to the permanent entity class called CAR is fixed at 2 and the entities are adjacent to each other in memory while the temporary entities are not necessarily adjacent and can only be accessed by using a pointer variable to the entity.

FIGURE 6.1   MEMORY LAYOUT OF PERMANENT AND TEMPORARY ENTITIES

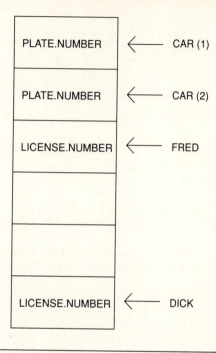

Releasing the space allocated to the permanent entities of class CAR requires only

DESTROY EVERY CAR

while releasing the space allocated to the temporary entities requires

DESTROY THE DRIVER CALLED FRED
DESTROY THE DRIVER CALLED DICK

6.2   Organization of Sets

In SIMSCRIPT, every set is owned by either the system or by an entity. The base information of a set is:

Pointer to the first entity in the set

Pointer to the last entity in the set

Count of the number of entities in the set.

If an entity is a member of a set, three additional attributes of the entity are automatically generated when the entity is created. These attributes are:

Pointer to the entity's predecessor

Pointer to the entity's successor

Membership flag (0 or 1).

A set is then just a collection of entities with inter-related pointers. To illustrate the organization of a set, consider the following definitions in the Preamble.

```
PERMANENT ENTITIES
    EVERY TEACHER OWNS A CLASS
TEMPORARY ENTITIES
    EVERY STUDENT HAS A GRADE.POINTAND
    BELONGS TO A CLASS
DEFINE CLASS AS A SET RANKED BY HIGH GRADE.POINT
                  .
                  .
                  .
MAIN
    CREATE EVERY TEACHER(1)
    FOR I = 1 TO 4 DO
    CREATE A STUDENT
    READ GRADE.POINT(STUDENT)
    FILE THIS STUDENT IN CLASS(TEACHER)
    LOOP
    CREATE A STUDENT CALLED NEW.STUDENT
    LET GRADE.POINT(NEW.STUDENT) = 3.1
```

Assuming the grade points of the four students were 2.5, 3.4, 2.0, and 3.9, then the organization of the set is shown in Fig. 6.2.

In this example only the first four STUDENT entities are included in the set called CLASS. The pointer variables P.STUDENT.CLASS for the first entity, S.STU-

FIGURE 6.2   SET ORGANIZATION

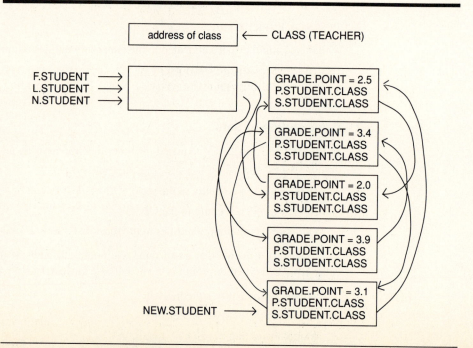

DENT.CLASS for the last entity in the set are undefined, as well as the pointers for the entity NEW.STUDENT. The variable NEW.STUDENT provides a path to the last entity created, if it is to be inserted later into the set.

Resources are a special case of permanent entities which have, in addition to user-defined attributes, two SIMSCRIPT defined pointers: a pointer to the set of entities currently using the resource (X.resource) and a pointer to the set of entities waiting for the resource (Q.resource). Each time a process requests a resource, a temporary Resource Request Entity (RRE) is created which has the attributes:

The number of resource units requested,

The priority of the request, and a

Pointer to the requesting process.

the RRE also has pointers to form sets of

RRE associated with the same process

RRE associated with entities waiting for the resource

RRE associated with entities using the resource

When an entity relinquishes a resource, the associated RRE is destroyed and the sets of RRE are updated to reflect the resource becoming available.

6.3   Events and Processes

In SIMSCRIPT, events are entities that have minimally the following attributes:

TIME.A: The time the event is scheduled to occur.

EUNIT.A: Code indicating if event is internal or external. If event is external EUNIT is the I/O unit used.

P.EV.S: Pointer to predecessor in this event set.

S.EV.S: Pointer to successor in this event set.

M.EV.S: Membership attribute; 1 if event notice is in the event set and 0 if not in the event set. (M.EV.S is set to 0 if an event is CREATEd but not yet scheduled).

In addition to these five attributes, an event notice also includes the attributes of the event defined in the Preamble. The user-defined attributes act as parameters that can be passed to the event routine when the event is executed.

In SIMSCRIPT, a process is an extension of the event entity. In addition to the five attributes associated with event notices, process notices include:

RSA.A: A pointer to the recursive save area for the process. This area contains the values of the local variables for the process.

STA.A: The current state of the process (Passive, Active, Suspended, Interrupted).

IPC.A: The process CLASS index.

F.RS.S: An attribute for pointing to a temporary entity for resource the process owns or is requesting.

6.4 Event Management

As in any discrete-event simulation language, the driving force within SIMSCRIPT is the discrete event. These events are scheduled in SIMSCRIPT using the SCHEDULE or ACTIVATE statement. When an event (a process is a special type of event) is scheduled a list of events must be updated to reflect the newly scheduled event. In SIMSCRIPT, there is actually a series of lists, one list for each type of event or process. The simulator examines the first element on each of these event lists and selects the one that is scheduled to occur first. Ties in scheduled event times are resolved by the order in which the event lists are checked. The order of checking the different event lists is by default, determined by the order processes and events are listed in the Preamble and, in the case of a tie, the event or process first listed in the Preamble is selected. We can call out a different order of organizing the lists of events by the PRIORITY statement

PRIORITY ORDER IS list of events and processes

For example

PRIORITY ORDER IS ARRIVALS, SERVICE AND END.SIMULATION

will force, in the case of a tie on event times, preference to go first to ARRIVALS, then to SERVICE, and last to END.SIMULATION, regardless of the order in which the events or processes were listed in the Preamble.

When all the lists of events become empty, the simulation comes to an end and is often the mechanism used to terminate the simulation. As we have seen in previous examples, however, the simulation will also come to an end by the STOP statement, leaving scheduled events and processes unexecuted.

7.0 SUMMARY OF STATEMENT SYNTAX, FUNCTIONS, SYSTEM CONSTANTS, AND VARIABLES

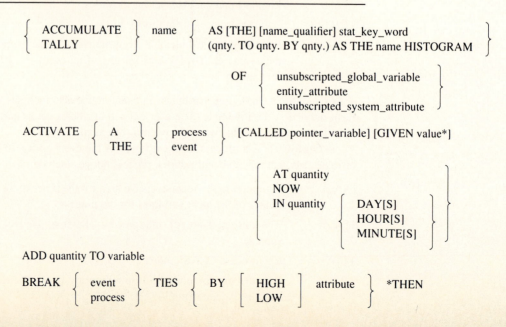

$$\left\{ \begin{array}{l} \text{ACCUMULATE} \\ \text{TALLY} \end{array} \right\} \text{name} \left\{ \begin{array}{l} \text{AS [THE] [name\_qualifier] stat\_key\_word} \\ \text{(qnty. TO qnty. BY qnty.) AS THE name HISTOGRAM} \end{array} \right\}$$

$$\text{OF} \left\{ \begin{array}{l} \text{unsubscripted\_global\_variable} \\ \text{entity\_attribute} \\ \text{unsubscripted\_system\_attribute} \end{array} \right\}$$

$$\text{ACTIVATE} \left\{ \begin{array}{l} \text{A} \\ \text{THE} \end{array} \right\} \left\{ \begin{array}{l} \text{process} \\ \text{event} \end{array} \right\} \text{[CALLED pointer\_variable] [GIVEN value*]}$$

$$\left\{ \begin{array}{l} \text{AT quantity} \\ \text{NOW} \\ \text{IN quantity} \left\{ \begin{array}{l} \text{DAY[S]} \\ \text{HOUR[S]} \\ \text{MINUTE[S]} \end{array} \right\} \end{array} \right\}$$

ADD quantity TO variable

$$\text{BREAK} \left\{ \begin{array}{l} \text{event} \\ \text{process} \end{array} \right\} \text{TIES} \left\{ \text{BY} \left[\begin{array}{l} \text{HIGH} \\ \text{LOW} \end{array} \right] \text{attribute} \right\} \text{*THEN}$$

CALL routine $\left[\begin{array}{l}\text{GIVEN value*} \\ \text{(value*)}\end{array}\right]$ [YIELDING variable*]

CANCEL [THE [ABOVE]] $\left\{\begin{array}{l}\text{event} \\ \text{process}\end{array}\right\}$ [CALLED pointer_variable]

COMPUTE name AS THE stat_key_word OF variable

CREATE [A] $\left\{\begin{array}{l}\text{temporary\_entity} \\ \text{process} \\ \text{event}\end{array}\right\}$ [CALLED pointer_variable]

CREATE EACH $\left\{\begin{array}{l}\text{permanent\_entity} \\ \text{resource}\end{array}\right\}$ [integer_value]

DEFINE routine AS [A] $\left[\begin{array}{l}\text{INTEGER} \\ \text{REAL} \\ \text{DOUBLE} \\ \text{ALPHA} \\ \text{TEXT}\end{array}\right]$ [FORTRAN] ROUTINE[S]

[GIVEN integer [ARGUMENT[S]] [YIELDING integer [ARGUMENT[S]]

DEFINE set AS [A] $\left[\begin{array}{l}\text{FIFO} \\ \text{LIFO}\end{array}\right]$ SET [RANKED $\left\{\begin{array}{l}\text{BY} \left[\begin{array}{l}\text{HIGH} \\ \text{LOW}\end{array}\right] \text{attribute}\end{array}\right\}$ *THEN]

DEFINE word TO MEAN string

DEFINE variable* AS [A] $\left[\begin{array}{l}\text{INTEGER} \\ \text{REAL} \\ \text{DOUBLE} \\ \text{ALPHA} \\ \text{TEXT}\end{array}\right]$ [integer-DIM] VARIABLE[S]

DESTROY [A] $\left\{\begin{array}{l}\text{temporary\_entity} \\ \text{process} \\ \text{event}\end{array}\right\}$ [CALLED pointer_variable]

DESTROY EACH $\left\{\begin{array}{l}\text{permanent\_entity} \\ \text{resource}\end{array}\right\}$

DO statement* LOOP

EVENT event_name [GIVEN value*]

EVERY $\left\{\begin{array}{l}\text{entity} \\ \text{event}\end{array}\right\}$ * $\left\{\begin{array}{l}\text{HAS A attribute*} \\ \text{OWNS A} \\ \text{BELONGS TO A set}\end{array}\right\}$ *

FILE [THE] pointer_variable
$$\begin{bmatrix} \text{FIRST} \\ \text{LAST} \\ \left\{ \begin{matrix} \text{BEFORE} \\ \text{AFTER} \end{matrix} \right\} \text{pointer\_variable} \end{bmatrix}$$
IN [THE] set

FIND $\left\{ \begin{matrix} \text{THE FIRST CASE} \\ \text{variable=[THE][FIRST] value} \end{matrix} \right\}$ $\begin{bmatrix} \text{IF} \left\{ \begin{matrix} \text{FOUND} \\ \text{NONE} \end{matrix} \right\} \end{bmatrix}$

FOR EACH $\left\{ \begin{matrix} \text{permanent\_entity} \\ \text{resource} \end{matrix} \right\}$ [CALLED pointer_variable]

FOR EACH entity_pointer $\begin{bmatrix} \left\{ \begin{matrix} \text{FROM} \\ \text{AFTER} \end{matrix} \right\} \text{entity\_pointer} \end{bmatrix}$ OF set [IN REVERSE ORDER]

FOR variable $\left\{ \begin{matrix} = \\ \text{BACK FROM} \end{matrix} \right\}$ quantity TO quantity [BY quantity]

GO [TO] label

IF logical expression
  statement*
[ELSE
  statement*]
ALWAYS

INTERRUPT [THE [ABOVE]] process [CALLED pointer_variable]

LET variable = quantity

LIST variable* [USING $\begin{bmatrix} \text{TAPE} \\ \text{UNIT} \end{bmatrix}$ integer_value]

LIST ATTRIBUTES OF entity [CALLED pointer_variable

[USING $\begin{bmatrix} \text{TAPE} \\ \text{UNIT} \end{bmatrix}$ integer_value]

NORMALLY MODE IS $\begin{Bmatrix} \text{INTEGER} \\ \text{REAL} \\ \text{DOUBLE} \\ \text{ALPHA} \\ \text{TEXT} \\ \text{UNDEFINED} \end{Bmatrix}$

PRINT integer LINES WITH variables THUS
{format layout}

PRIORITY ORDER IS $\left\{ \begin{matrix} \text{event} \\ \text{process} \end{matrix} \right\}$ *

PROCESSES [INCLUDE]

$\left\{ \begin{matrix} \text{THE SYSTEM} \\ \text{EVERY entity} \end{matrix} \right\}$ $\left\{ \begin{matrix} \text{HAS A attribute RANDOM} \\ \text{OWNS A set} \end{matrix} \right.$ $\begin{bmatrix} \text{STEP} \\ \text{LINEAR} \end{bmatrix}$ $\left. \text{VARIABLE} \right\}$

READ variable*

RELINQUISH integer-value [UNIT[S] OF] resource[(integer_value)]

REMOVE [[THE] $\left[\begin{array}{l}\text{FIRST}\\\text{LAST}\\\text{ABOVE}\end{array}\right]$] pointer_variable FROM [THE] set

REQUEST integer_value [UNIT[S] OF] resource[(integer_value)]
                                            [WITH PRIORITY integer_value]

RESERVE variable* AS quantity [BY]*

RESET [THE] [qualifier_name]* TOTAL[S] OF variable

RESOURCES INCLUDE resource*

RESUME [THE[ABOVE]] process [CALLED pointer_variable]

RETURN $\left[\begin{array}{l}\text{WITH quantity}\\\text{(quantity)}\end{array}\right]$

ROUTINE [TO] routine $\left[\begin{array}{l}\text{GIVEN value*}\\\text{(value*)}\end{array}\right]$ [YIELDING variable]

SCHEDULE $\left\{\begin{array}{l}\text{A}\\\text{THE [ABOVE]}\end{array}\right\}$ event [CALLED pointer_variable] $\left[\begin{array}{l}\text{GIVEN value*}\\\text{(value)}\end{array}\right]$

$\left\{\begin{array}{l}\text{AT quantity}\\\text{NOW}\\\text{IN quantity}\ \left\{\begin{array}{l}\text{DAY[S]}\\\text{HOUR[S]}\\\text{MINUTE[S]}\end{array}\right\}\end{array}\right\}$

START SIMULATION

SUBTRACT quantity FROM variable

SUSPEND [PROCESS]

THE SYSTEM OWNS THE set

TRACE [USING $\left[\begin{array}{l}\text{TAPE}\\\text{UNIT}\end{array}\right]$ integer]

UNTIL logical_expression

$\left\{\begin{array}{l}\text{WAIT}\\\text{WORK}\end{array}\right\}$ quantity $\left\{\begin{array}{l}\text{DAY[S]}\\\text{HOUR[S]}\\\text{MINUTE[S]}\end{array}\right\}$

WHILE logical_expression

WITH logical_expression

Note 1: Arguments marked with * can be repeated any number of times

TABLE 7.1
SIMSCRIPT LIBRARY FUNCTIONS

Function Mnemonic	Arguments	Function Mode	Description
ABS.F	q	Mode of q	Returns the absolute value of the expression
ARCCOS.F	q	Real	Computes the arc cosine of q $-1 <= q <= 1$
ARCSIN.F	q	Real	Computes the arc sine of q $-1 <= q <= 1$
COS.F	q	Real	Computes the cosine of a real expression given in radians
DAY.F	q	Integer	Converts simulation time to the day portion; q must be real
DIV.F	q_1, q_2	Integer	Returns the truncated value of q_1/q_2; q_2 0
FRAC.F	q	Real	Returns the fractional portion of a real expression
HOUR.F	q	Integer	Converts simulation time to the hour portion
INT.F	q	Integer	Returns the rounded integer portion of a real expression
LOG.E.F	q	Real	Computes the natural logarithm of a real expression
MAX.F	$q_1, q_2 .. q_n$	Real if any q_i is real, else integer	Returns largest q_1
MIN.F	$q_1, q_2 .. q_n$	Real if any q_i is real, else integer	Returns smallest q_1
MINUTE.F	q	Integer	Converts simulation time to the minute portion
MONTH.F	q	Integer	Converts simulation time to month portion
REAL.F	q	Real	Converts an integer expression to a real value
SIN.F	q	Real	Computes the sine of a real expression
SQRT.F	q	Real	Computes the square root of a real expression; $q > 0$
TAN.F	q	Real	Computes the tangent of a real expression given in radians
TRUNC.F	q	Integer	Returns the truncated integer value of a real expression
YEAR.F	q	Integer	Converts simulation time to the year portion;

TABLE 7.2
SYSTEM CONSTANTS

EXP.C	Real	2.718281828
INF.C	Integer	Largest integer value that can be stored
PI.C	Real	3.14159265
RADIAN.C	Real	57.29577 (degrees/radian)
RINF.C	Real	Largest real value that can be stored

TABLE 7.3
SYSTEM VARIABLES TABLE

Variable	Description	Initial or Default Value
EOF.V	End-of-file code; 2 indicates end-of-file encountered.	0
HOURS.V	Number of hours per simulated day	24
LINE.V	Number of the current output line	0
LINES.V	Number of lines per page	55
MINUTES.V	Number of minutes per simulated hour	60
PAGE.V	Number of the current page	0
PROCESS.V	If not zero, a pointer to the process notice of the currently executing process.	0
READ.V	Number of the current input unit	
RECORD.V	The number of records read from the current input unit, or written on the current output unit.	0
SEED.V	Array containing initial random number seeds	
TIME.V	Current simulation time	
WRITE.V	Number of the current output unit	

TABLE 7.4
SIMSCRIPT RANDOM VARIABLE LIBRARY

Function Mnemonic	Arguments	Function Mode	Description
BETA.F	q_1,q_2,q_3	Real	Returns a random sample from a Beta distribution q_1 = power of x, real q_2 = power of (1 - x), real q_3 = random number stream, integer
BINOMIAL.F	q_1,q_2,q_3	Real	Returns a random sample from a Binomial distribution q_1 = number of trials, integer q_2 = probability of success, real q_3 = random number stream, integer
ERLANG.F	q_1,q_2,q_3	Real	Returns a random sample from an Erlang distribution q_1 = mean, real q_2 = k, integer q_3 = random number stream, integer
EXPONENTIAL.F	q_1,q_2	Real	Returns a random sample from an exponential distribution q_1 = mean, real q_2 = random number stream, integer
GAMMA.F	q_1,q_2,q_3	Real	Returns a random sample from a Gamma distribution q_1 = mean, real q_2 = k, real q_3 = random number stream, integer
ISTEP.F	p,q	Integer	Returns a random sample from a look-up table without interpolation p = pointer to look-up table q = random number stream, integer
LOG.NORMAL.F	q_1,q_2,q_3	Real	Returns a random sample from a log-normal distribution q_1 = mean, real q_2 = standard deviation, real q_3 = random number stream, integer
NORMAL.F	q_1,q_2,q_3	Real	Returns a random sample from a normal distribution q_1 = mean, real q_2 = standard deviation, real q_3 = random number stream, integer
POISSON.F	q_1,q_2	Integer	Returns a random sample from a Poisson distribution q_1 = mean, real q_2 = random number stream, integer

RANDI.F	q_1,q_2,q_3	Integer	Returns a random sample uniformly distributed between q_1,q_2 q_1 = beginning value, integer q_2 = ending value, integer q_3 = random number stream
RANDOM.F	q	Real	Returns a pseudorandom number between 0.0 and 1.0 q = random number stream, integer
RSTEP.F	p,q	Real	Returns a random sample from a look-up table using interpolation p = pointer to look-up table q = random number stream, integer
UNIFORM.F	q_1,q_2,q_3	Real	Returns a random sample uniformly distributed between q_1,q_2 q_1 = beginning value, real q_2 = ending value, real q_3 = random number stream
WEIBULL.F	q_1,q_2,q_3	Real	Returns a sample value from a Weibull distribution q_1 = scale parameter,real q_2 = shape parameter,real q_3 = random number stream, integer

TABLE 7.5
STATISTICAL KEYWORDS FOR ACCUMULATE/TALLY STATEMENTS

Statistic	Accumulate Computation	Tally Computation
NUMBER	The No. of changes in X	The No. of samples of X
SUM	$\sum X(\text{TIME.V}-T)$	$\sum X$
MEAN	$\dfrac{\text{SUM}}{(\text{TIME.V}-T)}$	$\dfrac{\text{SUM}}{N}$
SUM.OF.SQUARES	$\sum X^2(\text{TIME.V}-T_L)$	$\sum X^2$
MEAN.SQUARE	$\dfrac{\text{SUM.OF.SQUARES}}{\sum(\text{TIME.V}-T_0)}$	$\dfrac{\text{SUM.OF.SQUARES}}{N}$
VARIANCE	$\sqrt{\text{MEAN.SQUARE}-\text{MEAN}^2}$	$\sqrt{\text{MEAN.SQUARE}-\text{MEAN}^2}$

TIME.V = the current simulated time
T_L = simulated time at which variable was set to current value
T_0 = simulated time of last reset for this variable
X = sample value of variable before change occurs

STD.DEV	$\sqrt{\text{VARIANCE}}$	$\sqrt{\text{VARIANCE}}$
MAXIMUM	Maximum (X) for all X	Maximum (X) for all X
MINIMUM	Minimum (X) for all X	Minimum (X) for all X

REFERENCES AND SELECTED BIBLIOGRAPHY

1. Russell, Edward, *Building Simulation Models with SIMSCRIPT*, Los Angeles, CA: C.A.C.I., 1983.
2. C.A.C.I., *SIMSCRIPT II.5 Programming Language*, Los Angeles, CA: C.A.C.I., 1983.
3. C.A.C.I., *SIMSCRIPT II.5 Reference Handbook*, Los Angeles, CA: C.A.C.I., 1976.

APPENDIX **D**

SELECTED STATISTICAL TABLES

TABLE 1
CUMULATIVE NORMAL DISTRIBUTION

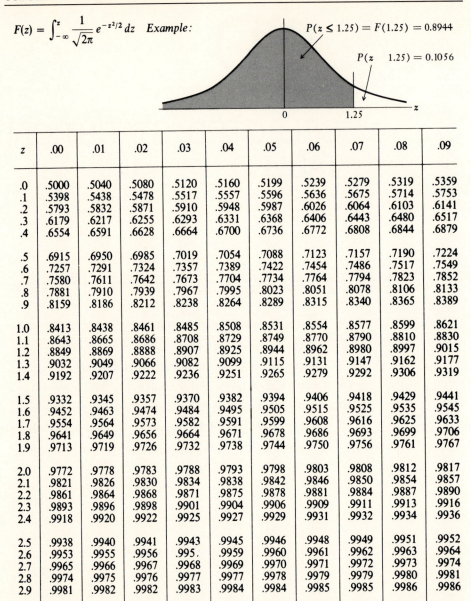

$$F(z) = \int_{-\infty}^{z} \frac{1}{\sqrt{2\pi}} e^{-z^2/2} \, dz \quad Example:$$

$$P(z \leq 1.25) = F(1.25) = 0.8944$$

$$P(z \quad 1.25) = 0.1056$$

z	.00	.01	.02	.03	.04	.05	.06	.07	.08	.09
.0	.5000	.5040	.5080	.5120	.5160	.5199	.5239	.5279	.5319	.5359
.1	.5398	.5438	.5478	.5517	.5557	.5596	.5636	.5675	.5714	.5753
.2	.5793	.5832	.5871	.5910	.5948	.5987	.6026	.6064	.6103	.6141
.3	.6179	.6217	.6255	.6293	.6331	.6368	.6406	.6443	.6480	.6517
.4	.6554	.6591	.6628	.6664	.6700	.6736	.6772	.6808	.6844	.6879
.5	.6915	.6950	.6985	.7019	.7054	.7088	.7123	.7157	.7190	.7224
.6	.7257	.7291	.7324	.7357	.7389	.7422	.7454	.7486	.7517	.7549
.7	.7580	.7611	.7642	.7673	.7704	.7734	.7764	.7794	.7823	.7852
.8	.7881	.7910	.7939	.7967	.7995	.8023	.8051	.8078	.8106	.8133
.9	.8159	.8186	.8212	.8238	.8264	.8289	.8315	.8340	.8365	.8389
1.0	.8413	.8438	.8461	.8485	.8508	.8531	.8554	.8577	.8599	.8621
1.1	.8643	.8665	.8686	.8708	.8729	.8749	.8770	.8790	.8810	.8830
1.2	.8849	.8869	.8888	.8907	.8925	.8944	.8962	.8980	.8997	.9015
1.3	.9032	.9049	.9066	.9082	.9099	.9115	.9131	.9147	.9162	.9177
1.4	.9192	.9207	.9222	.9236	.9251	.9265	.9279	.9292	.9306	.9319
1.5	.9332	.9345	.9357	.9370	.9382	.9394	.9406	.9418	.9429	.9441
1.6	.9452	.9463	.9474	.9484	.9495	.9505	.9515	.9525	.9535	.9545
1.7	.9554	.9564	.9573	.9582	.9591	.9599	.9608	.9616	.9625	.9633
1.8	.9641	.9649	.9656	.9664	.9671	.9678	.9686	.9693	.9699	.9706
1.9	.9713	.9719	.9726	.9732	.9738	.9744	.9750	.9756	.9761	.9767
2.0	.9772	.9778	.9783	.9788	.9793	.9798	.9803	.9808	.9812	.9817
2.1	.9821	.9826	.9830	.9834	.9838	.9842	.9846	.9850	.9854	.9857
2.2	.9861	.9864	.9868	.9871	.9875	.9878	.9881	.9884	.9887	.9890
2.3	.9893	.9896	.9898	.9901	.9904	.9906	.9909	.9911	.9913	.9916
2.4	.9918	.9920	.9922	.9925	.9927	.9929	.9931	.9932	.9934	.9936
2.5	.9938	.9940	.9941	.9943	.9945	.9946	.9948	.9949	.9951	.9952
2.6	.9953	.9955	.9956	.995.	.9959	.9960	.9961	.9962	.9963	.9964
2.7	.9965	.9966	.9967	.9968	.9969	.9970	.9971	.9972	.9973	.9974
2.8	.9974	.9975	.9976	.9977	.9977	.9978	.9979	.9979	.9980	.9981
2.9	.9981	.9982	.9982	.9983	.9984	.9984	.9985	.9985	.9986	.9986
3.0	.9987	.9987	.9987	.9988	.9988	.9989	.9989	.9989	.9990	.9990
3.1	.9990	.9991	.9991	.9991	.9992	.9992	.9992	.9992	.9993	.9993
3.2	.9993	.9993	.9994	.9994	.9994	.9994	.9994	.9995	.9995	.9995
3.3	.9995	.9995	.9995	.9996	.9996	.9996	.9996	.9996	.9996	.9997
3.4	.9997	.9997	.9997	.9997	.9997	.9997	.9997	.9997	.9997	.9998

TABLE 2
CRITICAL VALUES OF THE *t*-DISTRIBUTION

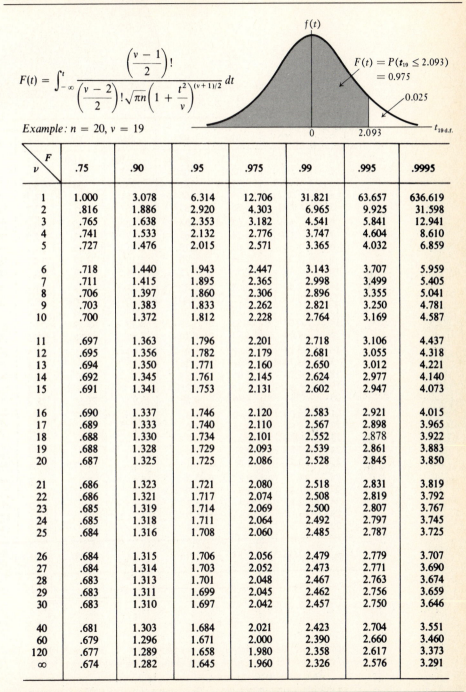

$$F(t) = \int_{-\infty}^{t} \frac{\left(\dfrac{v-1}{2}\right)!}{\left(\dfrac{v-2}{2}\right)! \sqrt{\pi n}\left(1 + \dfrac{t^2}{v}\right)^{(v+1)/2}}\, dt$$

$F(t) = P(t_{19} \leq 2.093)$
$= 0.975$
0.025

Example: $n = 20,\ v = 19$

F / ν	.75	.90	.95	.975	.99	.995	.9995
1	1.000	3.078	6.314	12.706	31.821	63.657	636.619
2	.816	1.886	2.920	4.303	6.965	9.925	31.598
3	.765	1.638	2.353	3.182	4.541	5.841	12.941
4	.741	1.533	2.132	2.776	3.747	4.604	8.610
5	.727	1.476	2.015	2.571	3.365	4.032	6.859
6	.718	1.440	1.943	2.447	3.143	3.707	5.959
7	.711	1.415	1.895	2.365	2.998	3.499	5.405
8	.706	1.397	1.860	2.306	2.896	3.355	5.041
9	.703	1.383	1.833	2.262	2.821	3.250	4.781
10	.700	1.372	1.812	2.228	2.764	3.169	4.587
11	.697	1.363	1.796	2.201	2.718	3.106	4.437
12	.695	1.356	1.782	2.179	2.681	3.055	4.318
13	.694	1.350	1.771	2.160	2.650	3.012	4.221
14	.692	1.345	1.761	2.145	2.624	2.977	4.140
15	.691	1.341	1.753	2.131	2.602	2.947	4.073
16	.690	1.337	1.746	2.120	2.583	2.921	4.015
17	.689	1.333	1.740	2.110	2.567	2.898	3.965
18	.688	1.330	1.734	2.101	2.552	2.878	3.922
19	.688	1.328	1.729	2.093	2.539	2.861	3.883
20	.687	1.325	1.725	2.086	2.528	2.845	3.850
21	.686	1.323	1.721	2.080	2.518	2.831	3.819
22	.686	1.321	1.717	2.074	2.508	2.819	3.792
23	.685	1.319	1.714	2.069	2.500	2.807	3.767
24	.685	1.318	1.711	2.064	2.492	2.797	3.745
25	.684	1.316	1.708	2.060	2.485	2.787	3.725
26	.684	1.315	1.706	2.056	2.479	2.779	3.707
27	.684	1.314	1.703	2.052	2.473	2.771	3.690
28	.683	1.313	1.701	2.048	2.467	2.763	3.674
29	.683	1.311	1.699	2.045	2.462	2.756	3.659
30	.683	1.310	1.697	2.042	2.457	2.750	3.646
40	.681	1.303	1.684	2.021	2.423	2.704	3.551
60	.679	1.296	1.671	2.000	2.390	2.660	3.460
120	.677	1.289	1.658	1.980	2.358	2.617	3.373
∞	.674	1.282	1.645	1.960	2.326	2.576	3.291

This table is abridged from Table III of Fisher & Yates: *Statistical Tables for Biological, Agricultural, and Medical Research*, published by Longman Group Ltd. London (previously published by Oliver & Boyd Ltd. Edinburgh) and by permission of the authors and publishers.

TABLE 3
CRITICAL VALUES OF THE CHI SQUARE DISTRIBUTION

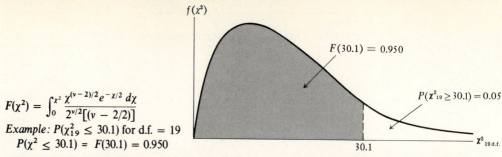

$$F(\chi^2) = \int_0^{\chi^2} \frac{\chi^{(v-2)/2}e^{-\chi/2}\,d\chi}{2^{v/2}[(v-2/2)]}$$

Example: $P(\chi^2_{19} \leq 30.1)$ for d.f. = 19
$P(\chi^2 \leq 30.1) = F(30.1) = 0.950$

v	.005	.010	.025	.050	.100	.900	.950	.975	.990	.995
1	.0⁴393	.0³157	.0³982	.0²393	.0158	2.71	3.84	5.02	6.63	7.88
2	.0100	.0201	.0506	.103	.211	4.61	5.99	7.38	9.21	10.6
3	.0717	.115	.216	.352	.584	6.25	7.81	9.35	11.3	12.8
4	.207	.297	.484	.711	1.06	7.78	9.49	11.1	13.3	14.9
5	.412	.554	.831	1.15	1.61	9.24	11.1	12.8	15.1	16.7
6	.676	.872	1.24	1.64	2.20	10.6	12.6	14.4	16.8	18.5
7	.989	1.24	1.69	2.17	2.83	12.0	14.1	16.0	18.5	20.3
8	1.34	1.65	2.18	2.73	3.49	13.4	15.5	17.5	20.1	22.0
9	1.73	2.09	2.70	3.33	4.17	14.7	16.9	19.0	21.7	23.6
10	2.16	2.56	3.25	3.94	4.87	16.0	18.3	20.5	23.2	25.2
11	2.60	3.05	3.82	4.57	5.58	17.3	19.7	21.9	24.7	26.8
12	3.07	3.57	4.40	5.23	6.30	18.5	21.0	23.3	26.2	28.3
13	3.57	4.11	5.01	5.89	7.04	19.8	22.4	24.7	27.7	29.8
14	4.07	4.66	5.63	6.57	7.79	21.1	23.7	26.1	29.1	31.3
15	4.60	5.23	6.26	7.26	8.55	22.3	25.0	27.5	30.6	32.8
16	5.14	5.81	6.91	7.96	9.31	23.5	26.3	28.8	32.0	34.3
17	5.70	6.41	7.56	8.67	10.1	24.8	27.6	30.2	33.4	35.7
18	6.26	7.01	8.23	9.39	10.9	26.0	28.9	31.5	34.8	37.2
19	6.84	7.63	8.91	10.1	11.7	27.2	30.1	32.9	36.2	38.6
20	7.43	8.26	9.59	10.9	12.4	28.4	31.4	34.2	37.6	40.0
21	8.03	8.90	10.3	11.6	13.2	29.6	32.7	35.5	38.9	41.4
22	8.64	9.54	11.0	12.3	14.0	30.8	33.9	36.8	40.3	42.8
23	9.26	10.2	11.7	13.1	14.8	32.0	35.2	38.1	41.6	44.2
24	9.89	10.9	12.4	13.8	15.7	33.2	36.4	39.4	43.0	45.6
25	10.5	11.5	13.1	14.6	16.5	34.4	37.7	40.6	44.3	46.9
26	11.2	12.2	13.8	15.4	17.3	35.6	38.9	41.9	45.6	48.3
27	11.8	12.9	14.6	16.2	18.1	36.7	40.1	43.2	47.0	49.6
28	12.5	13.6	15.3	16.9	18.9	37.9	41.3	44:5	48.3	51.0
29	13.1	14.3	16.0	17.7	19.8	39.1	42.6	45.7	49.6	52.3
30	13.8	15.0	16.8	18.5	20.6	40.3	43.8	47.0	50.9	53.7
z_α	−2.58	−2.33	−1.96	−1.64	−1.28	+1.28	+1.64	+1.96	+2.33	+2.58

NOTE: For $v > 30$ (i.e., for more than 30 degrees of freedom) take

$$\chi^2 = v\left[1 - \frac{2}{9v} + z_\alpha\sqrt{\frac{2}{9v}}\,\right]^2 \quad \text{or} \quad \chi^2 = \frac{1}{2}[z_\alpha + \sqrt{(2v-1)}]^2$$

according to the degree of accuracy required. z_α is the standardized normal deviate corresponding to the α level of significance, and is shown in the bottom line of the table.

This table is abridged from "Tables of percentage points of the incomplete beta function and of the chi-square distribution," *Biometrika*, Vol. 32 (1941). Reprinted with permission of its author, Catherine M. Thompson, and the editor of *Biometrika*.

TABLE 4A
CRITICAL VALUES OF THE *F*-DISTRIBUTION ($\alpha = 0.05$)

Tables (a) and (b) from M. Merrington and C. M. Thompson, "Tables of percentage points of the inverted beta (F) distribution." *Biometrika*, Vol. 33 (1943) by permission of the *Biometrika* Trustees.

The following table gives the critical values of the *F*-distribution for $\alpha = 0.05$. This probability represents the area exceeding the value of $F_{0.05, v_1, v_2}$ as shown by the shaded area in the figure below.

Examples: If $v_1 = 15$ (d.f. for the numerator), and $v_2 = 20$, then the critical value cutting off 0.05 is 2.20.

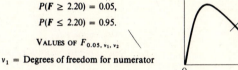

$P(F \geq 2.20) = 0.05,$

$P(F \leq 2.20) = 0.95.$

VALUES OF $F_{0.05, v_1, v_2}$

v_1 = Degrees of freedom for numerator

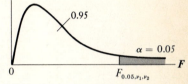

v_2 = Degrees of freedom for denominator

	1	2	3	4	5	6	7	8	9	10	12	15	20	24	30	40	60	120	∞
1	161	200	216	225	230	234	237	239	241	242	244	246	248	249	250	251	252	253	254
2	18.5	19.0	19.2	19.2	19.3	19.3	19.4	19.4	19.4	19.4	19.4	19.4	19.4	19.5	19.5	19.5	19.5	19.5	19.5
3	10.1	9.55	9.28	9.12	9.01	8.94	8.89	8.85	8.81	8.79	8.74	8.70	8.66	8.64	8.62	8.59	8.57	8.55	8.53
4	7.71	6.94	6.59	6.39	6.26	6.16	6.09	6.04	6.00	5.96	5.91	5.86	5.80	5.77	5.75	5.72	5.69	5.66	5.63
5	6.61	5.79	5.41	5.19	5.05	4.95	4.88	4.82	4.77	4.74	4.68	4.62	4.56	4.53	4.50	4.46	4.43	4.40	4.37
6	5.99	5.14	4.76	4.53	4.39	4.28	4.21	4.15	4.10	4.06	4.00	3.94	3.87	3.84	3.81	3.77	3.74	3.70	3.67
7	5.59	4.74	4.35	4.12	3.97	3.87	3.79	3.73	3.68	3.64	3.57	3.51	3.44	3.41	3.38	3.34	3.30	3.27	3.23
8	5.32	4.46	4.07	3.84	3.69	3.58	3.50	3.44	3.39	3.35	3.28	3.22	3.15	3.12	3.08	3.04	3.01	2.97	2.93
9	5.12	4.26	3.86	3.63	3.48	3.37	3.29	3.23	3.18	3.14	3.07	3.01	2.94	2.90	2.86	2.83	2.79	2.75	2.71
10	4.96	4.10	3.71	3.48	3.33	3.22	3.14	3.07	3.02	2.98	2.91	2.85	2.77	2.74	2.70	2.66	2.62	2.58	2.54
11	4.84	3.98	3.59	3.36	3.20	3.09	3.01	2.95	2.90	2.85	2.79	2.72	2.65	2.61	2.57	2.53	2.49	2.45	2.40
12	4.75	3.89	3.49	3.26	3.11	3.00	2.91	2.85	2.80	2.75	2.69	2.62	2.54	2.51	2.47	2.43	2.38	2.34	2.30
13	4.67	3.81	3.41	3.18	3.03	2.92	2.83	2.77	2.71	2.67	2.60	2.53	2.46	2.42	2.38	2.34	2.30	2.25	2.21
14	4.60	3.74	3.34	3.11	2.96	2.85	2.76	2.70	2.65	2.60	2.53	2.46	2.39	2.35	2.31	2.27	2.22	2.18	2.13
15	4.54	3.68	3.29	3.06	2.90	2.79	2.71	2.64	2.59	2.54	2.48	2.40	2.33	2.29	2.25	2.20	2.16	2.11	2.07
16	4.49	3.63	3.24	3.01	2.85	2.74	2.66	2.59	2.54	2.49	2.42	2.35	2.28	2.24	2.19	2.15	2.11	2.06	2.01
17	4.45	3.59	3.20	2.96	2.81	2.70	2.61	2.55	2.49	2.45	2.38	2.31	2.23	2.19	2.15	2.10	2.06	2.01	1.96
18	4.41	3.55	3.16	2.93	2.77	2.66	2.58	2.51	2.46	2.41	2.34	2.27	2.19	2.15	2.11	2.06	2.02	1.97	1.92
19	4.38	3.52	3.13	2.90	2.74	2.63	2.54	2.48	2.42	2.38	2.31	2.23	2.16	2.11	2.07	2.03	1.98	1.93	1.88
20	4.35	3.49	3.10	2.87	2.71	2.60	2.51	2.45	2.39	2.35	2.28	2.20	2.12	2.08	2.04	1.99	1.95	1.90	1.84
21	4.32	3.47	3.07	2.84	2.68	2.57	2.49	2.42	2.37	2.32	2.25	2.18	2.10	2.05	2.01	1.96	1.92	1.87	1.81
22	4.30	3.44	3.05	2.82	2.66	2.55	2.46	2.40	2.34	2.30	2.23	2.15	2.07	2.03	1.98	1.94	1.89	1.84	1.78
23	4.28	3.42	3.03	2.80	2.64	2.53	2.44	2.37	2.32	2.27	2.20	2.13	2.05	2.01	1.96	1.91	1.86	1.81	1.76
24	4.26	3.40	3.01	2.78	2.62	2.51	2.42	2.36	2.30	2.25	2.18	2.11	2.03	1.98	1.94	1.89	1.84	1.79	1.73
25	4.24	3.39	2.99	2.76	2.60	2.49	2.40	2.34	2.28	2.24	2.16	2.09	2.01	1.96	1.92	1.87	1.82	1.77	1.71
30	4.17	3.32	2.92	2.69	2.53	2.42	2.33	2.27	2.21	2.16	2.09	2.01	1.93	1.89	1.84	1.79	1.74	1.68	1.62
40	4.08	3.23	2.84	2.61	2.45	2.34	2.25	2.18	2.12	2.08	2.00	1.92	1.84	1.79	1.74	1.69	1.64	1.58	1.51
60	4.00	3.15	2.76	2.53	2.37	2.25	2.17	2.10	2.04	1.99	1.92	1.84	1.75	1.70	1.65	1.59	1.53	1.47	1.39
120	3.92	3.07	2.68	2.45	2.29	2.18	2.09	2.02	1.96	1.91	1.83	1.75	1.66	1.61	1.55	1.50	1.43	1.35	1.25
∞	3.84	3.00	2.60	2.37	2.21	2.10	2.01	1.94	1.88	1.83	1.75	1.67	1.57	1.52	1.46	1.39	1.32	1.22	1.00

v_2 = Degrees of freedom for denominator

TABLE 4B
CRITICAL VALUES OF THE F-DISTRIBUTION ($\alpha = 0.01$)

The following table gives the critical values of the F-distribution for $\alpha = 0.01$. This probability represents the area exceeding the value of $F_{0.01, v_1, v_2}$ as shown by the shaded area in the figure below.

Examples: If $v_1 = 15$ (representing the greater mean square), and $v_2 = 20$, then the critical value for $\alpha = 0.01$ is 3.09.

$$P(F \geq 3.09) = 0.01,$$
$$P(F \leq 3.09) = 0.99.$$

VALUES OF $F_{0.01, v_1, v_2}$

v_1 = Degrees of freedom for numerator

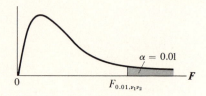

$\alpha = 0.01$

v_2 = Degrees of freedom for denominator

v_2	1	2	3	4	5	6	7	8	9	10	12	15	20	24	30	40	60	120	∞
1	4,052	5,000	5,403	5,625	5,764	5,859	5,928	5,982	6,023	6,056	6,106	6,157	6,209	6,235	6,261	6,287	6,313	6,339	6,366
2	98.5	99.0	99.2	99.2	99.3	99.3	99.4	99.4	99.4	99.4	99.4	99.4	99.4	99.5	99.5	99.5	99.5	99.5	99.5
3	34.1	30.8	29.5	28.7	28.2	27.9	27.7	27.5	27.3	27.2	27.1	26.9	26.7	26.6	26.5	26.4	26.3	26.2	26.1
4	21.2	18.0	16.7	16.0	15.5	15.2	15.0	14.8	14.7	14.5	14.4	14.2	14.0	13.9	13.8	13.7	13.7	13.6	13.5
5	16.3	13.3	12.1	11.4	11.0	10.7	10.5	10.3	10.2	10.1	9.89	9.72	9.55	9.47	9.38	9.29	9.20	9.11	9.02
6	13.7	10.9	9.78	9.15	8.75	8.47	8.26	8.10	7.98	7.87	7.72	7.56	7.40	7.31	7.23	7.14	7.06	6.97	6.88
7	12.2	9.55	8.45	7.85	7.46	7.19	6.99	6.84	6.72	6.62	6.47	6.31	6.16	6.07	5.99	5.91	5.82	5.74	5.65
8	11.3	8.65	7.59	7.01	6.63	6.37	6.18	6.03	5.91	5.81	5.67	5.52	5.36	5.28	5.20	5.12	5.03	4.95	4.86
9	10.6	8.02	6.99	6.42	6.06	5.80	5.61	5.47	5.35	5.26	5.11	4.96	4.81	4.73	4.65	4.57	4.48	4.40	4.31
10	10.0	7.56	6.55	5.99	5.64	5.39	5.20	5.06	4.94	4.85	4.71	4.56	4.41	4.33	4.25	4.17	4.08	4.00	3.91
11	9.65	7.21	6.22	5.67	5.32	5.07	4.89	4.74	4.63	4.54	4.40	4.25	4.10	4.02	3.94	3.86	3.78	3.69	3.60
12	9.33	6.93	5.95	5.41	5.06	4.82	4.64	4.50	4.39	4.30	4.16	4.01	3.86	3.78	3.70	3.62	3.54	3.45	3.36
13	9.07	6.70	5.74	5.21	4.86	4.62	4.44	4.30	4.19	4.10	3.96	3.82	3.66	3.59	3.51	3.43	3.34	3.25	3.17
14	8.86	6.51	5.56	5.04	4.70	4.46	4.28	4.14	4.03	3.94	3.80	3.66	3.51	3.43	3.35	3.27	3.18	3.09	3.00
15	8.68	6.36	5.42	4.89	4.56	4.32	4.14	4.00	3.89	3.80	3.67	3.52	3.37	3.29	3.21	3.13	3.05	2.96	2.87
16	8.53	6.23	5.29	4.77	4.44	4.20	4.03	3.89	3.78	3.69	3.55	3.41	3.26	3.18	3.10	3.02	2.93	2.84	2.75
17	8.40	6.11	5.19	4.67	4.34	4.10	3.93	3.79	3.68	3.59	3.46	3.31	3.16	3.08	3.00	2.92	2.83	2.75	2.65
18	8.29	6.01	5.09	4.58	4.25	4.01	3.84	3.71	3.60	3.51	3.37	3.23	3.08	3.00	2.92	2.84	2.75	2.66	2.57
19	8.19	5.93	5.01	4.50	4.17	3.94	3.77	3.63	3.52	3.43	3.30	3.15	3.00	2.92	2.84	2.76	2.67	2.58	2.49
20	8.10	5.85	4.94	4.43	4.10	3.87	3.70	3.56	3.46	3.37	3.23	3.09	2.94	2.86	2.78	2.69	2.61	2.52	2.42
21	8.02	5.78	4.87	3.37	4.04	3.81	3.64	3.51	3.40	3.31	3.17	3.03	2.88	2.80	2.72	2.64	2.55	2.46	2.36
22	7.95	5.72	4.82	4.31	3.99	3.76	3.59	3.45	3.35	3.26	3.12	2.98	2.83	2.75	2.67	2.58	2.50	2.40	2.31
23	7.88	5.66	4.76	4.26	3.94	3.71	3.54	3.41	3.30	3.21	3.07	2.93	2.78	2.70	2.62	2.54	2.45	2.35	2.26
24	7.82	5.61	4.72	4.22	3.90	3.67	3.50	3.36	3.26	3.17	3.03	2.89	2.74	2.66	2.58	2.49	2.40	2.31	2.21
25	7.77	5.57	4.68	4.18	3.86	3.63	3.46	3.32	3.22	3.13	2.99	2.85	2.70	2.62	2.53	2.45	2.36	2.27	2.17
30	7.56	5.39	4.51	4.02	3.70	3.47	3.30	3.17	3.07	2.98	2.84	2.70	2.55	2.47	2.39	2.30	2.21	2.11	2.01
40	7.31	5.18	4.31	3.83	3.51	3.29	3.12	2.99	2.89	2.80	2.66	2.52	2.37	2.29	2.20	2.11	2.02	1.92	1.80
60	7.08	4.98	4.13	3.65	3.34	3.12	2.95	2.82	2.72	2.63	2.50	2.35	2.20	2.12	2.03	1.94	1.84	1.73	1.60
120	6.85	4.79	3.95	3.48	3.17	2.96	2.79	2.66	2.56	2.47	2.34	2.19	2.03	1.95	1.86	1.76	1.66	1.53	1.38
∞	6.63	4.61	3.78	3.32	3.02	2.80	2.64	2.51	2.41	2.32	2.18	2.04	1.88	1.79	1.70	1.59	1.47	1.32	1.00

TABLE 5
CRITICAL VALUES OF _D_ IN THE KOLMOGOROV-SMIRNOV ONE-SAMPLE TEST

Sample size (n)	Level of significance for $D = \text{maximum} \, \lvert F_i - S_i \rvert$				
	.20	.15	.10	.05	.01
1	.900	.925	.950	.975	.995
2	.684	.726	.776	.842	.929
3	.565	.597	.642	.708	.828
4	.494	.525	.564	.624	.733
5	.446	.474	.510	.565	.669
6	.410	.436	.470	.521	.618
7	.381	.405	.438	.486	.577
8	.358	.381	.411	.457	.543
9	.339	.360	.388	.432	.514
10	.322	.342	.368	.410	.490
11	.307	.326	.352	.391	.468
12	.295	.313	.338	.375	.450
13	.284	.302	.325	.361	.433
14	.274	.292	.314	.349	.418
15	.266	.283	.304	.338	.404
16	.258	.274	.295	.328	.392
17	.250	.266	.286	.318	.381
18	.244	.259	.278	.309	.371
19	.237	.252	.272	.301	.363
20	.231	.246	.264	.294	.356
25	.21	.22	.24	.27	.32
30	.19	.20	.22	.24	.29
35	.18	.19	.21	.23	.27
Over 35	$\dfrac{1.07}{\sqrt{n}}$	$\dfrac{1.14}{\sqrt{n}}$	$\dfrac{1.22}{\sqrt{n}}$	$\dfrac{1.36}{\sqrt{n}}$	$\dfrac{1.63}{\sqrt{n}}$

Adapted from Massey, F. J., Jr. 1951. The Kolmogorov-Smirnov test for goodness of fit. _J. of Amer. Statist. Ass._, **46**, 70, with the kind permission of the author and publisher.

INDEX